Order in Chaos

FOREIGN MILITARY STUDIES

History is replete with examples of notable military campaigns and
exceptional military leaders and theorists. Military professionals and students
of the art and science of war cannot afford to ignore these sources of
knowledge or limit their studies to the history of the U.S. armed forces. This
series features original works, translations, and reprints of classics outside
the American canon that promote a deeper understanding of international
military theory and practice.

SERIES EDITOR: Roger Cirillo

An AUSA Book

ORDER
IN
CHAOS

The Memoirs of General of Panzer Troops Hermann Balck

HERMANN BALCK

Edited and Translated by Major General David T. Zabecki, USA (Ret.), and Lieutenant Colonel Dieter J. Biedekarken, USA (Ret.)

Foreword by Carlo D'Este

UNIVERSITY PRESS OF KENTUCKY

Scholarly publisher for the Commonwealth,
serving Bellarmine University, Berea College, Centre College of Kentucky, Eastern
Kentucky University, The Filson Historical Society, Georgetown College, Kentucky
Historical Society, Kentucky State University, Morehead State University, Murray State
University, Northern Kentucky University, Transylvania University, University of Kentucky,
University of Louisville, and Western Kentucky University.

Editorial and Sales Offices: The University Press of Kentucky
663 South Limestone Street, Lexington, Kentucky 40508–4008
www.kentuckypress.com

The German edition of this book was published as General der Panzertruppe a.D.
Hermann Balck, *Ordnung im Chaos: Erinnerungen 1893–1948*, 2nd ed. (Osnabrück: Biblio
Verlag, 1981).

Library of Congress Cataloging-in-Publication Data

Balck, Hermann, 1893-1982.
  [Ordnung im Chaos. English]
  The memoirs of General of Panzer Troops Hermann Balck / Hermann Balck ; edited
by Major General David T. Zabecki, USA (Ret.), and Lieutenant Colonel Dieter J.
Biederkarken, USA (Ret.) ; foreword by Carlo D'Este.
    pages cm. — (Foreign military studies)
  "An AUSA Book."
  Includes bibliographical references and index.
  ISBN 978-0-8131-6126-6 (hardcover : alk. paper) — ISBN 978-0-8131-6127-3 (pdf) —
ISBN 978-0-8131-6128-0 (epub)
  1. Balck, Hermann, 1893-1982. 2. Generals—Germany—Biography. 3. Germany.
Heer—Biography. 4. World War, 1914-1918—Personal narratives, German. 5. World
War, 1939-1945—Tank warfare. 6. World War, 1939-1945—Personal narratives, German.
I. Zabecki, David T. II. Biederkarken, Dieter J. III. Title.
  U55.B228A3613 2015
  355.009—dc23
  [B]   2015011481

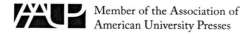

Contents

Photographs follow page 276

Maps

Foreword

Many of the German generals of World War II were superb battlefield commanders who not only understood mobile warfare, but also were masterful strategists and tacticians. Erwin Rommel, Erich von Manstein, Albert Kesselring, Hans Guderian, and Hasso von Manteuffel are among the well-known successful German generals that have garnered considerable attention for their exploits. Yet, one name is conspicuously missing from the list of successful generals: General of Panzer Troops Hermann Balck.

One of the means by which we learn is through a study of history and the lessons it teaches us. There have been few better ways to learn about World War II than to scrutinize the German generals who commanded the armies, corps, and other military units that fought so well against the Allies during the most deadly war in the history of mankind.

Shortly after the end of the war, the U.S. Army European Command Historical Division conducted a series of interviews and interrogations of those German generals who had been captured. The objective was to acquire a detailed knowledge of German military operations for the U.S. Army official history. It was also to gain a better understanding not only of an enemy that had fought tenaciously and well during the campaigns in the Mediterranean, the eastern front, and Northwest Europe, but of war. The transcripts of those interviews that number in the hundreds have been preserved and have proven invaluable to historians like myself who have studied and written about World War II.

There is much to learn from reading Balck's memoir. He was, as one of his translators, David Zabecki, once noted, "The Greatest German General No One Ever Heard Of." Although Germany produced a number of truly outstanding Panzer commanders during World War II, few were more successful or more accomplished than Hermann Balck.

Major General F. W. von Mellenthin, the well-known postwar author of *Panzer Battles,* served with and knew Balck well, and has said of him, "If Manstein was Germany's greatest strategist during World War II, I think Balck has strong claims to be regarded as our finest field commander."

Freeman Dyson, the famed physicist and mathematician, has written a book called *Weapons and Hope* that contains an in-depth assessment of Balck that goes even further. Dyson calls him, "Perhaps the most brilliant field commander on either side in World War II."

A classic example of Balck's skill as a troop leader and tactician occurred during one tank battle in Russia in 1942 while in command of the 11th Panzer Division. With no prior notice, Balck broke off an attack, moved his division twenty kilometers in a matter of hours in the dead of night, and counterattacked a Soviet breakthrough with such surprise that it not only foiled the attack but also destroyed seventy-five Russian tanks without the loss of a single Panzer.

Balck and General George S. Patton had much in common. Both were dynamic commanders who believed that offensive action was always preferable to defense. "It is quite remarkable," Balck once noted, "that most people believe that attack costs more casualties. Do not even think about it; attack is the less costly operation.... Nothing incurs higher casualties than an unsuccessful defense. Therefore, attack wherever it is possible."

The two leaders also believed strongly in the power and influence of personal leadership. Like Patton, Balck was a very "hands-on" commander who believed in being up front with his troops, both to control the battle and to uplift their morale.

Balck is rarely mentioned in the U.S. Army official histories and has been mischaracterized in the volume on the Lorraine campaign, while briefly in command of Army Group G, as "a strutting martinet." However, Freeman Dyson has a vastly different view of Balck and characterizes him as a soldier who never took himself particularly seriously. "He went on winning battles, just as Picasso went on painting pictures, without pretensions or pious talk. He won battles because his skill came to him naturally. He never said that battle-winning was a particularly noble or virtuous activity; it was simply his trade."

Few could claim greater success at their trade than Balck.

Moreover, because Balck was one of the few captured German generals who refused to participate in the U.S. Army debriefing program, the translation of his memoir into English has become an important and useful window through which we can gain a better understanding of German military leadership and some of its most important military operations during World War II.

Carlo D'Este
Author of *Patton: A Genius for War*

Preface

General of Panzer Troops Hermann Balck was the nineteenth of only twenty-seven soldiers awarded the Knight's Cross of the Iron Cross with Oak Leaves, Swords, and Diamonds, Germany's highest decoration of World War II. He was wounded a total of seven times in both world wars. U.S. Army general William E. DePuy once referred to Balck as "the best division commander in the German Army."[1] In his 1984 book, *Weapons and Hope,* physicist and philosopher Freeman Dyson wrote, "Perhaps the most brilliant field commander on either side in World War II was Hermann Balck."[2] And in his highly regarded book, *Panzer Battles,* German major general Friedrich-Wilhelm von Mellenthin wrote, "If [Field Marshal Erich von] Manstein was Germany's greatest strategist during World War II, I think Balck has strong claims to be regarded as our finest field commander."[3] Yet, Hermann Balck remains today a name known to only the most serious students of the military history of World War II.

Several factors explain why a field commander with "a record of battlefield performance unsurpassed anywhere in the history of modern warfare"[4] remains so obscure. Balck spent most of World War II on the eastern front, fighting the Russians. He spent only seven months, spread over four different periods, fighting against the western Allies. As the commander of an infantry regiment he led one of the key attacks that resulted in the decisive German breakthrough against France at Sedan on the Meuse River in 1940. Commanding a Panzer regiment in April 1941 he fought against the British and New Zealanders in Greece. As an acting Panzer corps commander in Italy he fought against the Americans during the initial stages of the Salerno landings in September 1943. And for a three-month period at the end of 1944 he commanded Army Group G in the Lorraine campaign. Most of what western readers learned about Balck in the years immediately following the war was based on the assessment of Balck by American official military historians that was neither fair nor accurate.

In the *Lorraine Campaign* volume of the U.S. Army in World War II series (the "Green Books"), historian Hugh M. Cole painted a bleak picture of the Army Group G commander with such statements as:

"Politically, Balck long held the reputation of being an ardent Nazi."
"From his earliest days as a junior commander he had built up a reputation for arrogant and ruthless dealings with his subordinates."

"Balck already had been ticketed as an officer prone to take too favorable a view of things when the situation failed to warrant optimism."
"He was, in short, the type of commander certain to win Hitler's confidence."[5]

Balck, however, was never a member of the Nazi Party, and he was not even close to being a Nazi sympathizer or an ardent Hitler worshiper. On 19 September 1949 the judgment of a West German *Spruchkammer* (denazification court) cleared Balck unequivocally: "These proceedings have found no causal connection between this man and National Socialism."[6] One of the key pieces of evidence offered in Balck's defense was a sworn affidavit written in November 1947 by former Colonel General Heinz Guderian. Cole's other charges against Balck are likewise unfounded. Mellenthin knew Balck well. He served as Balck's chief of staff for more than two years, and together they formed one of the all-time great commander-chief of staff teams. Writing in *Panzer Battles* in 1956, Mellenthin commented on Cole's distorted characterization of Balck, and the fact that other historians had picked it up and repeated it. Trying to set the record straight, Mellenthin wrote: "I regret that in that remarkable work, *The Struggle for Europe* (page 538), Chester Wilmont has followed the estimate of Balck's qualities given in the American official history, *The Lorraine Campaign* (page 230), where Balck is portrayed as a swashbuckling martinet. Apart from the comments on Balck I have no quarrel with the American history, which gives a very solid and on the whole impartial study of these operations."[7]

For many years after the war Balck did little to overcome his historical obscurity or even to defend his reputation. While still prisoners of war during the late 1940s, many of the *Wehrmacht*'s surviving senior officers cooperated willingly in the U.S. Army Historical Division's Foreign Military Studies program, writing monographs and participating in interviews. Even after they were released, many continued cooperating with the program well into the early 1960s. Balck was not among them. He simply refused to talk.[8] Thus, German officers already relatively well known to the western Allies, including Colonel General Franz Halder, Colonel General Johannes Blaskowitz, General of Panzer Troops Hasso von Manteuffel, General of Infantry Günther Blumentritt, and even Waffen-SS generals like Wilhelm Bittrich participated in the program, and in so doing were able to tell their own stories. Mellenthin himself wrote or contributed to five monographs in the series. Balck maintained his silence. He supported his family after the war by working in a warehouse as a laborer.

Near the end of his life Balck had a change of heart and started to open up to his former enemies. Mellenthin most likely had something to do with that. After the war Balck and Mellenthin remained close, and Balck even wound up working for his former chief of staff as a representative for the airline Mellenthin started in South Africa.[9]

The U.S. Army also rediscovered Balck in the mid-1970s, during the period of the American renaissance in classical military thought that followed the defeat in Vietnam. As the American strategic focus shifted back to Europe at the height of the Cold War, the U.S. Army's major challenge was to develop a tactical and operational doctrine for fighting outnumbered and winning against the overwhelming numerically superior tank forces of the Soviet Union and the Warsaw Pact. Balck, of course, was one of the undisputed masters of just that. In 1979 Battelle Columbus Laboratories interviewed Balck several times under a U.S. Army contract.[10] And in May 1980 Balck and Mellenthin together participated in a colloquium on tactical warfare at the U.S. Army War College, under the auspices of the Director of Net Assessment, Office of the Secretary of Defense. The senior American officers participating included retired General William E. DePuy, the former commander of the U.S. Army Training and Doctrine Command and principal author of the 1976 edition of *FM 100-5 Operations*; Lieutenant General Glenn K. Otis, U.S. Army, deputy chief of staff for Operations and Plans; and Lieutenant General Paul Goreman, J-5 (Plans and Policy), Joint Chiefs of Staff.[11]

German tactical doctrine, especially as it had been practiced by Balck against the Russians, had a clear influence on the development of the new American doctrine, called AirLand Battle.[12] From the mid-1980s through the early 1990s the study of Balck's December 1942 battle on the Chir River as commander of the 11th Panzer Division was a standard element in the formal course of instruction at the U.S. Army Command and General Staff College. It was held up as one of the best historical examples of the tactical principles embodied in AirLand Battle.

Fortunately, Balck maintained a detailed journal throughout his military career, from his earliest days as an officer candidate in 1913 to his final surrender to U.S. Army forces in May 1945. During the years following World War II he worked episodically to pull his journal entries together into a coherent narrative. The result was a book entitled *Ordnung in Chaos*, published in Germany in 1981, a year before his death at the age of eighty-four. Despite the renewed interest in Balck at the time, his memoirs have not been translated into English until now.

Perhaps the single overriding moral question about the German Army in World War II is how so many of its soldiers and officers could have fought so well for such a bad cause? Historians and philosophers have been pondering that question since even before the war ended. There may never be a conclusive answer, and Balck's memoirs certainly do not answer it. They do, however, offer important insights into the background, the experiences, the motivations, and the values of one of the most significant of those officers.

Freeman Dyson devotes considerable space to examining that question in *Weapons and Hope*. Dyson identifies two broad categories of Wehrmacht officers, distinguished by their basic attitudes to their professional duties. The one attitude he calls soldiering, the other *Soldatentum*[13]—the distinction between soldiering as a trade and soldiering as a cult. Dyson further develops his analysis using Balck as an example of the former. For the latter, Dyson's model is Colonel General Alfred Jodl, the chief of the Operations Staff of the *Oberkommando der Wehrmacht*—OKW, the Armed Forces High Command. Jodl, who was tried and convicted at Nuremberg and then executed, was the epitome of the military *Beamter* (bureaucrat). Comparing Balck to Jodl, Dyson wrote, "He was, unlike Jodl, a real Prussian. He fought as Jodl was not permitted to fight, in the front lines with his soldiers."[14]

Developing the contrast between Jodl and Balck, Dyson wrote that they were examples of two very different styles of military professionalism; the bureaucratic and the human, the heavy and the light, the humorless and humorous:

> Jodl doggedly sat at his desk, translating Hitler's dreams of conquest into daily balance sheets of men and equipment. Balck gaily jumped out of one tight squeeze into another, taking good care of his soldiers and never losing his sense of humor.[15] For Jodl, Hitler was Germany's fate, a superhuman force transcending right and wrong. Balck saw Hitler as he was, a powerful but not very competent politician. When Jodl disagreed with Hitler's plan to extend the German advance south of the Caucasus Mountains by dropping parachutists, the disagreement was for Jodl a soul-shattering experience. When Balck appealed directly to Hitler to straighten out the confusion in the supply of tanks and trucks, Hitler's failure to deal with the situation came as no surprise to Balck.[16]

Even after it had become clear to everyone that Germany had no hope of winning the war, Jodl continued to the bitter end because he had accepted Hitler's will as his own personal highest law. Balck went on fighting because it was his job and it never occurred to him to do otherwise. As Dyson wrote:

> I chose my two examples of military professionalism from Germany because the German side of World War II displays the moral dilemmas of military professionalism with particular clarity. Both Jodl and

Balck were good men working for a bad cause. Both of them used their professional skills to conquer and ravage half of Europe. Both of them continued to exercise their skills through the long years of retreat when the only result of their efforts was to prolong Europe's agony. Both of them appeared to be indifferent to the sufferings of the villagers whose homes their tanks were smashing and burning. And yet, the judgment of Nuremberg made a distinction between them. Whether or not the Nuremberg tribunal was properly constituted according to international law, its decisions expressed the consensus of mankind at that moment in history. Jodl was hanged and Balck was set free; and the majority of interested bystanders agreed that justice had been done.[17]

Dyson considers Balck a generally sympathetic character because he did not take himself too seriously. "He went on winning battles, just as Picasso went on painting pictures, without pretensions or pious talk." Balck had a natural and finely developed skill for winning battles, but he never came to believe that that battle-winning was an especially righteous or noble undertaking. It was his trade, and he was far better than most at it. Jodl, however, was unsympathetic because he set soldiering above humanity. He turned his soldier's oath, which he equated with blind loyalty to Hitler, into a holy sacrament. Jodl's sense of Soldatentum was far more important to him than saving what was left of Germany. Thus, Jodl in the end became infected with Hitler's insanity, and his ideal of Soldatentum lost all connection with reason, reality, and common sense.[18]

Dyson did write one thing about Balck that requires some additional comment: "He was accused of no war crimes."[19] In the strictest sense that is not an entirely accurate statement. During the years immediately following World War II, Balck was charged and tried in two separate incidents. The first was technically not a war crime. The second was, although the charge was trumped-up.

On 28 November 1944, when Balck commanded Army Group G defending the sector from Belfort to Metz, a divisional artillery commander named Lieutenant Colonel Johann Schottke was found staggeringly drunk in his bunker in the middle of a battle. Schottke did not even know where his batteries were positioned. Balck's units were under extreme pressure from Allied attacks along the entire length of his line. The failure of the artillery support in that one divisional sector only added to the Army Group G casualties. After checking the facts of the case twice, Balck ordered Schottke's summary execution.

Following the war the Schottke incident was investigated by the German denazification court. As the court ruled, "In the final analysis, however, this is not the matter for the Spruchkammer to pass judgment on. This court's only purpose is to determine whether or not this action can be judged as a Nazi terror act in the political sense. This clearly is not the case."[20] Noting that the armies of other nations would have acted with similar severity in such a situation, the court concluded; "It is, therefore, impossible to reach the conclusion the person concerned [Balck] acted in accordance with National Socialist policies."[21]

In 1948 Balck was tried by a civilian court in Stuttgart. He argued that his action had been taken in the heat of a crisis situation, and that under the circumstances he had acted completely within the framework of the German military code of justice. The court disagreed, ruling Schottke's execution unlawful. Balck was sentenced to three years in prison, and served eighteen months. Other German commanders besides Balck were tried by postwar German courts for similar incidents, including the widely respected Manteuffel.

While he was still in confinement from the Schottke trial, the French government charged Balck with a war crime for the destruction of the town of Gérardmer in the Vosges Mountains of Alsace. As Free French and American forces pushed eastward through the Vosges in mid-November 1944, the Germans were forced to pull back their front, leaving Gérardmer between the German line and the advancing Allies. As Balck later wrote, leaving the civilian population in the town "would have exposed them to high casualties and certain annihilation from our artillery fire." Rather than evacuating the local population to the east toward Germany, Balck decided to send them west toward the Allies, providing the evacuees with food and medical supplies. Balck then established a forty-eight-hour no-fire zone for his own artillery. Abandoned, Gérardmer was largely destroyed during the subsequent fighting.

In 1950 all the German leaders involved at Gérardmer were tried before a French military tribunal in Paris. The American occupation authorities refused to extradite Balck for trial, and he was tried in absentia. All those who were tried in person were acquitted. Balck, however, was convicted for the destruction of the town and sentenced to twenty years imprisonment—even though his actions clearly had spared the local population. As Balck later wrote, "My absence made it easier for the French to acquit those present, especially since during the pretrial depositions I had clearly admitted to the measures we had taken." Even after he was convicted, however, both American and German authorities refused to extradite him to France, and the sentence was never carried out.

Hermann Balck invites comparison with another of Germany's World War II generals. Field Marshal Erwin Rommel is undoubtedly the most famous and most celebrated German general of the twentieth century. But does his actual record of battlefield performance really justify his exalted reputation? Some military historians think it does not.

Balck and Rommel had very different backgrounds. Balck came from an old-line military family. His father, Lieutenant General William Balck,[22] commanded a division during World War I, and prior to the war he was one of Germany's best known tactical theorists. The elder Balck was a staunch critic of Chief of the General Staff Alfred von Schlieffen for his one-sided emphasis on envelopment. William Balck wrote a series of books on tactics, one of which was translated into English and used as a textbook in American military schools following World War I.[23] Hermann Balck grew up learning the military art at his father's elbow.

Born two years earlier than Balck, Rommel came from a family that had no special military tradition. His father was a school headmaster, although he did serve briefly as a lieutenant of artillery. It is exactly this lack of a military family background that makes Rommel's own career so impressive, especially considering that most of the key German generals of the two world wars were the sons of professional military officers.

As described here in Balck's memoirs and in Rommel's book *Infanterie greift an,*[24] their experiences as junior officers during World War I were amazingly similar. Both were among the earliest recipients of the Iron Cross 2nd Class and 1st Class. Rommel was wounded in action three times, Balck six. Both commanded infantry companies as junior lieutenants, and near the end of the war Rommel commanded an ad hoc battalion as a captain. For much of the second half of the war Rommel's Württemberg Mountain Battalion and Balck's 10th *Jäger* Battalion were part of the divisional-sized *Alpenkorps*. Rommel and Balck both fought at the battles of Mount Gragonza in October 1917 and Mount Tomba that November. In December 1917 Rommel was awarded the *Pour le Mérite,* Prussia's highest combat decoration. Balck was recommended for the *Pour le Mérite* in October 1918, but the war ended before the paperwork could be processed.

When Rommel published his book in 1937, it impressed Hitler, whose patronage contributed much to Rommel's meteoric rise during World War II. Rommel's record of battlefield performance during World War II rests on six weeks in May and June 1940 during the invasion of France as a Panzer division commander; his twenty-five months as a corps, army, and army group commander in North Africa from February 1941 to March 1943; and his six weeks as the commander of Army Group B in June and July 1944 during the Allied Normandy invasion. While he was in North Africa, Rommel was the primary German commander the Allies fought against during that period. In the process he acquired the nickname of the Desert Fox, and his name became a household word in Britain and America. The Battle of Gazala and the capture of Tobruk in May and June 1942 were the peak of Rommel's career. Not counting Rommel's four months in 1943 commanding an army group in Northern Italy, during which no combat operations were conducted, he commanded in combat for a total of twenty-eight months. He commanded one division, one corps, one army, and two army groups, none of which fought the Russians.

Balck also fought in France, as a regimental commander, and his attack across the Meuse at Sedan was the spearhead of Guderian's XIX Corps advance. Although the Nazi press controlled by Propaganda Minister Josef Goebbels trumpeted the crossing of the Meuse by Rommel's 7th Panzer Division at Dinant, it was Guderian's crossing at Sedan farther to the south that was the decisive penetration of the campaign. Balck, during World War II, commanded in combat for a total of thirty-six months, including two regiments, two divisions, two corps, two armies, and two army groups. Twenty-nine of those thirty-six months were against the Russians, and much of that in harsh northern winter conditions. And although Rommel was always outnumbered in North Africa, it was Balck who was the master at overcoming impossible odds. On the Chir River in December 1942 Balck with a single Panzer division virtually destroyed the Soviet Fifth Tank Army, despite superior Soviet combat ratios of 11 to 1 in infantry, 7 to 1 in tanks, and 20 to 1 in guns.[25] And at Budapest in early 1945, Balck attacked forty-five Russian divisions with seven German divisions. To the end of his life he maintained that he could have relieved Budapest if he had had two more Panzer divisions.[26]

Another significant difference between Rommel and Balck in their later careers was their attitudes toward General Staff officers. Rommel was never recruited to attend the *Kriegsakademie* or to join the General Staff, a fact that he greatly resented.[27] Balck, on the other hand, served in several General Staff assignments in the early 1930s, which qualified him for assignment to the General Staff Corps. Despite the fact that his father had been a General Staff officer, Balck on two occasions declined invitations for reassignment, saying that he preferred to remain a line officer.[28]

Although Balck had a healthy skepticism about what he considered the tendency for inbreeding within the General Staff Corps, Rommel largely disliked and distrusted General Staff officers. Mellenthin worked for both Balck and Rommel as a General Staff officer. When Berlin sent Rommel a small team of General Staff officers in June 1941, he initially "snubbed von Mellenthin and the other General Staff officers, ignoring their presence for a long time, saying: 'I don't need a staff.'"[29] The irony is that during his time in North Africa Rommel was served by one of the most brilliant teams of General Staff officers ever assembled under a single commander, including Mellenthin, Siegfried Westphal, and Fritz Bayerlein. Whenever Rommel ran into trouble in North Africa, it was usually after ignoring the advice of his staff.

Balck, on the other hand, valued competent and reliable General Staff officers. He forged tight and effective command teams with his two primary chiefs of staff of the war, Mellenthin and Major General Heinrich Gaedcke, who later served as a lieutenant general in the *Bundeswehr*. As Mellenthin later wrote of Balck, he never interfered in the details of staff work, giving his chief of staff full authority as well as full responsibility.[30] Nonetheless, Balck did not trust General Staff officers blindly just because they were members of the vaunted General Staff Corps. They had to prove themselves to him first, because he believed that General Staff officers had too much of a tendency to become inwardly focused and lose touch with the realities of war at the sharp end of the stick. That was one of the few things that Balck and Mellenthin did not agree upon fully. "Once he expressed his outlook on the subject by saying that on the staff one easily became 'secondhand,' as he called it. A man became smothered in routine office work. I cannot share my highly respected commander-in-chief's opinion in this regard, although we agreed in most other matters."[31]

Balck's memoirs are filled with his experiences with and comments on many of the major German figures of World War II. Balck held Manstein in the highest esteem, but he thought Field Marshal Walther Model was an erratic and meddling leader—and told him so. Like almost all of the Wehrmacht's senior officers, Balck had little use for most of the general officers of the Waffen-SS. The few exceptions included Josef "Sepp" Dietrich and Erich von dem Bach-Zelewski. Balck's positive comments on these two can be a bit jarring, considering how history has come to judge them. On the other hand, Field Marshal Gerd von Rundstedt initially opposed Balck's assignment as Army Group G commander because Balck had very little experience fighting Americans.

Guderian, the father of Germany's Panzer forces, was Balck's most important mentor throughout his career. Both Balck and Guderian started their military careers as officer candidates in the elite 10th Jäger Battalion. When Guderian joined the unit in 1907, his father, Lieutenant Colonel Friedrich Guderian, was the battalion commander. During World War I, when Guderian got in hot water for accusing his divisional commander of incompetence in an official after-action report, it was Lieutenant General William Balck who arranged for Guderian's transfer to another assignment, probably saving his career in the process.[32]

Balck's and Guderian's paths crossed many times during the interwar years, but their professional relationship probably was cemented during the May 1940 invasion of France, when Guderian was able to observe firsthand Balck's dynamic lead-from-the-front style of command, as well as his unusually wry sense of humor. As Guderian recounted his own crossing of the Meuse on 13 May 1940, he was midstream in an assault boat when "On the far bank I found the efficient and brave commander of the 1st Rifle Regiment, Lieutenant Colonel Balck, together with his staff. He greeted me joyfully with the cry, 'Joy riding in canoes on the Meuse is forbidden.' I had in fact used those words myself in one of the exercises that we had in preparation for this operation, since the attitude of some of the younger officers had struck me as rather too light-hearted. I now realized that they had judged the situation correctly."[33]

After the France campaign Balck's career followed Guderian's very closely. Although Balck had no experience in Panzer units up to that point, he was given command of a Panzer regiment for the Balkans and Greece campaign, followed by staff assignments in Berlin working with motorized and armored units, and finally command of a Panzer division. Balck's performance as commander of the 11th Panzer Division in Russia established him solidly as one of Germany's leading armored commanders.

In late December 1944, Balck was relieved of command of Army Group G after running afoul of one of SS chief Heinrich Himmler's political intrigues. Guderian, who at the time was the chief of staff of the German Army, made sure that Balck did not remain idle for long. Almost the same day he was relieved, Balck was reassigned as commander of the reconstituted Sixth Army, fighting on the eastern front.

Balck's relations with Hitler, his views on Germany's responsibility for World War II, and his general reluctance to address the Third Reich's barbaric racial policies and the Holocaust are among the most difficult parts of his memoirs. The modern reader will encounter much to question here. One always must keep in mind, however, that we are reading the thoughts and the memories of a man who was close to many of the central events of the Third Reich. Balck's memoirs, then, are both an explanation of how he saw things at the time, and how he came to understand them in the succeeding years. Much of his discussion of these key topics is inherently defensive. The fact that he twice brings up the "right or wrong, my country" defense—which he cites both times in English—is a strong indicator that he was still struggling with these issues as he was preparing his memoirs for publication.

Balck was never blinded by Hitler, as Jodl and many others were. But Balck also does not join the postwar chorus of German generals who blamed every failure on Hitler. In several cases, Balck gives Hitler credit for making correct decisions in opposition to the generals. In many other cases, however, he lays Germany's failures directly at Hitler's feet. Balck states very clearly that the Hitler of legend, the screaming and out of control *Teppichbeisser*—the carpet-chewing dog—was not the Hitler he dealt with many times. But in the end Balck does conclude: "Despite all my conscious efforts to evaluate Hitler with complete objectivity, I cannot escape the final verdict—he was our downfall. Beware of strong men who do not know the limits of their power."

Even as he was finishing his memoirs for publication Balck still did not quite know how to address the issue of Colonel Claus von Stauffenberg and the July 1944 plot to assassinate Hitler. Balck maintains that he knew nothing about the plot, and he admits to being glad that he was not drawn into it. But he knew Stauffenberg well, and he had great respect for him. Without specifically endorsing Stauffenberg's actions, he expresses an understanding for them, and in the end he refuses to condemn his old friend. "My opinion of some of the others involved in the conspiracy is not so positive, but I will always hold Stauffenberg in honorable remembrance."

Throughout the latter part of his memoirs Balck protests strongly that Germany was not the sole aggressor in World War II. As he continued to see it, even some thirty-five years after the end of the war, Germany was maneuvered into the conflict, particularly by Churchill and Roosevelt, who manipulated Poland and France. Balck ignores the evidence of the 1937 Hossbach Memorandum and the fact that it was Germany that attacked Poland, Norway, Denmark, France, Great Britain, Greece, and finally the Soviet Union. On 11 December 1941 it was Hitler who unilaterally declared war on the United States, even though Germany did not even have advance knowledge of the Japanese attack on Pearl Harbor. Balck's arguments and thoughts along these lines betray the complete lack of geopolitical understanding that was so characteristic of the German officer corps between 1871 and 1945.

At several points in his narrative Balck attempts to mount the same sort of *tu quoque* (you also) defense that was attempted so unsuccessfully at the Nuremberg Trials. At several points he accuses both the British and the Americans of treating prisoners of war brutally, even though the historical record is quite clear that the vast majority of German POWs in American and British hands testified otherwise. Balck even raises the old canard that Eisenhower at the end of the war issued specific orders to mistreat or even kill German prisoners. If he really believed that, Balck still did not regret the extreme lengths he went to in May 1945 to evade the Soviets and surrender his forces to the Americans.

In all his discussion of Hitler's pros and cons, Balck cannot seem to bring himself to face the reality of Hitler's brutal racial and occupation policies, the inherent corruption of almost all of the social and political institutions of the Third Reich, and the utter barbarism of the Holocaust. Like many of the Wehrmacht's senior commanders, Balck claims to have known little about the scope of the Holocaust for most of the war—even though anyone who lived in Germany after 1933 could not help but know about the Third Reich's virulent anti-Semitic policies. Only twice, once in the main text and once in a letter included in the appendices, is there any reference to the fate of the Jews or to Auschwitz. Balck staunchly defends the "Myth of the Clean Wehrmacht" that was championed so strongly and successfully by Manstein, Halder, Westphal, and others at the Nuremberg Trials. That myth held up for more than forty years after the war. Within the past twenty-five years, however, historical scholarship has exposed a high level of Wehrmacht complicity in the crimes of the Holocaust.[34]

In the final analysis, Balck is no different than the countless other soldiers and commanders of the past who found themselves on the wrong side of history at the conclusion of a war. Undoubtedly, most of the veterans of the Confederate Army in the American Civil War, including such revered figures as Robert E. Lee, Thomas "Stonewall" Jackson, and James Longstreet went to their graves believing they had fought an honorable war for a noble cause, regardless of the obvious flaws of the political and social system they defended.

Despite his inability to come to grips with these issues, the Hermann Balck that emerges from the pages of these memoirs is the essentially ironic figure of Dyson's good man who served a bad cause so well. Although Freeman Dyson is one of the leading intellectuals of the post–World War II world, he is no stranger to the realities of modern warfare. Between 1943 and 1945 he served in the Operational Research Section of the Royal Air Force's Bomber Command, developing analytical methods for the selection of bombing targets in Germany. As Dyson wrote of Balck: "The constant theme of his military career was learning to do more with less." And: "He was always inventing new tricks to confound the enemy in front of him and the bureaucrats behind him."[35]

Balck was a good man and an honest man, in addition to being a talented soldier and a brilliant combat commander. He also was a highly cultured man. His memoirs are full of references to history, architecture, and literary quotes ranging from Homer to Goethe. Yet, Balck wore his culture lightly, and it comes through in his memoirs with no sense of pretentiousness. Dyson wrote that if he had to choose an epigraph for a biography of Balck, he would take it from the old Anglo-Saxon poem commemorating the Battle of Maldon:

Thought shall be harder, heart the keener,
Courage the greater, as our strength lessens.[36]

David T. Zabecki
Freiburg, Germany

Dieter Biedekarken
Imperial Beach, California

Introduction

Fate propelled me into the world during an era of historical development in Germany that other peoples had long since passed through. Peoples pass through many levels in their development. The Germans, the English, the French did not exist in the beginning. Single tribes and personalities often united based on geographical conditions. Fighting erupted at the tip of the growth, which eventually led to fighting of all against all else. This is the state of particularism that forcefully forms into a unity of violence and cruelty. The developmental stages with all their unpleasant side effects are the same everywhere. In France it was the era of Richelieu and Louis XIV up to Napoleon; in England it was the period under Cromwell. After countless sacrifices unity is achieved and the development into a nation of world historic greatness can take its course.

Germany arrived too late. The right era and the right personalities may have been Wallenstein and Prince Eugene of Savoy. But the Habsburgs were not capable enough. Consequently, the development was postponed to our period, and with the same developmental phases. This is not meant to be an apology for what occurred during the Third Reich. An advanced culture and civilization should have and could have found other approaches. As a result, the end state for us was not, like in England and France, the development into a world power, but rather total destruction and collapse.

The following memoirs are based on journal entries that I kept from the first to the last days of both world wars. They consist of thoughts that I formed at the time. The reader will easily recognize critical thoughts that were added later. Often the journal entries are used verbatim.

The Balcks

The Balcks are a very old family. We come from the oldest of Finnish families. Around 1120 we migrated from Sweden to Finland. In 1308 Gregor Balck was the fourth Bishop of Aebo. Our ancestors settled on the estates of Balkis and Balkilax. Since that time we can trace our family completely. Our coat of arms is a blue bend on a golden field. The crest of an armor-clad arm rising from a cloud, holding an oak branch with a golden star, is a later Swedish addition. The family motto *"Frangi non flecti"* also comes from that period.[1] During the era of Sweden's imperial power we marched as Swedish officers all over northern and eastern Europe.

There were several Baltic and Russian branches of the family, and a Swedish branch which still exists today. A member of that branch in recent history was a General Viktor Balck, the best rider, swimmer, and fencer of the Swedish Army. He was one of the founders of the modern Olympic Games. His son was a naval officer and the adjutant to the Swedish minister of war.

In Germany, where we arrived before the Thirty Years' War, there were three branches of the family. One settled along the lower Elbe River and still exists in North America. Another was located in the Mecklenburg area, but has since died out. I come from the Hannover branch. A member of the Mecklenburg branch who was a high official of the treasury, *Oberfinanzrat*[2] Balck from Rostock, wrote the history of our family and our complete family tree going back to 1308. These records are kept in the state archives in Schwerin.

There are no more Balcks in Finland. By chance I came in contact with the current owner of Balkis and I have a picture of the estate, which now carries the Finnish name "Pelkis." The Baltic-Russian Balcks were especially interesting. At the time of Tsar Peter the Great they often played important roles. During the Great Northern War[3] a General Balck[4] seized and destroyed the city of Elbing. When the tsarevich, the son of Peter the Great, fled to Germany to escape from his father, he took the pseudonym of "Lieutenant Balck." One family branch was elevated to the nobility as counts. The last Count of Balck-Polew was the Russian ambassador to Paris in the nineteenth century. He had no male offspring. We are not, however, related to the Teutonic Order knight Hermann Balck.

The fate of the Countess Lopuchin, née Balck, was rather tragic. She was one of Russian Empress Elizabeth's ladies-in-waiting and was reported to be more beautiful than the empress herself. Accused of conspiracy by the jealous empress, the countess was cruelly flogged, her tongue was torn out, and she was exiled to Siberia. In 1762, however, she was pardoned by Tsar Peter III.[5]

The last tsarist police commissioner of Saint Petersburg was a General Balck who played a role in the Rasputin affair. This tsarist chief of police escaped the turmoil of the Bolshevik Revolution and lived in Belgrade between the two world wars. Other than him, no Balcks are known to have survived the Bolshevik Revolution.

My Family

After the Thirty Years' War our branch of the family settled in the *Altes Land*[6] along the lower Elbe River. The *Balcksee*[7] in that region still bears our name. For two generations we served as *Amtmänner*,[8] or what we today would call a *Landrat*,[9] in Rotenburg (Hannover) and in Isernhagen. The magnificent tombstones at the church of Isernhagen still bear witness to the work and the high standing of our family.

The son of the last *Amtmann* Balck was a student at the University of Göttingen when Lower Saxony was conquered by Napoleonic troops. Like many other young men from the electorate of Hannover, he hastily left for England and joined the 7th Line Battalion of the King's German Legion. Courage, a solid education, and his well-developed ability to draw helped him in short order to become an officer and a member of the duke of Wellington's staff, in which capacity he served in the Peninsular War in Spain and Portugal. There, with the family of Dr. Hume, Wellington's chief medical officer, the young Balck met and married Mary Grice, a friend of Dr. Hume's wife. My great grandmother, who was born on Barbados in the West Indies, was nicknamed "the Beautiful Creole." As it was customary for wives of British officers to accompany their husbands on deployments, my grandfather was born in Almeida, and his brother also was born in Portugal, in Coimbra. My great grandfather died young in 1812 in London.

After the Napoleonic Wars my great grandmother moved with her three children to Hannoversch Münden to live with her sister, who also had married a King's German Legion officer named von Windheim. They lived comfortably in Germany on their British pension. Unfortunately, my great grandmother died young, too, and her children were raised by her sister. During this time an odd change occurred. The duke of Cambridge had always shown particular interest in my grandfather, George. Every time the duke passed through Hannoversch Münden on the way to visiting his intended bride, a Hessian princess from Kassel, he ordered the two Balck boys to report to him at the post, where he would have them change his horses and where he assured them that he would do something for them one day.

Shortly after Aunt Windheim died, my great grandmother's friend, Mrs. Hume, the wife of Wellington's military doctor, approached the duke of Cambridge on behalf of the children. The duke arranged for my grandfather to move to England, arranged his adoption by Mr. Brigstock, court preacher to George IV, and bore the cost of my grandfather's education. And when my grandfather decided to enter the army rather than becoming a naval officer, as initially intended by his guardians, the duke purchased his officer's commission in the 93rd Regiment of Foot, the Argyll and Sutherland Highlanders. Even beyond that, the duke continued to provide financial support. He personally took care of my grandfather's academic education and introduced him to the premier British families.

My grandfather was at the start of a very promising career when he suffered a most unfortunate accident. During a parade on Barbados in the West

Indies he suffered heat stroke in the midday sun, and as a result lost his eyesight. Queen Victoria used her personal funds to obtain for my grandfather every possible cure and the consultation of every key European medical specialist. But it was all without result. My grandfather had lost his eyesight. He later married the widow of his brother, a Hannoverian officer who had died in an accident. She was the daughter of the Hannoverian Major General Lütgen. My grandfather retired from the British Army and lived in Osnabrück after the duke of Cambridge had secured special legislation making my grandfather a lieutenant colonel after the fact, thus permanently securing his financial affairs.

Adolescence and Parental Home

My father William[10] was an officer through and through. He was the last great tactical theoretician of the Kaiser's army, but he was also a pragmatist.[11] As a divisional commander, he received the *Pour le Mérite* and ended his military career as the governor of the Baltic Islands. As a brigade commander he was severely wounded near Warsaw in 1914.

His extensive military and general mentorship were priceless assets for me. From early on he sharpened my senses of historical and political thinking. From the age of ten on I rode with him almost daily, as much as my schooling would allow. What I observed and heard during these exercises made a deep impression on me, especially as my father always introduced me to all military questions. From early childhood, then, I grew up and was educated as a soldier. But I also learned something else from my father, something even more significant— a deep sense and understanding for the lowest ranking troops and the mistakes of our social class. From early on I had to participate as a silent listener when in the circle of friends and comrades the problems of the army and the people were discussed with grave concern.

My mother, Mathilde, came from an old and well-established family of legal professionals. Her father, *Landgerichtsdirektor*[12] Otto Jensen, had been one of the leaders of the Schleswig-Holstein uprising against Denmark and the right-hand man of the duke of Augustenburg. My grandfather also was a friend of the empress. We all looked up to him, awed by this giant patriarch. My grandmother came from a Danish officer's family. Although she had become completely German, her grandfather had been a Danish colonel. As the commander of Copenhagen he had defended the city and citadel against Admiral Nelson and Wellington—and, ironically, my great grandfather Balck. My mother balanced my father perfectly. I could not imagine a more happy marriage. She was gifted with a high academic education combined with common sense and an unusual pedagogical talent. She was a very deep influence even on my own children.

I was born on 12 December 1893 in Danzig. My father's various moves then led us to the Rhine, Berlin, Silesia, and from Posen to Thorn, where I finished school. Like all the Balcks, I was in constant conflict with school. In the subjects of history, geography, and German I was always far above average. In modern languages, mathematics, and natural science I was average. But when it came to the ancient languages I had no interest. It was only through my deep and thorough knowledge of antiquity, where my father had been my teacher and motivator, that I was able to barely maintain the necessary grades.

Soldier

Easter 1913 finally arrived. I had been accepted as a *Fahnenjunker*[13] with the Goslar Jägers.[14] I could not have picked a better unit. The officer corps and the troops represented everything that I had learned in my family home. I was completely comfortable in such an environment.

The battalion still was under the influence of its second to last commander, the father of Colonel General Heinz Guderian,[15] who had inculcated a sense of respect for even the lowest-ranking Jäger, freedom of all to express his opinion, toughness and justice while on duty, and the sense of achievement in one's accomplishments. My first commander, Lieutenant Colonel Bauer, knew how to manage and reinforce this legacy with a quiet, noble, but firm hand. The unit's noncommissioned officers corps was of extraordinary quality. Most were skilled hunters who were committed to nine years' service. Many had the *Einjährige*[16] or even the *Primareife*.[17] The officers corps was unique in its kind. Considering the small size of the Jäger branch, an unusually large percentage of its officers ended up at the highest levels of the army. These included Guderian, General Bodewin Keitel,[18] and General of Mountain Troops General Hans Kreysing. Numerous officers became division commanders. Joachim Eggeling, who served in the Goslar Jägers during World War I, later became the *Gauleiter*[19] of Saxony and Anhalt. General Stephanus was the only officer who refused to swear the Loyalty Oath to Hitler and resigned—without consequence. Almost throughout, our Jägers were volunteers. Serving with the Goslar Jägers was a special honor among the Hannoverian farmers and foresters.

A peculiarity of the battalion was the large number of *Einjährig Freiwillige*,[20] which annually approximated eighty. Since not all of them could be absorbed by the battalion, the selection for our reserve officer corps was easy. They came from all the professions, not only the foresters. To the largest extent possible, they were selected based on character. Accomplishment alone was not enough. In the test of war this selection process proved itself. There were always a number of one-year volunteers who passed the qualification to become reserve infantry officers, but declined the commission, preferring to remain NCOs in the 10th Jäger Battalion rather than become reserve lieutenants in some infantry regiment. From their ranks came many of our best officers that later received battlefield commissions. Almost all of them were tall farmers.

The Fahnenjunker received no mercy. Our training was militarily tough, but the bonding among the officer corps was very tight. What was created here, in terms of instilling values, was quite unique. My special mentor during that time was Lieutenant Hans Kreysing, who during World War II served as the commanding general of the Eighth Army.

In February 1914 I moved to the military school in Hannover. The city of Hannover at that time was quite a dangerous place for young, vivacious people. Anyone from a well-respected unit had access to unlimited credit. "Herr *Fähnrich*,[21] sir, this way and that way, please!" A flood of shady individuals was eager to take advantage of our lack of life experience. Naturally, we had been warned. But as always, this kind of warning made us just the more curious. To balance this, the commandants of the military school in Hannover were always selected based on their tough and hard-core attitudes. Our commandant, Lieutenant Colonel Waxmann, was the epitome of the Prussian officer. It was very much the toughest school I ever went through. We hardly had any free time. The pressure was so great that our teachers and instructors often stuck right with us, as their lives were no beds of roses either. But, too tough of an environment makes one callous. Excesses and breaking away to get a taste of freedom occurred like they never would have, had it not been for the mindlessness of the tough drilling. It was in a way an antiauthoritarian education.

Colonel Waxmann was clearly ahead of his time when it came to tactics. Throwing hand grenades was an activity he forced on us—one more reason for us to consider him a madman. His opinions about the defense corresponded exactly with what we later learned at the hands of the French. There were, however, two incidents of sharp altercation in front of us cadets when our tactics instructors, Captains Steuer, Rust, and Giese, openly rebelled against Waxmann.

Our tactical training area was between Hannover and Hildesheim, a place called Rusty Mountain. The village of Gross Giesen and the forest of Steuerwald lay close together and between them ran the Unsinnbach, a small creek. That area was strictly avoided in our tactical excursions.

The coming war cast its shadows. As early as 1913, when the French introduced three-year enlistment, my father told me that this meant war within the next two years. France would not be able to sustain the financial, economic, and human burden. The consequence would either be war soon, or acceptance of German political superiority and renunciation of revenge for Alsace and Lorraine.

Easter and Pentecost took me to Colmar in the Alsace region, where my father was a brigade commander. He gave me an introduction to the political problems of the local provinces, just as he had done previously when we lived in Thorn and Posen. My father understood how to win the hearts of the Alsatian people. Our instructional tour brought us to Metz, rounding out my new impressions of the eastern region. But the journey was overshadowed by signs of pending war. The assassination in Sarajevo was beginning to spiral Europe into crisis. We naturally did not speak of anything else. It would have been unnatural for young people who had chosen to become officers not to be enthusiastically waiting for the moment to finally prove ourselves.

I was lucky. Right before the outbreak of war I was able to visit with my father in Göttingen, where at the time he was leading a communications exercise as the chief of the Field Telegraph Service. And then the war broke out with an unbelievable wave of enthusiasm. All social class differences were swept away. Germany was a sea of black, white, and red flags.[22] I will never forget how a large crowd of people, mostly laborers, gave a standing ovation to General Otto von Emmich, and then marched on to the military school, celebrating us cadets with loud cheering as the future of the army. In earlier days they had been rather disdainful toward cadets.

The trust was justified. Of the 139 officer candidates at the Hannover War School, ninety lost their lives by 1 December 1916. Of those of us left in 1918, a good number were killed in World War II as general officers and division commanders. I am the last survivor today.[23]

1

1914

War Breaks Out

Much has been written about the reasons war broke out in 1914, and most of that based on the politics of the day. Much of what has been written is not very deep. The German-English differences were fundamental. In a letter to my father, the German crown prince wrote: "I am concerned with the ever increasing contrast between Germany and England. This concern increased when in conversation with King Edward VII,[1] who was always especially friendly to me, he openly expressed to me on several occasions that the differences had to be overcome one way or another. England would not allow the unilateral economic superiority of Germany for any length of time."

The fact that tsarist Russia was pushing for war with Germany and consciously drove toward it has been clearly proven by the publication of documents and files by the later Bolshevik government. According to Alexander Isvolsky, Russian foreign minister from 1906–1910 and ambassador to Paris from 1910–1917, "I am the father of this war." And according to Sergey Sasanov, Russian foreign minister from 1910–1916, "The peace-loving German Kaiser will ensure that we can choose the time for war to break out."

But what was the reason? Russia was a colonial land with vast estates in the hands of the landed barons, "the Boyars," who controlled a class of peasants whose lot only slightly improved after they had been freed from serfdom. Herein lay the seed for the coming revolution. After the unfortunate Russo-Japanese War of 1904–1905 one of the most important personalities of modern Russian history emerged as prime minister, Pyotr Stolypin. He concentrated his efforts on the right issue, the unjust land distribution. The Stolypin Reform created the independent farmers, the Kulaks. This was a large-scale reform and was very successful.

Naturally the land could only be taken from the landed barons. Their reaction came soon enough. When in 1911 Stolypin was shot and killed in the theater in Kiev, allegedly by a social revolutionary, the reform that had begun with such promise came to an end. That he had been on the right track was proven by the fact that no other social group was persecuted more by the Bolsheviks than the Kulaks.

As so often when an incompetent government is facing internal problems it cannot resolve, it seeks to overcome domestic failures through foreign policy successes. The decision to go to war had been made. Only Germany, which just recently had helped Russia by remaining neutral during Russia's war with Japan, was an immediately convenient adversary. "The road to Constantinople goes through Berlin." The German foreign ministry had continuously maintained that Russia would very likely seek friendlier relations. The Kaiser accurately countered, "The Slavs are now siding with England, by whom they were beaten in the Far East."

Germany, which could not make up its mind whether to side with England or Russia, was caught in between. Since World War I, Germans, as usual, have made Pan-Germanism partly responsible for the war. This fails to recognize the forces of Pan-Slavism in Russia, irredentism in Italy, revanchism in France, jingoism in England, and other "isms" elsewhere. It was a phenomenon of Europe's imperial age that simultaneously created the same stupidities all over Europe.

As for Germany's often blamed naval policies, they probably would have brought England to the negotiation table in the end. It is an irony that the German-English Colonial Treaty, which would have brought a great reduction of tensions and a resolution of the differences, was ready to be signed at the beginning of August 1914. "German-English relations were never better than in the summer of 1914," as Winston Churchill said in the House of Commons. And as Paul Cambon, France's ambassador to London, expressed among friends in May of 1914, "We have lost this game."

It would be interesting for the historian to analyze how German-English agreements drove the other adversaries to act quickly. It had to be now or never. As Kaiser Wilhelm II wrote after his abdication: "The French were afraid, even though for the moment they were assured of English support, that later the English would come to an agreement with the Germans at their expense."[2] In the final analysis, however, it seemed inevitable that at the decisive moment both the English and the German sides made mistakes, brought forth old resentments, and were not able to escape the traps of the previous years, including the Schlieffen Plan and English ties with France.

But these are all afterthoughts. At the time we were convinced that we had been attacked by our enemies and we were willing to defend ourselves. Somehow it leaked out that the 10th Jägers would mobilize in an accelerated fashion. To ensure that I did not miss anything, I took an overnight taxi to Goslar at the cost of 75 marks, only to learn that I had two more days. I was supposed to move out with a follow-on unit, the 2nd Field Battalion. There was nothing I could do about it. The only positive result was that I got to see my mother, who had come to Goslar for a few hours. Then she left. She later wrote my father, "Now he belongs to his comrades."

Liège

We loaded up on 4 August. Amid thundering cheers the train drove into the night. It was an earnest, sincere enthusiasm. The whole country felt that there was no other way; it had to be done. I never once saw anyone drunk during the mobilization phase. The movement through Germany was like a triumphal march; everywhere the same excitement. Germany was united.

On 6 August we off-loaded in Malmedy and continued on foot toward our battalion. Liège supposedly had fallen. We moved via Thieux toward Louveigné. In a forest the first shots rang out, our advance elements were in contact with Belgian *Franc-tireurs*.[3] The rumor that Liège had been taken was not confirmed. On the contrary, it appeared that things were not going right at the front. The supply trains of several regiments were flooding past us, all mixed up. People were telling the most horrific stories. We questioned a one-year volunteer from the field battalion who was sitting in one of the vehicles. Charging into a trench, he had received a rifle butt blow to his head, which knocked him unconscious. When the attack later advanced, he had been brought to the rear. But when we asked him about one officer or another, the answer was either "Dead!" or "Wounded!" With fixed bayonets we spent the night in the ditch along the road, numbed by the apparent defeat.

Scattered troops of the battalion arrived. They all talked about the heavy losses of mostly officers. They had stormed the Belgian trenches at night, but were then shot up by our own infantry. The mood of the troops was not really down. On the contrary, they all were mad at the Belgians. They were not real soldiers, and they maimed our wounded. After showing a white flag, they then fired on our exposed troops. Entire companies had surrendered to individual Jägers. And the Belgians were miserable shots, or such were the reports.

A battalion commander of Field Artillery Regiment Number 11 spent the night with us. We learned more from him. Six infantry brigades had been committed at night to take Liège. The most forward troops had already broken through and penetrated partially into the suburbs of Liège when heavy friendly fire forced them to retreat. The units had been completely disrupted. During the withdrawal the populace rebelled. Anyone who became separated from his unit faced potential death from ambush. Units marching through villages usually had their supply trains ambushed. Shots were fired from all the houses. When the battalion of Field Artillery Regiment Number 11 passed through Louveigné they were shot at from all the houses. The battalion commander set up one battery and destroyed the village. Horror stories upon horror stories, and all were believed.

On 8 August the situation became clearer. Liège had actually fallen. Singing, we advanced toward the field battalion, down the hill near Louveigné. A dark cloud hovered over the village with rising flames. That had been their summary punishment. In the town we encountered the first dead bodies of Belgian farmers, small people with grimacing faces full of anger and deadly fear. Cattle were running around without their masters. A few women squatted with the remnants of their belongings, staring with empty eyes. This was our first glimpse of war.

At noon we arrived at the battalion. Seven officers and 150 Jägers were dead, wounded, or missing, most of them through friendly fire. Liège has occupied my thinking repeatedly ever since. It had been a clear victory for the troops, but the mid-level and the higher leadership had not been up to the situation. Nobody except Ludendorff had shown the resolve to work through the crisis. Generals who later became highly proven leaders had failed here. What had happened? The troops had been deployed without training into this hasty attack. Night fighting was not the strong suit of the German Army. The mid- and lower-level leadership was not prepared for the required tasks. They were forced to learn on the battlefield.

That was the situation on 8 August. The Belgians were withdrawing to the west, the Germans to the east. In between lay the forts of Liège, still defended by their occupants. In the city of Liège itself, Ludendorff had a single brigade. His tough will and the recklessness of his personality had carried him through. This success was his alone.

The events of the next few days pushed us back and forth. Once again we passed through Louveigné. We were ordered to take all male inhabitants prisoner because shots rang out constantly during the night. We picked up sixty-two. In the parish rectory a bloody Hussar's uniform was found. The rectory went up in flames. Nobody thought of the possibility that the village priest might have been caring for a wounded Hussar. Despite a general sense of consternation, the prisoners were not shot, but hauled away to do forced labor.

I was a platoon leader in the 2nd Company, which I had joined. The platoon leaders along with me were Reserve First Lieutenant Nottebohn, who became a professor and noted food chemist in Hamburg, and Reserve Second Lieutenant Jung, who became the chief judge of the state court in Breslau and was also one of the defenders of that city in 1945. In 1918 all three of us returned to Goslar as company commanders, all wounded many times over. Jung and Nottebohn were among our best officers during the war.

Near Hermalle we crossed the Maas River on 14 August. Belgian government flyers were posted on the walls of all the houses, warning everyone not to approach us with weapons in hand. East of the Maas the poster warnings were a bit more ambiguous, urging the citizens to delay the advance of the enemy.

Onward into France

In the meantime we were attached to General Georg von der Marwitz's II Cavalry Corps. The French cavalry was near Ramillies Offues. Enemy bicycle troops occupied the hill. Dust was rising near the edge of a forest. Glimmering in the sunshine we could see a heavy concentration of French *cuirassiers,* still wearing chest armor and shiny helmets. Then things started to happen on our side, too, with machine gun fire reverberating and artillery firing. Like lightning the bicycle unit jumped off their bikes, dropped down, and started to fire. Horses reared as shrapnel exploded along the edge of the forest. Then we attacked. The French fired nervously, aiming too high. Then they abandoned their positions. On the hill they left some bicycles, rifles, and uniform items. The 29th Jägers took several prisoners, two artillery pieces, and two machine guns. As we stormed up the hill, a farmer fired from behind from the roof of his house on our advancing battalion. The farmhouse was set ablaze, and as I noted in my journal at the time, the farmer hanged himself. Those were the facts we were convinced of then. Today, I am certain that the puffs of smoke from the roof of the farmhouse were shots from French scouts who were aiming too high. But who knew then that the impact from an infantry rifle bullet created a sharp bang and a dust cloud?

A Jäger detachment was formed from the 10th, 4th, 9th, and 7th Jäger Battalions.[4] Our commander took overall command, and Captain von Rauch took over our battalion. I became the adjutant, even though I was still a Fähnrich.

On 19 August we made contact with the enemy again. French shrapnel hit the tightly advancing columns. I had to clear my way back to the battalion with drawn saber through the quickly withdrawing cavalry. Toward the evening we were positioned south of the Bois de Buis. Several times I rode across the battlefield from company to company through artillery fire, withdrawing cavalry, and French patrols.

Up until the fall of Brussels we received the latest Belgian newspapers every day. At first the Belgians reported they were winning near Liège, then west of Liège, then between Liège and Brussels, then near Brussels, and then it was over. We were most amused with the portrayals of morale. The feared German *Uhlans*[5] supposedly were giving themselves up by the hundreds because of hunger. We were portrayed as just a bunch of hoodlums that were kept together by the whip, and not wanting anything to do with war. Berlin was in revolution and the Kaiser had been murdered. The Belgian press, of course, had nothing but high praise for the Belgian and French soldiers. "What human beings! Such character!" wrote a correspondent about French soldiers near Dinant. A German prisoner was quoted as having said, "The Belgians, they're not just soldiers, they're lions!" A Belgian corporal reportedly killed single-handedly all the members of an entire German battery. Cannons towed by thirty-two horses had supposedly arrived in Liège. "A good prey for our brave soldiers." General Otto von Emmich supposedly had lost his *Pour le Mérite* for filing false victory reports . . . so on and so forth.

The German cavalry was moved to the right flank and the enemy withdrew from Belgium. We were fighting against French cuirassiers. Dismounted, they defended themselves in an orchard. Their shiny helmets and chest armor, red trousers, and high boots with knee pads hindered them from handling their carbines and fighting on foot. How irresponsible it was to send human beings into a war in 1914 with equipment that had not changed since the Napoleonic Wars.

On 24 August we seized Tournai, fighting against French territorial defense units. We captured one general officer, one colonel, and six hundred soldiers. The numerous enemy dead proved the superior marksmanship of our Jägers. Neither backyards, nor street fighting, nor poor terrain could stop the momentum of our attack. Shots rang out along the streets and impacted with a sharp bang into the houses behind us. We again heard cries that the Belgians were shooting at us from the rear. Supposedly shots were even fired at us from the steeple of the cathedral. In the confusion and tenseness of the street fighting and the anger about the supposed involvement of civilians in the fighting, a cannon crew grabbed a bunch of them and used them as human shields to move a gun forward. The human shield disappeared as the barricades and the houses crumbled under the close-range artillery barrage. I was able to prevent an artillery volley directed against the cathedral. Throughout my life architecture was my hobby. My war hysteria was slowly melting away.

Tournai

Once we were in the city we received the following order from the cavalry corps: "Take as hostages in Tournai the mayor and two hundred citizens, to include the highest church official plus twenty priests. Bring them to Ath. Disarm the citizens' militias; collect all the weapons; seize all the cash boxes; remove all the flags; destroy all the post, telegraph, and rail installations; demand 2 million francs in reparations; threaten to destroy and burn the city, to include all monasteries and churches. Execute this threat at the least sign of resistance by the citizens or in the event that German military personnel come under fire."

This order was given because some of the citizens had shot at German troops from the rear. The staff of the 10th Jäger Battalion was charged with the execution of the order. I picked two *Oberjägers*[6] and twelve Jägers from my old platoon as a security and covering force. The remainder of the battalion and the cavalry moved on and only my commander, Captain von Rauch, and I remained behind in the city, negotiating with the mayor. His face showed his shock. He finally wrote the note authorizing the tax collection. Policemen with bells ringing were sent into the streets. In the city hall a cashier's cage was erected as young and old arrived to pay. Only gold and silver was accepted, but that was easier said than done. Inside city hall a huge table was set up with our twelve Jägers sitting around it, and bags full of gold and silver were emptied out as the Jägers counted and counted. When it came to the silver we quit. We counted and weighed one bag, and then we estimated the weight of the other bags from that. The gold pieces, however, had to be counted individually. A cavalry supply unit coming through helped out. Any help was welcome. How easy it would have been for a 100 Franc coin to disappear into a boot. We could have never prevented it. But in the end it all added up correctly to the last cent. German ethics and morals probably never again rose to this level. No one ever thought of threatening disciplinary action before the process started.

There remained the two hundred hostages to be taken to Ath, among which was the very old and invalid bishop. I recommended to my commander to use a train, and we assembled an engine and three cars for the hostages. I got into the engine and the expedition toward Ath started to move. My commander took two automobiles full of gold and silver along the same route and informed follow-on units that the approaching train was not enemy.

We all linked up again in the market square in Ath. We cleared a house and then the hostages were brought in. Oberjäger Giessen along with his twelve men remained in Ath as the German commandant. The mayor of Ath was made responsible for the security and the rations for all. The gold and the silver were handed over to the commissariat of the IV Reserve Corps. A few weeks later Oberjäger Giessen caught up with us again. He had accomplished everything flawlessly, and he even had a letter of appreciation from the town of Ath attesting that he had performed his duties carefully and energetically, although all by himself inside enemy territory. The bishop and the mayor of Tournai also thanked him in writing, emphasizing how tactfully and carefully he had accomplished his mission. The commandant of the relieving garrison also wrote to us, praising our people. Those were our Oberjägers, all of them trained hunters and foresters. No better NCOs could be found anywhere else in the German Army.

The English

After we accomplished our mission in Tournai we were eager to move forward to our battalion. Behind us, the streets of Tournai were littered with French uniforms and weapons. The French territorial brigade had thrown away anything they could. We pressed on. At 1700 hours, three hours after the seizure of Tournai, we stood in formation. The II Cavalry Corps had the mission of cutting off the English retreat. Consequently we marched as fast as we could. At 2130 hours we crossed the French border. After another twenty-five kilometers we had a short halt of two and a quarter hours near Marchiennes. Then we set out again as dawn was breaking. At midday we had another four hours' rest, then we pushed on another eighteen kilometers. We finally bivouacked at St.-Hilaire, after having marched fifty-five kilometers within twenty-four hours.

Near Carnières we ran into supply units, we heard cannon fire, and we asked our way toward our battalion. West of Beauvais we found it, on the attack against the English. Their forward positions had been overrun, and the first English dead were in the otherwise empty trenches. In their khaki uniforms they were hardly distinguishable from their surroundings.

Gently and without cover, the hill in front of us rose to the crest line between the villages of Cattenières and Fontaine-au-Pire. There was no cover at all for the attacker. As our men closed in at seven hundred meters, there was still no sign of the enemy's main position. Only our dead and wounded were proof that he too knew how to shoot. Slowly the attack continued, as four hundred meters, and then three hundred meters separated us from the adversary. I was sent back to report to the commander of the cavalry corps, General von der Marwitz. I returned with the order not to continue the advance. The leading elements of the infantry were in contact. I was just behind the fighting positions of the battalion staff when the hill exploded to life. The English jumped up and stormed forward. They hit the ground after making short advances into our fire. Then from our side came the familiar order: "Fix bayonets and advance quickly." It was an unforgettable sight. Just as if one man had stood up, the German line raised, officers and NCOs with drawn sabers far in front. Everybody stormed forward in a rush and overran the English position. Recklessly we pushed toward the retreating enemy. Farther into the hinterlands, the road near Ligny was full of retreating English columns. Artillery took up positions among us and fired into the withdrawing adversary. Then it was all over. The utmost that human nature is capable of had been accomplished.

What had led to this assault? On the English side Field Marshal Sir John French, as he later stated in his report, had decided on 26 August to halt the fight "in order to prevent total annihilation." The English launched a number of limited attacks to facilitate breaking contact. The commander of our 1st Company recognized what was happening. Senior Lieutenant Kichheim was a veteran of the fighting in Africa. As the English reinforced their forward lines, Kichheim realized that if they managed to do that we would be lost. So, we started moving forward. On command, everybody jumped up and the adjacent units followed. We carried the day.

With just a few Jägers far ahead of his company, Kichheim ran into forty Englishmen and was hit in the neck by a bullet. The following day we buried 50 officers, Jägers, and Oberjägers of the 3rd and 10th Battalions, together with 150 English troops. Some 250 to 300 unwounded English prisoners remained in our hands.

We had fought against a tough enemy. In some positions he had fought to the last man, without giving up. And as soon as he had disengaged, he withdrew in a calm and organized fashion. The prisoners shook our hands: "You are great guys. We never thought you could do this." As a British General Staff report later noted about the attack of the 10th Jäger Battalion, "Losses did not stop the German infantry of 1914." Of course, we had fought on the side of the English against Napoleon, and "Waterloo" was inscribed on our cap badges.

The engagement at Fontaine-au-Pire remained a lesson for me throughout my entire career. A successful attack is less costly than a failed defense.

On to the Marne River

The battalion moved into the cuirassier barracks in Cambrai. When we left the next day the battalion looked a little odd. Almost everybody wore a small red, white, and blue feather hackle on his cap, which normally adorned the helmets of the cuirassiers in parades. White cuirassier gloves were also very much sought after for the march into Paris.

We marched behind the cavalry. Several French territorial divisions were thrown against us and were decimated. When things went against them, they just stripped off their uniforms and put on their civilian clothes. Back in Tournai we had run across a shoemaker who, in spite of the fighting and the noise, was sitting in his shop busily hammering on a boot. There was a lot of laughter when someone noticed that he was still wearing red trousers. During those days my commissioning paperwork to lieutenant finally reached me. I actually had been promoted when we mobilized.

The Jäger battalions that were attached to the cavalry were authorized a truck pool. We never saw ours. Only the 4th Jägers had theirs, but the vehicles were used for all kinds of purposes, not for moving the troops forward quickly. It is odd how the troops do not know what to do with a modern concept if it has not been trained for and rehearsed. What all these Jäger battalions could have accomplished if they, secured by their bicycle companies, had been moved forward by their motorized elements. The General Staff officer who had thought this one up was too modern and practically oriented for his time. Nobody understood him.

There was a similar example during the Franco-Prussian War of 1870–1871. The French *mitrailleuse*[7] was a weapon that gave the French the tactical upper hand over any enemy. For security reasons, however, the weapons were not issued until after the mobilization. Neither the troops nor their leadership knew how to use them. Their chance for victory had been gambled away.

The Battle of the Marne

On 4 September we crossed the Marne near La Ferté–Jouarre. Since the bridges had only been haphazardly repaired, we had to leave behind all nonessential vehicles. From a hill near Jouarre the Eiffel tower greeted us on the horizon. There was Paris and victory. Near Coulommiers we bivouacked in a barn with the staff of the 2nd Cavalry Division, which we were attached to. It was very interesting to listen in on the numerous incoming reports and radio transmissions. The big picture was beginning to form. We saw in our heads how the Second Army to our left was engaged in heavy fighting and how the French advancing from Paris were breaking into our right flank.[8] We followed the heroic fight of the IV Reserve Corps under General Hans von Gronau and lived through the excitement of how the corps of the First Army executed a forced march to provide him relief. The crisis was mounting, as we clearly could recognize. The cavalry of the First Army now stood alone in the gap that was created by the right flank inner move of the First and Second Armies. Slowly the enemy was coming to life. The English Army turned around and pushed into the gap.

Things had been calm near Coulommiers. We were alerted on the morning of 6 September and stood at alert on top of a hill south of Maupertuis, near a chateau and a road fork. A perfectly straight road ran south through a forest. Behind us to the left were a few large haystacks, and close by a herd of grazing goats. Again and again English cavalry patrols tried to observe our positions from the forest. Suddenly, the English horse artillery approximately fifteen hundred meters away moved forward on the road and turned toward the right. Some of the mounted gunners fell to our machine gun fire, but the English battery soon started to fire on us. We moved back to the hill north of Maupertuis. I was the last to leave our forward position and moved back on a bicycle, when all of a sudden I started taking heavy, close-range fire from among the herd of goats. Some Englishmen had hidden there all this time.

But the German advance was over and the retreat from the Marne began. (In 1940 I just happened to be at the same spot again. Everything was unchanged. The haystacks were still there, and so was the herd of goats. That time, however, we were not headed toward Paris; we were coming from there.)

Slowly we withdrew toward the north, as the English put increasing pressure on us. An infantry brigade with supporting heavy artillery arrived. The Marne front was to be held at all costs. Crossing a negligently unguarded and undestroyed bridge across the Marne, the English cut deep into our defensive lines, creating a new and dangerous situation. Undoubtedly the two cavalry corps under General von der Marwitz did not master the situation, which influenced significantly the decision to withdraw.

The German cavalry was committed incorrectly in 1914. It was too weak on the right flank and too strong in the Lorraine region, where it did not belong at all. Its true accomplishment was its offensive reconnaissance, attacking and pushing back every enemy cavalry patrol. The captured prisoners provided an insight into the enemy situation and resulted in significant reports to the higher leadership. The enemy's cavalry failed to produce such results. He was blinded by the aggressive attacks launched by our young cavalry officers. Consequently, the French Army command for the longest time did not realize the extent of the threat from the German right flank.

Some of the cavalry units were led brilliantly on the operational level. The operational leadership of General von der Marwitz was superb. Nonetheless, the troops' tactical proficiency and their equipment were inadequate. The units did not have enough machine guns and artillery, and had no field kitchens. Not used to fighting dismounted, the courageous cavalry regiments were doomed to failure when they were attacked along the Marne, and with huge consequences in the following days. The fact that the German cavalry shared these deficiencies with the cavalries of most other armies of 1914 excuses nothing. Only the English and the Russian cavalries were up to date. The latter especially was capable of executing a wide range of battlefield tasks.

Withdrawal

The die was cast. On 10 September at 0530 hours we stood-to in Coulombs, ready to march north. All the roads were clogged with supply trains and ammunition convoys that were all moving without orders. There was no getting through anywhere, and nobody knew what was going on. Only one thing was clear, the First Army was moving back. Around 0830 we slowly started moving. The convoys and the unit march columns moved forward side-by-side in jerks and halts. Added to this was the insufferable feeling of the unknown. There were no orders for reconnoitering, for trail parties, or for anything else. Finally, upon my insistence, we sent a bicycle patrol back to our start point. *Gefreiter*[9] Bertz returned and reported that the English had started to pursue us along a parallel course. Around noon they caught us as we were crossing a barren flat hilltop. English shrapnel started exploding right amid the columns and the convoys. We could see clearly the English gun crews servicing their pieces in an open, uncovered battery position.

Wild panic broke out among the supply clerks, and all efforts to bring them under control failed. Like a wild storm everybody rushed on, creating disorder in the organized formations. The heavy ammunition carriers of the foot artillery[10] raced across the fields. One soldier fell off the driver's seat and his head was smashed by a wheel. Others unhitched the horses, jumped on them two men at a time, and disappeared. I was able to stop an ambulance with my pistol drawn and force them to load a severely wounded *Feldwebel*[11] of the Grenadier Guards Regiment.[12]

The battalion was still a little farther behind. I rode back to meet them and redirect their route. Even here we encountered artillery fire, but one by one we got through. Our machine gun carriers often had to be pulled up the steep embankments with four horses. The English pushed hesitatingly at first, later more strongly with cavalry. Our 4th and 1st Companies that covered our retreat beat back every attack. Not a single Jäger who became separated from his unit considered giving himself up. In numerous small engagements they fought their way back to the battalion. Thank God the pressure of the English soon decreased.

In a village where the road split, I remained behind with several troops to redirect the ones that were separated. I acquisitioned wine and food and was able to revive the spirits of a fair number of these brave souls. The battalion reassembled in Ougly, in the forest of Villers-Cotterêts. Our retreat had been superbly covered by the 4th Company under Reserve Captain Richter, a forester in civilian life. We also had the 4th Machine Gun Detachment and a radio signal unit with us. We did not know anything about the friendly or enemy situations. As always in this kind of situation, one saw and expected the enemy everywhere. The signal unit was not able to establish contact, and our staff detachment was gone.

Finally, I was given an automobile and the mission to establish contact with anybody. I drove from hill to hill, observing as I went. I finally reached Villers-Cotterêts, where I found a scene of peaceful camp life. As I drove into the town, large columns of infantry were marching through. Our assumption that the First Army had been beaten was false. On the contrary, they had been victorious and only had to be pulled back because of the fatal gap that opened up between the First and Second Armies.

We almost had been annihilated only a few kilometers away from an intact infantry division. The infantry regiments I encountered had fought on the left flank of the First Army. They all looked very well. Their strength situation was better than ours, and we had believed that they had been almost completely destroyed. All of a sudden Oberjäger Wolters was standing in front of me with our complete supply train, which he had brought there without any losses. How he accomplished that was inexplicable.

"Supply train is ready, the meals from the field kitchen are prepared!" he reported. Soon the battalion arrived. The reunion with Wolters was a happy one. We bivouacked north of Villers-Cotterêts. Jäger August Bode from the 1st Company appeared in a tailcoat and top hat and started entertaining everybody. You could not kill the spirit of these men.

On 12 September we were in positions as the reserve of the II Army Corps at Terny-Sorny, near the Aisne River. The Battle of the Marne was over. Schlieffen's plan had failed. Right from the outset it had had two weak points. One was political. An attack through Belgium made conflict with England inevitable. Even Napoleon on St. Helena had said: "*C'est pour l'Anvers que je suis ici.*"[13] But the political element was not Schlieffen's strong point. Grand Admiral Alfred von Tirpitz thought as much, at any rate. Furthermore, the strategic thinking was driven purely by a Continental perspective, and England was not even considered to be a serious threat factor. A large portion of the responsibility for the failure lay with the leadership of the Reich. Chancellor Theobald von Bethmann-Hollweg—his memoirs speak volumes—had resigned himself to a military *fait accompli* in his highly compartmented and bureaucratic thinking. He avoided any kind of analytical debate concerning the military plans. One only had to compare the often sharp and difficult exchanges between Moltke and Bismarck in dealing with similar questions. Nor did the Kaiser play the role that was traditionally his, as umpire and balancer between civilian and military matters. Wars are won and lost politically, and we entered into this one handicapped by the most unfavorable political concepts.

The second weak point was that the Schlieffen Plan, even though it allowed for operational surprise, naturally had to lead to a rather difficult situation in the Paris region. The first supply crisis should have been anticipated there. The French infrastructure of Paris as a world metropolis offered all sorts of operational opportunities. The system of reinforced forts on the eastern city limits allowed the French to accept risk by leaving the front line between Belfort and Verdun uncovered. They superbly used that to their advantage, especially as the German leadership lacked the fortitude to overcome the crisis. It would have been quite possible to prevail, even after the serious operational mistakes made during the border battles and the withdrawal of two corps from the decisive right flank.[14] Schlieffen's warning "Make the right flank strong!" had been forgotten.

Would persistence in the Battle of the Marne have brought about the decision in the West? In hindsight the answer can only be "possibly," or "maybe." Even if there had been a clear victory, the railroad and the supply situation would have forced an operational pause in the action. This was especially necessary because the essential operational arm, the cavalry, had been marched to death and could no longer sustain the necessary operations deep in the enemy's rear. One thing is certain, however, the continuation of the Battle of the Marne would have left us in a much more favorable position to conduct future operations. It also would have been a tremendous moral advantage had we succeeded in breaking Paris away as the political center and the hub of the French infrastructure.

The withdrawal from the Marne had been initiated by Lieutenant Colonel Richard Hentsch, an extremely intelligent and gifted General Staff officer who had been sent as a liaison to the First and Second Armies by Moltke. The controversy surrounding him to this day centers on the following issues: What was his mission? Did he overstep his authority? Did he analyze the situation correctly? The issue was never whether he had been qualified to do this mission. Intelligence by itself is a beautiful thing in some professions. In military life intelligence alone is not enough. In fact, it can be downright dangerous, as it is often coupled with pessimism. Intelligence in the military arena requires a strong and decisive character as a balance. Hentsch did not have what Clausewitz had called the "harmonious union of powers."

A man like Hentsch was an excellent advisor to a leader, but not a leader himself. Ludendorff near Liège had been different. Personalities like Hentsch are militarily dangerous. Highly accomplished as a support player, they find themselves in a position sooner or later where they have to take responsibility and make decisions—and then they fail. The failure to heed similar alarm signals led directly to Stalingrad and Paulus.[15]

The problem of the talented support player was not a new one. Russian general Mikhail Skobelev once told his chief of staff, Alexei Kuropatkin, "You will always accomplish great things as the second in charge; God help Russia if you are ever put in charge." But during the Russo-Japanese War of 1904–1905 Kuropatkin was the man in charge.

The German situation in 1914, however, was a complicated one. Since France had fortified its borders between Switzerland and Belgium during the 1880s and 1890s, there was no room for operations in those sectors. The only available maneuver room was in Belgium itself, with all the known political disadvantages. What other choice was there? A frontal attack against the French eastern border would have shifted the decision from the operational level to the tactical level, with doubtful success and a high price in blood. Furthermore, the necessary, immense artillery assets were lacking for such an option. That plan was a nonstarter.

What remained was defense in the West and attack in the East, based on continuous fortification of the German western border. As shown during the Russo-Japanese War, and as the French later demonstrated to us, barbed wire combined with the machine gun gave the defense new and extremely strong capabilities. Politically this solution offered the possibility for France and the western powers to declare peace and, therefore, deny England the pretext to declare war, which it urgently needed to do. "A passive fending off of enemy strikes" would not have been in contrast to the classic teachings of Clausewitz. As a prerequisite, however, we would have to have had a unified, strong civil-military leadership that could have maintained things under perfect control. But such was completely missing on the civilian side. As Bismarck once said, "Just wait until you have a real bureaucrat as a chancellor; you will have some real problems then."

The Kaiser, who often was right on target, wanted to redirect the army at the last moment to march east, in order to keep England out of the war. But it was already too late. Missed opportunities could not be recovered, and the dead hand of Schlieffen still lay heavy on the course of world history.

Wisdom always comes after the fact. It is impossible to prove that England would have been kept out of the war if Germany had issued a proclamation toward France along the lines, "We will not attack, but we will repel any attack; and we will respect the neutrality of Switzerland, Belgium, Luxemburg, and the Netherlands." There is much to support such a theory, but there are many points against it, as noted in the letter from the crown prince to my father.

The main point I want to stress here is the necessity of a unified civilian and military leadership, and how flexible both must be to avoid getting sucked into unpredictable situations that turn previously established plans into disasters. Bismarck was able to do this. Always under the premise of a free rein in all areas, he was able to act in accordance with the situation and at the right moment.

The Race to the Sea

The following weeks were marked by the "Race to the Sea." Since no one could come up with a large-scale, unconventional, operational solution, Falkenhayn initiated a process of constantly reaching for an open flank. But since the French had a better and more intact railroad network, they were always able to get there first. Every envelopment we attempted ended in a blocked frontal attack.

After eight days of bivouacking without tents in the mud and rain as the reserve of the II Army Corps, we were withdrawn and set out to march in the direction of Chauny. Motor vehicles arrived to pick us up. With a sinister look on his face, a transportation officer got out of the lead car and reported that a French cavalry division had attacked Chauny and everything was ablaze and destroyed. As we advanced, however, we found everything very peaceful in Chauny. A small fire had triggered the shocking reports. And then another transportation officer stumbled in, saying that the rear commander was reporting a French infantry brigade advancing from Noyon toward Chauny. But that was unlikely, because the headquarters of the XI Reserve Corps was located in Noyon. Later we learned that the ominous brigade in Chauny turned out to be a column of prisoners. Rumors chased rumors. The more incredible it sounded, the more it was believed.

We were handed off to the IX Reserve Corps and were committed to heavy fighting the next day at Bethancourt, without artillery support. We took half the village with intense street fighting, after which our detachment commander broke contact. We then attached ourselves to the 7th Cavalry Division. A Bavarian infantry brigade arrived, preceded by some of the wildest rumors. We were quite disappointed that they looked just like any other human beings.[16]

On 21 August the Bavarian brigade was attacked in Lassigny by a Moroccan division[17] that was twice as strong. We were in an especially good position to attack the Moroccans in their flank, but our battalion commander did not budge and we eventually marched off toward the II Cavalry Corps. As darkness set in, a Pomeranian infantry division[18] arrived. They had marched the sixty kilometers in one stretch with just one two-hour rest period, an impressive accomplishment. The incident at Lassigny had some consequences. When we reported to the battalion commander in Plessis-en-Cachleux a written communication had just arrived from Major General Karl von Schoch, the commander of the Bavarian brigade: "How the Jäger Battalion, during the hour of the greatest danger, could abandon my 15th Regiment in order to follow an order that had been given without knowledge of the situation by Higher Cavalry Command 2 requires an explanation."

My company commander, Captain von Rauch, unshaven for weeks and sporting a sinister, graying full beard, jumped at the battalion commander, who was standing there in his pajamas, looking quite comfortable. Rauch yelled at him that he had compromised the honor of the battalion.

"Captain von Rauch, I will court-martial you!"

"Fine, then I can finally tell what was really going on."

All the pent-up anger of the last few weeks exploded from the upstanding von Rauch. Finally the battalion commander agreed to drive immediately to the

Bavarian general and to patch things up. That was a characteristic of the 10th Jägers—honest and candid to higher authority, even at the risk of being blunt.

The advance units of the Sixth Army[19] arrived from the Lorraine area just in time to prevent a large-scale envelopment by the French on our right wing. We continued marching north. Two French battalions were pushed south toward us by the Prussian 11th *Landwehr* Brigade,[20] which came from the Wedding district of northern Berlin. While we attacked from the south, we observed the Landwehr skirmish line moving forward from the north. We were establishing a cauldron, like in a hunt. Eventually the cavalry rode into the cauldron and cleaned it out with their lances. I then rode through the cauldron toward the Landwehr. Frenchman lay next to Frenchman. Our Landwehr soldiers were something else. How much use we could have gotten out of them if upon mobilization they had been equipped and manned in the same manner as the active and reserve units. This would have been possible without much effort.

The French had the advantage most of the time because of their better railroad net. The slowly arriving elements of the Sixth Army were thrown into the fight piecemeal as they were de-trained, and without being concentrated. They attacked, defended themselves, and attacked again until the lines became stagnant and trench warfare set in. We finally got hung up on the right wing of the I Bavarian Army Corps. Continued forward movement would have required reinforcements, and we should have been withdrawn under French pressure.

On 26 September we stood on alert at Flaucourt, near a sugar refinery with a tall chimney. Then artillery fire started hitting our covered positions. Someone supposedly saw signals from the high chimney being sent toward the enemy. A search found French soldiers in civilian clothes in the flu that led from the fireplace to the chimney. They were members of the home defense, allegedly on the way to their positions. A summary court-martial convicted them to death, and the sentence was executed. Everyone was convinced of their guilt, and still . . . for a long time I had a bitter taste about it. The witness statements were watertight. The judges were seasoned, calm, older officers, some of them with law degrees. Myself, I was never comfortable with the conclusion that they had been Franc-tireurs. I had a bad feeling about it, but at the time I would have sworn to the facts as they had been presented.

Years later I was sitting with a friend of my father's, one of our most experienced generals of World War I and an extremely intelligent man. Near Liège during night fighting in a forest, as he was at the point of a group of soldiers storming the Belgian lines with saber drawn, a soldier stumbled and stabbed him with his bayonet in the ribs. With the cry, "Fusiliers, take revenge for your dying general," he sank to his feet and awaited the hero's death that never came.

He told me this story and added, "In my brigade sector there were no more Franc-tireurs in Belgium."

All of a sudden it became so clear to me. Since then I have studied again and again the Belgian Franc-tireurs war. The Belgians were justified in their conduct by the Hague Convention on Land Warfare. But they have always declined to refer to this convention and insisted instead that the Franc-tireur war only existed in German imagination.

Studies of unfortunate events, such as in Leuven,[21] attribute the German reactions to nervousness and war hysteria. The counterargument is that any such hysterical reactions would have been impossible in the brilliantly trained and superbly disciplined German Army.

What then is the truth? War hysteria and the resulting panic can undoubtedly grab hold of the best and most disciplined troops, especially in the early days of a war. Nobody is immune. I was a witness to such events often enough. Reports and statements from participants should be considered with skepticism. On the other hand, it is impossible to dismiss hard evidence. Communication lines were cut and German soldiers suffered gunshot wounds. The latter clearly were inflicted by civilians, because shotguns were not normal issue in any army.[22] Near Leuven wounds from shotgun pellets were well documented. Clearly, civilians there had fired on German soldiers, and consequently all the other witness statements gained credibility.

Thus, I come to the following conclusion. A Franc-tireur war did take place in some areas, encouraged by the often unclear declarations of the Belgian government. But many, many instances of partisan warfare did not occur, and can only be explained by a war hysteria reinforced by the many Franc-tireur stories from the 1870–1871 war. Everyone was prepared for the worst and expected to experience it.

Back at Flaucourt, meanwhile, the Jäger battalions attacked Dompierre–Becquincourt. A wide flatland descended toward the twin villages. Slowly the attack gained momentum. The staff was positioned near a barn, from where we had good observation of our zone. We saw a general with his aide, calmly walking along the trenches under heavy fire. "He must have lost his staff and is lost himself," I said. "You know," Captain Wagner, our acting battalion commander that day, said to me, "Judging from his hand gestures, that could be Father Balck." He knew my father from Thorn. It was him. We were very happy. I was able to spend the afternoon with him. My father said, "I actually expected you to be in the front lines."

After my father left I resumed my adjutant tasks. Dompierre–Becquincourt was supposed to be taken by a night attack. The 4th and 9th Jägers would conduct a frontal attack while the 10th Jägers moved around from the left and took the town from the rear. Night was coming on. The enemy occupied farms on either side of us, but we bypassed them without triggering an alarm. After making a sweeping movement we arrived at the southwest entrance to the town without firing a shot. To the left and right we encountered high walls and hedgerows, which we had to work our way through. The 1st Company fell in on the road and we initially thought that the town was free of the enemy. Then flashes erupted from the entrance of the town and bullets whizzed through the streets. A French battalion deployed across the road in two lines and opened fire. Losses! Confusion!

I grabbed the rifle of a Jäger standing next to me and rushed forward. Four paces in front of the French line our attack broke down. I hit a wall to my immediate right and then crawled back on all fours. Uninterrupted, the French fire whipped along the street. Finally we all found each other gathered sideways behind a hedgerow. Of everyone who I had started out with, I was the only one uninjured. Cries like "Password Kaiser!" and "10th Jägers here!" were immediately picked up by the French and reverberated through the night. Finally everything was quiet. We heard steps in the street and then a French captain stood in front of the hedgerow. "*Rendezvous!*" he called out. A shot rang out and he dropped.

The 2nd Company was now storming ahead, and our group started to move too. We entered the farmhouses and cleared them one after another. Since Liège we had learned quite a bit. Out of one basement a Frenchman brought thirty of his comrades with him. We had the village, but we knew nothing about the 9th and 4th Jägers. In order to clarify the situation I was sent back to the Bavarian brigade, to which the three Jäger battalions were currently attached. I worked my way back and forth through French security and returned after a few hours with the information that the night attack had been cancelled shortly after we were in position to jump off. The order had not reached us in time, and now we were ordered to withdraw immediately.

By daybreak we were back in our initial positions with our walking wounded and sixty prisoners from a Nancy regiment. After collapsing into a death-like sleep, we were relieved by the 4th and 9th Jägers. We then worked our way toward Dompierre. Reserve Captain Richter, one of our best, took over command of the battalion. He immediately initiated the attack. The staff was in the most forward positions, and Dompierre was under heavy fire. Without firing a shot and at a quick pace, the battalion closed the nine hundred meters to the village. The enemy laid down a lot of fire, but it was all too high. Suddenly our forward line broke into a run, shouting. All along the front the butt ends of French rifles stuck up from the turnip field. They had no intention of engaging in a bayonet fight.

Becquincourt fell quickly. An open field lay in the direction of Dompierre. I crossed the field with one Oberjäger and found myself ten meters behind a tightly packed French trench. The French *Chasseurs Alpins*[23] were firing into the right flank of our advancing 2nd Company. From behind a gate I fired into the trench from the standing position. At first they did not notice us, then they turned toward me. But I had the advantage. Finally several rifle butts appeared in the air,[24] and they gave up. We then stormed down the village's main street as the fleeing Chasseurs Alpins emptied out into the middle of the street from the farmhouses left and right. Some we shot, but most of them surrendered. Dompierre was ours and the right flank of the I Bavarian Army Corps was secured. We had captured unwounded some five hundred men of the 11th and 5th Chasseurs Alpins, and we buried approximately two hundred more. The 11th Chasseurs Alpins had been virtually destroyed. They had put up a good fight.

Heavy artillery fire then hit the village, killing some of the wounded. We dug in and sent out patrols. The French artillery fired at us at just about the same time each day. In the evenings the regimental bands moved forward, and across the wide fields of the Picardy the sounds of the "grosser Zapfenstreich"[25] rang out majestically. On 18 October we started moving again. At Peronne we loaded up and started heading toward Lille.

Ypres

Near Ypres we attempted an envelopment one more time. On the German side the newly reorganized Fourth Army consisted of hastily trained war volunteers, reinforced by infantry units and artillery that had been used in the seizure of Antwerp. They met in a frontal engagement against English forces that were brought up from the Aisne River sector. But the flanks of the opposing armies had reached the sea. There were no longer any operational options. Decisions were reduced to the tactical level of attempting a frontal penetration against a well-dug-in and especially courageous and tough adversary. The question was whether the newly raised and totally inexperienced German units were up to such a task.

After an unbelievably wonderful rest break in Lille we returned to the army-level cavalry that attacked the English at Ypres through the gaps between our Fourth and Sixth Armies. We advanced swiftly toward the English positions through the overgrown terrain. The 1st Bavarian Jägers were to our left, and the 4th Jägers to our right. During the night, an English bicycle company launched a surprise attack. With his saber in his hand, their courageous leader, a Captain Peel, fell into our position. We found on him a regimental newspaper that described the composition of the divisions we were facing, and the English positions were clearly marked on his map. He also was carrying a detailed divisional order. But none of this made it up to higher headquarters, where it could have been analyzed and blood could have been spared. It all ended up as war souvenirs back home. Both sides were still very much like children at this point in the war.

Our advance was heavily flanked by high ground on our right. It had to be cleared first. That was done superbly by the Wedding column, our old friends the Prussian 11th Landwehr Brigade, supported by artillery fire and our machine guns. We were able to see every detail of the action. Scottish guard units with fixed bayonets glistening in the sun launched a counterattack. Supported by well-timed and -aimed artillery fire, the Scotsmen flooded back. Their officers drew their sabers and forced the troops forward, but our Landwehr troopers did not budge. The enemy dead lay next to more dead in front of their positions.

Three army corps replaced the army-level cavalry. The attack was scheduled for 30 October, led by the XV Army Corps. We were assigned narrow attack zones. Closely behind every battalion a battery was dug in, and following heavy artillery barrages we were supposed to attack at 0900 hours. The tension was intense. Nobody was familiar with this kind of attack. Our artillery often fired too close and into our own positions. At 0900 the Bavarian Jägers on our left were at the ready. But from the right an order was passed along: "Stand down until 0945!" Nobody knew where it came from, but a critical pause developed and the English started to get active.

My battalion commander sent me forward. I ran into my old 2nd Company and yelled into their position, "Everybody listen to my order . . . up and forward!" Not a Jäger lagged behind. In short order we overran three successive trench lines. We were in front of the fourth trench line when white flags appeared, and then disappeared, and then appeared again. As shots rang out, the commander of 2nd Company, Captain Radtke, collapsed right next to me. He had been shot dead through the heart. I was hit in the left hip. I stumbled and fell right in front of the Englishman who had shot at me, and I was able to kill him with a pistol shot as he was rechambering his rifle. Then the attack just swooped right over us. The waving of the white flags followed by the fired shots had enraged our soldiers. No quarter was given.

In hindsight the conduct of the English can be explained. It was not, as had been assumed at the time, an intentional ruse. Rather, it was an indicator of the crumbling resistance. Some of the English were ready to give up and raised a white flag; others were not and continued to fire. The consensus within the English line shifted back and forth erratically.

Artillery galloped forward and went into battery in the open positions between us. A reserve regiment moved ahead to the sound of music. Then one of the walking wounded escorted me to the rear. A medical NCO from my father's old brigade patched me up: "So honored to bandage the son of our old brigade commander." In the evening I arrived at an overflowing field hospital in Lille and a few days later I was on a hospital train to Leipzig.

Leipzig meant nothing to me. My mother lived in Hameln at that time. So, in Schwerte I had them take me off the train. Two Red Cross members loaded me onto a stretcher and put me in a freight car of a local train that brought me to Hameln. There they took me across the town to my mother's house. They rang the doorbell, the door opened, and I was home. My telegram telling her I had been wounded arrived after me.

Back Home

Germany was still beautiful then. Everybody supported the soldiers; everybody was proud of them. Everyone was proud to make sacrifices. There was no pessimism at that point. The people wanted victory. My wounds healed quickly. Shortly after Christmas I reported back to duty at the replacement depot in Goslar.

Our replacement battalion also had made history—of sorts. On the day of its activation it locked up the corps deputy commanding general in an arrest cell. It all happened because of the so-called *Goldautos*,[26] which were crisscrossing Germany to transfer gold from France to Russia. According to Kühlmann[27] in his memoirs, this scheme to circumvent all normal money transfer channels ran counter to all human logic, which is why it was so successful. But once the word got out, war hysteria became rampant. Every village was turned into a fortress, street intersections were occupied, and everybody was hunting down the money on wheels. Even the 10th Jäger Replacement Battalion got caught up in it. North of Goslar an Oberjäger along with a military police detail were manning a road intersection. They had been briefed specifically to be on the lookout for a prominent Russian spy in a German uniform. As a car approached they halted it and found an old general officer without an entourage in the back, and concluded that must be him.

"Your Excellency, your papers, please!"

"I do not have them. I left my mobilization orders at home. I am the newly assigned deputy commanding general of X Corps."

"That's impossible. You are the Russian spy."

Two Jägers got into the back of the car, the Oberjäger got in right next to the driver, and two Jägers rode on the running boards. When the party arrived at the barracks in Goslar they were met by the adjutant, who himself was a recently mobilized civilian.

"Deputy commanding general? That is utter nonsense! Why don't you just admit that you are the Russian spy. Be prepared to be executed."

"By thunder! Can't you call Hannover? They are expecting me there at any moment."

But when the call was put through to Hannover the answer was: "Deputy commanding general? No, impossible, there is nobody like that. Just keep him locked up. Something is wrong there."

Protesting to no avail, the cell was locked behind the general and a guard with loaded rifle was posted.

"Can't you call Blankenburg? Everybody knows me there."

After a number of hours another telephone call came from Hannover. There was a deputy commanding general after all. "Oh my God! What have you people in Goslar done?"

After a while a car pulled up in front of the guard shack with the mayor of Blankenburg, a uniformed policeman, and the general's daughter with his mobilization order. All doubt was gone; they had locked up their own deputy commanding general. How were they going to get out of this one?

The replacement battalion commander appeared in his service dress uniform, with the adjutant right behind him. The guard at the confinement facility stood at present arms. The key was turned in the lock, and salutes were rendered. Frosty silence. Without a word His Excellency got into his car and drove off.

There was little else pleasant to report about the replacement battalion. Everything was in the hands of overaged reserve officers who were full of energy and good intentions, but lacking in the ability to lead and manage the daily duties and to keep control of the organization. The incoming field troops were generally of low quality. The Oberjägers too were overaged, but they were vastly superior in the performance of the daily duties to their officers, and willing to use that to their advantage. The first indicators of an ugly *Feldwebel-wirtschaft*[28] were emerging.

I saw my father frequently. He had been severely wounded in Poland at the head of his brigade and was in a military hospital in Hannover. I started feeling the urge to get out again. Strangely enough, I wanted to get to Russia. We also were providing replacements for the 22nd Reserve Jäger Battalion in Poland. There I could take command of a company. My battalion was in Lille and the situation in the West was at a complete standstill. After some back and forth administrative haggling, I was off to Poland. The vastness of the East. Russia. The Russian people. A new, foreign world was calling to me.

2

1915

On the Rawka River

On 1 February the troop train left Goslar. We were stuck on it for days. In Leszno, where we sat for twenty-five hours, I had the waiting hall of the train station cleared and the floor covered with straw to give the troops a chance to stretch out. In Rzepin I bought meat with coupons. We already had been without rations for more than twenty-four hours. The supply situation was a long way from its standard high state of professionalism.

We finally arrived in Skierniewice, where the 22nd Reserve Jäger Battalion was resting. The unit had just changed commanders. The new commander was Major Hopfen, a mounted Jäger from Trier. His strength was that he cared about the troops. If there was anything lacking when it came to supplies, he would immediately rush off to division and not hold back on his opinions: "The Uhlan Regiment that is currently resting and not doing anything just received this or that. But my Jägers who have been in constant action are not getting anything! Why not?"

The staff of the 5th Cavalry Division was actually intimidated by him, because of his reckless support of his battalion. But we were not at that point yet. In February 1915 the rations were excellent. When we were in the front lines in the trenches everybody received an additional quarter pound of bacon as a so-called trench bonus, and the goods sent through the postal system easily fed the troops for another few days. In the summer, however, most of it spoiled . . . and later there was nothing left.

The XXV Reserve Corps, to which we were attached, was engaged in the quiet trench war along the Rawka River. It was one of the so-called *Kinderkorps,* like the ones that had to pay such a high and unnecessary blood toll at Ypres.[1] The XXV Reserve Corps had been sent east immediately and had more time to prepare and mature in easier fighting. It had then been engaged in heavy fighting near Brzeziny and, in coordination with the 3rd Guards Division, had broken up the Russian encirclement. The 22nd Reserve Jäger Battalion had had a substantial role in that. During the night fighting in the forests our reserve Jägers, war volunteers, short in stature and insufficiently trained, had overrun elite Siberian regiments whose members were twice the size and had twice the physical strength of our troops. We were all very proud of what they had accomplished.

In time, regular officers were assigned to the XXV Reserve Corps, and many of the overaged old guard disappeared. My father too had been reassigned to that corps, and he was severely wounded at the head of one of his brigades. He intended to fix the weaknesses of his units through his personal example. Our Reserve Captain Rockstroh, who was the commander of the 22nd Jägers at the time, accompanied my father as he was trooping the line outside the trenches under heavy enemy fire. As he later told me, "I finally jumped into the trench. I did not care if your father thought I was a coward. I could not do it." And Rockstroh was a courageous man, over fifty, a forester, who was not even of mobilization age anymore. He had volunteered out of a sense of honor and national pride. He never held back, although he continually let us all know that he hated war and was disgusted by it. His exemplary courage and sense of duty were worthy of even greater respect. Later that summer, when our attack failed during a heavy engagement, he never took cover, saying, "It would be shameful to come out of this unwounded." Shortly after, he was severely wounded by a shot in the stomach. He received the Iron Cross 1st Class for the breakthrough at Brzeziny, but he did not wear it. "I would be too ashamed in front of my Jägers, who did the same that I did." He was a unique person.

The corps commander, General of Infantry Reinhard von Scheffer-Boyadel, ordered me to report to him and invited me to dinner. I sat across from him, to my left was his chief of staff, Colonel von Massow, to my right the duke of Coburg.[2] His Excellency[3] von Scheffer toasted me, and when I got up, he also rose and said, "One must rise in honor of a knight of the Iron Cross 1st Class." In October 1914, I had received one of the first one hundred 1st Class Iron Crosses awarded.

The war at that point was calm and unthreatening. We were occupying various positions, mostly one to two kilometers away from the enemy. The only unpleasant place was called the "Witches' Caldron," a bridgehead across the Rawka River sixty to one hundred meters from the enemy that was constantly pounded with artillery fire. Fortunately, the Russians considered firing at night as a waste of state property and a punishable offense.

Although things were quiet during the day, a lively war between the trenches began at night. The Russians used every trick in the book, including confusing us with German speakers and conducting silent ambushes from the rear. It was not always easy to keep our troops alert. They were innocently unsuspecting. I tried time and again to be in the right place when incidents happened, and often was able to prevent the worst. We never lost a prisoner to the Russians; on the other hand, we frequently captured one. You could only shake your head whenever a scrawny war volunteer, who was nothing more than a child, came back with a huge Siberian who was following him dumbfounded and most willingly. But the prisoners were actually quite intelligent. Once, two Siberians were brought in. One was an older NCO with eight years of service, the leader of a patrol. When questioned, he stated that he was not allowed to say anything. Then all of a sudden he asked, "How much do I get for everything I know? Is it true that I can get money for my rifle?" When asked whether they received a bounty for bringing in a prisoner of war, he turned to a lieutenant and said, "I would get 50 Rubles for you." The other one was severely wounded. He spoke German and French and was grateful for the good treatment. His superiors had told him the Germans were animals.

Routinely one of the first questions we asked the prisoners was, "When will you start your revolution?" Not one of them comprehended. They all were absolutely loyal to the tsar. For us the question was motivated by the silent hope that our having to fight against the overwhelming Russian masses would end: "Sooner or later they will have to have their revolution."

News of important events spread quickly. When Przemyśl fell, the Russians manned their trenches and throughout the night they hollered, "Przemyśl is ours, Przemyśl is ours!" The losses inflicted on them by our instant response with artillery fire were probably not at all minor, but the Russians apparently did not care.

At the beginning of May our breakthrough offensive near Gorlice–Tarnow began. We had anticipated it for weeks, and it was hard for us not to act like a bunch of children. Toward the end of April 1915 we were sent to camp at the Warta River near Poznan. New divisions consisting of three regiments were formed from units that had been detached from the old divisions.[4] We were integrated into the newly formed 103rd Division, commanded by General Ludwig von Estorff, called "The Old Roman." He was an experienced veteran of the fighting in Southwest Africa.

In the Rear of Temesvar

On 27 May we departed the encampment near the Warta River. We passed through Breslau[5] and Oderberg among cheering citizens, but nobody knew where we were headed. Austrian troop transports headed to Italy crossed our path. The soldiers appeared to be in excellent condition. We speculated that we might be headed for the same destination. Near Marchegg we turned toward the east, passing through Budapest and Szeged. The Hungarians welcomed us with open arms. Their admiration for Germany was unlimited. They expected the most incredible miracles from us. Once we got past Szeged the direction would be obvious. If we turned left we would be heading into the Bukovina region; if we turned right we were going to Serbia. Everybody betted on Bukovina, but we turned right in the direction of Serbia.

Our first camp was in Antafalva, a large, clean, friendly Slovenian village. Then we reached the first German settlements and we crossed the Temes River. We would have done anything for our German brethren. In Titel on the Tisza River we were loaded into boats. Four large freight barges tied together and pulled by a tug brought us down the Tisza River and then up the Danube. As far as we could see everything was flooded. The Danube seemed even more majestic than usual. On our left the hills of Fruska Gora were covered with linden forests, easily recognizable by their aroma. It was an unforgettable picture. We unloaded in Ilok. Our destination was Erdevik, a half-German village in Syrmia. Anyone who ever heard of Syrmia knew about its industrious German population.

We were supposed to assemble and coordinate near the forward line that ran along the Sava River and the Danube. It was deadly quiet at the front line. In Mitrovica, right in the combat zone, life seemed rather peaceful. For two months not a single artillery round had impacted. So far, the result of the campaign was a perfect stalemate. The Austrian offensive had collapsed and the Czech regiments were blamed. The Serbs that had entered Syrmia, however, had been encircled and destroyed.

The Serbs were supposed to be courageous and tough soldiers, especially in the defense. The attack was not their favorite form of maneuver. Supposedly, they did not like to fight in the open flatlands. In the mountains, however, they were invincible. Their artillery apparently was an elite organization. The Serbian officers supposedly were well educated and supported the political ideals of their country, personally courageous, and always positioned at the most dangerous spot on the battlefield. The higher leadership, too, was apparently very good and did not fail, even in critical situations. Clearly, this was not what we had been expecting.

Movement to Indija (a small town thirty-five kilometers northwest of Belgrade) made it possible for us to visit Belgrade, or rather to Semlin. The Austrian area commander, General Phüllöps, had invited us. Looking across the river into Belgrade left a lasting impression. We were able to observe life in the streets as if we were in the middle of peacetime. Only the remnants of the railroad bridge over the Sava River and the two well-camouflaged naval guns close by reminded us that we were still at war. It was hard to tear ourselves away from those magical images. Naturally, we conducted plenty of training while we were there. It was a different battalion that got on the train on 12 July, well rested, well trained, and highly motivated. We had gotten along well with the local population and the allied army. A new, bigger world had opened itself up to us, and we were awed by the new things that we saw. But we also learned how to deal with it. It was a maturing experience. A cosmopolitan upbringing was not the strength of the German officer. When they were among themselves the Austrian officers referred to us with the somewhat ironic phrase "Prussian Charm."

Galicia

We were headed north via Budapest. Beyond Homona we saw the first signs of war: trenches, shell craters, burned-out houses. The fields and the harvest had not suffered much. Russian POWs were bringing in the harvest and were filling in the trenches. Galicia is a beautiful region; some of it reminded me of Thuringia. The Polish villages, however, all appeared impoverished. East of Przemyśl the flatlands started, interspersed by some rising hills. The Russians had only really destroyed the railroad infrastructure there.

We off-loaded in Zimna Woda, and then marched through Lemberg,[6] a city with horribly paved roads, some beautiful palaces, and run-down and extremely dirty houses with even dirtier occupants. We were rather disappointed by this area that was supposed to be known as the "tsar's missing crown jewel." We did, however, agree with the Russian general who had said as he was marching into Lemberg that he was looking forward to this city of beautiful women. We did, indeed, see some rare beauties.

We marched toward the north and joined the Austrian Army. As soon as we reached Ukrainian settlements the houses became cleaner and vermin-free. Near Sokal the Russians attacked. Disregarding losses from forced marching, we were committed forward. As the army operations order read: ". . . as long as the division can attack with single artillery pieces and companies. . . ."

The roads were horrendously sluggish and muddy. The artillery had to replace their horses frequently. Meanwhile, we pressed forward at a painfully slow pace toward the increasingly louder sounds of battle. As we moved forward, we passed Austrian battalions and batteries resting contentedly along the roads, which prompted some bitter catcalls. Then we were halted in Moschov. Our help was no longer needed. The Silesian and Moravian units of the Austrian Landwehr regiments had resisted successfully against multiple attacks by five Russian divisions.

The 32nd Infantry Regiment from Meinigen was assigned to the 103rd Division and one of its battalions had been attached to the 5th Cavalry Division for some time now. Since the 5th Cavalry Division was located close to us, we replaced that battalion and now became part of the 5th Cavalry Division.

On the Bug River

With our attachment to the 5th Cavalry Division we had hoped to be committed to more mobile warfare, but were highly disappointed. The Falkenhayn-like strategy was to try to roll up from the bottom the huge bulge in which the Russian troops were sitting, instead of tying the knot and choking them from the top. We were able to push the enemy back, inflicting heavy losses on him, but we also expended a lot of energy doing so. The fact that the three divisions on alert near Belgrade had to be brought east and thrown into the mayhem was not a sign that the Ninth Army leadership of the day was handling this correctly. The troops were aware of this and discussed it to the last man, hoping that Hindenburg and Ludendorff would be called to lead the army.[7]

The situation for us went back and forth along the Bug. Finally on 8 August we stood at Studianka[8] facing the Russians. From 1300 hours on things became deathly still in the direction of the enemy lines. Some of the villages went up in flames, a clear sign of a retreat. One of the patrols we sent out had not moved far enough forward, so I took them out again myself. Up to Studianka it was possible for us to conduct a covered movement through the high-standing grain fields. Then we reached a fifty-meter area without cover directly in front of the Russian position. We could not tell if it was manned or empty. As I advanced with my patrol on a broad front, a shot rang out and dirt kicked up in front of me. I hit the ground with my rifle stock to my cheek, when just behind me a runner named Brauner laughed out loud. He had accidentally pulled the trigger. It was a most uncomfortable situation.

Nonetheless, the question whether the position was occupied or not was answered and everything remained calm. But I could not resist. I continued on toward Vladimir–Volynskyi with a handful of soldiers. We reached the edge of the town along with our advance cavalry patrols. All the villages and the grain in the fields were burning. Smoke obscured the landscape and the town of Vladimir was a sea of flames. On the high ground beyond the town we could observe vehicle convoys of the inhabitants being escorted to the rear by Cossacks. Through binoculars I could see how the Cossacks occasionally used their Nagykas[9] to beat the people, who tried to duck the blows.

Vladimir fell quickly, but what we found bore witness to the way the Cossacks had terrorized the town. Nothing was left but burning embers. Before they left, the Cossack commander had summoned the elder of the Jewish community and told him they had orders to burn Vladimir down. He then asked how much the people would be willing to pay to prevent the burning of the town. But after a large sum of money was paid, all the women and girls were raped and the town was still burnt down.

From all the corners of the town we could hear the meek cheers of the liberated Jews. They brought tobacco, food, and anything else for our troops. That was the only time I experienced something like this. Even for the Russians this must have been an act of brutality above the norm. "We will do anything for the Germans," the townsfolk said, and they really did. When we turned Vladimir into a bridgehead, the people dug trenches voluntarily. After a short time, however, they resumed their old ways. Remembering that they had always been tradesmen, they started overcharging us.

The days in Vladimir were idyllic. We lay in our trenches and the enemy was far away. Only forward outposts were to our front. In the sector around us cavalry patrols from both sides moved back and forth, shooting at each other. One had to be careful in the somewhat obscure terrain. The Cossacks typically appeared with arrow speed and overran an inattentive guard post or guard relief, creating havoc with their beautifully designed Cossack sabers. Incidents occurred at night as well. Unexpected shooting from the direction of the adjacent unit woke me up one night. Approximately one hundred meters in front of me the Russians were shouting commands. As flares went up we saw four or five Russian cavalrymen. Ten paces in front of our foxholes shots rang out, hitting right into our midst. Horses reared as they turned around and collapsed, with their riders dropping. One of them was lying in the grass, quietly moaning, but when I reached him with our medic he was already dead. We had been hit by the Russian 3rd Uhlans. The next evening a Russian cavalryman came from the rear with his hands in the air. He had been the leader of the patrol. He had passed through our lines hanging onto the side of his horse, but then the horse was killed. He did not know anything about the whereabouts of the rest of his patrol.

Slowly the Russians moved back, and we followed. On 21 August we were near Rastow, in front of the Turja River. A Russian cavalry regiment rode off toward their own rear under our artillery fire. They withdrew expertly, keeping their losses to a minimum.

A large plain with no cover stretched all the way to the Turja. The Russian positions were on the other side of the small river. With dismounted cavalry and Austrian troops on our flanks, we attacked at noon on 22 August, supported by the fires of our three mounted batteries. As we were moving forward four artillery rounds exploded in front of us, tearing apart the leaders on my left and right. The Russians knew exactly where our officers were positioned. "Forward, Move! Move!" the officers yelled as we covered more ground. "Drop! Up! Move!" We inched toward the enemy. The soldiers followed the commands just like on the parade ground. But it was horrible whenever the rounds exploded in our midst. Since we were taking the most losses when we had dropped to the ground, and we were only taking artillery fire, I ordered the troops to rush ahead individually. The leading rifleman would dig for cover, then jump forward and the others would follow.

The Russian artillery fire became more sporadic and our losses decreased, but now we were within the range of the enemy infantry. We were hit hard from the left flank. We brought up two machine guns from the rear and put them into position on a small hill, from which they engaged the enemy on our flank. That helped. We moved forward faster. Four hundred meters away from the enemy we dug ourselves in. The adjacent units were far behind us. We had managed to advance more than a thousand meters into the uncovered terrain that descended toward the enemy. Night fell and it became chillingly cold. The next morning the enemy was gone.

We followed toward Kovel, which we reached the following evening. Three cavalry divisions were alerted for the night attack. Two of them were Austrian, but they did not participate. So in the end, only we, the Jägers, and the riflemen of the Hussar Brigade actually attacked. I was the commander of the reserve company. Ahead of us we heard the shouts and the firing and saw the burning houses. I was ordered to take a cluster of buildings that loomed in the dark. We took the objective and preempted a counterattack in the process. The next morning the enemy had disappeared. The estate had some good Crimean wine and sparkling wine, and we also had stormed a still intact bordello. The company was almost impossible to control that night.

We were now diverted to the north to cut off the retreating Russians from Brest-Litovsk, a hopeless undertaking. If you turn the sack inside out, you cannot tie it off at the top. The Falkenhayn-like strategy ended up having repercussions down to the lowest levels. We ran into the Russian rear guard and defeated them in a tough fight in a forest. I was hit in the back by a ricochet and collapsed with the dysentery that I had been suffering from for days. Along with a wounded Hussar officer I was hauled off in a cart driven by a Jäger. An ambulance was supposed to be waiting in Ratno. It really was there, but it had an empty gas tank. On we went toward Makary. Masses of refugees with mixed-in turncoats were streaming out of the forests and marshes, returning to the villages that they had been chased out of. There was nothing in Makary, so we went on to Malorita. Finally we arrived at a field hospital after three lonely days on the road. We were nicely received and then we were sent onward to Wlo-dawa in a mail truck.

A dysentery hospital is not a happy place, especially when it is located in crumbling, former Russian barracks that were built before hygiene had been invented. Even white linens and self-sacrificing care could not change that. My roommate was an officer in the Polish Legion,[10] so at least we had some interesting conversations. After ten days I had had enough. I was almost back to normal anyway, so I headed back to the front. After three days I reached my unit.

The 22nd Jägers had suffered heavy losses during a failed attack on a Russian rear guard position on 29 August 1915. The attack broke down only a few paces in front of the enemy. My company had lost sixty men. Among the fallen was a young protestant pastor, Franz Tongers, an East Frisian war volunteer from the town of Norden. His father was a teacher there. The man had been a true Christian. He helped his comrades whenever he could. He dug positions for them; he went on guard duty for them; he carried their field packs when they did not feel well. His worship services were always packed, even though I never ordered anyone to go. He spoke at the graves of our fallen comrades, gave advice in family and relationship questions, and took care of the soldiers' correspondence. He was an upstanding man who never hesitated to come to me and tell me what was right or wrong, or what should be done differently. Where he found the time and the energy to do all of this was a mystery to me. He turned down the opportunity to attend a reserve officer candidate course. He felt that as an officer he would not be able to do justice to his spiritual mission. When the Jägers got ready to storm the enemy positions, he was the first one to jump up and shout, "Let's go, they are escaping!" Those were his last words. Then he was hit by the bullet that killed him. In general, the pastoral service in the field was not well respected. But this man had been unique. You could not have found a better role model.

In the Rokitno Marshes

We pressed forward into the Rokitno Marshes, a sandy, swampy area the size of Lower Saxony and Westphalia together. The marshes were covered by alder trees and pine forests and were speckled with smaller and larger clearings. During the summer everything was dry and accessible. But when the snow was melting in the spring, it all turned into one big lake. The only features that stuck out were the roads and a few hills fifteen to twenty kilometers apart that the villages were built on. During the summers the villagers herded their animals into the forests and the clearings, and in the winter they withdrew to the villages. The cattle and the horses were small and tough. The pigs looked like their wild boar cousins.

The dark and foreboding villages were constructed from wood, using no nails. Only a wooden church with a green roof and a golden dome gave the whole image a little bit of color. Wooden crosses three meters high marked the cemeteries. Whatever the people needed they manufactured themselves, from earthen housewares to fur coats and brown shirts. Shoes were unknown to them; instead they wore sandals made out of birch bark. Only their knives and axes were made out of metal, which they used very expertly to cut and shape timber. There was very little farming going on, but a lot of beekeeping.

The land was dotted with estate manors. While the farmers were Belorussians, the owners of the estates were Polish nobility, who often were married to ladies-in-waiting of the Viennese court. Wolves, bears, elk, wild boar, and deer lived in the forests. As two of my Upper Silesian Jägers were moving forward through the forest one night, something big and dark suddenly moved in front of them. One of them yelled, "The devil, the devil!" and fell to his knees and started praying. The other one shot and dropped a huge elk. Many years later when I saw the Everglades in Florida, I was reminded strongly of the Rokitno Marshes.

We pressed forward into this terrain. At first only German and Austrian cavalry faced the Russian cavalry, mainly their 3rd Cavalry Division and 3rd Caucasus's Cavalry Division. They were excellent troops, brilliant fighters on foot as well as on horseback, and masters of the skirmish. We nicknamed their leader "Mad Arthur." We were dealing with the commanding general of the Russian Cavalry Corps, General von Güllenschmidt, who had made a name for himself operating behind Japanese lines during the Russo-Japanese War.

We were supposed to throw the Russians back behind the extensive north-south railroad line between Wilna and Kowno. Its loss would split the Russian armies in two, plus we would gain access to the line. The fighting was most peculiar. My company was attached to the 11th Cavalry Brigade. We fought in open forests with no other units close by. We could hear by the firing that they were somewhere. The enemy to our front were Cherkes[11] in long, black coats and tall black sheepskin caps, who would fire and disappear. If we followed we would run into well-placed machine guns firing into our flanks. At the same time we could hear the cheering of mounted and dismounted Cherkes and Cossacks. Our losses were small, but one really had to pay attention. As soon as we started receiving fire from the front, we instantly covered our rear with fire. That handled most situations. Once I was positioned with a squadron of the 8th Dragoons in a high forest. The Russians were storming at us from all directions. A giant Cossack came slashing into the infantry soldiers with his Nagyka, until he was shot. At the same time Cherkes attacked the mounted artillery battery to our rear, which shifted their trails and broke up the attack. The marsh that the Cherkes had crossed had been considered unpassable by us.

Often I found myself in an isolated position with my company, nobody to the left or right or rear. For a young officer it was excellent schooling and I was proud that we accomplished every task. The company received an unusual measure of recognition. The fighting intensified as we brought up our infantry.

Unfortunately, they were not used to this kind of fighting and not up to it. We dug ourselves in, forming a circle around Sheliesniza. For the first time in weeks my company was actually living under roofs and finally in the reserve. I even had time to read my Shakespeare. Then suddenly shooting and yelling broke out, as our infantry started falling back: "The Russians, we are encircled!"

I had a hard time organizing my people and getting them into position. We halted the withdrawing infantry soldiers in place.

"But our lieutenant told us to fall back."

"Well, ours told us to keep you right here."

With those words two Jägers knocked an infantry NCO flat. Directly behind us in Sheliesniza all hell broke loose, with artillery fire, burning houses, and yelling. To our front the advancing Russians were clearly silhouetted against the burning buildings. I was moving back and forth behind the firing line. Quite a few of our troops who were on the verge of losing their nerve had to be snapped back into focus with a kick of the rifle butt. As ordered, I withdrew toward Sheliesniza, and no enemy followed. At the edge of the village a mixed bunch of cuirassiers, dragoons, and infantry soldiers was standing around. Half the village had been taken by the Russians.

My company had not suffered any losses, but my copy of Shakespeare was taken by the Russians. At three in the morning we were moved back to Lubaczow, where we slept like the dead. The infantry, meanwhile, had counterattacked and retaken Sheliesniza. One of Crazy Arthur's runners fell into our hands. He just rode over to our lines. By the time it was over our total losses, missing, killed and wounded, came to approximately one hundred men and two machine guns.

The fighting flared up again around Kuchozka Wolja. Together with two infantry companies, my Jäger company was cobbled into a combined battalion and attached to the Hungarian 11th Honvéd[12] Cavalry Division. Flanked by Hungarians in dense forest, my company prepared to attack. The fusilier battalion to our right was commanded by the marvelous Hungarian Captain Gömörry. We completely surprised the Russians, speedily overrunning their positions and capturing three machine guns. We pursued them for three kilometers through the forest. We surprised and annihilated one company clustered around their field mess. In the hands of our Upper Silesians the entrenching tool became a battle axe. Again the Cossacks slashed into the retreating Russian infantry with their Nagykas, but were not able to stop them.

Then crisis struck. The wild chase had created chaos among all the units. Our infantry was not trained well for forest fighting. The Hungarian hussars were hit by a counterattack and fell back. Then we were hit by a counterattack from a Cherkes brigade. They charged toward us on foot like devils, brandishing their curved sabers, stopping to fire, and then charging on. Some of them carried lances. After a few minutes their deadly courageous attack stalled, broken up by the Hungarian artillery. But all efforts to rally the Hungarian hussars to move forward again failed, and we ended up falling back with the fusiliers to our initial positions. Actually, I had to make that decision myself. The Hungarians suddenly disappeared without notifying us.

After it was all over my company returned to the 22nd Jäger Battalion. It had been an exhausting time. It was very rare for a single company to be left to its own devices to operate for weeks. We received plenty of recognition. I was especially proud of the fact that my company did not have a single unaccounted soldier, and our overall losses were relatively low. A close-knit company welded together for life or death returned to its battalion.

Partisan War

The alliances were falling apart. Our forward posts were positioned along the Weslucha River. Whenever you stepped into the cold autumn night you could hear the wolves howling. My company was positioned behind the forward observation posts, again attached to the 11th Cavalry Brigade, which consisted of the Life Guard Cuirassiers and the 8th Dragoons. We had developed a great relationship with the regiments of the 5th Cavalry Division. They were all first rate. They had learned how to fight on foot and the excellent officers and soldiers always did what was necessary.

Two of the regiments stuck out in particular. The 10th Uhlans, superbly led by Count Bredow, and the Life Guard Cuirassiers, possibly Prussia's best regiment. Relations between the officers and enlisted soldiers in both units were excellent. If they came from the same region and had shared their youth together, they naturally remained on a first-name basis. The officers were to the last courageous and prudent. They accomplished everything with great calm. Everyone was consistently friendly and polite. The Life Guard Cuirassier Regiment was the standard for Prussian gentlemanly behavior and culture. Even the revolution did not affect them. The regiment stood together as a bulwark in the defense of Silesia against Polish insurgents.[13]

Back in Kuchozka Wolja, meanwhile, we busily improved our positions and collected winter supplies. We found numerous mass graves where the Russians had buried their dead from the previous fighting. The numbers of dead among the Russians could not be compared to our losses. Twenty-to-one was hardly accurate. Our designated quarters were in the large twin village of Kuchozka Wolja. A wide-open area separated the two parts. My company was positioned in the northern part. When the guard post woke me up at 0400 on the morning of 3 November telling me that South Kuchozka was burning, I thought perhaps one house might be on fire because of stored ammunition. But then artillery rounds started falling and hand grenades exploded. A few bullets whizzed by us. Then the brigade command post called: "The Russians are in the village. Send in everybody you can spare!"

I sent one officer with four squads, thinking that this would be a small patrol type of engagement, and I went back to my cup of coffee. Then the next phone call came: "Send all physicians and medical personnel." A man in a German uniform was picked up. He could only speak Polish and had been observed leaving town in the direction of the enemy. He turned out to be a totally disoriented labor reinforcement. One of his comrades wearing only a shirt and a bayonet stab wound in his butt was found five kilometers away by the cuirassier regiment in Pavlinov.

What had happened? South Kuchozka was built partly on a hill and partly into a valley. Our positions and wire obstacles followed the crest line. The troops were all positioned behind the wire obstacles. Only a labor reinforcement company had been positioned outside of the wire, secured by two guard posts. The unit had arrived later and nobody wanted to move them. We thought nothing would happen to them anyway. The townspeople had been issued black and white identifying armbands and were also working on the positions. Typically, the Russians had spies among the locals and knew everything about us. On the night of 3 November they were ready to strike. Several hundred Russians led by local guides with the black and white armbands split up as they reached the front of the village. One column entered the labor reinforcement camp. Stabbing everybody with bayonets, they cut through the wire obstacles and entered the town. Another column reached the artillery position, which fortunately had been repositioned the night before. From there they moved into the town, silently stabbing artillery and machine gun crews in their billets. Led by the locals wearing the black and white armbands, the Russians moved toward the officers' quarters and tossed in hand grenades. Other Russians went into the barns, cut down the guards, and set the barns on fire. The wounded were thrown into the flames. When we started to establish a resistance and formed a hasty counterattack, they broke off their attack with a whistle command, leaving behind six of their own dead and one seriously wounded. Our losses were around one hundred, fifty of them dead. Many of the wounded, who later died, had suffered five or six bayonet stabs. Seventy-five horses had burned to death. This brilliant surprise attack was conducted by the Russian Uhlan Guards.

In place of the labor reinforcements we received an infantry company. They arrived all excited, went into position, and then shot up a mounted guard detachment, who they thought were Russians. Higher headquarters quickly purged both the guilty and the innocent in this incident, but that could not bring the dead back.

The 5th Cavalry Division switched positions with an infantry division and ended up in the area south of Pinsk. We also changed commanders. In place of Major Hopfen the 22nd Jäger Battalion was taken over by Count Gilbert Hamilton,[14] a former Swedish Guard cavalry officer who had joined the German Army at the beginning of the war and who then served in the Life Guard Cuirassier Regiment. We were very fortunate with this nobleman as our commander. He had volunteered to serve the German cause out of a deep sense of conviction. He remained a faithful, paternal friend to me to the end of his life. He also remained loyal to the Kaiser, even serving as one of his adjutants in exile. I owe him much.

In the meantime, the Russians continued their partisan warfare, raiding the headquarters of the adjacent division, which had taken up positions in the village of Newel. The Russians knew this well through their organized intelligence gathering system and our inefficiency. Singing German songs, they entered Newel from the rear, beat twelve officers and more than one hundred men to death, and then disappeared with the divisional commander and the military chaplain. They had not dared to kill the latter because of the cross on his chest.

Now we started forming *Jagdkommandos*.[15] I was given one that was assigned to my company from the 5th Cavalry Division. It was formed on 7 December 1915, consisting of four officers and 130 soldiers. Many of the soldiers were from Upper Silesia. They were mostly first-rate people from the various cavalry regiments, but a few of them were the types the parent unit hoped it would never see again. My unit, however, had many who were particularly good, reliable, and courageous. I still remember some of them. *Wachtmeister*[16] Reiss of the Life Guard Cuirassier Regiment was from the German colonies in southwestern Africa. He was calm, collected, and honest. From the same regiment I had a Dutchman who had volunteered to fight with us. During World War II he wrote to me that his son was fighting in Africa under Rommel. And there was Sergeant Gralke from the 8th Dragoon Regiment, a typical Upper Silesian. He was faithful like a dog and had the natural instincts of an outdoorsman. He could smell the enemy. When he said that there is someone sitting behind a bush, it was true. As a point man on patrols he was untouchable.

Toward Pinsk there was a huge marshland, approximately ten to twenty kilometers wide and deep. Right in the middle there was a sand dune with a strong Russian outpost, which we estimated at company strength. We reconnoitered the situation forward of Pinsk without any local guides. I occupied a point four hundred meters behind the Russian position and observed them for days, with the never tiring Sergeant Reiss beside me. We learned every detail of the setup of their obstacles and dugouts, the placement and strength of their guard posts, and the timing of their shift changes. We also determined that they sent out their listening posts much too late in the evenings. For this raid I still had the Jagdkommando of the Guard Cavalry Division attached to me. I set out on 28 December with eight officers and two hundred soldiers. In the high reeds wading through knee-deep, ice-cold water I moved during the day as close as four hundred meters to the unsuspecting Russians. I left the Jagdkommando of the Guard Cavalry Division there and continued in the light of dusk with my own troops across the Russian line before they had it secured. Once we were behind the Russian lines we swung wide and turned toward our objective . . . and then all of a sudden we did not know where we were anymore. It was a horrible moment. I stopped all movement and tried to get oriented. I sent out a patrol into the most likely correct direction. After long minutes of fearful waiting Lieutenant Eberding returned and got us reoriented. He had spotted a Russian cutting wood out in front of his dugout.

Now everything went very fast. We answered the challenge of a Russian guard post in Russian. The man was very close to me, but Sergeant Gralke brought him down with a bayonet thrust to the neck. When we entered the enemy position they could not reach their rifles, which had been racked outside their dugouts. They threw hand grenades at us, and we in turn cleared the dugouts with hand grenades. It was a horrific job. A Russian emerged from one dugout with both his hands gone and the skin ripped off of the right side of his face. Horribly mutilated bodies were piled high in the dugouts. We pulled sixteen prisoners out of two of the dugouts. The other Jagdkommando, meanwhile, had charged ahead on my light signal and had entered the position at the same time. Unfortunately, there was a little chaos in the process. One huge dragoon guard cut into one of my people with his bayonet. Luckily the thrust hit the ammunition pouch and my soldier remained uninjured.

Peoples are different. The Russians conducting such an operation would not have made a single sound, and everybody would have listened to his superior. On our side the situation became quite frenzied. Once the fighting was over we started our withdrawal with the prisoners and our dead and wounded. We were guided by a telephone wire that we had laid for that purpose. By 0130 hours we were back in our positions. The surgeon, medical personnel, and vehicles were waiting for us.

Several days later I led another surprise raid of the village of Gorowachia. We had crossed the barely frozen Struma River and were already in the rear of the Russian lines when we were discovered. Reluctantly, and without having accomplished much, I had to give the order to retreat. The days of the Jagdkommandos were numbered. In a divisional zone of operations there might be one or two objectives worth a surprise raid. Anything beyond that is a waste of effort. Realizing this to be the situation in our sector, I requested the disbandment of the Jagdkommando. My request was approved. I returned to my own battalion and took over the command of the newly formed machine gun company.

3

1916

The Dead Front

Things became deadly quiet. Wire obstacles and improved positions had put an end to the search and destroy [Jagdkommando] raids on both sides. Our priorities now became the further improving of our positions and logistics. We collected mushrooms, planted vegetables, and raised chickens to provide the machine gun crews with a nice daily dietary supplement. The battalion tasked me with establishing a mess hall. I took an unorthodox approach to that task as well. I drove to Warsaw, where I enjoyed the Russian emperor's ballet dancers, saw Puccini's *Tosca* in Polish, and developed economic ties with a Jewish businessman who superbly delivered supplies on time to the new mess hall. The mess hall received a lot of attention. Our new division commander, General Eberhard von Hofacker, who was involved in every detail of daily operations, sent his logistics officer on several occasions to learn what I was doing next. Unfortunately, I could not possibly tell him about my Jewish connection, which was strictly prohibited.

I spent part of my leave with my father and his staff. He was now in command of a division on the western front. Other than that, there was not much going on. We were happily sitting in a bar in Pinsk, enjoying life, when we got the news of a Russian Army dispatch reporting the occupation of Pinsk and our complete annihilation. The evening became very festive at that point. That was about the only thing worth reporting that summer.

My old battalion, the 10th Jägers, had been fighting near Verdun and was then transferred to Romania. At that point there was no holding me back. I used every means available to get back to my parent unit. The farewell was not easy. I had become very attached to my troops. My fatherly friend, Count Hamilton, did not want to release me, but he understood.

To Romania

In Pinsk I shipped off my bag to Sibiu [Hermannstadt], Transylvania. Amazingly enough, it actually arrived there. Then I started my trip. The Hungarian railroad system was challenging. Designed to handle light traffic only, with single tracks throughout, curves that were too tight, and grades that were too steep, the system would break down under the slightest strain. That was compounded by the inability of the Hungarians to manage anything, and their efforts to reroute freight cars with valuable loads to destinations other than those planned. When called on it, they suddenly could not understand any German. I was a train commander through Hungary seven times, and each experience was incredible. One time a train loaded with horses was on a siding next to ours in Braşov [Kronstadt]. I invited that train commander to my car. "No, thanks, I am not leaving my car," was his response. "It has been uncoupled four times already, with my luggage disappearing every time I get off. I've learned."

The next morning I heard some horrific swearing near the station. There he stood with his passenger car, sitting all alone. All of his horses were gone and nobody knew where they were. "'Nem tudom,' no German, only Hungarian," was the only response he got.[1]

Finally I arrived in Caineni. I found the staff of the Alpenkorps and a few days later my battalion. They had bivouacked fifty-two times, mostly above the tree line. I hardly knew anyone anymore. Four times in and out at Verdun had taken a toll. Our old commander, Major von Rauch, was gone, and Kirchheim was the commander now. He remained with us until the end of the war. He was the best commander I had during the war. His instinctive tactical sixth sense was unique. Only once did an attack that he had ordered fail, and it was a situation where he could not have influenced the outcome. Despite all his personal courage and bravado, he had a failsafe sense for limits that could not be crossed unpunished. Details and minutiae did not interest him. Officers and enlisted alike followed him unhesitatingly. It was a pleasure to serve under him.

Into Wallachia

The major mission in Romania had been accomplished. The battalion had fought at the decisive point, at the Turnu Roşu Pass, and the strength of the Romanians had been broken. This time the "Romanian sack" had to be turned inside out. A choking-off operation along the line Braşov [Kronstadt]–Brăila was what was required at the operational level, but the terrain difficulties made such a maneuver prohibitive. So, as he would later do again in 1918, Ludendorff correctly decided to let tactical considerations take priority over operational ones.

I took over the machine gun company, which until recently had been led by my old officer candidate school commander, Senior Lieutenant Kreysing. He had been seriously wounded and it was not easy to be his successor. Once during a critical moment when I jumped in to replace a gunner who had been hit, one of the Jägers pulled me back and said, "This is our business. You are just like First Lieutenant Kreysing. We do not want to lose all of our officers." Such recognition felt good.

All of the fighting now turned into pursuit actions. Again and again the Romanian leadership cobbled together units by collecting up displaced troops and throwing them at us. It hardly ever took more than a few days, sometimes only hours, and the freshly reassembled enemy was dispersed again. One time I was crossing through the mountains with all of the battalion's pack animals— just my company and approximately seven hundred animals, separated from the battalion. We were heading toward a village where the main body of the battalion was also heading. It was already after nightfall. Shortly before we reached the objective we started taking fire from a Romanian position. I deployed my machine guns, pulled together half of the pack animal guides, turned them into riflemen, and attacked. Everything was going well when from our rear a trampling started. It became more and more intense and ended with seven hundred horses rushing in wild panic through us and into the enemy. Instinctively everybody stormed forward. The enemy, who must have assumed that the devil himself was coming for him, ran off. We spent the night in the forest in the wet, melting snow hunting for our horses. Except for maybe three or four, we managed to collect them all by the next morning as it was turning light. We had not suffered any human losses either. Another time we marched through the burning oil fields at Ploesti. Everything was black with soot. That day stayed in our memories for a long time as the "March of the Moors."

The pursuit continued through daily fighting on the southern slopes of the Transylvanian Alps. We were quartered in rich villages with nice homes, but our intense pursuits into the mountains took us through deep snow. For days on end we had to drag the heavy machine gun equipment up and down the mountains—then we had to bivouac in the snow. Our faithful pack animals hauled everything for us. The only trouble we had was with the pack animal that carried the liquor ration. He had the bad habit of losing his footing and dumping his load down the mountain, until the highly upset troops had a serious talk with the animal's guide.

We were greeted with loud cheers and applause whenever the local population recognized us as Germans. When they mistook us for Russians, they admonished us with very vivid gestures to be sure that we cut all the Germans' throats.

Newly arriving Russian troops could not turn the tide in Romania, and were beaten back. At Christmas we were sitting in deep snow, without a roof over our heads. Everywhere small Christmas trees appeared miraculously. In the starlit nights we could see the mountain silhouettes. On the slopes and in the valleys we could see hundreds of campfires and could hear Christmas carols everywhere. Along the Putna River, meanwhile, we started transitioning to trench warfare.

The serious crisis in the German Army leadership had been overcome by Hindenburg and Ludendorff. With their appointments to head OHL a collective sigh of relief ran from the front lines to the home front. Falkenhayn had never reached for the stars, and on several occasions he had not taken advantage of favorable situations on the eastern front. I am thinking primarily of the situation in December 1914 when the Russian armies had their right flank near Łódź and their back against East and West Prussia. Then there was the formation of the so-called "Children's Corps" and its deployment to Ypres at a strategically critical point; the approach to our offensive in Russia in 1915; Verdun; and the rift between the Austrians and us. These were all low points of our conduct of war.

I met Falkenhayn once when I was an officer candidate. He ate at our mess hall in Goslar. Because he had been a lieutenant together with my father, he asked me to join him. His sparkling eyes, his youthful attitude, and his friendly personality made a deep impression on me. I felt that I had been in the presence of a very important personality. That he was indeed a great soldier was evident by his superb leadership in Romania. He also proved that he was a great human being when he stepped down from the position as chief of the General Staff to take command of a field army. It was an example of serving his king selflessly. It is one of the peculiarities of military service that one can fulfill his duties extremely well in one position, and then fail at the next higher position, or vice versa.[2]

Nothing was going on militarily in the trench war on the Putna River. Both sides had reached the end of their strength. One could, however, find logistical challenges to deal with. I established a simple delousing and bathing facility. Initially, it was viewed somewhat critically because I had pulled troops away from digging fighting positions, but eventually the initiative was accepted enthusiastically. That was progress. Even at the beginning of 1915 the presence of lice was still handled in some units with punishment drills. Better methods were developed only after the lice remained unresponsive.

I also initiated the cooking of meals far forward for the machine gun crews in their positions, providing them with hot food at regular times, and not only at night. We also tried to improve the troops' living conditions. The huge wine supplies stored in all of the farmhouses were very difficult to manage and dispense, but that did not hurt our troops.

We were positioned very close to the Austrian 2nd Mountain Brigade, which was in sad shape. In 1915 our allies were still in a victorious mood after the end of the successful offensive against the Russians. The Austro-Hungarians had marched to Italy with high morale, hoping to be able to end the war there quickly. Their mood turned sour after the debacle at Luck and the aborted offensive in Italy. They replaced their officers constantly and the constant refrain we heard was: "We do not know why we are fighting this war. It is only for Germany anyway." All the Austro-Hungarian nationalities were represented in their officer corps, but attitudes diverged widely and often clashed. We were horrified to hear the continual mutterings such as: "Better an end with terror than this terror without an end."

We were horrified as well by things we saw. When we were stationed in Jarestea together with all of the supply units, one of their supply units had been in bivouac for three or four weeks behind one of mine. Every night their soldiers sat around the fires and got drunk until they just passed out. The officers, on the other hand, established a mess, where they were fed cooked meat twice a day. They had pastries, candy, cigarettes, and every night plenty of women.

Meanwhile, their soldiers were running around hungry and in rags. Almost daily one of them came into my area asking for bread. I saw Bosnian soldiers of the 8th Field Jäger Battalion picking up corn kernels off the road that washed up in the thaw. I thought they were collecting them for the horses, but one of them who spoke a little German explained that they were making their Polenta[3] with what they managed to scrounge. Naturally the Austro-Hungarian officers did not like to see how we fed our soldiers, how the relations between German officers and enlisted were, how we set up our quarters, and how our uniforms were well maintained.

"Does a state like the Austrian monarchy still have the right to exist?" we asked ourselves even then. Everything simply depended on good will and good organization. If you went to Budapest or anywhere else in Hungary you hardly could find any real restrictions, even though they were officially using food ration cards.

We did have our own abuses that were the signs of a long war. There was pillaging and a number of rapes. Bordellos were established only very late. Wherever that had been done early on, no problems existed. As St. Augustine wrote a long time ago, "Whoever chases the whores out of town drives everything into a morass of passion."

There were very few problems with the population. They were used to bending opportunistically through their experience of long Turkish oppression. Asian and European habits were interlaced. It was most peculiar to see a Romanian dressed in the latest European fashion all of a sudden sink to his knees and kiss your hemline, because he wanted something. Young Romanians frequently tried to pass through our lines to reach the newly forming Romanian Army behind the Russian lines near the Moldova River. Posters were plastered everywhere prohibiting such activity. The threatened penalty for such activity was summary execution. Our 2nd Company picked up a number of young Romanians, and our regimental commander ordered their execution. The company commander, Senior Reserve Lieutenant Nottbohm, reported back in writing that he would not follow the order, citing from the pertinent paragraph from the military criminal code that to do so would be a war crime. The regiment then obtained a war tribunal legal opinion that was read to us. The bottom line was that the order was not illegal and would have to be executed. The cited paragraph from the criminal code applied only to criminal acts that were easily recognized as such. The order was executed, but the episode was indicative of the libertarian spirit in the Old Prussian Army. One openly stated his opinion, the differences were clarified, and there was no retribution in any form.

Other than that, our time in Romania was uneventful. In Focşani I looked for the old castle of the Teutonic Order whose architecture and layout had very much interested me when I was a student in Thorn. But I could not find a trace of it. King Andrew I of Hungary had sent the knights there. The town itself had nothing of interest. Bucharest reminded me of a bad denture with a few gold fillings. The architecture of the farmhouses in the rural areas was interesting, though. European and Middle Eastern influences came together in an interesting mix. The overall impression, however, was one of a nouveau riche culture without real taste. A look at a castle and a farmhouse gave a true impression of the social tensions in the country. Free, well-to-do, and self-confident farmers dwelled only in the mountains, where there were no large estate holders.

An important political event about this time was the Peace Resolution passed by the German Reichstag. The initiative was completely rejected, and not only by the officer corps. The Reichstag no longer had anyone's respect anyway.

4

1917

Between Battles

On 12 April I returned from my leave. I had planned to transfer in Rudka for Budapest, but the connecting train was not running. The station master told me that there was a very nice train waiting on the other track which was going not to Budapest but to Košice.[1] From there it would be easy to get to Budapest. Along the way I could enjoy the views of the High Tatras, and see Košice, a very nice place. So, I thought, why not?

On the train I made friends with an Austrian captain. That evening we ate dinner in Košice. Hungary did not seem to have any food rationing. While Germans were going hungry[2] fighting to support the dual monarchy,[3] people here did not lack anything. Even so, they were still complaining about the war and how hard it was for them. My new friend was the same. In 1916 at the breakthrough at Lutsk he had commanded a company. He was its only survivor. All of his company's dugouts had sunk into the marshes and his troops suffocated. How he avoided suffocation, he did not say. But the bottom line of his wartime experiences was, "As soon as you hear the enemy's drums, leave, otherwise something bad will happen." He talked at great length about how he managed to make his life comfortable in the field. He was typical of the non-German Austro-Hungarian, pleasant, well educated, and able to converse intelligently about anything—as long as there was no danger.

Whenever I passed through Budapest I never missed the chance to go sightseeing in this uniquely beautiful city. From there I went on to Transylvania[4] and the Pedreal Pass[5] toward Focşani. Countless fortified churches sat on either side of the rail line. Each was unique, just as the builders had conformed it to the terrain for protection against the Turks. Mediaş[6] was an old, very German town with towers and battlements. Sighişoara[7] was situated high on a green hill, with an old massive church without a steeple and the old town in a circle around it. The steep, red roofs of the many fortification towers stuck out of the green fields like spearheads. On a plateau below, the new town had been built during a period later than the defiant old church. In its simple elegance the narrow tower of the city hall was somewhat crooked. None of us were really familiar with the old German culture of Transylvania. The war had brought this beautiful German land and the ties that bind back to life.

The only thing foreign in this land was the Hungarian signs—signs in German and Romanian were forbidden. The huge Transylvanian Alps were visible on the horizon. The ruins of an old castle that had belonged to the Teutonic Order bore witness to a little-known chapter in German history, when the Teutonic Knights had turned this area into a German land. After the Order was forced to withdraw in disgrace, they moved to Prussia.

The valley leads into German castle country. At Kronstadt[8] a valley opens up to the south, ending with a wall of mountains sloping toward Romania. This was favorable ground for an attacker coming from the south, but very bad ground for an attacker approaching from the north. Ludendorff had been right in not wanting to attempt a decisive attack here. Understanding the terrain along the border between Transylvania and Romania, you have to judge less harshly the initial withdrawal of Germany's allies. The Romanians held every piece of high ground that descended from two thousand meters down to six hundred meters within ten kilometers. Withdrawal from such an untenable position was probably the best course of action.

Training Period

My unit picked me up in Focșani and we proceeded to Alvinc[9] in Transylvania.

This was the period when America declared war. As I wrote in my diary: "What is symptomatic of the importance of this event is the fact that nobody is talking about it." I actually found out about it by accident a few days after the fact. Many considered it a ridiculous trifle that no one needed to be concerned about. Nobody had an inkling of the potential this giant had. Our thinking was purely Continental.

Alvinc was an ethnic Romanian town full of hostile citizens. They never failed to tell us how sad they were not to be part of Romania. Every one of them tried to take advantage of us, but nothing could change their poor opinion of us. We tried to make horses available to them; we helped with the harvest, but to no avail. They simply would not accept us. It was completely different for the troops that were staying in the ethnic German townships, where they were greeted as the liberators of Transylvania.

On 17 May we loaded up on trains and started heading toward the western front. We all quietly hoped to be diverted to Tyrol, but that did not happen. Moving into Bavaria, we traveled along the edge of the Alps. Everywhere we were greeted by cheers. In Ulm in Württemberg we received a friendly reception that I never would have expected after three years of war. Just as in 1914, everybody was out in the streets, raining flowers onto the train. When the train stopped in Pforzheim, people brought bread and beer to the train, even though everything was severely rationed. We knew once more what we had been fighting for. The homeland had restored our strength.

We finally off-loaded in Alsace[10] and started retraining to prepare for the fighting in the West. We rehearsed attacks near the Kaiserstuhl,[11] and my company was quartered in the town of Sasbach at the foot of Hohenlimburg Castle, supposedly the birthplace of Rudolf,[12] the first of the Habsburgs.

The 10th Jäger Battalion had close ties to the Alsace region. Not only had the unit spent a decade in Colmar and Bitche, but it also had many Alsatians in its ranks, and they were well treated. Only one defected, a Jäger named Huy who was a Lothringian[13] of French descent. All the others remained loyal to Germany and to the battalion. In 1918 one of our Alsatians shot an Oberjäger in a forward observation post who had been telling his troops that the war was lost and that it did not make any sense to continue. Reluctantly, the last Alsatians left the unit in May 1919, led by *Offizierstellvertreter*[14] Guirrlinger: "We have no choice," he said. "We have to go home. Otherwise we lose our homeland."

Alsatians were not supposed to fight on the western front. Every unit that was redeployed from the eastern to the western front had to report that all Alsatians and Lothringians had been transferred out. The 10th Jäger Battalion turned in a bogus report. I still had quite a few Alsatians in my company. According to regulations, they were not allowed to go back to their home villages on leave. I assembled them, told them about the policy, and then released them to their hometowns. They promised with a handshake in front of the entire company to remain on call and return within twelve hours notice. Not one of them broke his promise.

They were the best soldiers in Germany. The French Revolution had made it possible for them to move up. Rapp and Ney, to name only two of Napoleon's generals, were both Alsatians. Germany had nothing similar to offer in those days. Who could blame them for being sympathetic to the French cause then?[15] The last forty-five years, however, had been the best that Alsace had ever seen. The younger generation felt very much like Germans.

We were also garrisoned in Sundgau,[16] a quiet, beautiful landscape where not a single shot was fired. One of our most onerous tasks was the requirement to censor the mail of our own soldiers. It destroyed trust every time a superior did not handle this carefully. The older veterans were generally calm about the whole process. It was the young replacements who were always complaining. But in their letters they certainly fabricated the most incredible acts of heroism that never occurred here in the quiet parts of Alsace where no shots were fired.

Battle for Moldavia

I had the opportunity to take a short leave in the Champagne region to see my father, whose division was stationed there. Then we were loaded up and sent back to the eastern front. On 8 August we detrained in Focşani, Romania.

Despite the tense strategic situation that was draining Germany, OHL[17] decided to force Russia into collapse by inflicting a series of limited objective blows. The continuing revolutionary disintegration of the Russian Army seemed to make such a strategy feasible. Following a series of tactical successes in eastern Galicia, a sharp thrust in the area of Focşani was supposed to lead to the collapse of the Russian front there. The Romanian forces had not returned yet. They were in Moldavia, reconstituting and rebuilding under French general Henri Bertholet.[18] Ludendorff had high hopes for this offensive, and he gave it priority over the attack on Italy, which was still in the planning phase. By the time we off-loaded in Focşani the offensive was already in progress. To our front the artillery was firing fiercely, and the Alpenkorps[19] had moved forward across the Putna River. We passed through our own firing batteries, which were emplaced on both sides of the road. Vehicles and formations moved continuously in both directions. All of this was going on under strong Russian artillery fire, which amazingly enough caused little damage. There was nothing you could really do about it. All you could do was quietly march on, hoping that nothing happened.

At noon on 12 August the attack started across the steep and wide Şuşiţa Valley. Prussian and Bavarian Jägers descended into the valley. Wave after wave ran across the valley floor and ascended the opposite side. As far as the eye could see the valley was filled with advancing riflemen. The Russian infantry broke and ran. We increased the pace of the advance, but as always, the lead element got through and the follow-on elements got hit. The whole river valley was under Russian interdiction fire. Machine guns came coughing to life from somewhere, but we had to get through. Wave after wave went through the valley, with the dirt kicking up right and left and in front and behind us. Noise everywhere as we ran on and heard the pinging of the bullets around us. And then before we knew it, we were on the other side of the valley.

It was a powerful, morale-building sight, the valley full of exploding shells and shrapnel and advancing troops everywhere. Not one of them hesitated or looked for cover. There is nothing like the German soldier. One Jäger of my machine gun company carried his heavy ammo cans despite being shot through the arm, and he continued until the fight was over.

The Russians also must have seen it that way. They threw down their weapons and equipment and took off. What counterattacks they managed to launch quickly stalled under our counterfire. At the northern edge of Crucea de Sus we reached our objective. We did not take a lot of prisoners. They ran too fast. Only a few German-Russians from Odessa gave themselves up. The Russians seemed to have lost all motivation, as Kerensky apparently intended.[20]

On 14 August we continued the attack. The objective was to block the Oitoz Pass, which meant we had to conduct a wide, sweeping movement to the left. Our artillery hammered away, morning and afternoon. The battalion staff, with whom I was co-located, sat in a small, narrow ditch under heavy Russian fire. As we sat huddled closely together, clods of earth dropped on our steel helmets and the continuous roaring jolted the air. We could not even distinguish the individual detonations. Then there was a lull in the artillery fire and we all looked up. High above us in a nut tree sat a young Austrian artillery officer who was directing the fires of his battery and not paying particular attention to the Russian artillery fire.

When the battalion assembled, I went forward to my machine guns. We moved ahead swiftly. In Straoane the fleeing Russians were everywhere. The houses in the town were packed together so closely it was difficult to see anything. A huge Russian came out of one house screaming, the blood pouring out of his chest like a jet of water. Then he collapsed. From the left we heard the shout, "Russian counterattack!" Some troops came running back. Then Russians jumped out of the cornfield twenty paces away, bayonets fixed. A really tall one aimed directly at me, but I was faster. Two of my machine gun crews came running up, gasping for air. "Assume positions, firing direction toward the open field, half right!" As the ammo belts were inserted into the feeder tray, a row of Russian riflemen stepped into the open, hesitating as they saw the open field. A young Russian officer jumped ahead of the line, yelled something at them, and swung his saber. Then the machine guns opened up. As if hit by a single blow the Russians fell. No one escaped, and the Russian counterattack stalled. Right to our front, fifty meters away in a white house, something was moving. I knelt down next to a machine gun and pointed in the direction, when I was hit in the chest. I fell down and my troops pulled me behind the closest building. Coming from the half right a rifle bullet had hit my left side just above the heart, entered above the ribs, and lodged in my upper left arm.

My troops hauled me through heavy artillery fire back to the aid station. The number of Russian dead was enormous. Then I drove myself to the field hospital in Focşani, where they cut the bullet out of my arm. The surgeon wanted to send me to a recovery center in Râmnicu Sărat, but I refused to go. I wanted to go back to the front. But when he disagreed, I just got dressed, grabbed a taxi in Focşani, and went back to my unit.

Things had been rough while I was gone. When the battalion was getting ready to attack through the vineyards the next day at noon, the Russians were doing exactly the same—whether it was just a coincidence or they knew of our intentions, we would never know. Closely lined up, six to ten rows deep, they made contact with our thin firing line. Within mere moments the battalion lost almost all of its officers. Of the company commanders only Nottbohm remained uninjured, and thanks to his vigilance and courage the enemy's attack stalled. My machine gun crews also earned the highest praise. Their fire had cleaned up the Russians horribly. *Oberjäger* Seebode deserves special mention. He was one of the most courageous men I have ever known. He served in this war as a frontline soldier from the first to the last day.

Then something monstrous happened. As our forward line was holding, they sent the POWs to the rear. Those prisoners ran into the gun crews of the machine gun battalion of a mountain unit that was moving forward. The machine gunners opened fire and immediately spread the alarm that the Russians had broken through. One of our batteries limbered up and rushed away. The resulting wave of panic swept over everyone who was to the rear of our front line of troops. Some Austrian gun crews even abandoned their howitzers. One battery buried its breech blocks. A thick stream of refugees poured down the Șușița Valley. The divisional cavalry squadron tried in vain to stem the tide with drawn sabers. After ten to fifteen kilometers the panicked rout ended in total exhaustion. Throughout the whole sad affair my battalion, with hardly any officers and taking heavy losses, had held the line steadfastly. To their front the Russian corpses were piled high. Not a single man ran, not an inch of ground was lost. The battery of the German Alpenkorps also had stood fast.

Slowly things returned to normal from the chaos. I was riding forward with my arm in a sling, looking for my company's supply element. I found them in total disarray. The *Futtermeister*[21] had totally lost it. He had given the order to his men not to saddle up and to just save themselves. In his panic he had joined the flood of fleeing civilians, instead of extracting himself and the company's horses. Some of the pack horses and their saddles were lost. He really had it coming.

In the evening I took command of my company again. I passed over the spot where I had been wounded. I was looking for the young Russian officer who four days ago had so courageously pushed his soldiers forward. I did not find him. At the spot where I had thought he would be there was a small ditch. Had he been able to crawl back to it? I hoped so. Our positions were in the Valea Rea, a dull, barren valley. The ground was barren and rocky, with thin grass full of thorns growing along the hillsides that were cut by ragged and deep gorges.

On 29 August we attacked one more time. After ten minutes of a powerful artillery preparation everything was covered in dust and smoke. The earth was trembling and shaking. At 0700 hours we stood at the ready. We could not see out more than one hundred meters. The air was impenetrable. Making a fast sweep we quickly reached the Zăbrătău River, our objective of the day. Everywhere the Russians were fleeing, along with their supply trains. The enemy's artillery had displaced to the rear without firing a single shot. We had achieved a total breakthrough and the enemy in front of us was in complete disarray. But we had orders not to advance farther, and so we dug in.

There is a strange phenomenon known to anybody who has been on the front lines for a long time. Officers, enlisted soldiers, tough warriors who are not easily shaken, who react with a strange calm even under the heaviest fire, suddenly become very nervous and anxious. Their orientation becomes unsure, and before the day is over a bullet cuts their lives short. I had two runners. Paul was a quiet farmer from the Eifel region and Heublein was a forester from the Meiningen area. Neither soldier was ever afraid to be in the thick of it and was always ready to accomplish any mission. All of a sudden, Heublein became unsure of himself. It was so obvious that Paul remarked to me, "Lieutenant, the time has come for him."

Heublein never would have gone back to the rear, even if I had ordered him to stand down and stay with the pack animals. So I told him, "Heublein, go back to the supply train and get two machine gun bolts. We'll need them after the attack."

"Lieutenant, I cannot leave you now, we are getting ready to assault."

"It does not matter, the bolts are more important."

I thought I had done my best. I said to Paul, "Well, we have saved Heublein." Later a Jäger came up to me and reported, "Lieutenant, Heublein is dead. He is lying fifty meters behind the position, still clutching two machine gun bolts to his chest."

The same sort of thing happened to one of our best company commanders, Reserve Lieutenant Braun.

The next morning we were woken up by yelling that the Russians were attacking in close order. I was able to observe everything from the position of one of my machine gun platoons. The steep and densely overgrown valley of the Zăbrătău River was to our front. On the other side, a barren, coverless hillside gradually descended two kilometers toward the river. We could see individual Russians moving forward. They skillfully used every dip in the terrain for cover. Although our positions were under heavy fire, the Russians were having difficulty pinpointing targets. Group after group emerged from a wooded area along the horizon, often in tight four-man crews pulling a machine gun.[22] The ground was bone dry. In the bright sunshine you could observe the impact of a bullet at eighteen hundred to nineteen hundred meters.

The platoon leader correctly analyzed the situation. Offizierstellvertreter Mewes was one of our last remaining active duty Oberjägers. He concentrated the fire of his platoon on the four-man teams pulling the machine guns. He allowed them to move forward far into the barren river flats; then his two machine guns briefly barked. Rounds impacted around the enemy groups as they desperately tried to take cover behind their equipment. But in the end the Russian machine guns sat surrounded by their dead crews. Machine gun crew after machine gun crew stormed forward and was cut down after a few hundred meters. When the attack finally broke down we counted more than twenty Russian machine guns surrounded by dead bodies on the naked hill fifteen hundred meters to our front. Thanks to accurate observation, this was the most effective machine gun fire I ever experienced.

The Russians now became more aggressive. The fires of three artillery batteries started hitting Mewes's platoon, but his machine guns kept firing without interruption. I can still see Oberjäger Sohnekind as he stood out in front of his machine gun calmly clearing away the brush from the line of fire, as if he were back on the farm harvesting. Meanwhile, other soldiers reloaded ammunition belts until their fingers were bleeding. Again and again one man would come from the rear where the pack animals were, break through the enemy fire, throw two ammo cans at us, and then race back to bring more forward. By the time it was all over the platoon had fired more than ninety thousand rounds.

One afternoon I moved along the front line and as I came to the 2nd Company I called for Nottbohm. Suddenly, a rather disturbed face appeared out of a hole in front of me. I was shocked. I had not expected this from Nottbohm. "Man, get in here quickly; our own artillery is firing on us." And there it was, rolling in from the rear. A round of at least 150 mm detonated between us and the forward line, then another, and another. Yelling over the phone was useless. We had just made a connection when the line was destroyed. The only bright spot was that one of our artillery forward observers was huddling in the hole with us. We wholeheartedly felt that he deserved this unexpected pleasure.

At the first opportunity I got out of that lethal area and moved back to the ravine where the battalion staff was positioned. It was not an especially pleasant place either, because they were under Russian artillery from three sides. I had just reached the position when I heard the same terrifying rushing sound, followed immediately by the crashing noise of the exploding shell. Now, to top it all off, we were being fired upon by our own artillery from the fourth side of the ravine. The telephone line naturally went out immediately. Runners rushed off in all directions. But the eerie explosions did not stop. All rank and ethnic differences disappeared. Russian POWs, runners, officers, everybody was trying to take cover in any corner that looked at least partially safe. After thirty minutes it was over. We later learned that a 150 mm naval gun battery had fired without actual observation, using only map spotting.

A heavy rain poured down on us. A torrent of water swept us away with all of our equipment, and then the Romanians repeated the same kind of attack that the Russians had tried a few days ago. The first signs of the impending attack had been a number of defectors. One of them even brought his machine gun with him. Since we could not observe the impact of our bullets on the wet ground, the Romanians were able to break through our machine gun fire almost without losses. Then they reached the thicket and the ravines of the Zăbrătău River valley. From there they tried all day long to assault, over and over again. Each time they failed against the iron resolve of our 3rd Company. The dead piled up in front of their positions, sometimes three to four rows deep. I counted forty dead just at one critical point.

The offensive in Moldavia was over, but it had not achieved what Ludendorff had hoped for. Why? The supporting attack originally planned to come from Bukovina in the north toward our position in the south was cancelled because of a lack of forces. Furthermore, we had started the offensive before the most combat-ready brigade of the Alpenkorps had arrived. Consequently, this excellent brigade was thrown into the fight after it had been raging for days. The element of surprise was gone. The Russian-Romanian reserves and their strongest artillery forces had been massed in front of our axis of advance.

There is an iron rule of tactics: Do not start an attack unless all your forces are assembled. How often did we violate this basic tenet, me included. "*Klotzen nicht kleckern,*"[23] that is what the old Guderian[24] always hammered home. In this case, we had taken half measures and we underestimated the enemy.

Germans are impatient. Waiting is an art that is foreign to us. Actions like the one in Moldavia frustrate us. And still, the Moldavia Offensive was of the highest importance. It broke the remaining strength of the Russian Army. It now was no longer an effective combat force and it was falling apart internally to Bolshevism. Like so many politicians, Kerensky, the Russian head of government at the time, had no understanding of what was militarily possible with the means available. Instead of using his available forces to stabilize the domestic situation in Russia, he tried to relieve the strategic pressure on the western powers, and broke his own army in the process.[25] The end result was a victory for radicalism in Russia. At the decisive point Kerensky had thrown the wrong switch in world history. The English gave him a good pension after the war. He had delivered for them right on time.

Tyrolean Interlude

Whenever the Alpenkorps was loaded up, the rumor spread that we would be going to Tyrol. This time it was for real. On 10 September we loaded on trains in Focșani. I was in charge of the Alpenkorps' advance party. If one has never loaded up an advance party, one cannot even begin to imagine what it entails. The number of freight cars was fixed. But every type of unit showed up with at least twice as many horses, vehicles, and people and then tried to get on somehow. I was completely exhausted by the time everything was finally loaded. To make matters worse, everybody was suffering from dysentery. Bad weather, the constant eating of grapes, and unbelievably hot weather had brought everybody down.

In Craiova the train was divided into two, and naturally both sections left before everybody had returned from foraging. As usual, nobody had any idea about what was going on, "*Nem tudom. Nix Deitsch, Magyar.*"[26]

On the 12th we passed through the Iron Gate.[27] Even the Danube had shrunk to a trickle because of the hot weather. Steep, brush-covered, sunscorched mountains flanked the river. Some small islands in the river had medieval fortifications. One of them still belonged to Turkey, a witness of the former expanse of the Ottoman Empire.

On the 13th I received a telegram, "Convoy commander notified to report immediately to B.V.G. of 2nd T.L.[28] in Vienna." I got on the next fast train to Vienna, but the telegram had been a false alarm. Nobody wanted to see me, but I got to see Vienna, St. Stephen's Cathedral, the Schünbrunn Palace, the Belvedere Palace, and the great dance shows in the Variety Theater Ronacher. What a contrast there was between Vienna and Budapest, much to Vienna's favor. The people were friendly and nice. Everybody was very helpful and they did not try to take you, like they did everywhere else. The military bearing of the soldiers was also much better. After a slightly manipulated delay and with a bad conscience I continued on to Salzburg, where I hoped to catch the troop train; but I arrived twenty-four hours ahead of it. Salzburg too was wonderful. The old residential city greatly appealed to my interests in history and architecture. Eventually the troop train arrived. It had been rerouted accidentally through Ljubljana.[29] For once I appreciated the Hungarian lack of organization.

We finally off-loaded in Mattarello, near Trento, where we were totally reequipped. We received a huge number of machine guns, twelve alone for the machine gun company, and six for each Jäger company. I was put in charge of the machine gun training for the whole battalion. In the healthy Tyrolean air all the illnesses we had picked up in Moldavia faded quickly.

The positioning of the Alpenkorps in Tyrol was supposed to be a ruse, which naturally nobody had told us about. Our presence became known like a wildfire. Our 2nd Company had fought in Giudicarie[30] for some time in 1915, and now we were back there again. Some brave Jägers of the 2nd Company were clearly uncomfortable about returning to the area. Upon our arrival several of them laid low in the backs of the trucks. But the locals were not at all hostile. With no sense of rancor, mothers brought their "little Jägers" up to the trucks to show them off full of pride to their fathers.

The convoy was a triumphant procession in every respect. Military bands played in the towns and food was prepared. The front was dead quiet. Everywhere members of the Austrian high nobility sat on the mountaintops and pretended they were at the front. The officers even had their families with them. In short, it was an operetta war that could not have been any nicer. We were handed cleanly printed souvenir brochures with lots of sketches and other information. According to prisoner reports, the Italians were supposed to advance across the Chiese River with two battalions and attack Zanè.[31] The Austrians had evacuated Zanè and two other villages. Once in a while a completely obsolete howitzer from our side popped off some interdiction fire on the Chiese River crossing sites. We were supposed to reoccupy the three towns in a night attack and destroy the Italian force that had been blocked by the interdiction fire.

We advanced down the road in the darkness. The terrain did not allow us to move forward anywhere else. There was nothing in the first village, and we kept advancing. At the entrance to the next village we saw some movement and then a figure clad in white appeared. "If you please, dinner for the officers is ready." It was the cook of the local officers' mess. He knew the situation, and he was not concerned one bit.

The "battle" along the Chiese River continued. Orders were issued frantically, with the most senior officers personally issuing directives. Nobody was allowed to decide anything. High-ranking generals ordered individual patrols out and even briefed them personally. It was micromanagement of the worst possible kind. But there were also quite a few things accomplished. The positions were well prepared throughout. Every one of them was built into caverns, and well protected against fires. All the roads and the funiculars[32] were built mostly by female construction companies, who sometimes also improved the wire obstacles in front of the fighting positions.

Eventually everything climaxed into the preparation for an attack on Mount Vies. The transport of our equipment on a funicular proved impossible. We had to haul it up ourselves. We stayed overnight in the Malga Ringia. About the time we got there the carrier company coming back from the mountaintop arrived, all of them happy and strong women and girls who made the trip daily with a load of fifty pounds on their heads. It was a balmy night on the Malga Ringia—and that was the end of the attack on Mount Vies.

Days earlier our commander, Kirchheim, had been asked about the attack on Mount Vies by a waitress in Daone. She knew all the details and everything else worth mentioning about it. We were appalled. But the typical German is too dense to play along in a situation like that. The deception was perfectly organized. Our troops prepared for the attack, fully convinced it was real and expecting it to come off. Nobody could fathom that we were playing theater here.

We moved back toward Trento and then on to Pergine, which had been Italianized from its former German name, Fersen. Along with the Italianization came dirt and poverty. The old Renaissance palaces still stood as witnesses to the town's former wealth. As I entered my assigned quarters, I was swallowed up by a huge gate with a gothic hall behind it. It once had been a warehouse belonging to old German patricians. I walked up to the second floor and an ill-clad, dirty, old woman opened the door. I found myself in a big hallway with precious antique furniture everywhere and old engravings hanging on the walls. The old woman spoke only Italian. She disappeared and a young girl appeared, who seemed to be from a family of education and standing. Speaking German, she apologized that her mother had misplaced the key to my room. What a surprise! The mother of this house full of old engravings and precious furniture was this old frump who received me at the door.

From my room I could see the Fersen Castle and the magnificent alpine world. A few days later we were on a train again, heading toward the Isonzo River. On the wall of the train station there was a notice from the Imperial and Royal Austrian Railways warning, "Railway employees caught selling bread to prisoners of war will be fired and punished with conscription into the military." You could not have insulted the military profession more.

Eviva Germania[33]

In Arnoldstein in Carinthia we got off the train, crossed the Wurzen Pass, and arrived in Carniola.[34] The names of the towns were German, the population was Slovenian. The few remaining Germans, mostly belonging to the upper class, had no faith in the future. They knew the Slovenians were pushing them out, but they conceded, "They have fought a good fight." The landscape, including the jewel-like Lake Velden, lay before us in all its autumn beauty. We reconnoitered the advance route and the assembly area. There was not a single inch of land in this valley that was not covered with equipment for the offensive. One howitzer to the next, one mortar to the next. The valley was filled with fog and rain. On 20 October it snowed and rained, which offered the advantage of surprise, but which also could go completely wrong for us.[35] We marched across almost impassable mountain crests into the region of Gorizia. It was a horrible route, but thank God the rain had stopped. The troops in front of us along the route of march had thrown away all kinds of equipment, including machine guns, ammunition, pack saddles, oats, and bread. A few dead pack animals lay along the way. On the descent we had to chain up our pack animals. We spent the night in the most miserable huts. The next day, 22 October, was about the same, but the sun finally came out. The timing was perfect. Our advance had been covered in fog, and then at the right moment the weather turned good.

I had to ride forward again to reconnoiter. The roads were completely jammed. Twice I got stalled so badly that I could not move ahead or back. A distance that would normally comfortably take ten minutes on horseback took me an hour and a half. An Italian aircraft appeared overhead twice and we shot at it intensely. Actually, the enemy should have figured it out by that point. The two avenues of approach into the bridgehead at Tolmin[36] were already under artillery fire. I reconnoitered our assembly area as the artillery fire grew more intense. From Mount Mrzli Vrh the Italians were firing interdiction fire, and that night the fire grew heavy on both advance routes.

The battalion finally arrived, hours late. Thank God it was still under the cover of darkness. On 23 October we rested in the assembly area, taking only occasional enemy artillery fire. Early on 24 October the gas attack started. But rain also set in, raising questions about how effective the gas would be. Then at dawn the earth began to tremble, as an incredible preparation barrage commenced. Smoke, fog, and rain filled the valley, reducing visibility to less than three hundred meters. The Bavarian Life Guards Infantry Regiment to our front started the assault, and we moved directly behind them. The counterfire was minimal. The first Italian positions were completely destroyed by artillery and mortar fire. Some of the captured enemy gun crews were moving toward us. They were sent to the rear by the *Leiber*.[37] Even from a distance we could tell that the Italians were relieved that it was over for them. One battery commander was captured with his guns. They had been expecting an attack by two Hungarian divisions since the 18th; they knew nothing about German troops. "Hopefully you will be in Milano soon. Then at least this horrible war will be over."

The attack advanced and the main objective of the enemy positions on Hill 1114 was taken. The Leibers reported two thousand prisoners and twenty-five captured artillery pieces. We moved on along the endless serpentine paths under heavy artillery fire onto Mount Hasevenik, where we spent a bitterly cold night. On 25 October we were wakened by heavy artillery fire. I was hit on my steel helmet by a large chunk of rock, which knocked me down. On Hill 1114 the situation was still unclear. We moved forward through knocked-out batteries and heavy fires, but took no losses. A machine gun salvo ripped right over our heads. Our 4th Company was supposed to take an Italian position between the Bavarian Life Guards Regiment and the Bavarian Jägers. I reconnoitered forward to assess how to support that maneuver with my machine guns. In a maze of small hilltops I could see an Italian position in deep and heavily covered ditches screened with strong obstacles. My current position had recently been the headquarters of an Italian divisional staff. It had a well-stocked commissary. From there I could see the plain below and a network of excellent roads.

When the commander of the 4th Company, Lieutenant Müller, was killed right next to me, I also assumed command of the 4th. While I was still contemplating how to lead the attack, the Italians decided to make it easy for me. Along the whole front line white sheets popped up and three hundred men came running and jumping toward us. "*Eviva Germania, la Guerra finite, la Guerra finite! A Milano, a Milano!*"[38] Laughing, they slapped us on the shoulders. The only one real danger was being trampled to death by them. When I sent a few men over to the Italian position, a machine gun opened up. They would not let us approach, but they did let their own people go. A real hard head had to be over there still.

I committed two platoons to the attack, supported by four machine guns. Just then a Feldwebel Leutnant[39] of the Bavarian Jägers emerged from a ravine with his platoon. He was walking right into the enemy's fire. I yelled at him to stop. "I do not take orders from you," he responded in a thick Bavarian accent. His principled defense of his Bavarian turf rights cost him two dead and three wounded.

The Italian position finally fell. On the next hill crest we played the same game. Again, white sheets and deserters, and again a desperately defending Italian with a machine gun. One of my own gunners was having trouble keeping his piece in action. I jumped forward and took over the gun. Just as I had fired off half an ammunition belt, I got hit in the chest, hands, and back by an Italian machine gun salvo. According to the 10th Jäger Battalion official report: "... two grazing shots across the right hand, one across the left hand, one across the right side of the chest, one on the left shoulder blade. Everything minor." Even the most senior veterans could not remember anyone having that much luck, ever.

The following day I was leading my company with both arms in a sling. In the meantime, the Jägers had advanced toward the machine gun, which was being fired by an Italian colonel. As they took him prisoner he tried to pull his pistol, but he could not get it out of the holster. With tears running down his cheeks the only thing he could say was: "What a shame to be Italian."

"*Mort a te Cadorna*"[40] was written in large letters in countless spots in the Italian trenches. The Italians were completely demoralized. They fled toward the rear, leaving everything behind—artillery piece next to artillery piece, supply wagon next to supply wagon, and as many rations as we could have wanted. Prisoners by the thousands marched toward us, constantly yelling "*Eviva Germani! Eviva Germania!*"

Pursuit

We descended the steep hillsides and into the plains. The situation remained one of total collapse, with fleeing automobile convoys and at one position a battery firing off its last rounds. We could see the crews servicing the guns, and then it was every man for himself. White flares were being fired off to the right and to the left as far as one could see. They marked the forward line of our troops, aggressively advancing along a wide front. In San Pietro we crossed paths with the 12th Infantry Division's Upper Silesian regiments, totally drunk, loaded down with bacon, sausages, and chocolate, but still advancing. There was no stopping us now. The morale was fabulous. Everything had the aura of an event of world historical significance. Added to that, our losses had been minimal—only 224 dead, wounded, or sick in the entire Alpenkorps. The bag for the first day alone was forty howitzers and thirteen thousand POWs.

We reached the plains. Italy was supposed to be the best supplied front line of the Allies, and it certainly was. After a few days there were no more skinny horses in the company. My company became unrecognizable, with everyone decked out in the newest, best-quality Italian trousers, boots, and clothing. Our quarters were excellent, often in substantial castles. But then the rain came and it poured down without end. The water rushed down from the southern slopes of the Alps, which were only lightly forested.

The 14th Reserve Jäger Battalion ahead of us had marched through the Torrente Grivò without getting their feet wet. Then the water came rushing down with unbelievable power. The company in front of me still made it across the *torrente*,[41] but my company, the last in the battalion column, had the water up to our belts. The troops had to hold on to each other to prevent being swept away. It was an indescribably comical scene, with everybody carrying recently requisitioned open umbrellas forcing their way through the water. One pack animal at the end of the company was swept away with its guide. Feldwebel Wiederholt, my best and most courageous platoon leader, saved the guide at the risk of his own life, and received the life saving medal.

The next unit in line, the 10th Reserve Jäger Battalion, was not able to get across the torrente. Even though cables were strung across the torrente for the Jägers to hold on to, anyone who tried it was swept away in the raging waters. Eventually the 10th Reserve Jäger Battalion had to halt all attempts to make it across the Torrente Grivò. It had only taken about half an hour from the time that the water came rushing in to the point where it became impossible to get across. On the maps the Torrente Grivò was indicated as only a harmless trickle.

A little farther on the Tagliamento River was normally a small creek, but it too had become a raging river that held up the pursuit. A wagon loaded with heavy howitzer ammunition that had been pushed into the river to function as a bridge support was turned over. All of the roads were blocked with discarded military equipment, and several thousand Italians who also had been cut off by the flooding threw down their weapons. The rain had saved the Italian Army from total annihilation and Italy itself from total collapse—and it robbed us of victory.

The weather conditions meant a few days of rest for us. I took advantage to make a small detour to Udine, which had been cut off by a German brigade. Actually, no one was allowed to enter the town, but I finally got permission. It was the most maddening sight I had ever seen. Every window was broken; all the stores were looted; and there were heaps of broken glass everywhere. You could not even identify the original purpose of any of the stores. Everything was a black, tamped-down mass, covered with the stench of vomit and red wine.

In March 1918, I sat on a court-martial board in Mörchingen in Lorraine. A supply NCO from the logistics command of the Alpenkorps had brought goods back to Germany from Udine valued at 50,000 marks. He was caught in Munich. When he had arrived in Udine, tens of thousands of people were looting, half of them Italians and the other half Austrians. The NCO bought a truck full of fabrics worth 20,000 marks by paying 20 kronen[42] and one hundred cigarettes. Truck drivers were earning between 20,000 and 30,000 kronen on the road from Udine to Bled.[43] Along the railroad lines commercial companies had sprung up that were making incredible profits—thankfully all without German participation. But because the trucks were being used for other things, ammunition did not get forward.

Reaching a verdict proved difficult. The defense argued that when the man reached Udine, he saw tens of thousands of people looting and breaking into the stores. How could this one man stop anything? We finally acquitted the NCO, because in Udine the principle of "unclaimed merchandise" could be applied, and because the defendant had not acted with criminal intent. A decisive factor in the verdict was the fact that he was Jewish. He just had a different perspective on business matters. It was a somewhat convoluted rationale, because war booty technically belongs to the state. But the verdict was just. The judges, who even admitted to being anti-Semitic, concurred.

Taking a detour along the Via Venetia, I returned to my company. Everywhere it was the same picture of incredible collapse. Eventually an Austrian division was able to ford the Tagliamento River where it exits the mountains near San Daniele. We slogged on in the pouring rain, soaked to the bones. All the roads were covered with heavy mud. It took the entire column three days to march across the bridge. Everybody was nervous, tired, edgy, seeing every other fellow human as a personal enemy. It was nothing but rain, rain, and more rain. We would slosh ahead for three minutes, then stop for a half an hour, then move ahead for another minute, and then stop for an hour. This went on for three days and the rain just kept pouring down.

But soldiers are inventive. After a little while everybody had a chair and an umbrella and sat down happily during longer halt periods under the cover of the umbrella. When it came time to march on, they moved the couple of steps that the column would actually move, taking their chairs and umbrellas with them. This was the famous "night chair march" of the Alpenkorps across the Tagliamento River. We had often ridiculed the Italian commander in chief, Cadorna, who almost always canceled offensives because of bad weather. In cartoons he was always drawn carrying an umbrella. The man had been wronged terribly.

When after three days the endless marching and the Tagliamento lay behind us, the pursuit turned into a frontal push. The Alpenkorps followed as the second echelon. Even though the subsequent river crossings were conducted more expertly, the rain kept coming back in a deluge, and dry creek beds turned into large streams within minutes.

Monte Tombea[44]

Maintaining constant enemy contact, we followed toward the Piave River, which we reached near Valdobbiadene. The Piave at that point emerges from the Alps into the northern Italian plains. The front line, which had stabilized in the river flats from north to south, made a sharp right angle at Valdobbiadene and followed along the southern slopes of the Alps exactly from east to west. As a mountain unit, the Alpenkorps was naturally ordered across the Piave and into the mountains.

The Italians, meanwhile, had recovered with the support of the French and English divisions that had arrived to help them. We were hoping that we would be able to take care of the resistance along the Piave quickly, especially since Field Marshal Franz Conrad von Hötzendorf's South Tyrolean Army Group was standing ready to attack on the plateau of Sette Communi[45] near Asiago and Arsiero.

There was a footbridge exactly at the point where the front made a 90-degree right turn on the Piave River near San Vito. It sat between the front lines in no-man's-land. All of the approach routes were covered by interdiction fires. Kirchheim wanted to cross with four Jäger companies at the footbridge. He handed responsibility for all the pack animals to me. I was supposed to march them and my machine gun company northward on the eastern bank of the Piave River, and then cross farther upstream out of artillery range. But that route was also under fire and—even worse—subject to rock slides. Discounting any Italian action, which was possible but highly unlikely, I decided to follow Kirchheim over the footbridge. I went first, followed by seven hundred pack animals. Harassing fire in the mountains, where evasive maneuvering is impossible, does not exactly make for a pleasure walk on a narrow valley road. Marching slowly, stopping every few minutes for all elements to catch up, we reached Fener. It was an inferno like on the western front, but I was able to work my way around with the first twenty pack animals. Pack animal guide Number 20 had hesitated at every point along the way whenever I asked, "Has everybody caught up?" "All caught up!" he would answer; but it was not exactly so.

We had to go back. Close to the bridge most of the pack animals had turned left instead of right, and they were heading straight toward the enemy. Totally exhausted, I finally caught up with the lead animals, which by then were almost on top of the Italian positions. Turning them all around, we started back. This time, I stopped at the critical junction while under horrific fire and waited until the last animal had passed. By the time all elements had reassembled north of Fener and were safe and accounted for, we had had minimal losses. Three men had been killed by direct hits. But it was still a night of frustration.

The Mount Tombea massif with its foothills blocked the entrance to the plains. Taking this mountain was our mission. We moved into the mountain along narrow access paths, toward the two bridge locations under fire, where we crossed the torrente. Even weak artillery fire can turn a night march into hell. The path went straight up on the steep, razor-sharp ridges, slippery with wet snow. It was more than hell, because of the constant impact of mortar rounds.

There were no supplies coming forward, no bread. For days we scraped chestnuts out of the snow. There was no salt either. For eight days all we had was cold and saltless food, including the half-frozen chestnuts. Our only shelter from the weather was a thin, drafty tent half. All of this was enough to make this mountain a version of hell, even without the enemy's constant artillery fire. Our Austrian comrades called Mount Tombea "*Monte Paura.*"[46] There was nothing to add to that.

At night constant traffic moved along the narrow crest paths. Relief parties going up and down, carrier details, ammunition, mines, rations, wounded soldiers, everything and everybody moved back and forth in two uninterrupted lines through the most intense mortar fire. The descent was even more difficult than the ascent, because men constantly slipped and fell. Suddenly, there was a scream for a medic. The medics grabbed the man in the darkness and stuffed him into a tent canvas suspended from a tent pole. Then four men dragged the supposedly wounded man down the mountain. We did not leave our comrades behind. At the bottom of the slope the stretcher bearers collapsed with exhaustion ... but then the "wounded" man jumped up and disappeared into the dark. That was the only time I heard such human cries of utter anger and frustration.

Sometimes the shooting stopped. Heads popped up and you could see the Adriatic Sea on the horizon, Venice in the distance, and below us the town of Fener, built like it was made out of a wooden toy kit. "Run down to the local pub and get me a bottle of champagne," called Jung, our battalion adjutant, who was always good for a joke. One young Jäger actually got up and ran down to the town, returning with four hundred bottles of Marsala. The effect on our bodies, which hardly ever received any real nutrition, was devastating. The whole battalion was combat ineffective down to the last man.

The order to attack came as a relief. The Italian position was on a steep ridge. A narrow ridge ran toward the Italian main position. To the right the Leibers were supposed to attack to repel flanking attacks. Artillery fire was laid on the Italian position. The infantry assault was supposed to start at 0900, but nothing happened. Suddenly there was a raging crashing and whirring of splinters and rocks. Everything was covered in smoke and dust as shell after shell came in. All communications were out, and we had no word from the front line. Finally, a walking wounded came back from the 2nd Company. The Italians had moved into the gap between us and the Leib Regiment and had attacked our 2nd Company in the wire obstacles from behind. Our assault had stalled with horrible losses. All the officers had been killed and the 2nd Company flooded back into its initial attack position. The gorge was full of human corpses. The Italian heavy howitzer shells hit with incredible force. You could see clearly as the shells came in.[47] As they burst with a horrific bang the air was full of the shouts, "Medic, Medic!" At 1245 hours the Italian troops got on line for the assault. Even though some of our troops were retreating, a mountain gun from a Lower Saxony unit was pulled forward. Elements of the 1st Company under Feldwebel Falcke immediately prepared to counterattack. Our machine guns hammered away and finally threw the enemy back to his initial positions. Then help arrived in the form of a thick layer of fog that covered the mountain and facilitated the recovery of casualties and the withdrawal of our most forward elements.

One by one the casualties came stumbling back. One of them had gone mad and was crying like a child. Another had been buried alive and had lost his hearing, screaming all the time that he could not hear anymore. It was horrible. The Italians, however, never fired on retreating casualties that were walking or were being carried. They always stopped firing in such situations, which was absolutely unique in this war.

The 10th Reserve Jäger Battalion relieved us. We bivouacked in the valley near the railroad tunnel and the remnants of the battalion got some rest. That was the first and only time during the war that an attack by the 10th Jäger Battalion had been repulsed. The enemy artillery fire in our sector had just been too heavy, and the Leibers had been poorly positioned to protect our flank from the enemy. Consequently and understandably, the Leib Regiment had not attacked to cover us, but we never got the word.

In 1970 I returned to Mount Tombea. In my estimation, the attack should have succeeded if the staff of the Alpenkorps had considered committing the artillery of the adjacent division to our left. That would have choked off the Italians from the rear. Hardly any force could have withstood something like that.

We redistributed equipment in the bivouac area. Despite heavy losses, my courageous troops had not lost any equipment and had not left any of our wounded behind. Then we were hit with gas, as the poisonous vapors entered our railway tunnel. You learn who your friends are in such situations. As one soldier was trying to grab somebody else's mask in order to save himself, a runner came up to me, stood calmly at attention, and said, "Sir, your gas mask!" Only then did he put his own on.

"Monte Paura" was still holding us in its grip. We marched back up and relieved the 10th Reserve Jäger Battalion. We stayed up there for an extra day, and then we finally came down under orders. Inconveniently, our assigned rest area was situated to our left on the plains. We had to cross through the interdiction fire zone three times when we were relieved to go back to Vas. There we crossed the Piave River, which had been impossible to do in San Vito. Back on the other side of the Piave, we moved on difficult trails toward our left and front just short of Valdobbiadene, and from there straight away from the front line to Mareno, where our supplies were located. The total march was forty kilometers.

It was deathly quiet when we moved off Mount Tombea on 12 December—my birthday. In Fener it started up again, as we were subjected to raid after raid. The pack animals bolted from the designated holding area. We found them after many hours of tramping across the mountains. Daylight was gone as we pressed ahead under time pressure. I had ordered vehicles to meet us to pick up our equipment and the troops, but the Italian artillery had scattered them. Rain, mud, and a thick layer of sludge covered everything. Not a button or a rank insignia could be recognized. Desperate, on the edge of mutiny, the column pressed ahead, eyes glazed over, breathing heavily, muttering hard and angry words. As we were marching past the billets of an Austrian general officer's headquarters, a cook dressed in white, wearing his chef's hat and carrying a tray of freshly baked pastries, tried to shove his way through the column. I thought to myself, "This is not going to go well." At just that moment the cook was picked up and dumped on his head, and the tray of pastries was passed down the column. While the mud-covered cook sat on the side of the road, faces brightened, bodies straightened up, and marching along they sang, "Hurrah, I am a hunter of the 10th Jäger Battalion."

When we reached Mareno everybody collapsed into a death-like sleep. Then came the order, "Alert! Back to Mount Tombea!" We retraced our steps all over again, but when we arrived back at the peak we found that we were not needed anymore. We volunteered to stay one more day on this "mountain of horror" just to relax. Then we turned back and climbed down for good. The Italian campaign was over.

For the Record

Ludendorff had given priority to the offensive in Moldavia over the attack on Italy. As a result, we were dragged into the Italian rainy season, the immense impact of which nobody had had any clear idea about. Four to six weeks earlier the Tagliamento and the Piave would have been small creeks that could have been crossed easily at any point. The operational halt that had saved the Italians would not have happened. Originally, there had been no follow-on objectives. The intent had been only to relieve pressure on the Isonzo front with a short push. It is always a mistake, however, to push an offensive farther than originally intended.

Between the wars Ludendorff came to a gathering in Goslar of the 165th Infantry Regiment, which he had commanded at Liège. The officers stood on the parade field and were introduced to Ludendorff. "Where did you earn your *Hohenzollern?*"[48] he asked me.

"Near Tolmin,[49] your Excellency."

He looked at me musingly and said, "Ah, if only the Austrians had then . . ."

I wanted to say, "I thought we were never supposed to advance that far." However, the moment and my awe of this great soldier stopped me from showing the typical lieutenant's nerviness.

This time it certainly had not been the Austrians' fault. Their Germanic divisions and some of the others, particularly their Croatian and Bosnian regiments, had fought with the same boldness as did the first-rate German divisions of General Otto von Below's Fourteenth Army. General Krauss who commanded an Austrian corps, proved to be a master of mountain warfare and an outstanding leader of troops. Indeed, the attack of Field Marshal Franz Conrad von Hötzendorf's South Tyrolean Army Group near Asiago in the Sette Comuni did not punch through. But Conrad's forces had been too weak. Reinforcements were not able to reach him because of the sad state of the Austrian railway system. Some German units would have been able to reach him, but the consensus was that the Germans should not have been committed to the operation. The German High Command had made the correct decision in this case.

The question remains whether the Italian total collapse was predictable and calculable. It is most peculiar that German Intelligence in 1917 had predicted neither the French collapse of morale in the spring of that year, nor the Russian collapse, nor had it recognized or reported on the condition of the Italians. The total failure of this service did not allow us to see the potential for victory. If they had done a better job, many decisions made by OHL would have been different—I am thinking here especially of the resumption of unrestricted U-boat warfare. Victory would have certainly been ours if we could have prevented America's entry into the war, or even have delayed it.[50]

On the enemy's side, the rains that had turned the Tagliamento, the Piave, and all the other small streams into torrential, noncrossable rivers gave the Italians the time to halt the retreat of their army. Nor would the French and the English divisions have reached the Piave ahead of the Germans without those rainfalls.

There is another reason why the main Allied forces got to the right place at the right time. Shortly before the breakthrough at Tolmin an English patrol found a postcard in no-man's-land that a German soldier had lost. Written on it was: "We are enjoying well-deserved peace and quiet here in Austria, Heinrich." The card also included the field post number, which Allied intelligence was able to determine belonged to the Alpenkorps. The Allies then concluded correctly that wherever the Alpenkorps was, there would be the main effort. Certain indicators were already pointing to an offensive in Italy. That postcard from the field was the final piece of intelligence that contributed to the French and English divisions arriving at the Piave River just in time to stop the Italian withdrawal.

On the Italian side they did everything that any army would do to restore such a situation. Officers in the rank of captain and above that had abandoned their units were picked up in the rear areas and summarily executed without trial. Hemingway talks about this in *A Farewell to Arms*. In Albania in 1941 the Italian General Roni told me with some sense of pride. "What the French were capable of doing with their iron discipline, we, the Italians, did too."[51]

Italy for the foreseeable future had eliminated itself as a serious world power. But our Austrian allies also had shown such weakness that we had to be grateful that they were even able to hold the Italian front. They were hardly capable of any further serious, active participation in the war.

5

1918

Before the Decision

After my Christmas leave I rejoined my battalion near Bruderdorf, the area of the Battle of Lorraine in 1914. Every step of the way I passed French and German grave sites. The number of dead on the French side surpassed the Germans by a ratio of at least three- or four-to-one. In 1914 the French infantry had bled needlessly and anonymously, forcing the decision on the battlefield by attacking without regard for losses and in total disregard of the effects of modern weaponry. The limp French attacks during the Battle of the Marne and the subsequent Race to the Sea in late 1914 exhibited the same characteristics.

I asked Kirchheim for another Jäger company and was given command of the 4th. Up to this point every commander of that company had been killed, twelve in all; but I was not superstitious. Saying goodbye to my machine gun company was hard. Those were marvelous soldiers. But in leading a Jäger company one is a true leader, while the commander of a machine gun company is more of an organizer. And command, after all, is the most meaningful and valuable aspiration in the life of a young officer.

The coming great offensive in the West cast its long shadow.[1] A parade in honor of Hindenburg turned into a disastrous event of rain, snow, and hours of standing in the icy cold and muddy clay of Lorraine. Because my company was positioned in the second order we could not see anything. It was a huge disappointment. Instead of the formal parade, a casual visit to the soldiers' billets and talking to the assembled crowds would have had an incredible impact, but the military bureaucracy is archconservative.

Otherwise, we trained and prepared for the attack in the West. We were not assigned to the first wave. With tense anticipation we followed the reports about the first stage of the attack, the push toward Amiens. Morale was good throughout. The troops at the front wanted to win. The usual whining about wanting to be in the rear and wanting to be back home became less prevalent. The professional agitators grew more careful—they had to be. The rations were sufficient. They were certainly considerably better than at this time the previous year in the West.

Ludendorff's decision to attack in 1918 has since been criticized, because in the end it did not punch through, although there were some initial successes. Ludendorff wanted to defeat the English and the French before the Americans could be in position at full strength. He still trusted that the German army had sufficient energy to attack, but not the necessary strength to defend. This psychologically accurate assessment put him in agreement with the greatest of military leaders. During the attack there are always some individuals who propel the fight forward, with the masses following. In the defense, every individual, the lone fighters as well as the weak masses, must stand alone to maintain the defense. At this point in the war, most were no longer capable of such an effort.

Furthermore, a tactical turning point had been reached. Up to that point the defensive systems of barbed wire and machine gun, combined with our innovative defensive tactics, had always been one step ahead of the enemy, proving superior to even the most concentrated artillery barrage. With the appearance of large numbers of Allied tanks, the shifting of the balance of power from the defense to the attack became overwhelming. Barbed wire and machine guns were becoming obsolete and lost importance by the day. Countermeasures against the tank were not yet available in the necessary quantities. This presented an interesting variation in the classical debate about whether the attack or the defense was the stronger form of warfare. The answer, of course, is that every situation is different and subject to change. In 1943–1944 the German Army would once again have to address this key question.

The second major point of criticism about Ludendorff's offensives is that he emphasized tactics over the operational level. In other words, he did not want to expend his energy at an operationally critical location that was tactically strong, but rather he wanted to break through at a weak point, regardless of the operational value of the position. In doing so, he then intended to exploit the breakthrough to maneuver on the operational level. Here, too, Ludendorff may have been right, despite his many notable critics. What would have been the value of an attack at the operationally correct spot if it resulted in tactical failure?[2]

In the Italian province of Veneto, Austrian field marshal Franz Conrad von Hötzendorf attacked in 1916 and 1917 at the operationally correct spot, the Sette Comuni near Asiago. He intended to choke off the Venetian Pocket. The operations failed because the Italian positions were too strong tactically and could not be cracked with the means available. Ludendorff judged the situation in 1918 intuitively, and not based on dogma or theory.

Armentières

Near Armentières a new battle started on 2 April.[3] Operation MICHAEL had forced the English to shift strong forces to the south. But three weeks later the ground in Flanders had finally dried out and now was capable of sustaining large-scale attack operations.[4] Our push targeted two Portuguese divisions that had been put into the front line as replacements for the English forces that had been moved quickly to the south. As the Portuguese were neither very martially oriented, nor did they necessarily want to die for England, they were quickly swept away by the German divisions. They came toward us surrendering in droves, as we in the second wave followed the attacking lead divisions. We bypassed Armentières initially, as it was totally gassed. We were supposed to wait until the gas had dissipated, but then suddenly two battalions of the Alpenkorps were ordered to clear Armentières at gunpoint. The opposition in this case actually consisted of two of our own labor battalions that were supposed to clear and repair roads. Somehow they had managed to get into the city and were looting and drinking. There were sixteen deaths, all of whom had been drinking excessively and now lay dead in the wine cellars.[5] Some of the others had gotten into the factories. Almost all of them were wearing female corsets and tophats and were completely drunk. But the roads and bridges necessary to move the artillery and the ammunition forward had not been repaired and on the front line the soldiers were bleeding.

Other than that, the attack crept slowly across the broken terrain of Flanders that was marked by ditches and isolated farms. But the attack had already exceeded its culminating point. At the start only about four enemy batteries had been firing at us; a few days later they had fifty to sixty in action against us.

We were pulled out. For a short time we remained behind the front lines in a protected position. Everybody was involved in butchering and roasting livestock, and there was plenty of good wine and one cellar full of champagne. The entrance to the cellar was not easy to reach because of the heavy traffic in and out, and it quickly came under fire from English batteries. But not a single battle-hardened veteran could be scared off.

Mount Kemmel

Mount Kemmel lay threateningly on the right flank of the German attack, dominating for quite a long distance the flat lands to the north and south. Without controlling that high ground, we could hardly hold the salient we had driven in near Bailleul. The Alpenkorps was assigned to take it, and during the following days we took up positions on the outskirts of Lille and reconnoitered the ground. The battle zone was completely torn up. This was the area of the great 1917 battles in Flanders. Whole villages had disappeared. Craters lying right next to each other were filled with dark, smelly water. The Ploegsteert Forest was no longer there. Not a single tree was standing.

The entire country was one huge cemetery. The only thing growing there was barbed wire.

We received our operations order on Rossignol Hill. The objective to our front, Mount Kemmel, was the dominant terrain feature in Flanders.[6] To our right lay Messines Ridge, torn up by shells. There were no trees, no bushes. Only a few irregular reddish rises marked the spot where the village of Messines used to stand. We were briefed by the new first General Staff officer[7] of the Alpenkorps, Captain Günther von Kluge.[8] He told us, "This is only a local attack to deny the enemy Mount Kemmel; this is not a decisive breakthrough attempt." We were disappointed; we wanted to go to Calais; we wanted to destroy the enemy at the Yser River, and then take him from behind after we wrested Mount Kemmel from him.

The next day, 21 April, I was in Lille. I visited the citadel that had been constructed by Vauban, a masterpiece of the art of fortifications. Many captured English troops were inside the citadel, handsome looking and strong creatures. I spoke with several of them. In the past none of them had doubted that the English would be victorious. Now they said, "England has never been beaten and will not be now. But we also will not be able to beat the Germans."

On 23 April we moved forward in squad-sized elements to avoid observation from Mount Kemmel. It was a beautiful spring day. Since I had spent the whole morning observing the fall of shot of the enemy's artillery fire, I managed to get my company through unscathed. We conducted the relief in place of the frontline infantry, and I was able to look around the next day. We were closely interlocked with the enemy, sometimes only a few meters away. My right flank, however, was not tied into another German unit.

While there was little shooting going on during the entire day, around 2000 hours that evening heavy fire set in, which soon turned into a barrage. Shortly after 2200 smoke shells came in, followed quickly by machine gun fire and hand grenades. The 6th Company of the French 30th Infantry Regiment attacked from all sides into my right, wide-open flank. Holding this piece of terrain was absolutely essential for the security of the assembly area. I immediately counterattacked with the two platoons that were in reserve. I saw crouched in a hole the leader of the platoon on the right, Fähnrich Hümme, who I particularly liked. I gave him a swift kick and shouted, "Get up Fähnrich, no sleeping here." But I had kicked a dead body. Standing on the rampart, he had been leading his platoon's fight when the lethal bullet hit him.

My counterattack pushed the enemy back. The two platoon leaders of the French company were both killed, shot in the head. But the enemy still dominated our position with his machine gun fire. We were pressed for time. In two hours the 10th Reserve Jäger Battalion was supposed to relieve me, and I still had to reposition to the right. That required attacking and silencing the irritating French machine guns. Behind me some trench mortars went into position. I ordered them to fire onto the French machine guns. The platoon leader refused, saying he had orders not to fire until the actual attack. And besides . . . if he opened fire it would draw the enemy's fire onto his own position. Without hesitation I drew my pistol. "I will count to three, and then there will be a shot fired either from your mortar or from my pistol. One, two. . . ." A mortar shell came crashing down on the French machine guns. I was now able to accomplish the repositioning without further hindrance.

On 25 April I was in attack position behind the 1st Company of our battalion. At 0400 the gas attack began. Enraged, the French responded by laying destructive fire onto our attack positions at the maximum rate of fire. Then the fire started to slack and almost stopped.

At 0620 our trench mortars started to fire. Looking back I could see the whole horizon in an ocean of flames.

At 0703 hours I could clearly observe our zone. As a single man the battalion rose and stormed forward. Over by the 1st Company a machine gun rattled and they started taking losses. On the left things moved swiftly. Then, the French machine gun in front of the 1st Company was silenced, and the attack rushed forward like a torrential waterfall. The Ferme Lindenhoek fell, and French resistance started to collapse. Totally demoralized, they were either retreating or surrendering. I reached a ravine with my company and moved around the small Hill 95, where there was still intense resistance. We took it from behind. The French reserves, just getting ready to counterattack, threw down their rifles and shouted, "*Bons Camarades!*" As far as visible to both the left and to the right it was the same picture. By 1000 hours we had exceeded the day's objective by one kilometer. That was strictly prohibited because we had advanced beyond the range of our own artillery, which was dropping sporadic fire to our rear. On the hilltops along the horizon, near De Kleit and the Scherpenberg, one could see the fleeing French. Their batteries were taking off, singly and in groups, leaving abandoned guns everywhere. The enemy resistance ceased. The breakthrough had succeeded. I reassembled my company and marched forward singing in column toward De Kleit. Then the halt order reached us.

The company rested in the grass. Without meeting resistance, patrols moved up the Scherpenberg and toward De Kleit, bringing back cattle for slaughter. Right close to me stood our commander, Kirchheim, and the commander of the 10th Reserve Jäger Battalion, Captain Fischer, a 10th Jäger regular officer himself. Kirchheim, a bold, ingenious frontline soldier, wanted to go forward to the Scherpenberg. Fischer, brilliantly educated at the tactical level, emphasized the specific prohibition against overreaching the objective of the day. Our regimental commander was not there. We had no field communications with anyone, so we stayed where we were. It was not until midday and the afternoon that elements of the French 3rd Cavalry Division arrived on the decisive hilltops near De Kleit and the Scherpenberg, and barely closed the wide-open gap in the Allied lines. We had given away a potentially great operational success.

I have always viewed the Battle of Mount Kemmel as the decisive battle of World War I. If we had taken advantage of the great tactical success we had gained, and had used it for a push northward toward Poperinge, we would have gotten into the rear of the Allied forces there. Pushed against the sea, they would have been totally destroyed. If the enemy divisions positioned there had been taken out of action, the Allies would have had to establish a new front line running from St. Omer to Dunkirk. That would have required them to commit almost all of their remaining reserves. Most likely, it would have been impossible for Marshal Foch to shift over to a decisive counteroffensive after our next offensive, and the results consequently would have been unpredictable.[9]

The Battle of Mount Kemmel and, above all the failed opportunity to exploit that success, have never let go of me. In 1935, I wrote an article for *Militär-Wochenblatt*[10] about the Battle of Mount Kemmel, based on published documents which had been taken from the French. Ludendorff had not intended to make a decisive attack. He was playing a less risky game. He wanted to play it safe and postpone the decisive breakthrough for later. These were, perhaps, the first indicators of an impending crisis. One only wins through boldness, especially if everything is on the razor's edge.[11]

Almost daily Ludendorff got involved in the detailed preparations for the attack. Judging from the importance of Mount Kemmel, he suspected closely massed reserves behind it. Almost daily we heard his telephonic warning, "Taking the mountain will be easy, and then will come the counterthrust. Therefore, control the artillery tightly, and by all means reposition the artillery along the line Scherpenberg–De Kleit."[12]

This induced our Ia to talk of a limited local attack to take Mount Kemmel from the enemy. Once the objective for the day had been reached, he wanted to move the artillery forward and then take the Scherpenberg after another good artillery preparation. But as so often happens, the real enemy situation presented a different picture. German reserves were positioned behind Mount Kemmel, and the push of the seasoned regiments of the Alpenkorps had grown into a breakthrough within a few hours, and nothing but Ludendorff's timid carefulness and its incomprehensible effect on the staff of the Alpenkorps prevented the capture of the decisive high ground and the operational exploitation of this great tactical success.

A large number of after-action reviews cited the failure to move the artillery forward. It actually did end up in the wrong place. The attacking units were never assigned a follow-on objective, at least to the Scherpenberg and De Kleit, or even better, all the way to Poperinge. Reserve forces had been assembled right behind the Alpenkorps. The leaders were supposed to be forward near the front line, mounted on horses, in order to keep the push going and to give it a direction, just as Ludendorff had specified in his regulation on the offensive battle.[13] Elements of the artillery were to be attached to the infantry regiments right from the beginning and had orders to follow and support. But none of this ever happened. One mitigating factor for this failure was that the technical level of the communications at the time worked against flexible leadership on the battlefield—in fact, actually hampered it significantly. (Later, in 1940, when I was leading a regiment at a decisive point near Sedan, I had to think of Kemmel.)

We moved into a defensive line behind Kemmel Creek, at the base of the hill. In the twilight of the early morning the French 39th Infantry Division, without reconnaissance and in total ignorance of the situation, marched right into our machine gun fire. Their losses were horrible. The 39th Division had been alerted in Poperinge only at noon on 24 April. As our artillery attempted to bracket the French, it impacted right in the middle of my company. I was hit along with eight of my Jägers. Shell splinters tore through my right calf.

Two Jägers brought me back to an aid station dugout. Since the entrance faced the enemy, my stay there was not very comfortable. As a medic was propping me up right next to the entrance to help me conduct a certain bodily function, a French shell exploded. A splinter went straight across the medic's behind. He dropped me immediately and bolted. We later covered the dugout entrance with sand bags, but two more times shells exploded in front of the entrance. Finally, some litter bearers from the medical company came the following day, strapped me to a stretcher, and off we went. In the middle of the road in Kemmel Village we were caught by artillery fire. My litter bearers, four fat, goateed soldiers from the Baden region, left me on the road and disappeared. I lay there helplessly, strapped to the litter in the middle of the firestorm. When after half an hour the fire grew weaker, one after another of the fat goatees reappeared from the surrounding craters. "We never thought you would still be alive, Herr Lieutenant." I did not either.

After a horrible trip in an ambulance over torn-up roads, I ended up in a field hospital in Tourcoing. Fully realizing what would happen, I asked to have my personal belongings that were packed in a rucksack laid by my feet, so I could keep my eyes on them. "But, Herr Lieutenant, that's not very comfortable, I will set it right here next to me on the seat." Unfortunately, I agreed. I never saw my belongings again. But that was common. Even my father had his property skillfully stolen in 1914 by some helpful medics after he had been severely wounded as the commanding general near Warsaw. The only thing I really missed was a nice, handy edition of Clausewitz. Entertaining oneself during quiet periods on the battlefield by reading the great philosopher of war produced a strange sense of excitement.

Rest Period

My Jägers had soon figured out where I was and almost daily somebody came by and updated me. My injury turned out to be not overly severe, and when the battalion was relieved I sent for my dogcart, packed, told the nurse to give my regards to the physician, and disappeared. The battalion looked pretty mauled. Holding onto Mount Kemmel had been a bitter affair, but they had put up a good fight as usual. Although almost all the officers had been killed or wounded, not a square foot of ground had been relinquished. The hero of Mount Kemmel was the battalion surgeon of the 10th Reserve Jäger Battalion. He and a captured English medical NCO had walked the forwardmost lines daily, tending to the wounded. The Englishman had remained voluntarily. He appeared wherever there was any action. I can still picture him, a tall, strong man with a red face, red hair, and blue eyes, sparkling with passion. Eventually we had to turn him over to a POW camp.

The battalion surgeon, Dr. Samuel from Cologne, was a Jew. When the Battle of Mount Kemmel was over, his commander, Captain Fischer, recommended him for the *Hohenzollerschen Hausorden*,[14] which he was awarded. "I am an anti-Semite," said Fischer to his adjutant, "but I have to be fair." Dr. Samuel was one of probably only a handful of Jews who received this high frontline award. I am at least not aware of any others. After the war we invited Dr. Samuel to our get-togethers. He declined, explaining that his political convictions were different from ours.

We moved into beautiful quarters in Eine, between Gent and Oudennarde. It was a smiling, flowering countryside, with red brick houses, green gardens, hedges, and yellow, ripening grain fields. The Flemish inhabitants received us in a most friendly way. There were no communications problems between them and our Lower Saxons. "They're Germans," declared our Jägers.

I initially reported for duty in my dogcart, but shortly after I was lifted onto my horse and finally I was able to manage again. Our 1st Company found a large stock of Burgundy wine. Dutifully we reported this to the area commander, and the company commander received three bottles as a finder's fee. That bothered me. I complained and as a result every Jäger of my company received four bottles of Burgundy.

The influenza epidemic that was raging in 1918 was a peculiar experience. The 4th Company, 10th Jägers, never suffered from the flu while we were at the front. But I had a medical NCO, Sergeant Wehrstadt, who from August 1914 on had participated in every fight, every battle the battalion was involved in, without ever being wounded or getting sick. Right before the Battle of Mount Kemmel I sent him on home leave, against his will. I consciously wanted to spare him. But back in Brunswick he caught the treacherous disease and died.

Flanders had a lot to offer. Every weekend during our rest period I was able to roam through its old cities and I had a lot of contact with the people. I wrote into my diary at the time: "The Flemish are a real German tribe, a little stiff and austere, in a countryside still completely unpretentious. The cities, however, are very much Francophied. Had the Belgian government lasted another forty to fifty years, only the old people in the country would still be speaking Flemish. What will happen now? In my opinion, an independent Flemish state. It naturally would have to lean toward us, as they are opposed to the French and the Walloons. In the countryside this idea had a lot of adherents, but the cities were generally against it. Unfortunately, the countryside never had much influence in Flanders's glorious history. The cities set the tone. A German annexation would have been rejected even in the countryside."[15]

In mid-July we attacked near Reims, without success.[16] Keeping the attack a secret had failed. We were supposed to attack fourteen days later in Flanders.[17] However, as French officers who were captured near Reims knew of the day, the hour, and the extent of that attack, it was postponed. On 30 July we were moved to Tourcoing. On 8 August, the infamous "Black Day of the German Army," masses of Allied tanks broke through near Villers-Bretonneux, east of Amiens.[18] We were sent there.

The Turning Point

A war at its climax resembles a boxing match. Both contenders exchange hard punches. The outcome is uncertain until the last second, until an unexpected punch determines the outcome of the fight. Villers-Bretonneux was such a punch. It was a coincidence that this punch was delivered by the Entente armies. It could just as well have been delivered by us, despite the condition of total exhaustion all of the warring parties found themselves in by that point.[19] That, of course, would have required that we had not relinquished the initiative as we did at Mount Kemmel. We should have always retained the initiative and then followed up with strike after strike in order to exploit ruthlessly our initial success and not give the enemy a break. To what extent that would have been possible can hardly be judged now, and remains a hypothetical sand table exercise.

The big winners at Villers-Bretonneux were the enemy statesmen, especially French premier Georges Clemenceau. They had been trying their utmost to maintain the morale of their peoples and their armies, assuring them that the military, the necessary logistics, and the manpower were all up to the task. But on the German side there were no longer any responsible political and civilian agencies providing leadership in this war. The idea that war has to be led at the political level and would be won at that level never occurred to them.[20]

Up to the point of the unfortunate German offensive at Reims, the morale in the army was good overall. The frontline troops wanted to win and believed in the final victory. The agitators generally held back. There were, of course, dangerous symptoms. Twice Jägers in my company declined to take home leave, worrying about coming back with bad attitudes. It was depressing to hear the troops talk when they came back from leave. On the military trains agitators went from compartment to compartment, primarily targeting the officers. After 8 August the dam broke. As I noted in my journal at the time: "Had a meeting with Major von Wangenheim (10th Jägers). He had the same experience with the 'courageous' Saxons as we had. During the counterattack they had shouted out to his troops, 'War Prolonger!' One Saxon yelled 'Scab' after one of our sergeants in the train station at St. Quentin."

Only the home front could be blamed for this miserable situation. This horrible defeatism was our demise. Part of the blame, of course, lay with the officers of these units. But that did not help.

The German lines on the western front pulled back according to plan. A setback like at Villers-Bretonneux did not happen again. As I wrote in my journal near the end of the war: "The Entente has conducted these attacks with an incredible expenditure of materiel (tanks); but that is not the only reason for our defeat. In the past we had managed to deal with much greater material superiority ratios, and we developed highly effective, defensive measures against tanks. As a result, they lost their horrific effectiveness against us." The real reason had to lie somewhere else. Through the continuous propaganda at home, enemy agents, and—sad to say—the internal enemy of defeatism our troops acquired during home leave, their confidence in victory and the justice of our cause was undermined.[21] Enemy propaganda leaflets also had their effect. Often they were very cleverly designed.

The best German divisions had not borne the brunt of the enemy attack on 8 August. Those units had been mostly second echelon trench divisions, whose mission it was to hold the ground that had already been taken by the more hard-hitting attack divisions.[22] These lesser quality units had been positioned in exposed terrain under difficult combat conditions since March. Normally, the leadership of the officers should have overcome this difficult situation. But even the officers of these divisions were often second rate. Constant care and the constant example of enduring hardship and discomfort were missing. Compounding that, our peculiar views on enforcing military discipline had gradually resulted in no one any longer fearing punishment, which was rarely administered.

The signs of the creeping disintegration were alarming. The example of the Russian Revolution had been infectious. Soldiers returning from leave often explained that they were told in Germany, "It is all your fault. Just quit!" Rigorous intervention against those who did not want to fight or who engaged in propaganda was lacking. The most severe legal actions should have been applied against them. For too long those people were allowed to conduct their underhanded business. But even during this difficult time our battalion fought with its usual boldness. It never failed. The fighting was especially fierce around Épehy, where Kirchheim received a well-deserved *Pour le Mérite*.[23]

Our Jägers were doubtlessly far superior to the English troops. The latter made a poor impression. All were extremely young, freshly drafted in England, totally sluggish, tired, complaining about the conditions in their army, and complaining about the poor food. Wherever they faced machine gun fire their advance halted. The old, proud Englishmen were gone for good.[24] In one dugout we found the inscription, "Long Live the Irish Rebels; Down with the English Starvation Army!" Two to three squads of Jägers could easily defeat the same number of English companies. Nottbohm, who commanded the 14th Reserve Jäger Battalion, which only numbered forty troops, dislodged a fully manned English battalion from its position.

News of the Austrian peace offer had a bad effect on us. We did not believe in a negotiated peace. We believed that the war would last until one side broke, and then the other would be foolish not to take whatever it could.

Near the end of the war I was a member of a court-martial board. Two men from a recently arrived replacement unit had gone from position to position during an alert saying that the alert had been cancelled, thus preventing the replacements from going forward. For years those two had been categorized as indispensable civilian war workers and were well-nourished laborers from Halle. The court-martial convicted them to prison time, which they accepted happily. They knew that they would never have to serve their time. The prosecution had argued for the death penalty, but the verdict of the board was not unanimous.

Near the end of the war I was standing between two horses when a shell cut one of them down. As I crawled from under the dead horse, I said: "That would have served Captain Kirchheim right if I had gotten killed right here." I had been assigned to the battalion's leadership reserve pool because Kirchheim wanted somebody available to replace him as battalion commander if something happened. Our regimental commander had assured him that he would not request another replacement for him, and that I would be the one, despite my youth.

On 23 September the last of our Jägers came out of the front lines. I had made arrangements for all of them to get baths and I had a table set up with a white tablecloth in a barn. They were served soup, roast, and dessert. A rear echelon troop stuck his head in the door and yelled out, "The common man is bleeding at the front and the officers are dining back here." He probably had expected a better response to his comment. I often wondered what happened to him.

About that time we buried Captain Fischer, the commander of the 10th Reserve Jäger Battalion. He was a marvelous, highly educated soldier. I owed a lot to him from before the war, when I was still a Fahnenjunker. He was killed standing up at the edge of the trench, without cover, directing the attack against an English machine gun nest.

A 19 September message from our regimental commander, Lieutenant Colonel Bronsart von Schellendorf, documents the heroic fight that the regiment conducted:

> The 10th Jäger Battalion has a strength of 22 Jägers; the 10th Reserve Jäger Battalion has 32 Jägers. The 14th Reserve Jäger Battalion has a strength of 80 Jägers and six operational machine guns, excluding the battalion staff. We will try to equip the remnants of the first two units with three machine guns each. They are to be combined into one battalion under First Lieutenant Hornbostel.
>
> Therefore, the combat strength of the regiment has been reduced to two Jäger companies and one machine gun company. Aside from the numerical weakness, the majority of personnel is no longer combat effective. Approximately only forty men of the 14th Reserve Jäger Battalion have had four days of rest, the remainder are in a state of psychological as well as physical exhaustion, the likes of which I have not seen in this war.
> Signed
> Bronsart von Schellendorff

Even the enemy acknowledged us. One of the leaflets dropped on us read: "Members of the Alpenkorps, please start defecting like everybody else!"

Back to the Balkans

Replacements, machine guns, horses, and equipment arrived. The Alpenkorps was loaded up rapidly with orders to be prepared to conduct battalion-size operations immediately upon off-loading. Wild rumors floated around. Our potential destination ranged from Archangel to the Caucasus Mountains, to Salonika. Finally, we were on the train rolling on old, familiar routes toward the Balkans. Machine gun training, machine gun zeroing, reorganizing the company, all had to be done on the moving train. We even conducted live fire exercises during the long halts in Hungary. We emplaced one machine gun in front of the locomotive to prevent the train from leaving without us. We knew Hungary and its railroad system all too well. When we were past Belgrade and approaching Niš we started to feel more secure. We quickly forgot the western front as the beautiful country stretched before us. At more than a hundred meters you could not distinguish between a pig and a sheep. Both were the same size and had the same dark wool on their backs. They only tasted different.

Bulgaria had collapsed and the Bulgarian Army came rolling back home, aimlessly pillaging throughout the country. This signified the end, but even the end requires hard discipline, courage, prudence, and gumption from the highest general down to the lowest supply clerk. Otherwise everything ends in a gruesome catastrophe and unnecessary casualties, as happened to the Austrian Army in the Veneto.

When we entered Niš there were two trains loaded with clothing halted at the station. Our 2nd Company was detailed to guard them. Two Bulgarian companies in the area intended to seize the two trains and their contents and take them to Bulgaria. The situation was just at the point of breaking into a firefight when the Bulgarians decided to withdraw as more German troops arrived.

Bulgarian Collapse

The battalion reassembled in Mramor, ten kilometers south of Niš. Bulgaria as a country had collapsed. German and Austrian forces were assembling in the Niš–Pirot area in order to reorganize the German and Austrian units and to secure the southern border of Austria-Hungary.

The situation was unstable. Gangs and individual deserters were everywhere, and one prisoner claimed to be a Serbian soldier. The Bulgarian troops hardly wore uniforms anymore. They had resigned and accepted the inevitable. The young women and girls from the villages ran into the cornfields and hid there. They knew how wars were fought in the Balkans. The Bulgarians pillaged the whole country, rounding up all the cattle and piling the harvest into carts. What we came across there was unfathomable.

The new German High Command[25] ordered us to take all of the loot from the Bulgarians. We could not fight a war in a plundered land. The order was to collect up all the grain and to return all of the cattle to the local Serbian farmers. The Bulgarians were allowed to take only their assigned vehicles with them. My company established a bridge checkpoint at the Morava River, where I was supposed to control everything that crossed. As dawn was breaking on 5 October, a wandering mass of people started coming toward us. Near the front of the group a Bulgarian supply officer led one hundred carts filled with grain. Trying to negotiate, he took me aside and pulled back the canvas cover on one wagon with a dozen beautiful girls. He offered them to me if I would let him pass through with the rest of his wagons. Shaking his head, he moved along without his carts and only his bordello wagon. He just could not understand the world anymore.

Wagon upon wagon followed. Herds of looted cattle were pulled out of the line and not allowed to cross the bridge. Then came a column of fifty prisoners, each one shackled to a long chain with an iron ball. Gasping, they carried their heavy loads in their arms as they trudged forward. A Bulgarian officer came marching along amid large herds of cattle, carrying a gnarly cane. He was a former Chetnik.[26] With his long curls falling down to his shoulders and a huge beard reaching down to his belt, he was the very picture of a patriarch right out of the Old Testament. He hugged me and kissed me, as I was enveloped by a repugnant smell of garlic. The valiant Jäger standing next to me probably thought that he wanted to eat me, as my head disappeared in the huge beard. He threw himself between us with the courage of desperation. Even Jonah escaping the mouth of the whale could not have been happier and more relieved than I was.

We did finally reach an agreement. He was allowed to move on with one wagon and a few heads of cattle. Gratefully, he gave me a photograph of himself during his younger years in the Macedonian dress of a Chetnik, the belt stuffed with daggers and pistols. In his left hand he held an infantry rifle and his right hand casually rested on a few severed Turkish heads. It was a souvenir of the only man who ever kissed me.

On 6 October we marched southward with orders to deny the enemy a sector in the Jasjaza Planina. Masses of people moved toward us, with cattle herds following more cattle herds. To keep things simple we just let the Serbs have them. At that point only the horses and mules were of any interest to us. We confiscated all the mounts of a Bulgarian troop. That evening we moved into Prokuplje.

Mounted Jägers

On 7 October we reached the top of the pass at Jasjaza Planina, where I was supposed to block the enemy. The terrain was favorable, deforested, and dotted with a number of charcoal makers' huts. Made from freshly cut fir trunks, they were round, with a fire burning in the middle and the smoke escaping through the top. Several other companies were positioned to my right and left, several kilometers away, but we were not in direct contact. I had a mountain machine gun detachment under my control, giving me almost twenty machine guns. I kept tight control of everything in a large perimeter. Unfortunately, I was supposed to detach and move forward one platoon under an officer by the name of Lieutenant Wohlers to Zitni Potnuk, which was twelve kilometers away.

"Herr Lieutenant, can we ride? We have horses enough." Excited voices pressured me from all sides.

"All right then, but. . . ." They all stormed toward the captured Bulgarian horses and my happy troops rode off as "mounted Jägers." I rode along with them and made sure they were quartered in an isolated farm that was easy to defend. But I did not feel very comfortable as I rode back to my base position. The mood was too upbeat; but Lieutenant Wohlers was well tested and reliable.

It was noon the next day when I saw them again . . . but without the horses. The night had been quiet, and that morning they had mounted up. Unfortunately, a Serbian squadron approached them. The Bulgarian horses threw up their heads, whinnied, and took off toward the Serbian horses. It was too much. My Jägers jumped off the small Bulgarian horses, and once they had firm ground under their feet again they felt more stable. They grabbed their rifles and fought their way back to my position without losses. Wohlers had led brilliantly, calmly, and prudently. He was a farmer's son from Lower Saxony.

Serbs, Chetniks, and Old Wives

We made preparations to receive the anticipated attack from the Serbian squadron. We made our position appear dead, and we wanted them to come in right on top of us. But we noted many old women that were collecting wood in the forest. They came and they disappeared.

Then dismounted Serb riflemen started crawling carefully toward us. They knew exactly where we were. The old women had done their job perfectly. We had to play a different game, then. I ordered the troops to make a lot of noise that night. But the next morning all was deathly quiet one hour before dawn. Everyone was hidden. Then a single one of my machine guns started firing, and shortly after the crew one by one came running back to the main position across the pass. When the Serbs started shooting at them, my troops dropped the gun and bolted. That was too much for the Serbs. Shouting "Zivio, Zivio" from all sides, quixotic figures jumped up and stormed forward, swinging their rifles and pistols over their heads. Then my twenty machine guns opened up. After that encounter they left us alone.

During the following days the Alpenkorps withdrew toward the north. I had to remain in close contact with the enemy, hanging far back in the column. There was shooting all around us, as the old women continued to collect wood, even at night and on completely desolate hilltops. Below us, enthusiastic shouting broke out whenever the Serbian cavalry moved into the liberated villages. That night I received a blinker-light signal, "Is Lieutenant Balck there? What is the enemy doing?" I replied, "Lieutenant Balck is here! Enemy is doing fine." Days later I met up with our brigade commander, General Karl von Kleinhenz. "There you are," he said. "I have to thank you. It was a horrible situation. Everything was in flux. The division did not have contact with any of its elements and then came your blinker signal, '. . . enemy is doing fine.' Now, if elements that far forward still have that much of a sense of humor left, then everything is in order." General Ludwig von Tutschek, the Alpenkorps divisional commander, also got a good laugh out of the message.

The Serbs followed us very carefully. Our disengagement had worked. Then in Kaonik on 14 October as we were in a deathlike sleep: "Alarm, 1st and 4th Companies immediately back into forward position!" In a pitch-black night on a miserable path I found the area where we were supposed to go. I coordinated the location with the 1st Company, a house where their left flank post would be and where we could maintain contact. I positioned the platoons I had with me and then rode off to link up with another of my platoons; but when I got to where they were supposed to be, nobody was there. I searched and searched. Nothing. I rode farther on, but still nothing. In the twilight of the rising moon I saw three individuals in a clearing. I rode toward them, but then shots rang out. That clearly was the wrong address. I then started riding along a path where my people should have marched, but almost immediately I was shot at by a Serbian patrol. After an endless search I rode back to where I had left the rest of the company . . . and they were all there. The platoon I had been looking for had gone around in a circle and ended up again with the rest of the unit.

Just as I had resolved that one, another problem popped up. The blinker signal said, "Immediately make contact with battalion!" Meyer, my relentless messenger, ran back. He returned two hours later with the field kitchen. Suddenly the blinker signal stopped and we had no more communications. Once again I had to send Meyer back to the battalion command post. Angry, hungry, but still driven by his sense of duty, Meyer disappeared back into the night. But when he reached the village where the battalion staff had been located, it was empty. Finally, he found the battalion adjutant, Lieutenant Hinze, who told him, "You're supposed to move your company back to Kruševac immediately. Inform the 1st Company too."

"Yes, Sir! I would like to point out, though, that I may just collapse on the way back. I have been on my feet forever."

"Can you ride a horse?"

"Yes, Sir!" Actually, Meyer did not know how to ride.

"Orderly, dismount! Okay, Meyer, get on it and good luck."

But his boots hardly fit into the stirrups. So on foot again, with two men escorting him, Meyer staggered back to my position.

"Back to Kruševac," he told me. "There are no friendly forces in front of us anymore."

"Now, where exactly is Kruševac?"

"I have no idea either, somewhere back there toward the left."

As I formed up the company, the brave Oberjäger Kuenstel took off by himself into the Serbian night and wilderness, moving out with his rifle at the ready. Meyer and I moved toward the 1st Company to inform them. We were shot at along the way, but the 1st Company was nowhere to be found. Somewhere in the direction of Kruševac we could hear dogs barking. Was that where the 1st Company was? I had to make a decision. I rode back to my company and got them marching. We could not stay there until daybreak. I also could not leave anyone behind. Together with Meyer, I followed the rear of the company column.

After a while I halted the company and stepped into a building to check my map. It appeared that we were going in the right direction. But after we started moving again I lost track of Meyer. He had been with us at the last halt. Had he fallen out? At the pace we were keeping, it would have been no wonder. I halted the company and rode back calling, "Meyer, Meyer!" After a while I thought I heard a weak voice calling in the night: "Hallo, 4th Company?"

When I finally found him I said, "Meyer, where have you been? I have been looking for you all night."

"I have been waiting in the village for you, sir."

"Sure you were, and you fell asleep, right?"

I finally had everybody back together. At dawn we crossed the Morava near Kruševac and moved into positions on both ends of Jasika. The 1st Company had fallen behind and did not arrive until twenty-four hours later. They had to fight their way through the Chetniks and the Serbs. About that time the news we received from the home front was horrible. We listened to U.S. President Wilson's peace proposals and all became very quiet.

We dug new positions. There was plenty of meat in the countryside and the grapes were plentiful. The late summer weather was marvelous, but we did not take much notice of the beauty of the Serbian landscape, with its beech forests spread out like an English park. Although there was shooting everywhere, we suffered hardly any losses as long as we kept close control of everything. Occasionally, however, carelessness led to some unpleasant incidents. The pack animals that were bringing food for one company of a battalion of the Alpenkorps were attacked by women and children. Because of the heat, the animal guides had left their weapons in their nearby quarters and consequently could not defend themselves. The old wives disappeared into the forests with the pack animals and all the guides' clothing. Instead of the expected noon meal, twelve naked guides showed up at their unit. There clearly was a shortage of textiles in the Balkans.

We had no reliable intelligence about the enemy at this time, and therefore we had to take some prisoners. I was supposed to raid Kruševac, which lay in our sector of the front line. Reconnaissance had determined that such a raid was feasible. Replacements arrived, third-rate troops who had spent the entire war back at home where they had been assigned to X Corps. Along their way to the front they had raised red flags and had fired off all their ammunition. They arrived at noon. I made sure they were given a good meal. I allowed them to mingle with my troops for a while, and then I had them fall into a formation. I addressed them, "Tonight we will raid Kruševac and you are coming along!" Then I talked to them individually. From that moment on there were no more problems. They fought just like everyone else. The spirit of the Jäger had infected them quickly. I had not really needed them on the raid, but it was an old rule. Replacements were only valuable once they had been blooded.

We forded the Morava during the night and entered the town of Kruševac from two sides. The well-seasoned Feldwebel Falcke from the 1st Company captured a guard post. Our prisoner was not supposed to be a Chetnik, but a regular Serbian soldier. Once we had him we started heading back with no further complications. Except for the minor glitches that are common in such situations, everything had gone according to plan. I had broken off the operation at just the right time, before the enemy could initiate any counter actions. The whole thing had come off much to the frustration of my adventurous Jägers, who were still suspecting that there was an entire Serbian battery in the barracks at Kruševac.

On 22 October we resumed our withdrawal. The marvelous, mild late summer weather was replaced by cold and intense fall rain. We broke contact with the enemy by marching in a single day the incredible distance of more than sixty kilometers in the rain, over inhospitable mountain terrain, and on even more impossible paths. Again and again our rear guard elements skirmished with the increasingly aggressive Chetniks who were lurking everywhere. To give our pack animals some relief, we had loaded all of our supplies onto ox carts, the unfailing transportation mode of the Balkans. The only thing we had to remember was to give them time to chew their cuds, otherwise they would drop on us. But we were well experienced in the ways of the Balkans.

Once again my company was ordered to form the advance guard. The pouring rain was icy cold. We were happy to find some shelter from the rain in several pigsties along the route. We spent that night standing up and leaning against each other. Sitting down or even laying down in that filth was out of the question, despite our exhaustion. At dawn I received a blinker signal: "Back to Belgrade!" The company moved alone through the mountains. We could see neither enemy nor friendly forces. On 1 November the 4th Company, 10th Jäger Battalion, was the last German unit to cross the railroad bridge over the Sava River. We blew the bridge behind us. The Alpenkorps reassembled on the parade field at Semlin. I was able to slip into a horse track with my company. Laying next to me on the straw was the commander of the Bavarian Life Guards Regiment, Colonel Franz von Epp.[27]

Back through Hungary

By 1 November the divisions that had been pulled together to secure Hungary's southern border were of relatively poor quality. They mostly came from Romania and southern Russia. An Austrian officer from an adjacent division to our right, which swiftly disappeared to the rear, told me that one of the divisions had once been first-rate. The 9th Jäger Battalion had been in the Ukraine for a year and was now thoroughly infected with Bolshevik ideas. They no longer had any combat value. The adjacent 219th Division to our left was not much better.

That night I went one more time to the "Black Cat," a famous German guesthouse in Semlin. It claimed to serve the best wines between Vienna and the Black Sea. I remembered it from when I was there in 1915. The wines were still first class, but there was a lot of excitement. Croatia had declared independence. The ethnic Germans of Semlin, who were quite numerous, quickly repainted their German business signs in Croatian.

On 2 November we reached the Serbian village of Old Pazua. I was able to billet my entire company there only by force. Our field army headquarters had been out of communications with OHL for four days, and nobody knew what was going on. There was no mail service. There were rumors of a railroad strike in Hungary. What was going to happen next was a total mystery. Thank God the most maddening rumors did not become reality. It did appear that Germany had yielded to Wilson in all points. It was disgusting to think that our democratic politicians were now saying that they had to shoulder the guilt and the collapse of the old system. Why did the old system collapse in the first place? Only because some idealists and unscrupulous, overambitious people exploited the predicament of the government, which did not have a strong leader. The more severe the collapse, the greater the upheaval.

On 3 November there were indicators of total collapse. Austrian soldiers walked around without the national cockade on their caps, but with blue, white, and red ribbons instead. Numerous prisoners—Italians, Serbs, and Romanians—had been released by the new Croatian state. There was shooting everywhere. The country had gone crazy.

On 4 November we crossed the Danube near Neusatz-Peterwarden. Citizen militias were everywhere, and for some unknown reason they were constantly shooting in the air. From the latest newspapers we learned that the Austro-Hungarian Empire no longer existed. Both states of the new federation had reached an armed truce with the Entente. Judging from the conditions that the former Danubian monarchy and Turkey received, it looked damned little like rapprochement to us. Would this open eyes in our delusional homeland?

On 5 November we were subordinated to Mackensen's army group. We were supposed to fight our way back to Germany, together with the divisions returning from Romania. In the Serb village of Bekices our quartermasters were ambushed and stripped of everything. The regimental ordnance officer, Lieutenant Burandt, had led them well and fearlessly under difficult conditions against a superior force. For one last time the battalion developed the situation, as long lines of riflemen advanced toward Bekices, our bayonets reflecting the setting sun. The battle was short and intense. During the night we interrogated all the inhabitants and learned that we were in an allied country after all. A few criminals that had escaped from a prison in Budapest had established a regime of terror in Bekices. They beat to death the local mayor and a few of the dignitaries and disarmed everybody. We took care of them properly. In the next villages we reached the inhabitants welcomed us with white flags, bread, and salt.

The area we were moving through on 6 November had a peculiar ethnic mix of peoples that had flowed in after it had been depopulated during the Turkish wars. There were very few ethnic Hungarians. Communism seemed to be the order of the day. All the cattle in the village had been herded together and redistributed.

On 7 November the pending armistice was announced in the West. Our mood was quite gloomy, even though the situation was inevitable. On 9 November an Austro-Hungarian artillery regiment was disarmed at the entrance of East Beseke. Every civilian was armed. Nobody, not even the ethnic Germans, wanted to billet our troops. The only way we accomplished that was to move toward the doors with loaded weapons.

We marched to East-Verbacs on 10 November. It was a dismal, foggy day, which matched our mood. The Kaiser and the crown prince had abdicated. The

German fleet had mutinied. Kiel, Wilhemshaven, and Hamburg were occupied by the mutineers, and armed sailors were moving into Oldenburg, Hannover, and Magdeburg. The garrison in Hannover supposedly was still resisting the mutineers. So this was the grand finale. There was revolution in Munich, and workers' and soldiers' councils everywhere. Typically enough, the troops who had not done any of the fighting for four and a half years were the ones now making revolution. If a good portion of the army resisted the storm, everything would not yet be lost. The present poison had to be eradicated. The core of the German people was healthy enough to overcome the disease.

Billeting the troops caused all kinds of problems, even though the village was inhabited by ethnic Germans. Nobody wanted to house our troops, even in the pigsty. Only force could make the locals change their minds. The local people were saying to themselves, "The war is lost. We do not want to have anything to do with you." The uncertain future weighed heavily on them.

We read in the Hungarian newspapers about the negotiations between Mihály Károlyi, the new Hungarian political star, and the French commander, Franchet d'Espery. Károlyi was treated like a shoeshine boy. We quietly gloated over that.

The Alpenkorps was still holding together on 11 November. Only a few of the troops were trying to get home on their own, mostly farmers who were worried about their property. The Hungarians wanted to intern us. A Hungarian captain in St. Tomacs claimed to be selling exit visas to Germany. A few troops in the Saxon Division fell for the scam. After twenty kilometers they were pulled from the train, robbed, and interned. Then the Hungarian propaganda campaign kicked off: the Serbs supposedly were arriving today; all of the staff officers supposedly had gotten away in cars. The intent was to destroy the morale of the German troops by any means. But my soldiers were amazing. I was absolutely sure of them, and the situation in the other Jäger companies was similar. Everyone in St. Tomacs was actually expecting the Serbs. Serb banners, Serb flags, flower bouquets were prepared for the liberators. The local militia acted rather arrogantly.

The abdication of the Kaiser left our troops relatively unfazed. He was too far removed from them as a person. As a leader of his people he had been too detached. The people yearned for strong leadership, however. The Kaiser can be blamed for not providing that for his people, which is what did him in at the end.

On 12 November the Alpenkorps started to march to Silesia, a movement planned to last twenty-four days. The first night we were billeted in Obesce. As usual, I was going through the billets with my first sergeant, the marvelous, short, wiry Sitte, when a woman blocked Sitte's path with a dung fork. Her husband joined her, carbine in hand. I knocked him down with the butt of my pistol and grabbed his rifle. Sitte grabbed the dung fork, but he slipped and fell into a deep dung pit. Like Neptune from the waves, he reappeared with trident in hand from the horrible bath. Militia quickly appeared to help, but our Jägers were also right there and the tense situation quickly passed. Only Sitte remained dripping and foul smelling in the middle of a bunch of laughing Jägers.

On 13 November we refused a summons to turn in our weapons. From the latest newspapers we learned that all the dynasties had abdicated, but there were no major disturbances. Workers' and soldiers' councils were everywhere and OHL had offered its loyalty to the new government. But under the existing armistice conditions Germany would quickly approach famine conditions. The country's situation was never more serious. Famine would lead to bloody anarchy. Every decent German would now have to commit himself to the cause of law and order, no matter who was the head of the government, whether Liebknecht, Ledebour, Ebert, or Scheidemann.

The worldwide revolution supposedly took a hold of the Entente powers. Would world communism be our savior in the end? In all reality I believe that we still do not fully understand our era. Something big was happening here. You could actually feel it, but at the same time not really understand it. A new epoch in world history was about to start.

15 November was a rest day in Zenta, the place where Prince Eugene of Savoy had beaten the Turkish army decisively.[28] Our regimental commander had issued the order for each company to elect a council of trusted members. Our marvelous Jägers refused unanimously to support such an undertaking. The battalion was steadfast in its attitude. Nobody wanted that kind of change.

We reached Magyarkanizsa on 16 November. Looking at the power of the nobility from the middle ages to today, there is a pattern of powerful rulers in quick succession that elevate the power of their state by competing with their peers. The peak of this development was reached during the era of the absolute monarchs, Frederick the Great, Louis XIV, Charles XII, etc. After that, the individual power of the monarchs declined because of the lack of superior personalities. As time progressed, royalty increasingly struggled with their populace over the preservation of the crown's privileges. What we had in the end were no longer real kings. The great European revolution made obvious what had already happened internally.

On 19 November we moved out of Szegedin. In the end, the firm resolve of the Alpenkorps to force its way out if necessary paid off. But then came a really difficult hour when we had to leave our most faithful comrades behind, our horses and mules. For years we had taken good care of them and had pampered them through snow and ice, through barrages, the Alps, and the flatlands, while they always served us faithfully. Now we had to hand them off to the Hungarians for next to nothing. Every so often a shot rang out whenever a pack animal guide could not bear to see his horse in strange hands. We were allowed to take only sixteen horses with us; more than six hundred remained behind. It had been my plan to ride back to Germany with all of the battalion's horses. There were enough Jägers that had volunteered to ride along, but the first General Staff officer of the Alpenkorps, Captain Reitzenstein, advised against it. He was concerned that the Hungarians might refuse to give passage to the animals if we had to commandeer their fodder along the way. I knew Reitzenstein as a man of action. There was a special bond of trust between us, and I followed his advice.

We squeezed into just a few freight cars and then we started moving. Then we stopped and received a telegram from the Hungarian minister of war: "Continuation of transport only guaranteed if battalion fights against the Czechs."

We answered: "Will fight, but only against Hungary." The train immediately started moving again.

In Pressburg[29] the station commander wanted to disarm us. For the last time, the troops of the battalion picked up their rifles, occupied the train station, and detained everyone that was armed. The bitterness of our soldiers could hardly be curbed. The Czechs threatened us with an armored train, which they did not have. When they saw how mad our troops were they sent a telegram to their war ministry. The answer came back within five minutes: "Move them along immediately!" Twenty minutes later the train was on its way.

Flawless order ruled in Austria, fortunately.

On 23 November we crossed the Bavarian border near Salzburg and deloused in Rosenheim. The red cockade and the red gorget of a Feldwebel with the inscription "Soldiers' Council" were the only signs of change. Whenever our soldiers glared at those characters, they disappeared. We apparently were not welcome around there either. Otherwise, there was commendable order everywhere. The enlisted soldiers acted absolutely correctly toward the officers. Our first impression was that except for the red cockades nothing had changed in Germany.

On 25 November at 2000 hours our train arrived at the Goslar train station. We had expected to be met by the commander of the 1st Battalion, Major von Pappenheim. Instead, the Soldiers' Council was there. Kirchheim did not even look at those people. He ordered us to get off the train, and in old-fashioned order and firm attitude the battalion marched into its beloved old garrison town. The streets were mobbed with cheering people. It was quite different from what we had expected. The mayor greeted us in front of the town hall, delivering a lackluster speech appropriate for the times. What else could he say? And then we moved into badly prepared and sparse quarters, with no tables, no chairs, and no lights.

6

Retrospective on World War I

Before I continue with my memoirs, I would like to take a look back on World War I. For years I have been occupying myself with the analysis of its problems. I have read almost all of the literature foreign and domestic. The thinking of today is considerably different from our thoughts, our feelings, and our awareness in 1918.

Could we have continued the war? Contrary to our feelings then, today this question has to be answered with a clear "No." After the collapse of our allies the southern flank of the Reich was unprotected. The forces necessary to use against our newly emerging enemies were not available in the right numbers.[1] The loss of the Romanian oil fields was decisive. The lack of fuel would have forced a halt to the war by March 1919 at the latest. That was not sufficient time to achieve a military decision—not even if it had been possible to reestablish discipline in the army and on the home front. Even though the French, the English, and the Italians were in a similar state of exhaustion, Germany was at a turning point. Our morale inevitably would have declined, even after a short, possible improvement, because of the increasingly dire situation regarding materiel and having to fight the war on our own territory. In contrast, the morale of the Entente powers would have improved through rising expectations. Compounding all that was the unbroken power of the American Army. Nor did we have effective antitank weapons in sufficient numbers.

OHL [*Oberste Heeresleitung*] has been blamed for advising the government of the necessity of concluding an armistice in a hasty and totally unprepared manner. This charge shows a total ignorance of the nature of war. Only the events of the "Black Day" of 8 August exposed for friend and foe alike the true state of the German Army. The situation required very fast action, which Ludendorff accomplished in an objective manner, without consideration for embellishing his own legacy. This fast and decisive step saved the substance of the Reich and Germany from Bolshevism. A continued muddling through, which is all that could have followed, would have led inevitably to a total collapse. With a sense of responsibility and a correct assessment of the situation, a decision of rare significance had been made. The fact that the civilian authorities were surprised and unprepared was the consequence of a total lack of teamwork.

The Kaiser, the soldiers, and the civilian authorities were all equally guilty for the results.

The Stab-in-the-Back Legend

Few things have excited the German public to this day as much as the so-called Stab-in-the-Back legend surrounding the revolution that started in Germany that November. Depending on one's political perspective, the events of November 1918 are used to discredit the political opposition, whether on the left or on the right. Objectivity has no place in this process. Allow me to clarify a few facts here:

1. The so-called revolution had no effect on the outcome of the war. The war was lost. The revolution did, however, weaken Germany's position at the negotiating table. At the Allied War Council meeting of 25 October 1918 Foch, Pétain, Haig, and Pershing were willing to offer Germany reasonable conditions because they too were at the end of their strength. After 9 November, such concessions were no longer necessary.
2. The so-called Stab-in-the-Back was carried out by the independent social democratic movement. It started in 1917 with their backing of the naval uprising. For many far left-leaning elements, the cause for the war against Russia had disappeared with the collapse of the authoritarian tsarist regime. On the contrary, they now viewed the new Russia as a political ally and an accessory in the communist world revolution. The USPD [Independent Social Democratic Party] actually specifically took credit for the "Stab-in-the-Back." The managing editor of their journal, a Herr Thomas from Augsburg, stated during an election campaign rally of the USPD in Munich, "The 'Stab-in-the-Back' against the German front was the luckiest 'Stab-in-the-Back' of the revolutionary proletariat."
3. The Social Democrats, and specifically Ebert, had nothing to do with the "Stab-in-the-Back."
4. A stab in the back requires two parties, one that does the stabbing and one that allows himself to be stabbed.

What was it, then, that led to the tragic events of November 1918? In 1914 the German people had entered into the struggle for their future with incredible enthusiasm. The German people completely embraced the words of the Kaiser: "There are no political parties anymore, there are only Germans!" Everyone gave his best. Incidents where a mortally wounded German soldier would say something like, "I am dying for Germany, even though I am a Social Democrat," occurred frequently. I myself witnessed such in 1915 at the Rawka River. When at the end of August 1914 a Jäger had to be disciplined for an infraction, the loudly proclaimed opinion of his fellow Jägers was, "How can you commit such an offense in times like these?" The thinking of our upper leadership circles ran something like: "The German people are basically sound. We will not be able to avoid initiating a few reforms after the war, but for now everything has to remain the way it is. And besides, our administration is clean, good, and just."

Nobody seemed to recognize that a psychological high is naturally followed by a low, despite Schiller's old adage that "Enthusiasm is not a herring that can be preserved for a hundred years." When I talked to my father long before the beginning of the war about the necessity of enthusiasm in war he opined: "The enthusiasm is over after the first bivouac in a rainstorm. More important are a sense of duty, political attitude, warrior spirit, and esprit de corps."

Thus, nothing was done by the government. The only thing that happened was that judicial decisions were as lenient as possible, based on the rationale that the German people were so good. By the time everyone realized to their horror that the everyday reality was quite different, it was too late. What should have been done at all costs was to appoint a Social Democrat to one of the Reich ministries and introduce voting rights in Prussia. The people had a right to that much. But the Kaiser and the leaders of the Prussian administration were not willing to take such extraordinary steps. They assumed that since they governed matter-of-factly, caringly, and equitably, obedience was to be expected in return. They did not take into consideration the idea that when people have reached a certain level of political sophistication, this would not be enough anymore. One only accepts the state as one's own when one can participate according to one's abilities and has access to all state functions. The knights of the Teutonic Order experienced the indicators of such realities as early as the days of the Battle of Tannenberg in 1410. They had the best administration in medieval Europe, but the fact that they were outsiders could not prevent the local Prussian nobility and the *Bürgers* from changing their allegiance to the Polish king in hopes of being able to govern their own country under Polish rule.

Thus, the disaster of 1918 ran its course. A Clemenceau or a Lloyd George could have never made it in Germany. For legal reasons and to protect the immunity of the members of the Reichstag, the decision was made not to act against agitators of the ultra left, although they had only one objective, the foreign policy downfall of the German people. Immunity gave them the cover for any kind of agitation without risk.

The agitation of the far left was mostly directed against a pillar of the regime, the German officer corps. That such was unwarranted among the front-line troops is proven by the high blood toll paid by the active and reserve officer corps and the inner strength that almost all frontline troops maintained until the end. The rear areas were naturally more fertile ground for agitation. It cannot be denied, however, that in the final years before the war a certain *jeunesse dorée* ("gilded youth") element began to enter the officer ranks. They did not pursue an officer's career because of a calling, but rather because of social ambitions. This shift inside the officer corps is best described in a remark by Kirchheim: "When I went to Southwest Africa twelve years ago, the social events within the officer corps were geared toward the least well-off family. When I came back they were geared toward the richest."

But this rot was relatively small and still without influence. What was worse was the attitude of a peace obligation that crept into the field, where it did not belong. Many higher staffs set poor examples here.

Naturally, rations played a large role in the agitation. But it was less the irregularity of the meals, but rather the constant sameness that the field kitchens produced. This problem was not recognized properly. Wherever the officers avoided the constant mass-produced mush, there was discontent; where the officers ate from the field kitchen, there was no sense of revolution. Whenever possible or at regular intervals, I ensured everyone had cooked rations. No German soldier will turn against an officer who shares his joy and pain, death and danger.

The influence of the senior leadership at the general officer level strongly deteriorated during the war. The soldier in the hour of danger wants to see his general. Then he will follow him blindly. But the leadership was technologically tied to the telephone. Wireless communication was still in its infancy. Consequently, the general in order to avoid losing control was tied to his phone in the rear, much to his chagrin. The enemy propaganda called Hindenburg "Hintenburg."[2] Schlieffen's concept of the commander communicating by phone from the rear was compatible with the technological level of the time, but psychologically it was a grave mistake. Guderian was the first to tear the commanders away from the phone when wireless radio had reached the necessary capabilities.

A further reason for the decline in the credibility of the generalship among the troops was Ludendorff's habit of passing orders through the General Staff. How often did one hear the question, "Who is in charge of this division?"

The answer: "Captain So-and-So of the General Staff."[3]

"And, the division commander?"

"An old man who has no influence."[4]

Sometimes the opinions were even more critical. In all fairness, I must say that even though I heard such comments often, I never met a General Staff officer who said such things himself, and who tried to marginalize his commander for his own glory.[5] But the General Staff system as it was used by Ludendorff and all of his subordinates robbed the German Army of one of its main pillars of support. But this consequence was probably not at all clear to those involved in it. The German General Staff system had its origins in earlier times, when many generals were brave cavaliers and noblemen who needed a strong support system.[6]

Some leaders also believed that the army was the tool of choice against riots and other civil disturbances. All the troops should have to do is appear on the scene with shoot-to-kill orders, and everything would be back to normal. An army of conscripts simply cannot be used against the people during a popular uprising, especially in time of war when that army represents the full range of society's political groupings and the older age groups. This understanding gained during the Revolution of 1848 had been lost. Those leaders who relied on the admirable German discipline were taken completely by surprise when the 2nd Guards Division and other elite units refused to act against the people.

Ignorance and carelessness of our ruling circles, holding on to their privileges, and the stubborn trust in the authoritarian state and the discipline of the army made the Stab-in-the-Back possible. And thus, the murder victim himself can be blamed.

War and Politics

Wars are lost on the political level; but the soldier bears the brunt.

In 1805 incompetent politics missed the alliance with Austria and Russia and in 1806 led an isolated Prussia to Jena, without a chance against the victor of Austerlitz. Nobody criticized the politicians then, but tons of dirt were heaped upon the officer corps that had done all of the bleeding leading up to Jena and Austerlitz. It took one hundred years before Field Marshal Colmar von der Goltz was able to rehabilitate the reputation of the officer corps of that era.[7] At Tannenberg in 1410 the Grand Master of the Teutonic Order and eleven out of twelve of the knights grand cross were killed in the battle. This pattern repeats itself throughout history. It is no wonder, then, that the German officer corps developed its own way of thinking. The natural gap between the war fighter and politician deepened accordingly.

Prussian politics were especially depressing during the catastrophe of Napoleon's 1812 campaign in Russia. Instead of capturing Napoleon and the remnants of his army, as Napoleon himself had feared, he was allowed to escape through German territory with his shattered army, which he later rebuilt. It was only because of this act of madness that Napoleon's campaigns of 1813 to 1815, with their incredible blood toll, became possible. Thus, it should come as no surprise that soldiers have little respect for politicians.

Although Clausewitz taught that politics pervades and continuously affects the entire act of war, the controversy between Moltke and Bismarck changed the opinion of the soldiers. Briefly summing up Moltke's thoughts, once the field commander achieved a total victory, the politician could then build a new structure as a result.

The Kaiser once said, "Politics better shut up during war, until strategy allows it to talk again." That statement gave the final sanction to this twisted view of things. Glib courtiers like Bülow, or those like Bethman-Hollweg who were rigidly caught up in inter-departmental battles, were not competent enough to exercise political power. When the war finally broke out, it was not the statesmen but the dead hand of Schlieffen that determined the course of the world. As the war progressed, things only got worse. The statesmen provided no proper leadership, neither politically, nor economically.

Nonetheless, since business had to be taken care of, the void naturally was filled by the strongest entity, OHL, and at the time it had the support of every German. People from all walks of life sent numerous letters of encouragement to Hindenburg and Ludendorff. Even the bureaucrats were happy that someone else was dealing with the critical issues. Of course OHL was faced with tasks that it was not by nature equipped to handle, but nobody saw or wanted to see that.

The situation was similar at home, where practically the complete administration was handed over to the deputy commanding generals of the corps districts, who were neither schooled nor suited for such functions. To the best of my knowledge, nobody from the civilian authorities ever made even the slightest attempt to regain control. They were perfectly comfortable letting the soldier do everything and not having to bear any responsibility.

Only one person could have and should have effected changes, and that was the Kaiser. His grandfather, endowed with a highly developed insight into human nature, had achieved the balance between the military and the political leadership, and with his authority he had elevated the political element to its rightful position. But by the start of the war things were different. Although a highly gifted and colorful monarch was at the helm of the nation, he suffered from the disability of his crippled left arm, which he constantly tried to hide. He was broadly educated, influenced by his ancestor, Frederick the Great, and he primarily followed his accurate intuition; but he frequently was too weak and flighty to assert himself. His incomplete character development and lack of a work ethic made him prefer the slick, yes-men courtiers who paid homage to his authority. He selected personalities weaker than himself. The former *Rittmeister*[8] von Penz, Hindenburg's son-in-law and his aide-de-camp, once said of the people who surrounded the Kaiser: "They were wimps; we did not socialize with them; we felt we were better than they."

The Kaiser, however, could tolerate opposing views. The younger Moltke, when he was assigned as chief of the General Staff, asserted himself by clearly insisting on a halt to many of the abuses by the members of the Kaiser's inner circle.

An eyewitness to one such incident, a comrade from my regiment, General von Dallwigh, told me about a scene at the officers' mess at the Altengrabow training area: "I believe sixty members of the Prussian parliament, who were for the most part district administrators [*Landräte*], had voted against the Midland Canal, bringing down the proposed bill. They were the so-called Canal Rebels. During a dinner with three hundred officers of a cavalry division, the Kaiser toasted toward a Rittmeister, saying, 'Prost, your brother is one of those rebels too.' The Rittmeister answered loudly in the silent room, 'I wish Your Majesty had only such loyal subjects as my brother.' There were of course no consequences."

The shortcomings of the Kaiser became obvious during the war, and there were efforts to marginalize him. I deduced this from one of my father's letters from the field to my mother, which he wrote as a divisional commander. Such efforts are also mentioned in the memoirs of the chief of the Navy's Personnel Command (*Marinekabinett*), Admiral Georg von Müller.

All in all, one can say about the Kaiser that he was a colorful, multifaceted personality, who always wanted the good, who often decisively did the right thing, and even more often recognized it. I am thinking for example of his establishment of a research institute, the Kaiser-Wilhelm-Society (today known as the Max-Planck-Institute), and later on, his involvement in the development of wireless radio, where he intervened to end the competitive battles between two global companies. I also think of the dismissal of Bismarck, which often has been viewed as a mistake. Bismarck's intended solution of the social problem, pushing the workers into revolution, quelling of the revolts with the maximum power of the state, and then the rebuilding would have sent Germany into deep crisis. The young Kaiser did not play along; he correctly had something in mind along the lines of the workers being positively integrated into the whole of society. Unfortunately, his flightiness prevented him from pursuing this line to its ultimate conclusion; indeed, it ended with an ill-chosen remark about the "stateless vagabonds." Perhaps he recognized instinctively that Bismarck's strength lay in foreign policy and not in domestic politics, and that Bismarck was at his zenith. Owing to the timing of his dismissal, Bismarck retained his well-deserved glory and his place in the heart of the German people.

The war confronted the Kaiser with tasks that were bigger and tougher than he. It was his fate, not his fault. The absent political leadership during the preparation for war and during the course of the war was decisive and resulted in the war being lost. The soldier bore no fault here. It would have been necessary to juxtapose the strong personalities of OHL against a similarly strong political personality, a personality who would have been capable of leading the people as an alternate force. When Marshal Foch overstepped the boundaries that were set for him as a soldier, Clemenceau stepped in, saying, "Be quiet, this is France speaking now!" Germany did not have such a personality in the political sphere.

Were our war preparations sufficient? The coming world war was looming over Germany. It was bearing down while Bismarck was lying on his death bed. It was destined to be a fight against incredibly superior forces that was mostly on our shoulders, and not on the shoulders of our weak and unreliable allies. What was overlooked was the fact that in 1870 fifty-five German divisions had won against thirty-three French divisions, and that during the German Wars of Unification we maintained weapons superiority. Bismarck's politics were based on the needle gun.[9] "Your Majesty, introduce this rifle and you can determine where Prussia's borders end." Those were the words that the minister of war, Albrecht von Roon, used to recommend the purchase of the rifle to King Wilhelm.

But what about the inner attitude of the Prussian/German Army? Did they not believe that they could measure up to any army in the world? One army at a time, yes; but not all of them together. The decision was not made to build up and organize our military forces like that of France. When Ludendorff demanded such before the war, he was marginalized.

The statesman who would have been able to make the armament industry compatible with his goals did not exist. A horribly fragmented politics of defense was the consequence. An oversized fleet took resources away from the army.[10] To avoid conflict with the Reichstag, these necessary demands were not advanced. Nor did the Reichstag make any of the necessary requests. So, we marched into battle with the completely untapped productivity of the nation. Not even organizationally was anything done to establish a balance. Specifically, I am thinking here of the forming of another army corps from the many Reserve Jäger battalions during the initial mobilization. Attached to various conventional units, these elite units were useless and irrelevant to the conduct of the battle.

The tables of organization of the Landwehr brigades indicate just how haphazardly those units were structured. And this was done in full expectation of actually using them. Landwehr Corps Woyrsch is a typical example. Wherever the Landwehr was engaged, they fought a good fight. They were equal to regular French or Russian formations, often even superior. The same can be said of the *Ersatz*[11] divisions.

In 1915 we finally adjusted the divisional structure by adding a reserve infantry regiment to each brigade to establish a division of three infantry regiments; we also added a reserve artillery battalion to establish an artillery regiment.[12] Even earlier the German Military Mission to Turkey had taken the same steps to reorganize the Ottoman Army. The large increase in the number of machine guns issued to the infantry regiments allowed for a significant reduction in the strength of the infantry companies, which freed up well-trained soldiers for assignment to the Reserve and Landwehr units, thus making them more combat effective. And finally there was the blunder of the formation of the Kinderkorps, which robbed us of the most talented future NCOs and officers for years to come.

For whatever reason, the cooperation with the members of the Reichstag that Grand Admiral Alfred Tirpitz pursued on behalf of the navy was never attempted by the Prussian War Ministry. Nor was there any civilian preparation for the war, specifically in the area of food rations. The military, specifically General Wilhelm Groener, had suggested buying the Argentinian wheat harvest, but that initiative was rejected. The prevailing assumption was that whenever there was a war, the army would be right there, and the army would fix it. This failure of the civilian administration compounded the trend during the war in which everything gravitated toward Ludendorff's strong personality.

Military Leadership Failures

Much has been written about this topic. I just want to go briefly into the poor leadership in the West up until the Battle of the Marne, and in the East until the appointments of Hindenburg and Ludendorff. Initially one got the impression that the making of field commanders from scratch by the General Staff had failed. This, however, was not quite the case. The proper personalities were available in large numbers. I am thinking of Ludendorff, Seeckt, Hoffmann, Groener, Schulenburg, and many others. Only one wrong personnel decision had prevented the right man from being in the right position, thus erasing all the preparatory work that had been accomplished during peacetime.

The appointment of Erich von Falkenhayn as chief of the General Staff was a blunder. Maybe it can be explained by the Kaiser's timidity toward the somewhat gruff and self-confident greatness of the later OHL under Hindenburg and Ludendorff. The monarch did not want to be overshadowed by a victorious field commander. In any case, the Moltke-Falkenhayn period shows the critical importance of a personnel management system that understands how to put the right man in the right place. Such a system should never give preference to the soft, pliable, obedient man over the objectively right personality. The latter should be slightly critical, unrefined, and never easy to deal with, even gruff. The former, however, is more to the liking of the politician. Unfortunately, this lesson was not applied in World War II either.

Ludendorff

It is impossible to conclude a retrospective on World War I without considering this great soldier. His performance as field commander is history.[13] The accusation that he pulled all the strings must be evaluated in light of the failure of all the other responsible powers.

As former Royal Navy vice admiral Sir John Hughes-Hallet, and later a member of the House of Commons, said of civil-military relations in 1956: "I would like to emphasize here, that the only real danger of a military regime in Great Britain would be the result of a failure of the civilian and political institutions. Such a failure would create a vacuum which would be filled in time of war or in a national emergency by the army. In the long run, all of our constitutional safeguards depend on the existence of energetic and productive institutions in the political and in the civilian sectors and require them."

This was exactly the situation in Germany during the First World War. Much, too, has been written about Ludendorff's decision following the Black Day of 8 August 1918 to arrange for the government to stop the war. It saved us from a Kerensky-like experience and from communism. Ludendorff's postwar activities have been judged differently by history, and by me as well. His actions were those of the warrior mentality, of a soldier desperately fighting for his German fatherland, but failing to see that history had already passed him by and that he had expended all of his ammunition.

During the period of my captivity in 1945, I came across an affidavit about Ludendorff in the immediate postwar period by the industrial magnate Rehberg. Ludendorff reportedly was proposing that the German Army should come under French command at a ratio of 3 to 2 in favor of France. With every German division there would be a French officer, and with every French division a German officer, both of whom were tasked with making mobilization against each other impossible. The German naval fleet would come under English operational control. At a later stage Ludendorff envisioned an affiliation with the British Commonwealth.

Poincaré and Foch supposedly were strongly interested in this proposal. Be that as it may, Ludendorff's objectively realistic spirit anticipated what DeGaulle and NATO later accomplished. That the times were not right for something like this after World War I, and that it may have been a French ruse, as one could suppose according to Otto Gessler's[14] memoirs, is another story. I would imagine that Ludendorff suffered from the realization that he had allowed Lenin free passage to Russia, and thus had advanced Bolshevism. Consequently, he had judged the extent of the future Bolshevik danger correctly.

After 30 January 1933 Ludendorff wrote to Hindenburg: "By appointing Hitler to Reich Chancellor you have exposed our holy German fatherland to one of the greatest demagogues of all times. My solemn prophecy is that this unholy man will push our Reich into the abyss, that he will bring unspeakable misery upon our nation and that coming generations will curse you in your grave for having done this."

At the same time, a man like Theodor Heuss in his book *Hitlers Weg* [*Hitler's Path*] talked of Hitler's integrity and his trustworthy personality.[15] All these considerations again and again come to the accusation raised by the civilian side that "soldiers know nothing of politics."

However, the soldier is a factor in foreign politics. He understands something about it because he is used to dealing in an unemotional and level-headed way with the given power structures. Any kind of wishful thinking is foreign to him, unlike many politicians. In order to fulfill his mission, however, the soldier must have a unified people behind him, and therefore he urges cessation or at least the minimization of the internal strife for the sake of the larger foreign policy goal. But he overlooks the fact that this internal strife is often necessary to further develop society from within. Because he is hostile and unsympathetic to inner political party conflicts, he is accused of not understanding politics. Both sides should be more understanding toward each other.

7

1919

Revolution

Goslar suffered the same fate of all the German garrison towns: a ban on shooting, the appearance of sailors, the expelling of officers, the opening of the prisons, the looting of uniform and rations warehouses, and the election of a soldiers' council. Some of the old NCOs prevented the worst excesses. The situation in the Reich was completely unresolved. The SPD [Social Democratic Party of Germany] and the USPD [Independent Social Democratic Party], which was the former strongly left-leaning wing of the SPD, had formed a temporary government. In all reality, the workers' and soldiers' councils were governing, often in the wildest configurations. Everyone did what he wanted, without concern for the whole. Criminal actions often were the driving force.

Kirchheim had come back from Hannover, where he had tried to gain some understanding of the situation. On 26 November the battalion fell in for the last time, firmly controlled by its officers. The following day we elected a soldiers' council. My company elected me unanimously, and the following day I was elected to the grand committee by all the representatives of the frontline soldiers in a full meeting of the councils. So, now every day by ten o'clock in the morning I sat in the grand committee wearing my dress uniform, and took part in the governance of the city and county of Goslar. Our outgoing regimental commander gave me some advice: "You always must give those people the kind of advice that when they follow it, it will turn out wrong and work against the workers' and soldiers' council."

I decided to do exactly the opposite and act in a completely loyal fashion. The politics of Goslar could never be decisive. All that mattered was preventing more damage and keeping the option open for the reorganization of the 10th Jäger Battalion. My instinct turned out to be right. I soon established a relationship with the labor representatives based on respect, and I have been convinced ever since then that in politics trust and openness play an unusually large role.

The members of the workers' and soldiers' council were rather straightforward people who had the motivation to do the right thing and to maintain law and order. There were, of course, a few brawlers and bad elements, but they could not win against the organized laborers, who were firmly in control and who also were intellectually superior to the brawlers. The council chairman was a mason by the name of Schacht, whom I remember fondly. Financially the laborers tried their best to work selflessly and objectively, as far as I could tell. They gave me a great degree of access and everything seemed to be on the up and up. They worked especially well on food distribution. They knew the conditions. They had not started the revolution and probably thought deep down that it was quite superfluous, but they certainly were hoping that an inevitable world revolution would solve all the problems.

Once again my old 4th Company gathered for a farewell party. It was like old times. We stood together as one, untouched by the revolution. The overwhelming feeling was a desire to see the old order reestablished. At the time I wrote: "The whole thing is a brutal rape of the German people by a small minority of sailors, draft dodgers, and recruits. If we do not successfully and quickly establish order and permanent conditions, we will in just a few months have famine and Bolshevism in this country. The government in Berlin is too weak, because it does not hold any means of power. Salvation can only come from the field army, which has some of the best elements of the people."

Our men were separated from the army. The battalion marched to the train station with the band playing, officers in the lead. As they got on the train it was painful to see the departure of all these faithful companions, with whom for years I had shared happiness and suffering, hardship and death. The men felt it too, as I shook countless hands. A farmer from the Oldenburg region got off the train again, grabbed my hand, and said; "Herr Lieutenant, I thank you in the name of all my comrades for what you have done for our company."

Tears rolled down his face. Then the train disappeared into the dark. We had not imagined the demobilization happening quite like that. We stood there at the station feeling lost. The old days of our Jägers were gone. We faced a new and totally insecure world, and it was now up to us to shape it.

Chaos ruled initially. Consolidations of the remaining soldiers swelled my company to more than three hundred. Between twenty and thirty of them had served on the battlefields with me. The majority were recruits and members of inactivated units from all over the place. On 12 December the battalion refused to fall in for duty. One of the main perpetrators of the revolt was up on the roof of the school in which we were quartered, shooting onto the surrounding houses. Then he took off looking for me, but he did not get very far. The members of my old veteran cadre took care of him and gave him a painful lesson. The next morning I had everybody in formation and was listening to their demands, like leave, new uniforms, housing in barracks. Most of the demands were unrealistic because the supply rooms had been looted and were all empty. The main perpetrator of the previous day's revolt was brought forward, and I read out the charges against him. He was then taken straight to the train station and in clear terms told to never return to Goslar if he valued his health. A few others followed him. Later we learned that of the two worst agitators, one had been in prison for four years, and the other for two. In the end everything was brought under control by threatening denial of leave, rations, and pay.

Those events demonstrated, however, that I could rely 100 percent on the old veterans of my old company. The Reich and especially Berlin remained in total chaos. Impossible resolutions were proposed and passed. I wrote in my journal at the time: "If this resolution of the workers' and soldiers' council is passed, my work here will have been useless. I think I can say without exaggeration that it was mainly my doing that things were taken care of in a military manner; that radical chaos was prevented; that there is no voting on who the officers would be; and that disciplinary action was taken."

Naturally we continued to follow closely the events in Berlin. What happened there determined our fate. The attempt had been made to establish order in Berlin with a few divisions, but the troops wanted to go home. It was almost Christmas and they disappeared, which a weak and indecisive leadership did nothing to prevent. This was not the way to do it. In its current state the German field army was no longer capable of accomplishing any mission. Only new volunteer units, small in size and made up of quality people, would help the situation.

Ultimately the Christmas chaos in Berlin did have one good consequence. The independents left the government, which strengthened the government's ability to act. We hoped that action would follow soon. It was almost a joke that the same people who wanted to bring us eternal peace had to take up arms themselves after only eight weeks. Only now these people would have to realize how foolish it had been to destroy the army. The German people were defenseless, both internally and externally.

Parliamentary Deputy Gustav Noske had taken over military matters in the Reich. He had come with a good reputation from his time in Kiel.[1] In Goslar the events continued on. Fortunately we were able to separate quite a few people from the army. Being close to the madhouse situation in Brunswick, we initiated some precautionary military measures. Above all I was able to convince the workers' and soldiers' council to institute some strict military discipline.

On 9 January a number of delegates from the Hannover Workers' and Soldiers' Council showed up and started recruiting volunteers to go to Berlin and to the eastern borders. They had changed their tune completely and were now talking about how things would not work without officers. Only recently we had been scorned and any hoodlum could insult us in the street without fear of punishment. Now the officer corps was expected to pull the mired cart out of the muck. Kreysing's company and my company volunteered as a whole for duty in Berlin and the East.

Border Security in the East

While Kreysing and I tried to reestablish some sort of order in Goslar, Kirchheim traveled around Germany to get a feel for the situation. Just as we were ready to tackle new projects, he came back with a new directive to transform the 10th Jägers into the Volunteer Hannoverian Jäger Battalion for the border security mission in the East. Thus we avoided having to fight as Germans against other Germans. The ethnic Poles in eastern Germany wanted to leave the Reich, but they wanted even more. They wanted land where no Pole was living and that had never been Polish.[2] The Province of Posen[3] was aflame. Hindenburg with the senior army leadership had relocated to Kolberg. Germany's eastern border was to be defended with volunteer units against the Poles and Bolshevists.

On the evening of 25 January 1919 we left Goslar with approximately three hundred Jägers and moved toward the east. A few of the old, former officers came to the parade field as we were marching off, declaring that these troops were not real soldiers yet. We knew that too. What we did not know were the conditions that awaited us and how our men would deal with the new and unusual stresses. It would be a pretty tough situation that we were getting into. As a cautionary measure, I had distributed the old veterans of the 4th Company among all the railcars as we approached Sagan.[4] I knew who did not belong in our unit. In Sagan all the unreliable elements were taken off the train and sent home. The rest, we hoped, would last.

Everything had been well prepared in Fraustadt.[5] Unfortunately, we were billeted in the same barracks with a totally out of control "Red" security battalion. That would have to be changed first thing. The next morning we conducted drill and ceremony more rigidly than ever on the parade field, as our Red barracks mates lounged in the windows yelling, "You people are pretty crazy! Do not get caught in this! Tear off the idiots' shoulder straps!" and similar niceties. We conducted close-order drill for almost an hour. Then a whistle was blown and soon thereafter the "Heroes of the Revolution" quickly left the Kaserne. We had run the first battle and we returned to our old form. We received weapons, equipment, and new uniforms. Overcoats were the only things that could not be found for us in all of Germany, which made duty very hard in the -30 degrees Celsius air and in the face of freezing easterly storms. I often loaned my own greatcoat to one of the guards on duty. Later we solved the problem by taking the coats away from the Red units that were unwilling to go into combat, but naturally had coats. "You will not be fighting anyway, so why do you need the coats?"

The logic was clear and practical. It was a mistake that the riffraff in the garrisons had not been sent home right away. Most of them did not want to go, however. What they really wanted was an easy life in the barracks, the pay, and the pleasures. They were not even capable of cleaning the barracks.

We held a company party that welded everybody together even more tightly. Later in that evening a member of the Fraustadt Workers' and Soldiers' Council showed up in a Jäger uniform and started to agitate against the officers. He had picked the wrong audience. The soldiers hit him with some really strong counterarguments. Then one Jäger jumped up on a table and gave a short speech: "We need Oberjägers, sergeants, and officers. We will respect them. What we do not need is a workers' and soldiers' council!"

Throughout most of the Posen province the Polish revolution was winning, but the situation currently remained tense on the front line. The Poles had to deal with serious internal problems, including a lack of coal and a lack of fighting spirit among their troops. They only drafted their youngest people, who formed no more than roving gangs without artillery. The bitter cold often hampered fighting. But clearly they were trying to move the Polish border as far west as possible, with the Oder River being one of the objectives even then.

The fate of Posen weighed very heavily on all of us. Here in the middle of crisis and in the middle of an unfriendly Polish world, Germany was in a difficult situation. The troops wanted to fight, especially the 4th Aviation Replacement Detachment and the 6th Grenadier Regiment, which had been moved back to its home garrison in the area. The German population also rallied strongly. Posen had a clear German majority. A violent clash was prevented by State Secretary Helmut von Gerlach, a known pacifist who had been sent there from Berlin, and a senile commanding general who could not make a decision to fight. That was how Posen became Polish. The 6th Grenadiers then fought their way through to Silesia and became a rock in the waves of the Polish onslaught. To the south of Fraustadt near Rawitsch,[6] the Poles were on the offensive. There is not room here to describe every single skirmish, but I do want to highlight some representative excerpts from my journal.

6 February: "Alert! Transport toward Rawitsch. The local [Polish?] troops were even sadder looking than the ones in Fraustadt. They disappeared after the first shot was fired. Only the German local militias were any good. The reception in Rawitsch by the locals was marvelous."

7 February: "We attacked the small town of Sarne.[7] As soon as the Poles spotted our long lines of riflemen and took some fire from our supporting artillery battery, they all ran. My company entered Sarne from the rear. The jubilation of the freed local population was without end."

8 February: "We were resting when a new alert was sounded. A company of the 50th Infantry Regiment had left its positions and had gone to Rawitsch to go dancing. The chairman of the Workers' and Soldiers' Council, by the name of Krederlich, was in cahoots with the Poles and wanted to turn Rawitsch over to Polish control."

9 February: "Three companies of the 50th Infantry Regiment, each sixty men strong, were supposed to relieve us. Instead, only thirty-two men showed up. Consequently, we got no rest before our next mission."

10 February: "We attacked into Stwolno, with the 6th Grenadiers coming from the south and us from the north. The Poles did not respond to our attack. As I was moving south in the village, my runner and I suddenly encountered a well-equipped and orderly body of advancing infantry. 'Are you the 6th Grenadiers?' I asked.

"'Yes, Sir!' they responded as they moved along.

"But then one of my Jägers shouted, 'Herr Lieutenant, they all have the Polish Eagle on their headgear.'

"We were standing in the middle of the retreating Polish infantry. I immediately gave the order to fire. Some of them fell, but most disappeared in the rolling terrain. Their trailing elements, however, got caught in our fire and we captured several machine guns.

"The 50th Infantry Regiment relieved us. They complained loudly about having to go back into their positions, saying they would rather go back to Rawitsch. One of my platoons had remained behind in the important agricultural settlement of Wiesenbach. When we had received the alert notification, the 50th Infantry Regiment had left its positions and had withdrawn to Rawitsch, without having been attacked. They left behind two artillery pieces, which our 1st Company recovered the next day. My Jäger platoon in Wiesenbach had remained in position and saved the situation."

11 February: "Heinz Guderian[8] was with us. He was now a captain on the General Staff at the field army headquarters in Breslau.[9] The conditions were the same everywhere. There were three reliable battalions in the whole field army, the 6th Jägers, 10th Jägers, and 6th Grenadiers. The troops from Rawitsch were just about the worst. As soon as two good divisions could be pulled together, the intent was to take Posen from the north and south. But in the meantime those units did not exist. The fight at home was absorbing too much of our resources."

12 February: "Rawitsch was mopped up. All unreliable personnel were dismissed. Our people stormed into a session of the workers' and soldiers' council and declared it dissolved. They then handed all the money and the files over to the mayor, whom they quickly brought in. They tore down the red flag from the

top of city hall and raised the old black, white, and red colors. The whole town was in a delirious state."

13 February: "The towns of Rawitsch and Fraustadt each requested for us to remain there permanently in garrison. But then another alert order came in, and we loaded up to go to Bomst."[10]

14 February: "From Bentschen[11] southward there was a long row of lakes, only occasionally interrupted by a narrow outlet. The Poles used that route to break into the Brandenburg region. A German counterattack was launched by the well-seasoned 10th Uhlans, supported by the still effective remnants of the regiments from Brandenburg and Silesia, throwing the Poles back. A bridgehead near Neudorf was still in Polish hands."

In the evening I conducted a relief with my company in a narrow strait near Gross-Groitzig.[12] I had four machine guns from the 38th Fusilier Regiment with me. I knew this area very well. As a boy I had spent two years living with a local priest in the nearby town of Kopnitz. I used to roam the forests with a small gun hunting squirrels.

I was positioned all by myself with my company over a large area. One hundred men of the *Volkswehr*[13] were located nine kilometers to the north, a squadron of the 10th Uhlans was seven kilometers to the south, and the rest of battalion was behind me in Bomst, to which I had a telephone line. Somewhere in my rear there was a relatively large artillery unit firing preplanned interdiction fires all around us.

15 February: "A full moon shone down on the snow-covered fields. The night was bright as day. At 0430 hours a force of about fifty Poles approached our position, and we pushed them back. I was still able to request artillery fire on some key points, but then the phone wire was cut. From the village of Gross-Groitzig, three hundred meters east of our position, we suddenly started taking intense machine gun and rifle fire. Then we saw and especially heard the Polish columns moving toward us from the forest near Neudorf. I assessed it as a ruse because of the excessive noise they made. I moved with my reserve toward the southern front line, where the forest reached almost all the way to our position. About that time we also started taking machine gun fire from the west."

On my southern front a yellow star cluster went up. I had been right. The main attack was launched by a bunched-up mass seventy meters in front of my machine gun. It immediately broke down. At the same time from the north masses of Poles stormed forward. That attack too broke down under our machine gun fire. Our machine gun fire now laid down a hedgehog defense from all four directions. There was little cover anywhere. The air was full of red star clusters and interdiction fire, but not a single artillery battery was firing. A machine gun was firing in the distance, in the direction of Bomst. I had a bad feeling. In Gross-Groitzig everything was stable, but the Poles were now attacking on a wide front. Our artillery had been overrun and the fighting in Bomst was reportedly hand-to-hand.

The situation was muddled. I decided to clear our rear area first. A sand pit on a hill was the dominating terrain feature. Feldwebel Chraszler took two squads and the captured Polish machine guns up there, which put us on the enemy's north flank. That gave us some breathing space and covered our rear. A squad of scouts on bicycles rode off toward Bomst about the time a small milk wagon appeared from there. Everything now appeared quiet in Bomst. Realizing the situation, the Poles quickly abandoned their positions and withdrew toward the forest near Neudorf, but our following fire mopped them up horribly.

Our men had fought with spirit, just like during our best days, but our losses had been high. Half of our machine guns had been knocked out, the crews lying dead or wounded next to them. There had been no cover during the battle. Two of my troops had fought exceptionally well. One of my runners, Jäger Runge, constantly moved through the thickest fire. He was wounded twice, and then a third shot to his pelvis finally brought him down. Jäger Reiche stood for twelve hours in his foxhole in an exposed position, with an icy wind blowing over him. He fired and fired, while his comrades were killed or wounded all around him. He did not waver until he passed out from exhaustion. But just as bravely as we had fought, the courageous machine gun crews of the 38th Fusilier Regiment had put up a good fight.

The Poles had attacked with a reinforced company from the south and a strong battalion from the north. We counted 103 dead Poles in front of our positions, and we captured three machine guns. Unfortunately, our artillery and their observers had gone to sleep after laying down the initial interdiction fire.

18 February: "We stormed the Neudorf bridgehead." Then a truce was called by the Entente Powers and both warring parties were prohibited from conducting further operations.

The battalion could be proud of its accomplishments. Our successful fight had determined the future border of the Reich in our area. The enemy, too, had paid us quite a compliment by posting a bounty of 500 marks for the head of every Jäger, dead or alive.

Finale

The battalion was pulled back from the front line and went into ready reserve for the VI Corps near Glogau. Training and reconstitution were the priorities. Our strength soon went up to approximately one thousand men. But who were those men that came to us? The core came from the 10th Jägers, but volunteers from all over Germany joined us as well. The locals from the German-Polish border region proved especially useful. We also got many men from Upper Silesia who could only speak broken German. What motivated them?

For many, there was personal attachment to their old officers. Disgust with the impossible conditions in the homeland, joy in good soldiering, and the desire to rebuild a decent Germany were also driving forces. My company first sergeant was a Jew. In short, all elements of society were represented. A number of Alsatians also remained because they felt a nostalgic attachment to the battalion.

But along with these good elements, there were the bad ones. As we were moving out of Goslar, an old white-haired gentleman in a fur coat and top hat reported to us. "Herr Lieutenant, I was too old for the world war, but now in Germany's hour of need I also want to serve." I was touched and I signed him on as a clerk. Since I was not able to issue him a uniform right away, he performed his duties in his fur coat and topper and caused a lot of amusement in the battalion, especially by the stalwart salutes he rendered in this costume. But there was something about his saluting I did not like. It was a little too exaggerated, like he was hiding something. Long ago I had learned the art of reading the salutes of my men. My skepticism paid off and we caught him red-handed as he was trying to board a train with the company's payroll. It turned out that this patriot had twenty-seven previous convictions for fraud and theft. Such cases were relatively harmless. It was far more difficult to prevent the infiltration by the subversive elements.

Countless men, girls, and women talked to the troops and tried to influence them with the "Red poison." This was difficult to prevent legally, and much more dangerous to fight than open resistance. Perhaps it was the only real danger we faced then. The only effective countermeasures were solid arguments and dissociation from the population. As he crushed the Paris Commune uprising in 1871, French marshal Patrice de MacMahon issued orders to shoot any person caught talking to the troops. We did not go that far, of course, but there were countless fistfights between the troops and the disruptive elements.

I was sent back to Goslar on recruiting duty. Things were starting to look good there, too, after all the undesirable elements had been gotten rid of, but the Reich still looked like a madhouse. The Social Democratic movement had made an unmistakable shift toward the right. Herr Schacht, a mason and the calm and deliberate chairman of the Goslar Workers' and Soldiers' Council told me, "Democracy is nonsense. The German people are not ready for it. We first need an army again with good officers. The idea of eternal peace is crazy."

Nonetheless, the move to the right by the reasonable leadership was offset by the move to the left by the masses. The Social Democrats' determination to get votes at any cost now produced dire consequences. The regions that had never been Social Democratic before were now the most radical. In the countryside around Goslar the word was, "What can a majority Social Democracy do for us? The Spartacus League [*Spartakusbund*] is the only right one for us."[14]

At the beginning of March I traveled back to Silesia. But no trains were leaving Berlin anymore, because of the uprising of the Spartakusbund. Of necessity, I remained in Berlin as a quiet observer. Horrible acts of violence and chaos occurred daily. All units that were not controlled by officers failed. It was only the officers who saved the day for Germany.

On 8 March a train was supposed to leave for Silesia from the Görlitzer Bahnhof train station. I got an early start, but I lost an inordinate amount of time trying to find my gloves. They turned out to be lying openly in my room on a white tablecloth. Shaking my head, I left for the station. Why I had not seen the gloves right away was a complete mystery to me. The subway line went all the way to the Gleisdreieck station, and from there I had to walk to the Görlitzer Bahnhof station. As I got closer to the station there were more and more people milling around. Agitators were giving speeches. Naturally I was glared at, in my dress uniform and shoulder boards. Some people yelled, "Tear off his shoulder boards," and other obscenities.

As I got closer to the station the square was packed. I calmly walked right through the mob. Only one of them yelled at my back, "I would like to put a bullet right through your head, you pig!"

The government troops at the station were surprised to see me. "For goodness' sakes, how did you get through? Half an hour ago members of the Spartacus League tore up two of our people."

Looking for my gloves for half an hour had saved me from getting embroiled in that melee. I never understood it at all until about fifteen years later when an eye doctor explained to me that as a nervous overreaction it is possible to overlook small items on a white tablecloth.

The Finest Hour of the German General Staff and the SPD

While we were successfully trying to stabilize the situation in the eastern part of the Reich, big politics continued its relentless course. Signing the Versailles peace treaty or continuing the war was the big question.[15]

A new army was being rebuilt in the East and in the interior of the Reich. Could it stabilize the situation? Our self-confidence was limitless. All the preparations to march toward Posen and to reestablish the old eastern border had been made. Nobody doubted our success. We hoped passionately that the government would reject the peace treaty. Our signature on this shameful document seemed unacceptable and impossible.

"On 23 June 1919 at 2100 hours the eastern front is again in a state of war with the Entente and Poland." The contents of that message spread like wildfire from mouth to mouth. On 24 and 25 June nothing happened. We waited in vain for more news. On 16 June we had received orders to be prepared to march, but to where? Nobody knew. Rumors flew everywhere. The mood of the men and the officers was extremely tense. Everyone was ready to ignore the orders of the government in Berlin and to subordinate themselves to any leader who was willing to attack toward the East.

Then new information reached us. The Spartacus League and the radical left had decided to use strikes and sabotage in our rear to make further fighting impossible. That triggered fierce anger in the army. Later, when we were in action in Küstrin and Landsberg, the violent clashes in the Reich reached a new level of intensity. Then on 28 June Germany signed the dictated peace. Our world collapsed. Everything seemed to have been in vain. Many people left us and went back home or to the Baltic states. The troops felt deceived and abused. The names of Wilhelm Groener and Friedrich Ebert were only spoken in disgust. Any trust in the leadership was gone. Messengers hurried from unit to unit. During various meetings many argued for us to take our fate into our own hands. What was sacred to us and what kept us together was the loyalty to the old, beautiful 10th Jäger Battalion. But that loyalty was under severe stress.

This was a period of the most peculiar contrasts. But in truth, never before had the leadership of Germany and of the German Army been in such clear, firm, sober, and intelligent hands as during the time between the armistice and the signing of the peace dictate. What we did not know at the time was that since the days of the signing of the armistice at Compiègne,[16] two men had been on the phone daily working through the hopeless situation. On one side was the first quartermaster general of the German Army, Groener, and on the other the president, Ebert. The former was losing all control of the army, and the latter was in danger of losing control over the population. The one brought his position as a veteran officer to the table, the other his position in the SPD. Both of them knew that they had to sacrifice their personal honor and reputations. Both were more than doubtful whether their bases, the officer corps and the laborers, would follow and would understand.

A close examination of the details of this cooperation reveals a degree of collaboration between the military and politics such as had never occurred in Germany before—and would not occur again. No constitution and no laws achieved this collaboration. The decisive factor was solely the goodwill of two intelligent, patriotic Germans, ironing out the details and using all the means at their disposal to achieve a solution. Most likely neither one of them was aware at the time that they were contributing a classic chapter to the history of military and civilian cooperation.

The toughest hour came when the peace dictate had to be signed. It is surprising with how much sober clarity men like Groener and Ebert, and also Generals Wilhelm Heye and Hans von Seeckt, analyzed the situation and concluded that a taking up of arms again would mean the end of Germany. There was no emotion here, no patriotic surge; but the Reich survived and we were spared our own Kerensky-like episode. At the time, buckets of dirt were poured on Ebert's and Groener's heads. I as well thought that they had abandoned their honor, and I therefore feel it my duty now to state in hindsight that I regard both men as two of the most important names in German history.

But the dear price at the time was a total breakdown in trust in the army. Crying and waving their arms, the inhabitants in the East saw our train off, as we started heading west again. As we passed through Lehrte people threw rocks at us, accompanied by insults like "bloody dogs," and "bums." We were even shot at. This was how the Fatherland was thanking us. Doggedly we entered Celle, where quite a few of the locals learned the hard way that they could not insult a 10th Jäger without paying a price.

Back in Goslar

On 2 August 1919 we returned to Goslar and were merged with the existing units there into the Hannoverian 10th Reichswehr Jäger Battalion. When Kirchheim left us for another assignment, we lost one of the best officers that I have ever known. Whenever his tall, skinny figure appeared, calmly issuing orders while standing up exposed to enemy fire, just like he was on maneuvers, everyone knew he was a leader.[17] We all knew that his orders were always solid. There was never any doubt that any attack he organized would succeed. He was not interested in minutiae. He gave everyone the freedom to act. Enlisted and officers alike respected him to the utmost. Kirchheim also knew how to develop and retain good officers. He encouraged everybody's talent. There could not have been another unit of the old army like the 10th Jägers, where such a high number of officers had come up from the enlisted ranks, every one of them magnificent comrades and capable officers.

Reserve Lieutenant Heino Bosse was also one of the best officers I have ever served with. He started out as a one-year volunteer, and he once declined an opportunity to become a reserve officer in a line infantry unit to remain as reserve Oberjäger with us. During the war he quickly became an officer and commanded the 3rd Company for a long time. He was one of those magnificent, unmatched farm boys from Lower Saxony. He had been a farmer in Melverode, a communist town near Brunswick. After the war he was elected mayor, even though he had no political affiliations. Later, during the Third Reich, he was elected again, even though he was not a member of the Nazi Party.

Bosse's long-serving runner during the war became his dairyman after the war. Together they would pin on their Iron Crosses and go to the veterans' meetings. Whenever the dairyman would say in his thick, Low German accent, "Now we have to milk the cows," they would then put their Iron Crosses back in their pockets and return to the farm. In 1940 Bosse commanded a company during the crossing of the Bug River, and his runner was the same dairyman from the previous war. They were both hit at the same time by deadly Russian fire on the first day of the Russia campaign.

My duties changed as well. I became the adjutant of the battalion.

Memoirs only serve a purpose if they try to capture moods and events—in short, the atmosphere of the times they describe. Later additions are valuable and necessary to provide contrast. One should never give in to the temptation to give events a form that they did not have at the time based on later insights and improved knowledge—and to attempt to make oneself look like somebody who knew everything at the time. Undoubtedly there are people like that, but I am not one of them.

The Mood of the Times

A bad winter was behind us. Morale had been horrible. Ever since the signing of the peace treaty the trust in the government and the leadership had gone to hell. Everybody, officers and men alike, felt the insecurity of an unknown future. Who was going to be able to stay in uniform?[18] Everybody was looking for an alternative civilian career. Whenever someone thought he had found something, he grabbed it. This festered and affected the cohesion of the troops. And the big question was: "How could we possibly keep the Spartacus League at bay with a one hundred thousand-man army?"

Up to that point we had managed with approximately three hundred thousand men, and because we had been led politically and militarily in a disciplined manner—whereas the revolutionaries, although highly superior in numbers, had failed. They were without discipline and had a totally confused and indecisive political and military leadership. What would happen if those conditions changed? We only knew one thing for sure—we would with our lives and bodies have to bear the burden of the mess that had been handed to us by the politicians. We needed a leader. Hindenburg was gone. Ebert was not respected. Groener even less so. Where was the man we could trust?

There was one possibility—Hindenburg. Confidence in him remained unshaken.

Although when he resigned from OHL he had made it clear that he did not want to have anything to do with Groener and Ebert, the people still might have listened to him. Hindenburg should have gone to the troops; he should have talked to the officers and the enlisted and explained the military and political situation. He should have convinced them of the political necessity of the decisions that were made. He should have clarified that Groener and Ebert were not villains, but responsible, patriotic men. Noske, too, might have assumed this task. He still had the ear of the soldiers. Hindenburg, however, was old and firmly rooted in the old attitude that orders are given out at the top, and at the bottom no questions are asked; orders were to be followed, even against one's own convictions. That the times had changed, that soldiers were thinking beings, went unnoticed. Frederick the Great had once said, "If my soldiers would think, they would not follow me." But now the soldiers and the officers did think, and they felt abused, cheated, and lied to. The result was a breeding ground for the worst kind of militarism. And so the disaster ran its course.

The Kapp Putsch

On 13 March we were surprised by a military coup in Berlin. The Ebert-Noske government had been toppled. The new government was led by Wolfgang Kapp and General Walther von Lüttwitz. Our brigade alerted us to prepare for marching orders. The mood of the Goslar labor movement was depressed, but they did not intend to resist should the new government establish its legitimacy. Naturally, they had to follow the orders of their party and the labor union. We sighed a breath of relief. We had high hopes for Germany.

The 10th Reichswehr Brigade was assembled near Hannover. Our bicycle company was sent ahead to Hannover, and the rest of the battalion followed on foot, as the railroads were on strike. Almost all the requisitioned automobiles broke down just a short way outside of Goslar. Had it been sabotage? I was sent ahead to Hannover on the night of 14 March. Everything was quiet there. The 10th Reichswehr Brigade was under the impression that in this totally confusing situation it was a state within the state and it had to maintain law and order.[19]

I returned to the battalion. By noon on 15 March the staff and the bicycle company were located in Rethen, near Hannover. The rest of the battalion was approaching Hildesheim when we received an order from brigade sending us to Hildesheim immediately. The workers had taken control of machine guns and rifles that were stored at the county seat. The town was in the hands of uncontrolled, armed masses. The battalion staff turned around and started moving back to Hildesheim. When we reached Sarstedt we received a warning that armed members of the Spartacus League were approaching. The lead element of the battalion went into position. As a civilian informant on a bicycle was turning around right in front of us, a wagon that was following him dropped off a considerable number of armed men. Firing erupted, horses fell, and the troops took cover. Then women and children were driven out into the street, waving white sheets. Just in time we observed how behind this human shield some men were trying to put a machine gun into position. A short burst of fire over their heads scattered everyone. Then we stormed toward them, shouting. We captured five machine guns, a bunch of rifles, and twelve prisoners.

In Hildesheim we ran into a totally confusing situation. A new captain who had been transferred into the battalion and who lacked any kind of experience was at the point of the battalion. He was met by a delegation of the citizen militia who wanted to negotiate the conditions for passage through town. He was supposed to send a detachment to the union building where the confiscated weapons had been stored and render them inoperative. But when they got there Captain Kreysing, a naval lieutenant named Behrend who had been attached to us, and our armorer Lautenbach with two Jägers were trapped in the union building. The howling masses outside wanted to lynch them. The local leaders had lost all control. Fortunately, we were able to exchange our people for the prisoners we had taken in Sarstedt. We only managed to get them out the back door, through backyards, and over the fences because the head of the local communists physically covered our people with his own body.

But we still had to get control of the confiscated weapons. We knew that the machine guns had been taken to the union building. Circling around the local barracks, meanwhile, the howling and totally out of control masses were throwing rocks at our guard posts. The storm could break loose at any moment. Then shots were fired. At that critical point our commander, Major Pflugradt, gave the order to prepare to fire. In accordance with regulations, a bugle call was sounded and the mob was given three warnings to disperse. We were answered with screaming and more rocks. Then we opened fire and the dead and the wounded dropped. In the meantime, our follow-on companies with machine guns and the artillery pieces of an attached battery had reached the town and started patrolling the streets. The canal workers of the local branch of the Mittelland Canal, the main perpetrators of the revolt, ran away. A workers' delegation appeared within a short period and handed over the weapons and machine guns. They accounted for everything except one machine gun.

In the countryside, meanwhile, things were still running amok. Armed gangs roved around, disarming the citizen militias and looting. The citizen militias for the most part became ideal weapons' depots for the Reds. Eventually we were able to reestablish order everywhere. We disarmed the gangs and we reorganized the citizen militias and purged them of their unreliable elements. Within just a few days what had been a boiling witches' cauldron became a quiet and peaceful land.

We had been deeply disappointed by the *Bürgertum*.[20] They had failed completely. Again and again delegations appeared, pleading to stop the bloodshed; but as soon as the initial shooting stopped, they acted as if nothing had ever happened. The Reds, who had started a completely unnecessary revolt, were not confronted, of course. Lenin would have been very happy with his "useful idiots."

The Kapp Putsch was over. It had failed. Like many Germans, we welcomed the return of orderly conditions. But what was left was a Germany shattered to its foundations, with an abnormal distrust in its army and a Red army operating in the middle of the country and the industrial center, the *Ruhrgebiet*.

8

1920

Mad Romberg

In the middle of the night our troop train stopped outside a station at Buldern, on the edge of the Ruhr district. Somebody from the unit was supposed to get on the phone. Hientsch and I started walking between two tracks toward the station. There was a train coming toward us from the opposite direction. Just by chance I turned my head and saw another train approximately one hundred meters behind us. I pulled Hientsch to the side and we stood there clutching each other in the narrow space between the two tracks as the two locomotives met exactly where we stood. As they went by we slowly realized that we had escaped death one more time.

When we reached the station somebody there told us to go up to the castle, the baron was awaiting us. My commander asked what the baron's name was. "Baron von Romberg." If this was the famous Mad One, we had to be prepared for anything.[1] It was not him. He had passed away quite a while ago, but his son was trying hard to emulate his father. He met us at the gate with punch. He had been waiting to see who would show up first, the Reds or us. The Reds had been there the previous day and he managed to get them all quite drunk. They had parted with the comforting prospect that they would return and then, as sorry as they would be, they would have to kill him. Understandably, he was happy to see us. Besides, he was celebrating the fact that he had just received his one hundredth police citation and he therefore had sent a request to the local government at Buldern to post a policeman to watch over him. He was trying in his own way to deal with modern times. He had developed strong ties with the Red soldiers' council at the repatriation camp in Dülmen. On 27 January (the Kaiser's birthday) he had invited them to his castle, and then late that night they all sent a congratulatory telegram to the Kaiser in exile in Holland, signing it, "Your Majesty's most subservient Soldiers' Council, Dülmen." He also was full of stories about his father, which he told us with a great sense of humor.

The Ruhr Red Army

We provided cover for the deployment of a large number of troops to the Ruhr district. The idea was to wait until all forces were concentrated and to avoid piecemeal action. We were still feeling the aftershocks of the Kapp Putsch and the Hildesheim experience. Could we count on the German middle classes at all? Was not the Bürgertum just caught in the middle of the struggle between the two energy poles in this society, the army and the workers? I wrote in my journal at the time: "The labor movement is indeed a huge power that should not be underestimated; eventually a modus vivendi has to be found to deal with them." I also wrote: "A new sun is rising, 'National Bolshevism,' glistening, seductive, and dangerous. The road via Bolshevism is the shortest path to recovery for the German people, if the army and the workers pull together. The Bürgertum, with its lack of fighting spirit, very well might capitulate."

The Red Army wanted a fight. The Red movement in the Ruhr was well organized—no looting, tight discipline, and a well-organized military structure. Bolshevism had learned some lessons. There was a huge difference between the current and the initial uprisings at the beginning of the year, where everything ended up in looting. There must have been quite a few moral individuals within the movement. An alliance with such people should have been less and less of an obstacle.

In the morning hours of 25 March, Guderian had assaulted the repatriation camp in Dülmen with his 3rd Company. On the 29th we started our advance. Everything had been briefed orally. The adjacent units, even our other companies, knew nothing beforehand. Besides Guderian and me as the adjutant, only three other officers knew about the attack. Thus, we finally were fortunate enough to surprise the Reds. We had managed to outwit their excellent intelligence apparatus. The Red Guards fought an excellent fight. We took losses, but the enemy was destroyed. They attempted to mount a dangerous and well-coordinated counterattack with strong forces, but we repulsed it by our fire.

We took Haltern without resistance on the 27th. A mass of citizens flooded toward us, begging for protection and help. Of the numerous young men of draft age that had made it through to our lines, not one of them accepted a rifle that we offered them to participate in the fight against the Reds. Anyone not willing to fight will go under. But the Reds withdrew. They were done.

When the government decreed that anyone who had been wounded in the action would receive 1,000 marks, the reaction was one of exasperation. For us the old saying "*dulce et decorum est pro patria mori*" still had meaning.[2] While the officers shook their heads and smiled because they did not expect anything else from the government, the Jägers were mad. They felt humiliated. The military has a soul after all, and not everybody understands it.[3]

Orders to surrender all weapons always produced negative results. So the only hope was that lack of proper maintenance would render the weapons and ammunition useless before they were used again. On the political scene, meanwhile, there was a lot of back and forth. Initially military tribunals were announced; then cancelled; then reintroduced; then the imposition of the death penalty; then an amnesty; then the death penalty again. Nobody knew what was going on. Nobody really seemed to understand that the government of the Reich was not having an easy time of it. All this uncertainty among the troops only led to an undesirable form of vigilantism. The troops grew tired of always having to pull the chestnuts out of the fire, just to be insulted and never to receive a word of recognition. The word "strike" was in the air. On 9 April our advance halted.

On 17 April we conducted an operational review with the division commander, General Otto von Preinitzer. Continuation of operations required the approval of the Entente occupation forces, which had limited us to a strength of nineteen thousand men in the neutral zone. Thus, we had to withdraw forces from the zone.

The English occupation forces treated the Reds quite differently from the Reichswehr units, which were disarmed and interned. Red troops were not interned and sometimes not even disarmed. We had evidence that the English were giving weapons to the Red troops. During conversations between interned German officers and English officers they hinted that the reason was the difficulties with the labor force in England. The English government wanted to avoid the appearance of fighting the German labor movement.

Military tribunals manned by civilians were supposed to be established to render quick sentences. But the local judges resisted serving on them, for fear of exposing themselves. Civilian judges were then brought in from the eastern provinces, but even most of them did not want to serve.

We bid farewell to our commanding general, Oskar von Watter. He always had fought for the welfare of his troops in an upstanding manner. Nobody understood his dismissal. Watter had given the Reds a firm ultimatum. They were required to turn in a specific number of weapons within a short time period. When he visited our battalion he told us that the demands were unrealistic, but we had learned that lesson from Versailles. "Once the ultimatum has expired, I will hit them hard and clean them up."

In contrast, Prussian interior minister Carl Severing wanted to resolve the situation through negotiation. The military leadership and civilian leadership were pulling in opposite directions. Severing (the politician) was in a stronger position, so Watter had to go. But subsequent events proved Severing right. The Ruhr district remained calm and there was no further unnecessary bloodshed or new unrest. I see all this now in hindsight, of course.[4]

The operations in the Ruhr district now came to a complete halt. One clearing action in Wuppertal that was still pending was supposed to be taken care of by security police forces under civilian leadership. The security forces refused initially, because they were there to maintain law and order, and not to reestablish it. In the end they did the mission.

The Result

Looking back, I can now see that the government of the Reich had conducted some rather skillful politics. They hit where it was required. They granted amnesty, hit again, and granted amnesty again. In the end, lingering feelings of resentment and revenge were prevented and the future was not burdened with too much unnecessary bloodshed.

The military, of course, did not have much patience with such an approach. Their position was that the *vox populi* was not always the *vox jovis*.[5] Justified or not, the military felt that it had been abused. "National Bolshevism," as it soon became known, spread like an epidemic. At the end of April of 1920 (the exact date is not clear in my journal), Hientsch told me that he had heard from two of our former officers, Steinhoff and Helwig, the former from the University at Marburg and the latter from the academy at Clausthal. They independently had told him that for a long time the students had been unsure whether to support the Reichswehr or the Bolshevists. In the end they decided to throw their support to the Reichswehr.

The press at the time was constantly reporting rumors of an alliance forming between the communists and ultra-nationalist Reichswehr officers. General Hans von Seeckt carefully considered such an idea, but in the end he dismissed it. I often took the opportunity to talk to workers of the most diverse persuasions. The real communists were hostile to the military. They did not trust us. Only the followers of Syndicalism would have marched with us unconditionally. But they were a totally uninteresting splinter group.[6]

Ernst Haccius, who as the regimental adjutant had remained in Brunswick, asked me to give him my opinion on the situation. Haccius was one of our calmest and most respectable officers. His judgment was always especially valuable. He was killed in action in 1943 as the commander of the 46th Infantry Division in the Caucasus Mountains. I wrote to him:

Herne, 10 April 1920
My Dear Haccius,

Many thanks for your postcard of 4 April. I see that you too are contemplating the exact same questions that concern me and all of us here. The events of the last four weeks have made us all wonder. One thing is clear: the German Bürgertum has completely and utterly failed in Hildesheim, as well as in the Ruhr District. I think that its historic role is over. Lazy, cowardly, incapable of fighting, the German Bürger shakes in his boots in fear of losing his property and his fat belly, and so he lets events run their course. He is not worth fighting for. What keeps the institution alive at this point is the struggle between the two opposing poles, the army and the labor movement, or call it "Bolshevism." Without a doubt, you have to admire the energy potential and the will to fight of the German laborers.

Does the future belong to them? Yes and no. The answer is no as long as the officer corps as created by the Hohenzollerns makes a stand against them. It is yes as soon as we join in with them. The struggle that the German Army is going through right now is hard and hopeless. We do not have wide support among the people. We can be successful for a little while, but that will end. The example of 1918, where we likewise did not have popular support, should make us think. The economic demands of the workers are inconsequential to us. If they are just, then we can only welcome them as change. If they are unjust, they will simply disqualify themselves. Nobody wants to cut his own throat. Russia today is the best example. And as for the property of the lazy Bürger who does not want to fight himself, we should not have to fight for it. There is a lot wrong in our society that must be eliminated with fire and sword. No mercy should be granted. Whoever of the German Bürgertum and the higher society that still has some right to exist will surely survive.

So, to say it in clear language, we must use communism (the dictatorship of the proletariat) to reestablish reasonable conditions. The current muddling along cannot be a long-term situation. Democracy cannot maintain itself. According to its own label the labor movement is international. This makes no difference to us nationalists. The national movement is stronger and it will prevail. Look at Russia as an example. And besides, the German worker is so nationalistic that I do not see any danger in the internationalism. Deep in the inner circles of communism there is the popular notion of a war of revenge against France. If it came to a fight against France, they would all come together again. You hear this kind of talk every day. The popular view here sees our march against the Ruhr District as directed against the Entente. That tells you something about the morale of the people. But we will have to endure some hard times. Feelings cannot play a part in this.

We live in interesting times where everything old crumbles and new forces move up. Our old Germany is no longer. We will never get it back, not even an approximation. I have come to terms with this. But I believe in a new Germany emerging from its best strengths, even if the road there is covered with thorns. That is why I will remain a soldier, despite all the setbacks and the momentary tribulations.

So, my dear Haccius, this is my opinion concerning Germany's future. Grit your teeth and bear it. It is difficult to give advice to others. Everyone must make up his own mind. I have spoken about this with others. They had the same opinion as I, even though we had never spoken about it before. So, at least I have not dreamed this all up by myself.

I could still write a lot about this topic and everything related to it. One more thing, though. Just like the German Bürgertum, we too unfortunately must strike our Christian religion, at least in its current state, from the list of factors that can rebuild Germany. The church too has failed. The powerful force of Christian teachings has been watered down and is heading in the wrong direction. Our times are screaming for a reformer or a new religion. Socialism is really nothing but the dissatisfaction of the masses on a religious level.

But enough for now. We are doing well. The battalion is in better shape than ever and the men stand as one behind their officers. We can do with them whatever we must. They will follow us anywhere.

Best wishes,

We had taken a huge step closer to becoming Lenin's "useful idiots." At about the same time, Rudolf Nadolny, the director of the Eastern European desk in our foreign ministry who later became ambassador in Moscow, negotiated an alliance with the Russians. Soon thereafter, National Bolshevism got a new boost when Poland collapsed and Russian troops were approaching East Prussia.[7] At the time we were conducting an exercise in the Senne region, and General Hans von Seeckt, the new head of the Reichswehr, was there. Slender, elegant, with an impenetrable face, his few concluding words to us were as sharp as a dagger: ". . . and if the Russians cross the border of the Reich, then it is our task to throw them out again, and we will do this promptly."

A *Roi Connétable*[8] had spoken. His military appearance, his self-assured voice, the short, clear words, the unique aura that he exuded. . . . Nobody talked about "National Bolshevism" from then on. Once again we had a general at the helm that we could trust.

9

1921

The One Hundred Thousand-Man Army

The remnants of the 57th and 59th Infantry Regiments and the 8th Jäger Battalion had already been attached to the 10th Jäger Battalion. On 1 January 1921 we were reorganized as the 3rd Jäger Battalion, 17th Jäger Regiment, of the new *Reichsheer*. Originally formed as the Royal Prussian Hannoverian Jäger Battalion, the Goslar Jägers had made military history, well known throughout Germany. Highly competent officers from all over Germany had been attracted to the unit. Rommel had been a commander in Goslar. It was a special honor to be part of the Goslar Jägers. When we were reorganized we still had six out of nineteen officers from the old 10th Jäger Battalion—and if I remember correctly there were still 108 of the old Oberjägers and Jägers. Major Benno Pflugradt, who took command of the battalion after Kirchheim was reassigned, became the commander of the new unit. Pflugradt had received the *Pour le Mérite* as commander of the 1st Reserve Jäger Battalion. I remained as his adjutant. I was also assigned officially to the new Reichsheer as the first of all the first and second lieutenants of X and VIII Army Corps.

Things seemed to be stabilizing. We had to chase after Max Hölz[1] one more time, but there were no armed clashes. Otto Gessler, the new minister of the Reichswehr, visited us in Bitterfeld. He made a good and likeable impression, but Gessler later stopped visiting the troops. Wisely, he limited his involvement to the political side of his functions and made sure he covered Seeckt's back. By shielding the military from all political and otherwise harmful influences, he contributed greatly to the quality of the force. His job was not an easy one.

Germany in the early 1920s was dominated by the Interallied Control Commission, which supervised our disarmament. Goslar was an especially favorite target for these bureaucratic riffraff. Imposing controls quickly was all well and good, but what was supposed to happen if new disturbances or external complications arose? One hundred thousand soldiers were not enough for Germany. It was highly questionable whether the police could handle all the potential situations. We still had to rely on volunteers and unauthorized weapons, which we had to hide from the control inspectors. We had no intention of sacrificing our lives and the lives of our troops in a completely hopeless fight, whether an internal or an external fight.

Thus, numerous machine guns and associated pieces of equipment and ammunition were hidden away. We received inspection visits frequently, often at short intervals. It was surprising how well informed the Control Commission was. They sometimes stood directly in front of the walled-in hiding places, comparing what they saw to their blueprints. One time they made us dig out hollow spaces under the large earth deposits at the Rammelsberg Kaserne. The spot was absolutely right. Excitedly they dug up three huge chests. Unfortunately, the boxes contained only bricks and heather. We had placed them there as a subterfuge. They stopped their treasure hunt only a few meters short of the actual hiding place that contained several machine guns. As our troops hung out from the barracks windows and watched, they spontaneously broke into *"Deutschland, Deutschland über alles. . . ."* The French were mad and embarrassed. The English, however, laughed really hard, clearly feeling their allies deserved what they got.

But we wanted to know who had blown the whistle on us. So while our uninvited guests were staying in Goslar, some of our competent Jägers in civilian clothes kept them under surveillance. Once we thought we had the answer. "Herr Lieutenant," they reported, "the English major is receiving a lady in his hotel room. We will keep a close watch on the lady."

When she was trying to get on the train back to her hometown the police detained her. At first she protested her innocence and refused to make further statements. But then she finally caved in. She was a married woman from F_____ and claimed she had an affair with a Mr. Such-and-Such, a distinguished gentleman who had met her at the hotel. We did not believe a word of it and told her, "Get Herr X here now!" He finally showed up—with his wife and kids in tow. The reunion at the police station was more than dramatic. The gentleman, however, did look amazingly like the English major.

Change of Branches

Mobile combat, the operative mission of the cavalry, had always tickled my soldierly fancy. During the war I had spent a great deal of time working with cavalry units. The prospect of remaining in a subordinate position in Goslar after I had commanded companies for years was not for me, so I asked to be reassigned to the cavalry, specifically to the 18th Cavalry Regiment in Stuttgart. Southern Germany was foreign to me. After a short interlude in Celle, I reported to my new unit in early January 1922.

The regimental commander was Colonel Baun from Württemberg, who ran the regiment with an iron fist. We were always on duty. He had laid the foundation for the quality of the regiment. His successor was the exact opposite. Colonel von Kardorff had been a Guard Cuirassier, a Guard Uhlan, and aide-de-camp to the Kaiser. He was a distinguished older gentleman who never cared about details and who managed everything with a somewhat detached natural authority. Outside of the regiment he was viewed as somewhat of a lackadaisical character. In fact, he was anything but. He could control the most excitable individuals with a single glance. His insight into human nature and the way he treated people was unique. When meeting a total stranger, he could make a short remark or a gesture, and the individual addressed was clearly, accurately, and definitively judged. In 1945 he put an end to his life at his mother's grave site, only minutes before the Russians forced their way onto his old family estate.

I faithfully keep a special place in my memory for Colonel von Kardorff. Until the beginning of World War II, I maintained constant contact with him. Only once did he enter into a barracks of a squadron, and that was mine. I had two billy goats that were always roaming around the barracks, creating mischief and entertainment for everybody. Unfortunately they once noticed Kardorff as he every inch the nobleman walked across the parade field. The goats attacked him from behind. An intense duel ensued, cuirassier's saber against goats' horns. Afterward, I received a written order to report back immediately that the goats were gone. I had the heads of the two culprits stuffed and mounted on a plaque along with the regimental order, and hung it over my office door. Kardorff appeared on post, summoned me, and inspected the stuffed offenders. "Now that I have seen them, you might as well get rid of them."

The goat affair was never mentioned again.

General Reinhardt

The most striking personality I met in Württemberg was General Walther Reinhardt, commander of the 5th Division and commander of Military District V. As a colonel he had been the Prussian minister of war during the revolution. His time in that position had been controversial. Clearly he did not have the unfailing political intellect of a Groener or a Seeckt. His plan to make the eastern part of Germany independent and to rebuild the Reich from there was completely unrealistic. Fortunately, Groener and Ebert proved themselves to be stronger. Reinhardt was smart, an idealist of the highest caliber, and he had an ascetic bent. It is possible that those qualities made him less successful when it came to human leadership. He lacked toughness, something troops want. In the field of tactics he was superior, a modern soldier. He later might have made a perfect successor for Seeckt, an ideal complement. But Reinhardt had no such ambitions.

Reinhardt was with us often, and we enjoyed having this intelligent and reputable man around. One day we led him out to the beautiful patio terrace of the officers' mess, overlooking the wonderful Cannstatt Valley. Across the valley on a hillside rose the towers of a recently erected radio relay station that covered the whole southwestern region of Germany. It was a system designed to function even if there had been a total collapse of the mail and telephone services.

"So, what do you think makes the commander of this military district most happy when he looks around, my dear K.," said Reinhardt addressing Captain K., who had been commissioned from the enlisted ranks.

"Well, I would think the fact that you cannot see any soldiers around here," he responded in his thick Swabian accent. The breakfast that followed was a very pleasant event.

The 18th Cavalry

After a short time I was put in charge of the regiment's machine gun platoon, which was really a squadron. The unit later became the regiment's heavy squadron, which consisted of the machine gun platoon, signal platoon, gun platoon, and antitank platoon. Eventually I had approximately three hundred troopers and three hundred horses under my command. When I turned over the squadron in the fall of 1933 there was hardly a man in the unit who had not started out as a recruit under me, and hardly a mount that had not come to me as a young horse. It was a wonderful time. My superiors allowed me to command. I had very good and capable officers, who all became successful. Heinz Trettner even became the inspector general of the *Bundeswehr*.[2] I had close ties with the enlisted troops, just as I had had in Goslar with the Jägers. When I was going through rough times between 1945 and 1947 I received support from my old soldiers that I would have never expected in my wildest dreams.

The twelve-year service obligation that was forced on us by the Versailles Treaty was corrosive. Promotion opportunities were naturally minimal, along with a wide range of other personnel management problems we had to solve. Training courses to prepare for transition to civilian life, military leadership training courses, and other such innovations helped us to overcome the difficulties. For my part, I did my best and supported those of my soldiers who were qualified to become NCOs in other units. I therefore avoided having to deal with a dangerous group of unhappy and dissatisfied perpetual privates who were capable, but were stuck being privates forever. I also wrote truthful, not inflated discharge evaluations. There were organizations in the Stuttgart area that would hire any applicant with my signature on his evaluation, because they knew the man was exactly as I had described him in the evaluation. The Military District

V radio relay station, for example, hired only my people regardless, even if they had not had radio operator training. "Your people are at least soldiers we can rely on," they told me. "We can teach them how to send radio signals."

One dark chapter during this period was the influx of psychopaths into the army. The psychopath cannot succeed in the civilian career world. He is always a failure and he knows it. But he thinks that becoming a soldier might work for him. In the army he is given an order, and all he has to do is follow it. The leader leads you at all times and takes care of you. But once the loser is in the army, he realizes that the demands are especially high, and he realizes that he has failed there too. As a last resort, many turn to crime or suicide.

In later years when Germany's military build-up started, a remarkable number of the troopers from my squadron were promoted to the highest levels. Two of my old Wachtmeisters, Plapp and Lohmüller, were killed in action during World War II as regimental commanders.[3]

Tactical exercises took us through all of southern and middle Germany. On the average we could count on approximately sixty nights out in the field during the year, ranging from Berlin to Lake Constance. Wherever we stayed I made it a rule always to talk with our hosts about the economic, social, and political affairs of their towns. We, therefore, were able to achieve a cross-sectional understanding that could not be obtained any other way in Germany at that time. Once, when we had finished at the training area at Altengraben near Magdeburg, my squadron officers and NCOs and I rode all the way back to Stuttgart. It took fourteen days, sixty kilometers a day in the saddle, visiting all the important cultural sites of Thuringia and Franconia. Those are unforgettable memories.

The one hundred-kilometer marches by entire regiments were popular events at that time. Three days in a row, one hundred kilometers in the saddle, demanded quite a lot of us. But such techniques can be learned. Overall, our training maneuvers were very stimulating and battle-oriented. One such maneuver in the Rhön area concluded with a parade before Hindenburg. The entire cavalry division, six mounted regiments, dashed with thundering hooves at full gallop past the field marshal, in an unbelievable cloud of dust. And there at the place of honor, in a haze but clearly distinguishable like in a halo, stood old Hindenburg, unreal, iron-like, as if he were a stone monument.

Seeckt, Heye, and Hammerstein

The Reichswehr became a good army because it was led by an individual of the highest military caliber and not administered by an anonymous group. It was Seeckt who put his stamp on us. The trust that he had gained in political circles allowed him to screen the troops from any political influences, which was more than necessary considering the conditions that Germany faced at the time. The sad example of the Austrian *Bundesheer* justified our political isolation. Seeckt's strong suits were politics, his attitude toward the state, his operational background, his absolute discipline, and his ability to prevent any sort of spying on individual convictions. During World War II the operational training of the German Wehrmacht reached a peak unsurpassed by any other army at any other time. That was to the credit of Seeckt, who by building on Schlieffen's ideas administered that legacy in a masterful way.

The instrument that Seeckt had created was firmly in his hands. His authority was unquestioned and unflappable. It was unthinkable that his orders would not be followed. When Ebert in 1923 grew concerned about a military putsch and mentioned it to him, Seeckt could proudly declare, "In the Reichswehr there is only one person that could lead a putsch. That is me, and I will not do it."

Two of Seeckt's decisions stand out in particular. During the Kapp Putsch he declared, "Reichswehr does not fire on Reichswehr," very possibly saving Germany from a deep inner political crisis that could very well have resulted in only one winner—communism. His sharp intellect, which was accustomed to analyzing matters in a businesslike and objective manner, clearly saw that the Kapp Putsch did not have a chance of succeeding and that it would collapse within a short period. There was, therefore, no sense in spilling blood and creating obstacles for the future. Events proved him right, which still did not prevent some leftist politicians from criticizing him for refusing to resort to force. Germans, even if they are left leaning and pacifist when it comes to foreign politics, like to follow in domestic politics the old adage, "If you do not want to be my brother, I will simply kick in your head."

Seeckt made his second important decision in 1923. Ebert had given Seeckt the executive authority in the Reich. Seeckt at that point had the power of a dictator. The Social Democrats, the Centrist Party, and the democratic forces supporting the government were in a shambles. Communism had been defeated. The right was urging Seeckt to overthrow the government. And at that point the aristocratic Seeckt, the absolute master of Germany, went to the president of the Reich, the socialist craftsman Ebert, and reported the accomplishment of his mission and returned all of his authority back into Ebert's hands. Seeckt realistically understood that it would have been impossible to govern the country in opposition to the labor movement. But then what happened to the labor movement, to social democracy? The movement remained stagnant. In any other country Seeckt's truly democratic step would have caused an internal political turning point. But this was Germany, the country of obstinate doctrinaires.

I came into contact with Seeckt often. We flocked to his after-action reviews, during which he always gave a political overview at the conclusion. Twice during maneuvers I was his aide-de-camp for several days and was lucky enough to observe this outstanding personality up close. There is no light, however, without shadows. Even Seeckt's leadership had its flaws. He did nothing for the broader political education of the officer corps; he never clarified the military's relationship to the constitution. Blind obedience seemed to make such understanding unnecessary. It was taken for granted that one kept one's oath and no discussion was needed.

Seeckt's major military weakness was tactics, in which he had no interest. He was not a modern soldier. The cavalry kept their lances; the infantry retained the *Präsentiergriff*[4] and the *Exerziermarsch*.[5] This is why our infantry was more modernly trained at the end of World War I than it was at the beginning of World War II.

By the time Seeckt was forced to resign in 1926 after committing a political blunder, he had fulfilled his duty.[6] By that point he had given us everything he had to give. He was at the zenith of his glory. Everything from that point on depended on his successor, who had to keep developing the legacy. The appropriate successor could have been General Reinhardt. He was not Seeckt's political equal, but militarily he was a tactical genius and he would have complemented perfectly Seeckt, the strategist.

Unfortunately Reinhardt did not want to do it, so General Wilhelm Heye became Seeckt's successor. Heye had served with distinction in senior General Staff assignments on the eastern front. During the events at Spa when the Kaiser abdicated in 1918, Heye had exercised clear judgment and demonstrated the courage of his own convictions. As the military district commander in East Prussia he had all elements of the population from left to right convinced of the necessity of a defensive stance against Poland.

Unfortunately, Heye moved into the psychological realm and he wanted to create more modern forms of discipline. As a result, every black sheep in the army turned to Heye, who became known as the "Father of all Soldiers." The result was serious internal disruption in the army. When Heye finally offered a silver watch to anybody in the army who uncovered communist activities, he lost all credibility in the officer corps. The ability to lead human beings is not always directly proportional to other highly developed capabilities. Groener in his memoirs judged Heye quite harshly, and with some justification.

On the positive side, Heye pressed ahead with the development of modern arms and he accomplished a great deal that was not immediately obvious to the troops, but which paid off much later. Heye was succeeded by General Kurt von Hammerstein-Equord, a highly capable but notoriously lazy officer.

His Berlin-style flippancy did not go over too well in southern Germany. I had many encounters with Heye and Hammerstein. They could not hold a candle to Seeckt, but they still impressed me.

The State within the State

Among the accusations that politicians hurled at the military over and over was the charge that we were a state within the state. There is an element of truth in this. As long as both the right and the left formed their own paramilitary organizations and tried to pull the regular troops over to their side to support a coup, the army had no other choice than to isolate itself from all sides. On top of that, the army was spat upon from all directions, making it unlikely that we would align ourselves with those doing the spitting. The problem of the state within the state always comes back to the old issue that life consists of actions and reactions.

In 1923 social democracy missed a great domestic political opportunity, with Seeckt exercising his dictatorial powers in the most loyal way and relinquishing power to Ebert. There was a chance to recognize the military and change the attitudes toward it. But nothing happened. In contrast, the majority of the socialists, oddly enough, voted for the defense budget. An opportunity for a domestic political settlement was missed.

Philipp Scheidemann[7] once said, "The military must learn to follow the civilian authority blindly." Later in the National Assembly he also said, "You can see that we are about to grab these gentlemen [the officers] by their collars." Eduard David[8] said, "What we need to do most is to destroy the moral prestige that the officer corps surrounds itself with." With public statements of that sort, the MSPD[9] could hardly expect enthusiastic support from the military. On the contrary, they produced some excellent building blocks for the state-within-the-state. Too often it is forgotten that an army has a soul and a life of its own that cannot be trampled upon without consequences. If that happens, no one should be surprised by unintended consequences.

The Republic

Another area of conflict was the attitude toward the republic. The idea of a republic was new in Germany. There were no glorious examples for it in our history. On the contrary, the concept was tainted, rightfully or not, with the "Stab in the Back," the lost war, and the Versailles treaty. Reasonable individuals like Ebert wanted to let the wounds heal over time. Despite their socialist backgrounds, they only reluctantly supported the founding of the republic. But at the time neither violence, nor lip service, nor education seemed to work. The republican did actually prevail in the Prussian police force. Severing frequently praised the Prussian police as the republican model for the Reichswehr. That all came to an end, however, with the fall of Franz von Papen's government.[10]

Values are a tender plant. They take a great deal of time to develop. If the process is rushed, it fails. When many people sense a coming change, they will be quick to jump on the bandwagon. People's convictions are not rigid. They are quite changeable. The less time they are allowed to develop, the worse will be the train wreck when it comes. This is where Hitler later failed, too. A firm and clear character is far more important than the correct conviction. The former is recognizable and can be included in the equation. Convictions cannot.

The Prussian police failed because of these fundamentally psychological errors. For us in the military conviction was immaterial, but character was everything. The army had learned from the Kapp Putsch. It had drawn and internalized two important lessons: if an army gets involved in politics, it will self-destruct; and nobody in modern Germany can govern in opposition to the workers. There was only one way to make the republic popular, and that was to convince people by accomplished success. That route, however, was blocked.

Militarism

Militarism is an objectively unjustifiable overemphasis of military matters over the requirements of politics. As a popular catchword it has a deadly political effect that blocks effective thought and discourse. In the prisoner of war camps after 1945 a short and appropriate saying made the rounds to the effect that a militarist is a professional soldier who has just lost a war. At the highest levels politics and the conduct of war will always affect and interact with each other. The question of which of the two should be given preference in any given case will often be controversial, even though in most if not all situations the political arm must be the controlling element. A balancing authority is necessary, such as King Wilhelm during the German Wars of Unification. That authority could be a state president, a war cabinet, or a special commission. Exactly what form that authority will take cannot be mandated by a law. Each case will depend on the situation and the personalities involved.

Rarely has the question how militarism develops been studied, even though it is the really decisive question. This part of the problem of militarism is hardly ever examined. Politicians are most willing to blame the soldier, who in turn is used to remaining silent. That is why I see the problem of militarism thusly—the militarist comes into existence when the political arm fails, as was the case in Germany in 1914–1918, and when the soldier is abused. Naturally, war is too serious of a business to let politicians or soldiers mess with it like a bull in a china shop. But with the failure of politics, Chancellor Theobald von Bethmann-Hollweg created the militarist Ludendorff, and during the Thirty Years' War the Habsburgs created Wallenstein.

Politics Again

Even though we were screened off from politics, we nevertheless were politically interested. Actually, we followed foreign politics quite closely, being concerned about our hopeless military situation. Here was our one hundred thousand-man army facing armies on our borders numbering in the millions. Our enemies did not even have to mobilize. They easily could have squashed us with their peace-time forces. Even the smallest mistake in politics could well have cost us our lives. It was not a good feeling.

We had similar fears in domestic politics. One hundred thousand men were not nearly enough to deal with a civil war. The reliability of the police every-where was hard to judge. Should we rely on the paramilitary organizations? Each of those organizations came with their share of problems. Cooperating with the Red Front was out of the question. The *Stahlhelm*[11] organization would put us in direct conflict with the labor movement, even though they were the closest to us politically. The *Reichsbanner Schwarz Rot Gold*[12] took such a con-frontational position against us that any kind of cooperation with them was impossible. And nobody knew what the goals of the SA[13] were. Besides, we were looking for a quiet transformation, not a revolution.

What we knew of the developing communist power was impressive. I remember seeing a demonstration where good-looking, well-disciplined col-umns in the strength of a division marched through Stuttgart. I also saw much the same thing in Berlin. We knew that these people were relatively well armed. The parties that formed the government, the Centrists, the Social Democrats, and the Democrats, had lost much of their credibility. I thought Alfred Hugen-berg[14] was an especially unfortunate character. He had gathered together under the German National People's Party all the old forces that had supported the state. But rather than leading the way ahead, he tried to return everything to the way it had been. The future, however, lay before us—not behind us. Thus, Hugenberg did not creatively address the problem of the positive integration of the workers into the whole of society. But that was the key problem. Whoever managed to integrate the German workers owned the future. The Conserva-tives' slogan, "The worker does not care who he is governed by as long as the outcome is good and just," completely missed the mark.

Germany's inner political turmoil even divided families. Captain (later field marshal) Erwin von Witzleben, for example, was a monarchist, his wife a National Socialist, and his children were communists. Even two of General von Hammerstein's daughters were communists. Thus, for the German Army to avoid falling totally apart and becoming incapable of playing a national role, the only solution for us was the "state within the state."

The army's firm consolidation of its position, its sharp focus on the bigger picture, its elevated position vis-à-vis the political parties, and its independence from the influence of economic special interests were all factors in the military's almost automatic evolution from being a state within the state to becoming the actual power within the state—a power that could not be ignored. Naturally, our critics held all this against us, but they themselves had proved totally incapable of developing any other solution to Germany's social and political problems. They were the very ones who elevated us into this position.

Cultural Life

Commenting on life in the officer corps, Schopenhauer once wrote that one only talked about women, horses, and dogs. Well of course we talked about those topics. But I also must point out that life in the officer corps as I knew it during my whole period of service was characterized by an extremely high level of intellectual sophistication. Before the First World War the many reserve officers that came from all walks of life livened up the conversations in the officers' messes. The informal discussions touched on almost all subjects. Because of the informal nature of the conversations, civilians who happened to be present also contributed to the discussions, which in turn expanded the horizons of the soldiers.

Unfortunately, things were not quite the same during the period of the Reichswehr, but we nonetheless had many diverse opportunities. Stuttgart, with its many theaters and lectures, had a great deal to offer. We exploited such opportunities, which often ended in long discussions at the officers' mess. One of our favorite civilian venues was the German Gentlemen's Round Table, where gentlemen from all professions met each Thursday evening. The military was especially well represented. Everyone who attended was required to give a presentation and then defend it.

Duty obligations were demanding as well. Once every winter each officer was challenged to produce a paper, conduct a sand table exercise, or give a presentation. I usually gave presentations that dealt with operational issues. But we also were required to address civilian topics every other year. One year my friend Ulrich Kleemann gave an extremely good presentation on financial matters. Later, during World War II, Kleemann was the commanding general on

the island of Rhodes when it became necessary to replace the Italian government in 1943. He managed to stabilize the local currency with some very clever
measures, and thus maintained the peace among the restless populace. One
winter I prepared a rather substantial piece on "The History of the German
Labor Movement." The paper gave me a chance to deal in depth with the entire
body of socialist writing, and the personalities of Marx, Lassalle, and Lenin. In
preparation, I had a subscription to the social democratic newspaper *Vorwärts*
for a whole year. The paper was sent forward to the highest leadership levels as
an example of a well-crafted analysis.

Naturally the question of joining the General Staff came up. Twice while
serving in temporary General Staff assignments I achieved the necessary qualifications to transfer to the General Staff. The second time the chief of staff
of our 3rd Cavalry Division really wanted me to transfer. I, however, always
resisted strongly. I loved the frontline life, the direct contact with the soldiers
and the horses, working with living beings, and the hands-on training with the
troops. Becoming a second stringer, as so often happened in the General Staff,
was not for me.[15]

Besides, as a member of the General Staff I could not have pursued the
many diverse intellectual interests I enjoyed so much. Even my military interests, particularly military history, I was able to better pursue on my personal
time. As a General Staff officer one too often was drowned in bureaucratic
office work. I never regretted the decision.

I did a great deal of writing during those years. I turned my notes from my
war experiences into several articles. I also wrote an extensive treatise on the
Russo-Polish War, in which I believe I analyzed correctly the Russian operational concepts, which were based on exhausting the enemy's reserves by cleverly committing Russia's sheer human masses. By World War II the Russians
were still trying to do much the same thing. I was particularly interested in
questions of organizational psychology. Everyone at the time was opposed
to such thinking, and nobody wanted to provide personnel for the necessary
experiments. I went in the opposite direction and provided any number of personnel required for countless studies. Soon I became convinced that applied
psychological research provided an especially effective tool against nepotism
and against the infiltration of undesirable candidates into the officer corps. The
officer candidate year groups that were psychologically tested were of the best
quality throughout. They could not have been selected more carefully.

The personnel management system was further developed to a high level
during the period of the one hundred thousand-man army. One of the most
significant innovations was the introduction of order-of-merit lists. Every commander was required to evaluate and rank his officers. The division would then

consolidate all of its regimental lists. That process required getting to know your subordinates. The process for filling positions included ranking each candidate at the regimental level; inspection of his squadron by the division commander; participation in a divisional field exercise, to include a presentation; leading a unit; ranking on the divisional order of merit list; and passing a selection test by the command group. Those unsuited for the assignment always failed to make one of those cuts. No other army has managed to achieve what the thirty-six hundred-strong officer corps of the one hundred thousand-man army accomplished during World War II in terms of training, organizing, and developing tactical and operational leadership. This was largely the product of the Reichswehr's personnel selection process.

During this time I also received my first assignment in a foreign country. I was detailed to the Swiss Army with the task of evaluating pack animals in their cavalry units. During my time with the Alpenkorps in the First World War I had had extensive experience in this area. The Swiss gave me a delightful reception. I was quite impressed with what they were able to accomplish with their short-term enlistments and their militia facilities. Their enlisted soldiers were in the best physical condition and the officers were dedicated and capable. It was quite clear, however, that their highly developed military knowledge in some areas was a direct result of the fact that they had been on constant alert status during World War I. At that point, then, they were no longer really a militia force. A live fire exercise I observed was comparable to ours.

Political discussions naturally ensued, and it was pleasant to see that the Swiss officers with whom I dealt made an effort to balance the German and French elements of their national character. They did express a high regard for the Reichswehr and for German accomplishments during the war. Years later, one of those Swiss officers was attached to us and I spent some time with him during a maneuver. When we touched on politics again he admitted to very strong National Socialist leanings. When I expressed my astonishment to hear this from a Swiss, he responded, "We have not been separated from Germany all that long. We still are Germans."

10

In the Third Reich

30 January 1933

The Weimar Republic ended in perpetual crisis. In the end the choice was between Communism and National Socialism. All other parties had ruined themselves and had no more support among the people. The last attempt by Kurt von Schleicher[1] to split National Socialism and thus build a sustainable majority failed because of the hostile attitude of the unions. Democratic means were depleted. What remained was a choice between a military dictatorship and a civil war. No one wanted the latter, and in any event, it would have been impossible to conduct a civil war with a one hundred thousand-man army. It is always an unfortunate development when an army takes over as the political leadership, but it would have been one of those situations where the political element had to yield to the soldier. This meant either a Communist or a National Socialist government, and at that point only Hitler seemed to remain. The stupidity and hatred of the authors of the Versailles treaty had left Germany with inadequate means of power, resulting in this unwanted situation.

We regarded National Socialism with mixed feelings. On the one hand, we judged positively the fact that it had broadly succeeded in breaking the socialist labor movement and had established an opportunity for resolving the confusing state of domestic politics. But on the negative side, we did not know if National Socialism had the necessary qualified people to take over the government. Up to that point it had not been able to stand that test. The National Socialists managed to gain a foothold in the local governments only in Thuringia and Brunswick. In Germany political movements only achieve power when they get so large that they can no longer be ignored, rather than allowing them to gain experience on the local government level, which would give them the necessary education as professional politicians and the right sense of reality. And then we wondered why things went wrong.

Naturally we did not see things as clearly as the one man who was not a politician, at least not in the eyes of his opponents. On 3 July 1932, Ludendorff wrote in his own weekly *Volkswarte* magazine: "The violent coup d'état will come as it did in 1918; however, no delegate of the people will arrive in time to prevent the bloodbath. Instead of a people's delegate, Herr Hitler will arrive, who just like the previous delegates will claim to represent the popular will, but who will not be capable of quelling the bloodlust that he and his chief of staff[2] inculcated in the SA and the SS. After ten to twelve years the Germans will recognize that the revolution of 1932–1933 was a deceit of the people, just like the revolution of 1918, except an even bigger one."[3]

Why had Weimar failed? First and foremost there was the stupidity of the politics of Versailles, sustained by France with the goal of creating chaos in Germany, thereby turning it into a French-dominated zone of powerlessness in the middle of Europe. What the French politicians failed to see was that Bolshevism rather than France would be the only beneficiary of such a policy. Then as now, the words of Prince Eugene of Savoy remain true: "If you destroy Germany, you invite Asia into Europe."

The constitution of the Weimar Republic was itself a problem. It was a theoretical compilation of all the democratic ideals that would work only if all humans were angels. A constitution should bring to bear the positive characteristics of a people and counterbalance their flaws. If it does not account for real human nature, one should not be surprised by what follows. The inherent flaws of the German people were not accounted for by the Weimar Constitution. It was similar to the situation where the Belgian Constitution of 1830 was copied by many other young states as the ideal of a modern democratic constitution. It worked in those states only for the short run because the imitators themselves were not Belgian.

Social Democracy had its own unique history in Germany. For seventy years it had been allowed to agitate unchecked, making promises, all on the assumption that it would never find itself in a position where it would have to pay the piper. The movement had inherited its unholy legacy from Bismarck, whose ineptness in domestic politics had divided Germans into state-supporting factions and enemies of the Reich. Under Bismarck not even the position of a night watchman was open to a Social Democrat. After socialist leader Ferdinand Lasalle was killed in a duel in 1864, Bismarck's antisocialism laws crushed all national ambitions within the labor movement. Fortunately, Bismarck was prevented from pursuing his solution of bloody suppression of the labor movement by the young Kaiser, Wilhelm II. Nonetheless, the unfortunate legacy remained, and even the Kaiser eventually shifted to an anti–Social Democratic course. This basic criticism also applies to Bismarck's *Kulturkampf.*[4]

One can only wonder how the Social Democratic movement managed to produce so many creative statesmen at the top. I'm thinking here of Friedrich Ebert, Gustav Noske, Carl Severing, Giselher Wirsing, and Otto Hörsing, among others. But they could not prevail against the party's demagogical wing, like Philipp Scheidemann and others, and the majority of party functionaries continued on in their old ways. It was comfortable and there was a reluctance to shunt aside the "old warriors."

Groener once made an interesting observation about the Social Democrats. On 26 October 1917 my father wrote to me about a conversation he had with Groener, when they were both in command of adjacent divisions on the western front. "He [Groener] spoke in rather praising terms of the intellectual abilities of most Social Democratic representatives, something which was lacking with the Conservatives and the National Liberals."

After Hitler came to power we in the military did not at first notice any significant changes. Everything seemed to remain the same. Of course, we had not noticed that Hindenburg in later years had been leaning increasingly on General Schleicher, later making him the chancellor. The one change that we did notice immediately was that all those that had been kicked out of the army because of theft or other illegal actions were now pursuing their reinstatement or the applications for their pensions, claiming that they really had been separated because they had been loyal National Socialists. After 1945 a considerable number of these people approached me asking for affidavits confirming that they had left the military because of their anti-fascist activities. Unfortunately for them, I have an excellent memory. Spying on the political convictions of those in the military did not exist before or after the change in power. I do not know of any case where someone was kicked out because of his political conviction.

Farewells are always difficult. A long period of service as a squadron commander creates the strongest bonds with the people you worked with. The regiment's officer corps was also first rate. It consisted of members of all the German tribes, and proved the falsity of the cherished belief that each German tribe can only be led by officers from that same tribe.[5] What distinguished the officers of the regiment most was the absence of rumormongering and personal envy. We had a special sense of esprit, a real and sincere camaraderie—even though everybody was not necessarily friends with everybody else.

Divisional Adjutant

The chief of staff of the 3rd Cavalry Division, Colonel Gustav von Wietersheim,[6] came to Defense District III as the chief of the General Staff and initiated my transfer into his section, the newly emerging territorial staff of the 1st Cavalry Division. He was trying to position me and move me from there into the General Staff officer career field. Unfortunately, I had to disappoint him. At the decisive moment I asked to remain with troops.

At Frankfurt on the Oder River, where the 1st Cavalry Division was head-quartered, I was responsible for establishing area defense commands and similar organizations. After half a year, in the spring of 1934, the 1st Cavalry Division was restationed at Potsdam and I remained in Frankfurt with Lieutenant Colonel Maximilian Fretter-Pico,[7] the Ia,[8] to form the core of the staff of the newly forming 3rd Division. The division commander was Colonel Curt Haase,[9] from the Württemberg region. A man of high military skills and remarkable character, he was most supportive on personnel issues, which were mostly my area of responsibility. Unfortunately, he had the characteristically sharp and sarcastic Württemberg sense of humor that could come across as abrasive in northern Germany. He knew it and had told me, "Whenever you notice that I am about to say something inappropriate, just hiss lightly." Sometimes I could not hiss fast enough to prevent the biting but always perfectly telling comments. Haase displayed a lot of backbone when it came to dealing with the Nazi Party. Within a year a whole set of party functionaries had been expended against us. Haase once said to an *SA-Obergruppenführer*[10] who had just arrived in Frankfurt right after the Röhm Putsch[11]: "Just so that we are clear, I am a reactionary, which means I do not steal." Once again I had not hissed fast enough, but our visitor asserted sheepishly that he would try his best to see that this would not be an issue in his area.

East Brandenburg was a politically difficult region, and unfortunately we now had a lot to do with politics. Our small staff discussed all the problems. Frequently the initial discussions were between Fretter-Pico and myself during our early morning rides, and then later again with our divisional commander. The biggest political issue was a function of the fact that all the border security forces, which were local militia organizations, were subordinate to us, but the SA tried to meddle in everything.

Eastern Germany was an old colonial land that was different from the rest of the country in the way that land and property were distributed—a system perceived by many as unjust. When the class of large estate owners[12] becomes politically active and rules in an authoritarian fashion, tensions develop that easily can lead to revolution and the violent redistribution of land ownership. That is what happened in Russia. In the east of Germany the political contrasts were especially sharp and often bitter. The atmosphere was totally different from Germany west of the Elbe River. The fact that the former Prussian administration had been especially efficient, good, and just carried little weight now and did not particularly interest those elements that were still locked out of participating in government and administration. Even though the conditions had changed outwardly since 1918, the underlying resentments were still there. We had to deal with these conditions and work around them, because the border security mission deeply affected the daily life and social conditions of the local population.

The Röhm Putsch

At the beginning of 1934, relations with the SA deteriorated sharply. Their attempts to infiltrate the border security units, to assume military leadership positions, and to obtain weapons became increasingly violent. The SA was morphing more and more into a military organization, conducting exercises at the battalion and regimental levels. They formed engineer and signal units. The SA *Standarten*[13] units assumed the traditional lineages of old army units. We learned about a very secret organizational order from the highest command levels directing the SA to convert into a militia army.[14] In the spring of 1934 the SA activated special units consisting of hooligans and specially selected thugs. Undoubtedly, they were being organized for revolution. When one army officer happened to mention to an SA leader that he would be transferring to Küstrin that fall as part of the build-up of army units, the retort was that the "transfer would be more likely as a prisoner." Warning indicators also came from our border security units.

The situation became nightmarish for us. We expected an explosion at any moment, with supposed dates being thrown around. We no longer entrusted important orders to the mail system, and we restricted phone conversations to general daily business. Several times I traveled back and forth to the area defense command in Berlin with important messages and orders as a courier, each time by a different route. I was always met by an officer at a different location. In the beginning I only took a pistol with me, but later I always traveled with an armed escort. When the situation finally exploded at Bad Wiessee on 30 June, it was a relief for us. In his memoirs Field Marshal Erich von Manstein, who at the time was the chief of staff of the Area Defense Command III in Berlin, described the situation in similar terms.

Contrary to all expectations, everything remained calm in Frankfurt. There were no executions or riots in all of eastern Brandenburg. Under pressure from the alerted army troops and the SS units, the SA did not dare to put up any resistance. What happened then was a typical German about-face, where nobody had known anything; nobody had participated; and Röhm, who had only recently held godlike status, was now a long-known scoundrel. But we knew what had been said previously, and what was being said now.

Much has been written and said about the suppression of the Röhm Putsch. After 1945 a weak attempt was even made to depict the Röhm Putsch as resistance against Hitler and recast it as something positive. In historical terms, the

Röhm Putsch was an episode that every revolution will lead to inevitably. The driving, hard-hitting forces that brought the movement to power continue to press on, while the leadership that does not need them anymore and now wants to turn its ideals into reality has to restrain its own revolutionary forces. This is a problem that only can be resolved with ruthless use of force. In Russia a small, tightly organized minority of eleven thousand had won against the moderate masses of 150 million because nobody acted and Kerensky did nothing to help the advance of Russian politics. Thus in Germany, the emerging brown Bolshevism was eradicated. Naturally, there was bitter criticism from some quarters, mostly by the very people who had every reason to be thankful that the SA had been suppressed during the "Night of the Long Knives"[15] because they probably would not have survived it.

World history generally does not repeat itself, but in this case it perhaps did. There are parallels to Wallenstein's assassination, even in the details. In both cases, the elimination of the key personalities ran the risks of armed resistance and foreign political consequences. Both Wallenstein and Röhm had been operating in opposition to official policies. When they were eliminated physically, there was reason to fear that the regiments loyal to Wallenstein would intervene, just as we feared the SA's loyalty to Röhm. On the foreign political level, there was the fear in Wallenstein's case that Swedish-Protestant forces would take advantage of the situation to intervene; while in the case of Röhm the concern was interference by France.

A few years after World War II, *SS-Oberstgruppenführer*[16] Josef "Sepp" Dietrich was tried and convicted by the West German government for his role in issuing Röhm's execution order. This came as a surprise to people who knew the details of the situation. Dietrich was an upstanding human being. He was highly respected in the Wehrmacht. He was a good leader later in the war and he always tried to balance matters between Hitler and the Wehrmacht. I still hold him in high esteem.[17]

After the Revolt

After the suppression of the Röhm Putsch the air cleared for the most part. Röhm's demise was well received and the attitude toward the Nazi regime became increasingly rather positive in the Wehrmacht. We were aware of all the talk and chatter throughout the country, but the most common reaction was disbelief. Of all the gossip we heard, 70 percent was clearly false, 20 percent was exaggeration to the point of uselessness, and 10 percent may have been true.

A much more serious consequence was the fact that anti-Hitler feelings started to center around Colonel General Werner Freiherr von Fritsch. Many people started to believe that Fritsch would be the one to fix the situation; that he was keeping quiet for now, but he would strike; Fritsch was the man. In discussions among the staff, I occasionally mentioned that this could not possibly turn out well. Every member of the Nazi Party heard the same rumors, often in an even more malicious and distorted form. I remain convinced that the main reason for the nasty Fritsch Affair[18] that came later was the many idiotic rumors floating throughout the country. The result at the highest levels had to be mistrust, which was deliberately stoked by those who circulated the rumors. I learned my lesson during that period. From that point on I refused to give any credence to any political rumors and turned a deaf ear toward all such uselessness.

First Encounter with Hitler

An official letter arrived, addressed to Haase, our division commander. He called Fretter-Pico and me into his office and handed the letter to us, which announced that Hitler would be visiting Frankfurt. We were supposed to put the program together. Haase handed the letter to me and said, "Take care of this and tell me the evening before what is going on."

It was a pleasure to work for somebody like General Haase. I had a totally free hand. I drove to the district commanding general's headquarters, and to Hitler's administrative office, discussed everything, and then it all ran its course. Hitler refused to allow the local Nazi Party officials to participate. The security measures were interesting; they were simple and effective and relied mainly on the visit being a complete surprise.

We received Hitler at the train station with an honor guard company and then held a pass in review with a large element of the division. Then he visited the newly constructed barracks, in which he was very interested, particularly the concrete-reinforced roofs that provided protection against incendiary bombs. He had not known about that particular feature, and it was remarkable how quickly he grasped everything. Asking objective questions, he drew conclusions for civilian air-raid protection and residential construction, converted everything into numbers, and clearly formulated it all.

Then we had coffee in the Führer's train. Hitler became clearly more relaxed, mentioning in discussion the various Nazi Party leaders in Frankfurt: "Does Kube still act like a peacock?"[19] Hitler listened to our problems and he promised resolutions, which promptly occurred within forty-eight hours. Then we all had dinner in the officers' mess. I had arranged for everybody to be sitting at small tables. Besides the division commander, only young captains sat at Hitler's table. After dinner Hitler moved into a side room and sat at a large round table with all the best second and first lieutenants of the division. Hitler was very relaxed in this atmosphere and lost all his stiffness. The lieutenants were not shy either. Hitler spoke very openly about his recent trip to Venice to meet Mussolini, where *il Duce* had treated him particularly badly. "If he only had some kind of real misfortune, I would be happy about that," Hitler said. A Grand Tattoo[20] held in front of the division commander's quarters then concluded Hitler's successful and first visit with the Wehrmacht.

In the fall of 1935 my time in Frankfurt came to an end. I was assigned as the commander of a newly formed Bicycle Battalion of the 1st Cavalry Division. Haase also left Frankfurt. He assumed command of a division in Nuremberg, where his strong personality was needed to counterbalance the Gauleiter, Julius Streicher.[21] Hitler's earlier visit to Frankfurt factored in that move. I regretted parting ways with Haase. I had learned a lot from this brilliant, steadfast soldier.

Tilsit

Even though I had spent my final school years in Thorn, East Prussia was largely unknown to me. But I enjoyed going to "Siberia," and I never regretted it. My job was to stand up the Bicycle Battalion, which was the only one in the Wehrmacht. Certain experiences from my time with the Goslar Jägers gave me an advantage. I reported directly to the brigade. My brigade commanders, first General Erich Volk, then General Eberhard von Mackensen,[22] were ideal superiors. They mostly left me a free hand and were never stingy when it came to praise. I was able to enact all of my ideas about training and education, while reducing to a minimum the time spent on drill and ceremony. The maximum time was devoted to combat-focused training. The enlisted and the NCOs were almost all former policemen, and were thus completely unencumbered by the old routines. The officers of the unit quickly adjusted. The unit's replacements came partly from East Prussia, partly from the Rhineland, a particularly advantageous mixture. The East Prussian was considered dumb and stubborn. I found the contrary to be true. Seven hundred years of colonial regimentation created a human type that either said one thing and did the opposite, or did what he thought was right, or executed every order verbatim. The latter was the worst. But if you succeeded in breaking through this hard outer shell, you found a totally different human being, self-sufficient and instinctively doing the right things. The East Prussian was more in harmony with nature than anyone else in Germany and just as talented as any German. On top of that, he had an appreciation for authority and loyalty toward his officers. By playing on these strengths and not taking the formal kind of classroom approach, we got results.

I often heard my officers commenting: "We would have never thought that you can accomplish this with East Prussians."

Officer education followed the principles established by General Haase, and I gave special attention to the noncommissioned officers. No one was promoted into the NCO ranks unless he spent six months at the brigade's special NCO training unit. All of the brigade's regiments sent their prospective NCOs to this unit, which had the strength of a squadron and was led by Schwarze, an old police Wachtmeister, who had been accepted into the army at the same rank. He had such natural authority and skill in leading human beings that there never was a single disruptive incident, nor did I ever have to intervene. He was, a most unique case, later promoted from Wachtmeister to Rittmeister and put in command of a squadron. When I later established an NCO school for mobile troops in Warsaw, I had him transferred there.

This training produced an important side effect. The NCO who knows his business does not scream or mistreat his troops. If he understands the importance of making duty interesting, that eliminates a key cause of mistreatment. Another of the worst kinds of maltreatment occurs when a sadist and a masochist meet. A leader can be relatively powerless in dealing with this kind of erotic interplay. The only defense against this sort of problem is a good knowledge of human behavior, with which not everybody is equipped. Psychological analysis can alert the leader to such personalities and can prompt him to monitor and manage them accordingly. The third source of maltreatment of subordinates is emotional outbursts by people who are still young and imbalanced. The latter can happen frequently and it is best not to take it too seriously. A well-trained NCO is the best remedy for such cases.

Culturally East Prussia had a lot to offer. I offered sanctuary at the officers' mess for the men's social club that had been disbanded by the *Kreisleiter.*[23] They met there twice a month for presentations and discussions. Thanks to my connections with the German Club in Berlin, I was able to invite to Tilsit distinguished men like Ambassador Rudolf Nadolny.[24] My objective was to broaden the awareness of the young officers, to challenge them. I also encouraged hunting trips in East Prussia, although I always considered myself a friend of nature and not a hunter. Hunting was part of the duty obligations. Nobody had to take leave and we used military vehicles, although civilian clothes were authorized. The result was increased social contacts with friendly local families, and it also prevented anyone from getting into trouble from the boredom of Sundays in Tilsit. These initiatives saved me from a lot of unnecessary trouble and resulted in a highly motivated group of junior officers.

I had an interesting encounter at the castle of Count von Lehndorf in Steinort, where I met American ambassador Hugh Wilson,[25] who was accompanied by Dr. Rosenberg, the secretary of the German Club. I talked with Wilson at length about the question of the Sudetenland.[26] He favored the reintegration of the Sudetenland with Germany, as indeed soon happened. He explained that at Versailles, where he had been a member of the negotiation team, there had been a great deal of pressure to give the Sudetenland to Czechoslovakia.

Germans only have one enemy, and that is other Germans; and the Americans have an enviable lack of knowledge of things outside of America. One of the ambassador's aides tried to sound me out on the Blomberg Affair. I answered: "There is a lot of talk going on in Berlin, but we are not interested in it. We believe what Hitler says."

That, of course, was a "Right or wrong, my country" answer. Among ourselves, it was a different story. We judged Blomberg very harshly. His actions had hit us like a blow from a club. He had destroyed Hitler's high opinion of the officer corps, and everyone instinctively felt that irreparable damage had been done.[27]

We stood by Fritsch, but I did not believe that it would have been possible to act against the government in that situation. That would have amounted to a coup d'état against Hitler, which most likely would not have been supported by the enlisted soldiers and large numbers of the younger officers, the *Luftwaffe*, or the *Kriegsmarine*. Fritsch was too far removed from the mass of the soldiers, and soldiers cannot be ordered to do something like that unless their hearts are in it. This is a situation most civilians cannot understand, and probably never will.

During my time in Tilsit, I had two periods of service in a foreign country lasting from four to six weeks. One was in Finland and the other in Hungary to study their bicycle units. The Finns were especially good. I had the most favorable impressions and was well received by my Finnish comrades. My family, after all, had its roots there. One of my ancestors had been the fourth bishop of Finland around A.D. 1300. I gained valuable insights into winter warfare that I could apply in my battalion. From then on, a bivouac in -10 or -20 degrees Celsius lost its horrors for us.

Conditions had been very rough in Finland during their liberation from Bolshevism in 1917. Countless Finnish communists had been eliminated during the struggle, but in the 1930s their sons were now entering military service. Their political views were of great concern, and everything was done to instill in them a national pride in their fatherland. Part of this process was the "Border Baptism," in which the soldier was immersed in a river on the Russian-Finnish border and had to swear eternal enmity to Bolshevism and fidelity to Finland. The Finns honored me with a Border Baptism, an exceptional recognition for a German officer.

Even though they were at peace, bullets often strayed across the Finno-

Soviet border, and on occasion there was an exchange of fire during the "baptism" ceremony. When I was given my ceremony in German uniform two machine guns provided the cover, and everything remained calm. At another point along the border, a place called "Sisters Creek," both sides had painted the bridge red and white on their respective halves. As we stood on the bridge we could hear the Russian border guard phoning to the rear, *Germansky Offizier!* I came back to Germany with varied impressions of Finland.

The Hungarians were quite different. They practice a very strict but superficial discipline at the dog-training level that killed all initiative. Even though there was hardly any of the warlike influence remaining from Árpád[28] in today's Hungary, the Hungarians still retained the characteristics of a Steppe people. Time and space had no meaning for them. If something was scheduled for 0700 hours, it could happen at 0600, at 0930, or not at all. The only sure thing is that it would not happen at 0700. Despite their origins, the Hungarians had a certain softness and were highly sensitive to unfavorable weather conditions. Whenever a Hungarian soldier did not want to make a movement far from his post, he would report "strong enemy resistance" even though nobody was there. Battle reports frequently were falsified.

Command posts were usually established in a tavern far to the rear, which inevitably led to incorrect command and staff actions. The Hungarian General Staff officers were promoted quickly and ahead of more senior officers. I often heard the line officers saying, "Why should I do this? We have General Staff officers for this." The Hussar regiments were a rare exception. The effectiveness of the troops also increased significantly when a commander known as a hard charger was on the scene.

I submitted a very harsh report on the Hungarian Army, doubting their ability to conduct operations outside of Hungarian territory. The structures of the Hungarian state and society were still stuck in a feudal medieval system. The General Staff's director of the Foreign Armies Department at the time was Major General Kurt von Tippelskirch. Later, during World War II, whenever I ran into him he would tell me, "You were the only one who judged the Hungarians correctly. They are exactly as you described them."

Otherwise, the events in the Reich did not influence East Prussia very much. It was much like living on an island. The big news stories, the occupation of the Rhineland, the annexation of Austria, the incorporation of the Sudetenland, did not affect us in our daily routines. We consequently did not know anything about the troop alerts for a potential coup d'état during the crisis over the Sudetenland. I thought and still think today that something like that could not have been pulled off. A universal draft army cannot be used in domestic politics against a strong popular movement. Any attempt to do so creates a horrible crisis in which the army and the state get sucked into civil war and chaos. The politician always believes that all it takes is to win over one or the other general, who then issues his orders and everything runs its course. The impossibility of such was shown clearly by the events of November 1918. It would not have ended any differently in 1936.

At the Ministry

In the fall of 1938, I was transferred to the ministry as the operations officer of the cavalry branch. This office was being reorganized as I reported for duty. The Operations Branch became part of the newly established Mobile Troops Department, which was subordinate to the inspector of army motorization, Colonel Adolf von Schell.[29] I was given much independence in all my areas of responsibility. I dealt not only with cavalry matters, but also with motorized rifle regiments and reconnaissance battalions. At the time the old cavalry branch wanted to convert the cavalry division into a modern form of light division. I was handed thick files dealing with the light division concept. The files, in my opinion, reflected the German bias for purely operational thinking. The light divisions were fast and maneuverable, but they had no capability to hit hard. Their firepower consisted of an updated version of mounted artillery and accompanying machine gun sections. In real battle weapons with a solid punch always produce better results. From my own experience in the first war, I still knew what cavalry divisions were like. Although they were mobile and often exquisitely led, they stood little chance against a well-armed enemy. I thought it best to let the idea of a light division die slowly. The Poland campaign subsequently proved their uselessness, and they were reorganized into Panzer divisions.

The remaining cavalry units were bogged down with heavy equipment. The existing saddles and saddlebags were extremely heavy and robbed the cavalry of its mobility. I was able to break some new ground here. The new saddlebag was lighter when loaded than the old one had been when empty. It no longer sat in front of the saddle, but behind, where it could not pinch the horse. Machine guns and ammunition, which had been carried on the same horse with the trooper, were now carried by pack animals. I selected special mules from the mountain units for this function. They had the advantage of the appropriate physical condition and could not be misused as riding or race horses.

I also introduced some innovations in the area of organized sports. The traditional German equestrian tournament, which was of relatively little use, was replaced by combat-oriented mounted sports. The existing regulations for mounted units were based on the agile horse in close combat. That world did not exist anymore. What was needed now was a simplified regulation of horsemanship that concentrated on a horse capable of moving over whatever ground it encountered. By the time World War II broke out we had at least a few provisional mounted units that deployed with the new equipment.

I developed an excellent working relationship with Colonel von Schell. He held out the prospect of me taking over the whole directorate in the foreseeable future. That meant that I would have to get involved in the issues of the Panzer force. My working group had developed the regulations for the tactics of units equipped with *Schützenpanzerwagen* (armored personnel carriers). This regulation proved itself during World War II.

In the area of tank warfare I initially was only able to deal with the theory. In my studies I had noticed that during World War I the rate of breakdowns in tanks was quite high, while personnel losses were relatively low. What we needed, then, was a large reserve of tanks. The new crews could be easily made up from crews brought back from the front after their own tanks had been knocked out or had failed mechanically. Listening to a presentation made by Colonel von Schell, it became clear to me that our tank production was completely fragmented and without any significant output. We had built a tank army, without establishing the necessary tank production lines. Our tank force was hollow.[30]

I discussed this problem with Colonel von Schell. I estimated that we would need three thousand tanks to conduct a successful operation, three thousand more to bring it to an end after two weeks of operations, and another three thousand to consolidate our gains. We would have to build four to five tank plants with a monthly capacity of 200 to 250 tanks operating one shift, and upon mobilization add a second shift. The problem was that it was already too late. We should have started earlier. Another problem was that the level of steel production in Germany could not support this. In 1943, when it was really too late, this whole issue came up again, but I was not part of the discussions then. The consequences of a tank army without adequate tank plants became quite clear in the 1941 Battle of Moscow.

I also dealt with the question of an invincible one hundred-ton tank. I proceeded from the assumption that we always had weapons that were too light, and in real battle there always arose a need for heavy hitters. I have nothing against operational art, the great German strength, but sometimes one cannot win without a big club. At Stalingrad a few dozen one hundred-ton tanks possibly could have turned the situation around in the fighting for the city. The same could have been true at Leningrad as well.

But all such issues at that point were for me highly speculative, contingent on Schell's ideas about putting me into that position. What was a reality were the rather disconcerting power struggles within the ministry. Guderian's Inspectorate of Mobile Troops was in direct competition with Schell's directorate. Since both gentlemen had opposing views and nothing was decided at higher levels, the result was a rather unpleasant power struggle. Since I was close to both of them, I was forced into the not always easy role of mediator. My position was only easier because Guderian was receptive to any kind of open and strong argument. He only saw the facts and was not at all vain or sensitive.

Schell, unfortunately, had certain guidance from the General Staff to constrain Guderian. Even more unfortunately, the commander in chief of the army[31] did not like to make decisions and did not clarify his views and goals to everyone involved. These internal power struggles severely impeded development.

In my work I also had frequent contact with the chief of the General Army Office,[32] Colonel General Friedrich Fromm. I was soon on very good terms with him. He was a generous and clear organizer. Germany was lucky to have him in that position.

War Breaks Out

The beginning of World War II naturally occurred outside of my world. Nevertheless, I do have some after-the-fact assessments to offer. In the face of continuous publications by well-known revisionist American historians, the thesis of Hitler's sole guilt for the outbreak of World War II can no longer be sustained. Roosevelt's share in the guilt becomes clearer as time goes on, and the fact remains that Hitler never wanted the war with the western powers. He considered a strong British empire a necessity to maintain the continuity of western civilization.[33]

Another chief culprit is the French chief of the General Staff, General Maurice Gamelin. In France it had been the traditional procedure for generations to consult the highest ranking soldier before deciding to go to war. Depending on his answer, whether a successful war was feasible or not, the cabinet then decided. De facto, the decision over war or peace was in the hands of that one French soldier. If he failed, as did the French minister of war who in 1870 made the self-delusional declaration that the French army was over prepared, then the policy failed. In 1939 General Gamelin, against his better judgment, declared the French army fully ready for war. He did not want to go against the policies of the government. His "No!" might have avoided the war in the proper old French tradition. Strong personalities should be put in charge of a country's armed forces, even if they are rough and gruff and call a spade a spade. A highly educated, smart, but spineless personality, Gamelin did not belong at the top.[34]

Two things made it easier for England to go to war: the assurance that Italian foreign minister Galeazzo Ciano gave to the British ambassador in Rome that Italy would not participate, and the influence of the German internal opposition. Via numerous channels the English were assured that the National Socialist system would collapse within a few days after the English declaration. I personally know individuals who before leaving Germany for England praised Hitler loudly, but once they were in England were saying something completely different. As a soldier you have the duty to oppose such people. In the final analysis, it is the soldier who must pay the price with his own blood and the blood of his troops.

Unfortunately, one of the lessons from both world wars is that the average German who is not a direct member of the government thinks that he is free to cooperate with the enemy. The fact that the sons of such people are bleeding on the battlefield and performing their duties is one of those incomprehensible irrationalities of life. The phrase "Right or wrong, my country"[35] is unfortunately not in the German lexicon.

And Hitler...? He thought that he could play the same game with Poland that he had played with Czechoslovakia. Napoleon once said that one must change his tactics every ten years, otherwise they become ineffective. Today it is necessary to change much faster and more substantially. Poland would not fall the way Czechoslovakia did. In attempting to do so, Germany's intentions would be obvious, while the opposition would be far less predictable. But Hitler preferred to operate this way, instead of seeking alternate approaches. At this stage he already was displaying a certain stubbornness that later led to his huge military failures.

Another remaining question is whether or not the war at that point was inevitable. It is impossible to answer this one, since we human beings are not capable of lifting the veil that obscures the future. Anyone can answer that question according to his own convictions and argue convincingly, but such intellectual sand table exercises have no historical value.

The previous comments go straight to the weakness of German domestic politics. In Great Britain, on the other hand, it is common that in time of war the opposition stands loyally behind the government and supports it. Situations like ours were thus impossible there.[36]

11

World War II

Prelude

Hitler's tense voice on the radio was deeply excited as he announced to the German people the start of the war and the fact that Italy had remained on the sidelines. Events clearly had overtaken him. The reason for this could have been the fact that he had approached Austria, Czechoslovakia, and now Poland always with the same tactics. This time the enemy had been prepared. Hitler played with open cards against the enemy's hidden cards. A change in tactics toward Prague through a peaceful cooperation with the Czechs would have been quite possible, because of the Czechs' increased animosity toward the western Allies, and subsequently a change toward Poland could have created more favorable conditions.

Hitler never played the Russian trump card, his last political asset. In dealing with Poland, Russia should have been the lead card. Germany could have remained quietly in the background. The more active Russia was, the more favorable the situation would have been for Germany.[1]

The Mood

There was no enthusiasm whatsoever for this war among the majority of the people. But that was not necessarily a deterrent, because enthusiasm is rather a two-edged sword. So, right from the beginning the government of the Reich had to deal with the mind-set of the people and did not have the option of letting things run their course as they did in 1914.

On the surface the people were tightly unified, but under the surface the old internal political conflicts still festered and were just replaced by the no less competitive tensions between the party, the SS, the SA, the Wehrmacht, the Hitler Youth, the Labor Service, and the Labor Front. When I was the commander in Tilsit, a high party official remarked to me, "Your work must be a lot easier now that you no longer have the socialist agitation."

I answered, "If the political wisdom of the Kreisleiter culminates with the opinion that the military officer is reactionary and he therefore must disappear, then any change from the past is negligible."

Even though a large part of the leaders of the party and its subordinate enti-
ties worked loyally with the Wehrmacht, there were far too many who, driven by
their own inferiority complexes, believed they had to oppose the Wehrmacht.
Subconsciously, some of the officers recalled to active duty, mostly those in the
different branches of military administration, played directly into the hands of
those elements of the party. Once many of the recalled officers were safely back
under the umbrella of the Wehrmacht, and without regard to their oath, they
loudly declared that they represented the true attitude of the Wehrmacht and
the officer corps. For the most part, their opinions were such that they previously would have never dared to state openly. Their idle chatter was passed
along through the various party channels, often embellished, ultimately reaching Hitler's desk. Hitler, who was by nature mistrusting, was clearly influenced
by what he heard, which contributed to many bad decisions that in the end cost
a great deal of blood.

During that time I often thought about my first commander from 1914,
Major von Rauch. Without assets, having to rely on his small major's pension,
he refused any offer to return to active duty because of his convictions. He often
wrote to me that he was very concerned about the political and military developments. He did so without sounding mutinous and he was always respectful of
my position and the oath to which I was bound. He often prefaced his concerns
with the caveat, ". . . if you can comment in your position on this. . . ." He was a
true Prussian gentleman.

The Wehrmacht

The Wehrmacht was not at all ready for war. This fact was well known to Hitler and it speaks against him as being the one who was singularly responsible
for the war.[2] The Wehrmacht was still in a build-up phase. It had significant
weaknesses; above all it lacked a well-trained reserve force. Our totally modern
weaponry and innovative organizational structures were somewhat of an equal-
izer. The world's first modern tank army had been formed. Unfortunately, that
tank army was completely lacking its backbone, an adequate tank production
base. That tank army without an adequate number of tank plants remained an
empty shell despite increases in manpower and the accomplishments of the
leadership. This was a decisive factor in losing the war.

In contrast, German generalship and the General Staff had reached a level
of operational excellence unparalleled in military history. The Seeckt School
that was based on Schlieffen's concepts was bearing fruit. It had influenced
the entire officer corps of the old one hundred thousand-man Reichswehr far
beyond the domain of the generals and the General Staff. What we lacked was

a thorough foundation in tactical training, and that would take its toll during the course of the war.

Economically, the army could depend on the highly efficient German industry, provided that it could resolve the decisive quest for raw materials. That required extending the war beyond the borders of the Reich to catch up with global production capacities. An alliance with Russia and Japan could have alleviated this problem significantly.

The Political Leadership

Politically, Hitler was in complete control. His accomplishments up to this point had earned him a strong level of trust. People assumed that he could master the political situation and would tightly focus all the forces of the nation toward one common goal. It was also expected that the military and the political leadership would be unified. And it was expected that the political leadership would energetically protect the front line from any negative influences from the home front. That is what those who were willing to sacrifice their lives thought they had a right to.

Thus, the Wehrmacht approached all of its new tasks with seriousness and sincerity, convinced that it could accomplish them. The smart people who afterward claimed to have known all along that it was impossible were smart enough to remain silent for the time being. The majority of the officer corps deferred all misgivings about governmental system. "First we have to win the war" was the prevailing thought.

War Breaks Out

I, unfortunately, was sitting at the ministry and could only follow the events in Poland from a distance. After the conclusion of the Poland campaign I was sent to inspect the lesser quality Panzer divisions, to accelerate their reconstitution. Hitler wanted to secure his rear in the West as fast as possible. The troops generally did not understand the reason for the rush. They were perfectly happy to rest on their laurels after the victory in Poland. It was not always easy to get things moving in the face of resistance from some much higher-ranking officers, but in the end I worked through those problems.

1st Rifle Regiment

My assignment as the commander of the 1st Rifle Regiment in Weimar came as quite a relief for me. I would not have chosen any other regiment. In addition to the good reputation the regiment and its officers had, I had just outfitted this unit with the most modern equipment. Everything was armored and mobile. It was the most modern regiment in the army. The regimental adjutant, First Lieutenant Andreas Braune-Krickau, met me at the train station in Weimar. He was a strong, unique personality, with whom I worked well.

The 1st and 2nd Battalions of the regiment had been formed from the former 11th Cavalry Regiment. The 8th Company was the former 3rd Squadron of my old 18th Cavalry Regiment. Officers and NCOs were mostly Silesians and the enlisted were from Thuringia, with a certain percentage of Germans from the Sudeten region and from the Rhineland. The 3rd Battalion came from a motorized infantry division and consisted of soldiers from Hamburg and Lower Saxony. They all proved themselves beyond all expectations, and even those from Thuringia were far better than their reputation. In peacetime they were easy to mold and in war they were easy to lead, as long as they had officers who were fully committed. I have experienced over and over again that the positive and negative tribal characteristics of Germans complement each other well, as long as the mix is right.

The Waiting Game

Hitler wanted to turn against the western Allies as soon as possible after the Poland campaign. Operationally this was the correct course of action, but two important factors mitigated against it. Technologically our tanks were not prepared for the harsh winter conditions and the icy roads. A winter offensive could have easily destroyed the equipment without any enemy action. And second, the Wehrmacht was still not ready internally. That was clear from a visibly diminishing sense of discipline. As I noted in my journal then: "The disciplinary conditions in the homeland are not very impressive, especially on the trains. Everybody just loiters around. Salutes are rendered sloppily or not at all. There are similarities to 1918, except then the people were acting maliciously; now they are good natured but have grown lax about the unpleasant saluting ritual. Much damage was done by the removal of regimental insignia for security purposes. That killed esprit de corps and the soldiers became nothing but a gray, anonymous mass. The officer as the only bearer of discipline does not stand out anymore, because all sorts of people are now wearing officer uniforms for reasons of leveling down.[3] Commandants and area commanders are mostly old people who are not up to the task. Beware if a spark should fall on such dry tinder."

Hitler was fully aware of the first problem. An intense controversy raged between him and von Brauchitsch over the second problem, which gravely strained the relations between the two men. The conditions soon improved, however, with the introduction of leave schedules, special leave trains, and other measures. A war always requires a complete adjustment by an army. If you compared the Kaiser's army of 1914 to the Wehrmacht of 1939–1940, the latter looked rather good. The Poland campaign had not handed us any serious setbacks and there was no failure of the leadership. There had been no problems like the panic of the XVII Army Corps near Gumbinnen in 1914, the failure of the troops and their leaders at Liège, or the total breakdown of leadership during the Battle of the Marne.

We had become blind to reality and for the last twenty years we had been seeing anything that had happened in the old Kaiser's army through rose-colored glasses. Historical writing should be truthful above all. When it is written with an agenda, it can cause real havoc. The civilian population everywhere made an excellent impression. Serious, dutiful, willingly suffering the constricting consequences of the campaign, they were a great source of support for the troops, unlike in 1918 when they were a source of unrest.

The campaign plan against France changed. The initial plan was a rerun of the Schlieffen Plan, with the strongest wing on the right expected to overcome all resistance. Since the French and the English were also thinking along the old patterns, a frontal battle of both main forces would have taken place in the Dutch-Belgian region. In essence, that was exactly what Schlieffen had been trying to avoid, and we had to avoid it under all circumstances.

Major General (later Field Marshal) Erich von Manstein gets all the credit for developing under difficult conditions a completely different scheme of maneuver. Similar to Napoleon's plan for the Battle of Austerlitz, it was a blow at the pivotal joint of the enemy just as he was attempting to execute an encirclement. It was a complete departure from Schlieffen's scheme of maneuver, and I often thought of my father who even before World War I said again and again: "Schlieffen's doctrine is too one-sided and too formulaic. The solution cannot be found in a one-sided effort at encirclement only; but with today's mass armies it must be a breakthrough and an encirclement."

The change to the staging plan meant we had to reconnoiter the Dutch border area. We also had good intelligence from across the border. The Dutch troops were not at all impressive. A small part of the Dutch military was anti-German, the larger part was of the opinion that it was better to march with Germany. At the beginning of February 1940 my regiment was shifted to the middle Moselle and came under Guderian's XIX Panzer Corps. Things there were a lot more disciplined. The training was focused squarely on the coming actions. Up to the time of the breakthrough at Sedan we rehearsed everything in detail in both map exercises and field exercises on similar terrain, under combat conditions, including live firing and air support. The Moselle River was the training stand-in for the Meuse.[4] I was not satisfied until every man under my command was able to handle the rubber dinghies just like a combat engineer. I let the exercises run completely uninhibited to allow everybody to get used to independent thinking and acting.

It was the best preparation for an offensive that I had ever seen. As a result, we did not run into any surprises during the battle up to the breakthrough at Sedan. The trump card, however, was that when we stood ready to cross at the Meuse, instead of a long-winded order we received the short directive; "Act in accordance with War Game 'Koblenz.' Execute at 1600 hours today." And everything then went smoothly, quite a unique episode in military history.

Otherwise, we followed with suspenseful interest politics and the progress of the Norwegian campaign. For me personally there was a last-minute crisis. General von Schell, my last peacetime boss, became a ministerial secretary and he wanted me to succeed him in his military duties. Fortunately, this did not happen.

To the Meuse

The word came on 9 May. I was ordered to take command of the brigade and lead the advance guard of the division, which consisted of the 1st Motorcycle Rifle Battalion and the 3rd Battalion of my regiment. We crossed the border into Luxembourg on schedule. The border gates did not slow us down much. Our infiltrated informants stood next to most of them, having prevented them from being closed. I drove forward to one of the motorcycle rifle companies that was advancing at a point ten kilometers ahead of the advance guard main body and caught up with them at the Belgian border, just as they were preparing to dig in. Along the border lay the enemy bunkers that we were so familiar with from previous map exercises. They were silhouetted clearly in the terrain, but there was no movement. The Belgians seemed indecisive, almost as if they did not know there was a war going on. It was hard to believe. I immediately ordered the company to attack. The armored scout cars fired into the gun ports of the bunkers and the assault detachments moved forward. A Belgian tank or antitank gun tried to escape to the rear and the bunker crews started running. A few of the Belgians were cut down in our machine gun fire and we captured two machine guns, and five prisoners, including the Belgian platoon leader. It was all over in half an hour and we had broken through the Belgian border position with our surprise attack. Our losses were two killed and two wounded. The completely surprised Belgians had waited too long to engage with their weapons. They had been sitting in their positions for three months straight without

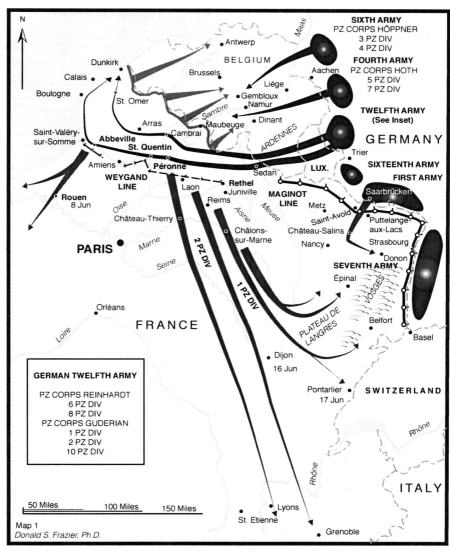

Map 1. The French Campaign, May–June 1940. (Map by Donald S. Frazier)

relief, and had degenerated into a rather ragtag mob. At that point the brigade commander returned from his home leave and I returned to my regiment that was still in the divisional rear.

Relentlessly we moved forward. French troops appeared and were cut up. On 12 May my regiment marched through Bouillon and crossed the Semois and the French border. Gottfried von Bouillon's[5] old castle looked down on us. We moved forward quickly in the face of light enemy contact. Horses, equipment, the dead, the wounded, and shot-up supply convoys lay everywhere. The French fought extremely poorly. Whenever we asked prisoners why they were fighting against us, the common reply was, "Because England wants us to; the rich want us to. We are not waging war; war is being waged with us." Their eyes would light up with hatred whenever England was mentioned.

We destroyed the enemy's forward bunkers according to plan and without losses and reached the exit of the Ardennes. The terrain was flat and without cover as it sloped down toward the Meuse River. My 3rd Battalion headed toward the Meuse on a broad front. I moved with the forward lines to ensure that the advance maintained momentum. When we reached the Meuse at 2300 hours there was nobody to our left or right. A French counterattack into one or both of my open flanks could have destroyed us, but everything remained quiet. Toward morning my other two battalions had come on line, which eliminated much of the danger of the situation.

On 13 May it was clear and sunny. The French artillery that day demonstrated its great effectiveness. Every movement we made was under fire and all traffic in the rear areas was affected. Although my regiment had already crossed the river under the artillery fire, the effect on the morale was strong. The soldiers hunkered down in their holes. I requested a Stuka[6] attack on the French artillery positions. Under Guderian something like that worked instantly. The effect was overwhelming. The French artillery was silenced and the mood of our troops turned into one of jubilation.

The Breakthrough

The attack was supposed to continue that day. Although I was skeptical, I prepared the regiment. The artillery had not caught up yet. Instead, there was a large-scale air attack with one thousand aircraft. Suddenly we received the classic order: "X time 1600 hours. Act in accordance with the established play book scenario."

For another two hours we waited with tense anticipation. The orders were perfectly clear, and there was nothing more to be done. At 1600 hours I was at the Meuse and we had our first crisis. The rubber dinghies were in place, but the engineers were not. At this moment the commander of the engineer battalion of the *Grossdeutschland* Regiment[7] showed up. "You are heaven sent," I told him. "Here are the dinghies, put us across."

"We are not trained to do that," he quibbled. "We are assault engineers."

We already knew how to assault. We did not need engineers for that. Thank

God I had trained all my personnel in dinghy operations at the Moselle River. We ended up doing it all ourselves, the river crossing and the assault.

The air and the ground shuddered from engine noises and the detonation of bombs. The French artillery remained silent and the enemy bunkers were silent. We attacked, just like on maneuvers. Prisoners flooded out of their bunkers, completely demoralized, and many of them senselessly drunk. When we broke through the first line of bunkers, Guderian showed up beaming. He had been the main proponent of such tactics, and had led the difficult struggle for their acceptance. The results were now proving him right. But he had laid all the extensive preparatory groundwork.

Once we were through the forward line of bunkers we still faced the enemy emplacements on the hills behind. Reports that our own artillery was firing on us came in from everywhere. That was not true, however. The French artillery had finally opened up. I committed my reserve battalion in the forwardmost position, telling them, "Let's go. Next orders briefing at that bunker up there on the hill."

Then I started moving forward. In such moments the leader has to expose himself. He must show a disregard for danger. But my regiment at that point was not exactly the model of a combat-ready unit. On the contrary, the attack was dragging. What was easy today could cost a lot of blood tomorrow. The day was coming to an end and we still had to reach the dominating terrain. I pushed and pushed, and by the time the sun was setting we owned the commanding hills and had destroyed the last enemy bunkers. The regimental staff had broken through with the lead battalion and we closed in on the key bunker, from which I had said I would issue my follow-on order. As we approached the bunker from the rear, the riflemen of the 2nd Battalion were storming forward. They were quite surprised to find their regimental commander already in the French positions.

We had accomplished a huge success. My totally exhausted troops fell into a leaden sleep. The enemy was gone and there was a huge gap in his lines. I thought back to Mount Kemmel, where we had achieved a similar great success, but no senior leadership had been at the point to follow through to a victory. It was my great good luck that I was allowed to lead at a point where I had seen others in the First World War fail so critically. I walked off a distance, thought about it, and made a decision. We had to advance another ten kilometers into the enemy. My adjutant, Braune-Kriekau, a resolute and courageous man with a keen military mind, said, "Sir, that would lead to the destruction of the regiment."

"No," I replied. "It will lead to the destruction of the French."

My battalion commanders insisted that it was impossible to move forward with the totally exhausted units. I did not budge. We would move forward after one hour rest. Battalion Richter was to remain and occupy the hills. The other two battalions staggered and hobbled forward into the black night.

Counterattack

A night that was not really one set in over the battlefield. At daybreak on 14 May I moved up to my forward elements in Chéhéry. There was no enemy anywhere. We had achieved the breakthrough. Our vehicles were still on the other side of the Meuse; all the equipment we had across had been hand carried. We had one antitank gun with us, which I had towed forward with my command car. The division's Panzer brigade was also still on the other side of the Meuse, and the troops were completely spent. Additional elements moved forward piecemeal, especially my somewhat rested 3rd Battalion, followed by individual antitank guns and ammunition. We still had to take the crossing sites on the Ardennes Canal, which were important for our turn toward the west. Elements of all kinds of units were thrown forward on any available vehicles moving toward Omicourt and Malmy. Even my command car was used for that. My personal adjutant, First Lieutenant von Kurzetkowski, moved forward in the forest near Vendresse, where he shot up an enemy battery. But then he was forced by enemy tanks to withdraw on foot.

Guderian and my division commander, Lieutenant General Friedrich Kirchner, with his brilliant Ia Major Wenck, arrived beaming. "Just hold out for another one to two hours and the Panzer brigade will be here."

Guderian's gumption was a guarantee for us to hold out in this crisis. Then a report came in from my units at Malmy-Chéhéry: "Strong French tank elements moving toward Chéhéry . . . our antitank guns cannot penetrate the French armor . . . we have to withdraw."

I responded, "The order is to stay in place. The regimental staff will stay also."

I sent forward an engineer company that had just arrived, not sure that would help. It could only be minutes before the French tanks overran us. We needed our Panzers. Then a motorcycle messenger arrived, reporting that the Panzer brigade had crossed the Meuse and would close with us within half an hour. An officer of an antitank company from the Grossdeutschland Regiment also arrived and reported that his unit would arrive shortly with 50 mm heavy antitank guns. Just as the French tanks were closing in on us slowly, we heard engine noises behind us. We thought those were the antitank guns. . . . but then two field kitchens pulled up right next to us. The devil himself must have sent them to taunt us.

But then the antitank guns finally arrived. The first gun went into position but was knocked out by the French tanks. The second gun went into battery and opened fire, setting one tank ablaze, then a second and a third. The French attack faltered, and the courageous antitank crews from the Grossdeutschland kept firing. At that point the Panzer brigade arrived and went straight into the attack. Dozens of French tanks were destroyed in short order, and the final count was fifty. We had overcome the crisis and not a single man of my regiment had left his position during the hellish episode. Consequently, our losses were minimal. Meanwhile, the staffs of the Panzer brigade, the 2nd Panzer Regiment, and the 43rd Engineer Assault Battalion were meeting at a road intersection in Chéhéry. I was hurrying to that location myself, but just before I got there a misplaced strike by our Stukas hit the group.

Coincidentally, the hill where we assaulted the bunker on the evening of 13 May was where the Prussian General Headquarters had its command post on 1 September 1870. It was there that French general André Reille delivered Napoleon III's surrender note to King Wilhelm of Prussia.

The Enemy Side

The French tried to stem the tide of defeat. Despite the horrible communications situation and the clogging up of all the roads caused by the masses of refugees, the commander of the French 55th Infantry Division, General Legrand, still managed to assemble forces for a counterattack. He committed two tank battalions and his 213th Infantry Regiment against my rifle regiment. But the chaos and the congested roads and villages delayed the counterattack for hours. He threw another infantry regiment forward, but that too dissolved completely in the general chaos and became completely combat ineffective. When a well-planned counterattack was finally launched and reached the forward German lines, our Panzers and antitank guns halted it cold. My regiment's exhausting night advance had paid off. Nonetheless, I still had to give General Legrand great credit for even attempting to launch a counterattack.

My regiment lay in deep sleep, strung out along the road, waiting for the vehicles which were still stuck far in the rear. During every peacetime maneuver I had driven home the point to the regiment that any machine gun that was not committed against ground targets or was not being transported would always be kept ready to engage in air defense. Thus, more than two hundred of my regiment's machine guns, augmented by a light anti-aircraft unit with 20 mm automatic cannon, were ready when we were attacked by a large number of French aircraft. With their machine guns blazing, the low-flying French planes raked over our positions. But when they were hit by our return fire, they hit the ground, broke up, and exploded. In just a few minutes that crisis was over and hardly any of the courageous French pilots could have survived.

Now we were finally left alone. I lay down in a garden and slept as if I were dead. When Braune woke me up he reported: "Everything has been prepared as ordered. We're ready to move out."

With a surprised look on my face I asked Braune what was going on and who gave the order?

"But, Sir, you gave that order just two hours ago."

I apparently had given the order in my sleep without realizing it. It had, however, been a pretty reasonable one.

The Final Resistance

The thrust of the 1st Panzer Division tore the French lines wide open. Our adjacent units had been lagging, but were now moving swiftly. On the French side any available reserves were brought up and thrown against the threat. In this situation Guderian executed one of his tactical concepts by turning the mass of his corps 90 degrees toward Amiens and the Channel coast before the majority of the trailing infantry division was fully forward and ready for action.

On the evening of 14 May my regiment moved toward the west into the emerging night. We took prisoner upon prisoner, all of them well aware of the propaganda line implanted by Goebbels, "We do not wage war; war is being waged on us."

On 15 May the advance guard, Battalion Richter, met the enemy, attacked aggressively, and got stuck in a confusing and uncomfortable situation along the edge of the village Ménil-la-Horgne. We were taking casualties rapidly, and we had to change the situation. In the meantime, my Battalion Studnitz on its own accord started to envelop the enemy to the right, through thick underbrush. In the dense forest my regimental staff encountered the staff of the Moroccan 2nd Spahi Regiment,[8] killing their regimental commander, Colonel Geoffrey. The captured Spahis pleaded for mercy, but their French officers remained calm and proud in captivity. Studnitz fought his way out of the forest, remounted his battalion, and then crashed through the retreating Spahis and a battalion from Normandy. Richter, meanwhile, took Ménil-la-Horgne through an encircle-ment, killing in the process Colonel Burnol, the commander of the Algerian 2nd Spahi Regiment. I have fought against all enemies in both wars and always in the hottest places. Rarely did anyone fight as well as the 3rd Spahi Brigade. Their commander, Colonel Maré, was wounded when we captured him. Includ-ing the two regimental commanders, twelve of the brigade's twenty-seven offi-cers were killed, seven officers were wounded, and 610 Spahis were killed or wounded. The 3rd Spahi Brigade had ceased to exist, sacrificing themselves for France. I issued special orders to treat the few surviving prisoners well.

We were near Bouvellemont, on a wide-open flatland facing toward the village. We were taking machine gun and antitank fire from its edge. Battalion Studnitz was positioned in a long line at the edge of the flats. The troops were completely exhausted. The rations were gone and there was nothing to drink in the extreme heat. Ammunition was low. While the losses of the preceding days had been minimal, they were now starting to add up. Every success we achieved had been paid for with the lives of some of our best troops, mostly officers.

I called the officers together and they told me that after a good night's sleep we would press on the next day. I cut them off. "Gentlemen, we will attack, or we will lose the victory."

It was a situation where no matter what you ordered, the soldiers were not going to move. So I turned around and said, "If you're not going, then I'll just take the village myself," and I started in the direction of Bouvellemont across the open field, fifty meters, one hundred meters. Then it all broke loose. Troops and officers, who just a few seconds ago could not move anymore, started to pass me. Nobody rushed from cover to cover, they all just stormed ahead. Their bayonets reflecting in the setting sun. There was no stopping them. With loud shouts echoing in the air, the thin, totally exhausted line of riflemen entered the village. Bouvellemont was ours. I had not miscalculated. No German soldier will abandon an officer who moves forward.

A battalion of the 15th Armored Rifle Regiment had been holding Bouvellemont. We destroyed that unit during hard street fighting at night, capturing eight tanks in the process. We had received reports that the 152nd Infantry Regiment of General Jean de Lattre de Tassigny's capable 14th Infantry Division had been sent forward toward Bouvellemont, but we were not able to determine if that unit ever entered the fight.

Pursuit

The last organized resistance of the French had broken down. Guderian paid us a visit on the morning of 16 May. He walked from company to company, talked to the troops quite informally, and read captured orders to them that gave them the idea of the sad condition the French were in. He had a personal, human, but soldierly touch that was devoid of exaggerated emotion, but still worked miracles whenever he spoke to the troops. Shortly thereafter, we moved out. The objective was the Oise River crossings near Ribemont.

We advanced through the withdrawing French troops. Some units were still in their garrisons. None of them seemed to be thinking about fighting. Occasionally enemy tanks tried to attack our columns and were quickly destroyed. Nobody bothered with the prisoners; somebody else would collect them up. An enemy motorized column tried to fight back, and in the process killed their own people who had already given themselves up. We took a bridge across the Canal du Nord just at the moment when English demolition crews arrived. They were the first "Tommies" we captured. We also captured a French major trying to escape dressed up like a female. His uniform trousers under the dress gave him away. "You know that I could have you executed right now without a trial," I told him.

He knew that, and he was clearly relieved when I told him that I would have done the same thing in his situation. I shook his hand as he took off the dress.

We had just taken the Oise River crossings on 18 May when an adjutant appeared with orders for me. I was to take command of the 1st Panzer Brigade immediately. On the afternoon of the 19th I arrived at Caulaincourt, the castle of General Auguste de Caulaincourt, who had been Napoleon's Master of Horse. The castle had been rebuilt after the first war, and during the renovation the very valuable memoirs of the general were found. My predecessor as brigade commander had suffered a total breakdown, caused by the horrific physical exhaustion and the constant tense situations. He had balked, complaining that it was impossible to cross the Somme and seize Peronne. We did just that the following day, and without a significant fight.

One of my subordinate units was the 1st Motorcycle Rifle Battalion, in which my son, Friedrich-Wilhelm, was a Fahnenjunker. It is always an awkward situation to have your own son under your command. For the father it is an additional heavy burden, and for the son it can easily be that he sees things in a slightly distorted light. I had therefore made sure that Friedrich-Wilhelm had been assigned to this unit, where I would not be in his direct chain of command. I had no way of knowing that I would end up commanding the rifle regiment in the same brigade; but now there was nothing that could be done about it. Friedrich-Wilhelm had developed brilliantly. He was the first German soldier to reach the enemy side of the Meuse. I saw him again for the first time during the war in the same place where in 1914 I had met my father for the first time during that war.

To the Channel Coast

Hitler's order to hold in place despite Guderian's sharp objection got us a little rest. On 20 May we marched on toward Amiens, the objective of our March 1918 offensive that we never reached. The sight of the cathedral ahead of us in the morning sun triggered some odd emotions.

Several sources have mentioned a run-in that I supposedly had with a senior officer at that point. I had occupied a bridgehead across the Somme River without a fight and was ordered to move from there toward Amiens. Another unit was ordered to relieve us in place. Their commander insisted on a formal battle hand-off procedure, as it had been the custom in the trench wars. There was no enemy anywhere in sight and I could not convince him to drop it. I simply ended the conversation brusquely, telling him, "I am moving toward Amiens. If the bridgehead is lost, then just retake it. That's what I would do. My field kitchens will still be here for a while to help you." There was no chance of enemy contact, and there were no significant enemy formations between there and Paris.

Amiens fell after a short fight and we developed a bridgehead on the south bank of the Somme River. The fighting was piecemeal, but in the process we destroyed a courageously attacking English battalion. At that point the enemy was among the least of our concerns. The number of POWs was growing. We constantly had some VIP or another coming through, even enemy VIPs: the aide of the English military attaché in Brussels, the area commander of Amiens who wanted to look after his house one more time, a Dutch officer who was supposed to withdraw money in Paris, aviation officers and a delegation from the French ministry of air that were supposed to get an aircraft factory operational after it had been abandoned by its workers because of our air attacks.

Amiens was a special liability. The staff of a battalion was appointed as the military government. For the most part only old people had stayed behind. The water pipes were all broken. The streets were full of dead bodies. The hospitals were full of wounded, but no doctors. The prisons were full of hoodlums and the guards had disappeared. And then a constant stream of refugees started moving into the city from all directions. "We were all directed by radio to come to Amiens" was the standard answer. And then these people, Belgians as well as Frenchmen, started to loot. Had the devil ordered all these people to Amiens? I had to sigh deeply. It was not the devil, but for several days Goebbels's propaganda organization had been using the radio to direct the French refugee columns across the few Somme crossings in order to create a traffic chaos to make Allied operations impossible.

On 22 May we were relieved in place and turned north in the direction of Calais and Dunkirk. There was hardly any resistance as we made a leisurely drive through the French rear area. At Desvres we did encounter determined resistance from a French engineer battalion. We broke through it, but unfortunately my best battalion commander, Major von Jagow, was killed in the process. His successor was Captain Eckinger, an Austrian, a tough, ingenious soldier. He was the first of a long line of well-trained Austrian officers that came under my command during this war.

My battle group was ordered to take the bridge across the canal at Bourbourg, Saint Folquin. After careful preparation by six artillery batteries and support by tanks, Eckinger's battalion forced its way across and established a bridgehead. They captured six guns and completely destroyed the enemy. Observing the attack from the roof of a house, I had the distinct impression that nothing was going right. Finally, I got down from the roof, sat down in my easy chair, and read *Le Figaro*. Sometimes you have to force yourself to trust reliable people who are leading at the front. In the end, everything worked out down to the second.

Then we were ordered to halt our advance and we could see bomber formations flying overhead to and from Dunkirk. The Luftwaffe was supposed to finish the enemy off, but the Royal Air Force [RAF] had other ideas. English fighter aircraft attacked us without interruption, as my command post building shook constantly. My son paid me a visit at that time. Over coffee and a jam sandwich he told me, "We have it much better up at the front. You guys are getting bombed too much."

The Battle of Dunkirk was over. The English had gotten away. At the time Dunkirk was not considered a turning point in the war. Of course, we should have advanced toward Dunkirk on the ground. Nobody could have stopped us. The rationale given for holding us up was to give the troops some rest for the follow-on missions, combined with the belief that the experiences of the Spanish Civil War and Sedan had proved that the Luftwaffe could finish the job on its own. The great lesson of Dunkirk was that a victory on the ground can only be won by ground troops, as valuable and indispensable as the air force might be. Also confirmed were Clausewitz's theses, "I do not want to hear about field commanders who think they can win without shedding blood," and "Humans are more valuable than materiel. Materiel can be replaced, human beings cannot." Acting in accordance with these principles, England lost Dunkirk but won the African campaign.

For the next few days we had some quiet time. Everyone relaxed. For my own victory reward I wanted to see Rodin's famous Burghers of Calais sculpture. When I visited the town I saw scenes of incredible destruction that reminded me of the extent to which victory can be misjudged. The formerly enemy coastal guns were already being manned by German sailors. Naturally, I also visited all the units of my regiment and thanked the troops. I was proud to be the commander of such a regiment.

Several interesting things were going on. My 1st Battalion had ordered a Dutch company that had moved into their area accidentally to guard the

POWs. The Dutch troops did a first-rate job and would not have minded fighting with us against the English. And what about the English? The French, the Flemish, the Walloons, the Dutch, nobody wanted anything to do with them. Near Gravelingen they allegedly had shot Flemish refugees and supposedly killed forty women, old people, and children just because they were annoyed by the Flemish dialect. If the hatred against England had been channeled properly, it could have stabilized Germany's western border forever. The French did not want to continue the war. Daladier and Herriot had the respect of the people, Reynaud did not.[9] Nobody wanted to fight for England and everyone thought the war was useless, displaying a total lack of political will.

The English were courageous soldiers and equals to us. Unfortunately, they treated prisoners brutally. A German air defense sergeant managed to escape after he was captured by them. They had tied him and his fellow soldiers up and laid them in a road ditch. The English that we captured, on the other hand, were impressive. Columns of their prisoners marched in formation whistling and singing. When our troops offered them cigarettes they declined. They were a proud people. It was too bad that Germany and England could not have come to an agreement.[10]

The Second Act

After the destruction of the French and English northern flank, which mostly included the enemy's best attack divisions, our follow-on mission was the destruction of the remaining French army. At that point an immediate invasion of England was completely out of the question, considering the unbroken power of the RAF and the nonexistence of any means of amphibious transport. And, of course, it was necessary to destroy the remaining French army to eliminate any potential bridgehead on the Continent. While strong Panzer forces were committed to break through on both sides of Amiens, we were assigned to a follow-on phase of the breakthrough at the Aisne River.

Toward the Aisne

Our movement led us through the destroyed and rebuilt battlefields of World War I. What the French had accomplished there was disturbing. On the surface everything appeared in order, but if there had been a prize for minimum taste and creativity the French would have won it. Using the old foundations everybody had rebuilt in any tacky manner he wanted to, without regard for taste. All the old angles and traffic traps remained. There were three basic models of war memorial which could be found cast in concrete, alternating in every village.

The movement toward the Aisne River was dull and dreary. The whole day long we sat in a convoy and ate dust. Nonetheless, there was some diversion. During a longer break I sat down in the grass a little off the road and was happy that I did not have to look at anything military for a while. As I was looking up, I stared into the barrel of a rifle. On my threatening shout the soldier, who was a member of my regiment, came to the position of attention. "Sorry, Sir," he said, "I just wanted to shoot that ox for the field kitchen." I had not noticed the ox that he was aiming at and which stood directly behind me. Later during the war the 1st Panzer Division was under my command frequently. Every time it was one of my units I sent the brave cook a bottle of liquor with a note: "With many thanks for not making me part of your meal plan." The last time I was able to do that was in 1945 in Hungary.

Breakthrough at the Aisne

The initial German attack was launched on both sides of the Aisne, with the intent of pulling General Maxime Weygand's[11] reserves in front of us toward the Somme. My battle group was to follow a few days later. During the actual breakthrough the Panzer divisions were this time in the second echelon. The task of making the breach was assigned to the infantry divisions. I was leading the left flank battle group of the division. West of Rethel the establishment of a bridgehead was successful, while east of Rethel the attack failed. During the night of 10 June we were ordered across the Aisne. The French had been fighting tolerably well. According to statements from POWs, they had been told that anyone retreating would be shot, and anyone attempting to surrender would be shot by his comrades.

On 25 May General Weygand had issued the following order: "The battle that will determine the fate of France will be fought without any thought of retreat from the positions which we are holding. From the highest army commander down to the platoon leader everyone must be driven by the fierce determination to fight to the death wherever he stands. As long as the leader leads by example, the troops will follow. If necessary [the leaders] have the right to enforce the obedience of the troops. . . ."

When later in the war Hitler in a worse situation issued a similar order, it was naturally considered a crime.

As a tactical innovation, Weygand added the fortification and defense-in-depth of every village. He exploited a national characteristic of the French, who have always understood with shrewd finesse how to turn townships into defensive positions and hold them heroically. We encountered this for the first time near Juniville. We had to take the town because it had a road junction that was necessary to control for our supply lines. Sooner or later you run into a position that cannot be bypassed. I ordered the motorcycle rifle battalion to attack with the expectation that everything would go smoothly. It did not. The battalion was unable to break through the strong resistance, even with artillery support. I then ordered the 2nd Battalion to make an enveloping attack around from the right and take Juniville from the rear. But as soon as everything was set to go, the French launched continuous tank attacks on our left flank and rear. Fortunately, the French attacks were only half measures and we were able to defeat them with direct field artillery fire.

Our 35 mm antitank guns were not much use in the fight because they generally could not penetrate the strong armor plating of the French tanks. My command post was in a small rectangular clump of trees. One tank circled us and chased us around the woods. My antitank guns fired thirty-six rounds and only missed twice. But the hits did not penetrate. Finally, when we managed to knock off one of the tracks we were able to fire into the less thickly armored areas. Even then only four or five rounds actually penetrated the tank. The crew finally bolted; every one of them was wounded.

Meanwhile, the fighting in Juniville was fierce. The town was expertly fortified. Machine guns positioned in shot-out windows and zeroed-in on a specific point were fired by pulley systems from remote covered positions, without anybody ever having to expose himself. Others were aimed to fire at stone walls in street curves, so that the bullets ricocheted along our approach route. Whenever we breached a barricade, it immediately came under mortar fire. Most of the enemy sat in basements, kept quiet, exposed themselves at intervals, and fired from the low levels into our troops. Most of our wounded were hit in the legs. Finally, we resorted to the age-old measure of setting the houses on fire. A newly arrived assault gun battalion also gave us support. By evening we had taken the town. We captured two hundred prisoners and the colors of the French 127th Infantry Regiment. The French had fought bravely. The heart of the resistance had been a captain, but I never did learn his name. In several sources I have been credited incorrectly with the "capture" of the colors of the French 127th Infantry Regiment. The French soldiers had been trying to burn the flag in a cellar after the color guard had abandoned it. When riflemen of my 2nd Battalion took the basement they pulled it from the flames. There was no fight for the flag.

Although we conquered Juniville, the division's main effort to our right had not been able to penetrate. The next morning I attacked with the entire regiment in a southerly direction. In front of us lay a wide-open plain without any cover. Both of the lead battalions were completely exposed, but we laid on strong artillery fire against the French positions. As the regiment moved in a wide sweep we started to take antitank fire. My troops simply dismounted and continued the swift attack on foot. Guderian was with me at my command post, observing the maneuver-like scene. Then the division's Panzer brigade advanced from the rear and gave the attack the final impetus. I immediately committed my mounted reserve battalion right behind the Panzers, and we broke through.

The Bridge at Étrepy

We pressed on through fleeing French convoys. There was no more stopping. At one point a French Negro soldier jumped out of a house and stormed toward us swinging a bush knife. One of my troops grabbed his weapon and split his skull with it. We continued our advance toward the south. Whenever we encountered any resistance one battery would stop and engage, while everything else kept moving forward. On occasion individual tanks put up resistance. One time I had stopped and had stepped away from my command vehicle when my entire staff was killed by a prematurely exploding round from one of our own Panzers.

On 13 June, as we approached the Rhine-Marne Canal, we captured the commander of a French tank regiment, caught by surprise just as he was stepping out of his quarters. I committed my battle group on a wide front along the Rhine-Marne Canal, intending to capture any bridge intact. Then I received the following message at my command post at Jussecourt-Minecourt (which I recorded in my personal journal that day): "Report from 2nd Battalion, 2nd Panzer Regiment at Étrepy. Bridge is intact but prepared for demolition. Request instructions."

I got extremely mad, jumped into my *Kübel*,[12] and drove straight there. Nobody had thought of the simplest of all actions in such a case, which was to get onto the bridge and cut the detonation cords. Instead, the tanks were clustered around the bridge. If it had exploded it would have been a mess. Cussing up a storm, I immediately put some troops from the 8th Company across the bridge and gave Lieutenant Weber, the platoon leader of the engineer platoon of our 2nd Battalion, the order to go onto the bridge and cut the cords. He took off with his head low. I followed him. I felt better when the wires on the first bridge had been cut. Weber then ran off to a second bridge, but shots rang out just as he was trying to cut the wires. Suddenly there was an explosion, then another. I thought at first that we were taking incoming artillery. The infantry fire increased. Even though the spot was only one hundred meters away from us, I could not see the situation clearly. I could not tell if the bridge had been blown. A short while earlier the Panzers had shot at an electric locomotive that had been passing by on the train tracks running on the far side of the river. A man in blue mechanic's overalls had jumped off the train. Had he been involved in the detonation?

Then all at once there was yelling and screaming as from all sides Arabs and Moors streamed out of concealed dugouts whining and pleading for mercy. "Tunis, Tunis" and "Duce, Duce!" they kept yelling. They were hunkering down everywhere, incapable of moving. Slowly they started coming forward until we had some two hundred of these "heroes" collected up. As soon as they realized that nothing was going to happen to them, they squatted together in a circle happily chatting away, throwing away their headgear and wrapping turbans out of towels.

The situation at the bridge also started to clear up. Thanks to Weber's lightning speed only part of the bridge had gone up and it was only slightly damaged. We then received the order not to cross at Étrepy under any circumstances, but I already had a bridgehead on the other side. I gave orders to repair the bridge and returned to my command post at Minecourt. I had just returned when Guderian arrived, highly relieved about the bridge. It was the only one we had captured intact. All others had been blown. Immediately we were sent across toward St. Dizier.

Wild Pursuit

We ran into chaos. A battalion of Tunisians on trucks ran into us and immediately surrendered without even an attempt to resist. The 2nd Battalion took an operational airfield. As night approached, I halted the attack on St. Dizier in order to avoid night street fighting. The overall outcome was already clear by that point. In the morning the enemy was gone. We had just made ourselves comfortable and were happy to learn about the fall of Paris when Guderian showed up, ordering: "Advance to the Swiss border. If possible, move as far as Langres today."

By 1300 hours we were back on the road. My regiment became the advance guard for the division. Again and again we engaged in skirmishes with displaced soldiers and the French 422nd Engineer Regiment, which was still putting up a good fight. As we took the village of Joinville there was intense artillery fire coming from our rear. A French freight train loaded with artillery ammunition had been approaching on the track along the road. Some of our units fired on the train to stop it, which worked, but it came to a halt diagonally across the road we were advancing on, the front of the train in a tunnel and the end on a bridge. The train was burning slowly and the shells started to cook off. We were completely cut off from the rest of the division. My adjutant, the unflappable Kurzetkowski, managed to cross under the train and got back to the division with the information. The division then had to take a time-consuming bypass through the mountains. The French engineer regiment, meanwhile, collapsed under our attack. At first there seemed to be many dead bodies laying around, but as our troops searched them many of them came to life, relieved at being able to surrender alive. There were casualties as well among the French refugees, whose misery was anonymous. But it was also good to see how my soldiers, who had just relentlessly overrun the enemy, were now only moments later handing out bread and chocolate to the refugees.

We were in the vicinity of Chaumont as darkness set in. We were taking fire from the town, but there was no real enthusiasm for attacking into a city at night, especially when everybody knew that the outcome of this campaign had been determined already. I took aside the commander of the most forward battalion, Captain Eckinger, and told him: "Tomorrow morning at 0800 hours the French cabinet is meeting. It has to open with the news that the Germans are in Langres. Politicians are hysterical and react to news like that."

Eckinger understood. We formed a small wedge consisting of a forward point tank, followed by Eckinger in his tank, then by the regimental staff. It was a nerve-racking trip. Occasionally we fired a burst with a machine gun or threw a hand grenade. Finally we were through and on the way toward Langres. We overran a roadblock and destroyed a French company that was trying to assemble. As we got close to Langres, I wanted to avoid street fighting. I sent two officers forward into the fortress as a truce parley, demanding the surrender by 1000 hours. In the meantime, I brought six artillery batteries into position and prepared the regiment to launch a pincer attack.

The business with the truce parley did not go quite smoothly. Some elements of the French forces were no longer under the control of their officers. Some of them were drunk, others wanted to resist fanatically. My two officers encountered a difficult situation, but they finally were able to get through to the commandant and negotiate with him. Fortunately, my 2nd Battalion noticed that something was not quite right and entered the city on their commander's initiative, which brought everything to a successful conclusion.

Langres is situated beautifully on a steep hilltop. I slept for two hours in remarkable peace in the wonderful garden of the officers' mess.

At midday we were on the march again, with our next objective being Besançon. Endless French convoys, artillery, supply trains, and motor and horse columns were marching from the north toward our left flank. Thousands of French came forward to surrender. Nonetheless we relentlessly continued the advance. As we overran French airfields, the returning French aircraft circled overhead like so many pigeons around their burning coop. We shot down some of those planes. That evening the Saône River finally put an end to the wild pursuit. The bridges across the Saône had been blown at the last minute.

The Saône River was a wide sector. With a lot of effort and good preparation my 3rd Battalion managed to get across the river and took Gray. The old but very courageous French General de Cutzon and his adjutant were killed in the process. Finally, the 1st Motorcycle Rifle Battalion reconnoitering on a wide front was able to find and secure an intact bridge and get across. The next morning the building where we were staying was rocked by incoming bombs, unfortunately our own. The aircraft were under the operational control of Army Group Leeb. We had no way to stop the attack, so we had to cross the Saône under the constant bombing of our own planes. Even though our losses were minimal, it was very disconcerting.

Finally, we managed to get across and were moving again toward Besançon, Julius Caesar's Vesontio, his main base in the conquest of Gaul, and once the old German imperial city of Bisanz. Smarter because of our experience at Langres, I decided to forgo the use of truce delegates and ordered the advance under artillery cover, with tanks and follow-on infantry converging from all sides on Besançon. My personal adjutant Kurzetkowski, who had gone forward to reconnoiter the bridge situation, came back on his motorcycle bleeding profusely. He had been ambushed by civilians and kicked to the ground, but he managed to pull his pistol and shoot his way out. I did not, however, take retaliatory actions against the civilians, nor had I at Langres.

We halted when we reached the far side of the town. The enemy had disappeared. I sat on the balcony of a small house, surrounded by flowering roses and fresh strawberries. It was an unreal environment after what we had been through. Night and day without a break we had fought and advanced, advanced and fought. Our rations often had consisted of some chocolate, and once in a great while a can of sardines. My regiment had more than done its duty. Fortunately, our losses had been much smaller than during our rapid advance from Sedan to the Channel. Rumors that France had capitulated were floating around. The final battle with the encircled French army's eastern group was still ahead of us, but there was no longer any salvation for France. Our host, a nice Frenchman, assured us again and again that nobody had wanted this senseless war. But at that hour Mars was still ruling.

Belfort

We were advancing again. At 1600 hours we started moving in the direction of Belfort. We were still at war, although France's soldiers did not want to fight anymore. The road led closely along the Doubs River. As soon as our forward elements arrived at a bridge it was blown. But since we never needed to cross the Doubs, the destruction was superfluous. At nightfall we were close to Montbéliard, the old Kingdom of Württemberg's Mömpelgard. The town was full of Frenchmen. If a fight erupted there, we would never make it to Belfort, which was where I wanted to go. I gave the order not to dismount and to just drive through the town without firing a shot. The clearing of the town was supposed to be done by the follow-on forces. Audacity usually triumphs. Masses of Frenchmen just stood around in the streets, even with horse-drawn artillery. Nobody bothered us. Some of them did not recognize who we were, and the rest just did not want to fight anymore. A civilian jumped on the running board of my car and yelled full of fear, "*Attention, les Allemands!*" ("Watch out for the Germans!)" I shouted back, "*Mais nous sommes les Allemands.*" ("But we are the Germans.")

"*Non, non, vous êtes pas des Allemands, vous êtes des Américains.*" ("No, no, you are not Germans, you are Americans.") He repeated his warning over and over again. When I finally yelled back at him in German, only then he realized his mistake and like lightning he jumped off and disappeared. Finally, we were through the town. One infantry and one Panzer battalion, two artillery battalions, and several smaller units followed. Overall it had required very little to take Belfort by a coup de main. My plan was to prepare to attack the heart of the fortress from inside the fortress ring, and then take each fort from within. It was the middle of the night and no shots were being fired. I did not know if Belfort still had artillery that we would encounter in the morning. It was a high-risk situation, and the sole responsibility rested on me.

The morning of 18 June started out dimly. I issued the orders, but then the divisional staff arrived. Somehow they had gotten through Mömpelgard. Major Wenck, the tried and tested Ia of the division, had also decided on his own accord to plan for a surprise attack on Belfort. He had set everything in motion and was now in position. The only information I had about my 2nd Battalion, which had the mission of clearing Montbéliard, was that it was involved in heavy fighting. To our front we encountered and quickly overcame a road block near a railroad crossing. Then we started taking fire from Fort Les Basses Perches. But after a few rounds from a heavy infantry weapon the fort fell quiet. Then everything went very fast, and Belfort seemed to be ours. We quickly collected at least ten thousand prisoners.

I invited the division commander to visit the famous Lion of Belfort statue[13] with me and pose for pictures. But just as we were turning into the inner city all hell broke loose. Shots were fired from all the buildings, and shots were fired from the citadel and several forts into the city. Then resistance flared up from the large French military post near the train station. I ordered the Panzers to drive through the streets and fire. One of our planes was circling the city. From all the fire that he was receiving we were able to assess how much we still had to deal with. My 2nd Battalion arrived after having cleared Montbéliard, capturing three thousand prisoners. Now we had the basis for a firm plan. One battery, the engineer battalion, and several Panzers were ordered to attack the military post near the train station. The heavy howitzer battalion set up inside the city. According to a carefully laid-out fire plan, my 2nd Battalion was to take one fort after another and finally the citadel.

The attack started at 1400 hours. I established my command post at Fort Les Basses Perches, at the place where my Uncle Schmidt had earned his Iron Cross in 1870. A beaming Guderian stood in my command post. Fort after fort fell after only short heavy howitzer shelling. Finally, the citadel fell. The whole thing came off without friendly casualties. The commander of the 2nd Battalion, Captain Eckinger, knew his business. The French barracks inside the city also capitulated, and finally all the people in the inner city. A second French regiment surrendered to my 3rd Battalion. Eventually, we assembled more than thirty thousand prisoners in a big meadow.

The effect of our heavy howitzers on the old forts had been devastating. The forts were the worst kind of death traps. At Fort de la Motte a shell penetrated a vault and killed a platoon of French infantry just by the overpressure from the explosion. An Alsatian soldier in one of the forts told us that they had planned to give themselves up but were prevented from doing so by their officers. Just as we attacked, they lowered the fort's drawbridge while the commander was on the telephone. At another place a captured French officer was sent back into the fortress with a capitulation message, and he was killed immediately as a traitor by his own people.

Finale

On 19 June we continued on into the Vosges Mountains. We did not encounter any significant resistance until we reached the crest overlooking the Moselle River valley. We did have quite a bit of a problem with single guns firing at us from open positions. Heavy howitzer fire and the fire from several Panzers that were moving forward along the road opened the way for us. Finally, the regiment deployed on a wide front took the position and old Fort Chateau Lambert. The enemy Chasseurs from the Pyrenees Mountains put up a good fight to the end. Their commander, an old colonel, cried like a baby over the weakness of France. I shared my breakfast sandwich with him and then had him escorted to the rear. Below us in the Moselle River valley the bridges near Le Thillot had been blown. During our morning stand-to on 20 June, French artillery fired on the pass again, but died down quickly. Almost all of them gave up without resistance. The French people were numb and exhausted; they could not go on anymore. They cursed England and their own government.

It finally ended for us at Travetin. A very elegant French major, with a flashy rear area appearance, came out of his headquarters and tried to chum up to us in a clumsy way. He was the only Frenchman I encountered during the campaign who found this to be necessary. But now it was finally over and we halted. I fell into a deep sleep in the bed of my French predecessor. Just then, I was awakened by a strong shaking to see the orderly of the French major staring at me in disbelief. He had overslept and he thought he was waking up his boss.

During the next few days we reached the Swiss border and the beautiful Jura Mountains landscape. It was raining hard, which flushed out the remaining French troops hiding in the forests. Nobody hindered us as we advanced into this new area. A delightful villa (a sanatorium) on an island in the Doubs River became my new headquarters. As I was sitting happily on the balcony in my shirt and trousers, eating my breakfast, a fully armed French machine gun company marched by below in very orderly fashion. Fortunately, we had already run telephone lines to the next village, where the French company was properly received and disarmed. Finally, I was relieved to see the arrival of the main body of my regiment.

Looking Back

The world stopped to breathe. Everything seemed like a dream. Reluctantly, without political objectives, and urged by England, France had entered the war.[14] To die for Danzig?[15] Hardly. Since no politician gave a political objective, the army leadership also had no operational objective. It was a standing political tradition in France that during a political crisis the clear question was posed to the highest military leader: "Can we go to war with reasonable assurance of winning?" Napoleon considered a 70 percent chance of success as the minimum necessary for him to attempt a battle or campaign. During the 1905 Moroccan Crisis General Jean Pendrézec, the chief of the French General Staff, had declared bluntly, "We have nothing to counter a German attack. It will be worse than 1870." And Foreign Minister Théophile Delcassé resigned. During the Moroccan Crisis of 1911 Prime Minister Joseph Caillaux asked General Joseph Joffre if France had a 70 percent chance. When Joffre answered no, Caillaux decided to negotiate.

In 1939 there was no tough military leader at the helm of the French Army. General Maurice Gamelin was only a second stringer. As General Jules Decamp once told Daladier, "You will not get a clear answer from him." Henry de Jouvenel, the French high commissioner of Syria in 1925, said, "Gamelin is a smart man, well-educated, well-versed in conversation. In short he possesses all the characteristics of a great military leader—except backbone."

Perhaps that was the very reason he was so well accepted among the politicians. Gamelin could not bring himself contrary to his convictions to say no clearly, which then brought about France's decision to enter into the war. General Weygand later opined that in 1939 the war was entered irresponsibly, without materiel, and without doctrine.[16]

The same was true of the French senior military leadership, vague and unclear. The army was administered, but not led. An army that is administrated and not shaped by the hand of a strong leader and imbued with his spirit to the last man bears the seed of its own destruction. French defense administration was pathetic as well. France spent billions on fortifications and the maintenance of obsolescent equipment, instead of putting the money into modern armaments. The Maginot attitude, "defense at any cost," had led the thinking within the French Army in the wrong direction. Forgotten was the warning, "*On ne perd que par la défense*" ("One only loses in the defense"). Forgotten were the words of Marshal Foch, who had adopted Frederick the Great's concept of "*attaquez donc toujours*" ("always attack"). As a result, an army marched onto the battlefield poorly equipped, poorly led, without political direction and consequently without operational goals, and with people who did not comprehend the reason for the war. The French approach, then, was the very antithesis of Guderian's famous principle, "*Nicht Kleckern, sondern Klotzen*" ("Do not dribble, pour"). The "Phony War" period of the winter of 1939–1940 further demoralized the French Army. Goebbels's propaganda slogans constantly played on the French troops:

"We are not conducting any war; war is being conducted against us."

"Only the plutocrats want war."

These phrases were known by every *Poilu*,[17] as the resentment grew against England. This worn-out mass was hit by an army that was commanded, rather than administered. The Wehrmacht was marked with the imprint of founders, foremost Seeckt, and operationally led with a purpose by a highly capable corps of leaders. A sound, objective personnel management policy had brought the most capable officers to the key leadership positions. Modern thinking had prevailed, particularly in the equipping, arming, and organizing of the Panzer force. The leadership, thanks to Guderian, was freed from the telephone line, and the German general was once again leading personally from the front.

The outcome was to be expected. As Gamelin later wrote, "What could you do with a bunch of soldiers that did not want to fight?" But it was him and the politicians who had created those soldiers. On a dead officer of General André

Corap's Ninth Army a postcard was found addressed to Prime Minister Reynaud: "I have taken my own life in order to let you, Mr. Prime Minister, know that all of my men were courageous soldiers, but that one cannot lead soldiers with rifles to fight against tanks."

Near Sedan the German thrust collided with two divisions that were completely and inadequately organized for modern battle. When the campaign was over one often heard the phrase, "The winner is Falkenhayn." In 1916 General Erich Falkenhayn had intended to bleed the French to death at Verdun, and break their physical power. Twenty-four years later the results paid off.

Operationally, Manstein had made a major contribution with his proposed breakthrough scheme of maneuver, rather than a rerun of the Schlieffen Plan. Hitler had accepted Manstein's plan over the reservations of the commander in chief of the army and the chief of the General Staff. Hitler then managed to win over the rest of the senior leadership of the army. After the war, when we were in prison together, Lieutenant General Walther Buhle, chief of Army Organization, told me that even Field Marshal Erwin von Witzleben[18] accepted Hitler's leadership qualities without reservation.

Guderian of course deserves special credit. He had created the Panzer force in the face of strong resistance, and he pioneered the concept of armored warfare. Without him, Germany's victories in Poland, France, and Russia would have been unthinkable. His concept of generals leading from the front by radio freed us from Schlieffen's desk-bound strategist.[19]

Lessons Learned and Consequences

It was not necessary for us to explore new concepts of leadership and tactics; we were on the right track. There were, however, lessons to be learned. With superior weaponry and good leadership anything is possible. Consequently, armament and personnel management policies were valued more highly than operational and tactical ability. This point of view, however, was not widely accepted. The opposing point of view credited the successes to superior German leadership. Hitler thought differently.

So far during the course of the war the relationship between Hitler, the commander in chief of the army, Field Marshal Walther von Brauchitsch, and the chief of the General Staff, General Franz Halder, had been dysfunctional. Communications had broken down. But for foreign policy reasons Hitler at that point could not bring himself to replace the commander of the army.[20] Guderian as commander of the army and Manstein as chief of the General Staff would have been one solution, but that arrangement never would have been acceptable to a politician like Hitler. Just as Kaiser Wilhelm for reasons of prestige had procrastinated over the appointments of Hindenburg and Luden-dorff during World War I, Hitler never would have allowed such a "Castor and Pollux" pair under him. Politicians always fear coups by victorious generals. Hitler wanted to see himself as the victorious military commander. In France, Léon Blum[21] had similar inclinations before the war. Consequently, everything remained the same in the important area of senior military leadership.

Politics

Dividing the Anglo-French alliance before the war had been completely out of the question. But when Churchill ordered the sinking of the French fleet at Mers-el-Kébir[22] he managed to do just that. The British evacuation from Dunkirk also deeply affected France's faith in the alliance. There was a favorable opportunity here for Germany to exploit, but Hitler did not take advantage of this situation any more than he had taken advantage of the Czech animosity toward England and France. But at the time, quite frankly, even I was not in favor of this course of action. I was all in favor of ending once and for all the fateful duel that had dominated European history since the death of Char-lemagne and the division of his kingdom. Separating France from its colonies and leaving France as a weakened third- or fourth-rate power would have been too dangerous—or such was my uninformed opinion at the time.

Rest Period

We spent almost half a year of peaceful quiet in God's most marvelous coun-try—first near Paris, where we were waiting for the victory parade that was sup-posed to follow after the settlement with England which never came, and then along the Loire River amid the French royal castles. I had always been fasci-nated by France, with its culture, its gothic style, and its castles. I took advantage of the opportunity to indulge my interests in architecture and history. I led my officers on numerous staff rides through all of France, all the way down to the northern border of Spain. These trips also served the purpose of getting them out of Paris. A rest and relaxation site had been established near Saint-Malo, where Brittany and Normandy meet and Mont Saint Michel rises from the sea. I was pleased to see that many more of my officers than I had expected were receptive to those great cultural experiences.

Meanwhile, the preparations advanced for Operation SEELÖWE (SEA LION), the amphibious invasion of England. On 1 September I wrote in my diary: "The preparations for the landing in England are apparently under way, but not with the usually expected intensity." From what I heard later on Hitler seemed to have been only halfheartedly committed to the invasion, and even then more as a ruse to mask his intent toward Russia. Hitler did not like the sea and easily got seasick. His interest in the navy, apparently, was of a purely technical nature. As Hitler's adjutant, Major General Gerhard Engel, later told me, that may have been the real reason SEELÖWE was abandoned. Could it have succeeded? Nobody can say for sure. General Buhle, one of our judicious General Staff officers, thought that it would. I am of the opinion that our Luftwaffe was not sufficiently strong to cover the sea movement against the Royal Air Force and the Royal Navy with the Napoleonic 70 percent probability of success. The fact that we would still have to face the core of the English Army that had been evacuated from Dunkirk did not make the odds any better.

The People and the Country

France returned to normal life, happy that the war was over. There was no sign of hatred, except against England. It was interesting to see how sparsely populated the country was. Half of the ground was untilled. The land was used only where it was comfortable and yielded good crops with little effort. France had evolved since 1914. In those days it was hygienically behind Germany, now it was our equal. The people were polite, friendly, but still proud and nationalistic. The more you got to know the French, the more you respected them and found them agreeable.

Along the Loire River my staff was quartered in Castle Rochambeau, which belonged to the family of the same name. The Rochambeaus were tall, blond, blue-eyed, handsome, and very nice people. They lived in a magnificent old castle. The servants, small in numbers, black, and completely different, lived in caves that were carved out as houses close by on the cliffs of the Loire. The Marquise, a fine old lady over seventy, returned from her refuge one day, determined to fight for her home. Her husband had died and both her sons had been killed in the first war. When we fulfilled all of her wishes in less than five minutes, she was happy and satisfied. During the three months we were there we never had any differences. Otherwise, the relations with the old French families were on both sides proper and correct, without injuring the French pride. Many of the older families had been generals and admirals for four generations and had an absolute understanding of all military matters.

Actually, there was one unfortunate incident during those months. A clerk from a temporarily attached staff had found the uniform of a deceased admiral in the castle. He put it on and made the rounds of all the bars with an accordion, and ended up drunk in a ditch. In tears, the sister of the deceased admiral stood in front of me, deeply hurt. I got very mad. We soon apprehended the colorful bird, and the beating he received was one of the best things I have done in my life.[23] The following day I personally returned the uniform and apologized.

Meanwhile, there was a great deal to be done. I took the opportunity to fix the regiment's logistical issues, which ran from beds for every soldier to resoled boots, white aprons for the cooks, fresh vegetables, stocked pantries, a swimming pool, firing ranges, and most of all the tools for the different trades.

By this time Operation SEELÖWE had been completely shelved and the division was transferred to East Prussia. There we encountered quite a bit of animosity from the old soldiers of World War I, officers as well as enlisted. There was quite a bit of tension. They were resentful that these young snots of the Wehrmacht had accomplished in six weeks what they had not been able to do in years.

When we left France, the relations with the population were good. There was no talk about resistance and partisan warfare. How did that situation change? A small group of Frenchmen, a handful of people, thought that the good relations were detrimental to the honor of France, and they wanted to do something about it. They decided to do something that would force the Germans to react, and consequently make their own people take a stand for or against. A harmless German soldier was thrown in front of a train in Paris. As expected, retaliatory measures were taken and the vicious cycle of partisan warfare started.[24]

12

Greece

3rd Panzer Regiment

When I walked into my office on 12 December 1940 my reassignment orders to take command of the 3rd Panzer Regiment lay on the desk. I was not at all happy to leave my great 1st Rifle Regiment, to which I had grown so attached over the last few years. Nor was it easy to leave my adjutant, Braune-Kriekau. He was energetic, independent, and always stood by his opinion fearlessly. You do not find an officer like that often.

On 17 December I arrived at my new regiment. I immediately liked what I saw. The unit's first commander, Colonel (later Colonel General) Josef Harpe, had similar ideas about training as I had; so I did not have to change anything. The regiment had been formed from the old 12th Cavalry Regiment; the officers and the NCOs were still mostly from Saxony. The enlisted were mostly from Vienna, but they had served the regiment quite well. The Viennese were technically competent and they obeyed their officers. Since the latter were far above average, my command functions during combat operations could be limited to keeping the troops communicating and coordinating everything.

My regimental adjutant, First Lieutenant Rämsch, knew the troops and the technology. He had a rare understanding of human behavior that was deeply rooted in his love for even the lowest ranking soldier. His completely objective judgment, regardless of his personal feelings, was especially valuable to me. He was devoted to the regiment, and later in the war he returned to it as its commander. He also had a similar connection with the Austrian citizens of our garrison town of Mödling.

The relations with the people of Mödling were good. We also had good relations with the local Party members, whose level of class was much higher than those in the old Reich. You could see that the National Socialist Party in Austria had evolved from the old imperial German Peoples' Party of Austria. The Kreisleiter in Mödling was an old officer of the Royal and Imperial Navy, who remained what he had been before he went into politics.

Old General Carl von Bardolff once visited my officers' mess. He had been the chief of staff of the Austro-Hungarian Royal and Imperial Army during World War I, and before that he was the chairman of Archduke Franz Ferdinand's military cabinet. He had been sitting in the same car with the archduke when he and his wife were assassinated in Sarajevo. It was quite an interesting evening. I always enjoyed hearing about the events of world history from a direct participant.

Heading South

Our follow-on mission was in the Balkans. Mussolini had foolishly attacked Greece, but was clearly rebuffed in Albania. We could not abandon him now, especially considering Churchill's long-standing concept of conquering Europe through its soft underbelly, the Balkans. On 5 March we rolled out heading south. All of Mödling was at the train station, seeing us off with enthusiasm. As we passed through Budapest everybody was yelling "Heil Hitler!" and giving the Hitler salute. The Hungarians were peculiar, highly emotional people. You really had to know them well to be able to understand them.

General Bardolff had told me that he thought the Hungarians had no mind for business. The Jews had filled that void, but they could only maintain their position as true Hungarians. So they became true Hungarians. The other ethnic groups, the Slovaks, the Romanians, the Rusyns, and the Serbs, were just poor, uncultured farmers. They could only move up by becoming Hungarian. For quite some time I had been of the opinion that Hungary had caused more damage to us in World War I, with their totally failed Hungarization policy, than had the Czechs through their treason. General Bardolff agreed with my analysis of Hungary.

The train advanced slowly through Transylvania and then Bukovina into Romania. The railroad systems had not improved since the last war. The train frequently stopped for anywhere from six to nineteen hours to allow oncoming trains to pass. I had an opportunity to meet with the local population during the long train stops. They were almost all impoverished Romanians wearing *opanci*[1] and hand-woven fabrics. They did not want anything to do with Hungary. "When will we become German?" was a question I heard often.

On 11 March we crossed the Hungarian-Romanian border. Across the plains of the Moldova River the train passed Focşani and the Măgura Odobeştilor Mountain, the old battlefields of 1917. We had to wait for twenty-four hours at the bridge crossing the Danube in Cernavodă. The Danube Valley with its majestic plains and the far hills of the Dobruja Region were relaxing to the eye after the Bărăgan Plain. For a long time we stopped, waiting for a locomotive near the old Trajan's Wall.[2]

"Bulgarians will not send a locomotive; Bulgarians receive poorly their new friends. Bulgarians bad people, no culture." That was the opinion of the train station master. There was a great deal of hatred between the Romanians and Bulgarians. We had been in Romania for two weeks. Once we crossed the border into Bulgaria the contrast was amazing. Sometime earlier I had been talking about Romania with the diplomat Otto Kiep[3] at my Berlin club. I thought that it would not be a good idea to take too much Romanian territory. He replied, "Just take a piece of the dung pile. It will still be a dung pile."

Bulgaria

Bulgaria was a completely different place. Tight order, good organization, and a friendly population greeted us enthusiastically. After two weeks on the train, a bath in Sofia was more than a blessing. I attended Easter mass in the Alexander Newski Cathedral, a grand, incredible ceremony with marvelous chants. One priest with a magnificent baritone voice stood out in particular. But I excused myself before everybody started kissing. Garlic is an indispensable staple in Bulgaria.

My regiment was quartered in the vicinity of Kyustendil. On one Sunday I managed to get away to the famous Rila Monastery. From village to village I saw the young men hiking to the dances. The sound of the recorder could be heard everywhere, and the men and women moved in quintuple time, dressed in magical old costumes that were different from town to town. It was an unforgettable image. The Rila Monastery had been the national refuge of the Bulgarians during the times of the Turkish onslaught. Without the Rila Monastery there would be no Bulgarian nation. Now it was in disrepair. Only thirty monks still lived there from a community that once numbered three hundred. The young do not want to become monks anymore.

The Bulgarians had worked hard and with a purpose since the last war. Now they wanted their payback. They wanted to control the Aegean Sea and they wanted Macedonia. They could not do that alone, so they put all their hopes on Germany.

The New Operation

The purpose of the new operation for which we came south was to subdue Greece in order to help Italy out of its predicament in Albania. We were not supposed to enter Yugoslavian territory because that state had just joined the Triple Alliance. That required an attack into the strongly fortified border positions of the Metaxas Line, between Lake Dojran, the Greek-Yugoslav border, and the Aegean Sea. The attack was supposed to be spearheaded by infantry and mountain divisions. The 2nd Panzer Division was to cross the Roupel Pass and follow on. We did not feel very comfortable with this plan, but suddenly the situation changed. The pro-German Yugoslav government in Belgrade was overthrown and the follow-on government sided with the enemy. That gave us the opportunity to push one Panzer division through Yugoslavia toward Salonika, even though the roads were poor. The thrust through the poorly fortified terrain west of Lake Dojran would achieve an envelopment and completely dislodge the entire Metaxas Line.

Toward Salonika

On 5 April the 2nd Panzer Division was near Petrich, prepared to launch the thrust west onto Strumica. After reaching that town we were supposed to turn south and move west of Lake Dojran, directly toward Kilkis-Salonica. My mission was to push forward on the southern bank of the Strumica River with one Panzer battalion, one infantry battalion, and one artillery battalion. It was a mild, beautiful night. In the bright moonlight we could see the mountains of Greece and Yugoslavia.

On 6 April at 0520 hours we were at the ready. The Yugoslavian border guards had fled and the Bulgarian border guards were happily shooting into the air, waving us through. The Yugoslav border was secured in a very odd manner. First there was a row of tight bushes, and then a dry fence made from twigs that made a loud cracking noise when anyone tried to cross it, and then a one-hundred-meter-wide open meadow. On the far side of the meadow there was a dog shed every fifty meters. There was only one human guard for every four to five guard dogs. It was primitive and simple, but impossible to sneak through undetected. Our troops from the Brandenburg Regiment[4] had completely failed to cross it the previous night.

Once we got across the border the roads usable for tanks ended. I had to get in behind our right column, which had been advancing faster on improved roadways and already had destroyed the Yugoslav 49th Infantry Regiment, capturing two hundred prisoners and sixteen guns. There was hardly any resistance. Yugoslavia, an artificial creation of the Versailles Treaty, fell apart at the first attack.

The bridges and the roads, combined with the rain and the bottomless mud, caused us more headaches. My battle group was supposed to swing out toward the left again near Megalasterna. But it took us hours to pull everything through the mud. I had driven ahead and was sitting in the middle of a field waiting for everything to close up. Slowly the first vehicle, then the first Panzer emerged from the mud, as the regiment followed piecemeal. Fortunately, there was no enemy. Salonika was close, but the damned mud near the border had slowed us down.

It was turning dark. I was sitting in my Kübel, sleeping, napping, and waiting. Suddenly I woke up with the bright headlights of two vehicles glaring in my face. I thought that they must be out of their minds, driving around like that in the middle of a war. I woke up the regimental clerk and told him, "Go straighten them out, will you?"

As he stood right in front of the lead truck I could hear shouting and confused voices. I was out of my vehicle in a flash and immediately realized that I was standing in the middle of a Greek company. I pulled my pistol, instinctively grabbed the rifle from the first Greek soldier, and started yelling at them. That did it. The Greeks immediately formed up, standing at attention. There were sixty of them and only six of us. We did have a submachine gun, but the soldier carrying it did not know how to use it.

In the meantime, I had managed to get the tanks, one rifle company, and one battery out of the mud. By that point the ground in the mud patch had been torn up so completely that nothing else could move. With the small force I had available I pushed on via Kilkis toward Salonika.

The Greeks Surrender

After we took Kilkis we received our follow-on order via the radio, "Change direction; position your unit behind Group Vaerst." The reason for the order was not transmitted.[5] We had enough gas to make it to Salonika and for twenty kilometers in and around Salonika. If I followed the order, which would have required a considerable detour, I would not have made it to Salonika. But if Group Vaerst got in trouble, I would have to support them. Naturally, at this point the whole wireless radio system failed completely. It was a hellish situation. Without knowledge of the situation, the outcome of the operation and the fate of the division depended on whatever we did or did not do. Finally, a long, encoded radio message came through. But the signal officer did not have the right code, which had gone into effect at midnight. Time-consuming radio messages flew back and forth. I finally lay down in a ditch along the road and forced myself to get some sleep. I was woken up with the report that the Greek East Macedonia Army Detachment had surrendered at midnight, and at 0700 hours we were to march into Salonika. The hardest and most nerve-racking crises are always the ones where absolutely nothing is going on.

The commander of the East Macedonia Army Detachment was sitting in Salonika when he received the report that "one thousand Panzers" were approaching from Paliokastro. Shortly thereafter he learned that "one thousand additional Panzers" were near Kilkis. At that point he lost his nerve, because he had considered a tank thrust impossible. But the situation for the Greeks at that point was not that unfavorable. They still held considerable sectors of the Metaxas Line and especially the important Roupel Pass. The Greek commander did not really know what was moving against Salonika. In fact, it was only elements of a division whose main body was still far behind at the border, stuck in the mud. Our Panzers positioned near Salonika only had gas for a few more kilometers, not enough for a real fight. No supplies would make it forward for forty-eight hours. Would the Greeks still have surrendered if they had known all that? The old adage is never to give up in war; the enemy is at least as bad off as you are. That was certainly true in this case.

Salonika

We entered Salonika on 9 April. The world had gone totally crazy. The city was packed with people shouting, "Heil Hitler, Heil Hitler, Bravo, Bravo!" Flowers were thrown into our vehicles. All hands were raised in the Hitler salute. Were we occupying an enemy town, or were we returning back home to a victory parade? Overall the Greek troops had fought brilliantly and quite tenaciously. They had been the toughest of all of our adversaries so far. They even fired on diving Stukas with their rifles. Their fortifications were cleverly designed. The fighting was more difficult than for the Maginot Line. Up to that point the Greek soldiers had been considered the worst in the Balkans.

Of course, we had to deal with the traditional ethnic and national hostilities of the Balkans. During the surrender the Greeks specifically requested not to be handed over to the Italians or the Bulgarians.

North of Salonika my regiment and staff were quartered in Nicopolis. When I opened my window in the morning I could see snow-covered Mount Olympus against the blue sky, hovering over the dense fog of the Warda Plains. It was overwhelming. I had seen a lot of the world. Nothing compared to Mount Olympus. So there I sat, pensively in awe, holding a copy of Homer that I had brought along. I never put him away while I was in Greece.

We had a much-needed halt for several days. The divisional headquarters asked me to find a German lady who owned an estate in the vicinity of Kilkis. Her late husband had been a Greek. She was over seventy and had been in the country for more than forty-five years, a fine, and tender, lovely lady. During the period that Kilkis lay between the fronts, the mobs started looting. The authorities were helpless. With her bodyguards, a White Russian and a Circassian, she went to town and managed to accomplish what the authorities had failed to do. She ended the looting and reestablished order by stepping out into the market square and declaring very succinctly that as soon as the Germans arrived, they would execute anyone that they found with looted goods. And then she told them just to return everything right back where they had found it. It was still an enormous accomplishment. Sitting across from her, I would not have thought it possible.

The battle losses in this sector had been minimal. We had more casualties from dog bites. At night countless dogs swarmed around the edges of every Greek village, protecting it as they had since ancient times against two- and four-legged thieves. They hunted in packs. One dog barked in the front and the others crept up quietly on their victim from behind and then pounced. One time only the high boots under my tanker's trousers protected me from becoming another of their victims.

Looking Back

The Greek head of state, Ioannis Metaxas, had built the fortification lines that were named after him in order to protect against a Bulgarian attack. Only the eastern tip of the country, the area around Alexandroupoli (earlier called Dedeagatch) remained outside the fortification line. The fortifications were very modern and offered complete protection against Stukas and heavy sustained fire. The weapons were protected by concrete or armor. The design more or less mirrored the Maginot Line. River sections, impassable mountain terrain, and artificial obstacles made the line even more complex. The whole layout was cleverly adapted to the surrounding terrain. They also used numerous false bunkers. The fires of all weapons interlocked. The line tied into the Aegean Sea in the east and to the Yugoslav border in the west, without any possibility of a bypass. It was an absolutely impenetrable obstacle for the Bulgarians, with their technologically inferior equipment.

The situation changed completely when Yugoslavia entered into the war on the side of Greece. The Yugoslavs were supposed to close the gap in western Macedonia between Albania and Lake Dojran. When the Yugoslavian Third Army dispersed within a day or two without much of a fight, the Greeks were left in a position where their only viable course of action was a total withdrawal of all their forces to the short line from Mount Olympus to the Adriatic Sea near Korfu, to link up there with the English forces. But the fortifications and infrastructure of this short line had not been developed for such a contingency, and the Greeks did not attempt to hold that line. Consequently, they lost not only the campaign, but the whole country.

The English had arrived in Greece with two divisions, one from New Zealand and one from Australia, a tank brigade, and an air element. They were located in a very favorable position at the Vardar River (the Greek name is Axios), intending to catch the 2nd Panzer Division in its flank as it was moving toward Salonika. Considering the condition of the division's lead elements,

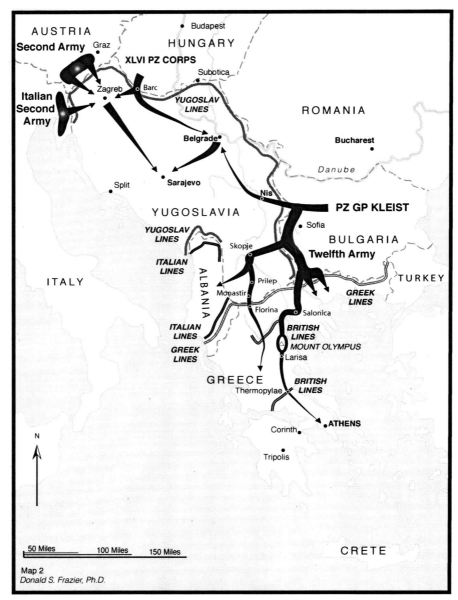

Map 2. The Balkan Campaign, April–June 1941. (Map by Donald S. Frazier)

there was no doubt who would have been successful. But instead, the English corps just stood by without intervening as the East Macedonia Army Detachment was destroyed.

On the German side our knowledge of the layout of the Metaxas Line was nebulous at best. German and Bulgarian intelligence had failed completely to identify the improvements that had been made to the positions. Had we known all that in advance, we most likely would have developed a different scheme of maneuver.

Two Austrian mountain divisions performed exceptionally well during this battle, the 5th under General Julius Ringel, and the 6th under General Ferdinand Schörner. Before the other divisions attacking the Metaxas Line had achieved their objectives, those two divisions took the western flank of the line, and during the subsequent pursuit they destroyed the Greek reserves. The 2nd Panzer Division, whose appearance near Salonika had caused Lieutenant General Konstantinos Bacopoulus to make the decision to surrender and thus brought about the final outcome, had nothing to show other than marching efforts, albeit under incredible difficulties.

The New Situation

Now that it was too late, the Greek Army's leadership tried to pull back their troops toward the short axis running from Mount Olympus to the Adriatic Sea. They were completely destroyed by the German units that had rushed through southern Serbia. As always, the English divisions were like rocks in the surf, refusing any kind of coordination with the Greeks, and conducting their own naval evacuation. Initially they intended to stop the German advance by holding the Mount Olympus line and farther toward the west. They believed such a course of action would be feasible, considering the incredible defensive advantage of the mountainous terrain and the traditional toughness and courage of the British soldiers.

On the German side our objective was the destruction of the English forces, which would result in the conquest of all of Greece. The Twelfth Army initiated the pincer movement against the British Expeditionary Corps. On the German left wing the 2nd Panzer Division was supposed to attack on both sides of Mount Olympus, with the 6th Mountain Division attacking across Mount Olympus, thrusting toward Thessaly. Larisa was the objective for all forces. I commanded the left column initially, with Panzer Battalion Decker, one artillery battalion, and one motorcycle rifle battalion subordinate to me.

Toward the Tempe Valley

In his great play *Faust,* Goethe set the classical Walpurgis Night in the Tempe Valley. Mephistopheles opened with the question, "Are any Britons here? They are always traveling, to track down sites of battles."[6]

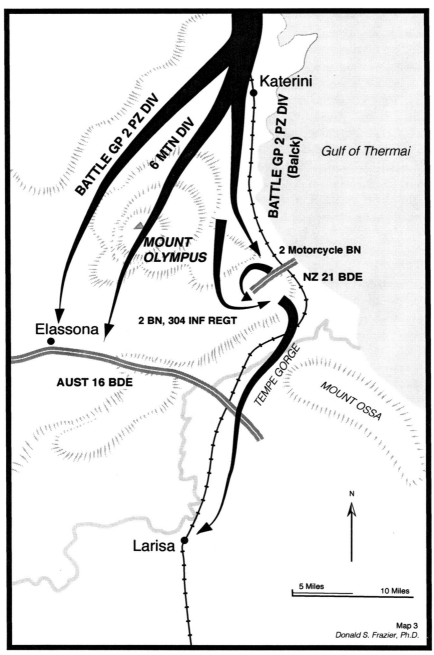

Map 3. Battle of Mount Olympus, 6–30 April 1941. (Map by Donald S. Frazier)

The same question was on my mind as I approached Lieutenant Colonel Decker, the commander of my lead battalion which was just attacking Panteleimon, an old Venetian fortress that lay between Mount Olympus and the sea on a blocking mountain ridge. The British were there. It was clear that our frontal attack was bogging down. We could not observe the enemy in the jagged, bushy terrain; the Panzers could not mount a reasonable attack; and our artillery fire was relegated to complete ineffectiveness.

I halted the attack temporarily, reconnoitered, and determined that our present course of action could not succeed. I let the tanks conduct another feint attack. In the meantime, I pulled out the motorcycle rifle battalion and sent it through the mountains to envelop the defending New Zealanders. When the 2nd Battalion, 304th Rifle Regiment arrived, I sent them around even farther to the right. That unit's left flank man was supposed to march along the ridge that ran toward the enemy. The battalion itself was to move beyond the ridge, and without letting the enemy push them back, penetrate deep into their rearward lines. "Do not end up in front of the enemy, under any circumstances," I ordered, "even if your adjacent unit is crying for support."

We spent the night moving forward through horrible terrain. At 0900 hours on 16 April we were to be ready. Shortly prior to that I had formed up the Panzer battalion, one rifle company, and one engineer company to fix the enemy frontally, while the artillery brought the ridge under fire. We took heavy counterfire as the attack started. The tank in front of me hit a mine and exploded. As a piece of paper came flying back from the smoke cloud, Rämsch caught it. It was a picture of a woman. Then from the smoke an uninjured lieutenant emerged who had commanded the destroyed tank. We handed him the picture of his wife. In total surprise he said, "But I have it here in my breast pocket. . . ." It was not there anymore. Who knows how such things happen.

And then it was all over. Under pressure of our envelopment the New Zealanders abandoned their positions, leaving all their equipment behind and disappearing toward the rear. That was done, but there was still hell to pay. The mule path that we had been moving forward on had to be reinforced to handle tanks and wheeled vehicles. That took time, a lot of time. Meanwhile, a number of recon patrols mounted on quickly requisitioned donkeys rode toward the entrance of the Tempe Valley.

It took twenty-four hours, until 1100 hours on 17 April, before we managed to get anything across that damned mountain. Then we moved into the Tempe Valley Pass. To our left and right the rock walls went straight up for three hundred meters, and the Pineios River raged through the middle of the valley. On the opposite side of the river there was a road, but it was out of our reach. Railroad tracks ran on our side of the river. There was no enemy for the time being. At all costs I wanted to prevent getting caught bunched-up in the valley by enemy artillery. The results would have been horrendous.[7]

I took only one tank and one rifle company forward with me. We continued on over the railroad tracks. We were able to get through the first tunnel, but just short of the second tunnel the track bed had been blown up, and the tunnel entrance was damaged as well. A freight car sat trapped between the two positions. The Tommies sat on the far side, shooting into the tunnel. That was as far as we could go. The river was torrential. It was the Centaur Chiron who said, "Mount! I may freely ask then and respond. Where are you bound? You stand here by the banks. I am prepared to carry you beyond."[8] But Chiron was not there for us. It was still two weeks before Walpurgis Night.

We had to risk it, even without Chiron. Two lieutenants in undershorts and high boots dived into the whirlpools of the Pineios. They came back and told me it just might work, and I decided to risk one Panzer. The behemoth moved down the steep railroad embankment and into the water and then the driver stepped on the gas. The water came over the turret, but the exhaust stayed clear. It worked. Two more tanks followed, then everything stopped because of an explosion in the roadbed on the far side of the river. Fifty Australians that were ready to give themselves up had run into the mountains when somebody inadvertently fired on them by accident. In the meantime, I sent the rifle battalion outside the pass across the Pineios to repair the road damage on the far side.

As night came on, the air was full of balsamic spring fragrances, a nightingale was singing beautifully, and the English artillery was firing full force into the pass. Rock avalanches fell from both sides of the valley, increasing the effect of each round tenfold. Thank God I had halted my main body at the valley entrance.

On the morning of the 18th we pressed on. Every half hour a tank made it through the river. We lost two tanks in the water, and the riverbed was churned up. We had to shift the location of the ford frequently. As soon as a platoon assembled on the far side, I sent it to the western exit of the valley. In the late afternoon we were ready. I had enough tanks, one rifle battalion, and one 100 mm artillery battery massed at the exit. We attacked. The Australians defended themselves desperately, but they had no tanks, and their antitank capabilities were limited since they had counted on the rough "No-Go" terrain. The enemy was caught totally by surprise, wondering where we had come from. Echoing Goethe's pygmies on that classical Walpurgis Night . . .

Do not ask us how we got here,
For the fact is we are here![9]

We broke through line after enemy line. Their trucks went up in flames left and right, and we destroyed what few antitank guns they had. We were taking heavy fire from the decisive Hill 214, but we punched through it. Completely thrown back, the enemy dispersed. When we could see no more targets in the tanks' gun sights and we started to encounter mines, I halted the attack. The 6th Mountain Division was not close enough to us yet, but we could hear the sounds of battle from their direction. My troops all fell into a well-deserved sleep. Through their incredible efforts we had overcome obstacles that the English had considered impassable. As one of their captured intelligence reports later read, "The 3rd Panzer Regiment knows how to cross terrain which we consider 'No-Go' for tanks."

We had fought against the Australian 16th Brigade and the New Zealand 21st Battalion. New Zealand's official World War II history praised this unit highly:

> The 21st Battalion had the misfortune to be detached from the Division during the commencement of the Greek campaign, and came under another formation, and in the heavy fighting bore the brunt of an attack in which they fought with determination and great courage. They were overwhelmed by greatly superior forces and scattered; their losses were heavy. In light of the full details which history has now revealed, I wish to pay a tribute to the rearguard action that the 21st Battalion fought from the Tempe position where they suffered so heavily.[10]

We too willingly praised our courageous enemy. Imprisoned New Zealanders acted with dignity, refused to make any statements, and firmly believed in the victory of the Empire. Unfortunately, the main body of the English forces escaped. We had destroyed only what had been in front of the left column of the 2nd Panzer Division. They had not committed their tanks anywhere. In Larisa we found only one English light tank that had broken down with mechanical problems. The original reports of enemy tanks destroyed actually had been trucks. That was a mistake easy enough to make in the dusk.

Larisa

We were rolling toward Larisa bright and early on 19 April. When we reached the town we found complete English supply depots that had been abandoned. Our first supply aircraft soon started landing at the airfield. A few hours after us the lead elements of the 6th Mountain Division arrived. They had accomplished an incredible marching distance and were bitterly disappointed to find that we had beaten them to the objective. Earlier Larisa had been destroyed in an earthquake. The following day, after the dead and wounded had just been recovered, the Italians bombed the town. Not a building was left unscathed. But from those ruins the lavish splendor of a southern spring bloomed forth, accompanied by swarms of Eurasian Hobbies feeding on the insects.

During the follow-on advance our division reverted to the second echelon and was held up by the excruciatingly slow and horrific traffic congestion on the route to Athens. The road had been blown up, but the English had abandoned everything. In the air our aircraft all vectored toward the English port of debarkation. So far, the Royal Air Force had not attempted to intervene. Had they done so, they would have had plenty of targets of opportunity and we would have learned a hard lesson on how not to take Panzer divisions through mountainous terrain.

We had the leisure to ponder these thoughts at Pharsalus, where the decisive battle between Caesar and Pompey had been fought. In order to throw forces against Pompey's superior mounted troops, Caesar had turned the soldiers of his famous X Legion into mounted troops, but not with much success. When I looked out from my vehicle I could see the plains covered with the soldiers of my regiment who, like Caesar's legionnaires, floundered around ineffectively on various forms of four-legged transport. Perhaps the place really did have something like a *genius loci*.[11]

The population had fled. In the old Balkans tradition the young and pretty girls and the women and children had been sent into the mountains. The locals were quite surprised that we did not conduct war in the old Balkan tradition, but rather in a civilized manner. West of Athens the pursuit came to an end.

Back and Forth through Greece

Again, just as in France, days of endless pleasure followed the exertion of combat. Every man in the regiment got a chance to go to Athens and see the Acropolis, where I arranged for expert guided tours. Previously, I had an image of the Acropolis as an unplanned cluster of beautiful buildings, but what I finally saw was quite different. Nowhere had I seen a finer use of space as there and later at Delphi. The visitor's eye is led consciously through the architecture, from building to building, from highlight to highlight. The master accomplishment was the positioning of the Temple of Athena Nike oblique to the axis of the Propylaea. It was so much more different than the architecture of Rome.

Naturally, I went to Marathon ... but I did not think about Miltiades (the Younger), but rather about an unknown master armorer from Athens. Up until the Persian Wars, the Greek warrior carried a small round shield with a grip in the middle. With this shield he could block enemy projectiles launched from afar, but he needed a lot of space for this activity. The master blacksmith had the ingenious idea of adding a second handle to the shield through which one could slip his arm. That meant the shield could be bigger. It now covered the whole man, and now the Greeks could fight in a closed, tight phalanx. That formation allowed them to cut through the loosely deployed Persian masses like a knife through butter. Since the Persians stayed with their antiquated equipment up to Alexander's period, the Greeks won every time and Western Civilization did not go under. On a visit to South Africa after the war I learned that Shaka, the great Zulu chieftain, won his victories with the same technology, and thereby established his empire.

Delphi was another place I went to see. Without fail I wanted to visit the place where the most profound saying of Greek antiquity was once engraved: "*Gnothi Seauton*"—Know thyself. I also visited the Peloponnese and Acrocorinth, where the two Greek goddesses met, Pallas Athena coming from the north, and the erotic cult of the Middle Eastern Aphrodite. All the old tales from mythology came to life for me here in this country. I then went on to Mycenae, Tiryns, and across country toward Olympia and Patras. That was a route that my parents had done in 1908 on horseback over mule tracks. They were accompanied by one of my father's Greek students at the Kriegsakademie, then-Captain Metaxas, the same Ioannis Metaxas who as the head of the Greek government died shortly before our campaign started, and after whom the Metaxas Line had been named.

Goethe in Greece

Goethe had never been to Greece. Nevertheless, when we left Sparta, driving across the fog-bound Eurotas River Valley, and the ruins of the medieval Venetian city of Mistra slowly rose from the swirling mist, I felt like I was in the middle of *Faust*, Part II.

> "Yes, it darkens of a sudden, lifting mists unveil not brightness,
> Gloomy gray and dun of stonework. Masonry confronts the
> Vision. . . ."[12]

And he described the scene:

> Inner Courtyard of a Castle.
> Surrounded by Opulent and Fanciful
> Medieval Architecture.[13]

The only difference was that Faust did not appear "at the top of the stairs in knightly court garb of the Middle Ages."[14] Instead, an old, blind abbess supported by two nuns invited me to enter the convent. She was a noble apparition. She told me, "Tell the Führer to make Greece into a German protectorate, a German province. We will endure it. But he cannot ever turn us over to the Italians." Then she disappeared.

Although Goethe had never been to Greece, somebody surely had told him about Sparta, the Eurotas River Valley, and Mistra. I could not imagine a more accurate portrait of this area than the one the poet had drawn in the second part of *Faust*.

Patras

I finally linked up with my regiment again in Patras. The town had one problem. It was not the Greeks, but rather the Italian POWs who earlier had been captured by the Greeks. The Italian Navy had moved into the harbor with minesweepers, and at night the sailors were giving the locals a hard time. The Greeks suffered silently, with pent-up hatred. Not a single shoeshine boy would shine an Italian's boots. I visited the Italian naval captain to discuss the locals' complaints. He was not surprised at all, suggesting that the situation could be worse. He promised to improve the situation, but in turn he wanted to have a nearby prisoner camp full of Italians moved to Patras. I turned him down. That was the last thing we needed. The freed Italians would have turned Patras upside down.

On the evening of 10 May I had the Italians over for dinner. In their honor we had erected a flag pole with an Italian flag. One of the local farmers, who was there to sell us chickens, saw it and jumped to the wrong conclusion. He grabbed his chickens and started to leave, saying, "No chickens for Italians, only for Germans." It took quite a bit to convince him that we were Germans and for him to leave the chickens.

The Greeks played rather clever politics. Every Greek told every German soldier how much he admired Germany and how much he disdained the Italians. The Greek authorities overloaded us with complaints against the Italians, apparently ignoring any wrongdoing on the part of Germans. But our troops definitely were not choirboys, and there were instances of misconduct. I asked the Greek prefect to come and see me and told him that while we were sympathetic to the Greek complaints, they had to remember that the Italians were our allies. Any insult against the Italians would force us to take their side automatically. Naturally, I worked at fostering good relations with the Italians.

On 16 May we boarded troop ships and sailed, escorted by two Italian destroyers. We passed Ithaca on 17 May and woke up the next morning in the harbor at Taranto, Italy, where troop trains were waiting for us. On 21 May we off-loaded in Nuremberg.

Bitter Aftertaste

Both ships that had brought us from Patras to Taranto hit mines and sank on their second trip. They had not been escorted by the Italian Navy on that trip. The losses were substantial. The life preservers had been thrown into the water before the ships stopped, and by the time the men got into the water they were beyond reach. Even most of the good swimmers drowned. They immediately had started swimming back toward Ithaca, confident that they could cover the few kilometers easily. Almost all of them succumbed to hypothermia. The Greek coastal inhabitants did what they could to help, and were able to rescue many soldiers from a watery grave.

13

Russia

The Great Turning Point

I had just been appointed the commander of the 2nd Panzer Brigade when I was called to Berlin to report to General von Schell, to the Organizational Directorate headed by Lieutenant General Walther Buhle, and to Colonel General Friedrich Fromm, who was the de facto minister of war. I had resisted vigorously all efforts to get me to come back to Berlin to work on the issue of organizing the motorization of the whole army, but my luck eventually ran out and the problem finally caught up with me again. On 7 June I returned from Berlin, and I recorded in my journal the summary of my conversations with those three gentlemen:

"We are at a decision point in the war. England has been driven out of Europe, but is still sitting in the Mediterranean. Our follow-on mission will have to be their complete removal from there in order to control the oil of Asia Minor, the cotton of Egypt, and the considerable treasures of Africa, and to be able to transport everything safely across the Mediterranean. This conflict will be difficult, time consuming, and can only be conducted with minimal forces. But with our overall superiority in materiel and personnel, success should not be in doubt.

"What do we do with the rest of the overwhelming mass of the Wehrmacht? England will not return to the Continent, even with American assistance. That would be suicide for them. To keep Europe subdued, we only need minimal forces, since almost everyone has accepted the New Order, some of them most agreeably.

"The remaining problem is Russia. Its existence forces us to maintain a strong army in the East. At the present time we are so superior to the Russians that they cannot seriously compete with us. For this reason, they supply us with almost more than we can accept, and they steer a demonstratively friendly pro-German course. What will the situation be, however, when Russia believes that they are materially strong and Germany has a crop failure or is attacked by America, or everything happens at the same time? Then Russia will pursue its political goals against us with all means. In other words, it will attack us together with England and America. The tight encirclement [of

Germany] that we have destroyed will be replaced by a more dangerous wide one.

"For us the only course of action must be to attack Russia as soon as possible, to destroy it, to gain control of the Baltic States, the Ukraine, and the Caucasus, and then to turn our attention calmly to the Anglo-Americans.

"The other tasks, like the fight for the Mediterranean, the occupation of Europe, the battle for the Atlantic, can be accomplished in passing. An English invasion of the Continent is not imminent. France is no longer materially capable of land warfare—and besides, through our clever politics they have been won over because the brutal English policies (Mers-el-Kébir) brought them into our fold.[1]

"It is a disadvantage that public opinion in Germany will not understand these lines of thought. [The attack on Russia] will have to be a purely cabinet-led and preemptive war. Furthermore, the supply of Russian oil and wheat will be interrupted and will probably not resume until year's end. Both issues can and must be accepted as reality.

"Once Russia is subdued, an encirclement and blockade of Germany becomes impossible. And at that point we can ignore any ups or downs in the public opinion on the home front. We will have free reign then to crush England. Perhaps rapprochement might even be possible."

A few days later, on 12 June, I noted, "Once again the problem with Russia. It would be, of course, a political achievement of the highest order to involve Russia actively in the fight against England." Now, after the fact, it is impossible to determine if such would have been possible.

The Death of the Kaiser

On 9 June, Kaiser Wilhelm II was buried in Doorn, Holland. A tragic life came to an end. He was extremely gifted, always intended the best, always sensed the right thing, but he was never a leader. The level of his intellect was not equaled by strength of character and personality. Compounding that was his lack of understanding of human nature that prevented the right individuals—Tirpitz, Gallwitz, Goltz—access to the right positions of power, but instead put completely incompetent individuals—Bethmann-Hollweg, Moltke (the Younger)—into the highest positions. I do not blame the Kaiser for his failures during the early stages of the revolution. The game was already over by that point, and he was not the right man himself to take the helm with a firm hand. In the eyes of the people his flight to Holland made him and the monarchy look weak and outdated, a factor that German domestic politics will always have to account for. The German monarchy was over for all times.

But because of the Kaiser's sincerity and upstanding morality, we should be grateful that he lived to see Germany's recovery, and—that he was spared knowledge of the greatest catastrophe in German history.

Russia

The war against Russia started on 22 June 1941. I was not happy being left out of it, sitting around passively, just patching up tanks. I had an idea of what was to come. I understood the situation and had given it a lot of thought. You can look at the Russian problem from several different perspectives. I want to approach it from today (1979).

Russia had been a problem for Germany since the Wars of Liberation.[2] "In a hundred years Europe will be either French or Cossack," Napoleon had said to General Armand de Caulaincourt[3] as he hurried out of Russia on a sled, on his way from Vilnius to Paris.

"Only in times of internal confusion can Russia be defeated," reasoned von Clausewitz.

And General Joseph Radetzky, Austrian field marshal Karl von Schwarzenberg's chief of staff during the Wars of Liberation, saw Russia as the greatest of worries. No other politician or statesman had, like this great soldier, recognized the Russian threat and articulated it in such a clear, precise manner. His assessment remains valid even today. As a countermeasure to the Russian threat, Radetzky was one of the earliest proponents of the concept of the citizen in uniform as part of a free citizenry. Tragically, instead of this political and military genius, a reactionary like Metternich ended up steering the course of Europe.

Bismarck, contrary to popular belief, was not an unconditional friend of Russia. During his day the German operational plans were directed against Russia, and not against France. A Russian proverb says that one should watch people's hands, not their mouths.

Seeckt, even years after his dismissal, declared in his clear, precise way, "Russia cannot be defeated." But clear-thinking soldiers were not the only ones who recognized and grappled with the Russian problem. Joseph Victor von Scheffel in his 1851 poem "The Trumpeter of Säkkingen: A Song from the Upper Rhine" wrote:

And whenever the last scion
Of the Germans on the Rhine-shore
Has been gathered to his fathers,
Then will others walk and muse there,
And in gentle foreign language

Murmur the sweet words: "I love thee!"
Do you know them? They have noses
Somewhat flattened out and ugly;
By the Ural and the Irtish,
Now their ancestors drink whisky,
But to them belongs the future.

Only the German Social Democrats were staunchly anti-Russian—not for reasons of foreign political insight, but because of domestically motivated political reasons. They wanted to topple the autocratic, tsarist system. What that would mean as a consequence nobody knew for sure, but certainly not a socialist heaven.

The mass of German citizens saw Russia as the ally and good friend who during the Seven-Years War and the Wars of Liberation and in a selfless alliance with Bismarck faithfully stood by us. That we actually had to thank England for our successes then was beyond the comprehension of the average German. After all, how important could a maritime power be?

The Germans had only nebulous memories, based on a few direct contacts with Russians. My parents' old cook remembered hearing her grandmother call the Russians bad people. And once in a while you could still hear that it was better to have the French as an enemy than the Russians as friends. But as Scheffel's tomcat Hiddigeigei from "The Trumpeter of Säkkingen" was singing as early as 1857:

Harmless tribe! Your lyric madness
You'll continue, while there yonder,
In the East, the clouds are gathering,
Soon to burst in tragic thunder.[4]

Russia in World War I

World War I brought about the total collapse of Russia. Popularly that was credited to the superior German art of leadership, to which the stupid and uneducated Russians were obviously not equal. And that is the way it always will be, very comfortable thinking. Reflection was clearly discouraged. The reality, of course, was quite different. Clearly, the Russian generals and soldiers were not equal to the German art of leadership and the independent thinking of German soldiers. But the true reasons lay deeper.

In 1914 the Russian army had only one basic set of equipment, and as soon as that was lost it could not be replaced. Russia was losing machine guns,

guns, ammunition, and rifles in unimaginable numbers and the Russian soldier had to fight without equipment against a well-equipped adversary. Before the Murmansk rail line was completed, thirty-four thousand rifles were transported every month from Murmansk to Saint Petersburg laboriously on reindeer sleds. Often only the first wave of Russian infantry had rifles, and the follow-on forces had to grab them from the dead.

Russian artillery was scarce. The conduct of nighttime artillery firing was punished at times by court-martial as a waste of state property. The losses of the courageously attacking Russian infantry ended in indescribable mayhem. There were no rifles for replacements to train with. For months at a time the recruits were kept busy with stupid exercises—whole days, for example, were spent practicing saluting. All that gave the looming revolution a breeding ground that could not have been better. The fate of the tsarist empire was sealed when the English failed at the Dardanelles to open the supply lines to Russia. Russia was decisively defeated at the Dardanelles, not at Tannenberg.

These conditions never could have been mastered by a self-serving ruler like Tsar Nicholas II. The most amiable weakling in Russian history sat on the tsarist throne, dominated by fuzzy mysticism and the monk Grigori Rasputin. Objective decisions were never made. A level of corruption unlike any other in history pervaded all areas of the state. Personnel policies extended far beyond your normal cronyism. The tsar's *Hofjägermeister* [court hunt master], Rudolf von Stackelberg, once described Nicholas to my father as malicious. It was not surprising, then, that such an edifice should collapse when going up against the German Reich. What was surprising was that it even lasted until 1916–1917. The courage of the Russian soldier could not change the final outcome.[5]

In Hitler's Eyes

Hitler had recognized the threat that Russia and Bolshevism posed much more clearly than his western adversaries. The conclusions he drew were influenced by his experiences as an infantryman on the western front in World War I. His experience in that war formed him. He was not able to let go of that experience, but he also was not able to move beyond it.

Hitler's judgment of Russia, therefore, was that of a typical infantryman from the western front of 1914–1918. In other words, the Russians were a dumb, stupid mass, badly led, with corrupt leadership, and technologically inferior. At the first hard blow their system would collapse. The Russian people, an earthen clod without head or feet and never having governed themselves, would after the defeat accept German rule willingly. Whatever Hitler read or heard to the contrary he was skeptical of and most often rejected. This, in my analysis, was the major reason for the preemptive war against Moscow.

Hitler later said, "In Russia we faced a people and not a system."

And to Guderian he also remarked, "If I had known that the numbers on Russian tank production in your book were right, I would not have started the war."[6]

There was a rumor prevalent in highly respectable Wehrmacht circles that the chief of the *Abwehr*, Admiral Wilhelm Canaris, reported to Hitler lower numbers on the Russian arms production than the figures that had been developed by his department.[7] I cannot verify that rumor.

The fact remains that Hitler entered the war with inaccurate economic and political requirements and without the personal experience of the wideness of the Russian spaces. If fate had sent Hitler as an infantryman to the East during World War I, his decisions might have been different.

And the Truth

In 1943 or 1944, when I was the commanding general of the XLVIII Panzer Corps, I was together one day with other gentlemen of the army high command. After dinner the ladies of the Russian theater came in to dance with us. They had all been checked out and were fanatical anti-communists, we were assured. An intelligent, German-speaking, somewhat older actress sat down next to me. After a short while as we were conversing she said: "I am naturally a convinced communist. The Bolshevik revolution has liberated us women from the slavery of the church and the husband. Now we are free human beings. We get married for love and to whomever we want. That is the difference between us; you do not marry for love but for financial and business reasons."

I was rather shocked. But I did not betray the lady's trust and kept her disclosures to myself. When I was still in Tilsit, I had been able to convince the former German ambassador to Moscow, Rudolf Nadolny, to give a talk to the officers. Hearing Nadolny talk was not only living history, he was also an acknowledged expert on Russia and he had headed the Eastern European Department of the Foreign Ministry at the end of World War I. He described Russia to us just the way we later experienced it ourselves. As he warned all of us then, they are a steadfast people.

During the conversation some members of the Slavic Institute of the local university barged in saying that the ambassador did not know what he was talking about. They assumed that he had just sat in his embassy, did not get out, and only heard what he wanted to hear. According to them they had access to real sources at their institute; they had conducted interviews with endless numbers of immigrants and refugees and returning migrants; they knew what was going on. The truth, according to them, was exactly the opposite of what Nadolny was saying. But since all refugees or returning migrants were automatically suspected of Bolshevist tendencies, they naturally tended to draw a much bleaker picture of the Russian conditions for their own protection.

The analysis of intelligence is probably the most complicated sphere of human action, one that requires a limitless amount of experience, knowledge of human nature, languages, geography, and character analysis—all skills that are more than rare. The Slavic institutes in the universities had an ominous influence because Hitler listened to them, and these institutes only presented what Hitler wanted to hear. *Quidquid delirant reges plectuntur Achivi,* or "The soldier has to suffer for it."[8]

In the High Command of the Army (OKH)[9]

The *Sparkommissar*[10]

After a lot of pulling and pushing back and forth I finally had to go to Berlin, where I was confronted with a daunting series of tasks. The wear and tear on our motorized equipment in Russia was immense and it could not be replaced. Our stocks of both fuel and rubber would be exhausted in the fall. But Hitler wanted a highly motorized army in 1942. So that meant conserving motor vehicles wherever possible to get us through the shortfall. The shortage of rubber was solved by two blockade runners, and the shortage of fuel by switching to synthetics. What remained was the need for motor vehicles.

When I reported to Berlin, I received the news that my oldest son had died a hero's death. He had been killed leading his platoon in a most exemplary manner, from the front.[11] Under such circumstances, the mountain of work and the responsibilities that awaited me were quite welcome. I immediately selected knowledgeable assistants. The first two were my highly accomplished regimental adjutants. I knew they understood the troops and their needs without asking a lot of questions or consulting additional advisors. In some cases we got officers from line units upon whose judgment we could rely. The next thing I obtained was a directive signed by Field Marshal Walther von Brauchitsch, the commander in chief of the army, giving me near-dictatorial powers for all departments within the war ministry. Without having to negotiate with anybody, I could issue any necessary order without much ado.

My new assignment required me to spend half my time at the ministry in Berlin and half my time at army headquarters in Rastenburg. I commuted back and forth by plane and by car. On one flight Colonel General Friedrich

Fromm came with me to report to Brauchitsch. The army wanted to reactivate the rocket development program at Penemünde, which Hitler had cancelled two years previously. In my presence Brauchitsch told Fromm, "Okay, let me have [the report]. I will present it to [Hitler] one more time. It is frustrating. Instead of these high losses during bombing attacks on England that do not do very much, we would have only had to push a button."

By the conclusion of my assignment as Sparkommissar I had conserved more than one hundred thousand motor vehicles with their associated personnel. In addition, we inactivated numerous redundant units, including many reconnaissance units, engineer platoons, etc. Unfortunately, those actions came too late. They should have been carried out before the start of the Russia campaign. The motor vehicles that had been lost were gone forever, and my efforts could only affect the standing-up and equipping of new units. In the process I did get to know the army very well in all of its intricacies. After four months on the job, at the beginning of November, my assignment ended.

General of Mobile Forces at OKH

At the beginning of November I was assigned as General of Mobile Forces at OKH.[12] When I reported for the last time to General Fromm, who was also the commander of the Reserve Army, I was happy to hear him tell me, "Normally the combat arms senior officers of OKH have no place with the reserve forces; I do not want them there. With you it is different, though. You can go there anytime and order them to do what you think is right."

I did not get much of a chance to do that, my work did not allow the time. Then I reported to the commander in chief of the army, Field Marshal von Brauchitsch, who had always been very supportive of me. I also reported to the chief of the general staff, Colonel General Franz Halder, who told me verbatim: "I want you to prepare with a grand vision for the war that our grandchildren will have to fight. In this war the victory of the land battle cannot be taken from us anymore." I was a little shocked.

Guderian

A few days later I was sitting on a plane to Orel to see Guderian, who was the commander of the Second Panzer Army.[13] I wanted to get oriented on the real situation and find out where I should start my work. I knew that I would get the true, unvarnished picture from Guderian.

He and I agreed completely on what had to be done and what the objectives should be. We then drove to the front for three days. The situation was a little different from what I had expected from Halder's remarks. We passed the 296th Division, which was at full strength and fully equipped, marching to the front lines. It was an impressive sight. On the road to Tula we saw abandoned Russian tanks, including their new T-34. The T-34 was completely impervious to our weapons, and it mounted a first-rate main gun. Nearby we saw one of our own PzKpfw[14] IIIs, which had been torn apart by just one Russian tank round. The Russians could not handle their own marvelous equipment, and their tanks had been abandoned because of technical problems.

Two divisions (from Frankfurt and Mainz) of III Corps had been destroyed. But a third division from Würtemberg, even though it went through the same experience, came out looking exactly as it had on the day it went in. A Russian battle group had been encircled east of Stalinogorsk (now Novomoskovsk). The following night that unit, a Siberian division, broke out of the encirclement. With their leaders up front in tanks, the unorganized mass of troops followed like a herd. In the process, two battalions of our 25th Motorized Infantry Division, which still had nine and seven rifle squads respectively, were overrun. There were so many Russians that even the machine guns could not finish them all off.

The Russian escape route was lined with their dead for kilometers. Our troops had vanished in the human waves. But when we reached our positions our troops all looked very good. Guderian walked from man to man, speaking with them informally. He made quite an impression on them, the army commander out there on the front lines during their hour of crisis. But I could not help noticing that the troops were at the limits of their strength. As a result of their numerical weakness, they constantly ended up in the most difficult crisis situations, which were then resolved by throwing in our best troops. But as those troops were killed, the toughest core of our army that we could not do without slowly but surely vanished. The Russians had left ninety-four guns and seventeen tanks in the encirclement perimeter. During World War I they saved their materiel at the cost of human lives. Now they did it the other way around. Was it a symptom or a coincidence?

The XXIV Motorized Corps was commanded by General of Panzer Troops Leo Geyr von Schweppenburg, my old comrade from the 18th Cavalry Regiment. He spoke gravely about the condition of his unit and asked me to report to higher headquarters accordingly. The corps formed up that day (26 November) with three divisions in three columns near Tula. With the three divisions equal in size to only three reinforced battalions, the movement naturally ground to a halt. They spent the night in Yasnaya Polyana, Leo Tolstoy's estate. Everything was done to keep the place intact. One officer was detailed as a guard. No billeting was allowed.

On 27 November I had my last meeting with Guderian in Orel. He believed he could still take Tula, but that was the limit of what he could do. He also asked me to describe the condition of the troops to higher headquarters. On the way back I stopped at Smolensk and had dinner with the commander of Army Group Center, Field Marshal Fedor von Bock. It was an interesting evening. After my return I spoke with General Buhle, who immediately informed Halder of my observations. On 30 November I reported to Brauchitsch and gave him a rather blunt assessment of the condition of the force. A sick, broken man sat in front of me, but he assessed the situation much as I did. Hitler, meanwhile, was demanding more and more attacks, because he believed that the last battalion thrown into the battle would determine the outcome. Thus, the piecemeal dribbling would continue, not resulting in anything. Brauchitsch, who normally was self-controlled, broke down, "Why don't you go and tell him yourself? We are finished."

I was deeply shaken. Napoleon had tried to do something similar at Eylau (now Bagrationovsk) in 1807, and the instrument broke in his hands. The only viable course of action was to suspend the operation and transition to the defensive.

The Great Crisis

The great crisis that was looming during my visit with Guderian in Tula and Kashira broke out in full force. The Russians attacked with everything they had. They had little artillery and fewer tanks, but they had people, whoever they could muster without regard for their ability to regenerate their army. Workers from shut-down industrial plants were formed into battalions, prisoners into companies. We ended up in a number of very bad situations because our personnel strength was completely down and our equipment was worn out. We were beyond the possibility of victory and now it was just a matter of holding on.

On 19 December, I was called in by Brauchitsch. He had been fired. Hitler assumed direct command of the army himself. The mood was gloomy. Halder spoke warmly to us about Brauchitsch's accomplishments. Then we went to see the field marshal. Brauchitsch had aged and looked tired. He forbade any kind of speech, but he himself spoke clearly and well. He said that his heart could not take the stress any longer and that Hitler had now taken over personally as supreme commander. The army hopefully would now receive everything it needed. Addressing Halder, Brauchitsch cordially thanked him.

It was touching. The end of a man, whose only mistake was that he could not deal with Hitler. Brauchitsch was not to blame for the current crisis situation in the army. On the contrary, he had always predicted it. And now a highly accomplished man would disappear. Clearly recognizing the situation, he often had asked to be relieved. He knew that there had to be trust between the highest level of the political and military leadership. Hitler had always refused to accept. Now we were facing the consequences of an unresolved personality conflict that had been intolerable for a long time.

Brauchitsch, who had been my commander in East Prussia, had always been especially benevolent toward me. I owed him very much. Silently he shook hands with all of us one more time as we looked into his clear eyes.

The Crisis Near Moscow

There was extremely heavy fighting. What was the situation in the front lines? Had a catastrophe already occurred? Was it in the making? Would we be able to weather it? Those were the questions that bothered all of us. Officers of OKH were ordered to the front lines, to give moral support. They were given a wide range of authority to stop any rearward movement. Hitler had forbidden any kind of retrograde action, and that decision was to be made clear. I was sent to the Third and Fourth Panzer Armies near Moscow. Halder gave me an initial orientation. He described the situation in a classical manner. The overriding objective, which was total victory and the complete destruction of the Russian Army, had failed. Now the Russians were on the offensive. Considering the conditions of the Russian winter, any withdrawal on our part would result in a catastrophe of Napoleonic dimensions. Halder now seemed completely rejuvenated. He spoke to me about the *feu sacré* [sacred fire] of the combat commander that one now had to exhibit.

By way of Vilnius, I arrived on 23 December in Smolensk at army group headquarters. Bock was replaced by Field Marshal Günther von Kluge. Bock had wanted to withdraw back across the Desna River under pressure from the Russian counterattack. But the onset of the Siberian winter would have meant the dissolution of the army group. For a few days destruction and defeat loomed over Germany.

Kluge made a very energetic and clear impression. On 24 December, I arrived in Gzhatsk [now Gagarin after Yuri Gagarin] at Colonel General Erich Hoepner's Fourth Panzer Army. The army was still standing, but how? During the retreat from Moscow masses of materiel had been left behind because of the lack of fuel. The troops were totally spent. The individual divisions were mere shadows of their former selves. The 160th Division, for example, had eighty riflemen left. Everything was drowning in snow. Communications were miserable. Lateral movements were impossible.

The staff, officers, and enlisted celebrated Christmas together. Hoepner spoke firmly, sincerely, and with confidence. He was a powerful leader. I sat next to him. He said that the hardest challenge of leadership came in situations where one had to muster all his personal powers to appear upbeat and confident in order to give his subordinates strength.

The withdrawal from Moscow had not been easy. Unsurprisingly, there had been incidents of disintegration at certain points. Although the troops had given their best, they did not accomplish their mission and now they had to go back. The following day I went on to the VII Army Corps, where Hans Krebs, an old member of the Goslar Jägers, was the chief of staff. I could expect to receive thorough overviews and analysis from him. Slowly I drove through the Russian winter landscape, past the 1812 battlefields of Borodino. I could still see the heaps of earth from the Russian positions. There was sunshine but no wind in the -5 to -20 degrees Fahrenheit weather. The smoke from the villages rose straight up in long, solid columns, high into the sky. It was a picture that could have been inspirational, were it not for our desperate situation and the Napoleonic memories. Thoughts of the dutiful, courageous German soldier weighed heavily on us.

I immediately went to the forward lines with Krebs. The troops looked pretty worn out, but were still in good spirits. With some imagination I could recognize the beginnings of dug-in positions. Nobody wanted to retreat. They had experienced the consequences themselves. They felt vastly superior to the Russians. But a few troops here and there can get pretty lonely, and the Russians always arrived with a hugely superior force. What we needed mostly was people, especially officers and NCOs, along with better antitank weapons.

The reaction to Hitler taking direct command was having a surprising effect. "Everything will be good, now that the Führer has taken over," could be heard over and over again. Even Krebs commented, "I would have never thought that even today this could have such an influence."

On the evening of 26 December I was back in Gzhatsk with Hoepner. We sat together for a long time in the evening. Hoepner considered the armored thrust toward Moscow to be unfeasible—bad terrain, too weak a force. He complained heavily about the senior leadership. At the army group level Field Marshal von Bock did not issues orders, only recommendations. Consequently Field Marshal von Kluge at Fourth Army remained aloof. The enemy forces, meanwhile, were concentrating on the Fourth Panzer Army. So far, Bock had done nothing to plug the hole along the Tula–Kaluga line. He was incapable of asserting himself against Guderian, who did what he wanted. During this conversation we received the news about Guderian's relief. It hit us all very hard. He was made the scapegoat for the disaster on the southern flank of the Fourth Army.

On 27 December I made a trip to the XLVI Army Corps. General Heinrich von Vietinghoff appeared firm and in good spirits. As long as he had the 5th Panzer Division and the Waffen-SS Division "Das Reich"[15] he would be able to support the units on his flanks. The 5th Panzer Division had just returned from home leave, fully equipped and refurbished.

On the 29th I was back with Kluge and had dinner with him. Then I met with Hitler's senior adjutant, Lieutenant General Rudolf Schmundt, and discussed with him the results of my multiple visits to the front. He said to me, "We must go see the Führer immediately. He needs to hear this."

Guderian's Farewell

Guderian's relief hit everybody very hard, especially the Panzer force. Kluge talked to me about it for a long time. He had been forced to take that action because Guderian had not been completely honest with him. Guderian had assured Kluge that he would hold a certain line, even though the troops of his 4th Panzer Division were already falling back from that position. Kluge cited two other similar instances in Guderian's previous conduct of the operation when he supposedly had not played with open cards.

I also blame Bock to a certain extent. As army group commander he had not issued any orders, and as a consequence Kluge's Fourth Army did not attack Moscow. Bock also did nothing to close the gap that had developed between Tula and Kaluga as a result of Kluge stopping his movement. Nor had Kluge done anything decisive; he had ordered only a few half-hearted actions. And Guderian himself? I made the following notes in my journal during my last visit with him: "Psychologically, Guderian leads masterfully, however, he increasingly depends on the moods and weaknesses of his troops in making his decisions. The troops like this situation. They feel understood. This is not, however, conducive to the tough decisions that a field commander who demands the most must make."

I pushed these thoughts aside, because Guderian indeed had always accomplished what he intended to accomplish with his masterful manner of human leadership. But Hitler judged similarly. On 20 December he had told Guderian, "You are too close to the events. You let yourself be affected too much by the suffering of your soldiers. You have too much compassion for the soldiers. You need to distance yourself more."

Guderian was, as I judged him, a good and honorable man. The inner core of his personality was sensitive and empathetic. But as he knew that this could bring danger, he often forced himself, driven by his hot temper, his love and sense of duty for Germany, to be hard and ruthlessly open, appearing unstoppable. Military and moral courage were developed in Guderian with equal intensity. Naturally, he had made a lot of enemies, who weighed in against him when the crunch came.

Shortly before my visit with Guderian in Orel he had been discussing with OKW the withdrawal of some units for reconstitution in Germany. When I was in Orel everybody's thinking centered on that. Individual units had already been pulled out for transport back and Guderian spoke openly with the troops about it. On 25 November he spoke to the two battalions of the 25th Motorized Infantry Division, which had borne the brunt of the Russian breakthrough. The news of the pending withdrawal spread like wildfire. How that happened remains a mystery.[16]

Poor personnel policy was another major factor that made this bad situation worse. The Personnel Branch knew that Guderian did not easily fit in. It also knew that the relationship between Guderian and Kluge had not been good for many years, which made it impossible for these two good soldiers to work together. Placing them in such a position could only lead to a disastrous clash. That crisis occurred near Orel, to the cost of the common soldier. These two able soldiers would have served better elsewhere, where they could not have clashed with each other.

Guderian told me that Kluge once challenged him to a duel, but Hitler had prohibited it. Guderian never forgave Kluge for his relief from command. At a meeting a few years later in the Führer's headquarters Kluge stepped up to Guderian and instinctively offered his hand, as he always did to everyone. Guderian saluted and ignored the offered hand. Instead of silently dismissing the gesture, Kluge asked, "Why don't you shake my hand?"

Guderian responded, "I salute the uniform, not the person."

Briefing Hitler

On 30 December I was back in Rastenburg and the following day I briefed Hitler. It took more than two hours, during which time Hitler hardly spoke. He only occasionally asked a question. I pleaded with Hitler not to withdraw under any circumstances. Operations were completely impossible in the snow that was two meters deep, and in the -58 degree Fahrenheit weather river crossings and the building of positions were impossible anywhere. This was a crisis that could not be solved operationally. Front lines were being held wherever we could manage to get just one tank and twenty men to one decisive point after days and days of trying. The demand to hold under such conditions might sound brutal, but in reality it was the greatest clemency. I was further able to give my assessment to Hitler about the Russian tactical developments of missile launchers, assault artillery, tanks, and the mass commitments of poorly trained infantry. I also expressed my concerns about tank production, stressing the crucial need for more.

I gave him the number of tanks that were delivered to the troops in December. Hitler said, "You are wrong, it was . . ." and he gave twice the number. Taking the plunge I replied, "My number is right. Your numbers have both the December and January production combined."

OKW chief Field Marshal Wilhelm Keitel, red faced and with his moustache quivering, interjected, "My Führer, now this is a grave accusation against me. . . ." Hitler made an interrupting gesture and Keitel fell silent. Later, Keitel did not throw it up to me, which I thought was quite decent of him.

I also pushed for the immediate fielding of shaped charge rounds, which were especially effective against armor. They were supposed to be the great surprise for 1942. I had a good rapport with Hitler and I hoped to have some influence on the decisive question of tank production. I apparently got Hitler's attention, because he immediately summoned Minister for Armaments Fritz Todt. After briefing Hitler I reported to the army chief of staff, Halder, who I found to be very upbeat and confident.

In the evening I met with General Buhle, the chief of the Organizational Directorate. He had been transferred to OKW as the chief of army affairs. I noted in my journal, "Hopefully, Buhle will now assert himself so that the Army gets what it needs. It is high time."

At the beginning of the New Year, Buhle, General Friedrich Paulus, and I sat over a map and brooded about an order that was supposed to align operations and the reequipping of the Panzer divisions.

Reflections on the Battle for Moscow

Much has been written about the battle for Moscow, and I do not want to repeat it. Deliberations about whether various operational decisions could have led to success may be rather interesting, but they also are a sure sign that the force had been expended and the culminating point[17] of victory had been surpassed. The indicators of a healthy, promising operation are the ability of the available, participating forces to resolve tactical and operational errors and personnel glitches. Such errors are then not apparent and can be ignored, because they have no negative consequences. Such had been the case in all of our previous campaigns in Poland, France, and the Balkans. Thus, the question is not what could have been done differently operationally, but what we could have done to infuse new forces to avoid exceeding the culminating point.

I cannot judge whether or not effective personnel actions could have been taken in front of Moscow. Plenty of personnel were available as the crisis unfolded. The materiel factor was more important. Following the campaign in France, Hitler had encouraged equipping the PzKpfw III with the long-barrel 50 mm main gun rather than the short-barrel 35 mm gun, and the PzKpfw IV with the long-barrel rather than the short-barrel 75 mm gun. I remember listening in on a conversation between General von Schell and Colonel General Fromm when they decided contrary to clear guidance to use the short-barrel guns, because it was more difficult to move through forests with the longer guns. They believed that the tube of the main gun should never extend beyond the edge of the tank's hull. The consequence was that our tank guns at Moscow could not penetrate the Russian armor.[18] When we refitted our Panzers with the longer-barrel guns during the winter of 1941–1942, the Russian tank superiority ended. That by itself might have produced different results at Moscow.

Years earlier, during a discussion about tank issues I had with then-Colonel von Schell, I told him that the material losses of tanks had been high in the last war, but tank crew personnel losses had been minimal. We would need six thousand tanks for an operation that would be used up after a certain amount of time. But the majority of the tank crews would still be available. If we had six thousand additional tanks, we could give them to those crews and the Panzer divisions would be able to maintain their original strength and combat effectiveness. The cycle could even be repeated. What we needed to abandon was our practice of fragmented and low-rate production. We needed more factories. We had built a tank army without the necessary tank production. Schell thought that three times six thousand tanks was impossible, and besides, it was too late now. We should have started much earlier. I did not have the authority then, but in my mind I postponed the issue to a later point when I would have more influence over the process.

On my trips to the front I came across ad hoc units that had been thrown together with tank crews which had lost their tanks. Not trained for static warfare in trenches, they suffered heavy losses in their black uniforms in the white snow. Later, these old tank crewmen were desperately needed.[19]

We did not recognize the incredible possibilities for reconstitution in a modern tank army and we never resolved the dilemma of a tank army without adequate tank production. We lost the war because of this. At Moscow one to two thousand new tanks could have produced different results. In the whole history of warfare there is no generalship, no General Staff at the operational level that was the equal of the Germans in World War II. Unfortunately, that resulted in our attempts to solve all our problems on the operational level, even when there was no operational solution. That was the case in front of Moscow.

Twice I had tried to get from the headquarters of the Fourth Panzer Army to reach the subordinated corps headquarters. I only managed to do it on the third try. I then attempted to get from the Fourth to the adjacent Third Panzer Army, but had to give that up altogether. Someone once commented to me, "You folks at OKH must believe that summer has broken out in front of Moscow." At army group headquarters I listened in to a telephone call during which Field Marshal von Kluge tried unsuccessfully to get a general officer moved to a field army headquarters as the new commanding general. At that point I knew that operational decisions had absolutely no value anymore. The decision over a battle won or lost had moved from the operational level, beyond the tactical level, down to the simple question of whether one tank, one antitank gun, or twenty soldiers could be moved to a threatened position.

The decision to hold at any price and not give up an inch was obvious, given the situation. As tempting as frontline adjustments appeared on paper, the reality was that equipment, rations, and often the wounded were lost in the process. The conserving of significant forces rarely resulted, because the shortening of the front line also gave the enemy an advantage. Once the new position was established, the old game started all over, and looking toward the rear and toward another shortening of the front line started anew. In the process, the morale of the troops that had just lived through a horrible withdrawal would deteriorate even more. Hitler recognized this, but from that point on he was very skeptical of any operational actions. In the long run, that was very much to our detriment. But at that point in time and in that situation, I was convinced that there was no other solution but to hold at all costs. Anything else would have resulted in death and destruction.

Several accomplished generals, particularly Guderian and Hoepner, became victims of this solution. But the guilt ran deeper. Brauchitsch had not demanded unconditional obedience from the generals. Schlieffen had demanded a turning movement by the entire German Army that was supposed to be executed just as if it were done by a battalion. He had recognized that in the endless battle front of modern mass armies, independent operational decisions by army-level commanders were rare and that they could jeopardize the whole. Brauchitsch, however, had allowed too much leeway. Hitler, in contrast, believed that he had to reestablish unquestioning obedience. At that time there was a lot of support for that point of view.

Wars and sometimes even battles are won or lost politically. Moscow had been such a battle. The fight against Russia required the concentration of all forces. Hitler neglected to involve Japan or even to keep the Japanese updated. Instead, Japan pursued its own path in the Pacific. There would be time for that after the defeat of Russia. The fact that we did not involve Japan in the

Far East against the Soviets allowed the Soviets to use their easternmost forces against us at Moscow at the decisive moment. Hitler's failure to combine the two nations against Russia ultimately led to their joint defeat in World War II. It was similar to World War I when the German chief of staff General Erich von Falkenhayn attacked the French at Verdun in 1916, while the Austrian chief of Staff, General Franz Conrad von Hötzendorf, attacked Italy. The irony is that Hitler the politician lost the Battle of Moscow, while as a military leader he saved the German Army temporarily.

The Conclusion of the Winter Battle

The Winter Battle was slowly ebbing away. It was interesting to see how the sudden beginning of the winter with its incredible masses of snow from one day to the next changed the art of war from a highly modern, equipment-driven process to a much more primitive form. Every man with one rifle, two hundred rounds of ammunition, one landmine under his arm, rations for four days, no artillery, and only a few mortars was the equipment of the Russian shock armies. With that they were superior in winter fighting to our well-equipped but immobile divisions. That was exactly how fifteen hundred Finnish snow-shoe-mounted troops stopped and decimated a Russian invasion army. During World War I the Finns had used the same primitive methods to destroy a Russian division.

But the Russian leadership was not able to manage their local successes at the operational level, or to mass their forces to destroy our Army Group Center. Their shock armies petered out in the endlessness of the eastern steppes, where they eventually came to a halt somewhere and then started to live off the land. And thus the battle was decided. Such tactics could only produce success if the Russian shock armies were firmly directed toward a single objective, and if the Germans cooperated by withdrawing, losing all of their equipment, and letting panic break down their unit cohesion. But we stood firm wherever we were, and the Soviet shock armies dissolved. The Russian tactics failed.

By the time winter was over both opposing forces in many sectors were closely entangled and exhausted, directly opposite each other. By holding on, by using strongpoints, and by launching immediate counterattacks into the Russian masses we had mastered the situation. Hitler had been right in this case. Would he also be right later on? Typically, he did not change his methods that were successful initially, but which later turned out to be disastrous under different circumstances.

"You should change your tactics every ten years," said Napoleon. "Otherwise the enemy will figure them out." But in our times things moved much faster. What had been right yesterday was wrong today and led to ruin. Thus, Hitler failed to understand the uniqueness of the Winter Battle. My journal entry of 15 January indicates the lack of influence that Hitler's thinking had on me at the time:

"Undoubtedly it was correct to try to finish off the Russians in pursuit. The same people who criticize this course of action now would have likewise criticized halting in the fall and constructing winter positions. They would have urged pursuit. But this was not the decisive mistake. The decisive mistake was not to push reserve forces forward immediately, reserve crews, tanks, etc., in order to maintain the momentum of the attack. When it was too late, the necessary forces were suddenly available. Who bears the blame for such negligence? Brauchitsch did not, without a doubt. It was Hitler's fault. He so easily took the second step before the first one, and then neglected the necessary follow-on action. This is how we had prepared to conduct all kinds of operations, the war against England,[20] the offensive in the Caucasus, war in the Middle East. Instead of completing one thing and taking it to the end, we already moved on to the next. So we exceeded our culminating point."

Halder once asked me, "Are you a humanist?"

I acknowledged that I was.

"Do you know what 'hubris' means? That is our problem."

People and Soldiers

Quidquid delirant reges, plectuntur Achivi.[21] That verse from Virgil's *Aeneid* has stuck with me all of my life. An examination of the events of the winter of 1941–1942, therefore, would be incomplete without also remembering all the people involved, the German and Russian soldiers and the civilian populace. As I saw the situation at the time . . .

25 December, near Moscow: "The population is eager and works as they should. They have learned to obey. In some regions there is already famine. Quietly and apathetically the situation is accepted. When asked in the fall, 'Why don't you work your fields?' They answered, 'It makes no sense; our food will only last until April anyway. We will not live to see the next harvest. Now that your soldiers eat our stored food with us, it will only last until February.'"

Between 1919 and 1929 it was the same. Then 40 percent died of hunger, now it would be 60 percent. Numbly the people acquiesced to their inevitable fate. Their indifference toward fate and death was beyond conception. The younger generation was communist, the older ones were completely apathetic.

A regimental comrade, Radowitz, told me on 2 February that some of our troops who had remained back in Rostov during our withdrawal had been hidden by the local citizens from the Bolshevists and finally reached German lines in disguises.

All comforts—any kind of pleasure—had been abandoned by the Russians for their arms build-up. But even at this lowest of standards the people still had the minimum and were well fed. Here and there one even saw a better dressed woman. There was absolutely no décor in the living areas. The art was gigantic *kitsch*. Everywhere there were the same stucco statues of Lenin and Stalin. The architecture was a poor imitation of American styles. Russian family life, however, was completely different from what we had imagined. There was no prostitution. Discipline and morality within the family were highly valued.

On the German front line the Hannoverian 73rd and 74th Regiments, which had a combined strength of only three thousand to four thousand, overran much larger enemy forces. They brought in one thousand prisoners and counted more than five thousand enemy killed.

Wachtmeister[22] Kuhfall, a forward observer from the 7th Battery, 268th Artillery Regiment, was shot through the lung but remained in position until an officer replaced him. When he heard at the aid station that this officer had been killed, he immediately went forward and, despite his severe wound, started directing fires again.

One NCO of the 384th Infantry Regiment self-described his condition as healthy and fully combat ready, even though he had twenty-eight festering boils from lice.

One soldier in the 364th Infantry Regiment was standing guard, writhing with pain from joint rheumatism. When asked about it, he stated that he had had three days of rest coming, but because there were so few of them he just had to go back on duty.

As one of my officers reported to me after a visit to the front lines, one private in the 432nd Infantry Regiment was standing guard with his festering feet wrapped in rags because they were so swollen they could not fit into his boots. Otherwise he appeared crisp and upright. He said, "We are only five men left in the squad. If I fall out, the others have to stand guard even more frequently."

This active German heroism was countered by a more passive Russian heroism that, nevertheless, had to be valued at the same level. To reinforce the partisans and their forward positions the Russians dropped soldiers at a height of ten to fifteen meters from low-flying, old, slow airplanes without parachutes into the deep snow: 15 percent died, 30 percent were injured, and only 55 percent remained fit for action. There also were frequent reports of cannibalism among separated and encircled Russian units, but I personally never saw evidence of such.

My staff advisor for armored trains, Lieutenant Colonel von Olschewski, reported from the rear: "Everybody has caught the Russian illness of indifference, 'Nichevo!' The insightful ones say that this is caused by the monotonous steppes." A senior German railroad official refused to transport wounded soldiers in his official car that was running well-heated, right behind the locomotive. When Olschewski attempted to intervene, the soldiers declared, "If the man has to be forced to do the right thing, just forget it. We are better than that."

My Functions as General of Mobile Forces[23] at OKH

Because of my trips to the front, I knew the situation and I knew what had to be done. The answer was tanks, tanks, and more tanks. Since I knew the inner workings of the ministry, where the powers-that-be mostly neutralized each other, I tried to put some leverage where I knew I would get some results, directly with Hitler. I made a good start at the end of December and from then on I never hesitated to take that route. Hitler's senior adjutant, Schmundt, supported me continually. I just had to call and give him an outline of my main points, and I was sure of being able to see Hitler within eight to ten days. It obviously was essential to present only the real bottom-line issues to him, and only concentrate on my own area of responsibility.

I believe that with this process I was successful in steering Hitler again and again toward the central problem of tank production, and that it kept his interest in the issue alive. All other issues became secondary. It was also important that Colonel General Fromm, who was for all intents and purposes the minister of war in Berlin, was kept abreast of things and never had the feeling of being cut out. He always trusted me completely. He had too much insight as a soldier and was much too generous to interfere because of any interdepartmental jealousies.

The next area that I concentrated my energy on was the problem of the NCOs. Much more than in earlier days, the NCO was the heart and the foundation at the small unit level. I initiated an NCO academy for the mobile forces at the Rembertow maneuver training area near Warsaw. For the commandant and the instructors I drew from the officers from my old 1st Bicycle Battalion. I had trained them in peacetime when I was their commander, and they knew exactly what I expected. But it was difficult to sell this initiative. Colonel General Halder, for one, wanted to authorize only a two-week course. Finally he agreed to three months, which I then quietly extended into a six-months course as I originally had requested. A modern NCO cannot be trained in less time than that.[24]

I also wanted to start a battalion commander's course at Versailles, similar to the one conducted by Tank Brigade West. Considering Warsaw and Paris, I was drawn to the idea of bringing the course participants from the East into a culturally somewhat more sophisticated atmosphere. The preparations for the school had been completed in Paris by the time I left to assume command of a division. And, of course, there were regulations to edit and publish, which were useful for disseminating lessons learned.

In the course of all these actions I traveled to both Warsaw and Paris. What I saw there was not pretty. I could never quite understand why supply and logistics activities supposedly only functioned among the pleasures of the big city. The speed and effectiveness of the logistics system was not at all optimal in such environments. Much got lost en route and never arrived where it was needed, with the troops.

My assistants were all competent, hand-picked officers. My adjutant was Hans-Georg Lueder,[25] who once stood up to me openly and courageously when I was heading in the wrong direction. Later, when I was an army commander, I picked him for my adjutant again. I never had much use for yes-men. My chief of staff, Colonel Krahmer, and I went far back together. One day he reported to me very formally and stated that he was not a National Socialist. All I could tell him was that I did not care about that. Because of the sense of duty we both shared as officers, it was completely irrelevant. And that was that.

Another of my officers who stood out was my staff advisor for cavalry issues, Lieutenant Colonel Helmuth von Pannwitz, who later became the commanding general of the 1st Cossack Division.[26] He was extremely knowledgeable about the peoples of the East and expanded my horizons on this topic immensely. I had chosen him because during peacetime in East Prussia he had already come to my attention for his sincerity and the soundness of his opinions. He was an officer who distinguished himself by his deep love and understanding of the simple frontline soldier and the peoples of the East. When necessary, however, he was capable of indomitable harshness. He spoke most of the Slavic languages fluently. I gave him full rein to develop his plans to recruit the Cossacks.

Later near Stalingrad, Pannwitz came through my divisional headquarters on his way to meet Hitler to receive the Oak Leaves to his Iron Cross Knight's Cross. He asked me whether he should give Hitler his opinion about the peoples of the East. I told him, "Hitler talks interestingly and fascinatingly. Just interrupt him in the middle of a sentence and tell him, 'My Führer, I have to tell you something . . . ,' and then just take off without timidity. He listens to people that come from where the action is, who speak from experience, and who are personally courageous."

The conversation went as expected. Pannwitz did just as I advised him, and

Hitler listened. Pannwitz had an equally developed sense of moral courage, as well as military courage. He was totally blunt and was not afraid to say that our policy toward the East was wrong and that there were no subhumans in the East. Afterward Pannwitz became the commander of the Cossack brigade that was being formed, which he later developed into a Cossack division, and then a Cossack corps.[27] It was the only unit of Eastern Europeans that completely lived up to our expectations. At the end of the war Pannwitz refused to abandon his Cossacks. He voluntarily transferred with them from British detention to Russia and certain death, of which he was completely aware.[28]

Pannwitz frequently went back to Hitler and always pushed through whatever he needed. An officer in the Organizational Directorate later told me that Pannwitz would never leave until he had everything accomplished he had set out to do. Even at that he was unique. After his first talk with Hitler there was a noticeable change in attitude toward the peoples of the East, although Pannwitz alone was not the cause. The time was right and the situation was heating up for us, but by then it was far too late.

Nobody at OKH was happy with Hitler taking direct command of the army. As the head of state he was overtaxed, and he had stepped from his high level of leadership down to a level where he lacked the necessary knowledge and skill. The war did not allow him the time he needed to become an expert. As a temporary solution Hitler's assumption of command had been justifiable and even necessary; but as a permanent solution it was wrong.

During one of many evenings I spent with Colonel Claus von Stauffenberg we discussed these matters. In the course of one conversation he suddenly said to me, "Colonel, I have a peculiar solution here. Himmler should be made commander in chief of the army. Then he could not just put all of his efforts into the SS, but would have to take care of the army as well."

That conversation shows how little we were able to look really deep inside the characters and the issues of that time. Although our discussion at the time was little more than a dinner table conversation, Stauffenberg typically loved to throw such thoughts unexpectedly into a conversation in order to clarify his own thoughts in the process of the discussion that would instantly follow.[29]

14

1942

Between Smolensk and Stalingrad

Preparation—The *Via Sacra*[1]

The build-up of a powerful mechanized army for 1942 was more than difficult. Endless amounts of materiel and countless tanks, trucks, and weapons had been left behind during the withdrawal from Moscow. I estimated the loss equal to at least one or two armies worth of equipment. This indicates what would have happened to us if the withdrawal had not been brutally halted. A further foul-up was the so-called Via Sacra.

On 16 October a close associate of mine, Major General Alfred Baentsch, earlier the chief quartermaster and now commander of the 82nd Division, told me about it. In December 1941 Baentsch had witnessed the following conversation between Hitler and Major General Adolf von Schell, the plenipotentiary for military automotive engineering.

> Hitler: "Do you have 10,000 trucks?
> Schell: "Yes."
> Hitler: "Can I have them in Warsaw by December 22nd?"
> Schell (without thinking): "Yes."

The ten thousand trucks were mostly pulled out of France, loaded with urgently needed equipment, and organized into companies transporting 250 tons each. They were then driven across Germany by inexperienced drivers, mostly Hitler Youths, only to keep the deadline. But only wrecks arrived in Warsaw. The companies that had carried 250 tons each were then reorganized into companies carrying 60 tons. What actually reached the front lines was junk. The ten thousand trucks had been wasted.

It is interesting to note that Hitler did not draw any consequences from this experience, just as he never initiated any actions against those directorates that had not followed his orders concerning the installation of the long guns into the tanks.

A case similar to the trucks had happened with some tanks. Sixty desperately needed tanks, an entire month's production at the time, had been driven by untrained personnel, some of whom were Hitler Youths, with their brakes locked from the off-loading site at a railhead to the front lines. They ended up as junk along the roads. Of course, the winter was blamed for that. I then personally tested frost-proof loading techniques. Only slowly did we realize that the winter conditions could not be blamed for what happened to the tanks.

Under such circumstances the vehicle upgrades that I had ordered at the time when I was the "Agent of Frugality" proved very helpful now.

It was particularly difficult to extract the tank divisions from the sector of Army Group Center. In order to block the withdrawals, Field Marshal Günther von Kluge dissolved all the order of battle organizational structures. Certainly such had happened before under the pressure of the moment. But now it turned out to be a marvelous instrument to resist the extraction of every tank unit. A supreme commander of the German Army in the proper sense did not exist anymore, and for different reasons not all the details could be presented to Hitler. Colonel General Franz Halder[2] had only limited command authority and certainly not the necessary overall authority. Much disagreeable and often sternly written correspondence went back and forth and much precious time was lost. That—after all that—everything still went off on time seemed like a miracle.

Hitler demanded the establishment of two new tank divisions at home. The ministry declared that was impossible. When I met with Colonel General Friedrich Fromm[3] I suggested to him that the two divisions could be built around the two tank regiments of Panzer Brigade West. The infantry regiments could be formed from individual companies of the Army in the West (*Westheer*),[4] consisting of personnel from selected young age groups that were available in the West. They then could be replaced in the West by recruits. Artillery units could be made up of older soldiers from the West and the same with engineers. Whatever was still missing would have to be acquired from various sources.

Thus, the 22nd and 23rd Panzer Divisions were established. I had made it a rule not to interfere with personnel issues. There were always more important problems to resolve. As I later had to admit, that was an unfortunate decision. Such units, especially as they were formed using a lot of tricks, would have required only the best divisional, regimental, and battalion commanders, who through the power of their personalities could overcome any adversity. That factor had been ignored by the Army Personnel Department. Here I should have intervened and I feel partly responsible for the misfortune that fell to the 22nd Panzer Division in the Crimea.

There the unit had been designated to attack across the narrows near Feodosiya in the direction of Kerch. The 22nd Panzer Division had arrived piece-meal and the leaders did not know their troops. The division was practically thrown into the battle piece by piece, directly from the railhead and formed up only while it was being committed to action.

That process, unfortunately, was not uncommon and always ended in disas-ter. The divisional commander wanted to wait, but he was put under huge pres-sure by the overall commanding general: "If you do not attack today, we lose the Crimea tomorrow."

"I will attack then," responded the divisional commander. But instead of attacking through an existing bridgehead across one part of the marshy zone, the division was lined up across the whole marsh and then got bogged down and suffered heavy losses.[5]

I was sent there to evaluate the situation and was deeply moved by what I saw and heard. I talked to almost all of the tank commanders and officers. Even though many of them had made every possible tactical blunder, a large part of the blame lay with the inadequate personnel situation. An experienced, tough divisional commander would have found means and ways to postpone the attack until the division was completely assembled and probably would have attacked in a different manner. With a "*Pater, peccavi*"[6] from me, nothing could be changed either.

I got to see very little of the Crimea. I turned down an excursion to Bakh-chisaray to the old architecturally interesting residence of the khan of the Crimean Tatars. The purpose of the trip was not really appropriate, and I also purposely did not want to use up any more gas, which was hard to come by.

The 22nd Panzer Division later successfully participated in capturing Kirzhach and was then committed in the first counterattack at Stalingrad as part of the XLVIII Panzer Corps, where it suffered heavy losses and was dis-banded. The disbanding of the 22nd, or rather its merging with the 23rd Panzer Division, was necessary because it was logistically impossible to reconstitute both divisions. It was better to have one complete division than two rumps. All other options would have been wrong.

The Outlook for 1942

On 3 March I noted in my journal: "An interesting question is what are the Russians capable of doing in the spring? This is the decisive question of the war. Having been underrated up to this point, they are now overrated. The most unfavorable intelligence for us indicated that they will add sixty new divisions and thirty-five tank brigades. That seems exaggerated. For the time being they have nothing with which to exploit their initial successes. What they are throw-

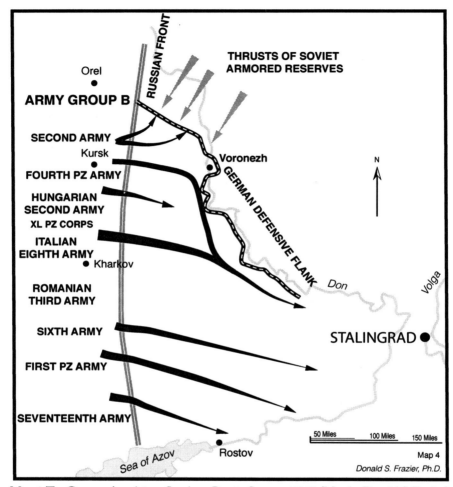

Map 4. The German Attack into Southern Russia, Summer 1942. (Map by Donald S. Frazier)

ing into the fight is old people and whatever else they can muster—Moscow policemen, for example. I believe that they too are stretched very thin and since the beginning of the year they are scraping the bottom of the barrel. In other words, they are running out of options as well. One thing is clear: if we can grasp the initiative again, they will be finished."

Those comments show how one can be totally off in one's analysis. Enemy estimates are some of the hardest things to do.[7] There is no such thing as a wrong estimate, and no blame can be attached. One of our most capable and energetic intelligence officers, who had been a Fähnrich[8] in my former squadron and who I was friends with, came up with the same conclusion: "The Russians are finished." He was a Baltic German and spoke Russian as fluently as German, but he despised the Russians deeply and did not think them capable of anything.

For the intelligence service the same is true now as what Goethe said about the writing of history: "One must start with the positive and then if one in the course of the work gets to the negative, one is right there. If one starts out with the negative, one remains there." That was the failure of this outstanding officer. The Personnel Department had not accounted for this and had been lulled by the exemplary traits of this gentleman. In all other areas his achievements would have been first rate.

Our Allies

Our allies played a major role in our plans. On 4 January Colonel General Friedrich Paulus[9] had hoped to bring another forty divisions forward along with the Finnish units. We had, after all, managed to get almost all of Europe involved in the fight against Bolshevism. But the main problem was that the allied units, unfortunately, were of differing quality, and we were not able to give them modern equipment.

The best were the Finns, then the Croats, the Flemish, the Walloons, and the Dutch—the latter organized in the 5th SS Panzer Division "Viking." The Slovaks, Italians, and Romanians were adequate, if they were not burdened with missions too difficult for them. The allies who least met our expectations were the Hungarians. My disparaging verdict from World War I and my assignment to the Hungarian Army were shared by the assessment of General of Infantry Kurt von Tippelskirch, the General Staff's former chief of the foreign armies section. A certain amount of blame also goes to Hungarian regent Miklós Horthy and his unclear policies. In 1945 a Hungarian division commander under my command told me that he had a strict order from Horthy to subordinate all other missions to the only important one, to bring the division back to Hungary in one piece.

One cannot conduct a war with that kind of thinking. Hungary's curse was the "Hungarian globe"—in other words, looking at Hungary as the center of the world. All others were expected to conform to Hungary's decisions. I credit the good attitude of the Slovaks to the politically unambiguous attitude of their leader, Jozef Tiso, who in 1945 told me, "A small country like Slovakia cannot conduct its own foreign policy. It all depends on making a clear decision and then sticking with it."

During the withdrawal of the Hungarian mobile corps at the beginning of the winter of 1941–1942 the Hungarian officers were disgusted. They felt that it was a stain on the reputation of Hungary to leave the Germans alone during this heavy fighting. Interestingly enough, Horthy relieved two higher generals, Henrik Werth and Dezsö László, because of their pro-German attitudes.

Commander of the 11th Panzer Division

On my last day at OKH[10] I went to see Hitler's adjutant, Major General Rudolf Schmundt, one more time and proposed the reinstatement of General Heinz Guderian. Unfortunately, Hitler was still completely against it. Only somebody who knew both personalities without bias would be able to understand the situation. Shortly before Guderian's relief there had been a severe confrontation between the two. Guderian in his forthright manner had not backed down. Hitler stated afterward, "I was not able to convince this man." As an insider I would interpret that as the admission: "He did not fall under my hypnosis."

The incident created the irreconcilable rift. I could only carry out my duties as the General of Mobile Forces at OKH if I had the recent frontline experience that would give me the necessary moral authority. That was the official reason I gave when I requested General Halder to reassign me to the front as a divisional commander. The unofficial reason was that I had had enough of OKH. I had always considered myself a soldier first and not a pencil pusher. During wartime I did not want to be the latter. Thus, I was given command of the 11th Panzer Division, a unit that really only existed as remnants, although it once had a good reputation. Making matters difficult but in some ways easier was the fact that my predecessor[11] had so thoroughly alienated all of his subordinate commanders that twenty-two regimental and battalion commanders were then home on sick leave. I received a thick folder in which my predecessor had documented the conflict between himself and the commander of the division's 61st Motorcycle Infantry Battalion, Lieutenant Colonel Paul Freiherr von Hauser, an Austrian. The dispute was over the legitimacy of Hauser using the noble title of *Freiherr*.[12] In Austria the nobility had been abolished. I had the folder destroyed and addressed Hauser right from the beginning as *Herr* von Hauser and found him to be one of the best and toughest soldiers of the entire war. He was a commander who stood out, even among the elite of the 11th Panzer Division. Hauser ultimately became the last commander of the Panzerlehr Division.

The 11th Panzer Division was currently in positions east of Smolensk, engaged in a defensive battle against partisans. I had brought the Motorcycle Infantry Training Battalion from Germany in order to give this well-equipped training unit an opportunity to gain some combat experience. But Field Marshal von Kluge immediately ordered this valuable unit to remain near Dorogobuzh. In the back and forth haggling I managed to maintain the upper hand. Von Kluge had with minimalist and detailed measures won the Winter Battle, something that a commander more inclined to a broader stroke approach might not have been able to do. But his resistance at this point to releasing any units made it close to impossible to start new undertakings. He was "smart as a whip, had reckless energy, but was small minded."

Saying farewell to warfare against the partisans was no loss. Every soldier hated it. The commander of the rear army area, General of Infantry Max von Schenkendorff, who we came under, told me, "You can only overcome the partisans if you have enough troops available. But even then, their elimination is questionable. The nature of the country favors the criminal mind and the Russians are used to living off the land and have always avoided political pressure. They will stop by themselves when Moscow has fallen and the desire of the people for peace and quiet turns against the partisans.

"The ruble is no longer a valid currency. Money has no value. The Russians are numb when it comes to the threat of heads rolling. One should use schnapps and tobacco as payment and try to get the weapons out of the country. A lot wrong has been done. For one example, fifty thousand prisoners were sent on furlough for the harvest. If they had been called back after the harvest at the beginning of November they would have probably come back. Now nobody will come back. (*Relata refero*—This is only hearsay.)"

After attending a good art history lecture in the cathedral at Smolensk, I moved southward to Kursk. My movement was dogged by rain, impossible trails, breakdowns, no fuel, twenty-four-hour convoys, and towing and changing vehicles. The troops were not doing much better. In Bryansk I stayed in a soldiers' convalescent home. When I did not use proper blackout procedures at night, I was promptly scolded by the head nurse, a Baltic-German Baroness von Wolff. After the war in Stuttgart I was able to thank this wonderful lady properly for her strict training discipline. She became a frequent and welcome guest in my home there.

The Readiness of the Division

Despite all the efforts some areas still looked dismal. Personnel and weapons were at 100 percent. Motorized vehicles were still 40 percent short. I had to initiate emergency measures. Artillery batteries were formed with six guns each,[13] and thus the number of batteries was reduced. The 111th Panzergrenadier Regiment was made mobile—actually not quite mobile. The men had to march or were made temporarily mobile by assigning them to a motor column unit.

Certainly the commander of my 11th Panzergrenadier Brigade[14] was right when he said that we had never before entered into an offensive so poorly equipped. But the majority of the units that were set to attack at the lower Volga and the Caucasus were finally fully equipped. It was an organizational masterpiece that we were capable of attacking at all after the last winter. And the Russians were not any better off.

The division was ordered to cover the major offensive of Army Group South on its left flank, move toward Voronezh, and break through the Russian positions along the Tym River.

After several days of thorough reconnaissance, questioning prisoners, and meeting with the artillery and the adjacent units, everything was set. I did not issue a written order, but rather oriented all the commanders using a detailed map exercise and a terrain walk. That technique had the advantage that all doubts could be cleared up immediately and wrong interpretations and misunderstandings came to light right away. My General Staff officer Ia,[15] the very capable Kienitz, unfortunately summarized everything in a written order and sent an unsolicited copy to the corps headquarters. He received it back well edited. All I said was, "There you go. Why did you have to go straight to your prince?"[16] We did not, however, change a thing. And never again during this year of unclouded and magnificent cooperation did we publish anything in writing.

In the meantime nature provided us some security. It rained and rained, turning the roads into a soapy mess.

Toward Voronezh

On 28 June at 0200 hours in the morning I was at my command post. The world was quiet and peaceful. Not a single sound interrupted the silence. The blooming pastures gave off a nice aroma. At 0215 hours an artillery barrage of incredible force broke loose. Dust, smoke, and thunder covered everything. Fifteen minutes later a Russian battery answered. Their fire landed somewhere harmlessly in the fields. Soon I could see our riflemen everywhere climbing up the enemy hillsides. At 0900 hours the first bridge was ready and I was able to cross and drive to the 539th Infantry Regiment, which had been attached to me. The regimental commander was beaming. Against his expectations his troops, all of them originally classified as *uk-gestellte*[17] laborers deferred from military service, had fought magnificently.

Then I went to one of my own infantry regiments. I walked along the forward lines while the troops were being engaged. Every officer and NCO jumped up and while standing at attention reported to me under enemy fire, just like during a peacetime inspection. From that moment on I had control of the division. Then I got back into my Kübelwagen[18] and accompanied the Panzer regiment that was moving toward Mikhaylovka.

It was an intoxicating picture, the wide, treeless plains covered with 150 advancing tanks, above them a Stuka[19] squadron. At the next river section, at the Kschen, we ran into new resistance. I halted the attack and made sure nobody was bunching up. Then I went back through the high rye fields to our vehicles with my adjutant, Reserve Major von Webski. Once in a while a Russian infantryman would pop up in fields of high grain, look around shyly, and drop back down again while moving eastward.

Massive, heavy artillery fire was dropping all around us. In the middle of a sentence Webski dropped to the ground, hit by a shell fragment in his left temple. Instinctively I pulled his hand away from his wound and bandaged him. He fought me and said, "Sir, you have more important things to do right now. I can take care of myself." Then he lost consciousness. I handed him off to my aide, who took him back to the rear. A few days later this marvelous man passed away without ever having regained consciousness. One of the points that he had always stressed over and over was the necessity of wearing a steel helmet, because of the high mortality rate of head wounds. He had not been wearing his steel helmet when he was hit. Otherwise, who knows. . . .

That night I stayed put where I was, because it was unlikely that we would have found our way back to the command post. Besides, I had everything under control by radio. We pushed the vehicles together like circled wagons and fell asleep. Suddenly there was horrible yelling and screaming. "The Russians!" Everyone grabbed his weapon. A motorcycle messenger had run over some Russians who had settled down nearby, and now with horrible screams they were all torn from their sleep.

Minor Events

Rain, rain, and more rain. Everything was soapy. Laboriously everybody was sloshing forward. On the Kschen River our Stukas mopped up the opposing Russian tanks.

But the Russian fighter planes were also zeroing in on the 11th Panzer Division. Just as I was poring over a map with my chief of staff in my command car, a strafing round shot right between us into the map. Shortly after that supplies and our supporting infantry division arrived and we moved on. My 15th Panzer Regiment moved forward with unbelievable speed, disappeared over the horizon, and was not to be seen anymore. I drove after them for two lonely hours along the clearly marked tracks. I caught up with them as they were establishing a strongpoint six kilometers in front of the Olym sector.

A shortage of fuel had ended that push, but the Russian front had been penetrated completely. Naturally the infantry divisions lagged far behind the Panzers on the left and on the right. On the morning of 1 July I had enough forces together, and most importantly the necessary fuel, so that I could position my Panzer regiment on the Olym crossing near Naberezhnoye. As I was following the unit I saw a tank in a field of high grain. I drove toward it intending to ask the position of the regimental staff. When I was about two hundred meters away I recognized that it was a Russian tank. When I finally arrived at the Olym the last hand grenades were being thrown and then we went up the next hillsides quickly.

I stayed at the Olym and let the rest of the division move up to the seized bridgehead. Engine noise and antitank and machine gun fire broke out, as seven Russian tanks were trying to break through our lines from the rear in order to reestablish contact with their own lines. Six of them broke down under our fire. The seventh raced forward at high speed and did not notice the twenty-meter drop at the bank of the Olym. It flipped over in the air and dropped into the torrents of the river.

As we were driving through the steppes along the open flank of the division, a Russian jumped up in front of us. My escort officer pointed at him. He only snapped back to reality when I shouted, "Oh my God, get your pistol out!" The Russians could be like wounded animals when you caught them. Whoever shot first under such circumstances would win. This one for a change was harmless, but we were alone in a Kübel, without an escort.

Finale

To our right the main effort toward Voronezh was moving forward. As we were protecting the left flank, we were hit by a series of Russian tank attacks. The fighting raged back and forth. At one time the tank battle was circling around my command car just like a carousel. From the vehicle's roof I had a grand view, and I was able to direct the battle from there. Gradually the adjacent units came up and we moved into a defensive line. One Russian tank attack after another rolled up against us every day. We shattered them one attack at a time before they even reached our front line. The area looked like a tank cemetery. Various models were out there, even English ones. My division so far had destroyed 160 Russian tanks with minimal losses. The long 50 mm and 75 mm cannons that had finally been retrofitted onto our tanks gave us back full superiority over the T-34s. We could stand up against them. But the Russians were good at setting up traps. Some of their light tanks would pretend to bolt in front of us. If we followed carelessly we would end up in a minefield and caught in a crossfire from the left and the right by camouflaged antitank guns and heavy tanks.

I was able to hand off a secured sector to the infantry unit that relieved us. But they were in bad shape. As I noted in my journal, it was "One antiquated outfit, not up to modern warfare. As is so often the case, such a unit lacks self-confidence, and no proclamation from the Führer can restore it. Only adequate equipment can do that."

I had made a specific arrangement with my chief of staff regarding leadership. He stayed with the divisional staff at a set location that was a little removed from the immediate battle action, maintaining contact with the higher headquarters and the adjacent units, and directing reinforcements to the front. Simultaneously, I remained mobile, leading from the front by radio or by personal orders. I was always at the respective key spot and could shift my position quickly.

I continued that command technique throughout my tenure as a division commander and never regretted doing so. I still consider the often practiced approach wrong in which the division commander and his chief of staff ride together in one vehicle. A vehicle breakdown or a battle accident can cripple the entire leadership structure in a stroke, and the inevitably greater radio traffic required by this method restricts mobility.

Although the losses during these actions were minimal, I was especially hard hit by one piece of news. During the campaign in France I had told the Fahnenjunkers[20] in my regiment that their shoulder boards[21] were waiting for them beyond the Maginot Line. Their losses had been disproportionately high. I did not want to make this mistake again. There would be time enough to die a hero's death as an officer, and then it was almost inevitable. I had issued clear orders regarding the deployment of the Fahnenjunkers to make sure that they received a certain amount of frontline experience, but that their losses would be manageable. So far that had worked out. I now had sent them home intentionally before the offensive, either on leave or to the basic officer course. In Bryansk the train they were on was caught in a bombing attack at night. Of my seventy young men, twenty were dead and thirty-five wounded. One should not try to manipulate destiny.

After we had been pulled out of the line, I walked with my chief of staff one more time back across the ground of the breakthrough at the Tym River. Comparing our initial assessments with the actual situation we had faced, we had been 99 percent correct, thanks largely to defectors from the other side. Walking the battlefields became a quiet but intense retrospective, especially when I had to ask myself at every grave if this could have been avoided or made more tolerable with a different approach.

Looking at the big picture, the results were not completely satisfactory. The Russian tanks had suffered heavily during their counterattacks, but the bulk of their divisions opposing us had evaded us masterfully. Using the fields of high grain and the countless deep ravines, they had managed to withdraw. We took a few prisoners and did not capture any guns. I saw only one anti-tank gun that they left behind. The blood losses of the Russians had not been excessive at all.

Heading North

We actually had been expecting to move south toward the Caucasus, but then the orders came sending us in the opposite direction, to the Second Panzer Army in Orel.

As a result of the previous Winter Battle, the positions in that sector were distorted in an unfavorable shape, all interlocked, entwined, and indented through the vastness of Russia. Realignment was necessary to free up extra forces. Such a shift could be accomplished toward the rear or toward the front. If we did it toward the rear, the message to the Russians would be clear that we did not intend to operate in that sector, and that would allow them to shift their forces at will, especially toward the south in front of our attack positions. If we aligned forward we could destroy their forces and leave them in the dark operationally. The apparent threat to Moscow would tie up their forces in the center, where they would not threaten us operationally.

The Battle of Sukhinichi

On the inner wing of the Second Panzer Army and the Fourth Army the Russians had managed during the winter to establish a deep salient that we sealed off with a great effort. Since then the Sukhinichi Bulge had been depleting our strength. Our intent was to attack it from three sides, destroy the forces inside it, and establish a shorter, less exhausting front line.

But then the Russians achieved some success at Rzhev, a situation that could have been deadly to us. The forces designated to attack into the salient from the northwest were then pulled out and deployed to the north.

After careful preparation the 11th Panzer Division attacked on 11 August. By that evening we were approximately in the center of the Sukhinichi Bulge. To our left, the XLI Panzer Corps attacking at the base of the bulge had only made insignificant progress. Its Panzer divisions had not yet been retrofitted with the improved main guns. The Russians, however, were totally surprised as usual, and initially panicked. The operations order of the infantry corps that my division was attached to directed us to continue to attack northward and then establish some maneuver space for the Panzer corps by striking southward. Additionally, I was to keep open the gap to the rear. Since all of these missions were too much for one division, I decided after a sharp confrontation with the corps staff to strike initially with all of my available forces toward the south, in order to link up with the XLI Panzer Corps. That was successful. The Russian forces in that area were completely annihilated. Now we had our hands free to strike toward the north.

In the meantime, the Russians woke up and were rushing toward us with the strongest forces from the north. Without interruption their aircraft, their artillery, and their Katyushas[22] were hammering at us. Then to our surprise the fully equipped 9th Panzer Division passed right through us. Why we had not waited to attack until they had moved up could not be explained. If they had been next to us on the day of the breakthrough, it would have been easier to exploit the total surprise of the Russians, but now it was too late. The Russians had used the time wisely.

The 11th Panzer Division now became part of the XLI Panzer Corps, which we welcomed. Our association with the infantry corps had not been a happy one. Instead of leading us, we only heard complaining: "Why isn't the 11th Panzer Division there yet?" Finally I radioed, "Request immediate visit by the commanding general by plane." That had shut the corps staff up, and when he finally arrived he landed to our delight in a hail of Katyusha fire that was quite intense.

The heavy fighting continued, during which we made daily gains against newly committed Russian units, but only painfully so. For days the heavy fighting raged without decision in the primal forests of the Zhizdra. By 19 August it became clear that our offensive had ground to a halt. As the heavy fighting continued I made the following entries in my journal:

21 August: "The Russians are attacking from everywhere. Suddenly they have a lot of artillery. All attacks have been completely repelled, except by our adjacent unit on the right."

22 August: "I was supposed to pull out the troops of the 20th Panzer Division, but also continue to spearhead the attack. That was crazy. Insane phone conversations with the higher headquarters. Additionally, there was the constant pressure that if a clear decision was not reached within the next half-hour, a catastrophe would befall us with unnecessary losses. I finally was able to assert myself. Just as it turned dark we moved back into a short, defined line."

23 August: "Again endless attacks. Prisoners are telling us that the slogan 'Victory or death!' has been put out. But the victory belonged to us and death belonged to them."

24 August: "Repelled strong attacks. Stalin's order was to hold at all costs. Smart propaganda among their people trumpeted the second front in France."[23]

A Russian battalion was supposed to attack at 1400 hours. However, it was delayed until 1800 hours because of the passive resistance of their troops, who then killed a political officer and defected. There would be more coming over, but the process of defecting was too difficult. If they tried to come over without a weapon they would be shot by their own people. If they came over to us with a weapon, we naturally would shoot them. We were too leery of their continued use of ruses.

At one point a unit of about fifty Russians was advancing against our positions through the high grain. Suddenly one of the Russians started to shoot his own comrades with his machine pistol and used the confusion to defect. He was a former tsarist officer candidate who now enthusiastically demanded to fight with us against the Bolsheviks.

25 August: "Fragmented Russian attacks were destroyed one after another by the concentrated fire from our divisional artillery. My superbly led 119th Artillery Regiment proved to be a wonderful main effort weapon. A winter position is being established in the rear, to which we are to withdraw slowly."

26 August: "Trouble at the adjacent unit on our right. I'm distrustful of such reports. Often they just want tank support, which they then commit incorrectly and turn them into battle losses. I therefore sent out a recon scout team to the adjacent division to clarify what was really going on. They first were to move up to the forward line and only then to the divisional staff in order to develop an unbiased picture. After two hours I received a classic message: 'Forward line is holding. Regimental commanders gone nuts. Division commander drunk. Leutnant X.'"

God protect the lieutenants of the German Army. Nobody on earth can replace them.

27 August: "Newly attacking Siberian troops have been repelled. We have to maneuver without reserves. The only reason we can get away with it is because our troops are so far above average."

29 August: "Yesterday's calm was a bluff. At 0130 hours all hell broke loose with fighter planes, artillery barrages forward, and harassing fires on all routes in the rear. Soon the reports started to come in. Tanks broken through everywhere and striking deep into the rear. Horrible moments, without a reserve. The first impression was everything had gone to hell. Then things started looking up. Somebody reported two Russian tanks destroyed, then seventeen tanks. Finally the picture clarified. The forward lines had held mostly, but several Russian tanks had broken through."

I had kept First Lieutenant[24] Piontek with the rest of my tanks on alert in the rear. Now I ordered him to go. He nicely managed to clean up the situation and to destroy the enemy tanks. Then we dealt with the bulges in the main line of resistance.[25] By the evening everything was in order. We were lucky that we had been able to separate the Russian infantry from their tanks immediately with machine gun fire and artillery and then destroy them both separately. In the evening I could see that my division had achieved a huge success. We had destroyed ninety-one enemy tanks, which made our total kill 501 since the beginning of the spring offensive. The Russian attack had been led by approximately two infantry divisions and three tank brigades of the IX Tank Corps. Hundreds of dead were lying everywhere.

We had not lost a centimeter of our position. The 11th Panzer Division was mentioned in the Wehrmacht daily report. Our number of destroyed enemy tanks was never equaled by any other division during the war. It was a huge success, but it was a fight that did not leave me satisfied at its conclusion, because of the stress and strain it inflicted. Our losses had not been minimal.

30 August: "A quiet day today. An older Soviet political officer defected today, something that had never happened before. He said he could not go on any longer, he could not stand the endless slaughter. Today in the afternoon a Soviet tank defected, with its gun tube elevated and a white flag flying. That was new, too."

Even though the division's leadership had worked out perfectly, the main credit must go to the courageous men in the front lines. Above all it was Lieutenant Piontek, the adjutant of the 15th Panzer Regiment, who led the tanks of the divisional reserve from one successful action to the next. Unfortunately, army group headquarters refused to award him the *Ritterkreuz*[26] because he had acted on orders rather than on his own initiative. Then there was Senior Corporal[27] Alois Assmann of the 61st Panzerjäger Battalion.[28] Wounded and only superficially bandaged, he destroyed eight tanks in one hour, during which time he had to turn his antitank gun around twice during engagements because enemy tanks were also approaching from his rear. He did receive the Ritterkreuz.

One of my lone tanks saw three T-34s approaching, destroyed all three, but also caught fire itself. The crew bailed out, rescued their wounded, returned to the tank and extinguished the fire, and then brought it back to our own lines.

One rifleman rushed up close against one enemy tank, ignited an explosive charge with a match, and saved himself at the last moment by jumping for cover before the tank blew up.

1 September: "The last few days have been relatively quiet. I was up front with the troops. I saw tank sitting next to tank, shot up or destroyed by raiding parties. The terrain looked like one big massive tank cemetery. I had never seen anything like it. The division can be proud of itself. The equipment of six enemy

tank brigades is scattered along our route of march, as well as in front of and even in our positions. We simultaneously destroyed the same number of enemy infantry divisions. Unfortunately, none of this translated into an operational success. But at least it looks like our counterattack broke off the Russian offensive."

3 September: "Two somewhat wild days. Yesterday I was in the front lines There was heavy fire. At noon the Russians attacked along the whole front. We stopped them completely in front of us. Again, there were hundreds of dead everywhere to our front. Unfortunately, the right wing of the 9th Panzer Division could not hold and the enemy broke through deep into my left flank and rear. Toward the evening we had taken care of that situation, too, except for one small bulge on the left flank. We destroyed thirty-five enemy tanks. Naturally, we too suffered losses that weighed especially heavily at this point.

"At night we harassed the Russians with loudspeakers. The defected political officer and other higher ranking Russian soldiers spoke back to their own lines. In the end we had forty-eight more defectors.

"Today at noon the bulge on the left wing was supposed to have been cleaned up in coordination with the 9th Panzer Division. Strong Russian artillery interdiction fire prevented us from accomplishing that mission completely. While that action was still under way, the left wing of the adjacent unit on our right collapsed. I had to decide to abort the attack on the left and throw my Panzer regiment against my right flank to stabilize the situation. The action is still going on as I write this. Slowly one reaches a state of psychological equilibrium that cannot be shaken by anything. Today during the height of the crisis we were laughing and bantering in our command vehicle. Hopefully, the Russians will soon stop these senseless attacks."

In the evening all the towns around us were in a state of chaos. The Russians had crashed into Kolosovo, and we were not able to clean up the mess completely. The commander of my Panzer regiment had nothing left to throw against them. Eventually I was able to help by making a slight adjustment of the main line of resistance. By midnight it was all over.

4 September: "Same routine as yesterday. First there was trouble in Kuvshinovo, where we destroyed ten tanks. That was followed by heavy attacks in Kolosovo, with the usual breakthrough and subsequent clean up. Thank God I have first-class artillery that always responds at the right time."

5 September: "Today at 0400 hours there was something new—a mass attack on Kolosovo in the early morning dawn. I had anticipated something like that. They had fired an artillery barrage with twelve batteries between 0300 and 0400 hours. Then the attack broke down rapidly.

"Now finally it is calm. Did they have enough? My troops are pretty worn out. I would like to take them back to the winter positions as soon as possible.

But higher headquarters does not want to pull back yet. This is a very exhausting form of fighting.

"We undoubtedly kicked the enemy's butt really hard. But with utter ruthlessness they threw human wave after human wave against us. Their officers stayed in their rear and shot their own troops from behind when necessary to keep them advancing. This happened frequently. But our loudspeaker propaganda produced good results. We took in many defectors, 150 collected by one of my battalions alone. Some one hundred more defectors in the same sector were mowed down by a Russian tank just as they were coming across. The Russians also abandoned three of their tanks yesterday. We put them to use immediately.[29] All of this indicates strong demoralization. But the enemy's leadership is too brutal. Up until now they have managed to crush all signs of weakness in their own lines. Will this keep working in the long run? I doubt it."

10 September: "For a few days now we have been pulled back a short distance. Our forward line had finally been withdrawn to form a shorter main line of resistance, which we had been improving for the last several days. That was a relief for the troops. They were quite worn out. The following report excerpt is a typical example of what they accomplished: 'the 61st Motorcycle Infantry Battalion had been engaged in combat action for three continuous weeks without relief. Within six days it destroyed eighty-five enemy tanks, fifteen of them in close combat action. The forward line of the battalion was often overrun by the tanks. The trenches that the enemy penetrated into were retaken every time through desperate counterattacks, man against man.'"

From 14 August through 9 September that battalion launched eight attacks, repelled forty-two enemy attacks, and launched twenty-three hasty counterattacks.[30] By the hundreds the dead Russians lay in front of and in the battalion's position.

And now the downside. The battalion's surgeon, Dr. Hellweg, wrote in a report on 4 September, "The health condition of the troops has deteriorated drastically. The troops are extremely exhausted. Their leaders can no longer motivate them. Everywhere there are cases of total exhaustion and weakness. Since food can only be brought forward at night, the troops have not had a warm meal in weeks. Add to that the effects of hypothermia in the trenches and foxholes. Infectious colds of the bladder and diarrhea are extremely common, without the possibility of treatment. Since the beginning of operations on 11 August the troops have not been able to wash themselves. They are dirty and covered with lice. Illness associated with poor hygiene is widespread."

That the battalion had accomplished so much under such conditions is to the credit of its commander, the tough Austrian Captain Freiherr von Hauser. But he was not only tough, he was also caring and skillful. He led from the front, conducting numerous, rapid, and unpredictable counterattacks, so that his unit was never taken under flanking fire and his soldiers were always able to counterattack from secure positions. Also, the battalion's very busy and caring surgeon, Dr. Hellweg, never wavered and made a major contribution to the unit's success. Dr. Hellweg was the best military surgeon that I knew in both wars. His name deserves to be remembered.[31]

Between Battles

The 11th Panzer Division was finally pulled out of the line. It left the field as a battle-hardened unit that had not known failure, only victory. Our losses had been heavy because we were almost always on the defensive. But the division's core held firm, and we received an unprecedented recognition. An after-action order of the Second Panzer Army read as follows:

Panzer High Command 2   Army Headquarters, 9 September 1942
The Commander in Chief

To the 11th Panzer Division:
    After the victorious conclusion of the fighting in the Voronezh Sector the division had been attached to the Second Panzer Army to assume a special attack mission.
    Faithful to the reputation that preceded it for outstanding combat accomplishments, gained in countless battles, the division once again has conducted itself in an outstanding manner. Committed in the most forward lines, it was the first to break through the strong and tenaciously defended enemy positions and it remained the pacesetter during the thrust toward the Zhizdra.
    Likewise during the ensuing, heavy defensive engagements, the division despite high enemy numerical superiority and heavy losses managed time and again to prevent an enemy breakthrough by launching counterattacks under the most difficult conditions.
    With the departure of the division from my command, I want to express my special thanks and full recognition to the officers, officials,[32] noncommissioned officers, and enlisted soldiers for your outstanding accomplishments. I am convinced that in the future the division will accomplish all missions with the same energy and motivation. I wish you success and soldier's luck.
    Signed Schmidt[33]
    Colonel General
    Commander, Second Panzer Army

Bryansk

The division's regiments were resting near Bryansk. I had entertainment organized for the troops. The old warriors were sitting in the theater. Full of expectations, their eyes were focused on the stage. An actor came out emphatically singing his song:

"Oh, what fun it is to be a soldier . . . !"

A booing and jeering chant swept through the audience. The actor recovered quickly and countered with another song:

"That cannot possibly rattle a sailor . . ."

The front line and the rear will never understand each other. This bordered on sabotage, but I laughed my heart out.

The division was billeted nicely in clean workers' quarters. The workers lived well, at least by eastern standards. The farmers did not. That was true for the Russian military, too. The majority of the Russian farmers served in the infantry, were badly fed, and often fought badly. The industrial workers served in the tank corps and as aviators and were better fed and fought better.

A doctor that had been on duty here for a long time told me that it had not been possible since we had gotten here to establish a brothel, neither here nor anywhere else. Since 1933 the family had been the official center of German life. Honoring your parents was expected, grandparents were addressed with the "formal you."[34] Sexually transmitted diseases were unknown. Of the thirty unmarried girls employed in the sector, twenty-eight were virgins.

Back South Again

The division rolled out by train, southward toward Stalingrad. I had driven on ahead. When I reported to the army group headquarters in Starobilsk I was told that all transports had been stopped at Voronezh. What exactly was going on there was unknown.

Throughout the fertile country, harvest and fall planting was going on. Then we continued moving back north again, to the Second Army. Nothing was going on there either, and the division got some well-deserved rest. The sensible commander in chief, General Hans von Salmuth, left us alone, and his chief of staff, my old comrade Major General Gustav Harteneck, took excellent care of us. After the incredible successes of our southern offensive there was a lot of talk about a separate peace with Russia. But that was wishful thinking. Unfortunately, we totally misinterpreted our successes.

Calm Days, Partisans, and the Rear

We were moved north into the area around Roslavl as a last resort reserve for OKH. The Russians supposedly were preparing an attack. Roslavl was full of rear-area types and supply units, approximately thirty thousand men. I had dinner with the commander of the rear area. He had opened a "house of depravity," with great food, a string quartet, friendly female artists—all just for a select circle. The man knew how to live. The Russian service girls naturally had all been checked to ensure they were anticommunist and they did not know a word of German. *Sancta simplicitas!*[35]

All military plans were discussed openly there. Roslavl was close to a huge forest area that was full of partisans. The lover of a Russian major who was serving with us was our primary source of intelligence on the partisans. According to her reports there were several thousand partisans in the forest in well-developed positions and numerous bunkers. If they attacked it would be impossible to hold Roslavl, and such an attack was to be expected any hour. Only a few thousand men were available for the defense. I was sitting on a powder keg.

At the Fourth Army headquarters of Colonel General Gotthard Heinrici, things were run with more discipline, in a clear, objective, and determined manner. The presence of the 11th Panzer Division was an opportune chance to clear the partisans out of the Roslavl forest. Considering the conditions in Roslavl, I requested that no specific orders be issued and that I be given a free hand. This was granted immediately.

Nevertheless, it was still like knocking down a hornet's nest. I received calls and offers of help from all sides. The "rear echelon heroes" did not want to miss out on the opportunity to improve their rations by trailing in the wake of a Panzer division. The worst was the call from a chief surgeon of a military hospital. He offered to accept the potential wounded of the division in return for two milk cows. He did not expect the answer he received.

I let some time go by for emotions to calm down. I issued a warning order initiating movement in the opposite direction, toward Smolensk–Rzhev. Then I sent out an advance party toward the north and alerted the division to be prepared to march either north or south. Finally I deployed my forces in concentric circles around the forest. In order to maintain immediate situational awareness, I moved with the most forward elements of the infantry that combed the forest. Initially one of my reconnaissance teams had one engagement, and we took several small camps and small ration caches. On the first day we captured approximately 150 men. On the third day strangers started appearing in the surrounding villages. It had gotten too cold in the forests for the partisans. From that point on they were easy to capture. They never had more than three thousand or four thousand men. They had not let anybody into their camps and their ration supply had been decentralized with the local farmers. Every one of them had been forced to establish a small cache, hoping too that we would not take it away from the farmers. One camp had a bakery. We also found two improvised airstrips with an airplane, with which they maintained liaison with Moscow.

I took control of the food supplies. The farmers were only allowed to draw small quantities, and the partisans therefore lost their base support in the area. They had lived safely and quietly behind the bogus intelligence that the mistress of the Russian major had passed on to us regarding their strength, their fortifications, and their intentions. Needless to say, the lady in question disappeared from that day on, never to be seen again.

The partisans had managed to survive so long because we had only been able to muster old and incapable troops against them. And they were no match for the partisans. When one such unit was committed against the partisans, the officer of the guard shot and killed one of his own sentries at night, which triggered a spasm of shooting and increasing ripples of machine gun fire, grenade launchers, and hand grenades. Finally, after hours of "bitter fighting," they finally realized that they had been playing a "lion's game." Two lions, as the fable went, entered the forest and ended up full of rage eating each other. The net result was two more Germans were killed and many more wounded. No partisans were involved in this fiasco. But when despite everything that unit submitted a mass recommendation for the Iron Cross, the sad truth of the affair came to light.

Otherwise the partisan war was conducted with a great deal of cruelty. Cases of cannibalism were credibly reported.

From Stalingrad to Kharkov

To the Quiet Don

I read in the Wehrmacht report that the Russians had broken through at the Great Bend in the Don River, and that countermeasures had been initiated. We were the countermeasures. My command car was sitting on a rail flatcar, while in cozy comfort we rolled along in the train toward the next huge mess. "There is one thing we must be clear about," I wrote in my journal, "obscure conditions, Russian breakthroughs, uncontrollably fleeing allies, and a division arriving piecemeal. This will be our lot. It will cost us dearly."

I had no illusions. The positive side was that the 11th Panzer Division was combat experienced and confident of victory. Personnel and equipment were at 100 percent strength. We were fully mobile. Unfortunately, Field Marshal

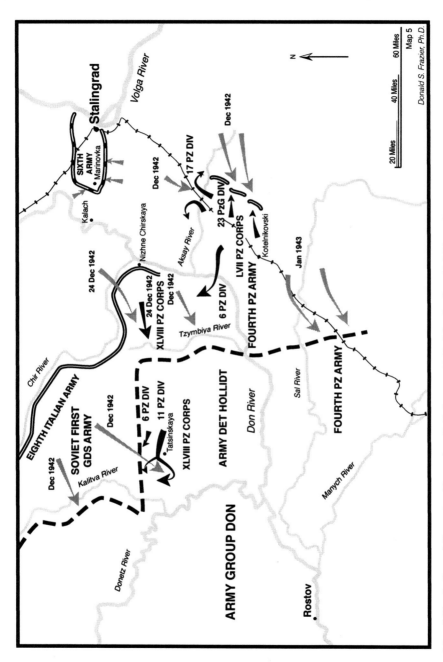

Map 5. The Stalingrad Campaign, December 1942–January 1943. (Map by Donald S. Frazier)

von Kluge had managed to detach the 3rd Battalion of my Panzer regiment. It remained in the north and was rusting away because of a lack of maintenance resources. As part of the division it would have been a great value. The technological aspects of warfare must be managed, too. Unfortunately, I was not able to get my way this time.

A few weeks previously Hitler had issued a very sensible order. Considering the certain difficulty of the coming winter, all commanders who were not up to handling the stress were to be relieved and replaced. I did that with commanders of one regiment and one battalion, much to the benefit of the troops. Now I felt I could rely completely on any of my commanders.

On 27 November the divisional staff was in Millerovo at the army group headquarters. The situation had calmed down a little. Along the Chir River a weak front manned by quick reaction forces was able to hold the line because the bulk of the Russian forces were tied down at Stalingrad. In the evening I went to see General of Infantry Kurt von Tippelskirch, who was babysitting the Italian Eighth Army. I wanted to develop a better picture of the situation. He welcomed me with the words, "I still often think of your excellent report on Hungary. You were the only one who dug below the surface and correctly analyzed the people." But Tippelskirch harbored no illusions about the reliability of the Italians.

Stalingrad was being held as a fortress. The Russians had broken through the Romanians from both sides and had encircled the German Sixth Army. Now we were preparing for the relief action. Field Marshal Erich von Manstein was now commanding the new Army Group Don and was in charge of the operation. The Romanians had taken off running like rabbits. You could not really blame them. Marshal Ion Antonescu had formed more divisions than he could equip and, most importantly, more than he had competent officers for. So, the end result was a bunch of ragtag units. Now the mess had to be cleaned up. I expected the Russians to continue to attack our allies along the middle Don in order to draw away our reserves that were assembling for the counterattack.

28 November: "Yesterday the storm was howling across the steppes and today there was a marvelous sky across the wide, beautiful land. Here everything was more friendly and clean looking than up north. Our village was quite nice."

You had to hand it to the Russians. Their leadership at the strategic-operational level was excellent. They had managed together with the Anglo-Americans in North Africa[36] to launch a major offensive in two decisive locations at the same time. Hats off to their clear vision, consistency, and organizational talent. It will always stand as an example of what a hard, brutal leadership under unfavorable conditions can wrest from even an unwilling people.

1 December: "Alarm at night."

We were supposed to move immediately to Morosowskaja to support the Romanian Third Army, where the situation was on fire. I managed to postpone the move by twenty-four hours, and then I drove there with Kienitz. The commander, Lieutenant General Petre Dumitrescu, was handsome in appearance and had a most impressive personality. The Romanians themselves said of him that he "looked like a European." He carried the fate of a beaten battlefield commander with much dignity. For two days now Colonel Walther Wenck,[37] formerly the Ia[38] of the 1st Panzer Division, had been serving as the chief of staff there. With the help of construction battalions and rapid response forces they had managed to establish a new front line along the Chir River. But along the sixty-kilometer front line they had only one lone field gun and one mobile field howitzer. Since the Russian priority was to break the resistance at Stalingrad first, the Chir front line had been able to hold, and hopefully would continue to hold until our deployment was complete.

The primary thing to worry about was whether the Russians to our rear on the middle Don River would be able to break through along the boundary between the Hungarians and the Italians. That was where the Russian forces were assembling. We set our countermeasures in motion, but would we have enough time? Our railroad network in Russia was not at all capable—and it never would be.

The Russian I Tank Corps

7 December: Even before we arrived the 336th Infantry Division under Major General Walter Lucht had arrived at the Chir and had been committed along the river line. While I was reconnoitering at the Chir the bad news came in that the Russians had broken through the advance lines and were at the deep left flank of the 336th Infantry Division. I drove immediately to Warche–Solonowski, where the staff of the 336th was located. They made a calm and amiable impression. I established my divisional command post right next to theirs. That was against all the standard procedures, but it worked out perfectly in the end. Both divisions now came under the XLVIII Panzer Corps, commanded by General of Panzer Troops Otto von Knobelsdorff. His chief of staff was Colonel Friedrich-Wilhelm von Mellenthin. An exceedingly harmonious relationship between Mellenthin and me developed that would last throughout the rest of the war.

On 8 December everything was ready for the attack. It was critical to be an hour earlier than the Russians at the decisive point. That was the rule we followed almost daily from there on out. Unfortunately, the situation was so critical at that point that I could not wait until I was able to commit the whole division together.

In order to screen the 336th Infantry Division, I had established a blocking position made up of air defense units, engineers, and antitank guns. It was rather obvious that the Russians intended to overrun the 336th Division. When the Russians got ready to attack the next morning we were right there. They did not suspect our presence. The 15th Panzer Regiment, under its tested commander, Colonel Theodor Graf von Schimmelmann, was followed by the 111th Panzergrenadier Regiment. Both of my regiments hit the Russians in the rear, just at the moment they were starting to advance to the East. First they annihilated a long column of mechanized infantry, and then the mass of the Russian tanks that were attacking the 336th Division. I positioned my approaching 110th Panzergrenadier Regiment toward Sovkhos 79,[39] where another significant number of Russian tanks were cut off in the valley. We could see tanks, trucks, and Russians running back and forth nervously. By that evening the Russian I Tank Corps had ceased to exist. Fifty-three Russian tanks had been shot up on the steppes.

Sovkhos 79

As I drove through Sovkhos [State Farm] 79 a horrible picture unfolded before me. The supply units of the 336th Division had been staged there. By the hundreds our brave soldiers had been brutally slaughtered. They had been surprised and destroyed by the Russians in the early morning hours.

That scene made one basic fact clear. This was all about the existence or nonexistence of our people. Would it be possible in the face of this extremely tense situation and the endless Russian onslaught to protect the Fatherland? We believed and hoped that we could. I summarized the situation in a divisional order of the day, one of the very few that I ever published:

11th Panzer Division
Staff Section Ic[40]

Comrades,

The Bolshevist cruelties at Sovkhos 79, where several hundred German soldiers were slaughtered by the Russians, will remain in our memories forever.

The interrogation of the prisoner of war, Sergeant Ivan Jakovevich Kurilko, from Kharkov, born 1918, 1st Company, 346th Tank Battalion, 157th Tank Brigade, resulted in the following information: At a meeting shortly before 19 November 1942 (in preparation for the brigade to attack the Romanian Third Army) at which all brigade and bat-

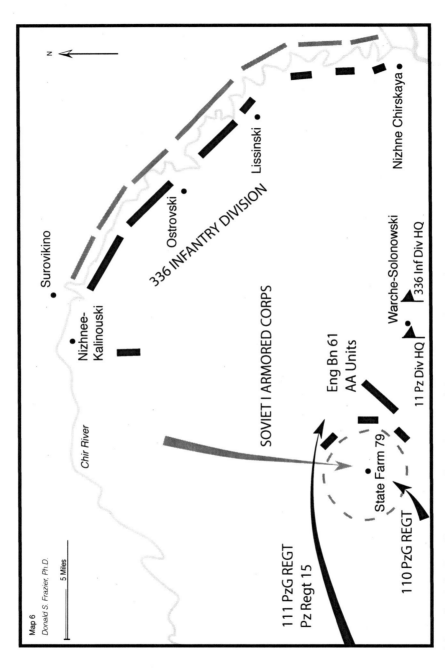

talion commanders were present, two Romanians were brought before them who supposedly had deserted. Those assembled were told that these were Romanians, and that Romanians were to be taken prisoner. They were ordered, on the other hand, to take no German prisoners.

They were ordered not to shoot Romanians in front of Germans, but to shoot Germans in front of Romanians. This statement corroborates what we have seen with our own eyes at Sovkhos 79. It is also consistent in all details with the repeated announcements in the Anglo-American press calling for the complete eradication of the German people.[41]

In total contradiction to this, as all of you know, is the dishonest Russian propaganda that promises German defectors and prisoners safety and return to the Fatherland after the war.

Comrades, the tough days of fighting that are behind us now show us anew that this is about the existence or nonexistence of our people. If in the future you waver in your courage, should you grow weak during the bitter fighting, always remember the Anglo-American hate tirades, the slogans of the 157th Russian Tank Brigade, and the horrible sights at Sovkhos 79 that prove to us without a doubt the fate that will await us if we do not win this fight.

Signed
Balck.

Based on this order, claims were later made that I had ordered the shooting of all Russian prisoners. I never again released such an edict. Its sole purpose had been to show everybody what our situation was in the big picture and what was at stake. I found other ways to tell my people the truth.

On the Chir River

The 336th Infantry Division was positioned solid as a rock on the Chir River. Everything depended on it holding fast, even in the most desperate situations. It was the shield and the pivot for all of the operations of the 11th Panzer Division. The 336th understood its mission completely. Showing strong nerves, the 336th mastered every crisis it faced. That made it possible for the 11th Panzer Division to attack the Russians with concentrated force anywhere they broke through. General Lucht never lost his nerve. He never in a crisis interfered with the units of the 11th Panzer Division. Without this shield, the successes of the 11th Panzer Division would have been unthinkable. The tight cooperation between the two divisional staffs bore unimaginable fruit. Unfortunately,

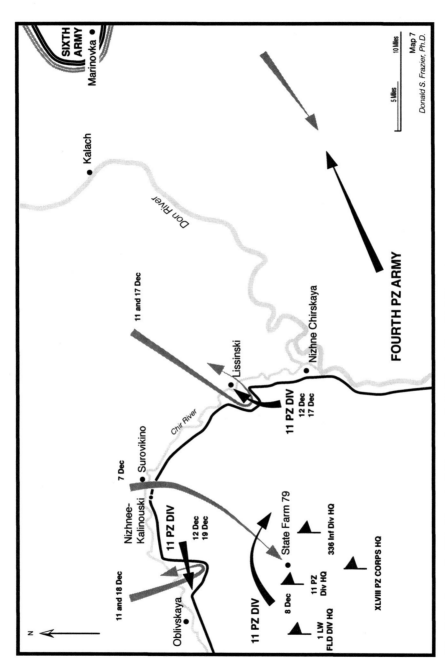

Map 7. Battles on the Chir River, 8–19 December 1942. (Map by Donald S. Frazier)

the equipment of the 336th Division was sparse. It was especially too short of antitank guns for its mission. That, of course, only made their achievements all the greater.

From 9 December through the 17th the days were all the same. The Russian forces would break through at location X. We would counterattack, and in the evening everything was back to normal. Soon, another report would come in of a deep breakthrough at the position of some rapid reaction force. We would turn around with lights blazing, tanks, riflemen, artillery driving through the winter night. We were ready the next morning at dawn. Positioned at the Russians' weakest point, we would bear down on them in surprise and destroy them. The following morning we would play the same game ten or twenty kilometers farther to the west or east.

It was a complete mystery to me when the soldiers actually slept during those nine days. One tank crewman had added up the hours of sleep he had gotten during those days. Even if I had doubled the count it still would have been totally implausible. At the same time the fighting was not as easy as it may sound here. Quite often elements of one of my units were overrun by the Russians, encircled, and had to be extracted. Additional enemy forces always tried to exploit any successful attack. But our losses were not that high because we used surprise to our advantage. "Night marches save blood" became the slogan in the division. I often yelled to the men, "What do you want to do, bleed or march?" "Let's march, Sir," came the answer from the tired and worn-out faces.

With delight we followed the initial successes of Colonel General Hermann Hoth's Fourth Panzer Army. The more enemy forces we drew toward us, the easier would be the mission of the Fourth Panzer Army. "Is our adversary the Fifth Tank Army still there, or did they march off against Hoth's army?" That was the daily critical question. Then a report would arrive: "Tanks broken through at X," and the reaction would be, "Thank God, they are still here." We developed a unique system for issuing orders. My General Staff officer Ia, the brilliant Major Kienitz, sat in one position a little toward the rear and maintained radio contact with me, the higher headquarters, and everyone else. I remained highly mobile, moving to all the hot spots. I usually was at every regiment several times a day. While still out on the line during the evening I drew up the basic plan for the next day. After communicating by phone with Kienitz, I drove to every regiment and gave them the next day's order personally. Then I drove back to my own command post and spoke by phone with the chief of staff of the XLVIII Panzer Corps, Colonel von Mellenthin. If the commanding general Knobelsdorff concurred, the regiments received the short message: "No changes!" If changes were necessary, I drove at night one more time to all the regiments so that there would not be any misunderstandings. At daybreak I was always back at the decisive point.

The Russians fought fanatically at times. One Russian tank that had been hit was sitting behind our front lines for days, and I passed it frequently. Then a German staff car stopped next to it and the crew got out to take a closer look. Suddenly the turret cupola opened and a Russian popped up, threw a hand grenade, and disappeared back inside the tank. The Russian tank was finally destroyed with a shaped charge, but the Russian crewman had to have been waiting for his chance for several days.

The new 1st Luftwaffe Field Division[42] arrived in the sector. It was magnificently equipped and had good and willing people, but they had no real training. They were absolute military novices. During any action they did not even have the capability to maintain their supply of rations and ammunition. After a few days the division evaporated, an ego toy of Göring, who wanted to form and control his own ground divisions, rather than subordinate them to army operational control. Virgil's proverb, *Quidquid delirant reges plectuntur Achivi*,[43] was a fitting description of these brave troops. Göring had been popular once, but by this point in the war he had lost all of our respect and he would never regain it.

My troops were outstanding. During those days I saw nothing that did not make me proud of them. Even the attitudes of the wounded at the aid stations were exemplary.

The Soviet Motorized Mechanized Corps

The 11th Panzer Division had just stopped a deep Russian breakthrough with a swift counterattack when an order from corps headquarters arrived: "Suspend current attack. Russian forces broken through in-depth twenty kilometers farther west." That was the usual in the evening. I answered Mellenthin: "Fine, we will clean up right here first and then we will take care of the other problem."

"No, General, this time it is more than critical. The 11th Panzer Division must go there immediately, every second counts."

"Okay, we will take care of it."

So we halted our attack, refueled immediately, and distributed rations. I issued the warning order: "Get ready to move in the direction of Nizhnee–Kalinouski. Twenty kilometer march distance. Drive with headlights on. On 19 December in the morning you will be deployed as follows: the 111th Panzergrenadier Regiment secures the right flank of the attack against Nizhnee and Kalinouski; the 15th Panzer Regiment penetrates into the enemy left flank; the 110th Panzergrenadier Regiment deploys on the Line A–B against the Russian attack, artillery, . . . etc."

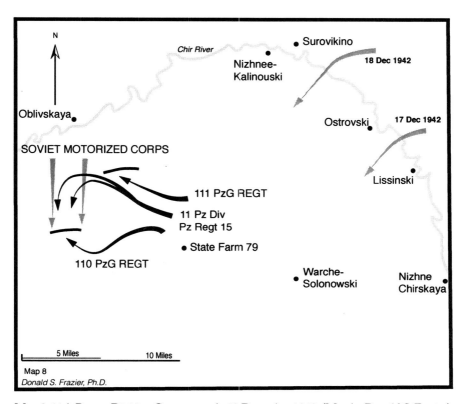

Map 8. 11th Panzer Division Counterattack, 19 December 1942. (Map by Donald S. Frazier)

Tanks, infantry, and artillery all lumbered off into the dark night. At 0500 hours the Russians arrived. Their tanks and other formations were rolling past us toward the south. Then Schimmelmann[44] released Captain Karl Lestmann's element.[45] Just like in a training area, our tanks pivoted around and followed the Russians. The Russians had no idea that the tanks following their columns were German. In just a few minutes Lestmann's twenty-five tanks destroyed forty-two Russian tanks without any losses. Then they disengaged and prepared in the hollow of a valley for the second Russian wave. As the Soviet tanks moved across the crest of the ridge our guns fired from below. Again, the fight was over in a few minutes. Twenty-five German tanks had shot up sixty-five Russian tanks without a loss. The accompanying Russian infantry escaped initially, but then a Russian relief attack broke down with heavy losses. The Soviet Motorized Mechanized Corps had also ceased to exist. Shortly thereafter I moved among the still burning enemy tanks, thanking my courageous troops. Gone was the strain of the previous days, as the smiling faces of the unbeatable force peered out from their turrets.

On the 21st the division was in defensive positions when at 0200 hours Kienitz woke me up. All hell had broken loose from all directions. The 110th Panzergrenadier Regiment had been penetrated and the 111th Panzergrenadier Regiment overrun. The 15th Panzer Regiment radioed that the situation was very critical. In the bright light of a full moon the Russians had attacked with tanks and infantry right at the seam between the two Panzergrenadier regiments.

Much of the situation had already been consolidated by the time I arrived at the scene. I immediately threw the tanks and Hauser's motorcycle riflemen into a hasty counterattack to close the gap between the two regiments. By about 0900 hours everything was pretty much back in order. Russians by the hundreds lay dead in front of and in our positions. Our defense had been a solid success, but not without the cruelties of war. Russian tanks had crushed some of our wounded on the ground, who then froze in that position. When my troops saw what had happened they became uncontrollably mad, which is quite understandable.

Our losses had been considerable. It was not an easy time to be a commander. Even if the old eastern front proverb held that if the day starts out miserably, it usually ends with a major success, it still was never easy in the face of the flood of bad news messages to remain calm and focused. There were times when I thought that the division actually had ceased to exist.

But the situation along the Chir River had been stabilized, and all was now quiet. All of the subordinate corps of the Soviet Fifth Tank Army had been eliminated, one after another, and mostly by the 11th Panzer Division. If the Fifth Tank Army had attacked with all of its corps simultaneously across the Chir we could not have stopped them. We would have been overwhelmed by the Russian masses. But the Chir line held. Part of our success was a function of the poor training of the Russian troops. We had been able to manipulate them. On 12 December the 11th Panzer Division was again mentioned in the Wehrmacht report.

The Dike Breaks

There was no relief in sight for the 11th Panzer Division. On 23 December we received a most cordial farewell from the XLVIII Panzer Corps, from Knobelsdorff and Mellenthin. We had had a very positive association with that corps, based on trust and honest camaraderie. I also had a farewell drink with General Lucht at the courageous 336th Infantry Division, and then we moved off quickly to Morozovsk, to the Romanian Third Army.

That was some situation we encountered. Paraphrasing Queen Elizabeth on the Spanish Armada, I could only say: *Stalinus afflavit ac dissipati sunt.*[46] The Italians had been swept away and the Russians unopposed were thrusting south with multiple tank corps. Hitler had ordered Morozovsk held at all costs.[47] One Russian tank corps was advancing from the north toward the town, with our fire brigades[48] in its path. The Russians also were feinting an encirclement of Tatsinskaya on the left. The situation was desperate and the only hope was my tired and worn-out division, which was arriving piecemeal. I strongly voiced the opinion that the situation was so hopeless that only boldness could overcome it—in other words, an attack. Any defensive solution would result in destruction. The first order of business would be to destroy the enemy's western column, in order to clear our rear area. Our fire brigades would have to hold out for one more day. There was no other alternative. Thank God the German chief of staff of the Romanian Third Army was Colonel Wenck, a man of strategic vision and strong nerves and the old Ia of the 1st Panzer Division. He agreed with me completely and the glorious old Lieutenant General Dumitrescu accepted the responsibility completely.

The Russian XXIV Tank Corps

Without waiting for reports, I decided to advance immediately to the position where the Russian tank corps had advanced across the Bystraga sector. We would certainly hit something there. Everything else would just have to fall into place.

24 December: It was a ragged bunch of German forces that punched into the Russians' flank and rear that morning. I had only twenty tanks, one battalion with the strength of a company. But I also had the mass of my still intact divisional artillery. Everything else was on the road moving up. But what would have been the additional benefit of four more battalions, each with the strength of a single company and hardly any heavy weapons left? Nonetheless, I had hardcore soldiers with me, and we knew what we wanted.

I drove closely behind the lead tank. We encountered no enemy forces short of Skasyrskaya. It was therefore clear that the Russians were farther along, at Tatsinskaya. Reports started to come in confirming this. We took Skasyrskaya in an intense fight against a Russian battalion supported by tanks. That in effect cut off the Russian main route of retreat. I issued orders over the radio to deploy my rearward regiments that were now arriving in the sector concentrically toward Tatsinskaya. Meanwhile, I monitored by radio the enemy's reactions. The Russian XXIV Tank Corps radioed to its units: "Enemy tanks in our rear. All tanks assemble on me at Hill 175." That location was exactly where my plan would put them in a pocket. Thanks to their cooperation, we had the Russians encircled inside of the pocket by the evening. They formed a huge "wagon fort" right around Hill 175. Unfortunately, it was too late at that point to fire our artillery effectively against them.

In the evening I was sitting comfortably together with old Dumitrescu, who by now was quite relaxed and relieved. The fire brigades had all held their positions as well as they could and our own 6th Panzer Division was arriving. The Russians were stunned and hesitant along the whole front.

25 December: We tangled with each other all day long in the pocket and pushed the Russians into Tatsinskaya, but in the end we could not crack the pocket. There apparently were many more Russians inside the pocket than there were Germans outside of it. In the evening they were preparing for a new attack, with which I had very little to oppose. Thank God I had received operational control of one regiment and the assault gun battalion of the 6th Panzer Division to break the Russian stronghold. The next day was not going to be easy.

26 December: A day of rage. At first everything went very well with Hauser. In coordination with Lestmann he took Krujkoff at night. Now we knew for sure that there was nothing of significant strength left in our rear. Nothing went right at the pocket, however. The assault gun battalion did not arrive. It had lost its way and was unavailable for an entire day. Since I only had eight operational tanks, I was not able to crack into the Russian stronghold by myself. We could only shake our clenched fists at them in frustration. Tomorrow would be another day.

27 December: Our concentric attack on Tatsinskaya was starting to strangle the enemy, but his resistance was still significant. At least we were wearing him down significantly. We had destroyed twelve enemy tanks, but it was hard to estimate what they had left in the cauldron. At the minimum they still had one tank brigade with strong infantry forces, most likely the 24th Infantry Brigade. The XXIV Tank Corps headquarters also was certainly trapped in there. We intercepted a radio transmission to them: "Hold out. Five infantry divisions are coming."

Very close to us a Russian plane landed, took off again, and was then shot down. The two pilots were killed. Their charts and papers did not contain anything of importance. Perhaps they had been trying to extract the commander of the XXIV Tank Corps from the pocket. They had landed exactly where his command post had been located two days earlier, and where mine was now.

28 December: "Today the pocket exploded. Of course, the events played out differently than we had anticipated. Yesterday in the bright moonlit and starlit night I had pushed on everybody to continue to attack. This morning at 0500 hours I was about to drive to the front when my aide reported to me that the Russians had broken out toward the northwest. That figured." Our night

attack hitting them from all sides had forced them to take that action. Elements of the Russian forces had broken out in the sector of the 4th Panzergrenadier Regiment.[49] I drove forward. From all sides my regiments were entering the town, breaking the remaining resistance. Only about twelve Russian tanks and thirty trucks had managed to break out of the pocket. Everything else was destroyed, dead Russians were everywhere, only a few escaped. That was the end of the XXIV Tank Corps. We also hunted down and destroyed the twelve tanks and thirty trucks. The trucks got stuck at a creek, and we burned several of the tanks. We had accomplished all of this with a spent division that started with only twenty operational tanks. By the time it was over we had eight to twelve tanks still running, but otherwise our losses had been relatively minor.

The troops had been marvelous. Despite unbelievable hardships the morale was excellent. Of course, the incredibly well-stocked supply depots in Tatsinskaya where everybody had been able to resupply themselves contributed to that. Wherever I drove the troops threw chocolate, cigarettes, and salami into my car. "We have to take care of our general too!"

We could never be beat with soldiers like this. Whoever has lived through such a completely hopeless situation and has seen how certain defeat was turned into a victory could never doubt the victorious outcome of this war.

The area was now operationally calm and we were scheduled to be withdrawn. The Russians had taken a bad hit here, and there would be a crisis somewhere else. We left the area with a great deal of satisfaction. The 11th Panzer Division had the singular fortune to take on an enemy twice its strength and win a Cannae-like battle. The Russians had been led by their own Terrentius Varro,[50] who played his part nicely. Maybe it was also an omen that my divisional staff had the codename designation of HANNIBAL.

As soon as we had seized Tatsinskaya, the customary reports about the Tartars came in. Fresh strong enemy forces were attacking near Skasyrskaya. I quickly turned the division around. By 1145 hours the 15th Panzer Regiment and the 110th Panzergrenadier Regiment under the steadfast Colonel Albert Henze had attacked and thrown back the Russian 266th Infantry Division, which the previous night had marched blindly into Skasyrskaya, ignorant of the overall situation. By this time we were very experienced in executing turning movements.

Happy New Year

On the last day of the old year the 11th Panzer Division held a broad front in the Titzul sector. I had reorganized the division to address disparities between supply elements, vehicles, and combat power. I dissolved the Panzerjäger[51] battalion and organized both the Panzergrenadier regiments into one battalion each. The intent was to make the division more mobile and harder hitting. Now we were no longer slowed down by countless extra vehicles moving as a separate formation.

I drove to all the regiments to ensure that they understood the reorganization and that the implementation would be completed by the next morning. "Guys, today is New Year's. The Russians will take advantage of it, so just cancel the New Year's brouhaha for once and remain alert." That was my final warning.

"But, of course, Sir." Happily they waved as I left. I could still hear in my mind the greeting of the marvelous Colonel Alexander von Bosse: "Hello, hello General, Sir, Happy New Year."

The divisional staff had set up the command post at the Don River bridge, even though it certainly did not belong there. We destroyed one Russian tank almost in our quarters. Russian planes bombed the bridge that night. It was not light yet outside when Kienitz stood at my cot with a somber face. "All hell has broken loose again. The division was overrun tonight. We do not have contact with anybody."

So, the damned New Year after all. Now it appeared to me that there had been the smiles of Augurs on all the faces as I delivered my parting warning.

But that could not be helped now. I got into my Kübel and drove off. A short distance from town I ran into five of my tanks. I transferred to a tank and took off with them. They did not know anything about the situation. Then I ran into a battalion of the 15th Panzer Regiment. The situation was still unclear, so I gave the order to move forward and attack the next village. There we found a Panzergrenadier regiment that had established a strongpoint against Ivan. Our attack resolved that immediate crisis. Then it was on to the next village. It was the same picture there. Schimmelmann stood next to his tank and dryly reported, "They did celebrate New Year's after all." Finally the rest of the division arrived.

When we were able to assess the battle damage we found that nothing much had actually happened, except that the Russians had suffered senseless losses. Alcohol in a good unit is totally harmless; in a poorly led one it spells catastrophe.

Hermann Balck's great grandfather, the Hannoverian Major General Lütgen.

Hermann Balck's father, Lieutenant General William Balck.

Hermann Balck as commander
of the Sixth Army, 1945.

Hermann Balck's son,
Friedrich-Wilhelm Balck,
was killed in action in
June 1941.

Hermann Balck's son-in-law,
Senior Lieutenant Hans-Heinrich
Schlenther, was killed in action at
Stalingrad.

Hermann Balck as a child in his parent's house.

Hermann Balck (*seated middle*) as an officer candidate, 10th Jäger Battalion, Goslar.

Hermann Balck (*second from left*) as watch commander, Dom Kaserne, Goslar.

Balck's officer candidate tactical officer, Lieutenant Hans Kreysing, 1913.

The Guderian family (*left to right*), Heinz Guderian, Lieutenant Colonel Friedrich Guderian, Fritz Guderian, and Clara Guderian. Photograph taken in Bitsch, Lorraine, while Friedrich Guderian commanded the 10th Jäger Battalion.

Officer Candidate Hermann Balck, Christmas 1913.

Hermann Balck and his father in 1914.

Prince Leopold of Bavaria (*third from the left*), commander of Army Group Prince Leopold, visiting the 10th Jäger Battalion.

Captain Heinrich Kirchheim, commander of the 10th Jäger Battalion, wearing the *Pour le Mérite* and Alpine Troops Edelweiss badge.

Officers of Volunteer Jäger Battalion Kirchheim pulling security on Germany's eastern border in the autumn of 1919. Hermann Balck is the third from the left in the front row, and Heinrich Kirchheim is seated in the center of the front row.

Balck and his father, who was then the commander of the 51st Reserve Division. Note that both are wearing the Iron Cross 1st Class.

Rittmeister (Cavalry Captain) Hermann Balck, commander, 2nd Squadron, 18th Cavalry Regiment.

Adolf Hitler and Minister of War Colonel General Werner von Blomberg visiting Balck's unit at Frankfurt am Oder in 1935.

Balck as the commander of the 1st Bicycle Infantry Battalion in Tilsit in 1935.

Balck's unit loading in Patras, Greece. *Left to right*: Unidentified escort officer; Hermann Balck; Lieutenant Rämsch (Balck's adjutant); Field Marshal Wilhelm List; and Lieutenant Colonel Decker (Balck's successor as commander of the 3rd Panzer Regiment).

Lieutenant General Albert Henze, commander of the 110th Panzergrenadier Regiment when Balck commanded the 11th Panzer Division.

Colonel von Bonin, Balck's chief of staff when he commanded the XIV Panzer Corps in Italy, 1 September 1943.

Staff of the XLVIII Panzer Corps during the battle at Brusilov in 1944. *Left to right*: Major Erasmus, operations officer; Hermann Balck; Major Kaldrack, personnel officer; Colonel Friedrich-Wilhelm von Mellenthin, chief of staff.

Balck speaking with SS-Oberstgruppenführer Joseph "Sepp" Dietrich.

Balck in a situation conference with General of Panzer Troops Erhard Raus.

Balck as commander of Army Group G, with Field Marshal Gerd von Rundstedt, Commander in Chief West, and General of Panzer Troops Otto von Knobelsdorff, commander, First Army.

Balck in his command car as commander of Army Group G.

Situation conference. *Left to right*: General of Infantry Otto Wöhler, commander of Army Group South; Colonel General Heinz Guderian, chief of the Army General Staff; General of Infantry Hans von Greiffenberg; General of Panzer Troops Hermann Balck, commander of the Sixth Army.

Major General Helmut Staedke, Mellenthin's successor as chief of staff of Army Group G.

General of Panzer Troops Hasso von Manteuffel.

General of Panzer Troops Walther Wenck.

A German Panzer negotiating its way through thick Russian mud during the late autumn of 1941. (National Archives, NARA0509033j)

A German machine gun crew in a street in the suburbs of Stalingrad. (National Archives, NARA0509018j)

15

1943

Nothing New in the East

Nothing changed much between 1 and 23 January 1943. Our first reinforcements arrived. The Russians had been hit really hard and in some ways the situation had stabilized. But according to my journal there were only three days during that period we did not fight and, of course, days off did not exist.

The engagements mostly followed a common pattern. The Panzergrenadier regiments moved into an extended position, and the Panzer regiment attacked to the front of them and destroyed everything that moved toward us. Then we would have some peace while the Russians turned toward an adjacent unit, which I then supported with the Panzer regiment. Thus, a peculiar pattern emerged with something like the adjacent units fighting a downstairs war, while we were fighting upstairs. This process worked well. I naturally spent a lot of time at the adjacent units to coordinate the support. Colonel General Karl-Adolf Hollidt had replaced Dumitrescu. He and his chief of staff, General Walther Wenck, had been at General Friedrich Mieth's IV Army Corps when I provided some support to that unit. After that, Hollidt thought that the 11th Panzer Division should now come under Mieth's corps. Mieth, however, vetoed the idea, saying that coordination was now working so well that it could only get worse if the command relations changed. I was pleased by that decision, even though I have to admit that pure self-interest required me to commit all means at my disposal to support the units on my flanks. Following are some excerpts from my journal:

8 January: "The Russians have broken through the unit on my left. Why? The troops are really worn out, far beyond good or bad. Also, they might not have received clearly the order that we were supposed to hold at all costs. And finally, you just had to consider what we had available there—battalions made up of soldiers in leave status, supply clerks, etc. Despite all that, what we managed to accomplish will remain forever an unforgettable achievement in the pages of German military history. It has been a battle unlike any other.

I decided to push north on this day to give the unit on my left a little more breathing space. As usual, the Russians attacked at 0300 hours. Every unit in my sector was holding, but the Russians kept advancing on my left and were soon into the center of the operational sectors of the divisions on my flank. Then the immediate counterattack by the Panzers and the motorcycle infantry took effect. For sixteen kilometers my Panzers advanced into the enemy's flank, overrunning everything in their way. My motorcycle infantry made good progress, but the German division to my front, which actually consisted of only two reinforced battalions of soldiers in leave status, was screaming for help. The Russians had gotten really close. My Panzers, however, were positioned on the far side of a long, steep canyon, and their route of withdrawal was in danger of being cut off. Reluctantly I decided to recall the regiment. Tomorrow would be a difficult day. I did not know yet if my Panzer regiment would be able to return intact. They were calling for fuel. There was also some concern whether or not "Division G" could hold. I had talked to G[1] for about an hour today. He was like a sick horse. He was finished. Even though he was senior to me, he was asking me for orders. I referred him to his corps commander. The communications lines to army headquarters had been cut, but I finally got through to army group headquarters. It is never easy to remain steadfast in such situations. If I could get my Panzer regiment out of its tight situation, I had hopes of making it through tomorrow.

9 January: My Panzer regiment made it back safely. Their thrust deep into the Russian rear had its effect, and they did not budge at all that day. I took advantage of this and cleared a town in the south that they had taken from one of our disastrous makeshift units. We destroyed three enemy battalions in the process.

Unfortunately, G got nervous at daybreak and sent out all sorts of doomsday messages and interfered with my movements. That caused some unfortunate delays, and consequently I did not get quite as far as I had intended. But the day was still a complete success. Now the 7th and the 23rd Panzer Divisions were in position to attack the next morning from the north. For some peculiar reason the Russians were only attacking with infantry. They apparently had no fuel and serious supply problems, because Stalingrad was blocking all flow of their supplies.

10 January: The daily situation reports did not accurately describe the situation. On a forty-kilometer-wide front line three German battalions with a combat strength of 150 men each were being attacked by a Russian corps. Whenever the Russians broke through, hastily assembled reserves then overwhelmed and ejected the attackers. Every day it looked like everything was drowning in the red flood, but by the evenings the Russians were reeling back, beaten. Here and there individual German troop units failed, which was not surprising considering that many battalions were made up of bakers and other rear echelon elements that had no real combat value and were not even capable of supporting themselves.

As for my own troops, the incomparable Hauser with his 61st Motorcycle Infantry Battalion was down to only two companies. Attacked by a regiment, he held the enemy with one company and hit them in the flank with his other company. The Russians fell back, and Hauser received a well-deserved Iron Cross Knight's Cross. It is impossible to reward such troops adequately. When I visited the motorcycle infantrymen everybody was happy and cheerful. As the situation allowed, I was able to assemble them in the forwardmost line and thank these faithful men personally. They looked audacious, unwashed, and unshaved. For days they had been sleeping outside in sub-zero Fahrenheit temperatures, but they were quite alive and feisty. With such soldiers and officers you could do anything. Hauser took good care of them. Behind the front he established warm-up trucks with iron stoves, and at regular intervals everybody had an opportunity to thaw out for two hours.

At about the same time the totally exhausted and cut-off 336th Infantry Division got up and attacked due east. The Russians were pushed back everywhere. Active defense was our great strength. Without it we would have long since drowned in the red masses.[2] It was about that time that Pannwitz came through my headquarters, as I described earlier, on his way to Hitler's headquarters to receive his Knight's Cross. He had done magnificently with Romanian troops at Stalingrad.

The Fate of the Caucasus Front

Operations now focused on the control of Rostov. That was the bottleneck through which our withdrawing Army Group Caucasus had to pass. The Russians were closer to Rostov than was Army Group Caucasus. Even though some new units had arrived, the covering force near Rostov that was supposed to screen the withdrawal of Army Group Caucasus was pretty thin. Our major advantage was that we were still holding at Stalingrad, and that in turn tied down significant Russian forces and blocked their supply lines. Combined with our intense strikes, the Russian movement from the Don River Bend toward Rostov was reduced to a snail's pace. The situation along the Manych River was different. Strong Russian forces had penetrated the Manych line and were advancing toward Rostov. On 22 January the 11th Panzer Division reached Rostov and we finally were given a so-called rest day.

The III Guards Tank Corps

All elements of the 11th Panzer Division crept slowly across the jammed-up Don River bridges from the European to the Asian side. Together with the 17th Panzer Division and the 16th Motorized Infantry Division,[3] we were to destroy the spearhead of the enemy attack that was approaching Rostov from across the Manych River. By the time we finally reached our jump-off positions we had run out of gasoline. I drove up to the lead unit in a rage. But that, of course, did not get us any fuel. The Fourth Panzer Army urged us to speed up, but that did not do it either. Everything behind us was hopelessly congested. I finally allowed the troops to move into quarters and wait for fuel.

The next day, 23 January, matters improved. At 0500 hours we were rolling again. By 0700 hours we had penetrated two Russian positions, along with the 16th Motorized Infantry Division. When I stopped in my Kübel in the newly taken position, somebody yelled out, "That Russian there is still alive!" Seconds before the Russian could wreak havoc with his machine pistol, my quick-witted adjutant jumped him in the snow and took him out. We continued the attack until we came to a halt in front of Manychskaya. The Russians were radioing for fuel, reporting that they had only fifteen tanks left.

On 24 January we reached the Manych crossing site at Manychskaya, which was held by the Russians as a bridgehead. Their tanks were dug in and they held out against our three attempted attacks. Our troops had long since learned how to fight such battles, and our losses stayed relatively small. Instead of remaining in their positions, however, the Russians had a tendency to run away from our tanks and suffered horrific losses under our fire.

On 25 January I attacked Manychskaya again, using a very carefully developed fire plan and timeline. To lure the Russian tanks out of their entrenched positions I directed against another location a substantial and long fire preparation with all available batteries firing mixed high explosive and smoke rounds. The scout cars, armored personnel carriers, and trucks then feinted a strong attack in the smoke. Sitting up on a hill I observed how the dug-in Russian tanks came to life, left their positions, and drove toward the rear of the position of the ruse attack. Quickly, then, the fires of all available artillery were shifted to the location of the actual attack. Only one battery continued to fire smoke rounds in the direction of the feint attack. Then I launched my tanks.

The Russians collapsed. We caught their tanks from the rear, destroying approximately twenty-two. Their infantry launched a series of senseless counterattacks, and then was destroyed while retreating. My motorcycle infantry and tanks pursued the fleeing enemy until late at night. The III Guards Tank Corps had been destroyed. Our losses were one killed and fourteen wounded. It had been one of those rare actions where I had managed to control both the enemy and my own troops according to a firm plan. Nonetheless, we could not quite enjoy this success, even though it was so decisive for the overall situation. In the evening of that very successful day I wrote in my journal:

"Stalingrad weighs heavily on all of our minds. A heroic fight beyond comparison is coming to an end there. It remains questionable if we will still be able to extract the remnants of the Sixth Army. Supplying them is very difficult because they have lost all their airfields. On the other hand, they continue to block all the Russian lines of communication and are blunting the force of their southern wing. The question arises if it would not be better to abandon Stalingrad. I believe extraction would have been possible if the Italians had held their lines. If the extraction does not succeed, and that is very likely now, those troops are lost. How many? Nobody knows for sure. They naturally are exaggerating their reporting numbers for supply accountability, so that the difference of several tens of thousands is likely. Approximately forty thousand wounded have been flown out. Many have died. But there are still large numbers remaining. But we must remain hard during these changing wartime situations. Changing situations have always existed. However, with million-man armies, the numbers are naturally higher than during Prussian times."[4]

A Rifle Corps

There was no quiet time for anybody, and especially the 11th Panzer Division. On 28 January we were assigned to the LVII Panzer Corps. We absolutely had to hold, as behind us the First Panzer Army was withdrawing [from the Caucasus] toward Rostov. The divisions of the LVII Panzer Corps were like islands in a sea of red waves. The likely encirclement of the LVII Panzer Corps was looming, with the Russian masses approaching from the flanks and rear. I decided to advance on a broad front of four columns on the morning of 29 January. I gave the appropriate orders, and sent Kienitz to the corps headquarters. He had instructions to report to higher headquarters that changes were no longer possible.

I spent a cozy evening in the small house of a teacher. A clever device fed sunflower seeds into her stove, filling the room with a comfortable warmth. A balalaika hung on the wall. It had the most beautiful sound I ever heard. The people and the land here were different than in the North. The treeless countryside, showing all the contours in an even more pronounced way, had its own charm, especially when the setting winter sun covered everything in a violet light.

The inhabitants were not excited about the approaching Reds. We were in the lands of the Don Cossacks. Everything was clean and refined. Oddly enough, those people did a lot of painting. Almost every third or fourth house had an amateur painter. They seemed to concentrate on three primary themes. The most common one was a manor house set in the middle of a well-kept garden full of flowers. A lady in a formal dress sat in the middle of the garden feeding the swans, while doves brought her letters or roses. Another theme was the duck hunter; and the third was the "Bogatyr," the hero of the ancient legend.[5] The buried soul of a people? Who knows?

As the morning of the 29th broke I drove out to my left column, my Panzer regiment. When I got out to where they were supposed to assemble, they were not there. The only thing I found was a sack of straw with a wolf standing next to it. He took off as soon as he saw me. Finally, after a long delay, I saw a long line of tanks, looking more gigantic than normally as they emerged from the fog and the snow. Then Schimmelmann drove up in a staff car. As he got out he reported to me, "Lestmann, as you know, received the Knight's Cross yesterday, and they are all still drunk. The two of us will have to lead the advance party."

There was nothing we could do about it, so we both drove ahead of the tanks, crisscrossing and taking turns leading, while the herd of elephants followed faithfully in our tracks. When after a long march we approached the village of Kamenyi, Schimmelmann said, "Others can take over now; I think we will be all right." He was correct.

As the tanks advanced through the fog and the snow down into Kamenyi, all hell broke loose. Within ten minutes we had captured thirty-two guns and destroyed a very surprised antitank brigade. Then the general conflagration broke out all along the front line. The Panzers and attacking infantry destroyed the Russians, battalion after battalion. By nightfall we had the remnants of an infantry division and two rifle brigades encircled southwest of Metschetinskaja.

I spent most of that night making telephone calls. Army headquarters wanted us to move north, because a new crisis was emerging there. I argued fiercely for cleaning up my present situation. They finally conceded. On 30 January at 0500 hours we were at the ready. It turned out to be a successful day. We completely destroyed whatever was facing us or had already been encircled. The members of the enemy divisional staffs tore off their rank insignias[6] or committed suicide. When in the evening we were able to assess the results, the 11th Panzer Division had captured the following in two days:

17 antitank guns, 47 mm
81 antitank guns, 76.2 mm
3 field guns 105 mm
4 field guns 120 mm
2 infantry guns
92 antitank rocket launchers
24 infantry mortars

The Russian 248th Rifle Division and two additional rifle brigades had ceased to exist. We also captured several thousand prisoners and twenty-two camels. We were in Asia and camels were pulling the guns here. The prisoners included old men and children with little training.

On 2 February my division was pulled out of the line. "I reported one last time to General Friedrich Kirchner, the LVII Panzer Corps commander, my old division commander from the 1st Panzer Division. In those earlier days we had not always gotten along, and there was still some bad blood between us. But in the current situation it was more important to focus on our mutual interests and responsibilities. It was a pleasant meeting."

Twenty-one years later I received on 3 February 1962 a note from Colonel General Hermann Hoth, stating, ". . . without the 11th Panzer Division we [Fourth Panzer Army and First Panzer Army] would not have gotten out."

It was a difficult war. The Panzer divisions were covering forty- to eighty-kilometer fronts and had to hold those lines against overwhelming enemy superiority. We managed because of our superior leadership and high mobility, but it took a toll on our equipment. After very little maintenance for a period of weeks the vehicles started to malfunction in large numbers. The resulting horrible surprises made it impossible to be sure that anything would go according to plan. At the completion of the current operation we were supposed to receive a period of rest, but the old warrior in me remained skeptical.

Stalingrad

The battle for Stalingrad that had overshadowed everything else came to an end. As I wrote in my journal at the time, "The heroes of Stalingrad have given their lives to buy the time necessary to open up the new front." The German forces at Stalingrad had tied down the majority of the Russians, blocked their supply lines, and thus established the conditions to establish the new front line necessary to withdraw our armies from the Caucasus, and to stabilize the horrible situation that our allies left us in by withdrawing without much of a fight.[7] Was all the sacrifice worth the outcome? This question has been examined repeatedly, and rarely has it been addressed objectively because of bias and political orientation.

In the winter of 1941–1942, Hitler's order to hold in front of Moscow had undoubtedly saved the German Army. But what had been right then was wrong in late 1942. Hitler had a tendency to use over and over again any measures that had proved successful once. He was quite obstinate in this sense. In contrast to the situation of the previous winter, the problem at Stalingrad could only be resolved at the operational level. The situation then was a classic model of the type of problem the German General Staff was the master of. It required only one order: "Field Marshal von Manstein, take charge of the forces from the Caucasus to Voronezh and reestablish the status quo ante."

But Hitler could not and would not give such an order. Without doubt the dictator's fear of having to stand in the shadow of a successful combat commander had something to do with it. And within the Nazi Party, Göring and Himmler especially were opposed to any such course of action.

Since the previous winter, Hitler had been opposed to operational art.[8] Mistrusting as he was, he was afraid that the end result of an operational solution would be withdrawal, certain defeat, and his own demise. Another key reason was that Hitler saw himself conducting an economic rather than a military war. He saw the advantage of controlling the Caucasian oil fields and the Donets Basin, and the disadvantages for Russia if those resources were lost.

World War I had influenced Hitler's thinking and his objectives. Back then, when defensive weapons were stronger than offensive weapons, hold fast orders were feasible, especially considering that divisional sectors were only three to five kilometers wide. The same order in the 1940s, when the offensive weapons were superior and the frontline widths ran from twenty to forty kilometers, was impossible to execute regardless of any level of leadership expertise and courage of the troops. Russian human waves and massed tanks swept everything away. Hitler could not accept that reality. Thus, the German military leadership had its hands tied. But rather than revisit a detailed review of the events, I want to describe the more fundamental reasons for the disaster as I saw them.

One question remains to be resolved: were the supply operations for Stalingrad correctly organized? It is not a case of perfect hindsight to state that sufficient fuel, ammunition, and rations should have been stocked in Stalingrad itself. Such supplies had no value sitting behind the Chir River. Considering the faulty logistics organization, the dangerous situation in which we found ourselves at Stalingrad was predictable.

Paulus

Aside from Hitler and Manstein, Field Marshal Friedrich Paulus was the third key figure in this drama. I had known him for several decades. During World War I in the Alpenkorps he was the adjutant of the 2nd Jäger Regiment, to which my 10th Jäger Battalion belonged. Paulus generally had no contact with the officers of the subordinate Jäger battalions. He was overshadowed by the forceful personality of our regimental commander, Lieutenant Colonel Bronsart von Schellendorf, a typical aristocrat from Mecklenburg. There was no sign of an independent mind in Paulus. He always had the exact same opinion as his regimental commander. Bronsart von Schellendorf finally relieved him for failing to demonstrate the necessary resolve in a tough situation. After that, Paulus's career as a General Staff officer on the staff of the Alpenkorps started.

Paulus and I served together in Stuttgart for quite a while between the wars. He was a company commander in the 13th Infantry Regiment; I was a squadron commander in the 18th Cavalry Regiment. We also spent some time together on several General Staff rides, and once during a maneuver as escorts for Seeckt. The Paulus I knew in Stuttgart was very different from the person I had known during the First World War. I came to see him as smart and highly educated, but also as a shy and sensitive human being. Above all, I considered him a noble and honest individual. Since our Stuttgart days we ran into each other frequently at OKH.

Paulus spent almost his entire life serving in staff positions. He never had made a decision on his own. He just received decisions and then passed on orders to be executed. He was a typical man in the background, irreplaceable and of the highest quality when led by a strong hand, as for example by Reichenau. But Paulus was the man who ended up in a messy situation because of Hitler. It was a situation in which the only thing that counted was your own inner strength. As the weak man that he was, he remained true to what he had always done; he presented facts, asked for decisions, and then turned them into orders for others to execute. Nor had Paulus been properly groomed for command. He moved from being a chief of staff of an army immediately to army commander. He skipped the positions of regimental, divisional, and corps commander.

Paulus cannot bear all the blame for Stalingrad. Stronger and tougher soldiers could well have failed in such chaos. Would the Sixth Army have been able to break out of the Stalingrad Pocket? To where could it have moved? Reserves that could have relieved the Sixth Army did not exist. The assembly of the necessary reserves on the opposite bank of the Don River Bend had been neglected for too long, until there was no longer sufficient time to do so. The danger in any attempt to break out of an encirclement is that the troops, or at least a large portion of them, will lose their cohesion, and a mentality of "Save yourself at all costs!" takes over. In this case, any routed mass of combat ineffective human beings would have quickly been destroyed by the Russians in the vicinity of Rostov. I had seen this scenario play out during numerous Russian breakout attempts from encirclements. I had a good appreciation for the difficulty of such an operation, and what the proponents of a breakout would be saying after the fact. And what would have become of Army Group Caucasus?

In the hands of someone like Hoth, the commander of the Fourth Panzer Army, the five Panzer and three motorized divisions in the vicinity of Stalingrad, even though they were not at full strength, could have destroyed any Russian attempt at encirclement. Here for once, the organizational structure was the decisive factor in success or failure. The second opportunity for a breakout was when Hoth's Fourth Panzer Army attempted a relief attack and got as close as forty kilometers to Stalingrad. Any breakout attempt at that point, of course, did run the risk of disintegrating into a panicked rout. In any event, it was never attempted because supposedly there was only enough fuel in Stalingrad for the tanks to go another twenty kilometers. Based on my own experience with fuel reports, I think the tanks could have made it another forty to fifty kilometers. Fuel reports almost always underestimated, but Paulus apparently accepted the reports at face value, rather than checking himself.

Be that as it may, no hindsight wisdom can change the fact that inside the pocket everyone from field marshal[9] to the lowest-ranking man did what he could do. Only someone who has never borne the responsibility of such decisions would cast stones at these men. We held them all in awe, and even then we knew that they had saved us.

The disasters at Stalingrad and North Africa happened at the same time. The flood was reversing against Germany. It was a serious warning not to conduct operations beyond one's own limits, when secure supply lines and the rapid movement of reserves from far in the rear to a sudden point of crisis were no longer possible. Both Stalingrad and El Alamein were far beyond such limits.

The Destruction of Popoff's Fifth Shock Army

The Situation

Immediately north of Field Marshal Erich von Manstein's Army Group Don, the Italian Eighth Army and Hungarian Second Army of Army Group B had withdrawn without putting up much of a fight. They left their artillery and heavy weapons behind. The troops threw away their rifles. Some of the staffs just drove off. In short, a huge hole in our lines opened up all the way to Voronezh, into which the Russians poured without resistance and cut off Manstein's army group. A second, much larger "Stalingrad" was looming. Thank God Manstein had the authority to maneuver more freely and thus thwarted the Russian shock armies. Manstein managed to develop a contiguous front line along the lower Don and Donets. Behind this rather fragile shield the army group pulled the First Panzer Army under General Eberhard von Mackensen out of the Caucasus and to the north, deploying it against the southern flank of the Red Army, which was advancing in our rear. Meanwhile, we assembled another force to commit against their northern flank.

Our Allies

During those days we naturally did not think very highly of our allies. Fairness requires me, however, to explain some matters. I knew all three of them, the Italians, the Romanians, and the Hungarians, mostly from my frontline experience in World War I. The impressions I formed then remained generally valid and unaltered. I respected the Romanians, more than the others. They were courageous, but they did not have modern equipment. They had too many units, but not enough officers, and even the greatest amount of courage did not help. Nonetheless, the war still had a certain amount of purpose for the Romanians.

The Italians were never good soldiers, with the notable exception of certain units like the *Alpini* and some *Bersaglieri* regiments. Napoleon had spoken rather disparagingly about the Italians. The Russian campaign was for them a misunderstood cabinet war in which they thought they had no part. Nor were they used to the climatic conditions in Eastern Europe. None of these factors increased their enthusiasm for the war.

The Hungarians were similar to the Italians in terms of their combat value. The enlisted soldiers of the Hungarian Second Army were drawn mostly from Hungary's recently regained territories. Almost all of them had returned to Hungary reluctantly because of its misguided Magyarization policies.[10] Also, the Hungarian units received rather ambiguous orders from Miklós Horthy, the regent of Hungary, who played both sides. What were these troops doing on the Don River? Fighting for a Hungary that they despised? Despite a lot of goodwill among their officer corps, I always judged the Hungarians as being capable of fighting only in the Carpathian area, and only against Romanians and Slovaks.

Their liability as a military force was compounded by the fact that all three nations wanted to fight in their own armies only, and they did not have any modern equipment. Their respective heads of state who insisted on maintaining their own armies were ultimately responsible for the deaths and imprisonment of thousands of the poor devils. *Quidquid delirant reges, plectuntur Achivi.*

That we even counted these units as a factor in the correlation of forces can only be explained by the fact that we were intoxicated by the idea of forty extra divisions and we totally misjudged the discounted value of their defensive capabilities against modern weaponry. The attack had become the stronger form of combat, and the three allies could never stand up to it. It would have been better if they had been formed into regimental-sized units with artillery and engineers and subordinated to individual German divisions. Used as relief forces or to spell German units in the line, they could have served some purpose. Or, we should have done without them completely and have based our operations at a much lower level of risk. In the end, what we did was add several more points of catastrophic vulnerability to an already overstressed situation. Hitler's policy had done substantial damage.

Toward the North

The 11th Panzer Division moved north behind the First Panzer Army. We were to push north from Kostiantynivka along the western bank of the Krivoy Torets River. The division advanced painfully northward through miles and miles of workers' housing areas, fighting house to house. Our opponent was a unit we knew well from the battle of Sukhinichi, the III Tank Corps, followed by the IV Guards Tank Corps. Both corps were worn out. After several days we had managed to fight our way through the twenty-four-kilometer-long line of housing areas. It had all been pure street fighting, during which the combat took an unfortunate turn. I had attacked before every one of my units was assembled. I did exactly what I had so often criticized others of doing. The division's first failure was my fault.

We approached the industrial town of Kramatorsk, which we failed to seize. Every day we tried to take it from a different direction. Even though the control of Kramatorsk was of decisive importance, I avoided getting drawn into street fighting. Considering the Russian expertise at such fighting, it would have resulted in getting the division tied down unnecessarily. If an objective like Kramatorsk did not fall to the first attack, or even after changing the direction of attack, it was better to bypass it.

During those days we were able to determine the enemy's intention by monitoring his radio traffic. The Fifth Shock Army was to push southwest and position its corps according to assigned coordinates. The III Tank Corps had read the coordinates wrong and had marched southeast instead of southwest, where we defeated it. The III Tank Corps also dragged the IV Guards Tank Corps behind it and into the maelstrom. Now the army commander, General Markian Popoff, attacked with extreme force. He managed to extract the IV Guards Tank Corps and turn them toward the southwest. The X Tank Corps, meanwhile, was still in Kramatorsk.

Even though the 11th Panzer Division failed to take Kramatorsk with a pincer attack, we were able to destroy a fast-approaching Russian infantry division and keep the X Tank Corps and the remnants of the III Tank Corps bottled up inside the city. Almost all of the enemy's tanks had been destroyed. The Russians, meanwhile, were still interpreting our probing attacks as break-out attempts from the encirclement they thought they were forming around us, while we in fact were encircling them.

I had always argued for bypassing Kramatorsk and advancing south of the city into the rear of the Fifth Shock Army. Unfortunately, the leadership of the XL Panzer Corps, to which I was attached, did not concur with that course of action. They believed that we would not be able to complete the advance because of the deep snow. The Russians too considered the snow to be an absolutely effective flank protection.

Now the staff of the XL Panzer Corps was moved south around the other side of the forming encirclement, and I was assigned to the First Panzer Army. I drove to the army headquarters and presented my estimate of the situation. Mackensen, who never risked a unit unnecessarily, concurred with my assessment, saying, "With a unit like the 11th Panzer Division you can take such a risk." Thus, on 18 January I was able to withdraw my division from the fight for Kramatorsk, which the Russians took as an indicator that they were winning.

After commandeering every snowplow I could find, we launched on the morning of the 19th. The plows led the way, driven by an assortment of old rear-area souls. I had an energetic officer on every plow, followed by motorcycle infantry, then tanks. The division headquarters followed closely behind the plows. Other snowplows followed to keep the route of advance open.

After two hours we stood astride the Russian avenue of approach. The enemy was completely surprised. Initially we only encountered recovery tanks and repair details. Then we pushed farther south. My Panzers entered the village of Novotroitsk on a broad front. I parked my Kübel next to Schimmelmann's tank and then sent my IIa,[11] Major Kaldrack, to ask Schimmelmann to come over and ride forward with me. Kaldrack came back saying, "Sir, the *Graf*[12] said that there is still heavy fighting going on in the village, and whether you would not rather join him in his tank."

"Nonsense, you cannot see anything from a tank. I want Schimmelmann to come with me."

Kaldrack came back again, "I am supposed to report from the Graf that if the general does not behave and come forward with him in his tank, he will not go."

What else could I do but laugh and jump in Schimmelmann's tank. The thrust of the 11th Panzer Division meant the end of Popoff's Fifth Shock Army. Attacked from the rear and completely surprised, the IV Guards Tank Corps was the first to break apart completely; the others followed. By the time my division finally pivoted toward the north, there was no more fighting, only pursuit, during which we passed, cut off, and destroyed one Russian combat group after another. When we reached the Krivoy Torets River near Barvenkovo, the Fifth Shock Army had ceased to exist.

Barvenkovo, which was strongly reinforced, fell through an attack into its rear. I let my 15th Panzer Regiment, together with the 7th Panzer Division on its right flank, break through and take Barvenkovo from behind. The 7th Panzer Division was more than happy to add my Panzers temporarily to its strength. Rigid and inflexible attack zones should be avoided in a tank war.

The point of decision now shifted toward Kharkov, and the 11th Panzer Division was now ordered to that hot spot. Prior to leaving we received an especially warm farewell memorandum from General von Mackensen:

First Panzer Army   Army HQ, 2 March 1943
Telegraph Message

To the 11th Panzer Division,
    Following four weeks of the hardest winter attack operations, the 11th Panzer Division is assigned follow-on missions and is now released from the operational control of the First Panzer Army. I greatly regret having to let this outstanding division and its much proven commander move on. This brave division has repeatedly in this winter battle added success upon success, fulfilled all of its missions, and has operated at the peak of its performance capabilities. The division was committed deliberately by me and its commanding general to the critical points of the operation. It was, therefore, the soul of the attack of this army, specifically securing not only the necessary space, but also destroying the enemy forces. The 11th Panzer Division has proven itself repeatedly to be the master of such situations. It is with great pride that I express my high and grateful appreciation to the division and wish it and its commander further battle success in the name of the whole Panzer army. And most especially I personally salute you with the words,

Farewell until we serve together again,
Signed von Mackensen,
General of Cavalry

The Crisis of Trust

The fall of the Sixth Army in Stalingrad naturally had its consequences. Recording the mood of the times, I wrote in my journal:

8 February: "There is a feeling of numbness. Mechanically we execute order upon order; but there is an end in sight. The III Tank Corps that we destroyed over the course of the last three days had nineteen tanks left when the battle started, and only four of those escaped. Everything else was destroyed. Tomorrow the IV Guards Tank Corps is supposed to arrive on the scene. It still has thirteen tanks, so the fighting is clearly moving to an end state. The Russians are running out of the forces to continue operations with any real punch."

10 February: "Today Kaldrack came back from OKH. The tension between Hitler and the generals is quite strong and spread throughout every senior staff

section. Paulus had sent Hitler a last message saying that he should listen more to his military advisors. The offensive into the Caucasus was an overreach of our strength. The clearest indicator of an overextension is always that small mistakes become decisive; small mistakes that happen by the dozen have no consequence as long as your strength is still sufficient.

"We have to play for low stakes for now; but at some point in the future there might be opportunities to do more again. There is, however, only one right thing to do now, and that is to stand as one behind our leadership without complaining loudly and destroying trust. The division of labor between Hitler and the generals will self-correct. Manstein would be best as commander in chief of the army."

17 February: "Visiting higher headquarters is not very pleasant right now. All you hear is constant criticism of our most senior leadership. There may be a lot to criticize, but the complaining will not improve matters. Our situation is certainly not pretty, but we will manage if everyone remains positive. That is what we are lacking. It is a shame that there never developed any real sense of trust between Hitler and the generals. That is the source of all our ills. It started with the Blomberg Affair and our attitude toward the Nazi Party and all their reactionary gibberish. Brauchitsch never took a clear stand politically, and he failed because his own uncertain position robbed him of any credibility with those above or below him."

During the previous winter Hitler had saved the army in spite of the generals. But what was right in the previous winter, stubbornly holding on because the snow made any kind of operational options impossible, was a major mistake this winter, because operations were possible in the more favorable snow conditions. Unfortunately, we make those kinds of mistakes and are therefore always too late and always behind the decision curve. Thus, the sharp criticism from the generals was justified in this case. The solution that everyone in the army was looking for was the passing of the command in the East to Manstein. We could no longer afford to indulge in nonsense.

Ironically, Hitler during the first years of the war always made decisions of great audacity; but by now he had become hesitant and he only made half-hearted decisions. He stubbornly insisted on holding gained territory, even when the situation made it necessary to yield ground. Perhaps he became insecure because deep inside he knew that the limits of German strength had been pushed beyond the culminating point, but he could not accept the fact. Regardless of what the answer was, we had reached a critical high point of our history and of the war.

We underestimated the Russians. In 1942 they intentionally evaded us. No doubt they did so under our pressure and to a much greater extent than they had intended; but their counteroffensive was well planned, well prepared, and brilliantly executed. Wisdom *post festum*.[13] I also underestimated the Russians considerably. Now we had to prepare to fight on the defensive along the shortest possible line, and pay a high price in the process.

Farewell to the 11th Panzer Division

While in the Kharkov area my reassignment orders to the Leaders Reserve[14] caught up with me. My time as a division commander was over. It was time to say farewell. At such a juncture it is certainly appropriate to take stock. The first question a soldier must ask himself is: "Were successes and losses in the right proportion?" During the first part of our advance on Voronezh we suffered only minor losses. The fighting and the losses in the Sukhinichi Bend had been heavy, but our losses were far lower than those of the enemy.

The conditions during the current winter were different still. Below are the division's statistics for the period between 7 December 1942 and 31 January 1943—in other words, for the two months from the Chir River until the end of the fighting east of Rostov:

	enemy losses	11th Panzer Division losses
tanks	225	16
scout vehicles	12	4
guns	35	0
antitank guns	347	12

Our losses and breakdowns in motor vehicles had been high. We lost 745 motor vehicles, of which 450 were being repaired in maintenance shops; and we lost 280 motorcycles, of which 100 were being repaired.

The enemy's personnel losses were estimated at 30,700 dead. This high number was the result of the Russians' tactics and organization, which consisted of untrained human waves supported by numerous antitank guns, but with hardly any artillery or any other heavy weapons, committed in tightly packed formations against our fires or against our tanks. Added to those killed in action outright were those who later died from wounds. Were the estimates of the enemy dead correct? I really cannot say for certain. In the excitement of success troops will always exaggerate these numbers. That is most likely the case here, too. Our own losses during this period were as follows:

Killed in Action:	215, including 15 officers.
Wounded in Action:	1,019, including 47 officers.
Missing in Action:	155, including 3 officers.

The day I relinquished command, the division destroyed its one thousandth enemy tank since I had taken command. But here again, there remains that small question mark. The discrepancy between our own losses and the enemy's can be explained by the badly trained Russian units and their lower-level leadership, which was not up to task. They went up against Graf von Schimmelmann and his tank regiment, one of the most combat-effective units I ever encountered. The vastness of the steppes and the lack of follow-on forces on both sides combined to bring out the natural superiority and the self-reliance of the German soldier in a way that was not often seen.

The 11th Panzer Division had been formed on 1 August 1940 from the 11th Infantry Brigade, which originally had been formed on 1 December 1939. The division's main units were the 15th Panzer Regiment, and the 110th and 111th Panzergrenadier Regiments. The division was assigned in December 1940 to the XIV Army Corps (Motorized) as part of the Twelfth Army of Army Group B in Poland. It served with the Twelfth Army in Romania and Serbia and then under the XLVIII Panzer Corps in action at Zhytomyr and Uman. It was part of the Sixth Army for a short while at Kiev. Subsequently, as part of Panzer Group Four [later renamed Fourth Panzer Army] it pushed as far as Vyazma and a short distance in front of Moscow. During 1942 it saw action near Gzhatsk [now Gagarin], Orel, Voronezh, and at the Don and Donets Rivers. From February to June 1943 the 11th Panzer Division was committed near Kharkov. It then passed through Belgorod, Poltava, Kremenchuk, Cherkasy, and Chişinău back toward Iaşi. In June of 1944 the division was transferred to the West, where it served under me when I commanded Army Group G.

But now it was time to say farewell. I managed to visit almost all units one more time and to thank the troops and the officers. I could with good conscience recommend all of my regimental commanders for divisional command.

Theodor Graf von Schimmelmann became a general officer in Jutland. His ancestry, family connections, and language skills particularly suited him for that assignment. I would have liked to see him as a divisional commander. His leadership abilities were unique and desperately needed in a longer war. Unfortunately, my successor[15] had problems with his rather bold but fitting sense of humor and his nonchalant manner, which he also used with his superiors. I never missed a chance to visit with Schimmelmann after the war.

Albert Henze, the quiet, calm, steadfast commander of the 110th Panzergrenadier Regiment did become a division commander. He was captured by the Russians in the Courland Pocket. He remained always upright and courageous and he went through the inferno as the gentleman that he was, admired by all who were with him.

Paul Graf von Hauser, the commander of the 61st Motorcycle Infantry

Battalion, became as a colonel the last commander of the Panzerlehr Division in April 1945. There was not a better officer for that assignment. Smart tactically and highly educated, he combined a strong will, courage, and intellect. He had what Clausewitz called that rare *Harmonie der Kräfte.*[16] During the capture of Berlin Hauser was reported to have been shot and killed by the Russians. I saw the detailed reports from the alleged eyewitnesses. As I write this, however, he is alive and living in Vienna.

Colonel Schmidt was the seasoned commander of my artillery regiment. Together with his excellent staff, he always knew how to mass fires quickly on the decisive point, thereby contributing to the success of the division time after time. He did not survive the war.

Alexander von Bosse, the Baltic-German commander of the 111th Panzergrenadier Regiment, was Russian-educated with native fluency in Russian as well as in German. He became the commander of the 1st Cossack Division. Through sheer coincidence, he had erroneously been declared dead, which prevented him from being handed over by the English to the Soviets with other Cossack leaders. During my farewell visit with him he raised his glass and said, *"Herr, bleibe bei uns, denn es will Abend werden."*[17]

It was hard to leave my staff behind. Kienitz, my faithful and proven operations officer Ia, stayed with the division. He died shortly after the war. Kaldrack, my division adjutant, was killed defending his home estate in Pomerania. Knorr, the assistant Ia and later the division adjutant, became a state attorney in Bamberg. How often did he brighten my serious hours with his sense of humor. My security detail officer was killed as a tank commander soon after I left. I cannot mention them all, but I must thank them all.

The Leaders Reserve

My tour of duty as a division commander was over. The follow-on assignment to the Leaders Reserve was intended as a needed time for recuperation. Even generals get worn out. Also, an officer's time in the Leaders Reserve was used to evaluate his capability for assignment to the next higher position.

Upon leaving the eastern front I notified both Manstein and Hitler. Both of them had the time to see me. Manstein was in the process of analyzing past operational possibilities. Hitler was in a somewhat plaintive mood, regretfully considering his plans for western Asia. He talked about economic considerations. It was a repeat of the old tensions that had existed between Bismarck and the General Staff. As early as 1866, Bismarck was being called "the Traitor" by the General Staff. But back then when diverging opinions emerged, the king was the supreme authority who decided at his level. These days the decisions were not made by an executive council, but rather by a single person, Hitler. And he was also the personification of the National Socialist Party. The senior ranking statesman should not have to step down to the levels of army leadership, economic strategy, and politics. He should be above all of that.

Other than that, Hitler, who had a great deal of respect for the 11th Panzer Division, was very interested in everything that I had to say about the troops, the enemy, and the country. I met with him for almost an hour.

At the end of my assignment I received 1,500 Reichsmarks in foreign currency for a vacation with my wife in Slovakia.[18] However, I spent the 1,500 marks one evening in the fall of 1944 when the 11th Panzer Division was again under my command in Lorraine. We had a huge party for all the old members of the division who had fought under me in Russia.

16

The Gross-Deutschland Division

I was just about to depart for Slovakia when I was called off the train. I was assigned to command one more time, this time in the coming battle for Kursk as acting commander of the Gross-Deutschland Division. On 4 April I found myself back in southern Russia, in Poltava. The attack, however, was delayed repeatedly. We spent a quiet time in a beautiful setting that reminded me of Pomerania and Mecklenburg. I was able to do quite a lot with the division on training matters. The division surgeon initiated for his physicians a small front-line medical school that I enjoyed supporting, and without a doubt it contributed to motivation and the exchange of lessons learned.

The Gross-Deutschland Division had enough equipment for two divisions, much like a Waffen-SS division. This did not make it more combat effective, but rather more cumbersome and more difficult to command. The idea was to establish both an army and a Waffen-SS corps with two to three such divisions each as a reserve for the senior command level. I was slated to command the army corps and was first to gain some experience with the Gross-Deutschland Division. I considered the overstuffing of the division with equipment to be a mistake. The excess was easily destroyed by enemy fire without increasing the division's effectiveness, and that excess equipment was then not available elsewhere. I reported my assessment back to higher headquarters in the clearest terms, which created considerable trouble, especially with Guderian. Fortunately, the idea of a super corps remained wishful thinking; but the over-equipping of the division never stopped.

Thoughts and Conversations

Naturally the quiet days leading up to the battle of Kursk gave me an opportunity for discussions of all kinds. As I recorded in my journal at the time:

2 May: "Our situation after the winter campaign has stabilized. Russia has been weakened. Japan may be able to reach a conclusion to its operations in China and then hold on to what it has elsewhere, but nothing more. A Japanese intervention against Russia is not possible at this point.

"Our other allies all have all but quit, except the Finns and the Croats. The others at best can only be used for missions of the third order.[1]

"Norway and the Atlantic coast are fortified in a manner that will make it difficult for English operations.[2]

"The situation in the Balkans is aggravating. The Italians have not been able to stop the guerilla warfare, tying down strong forces and practically inviting English landings.

"English landings are a question of tonnage and that depends on the outcome of the U-boat war. If we are successful in maintaining the campaign up to the point where the Anglo-Americans are not able to stage large-scale landings, we can be less concerned about it.[3]

"Finally, there are the Allied air attacks on the homeland. They have quite a demoralizing effect. I see danger there, especially since there is no remedy at this time.[4]

"What now? The thought that immediately comes to my mind is not to let the Russians off the hook, not to give them any time to breathe. But there will not be any major German offensives, because there are no forces available.

"We should have considered countering the Anglo-American operation against Tunis by cutting off the Mediterranean at Gibraltar. But that chance has been missed, and now [Spain's leader Francisco] Franco has become understandably cautious."

5 May: "Today the commanding general of VIII Aviation Corps, General Martin Fiebig, visited with me for quite a while. We discussed Stalingrad. He was of the opinion that Paulus's leadership had been poor. Fiebig had been inside the pocket quite a few times. Paulus, a broken man who could no longer make a decision, who always saw the same problems, did not want to risk anything and thus lost everything. I know Paulus very well from serving with him in the first war. Nobody then, even when he was still healthy, could have guessed that he would be an army commander. By 1943 he was suffering from a stomach illness. Intellect alone cannot compensate."

6 May: "Italy is not doing at all well domestically. An insider told me that Mussolini was sick and a broken man. The Italian Army and the people are against the war. Here in Russia the Italians have openly taken a position against us. In the Gross-Deutschland Division's area of operations Italians who had fought with us previously have been found among dead Russians. Italy is certainly our weakest point. If Mussolini is killed or dies—they call him the 'Coal Thief' now—we have to expect a military dictatorship or efforts to negotiate a separate peace accord."

9 May: "The fighting at Tunis is coming to an end. Again, we are losing the best divisions and irreplaceable personnel. Was that necessary?[5]

"The Kursk Offensive was postponed again and again. But with reservations, I think that is the wrong decision. The Russians are getting stronger and stronger, but we are able to build up at the same pace. We are trying to play it safe. That is quite understandable after the experiences of 1941 through 1943, but war is only won by the side that acts decisively. The side that wants to play it safe will lose inevitably. Just look at France.

"During the many meetings leading up to the offensive Manstein was very convincing, conducting a tactical and operational analysis that could be called classic. It is too bad that he is not destined for the top."

27 May: "We have had some trouble with partisans. But the degree of effort and magnitude of success are not well balanced for the Reds. At night partisans are dropped into our lines, and during the day we capture them. Some of them are harmless creatures who are not capable of executing their mission and are just glad that the war is over for them. Others, however, are fanatics. One group of eight fought us to the end. The last one, even though wounded, put a hand grenade under his head and pulled the pin."

On 10 June the actual division commander, General Walter Hörnlein, returned to the front. I flew home and then spent some unforgettable days in the High Tatras. That was the last time I was able to enjoy my apartment in Berlin. After I visited my mother in Wiesbaden, Allied bombs destroyed our home in Berlin.

The Homeland

Naturally, the mood and the situation back home in Germany were extremely interesting. The common man, firmly led, was the most loyal son of the Fatherland. The reactions of many people on the day after a bombing raid were exemplary and quite similar to those in the front lines. It was different, however, with some of our former leading classes. They still denounced the actions of the Social Democrats—they really meant the independents and the members of the Spartacus League—during World War I, because in such times the only thing you could do was to rally in unison behind the government, regardless if you agreed with it or not. Anything else was considered treason. But now the exact opposite was true. There was the belief that cooperating with the enemy was acceptable so long as you were not a member of the government. The role of domestic politics was a major factor here, and the result was a most unreliable segment of the citizenry. Ironically, however, the sons of that class of society, regardless whether they were general officers or lieutenants, fought on with incredible courage.

In my own circles I did whatever I could to neutralize this trend. Ultimately, I owed as much to the troops who suffered and died in the white hell of Russia without complaining and with courageous heart. At my club in Berlin

I gave an informal talk on the fighting and the accomplishments of the army. I knew there were gentlemen sitting at my table who were following a path that I considered wrong. I wanted to clarify that in case of an attempted coup d'état nobody could count on the armies in the East. As I gathered after the war from the writings of Ambassador Ulrich von Hassell, he had not understood what I was talking about.[6] Perhaps he was too clever.

Many people in Germany still did not understand the significance that the people and the workers had gained in recent years. The thinking was that it made no difference to the people who governed them. A great deal of damage was done by some officers who had been relieved in the East and who, instead of keeping quiet, loudly claimed that they had gotten themselves out of the current mess because of their own strength of character. Nonetheless, many relieved officers did bear their fates with soldierly dignity and understood that it was better to remain silent.

In every war there are shifts within the officer corps. One cannot blame anybody if the events become too much for an individual. The transition from a traditional form of warfare to armored warfare; the tremendous demands made by the vastness of the space in the East; the Russian winter; and the lack of relief forces were some of many factors of gigantic proportions. A general in World War I still had to lead from his desk using telephones, as Schlieffen described it in his little treatise about the modern Alexander. Since then, wireless communication and motorization created the need for a different type of general. Not all of them could keep up, especially not the desk warriors and the second stringers. This completely new and at the same time age-old psychological environment required the closest communication between the general and the soldier on the battlefield. The soldier only respects the leader he sees right next to him in battle.

All of that was hard to accept for many otherwise first-rate officers. In their own eyes they had given their best—and they really had. But it was a typically German reaction that all these currents flowed into domestic politics. Such would have been impossible with a king and emperor as the head of state, but with the "Bohemian Corporal"[7] it was a different story. What made the situation worse was that supposedly everyone responsible for managing the desperate situation in the East was a Hitler-dependent yes-man. That too was typically German.

To Italy

At Bendler Strasse[8] General Rudolf Schmundt briefed me on my new interim mission. I was supposed to replace General Hans Hube as the commanding general of XIV Panzer Corps while he was on a four-week leave. The corps was positioned near Naples. So far so good, then came the clincher. "Hitler sends you the following message: 'All military and civilian directorates in Italy are misinterpreting the situation in Italy. Italy is not—as they believe—a faithful ally, but is preparing to defect. Italy will do so combined with an attack on all German troops and staffs. It is your mission to take over command of all available German troops in the event of the loss of your next higher level of command and, disregarding any previously made deals, act to stabilize the situation. There will not be another Stalingrad or Tunis in Italy. [In the event that Italy defects] you have complete freedom to act. You are not authorized to disclose to anybody this special mission, and it is therefore only issued to you orally.'"

While I was still trying to figure out if I needed to ask more questions and get further clarification, Schmundt hit me with a question from Hitler:

"Do you believe that the offensive near Kursk will be successful?"

Still trying to come to terms with my new orders, I answered with a counter question, "Why should it not succeed? So far, every well-prepared attack has succeeded."

Afterward, I blamed myself very much, and still do so to this day. What I should have said was, "Do not attempt this offensive. Both sides have their cards on the table much too openly." Would that answer have changed the decision to attack at Kursk? There is no way of telling.

On 2 September, after a flight over the old battlefields of 1917 on the southern slopes of the Alps, I landed in Rome and reported to Field Marshal Albert Kesselring in Frascati. The mission of the XIV Panzer Corps was to prevent enemy landings in the Gaeta–Paestum zone. Hube handed off the corps to me on a country road where our paths crossed. The corps staff was located inside a small forest of chestnut trees. The Allied air superiority was clear and it determined all of our actions.

The corps chief of staff was Colonel von Bonin, with whom I worked well on a personal as well as on an official level. Unfortunately, like almost all senior officers in Italy, he was still depressed by our defeat in Tunisia and our futile defense of Sicily. Even though the evacuation of German forces from Sicily, in which Bonin played a key role, had been a masterful operation in terms of leadership, there was still too much of a tendency to overestimate the Anglo-Americans and correspondingly to underestimate our own capabilities. Additionally, there was a strong antipathy toward Kesselring's leadership. I was never quite able to figure out why. Objectively, the only criticism that could be leveled against him was that he had not dispersed our air forces at the right time. Our aircraft in Sicily had been operating on airfields as if in peacetime, and as a result many aircraft were needlessly destroyed.[9] I could never confirm the reservations against Kesselring. On the contrary, the old, lingering antagonism between Kesselring and Rommel may have had much to do with it.[10]

Between 3 and 5 September I visited the corps' subordinate divisions, the 16th Panzer Division, the Hermann Göring Division,[11] and the 15th Panzergrenadier Division. Unfortunately, the divisions consisted mostly of recruits. Meanwhile, we made all the preparations necessary to take over immediately all the Italian coastal batteries in our sector. Pompeii was nearby, but at the time we had better ruins in Germany. The ancient Greek temples at Paestum came close to the harmony of dimensions of the Parthenon, or possibly even surpassed it. I ordered the artillery to modify its deployment so that the temples there were not in the line of fire.[12]

On 5 September I intended to fly out to the 16th Panzer Division one more time. The pilot, however, was not able to lift the Storch[13] off from the short airfield. He crashed the aircraft into a stand of poplars at the end of the field. Typically, the pilot was unharmed, but I broke every rib in my body. The Luftwaffe had been more than negligent in assigning to a corps commander a Storch that had engine problems and a pilot, as I later found out, who clearly did not know his trade. Banged up as I was, I hoped to be back in action after a few days, and thus I hung onto command.

The attitude of the Italians was mixed on 7 September. One Italian captain of the General Staff approached us and reported that they would turn against us in the event of Allied landings. Most Italians at that point just wanted peace, and the army generally blamed Mussolini for starting the war totally unprepared. At that time, however, there were still strong Fascist elements in the army and among the people that were pushing the war. But there were also strong communist elements among the Italians. Just within the last year Neapolitan troops in Russia had greeted Russian prisoners of war that were led through by one of our units with rousing yells of *"Camerati sowietici."*

In general, however, the attitude of the Italian people was not unfriendly. Aside from some isolated acts of sabotage, there were also many indicators of honest cooperation and shame over the poor conduct of their troops. In Sicily the Italians had not fired a single aimed shot.[14] On 8 September our aerial reconnaissance reported heavy Allied concentrations departing from Palermo and Bizerte. Their entire landing fleet was waiting out of sight of the coast, in front of the Gulf of Salerno.

Betrayal

9 September. The church bells were ringing. Italy had declared an armistice, which actually was militarily insignificant. They already had stopped fighting.

Thank God all the necessary preparations had been made so that I could keep my special mission orders to myself. The operation to disarm the Italians started while the Allied landings near Salerno and Paestum were under way.

The Italian troops for the most part were happy. Unfortunately, General Ferrante Gonzaga, commander of the 222nd Coastal Division, and two regimental commanders were shot and killed during the operation. When the order to disarm was handed to Prince Gonzaga, he pulled his gun. The gesture was interpreted as a hostile act by the German security detail. Possibly the prince had no intention of shooting when the officer handed him the order to disarm. Perhaps he was simply making a Mediterranean gesture, but it was one that was beyond the comprehension of the security detail. Because the prince was a nephew of the pope, the Vatican asked for more details. I insisted that we respond with complete, total openness. The facts of the case were objective. The Vatican did not at all make any accusations and accepted the answer. Any attempt at a cover-up to make it look like an accident would have led ultimately to a loss of credibility.

During the disarmament operation one Italian officer told us that he could only hand over his battery once he had fired it. "Why don't you aim 50 meters to the right and fire into the air?" He did that and then surrendered his battery. Another battery commander shot himself. His people cried and wailed for him, and started a huge lament. Then they happily dispersed. They could not even be induced to bury the corpse. Within just a few hours the disarmament operation was over. We used hardly any combat troops, even though the Italians outnumbered us by a large margin.

The Big Picture

The German Perspective: Although we had expected Italy to defect, we were still uncertain how that would affect things. Considering the heavy sacrifices that Germany had made for Italy, we hoped it would be done in the least damaging manner; but we were also prepared for the worst case. We anticipated the Allied attack. On 3 September they already had crossed the Strait of Messina to land on the mainland in the south. We also were certain they would conduct a second landing farther up the peninsula, most probably around Naples.

The Italian Perspective: The preparations to switch sides were made with great deceit and disloyalty. The Italians presented their German allies with a web of lies filled with words of honor. They hoped that the German troops could either be disarmed or at least isolated to the point that an organized resistance was no longer possible and that they would become easy prey for the Anglo-Americans. In so doing, the Italians hoped to present themselves as equal partners to the other side. The extent to which the Italians overestimated the price of their treason was betrayed by the demand of General Rizzio, the commanding general of the Italian Seventh Army, to assume command of the Anglo-American forces.

The Allied Perspective: The Allies rated German combat effectiveness very highly, but they also firmly believed that the Italians would fight on the Allied side. During a meeting of the Allied commanders on 23 August, however, British general Bernard Montgomery declared that he considered Italian cooperation to be a complete hoax. The Italians, he said, would not fight; and even if they did, they would suffer a decisive defeat. Thus, the Allied plan called for Montgomery's British Eighth Army to land with its V Corps at Taranto and Bari on 9 September and advance toward the north along the eastern coast of the boot, while the British XIII Corps would cross the Strait of Messina on 3 September and march along the western edge of the boot toward Naples. The U.S. Fifth Army would land in the Bay of Salerno on 9 September.[15]

The Distribution of German Forces

The German forces in central and southern Italy came under the Tenth Army, subordinate to Field Marshal Kesselring's Army Group C. The Tenth Army's lead units were my XIV Panzer Corps near Naples, the LXXVI Panzer Corps facing the British XIII Corps, and the 1st Parachute Division near Taranto. We also had a strong group of two divisions deployed near Rome, and one Panzergrenadier division and one Waffen-SS brigade in Corsica and Sardinia. In northern Italy Rommel's Army Group B had six infantry divisions, two Panzer divisions, and one mountain brigade. Both army groups reported directly to OKW, which made unity of command and concentration of forces in Italy impossible.[16]

The Battle of Salerno

While the disarmament operation against the Italians had gone smoothly, the American VI Corps was landing near Paestum and the British X Corps near Salerno. The 16th Panzer Division was engaged in heavy fighting. It suffered heavily under Allied naval gunfire, with which we had nothing to counter. I credited one further factor to the success of the landings. Without my knowledge loudspeakers had been set up on every base in the coastal zone, with which the Americans were urged to surrender. Naturally they did not do that. No reasonable human being should have expected such. This foolishness gave the Americans time to cross our kill zones without encountering any resistance.

"I do not want to know about battlefield commanders who want to win without spilling blood," Clausewitz had written.[17] Some all too clever people had wanted to resolve without a fight a situation that could only be resolved by a fight. Not a single senior officer intervened. I only learned of it much later. In his memoirs the American commander, General Mark Clark, noted the incident and was quite amused by it.

By the evening of 9 September the English at Salerno and the Americans at Paestum had managed to establish a large enough beachhead, although there was a large gap between the two Allied positions. By the following day it was clear to us that there would be no further landings at any other coastal sector. My corps could now be committed to the counterattack. The Hermann Göring Panzer Division advanced toward Salerno, where its attack made reasonable progress. The 16th Panzer Division was set to thrust into the left flank of the Americans, and it was given everything that could be shifted from the 15th Panzergrenadier Division.[18] The 15th Panzergrenadier Division was left holding its sector with only a skeleton observation force. The Tenth Army, meanwhile, prepared to launch the LXXVI Panzer Corps against the right flank of the Americans, spearheaded by the 29th Panzergrenadier Division. Our most dangerous adversary at that point was the enemy's naval gunfire.

On 11 September our initial actions started to show results. The thrust against the American left flank into the gap between the Americans and the English hit their weakest spot, as we had intended. A 170 mm field gun battery concentrated its fire on the enemy warships, and hit one of the American cruisers.[19] Unfortunately, the battery only had sixty rounds. The remainder of its basic load of ammunition had been left behind at Regio. A Luftwaffe convoy was supposed to bring it forward later, but they ignored the orders of senior army officers.

12 September brought us some considerable success. I was back to normal enough that I was able to visit the front line, although in considerable pain. The 16th Panzer Division seized Montecorvino, Battiplagia, Pesano, and Altavilla. The Hermann Göring Panzer Division pushed the English forces almost back to the edge of Salerno. On the American side General Clark faced the possibility of being pushed back into the sea, and for a time he seriously considered destroying all of the supplies that had been landed.

On 13 September we received reports that the LXXVI Panzer Corps had pushed the enemy back and was starting the pursuit. That information, however, turned out to be incorrect. A liaison officer sent to the LXXVI Panzer Corps was shot up by enemy fighter planes. Further radio traffic from Tenth Army headquarters reported that the Americans were preparing to reembark on their ships. On the American side the crisis had reached its peak. The commander of the U.S. VI Corps, General Ernest Dawley, reported that his lines had been penetrated and he did not have any more reserves. Upon Clark's question what he could do, he answered, "All I've got is a prayer."[20]

Clark assessed his own situation as being completely at our mercy. With everything he could muster from all sources, to include quick reaction units and his two military bands, he was finally able to stop our armored thrust three kilometers away from his army headquarters. In the evening of 13 September Clark assessed the results of the day: "We narrowly escaped disaster."[21]

Both sides were looking to the south with anticipation. Clark was expecting Montgomery and his XIII Corps, and I was anxiously awaiting the 29th Panzergrenadier Division. On 14 and 15 September we had more significant successes, but not enough to reach the point of decision. On 16 September we finally had to abort the fighting because the British Eighth Army coming up from the south had reached our left flank.

The final results were not at all satisfactory. My XIV Panzer Corps believed it had fought well. Without concern for its flank and rear security, the corps had thrown all available forces against the enemy's weakest point, the gap between the English and the Americans. Could we have won if it had been possible to bring forward the LXXVI Panzer Corps in whole or even partially? I cannot judge. We certainly could have won if OKW—meaning Hitler—had decided to commit the many divisions that were sitting idly in northern Italy. A successful defensive operation against the three widely scattered and unsynchronized allied landing forces would have been in the realm of the possible. The consequences could have been far reaching.

But Hitler at that point was having a hard time bringing himself to making complete decisions. He also always gave two elements the same task. *Divide et impera!*—Divide and rule! That, of course, was total nonsense in the realm of military operations. The matching of the right individuals to the tasks at hand was never the strength of our personnel policies, and we often paid the price for it.

The Italians

Even though we completed the disarmament operation within a few days, there were quite a few incidents after that. Cables were cut, the staff of the Hermann Göring Division was raided, and similar incidents. But we always reacted immediately and decisively. The Italians continued to secure our telephone lines, and the clergy, some of whom had called for the expulsion of the Germans, were now urging the exercise of Christian patience. I was constantly reminded of the expeditions to Rome by the various German Kaisers throughout history.[22] The

Italians always cowered before the armies of German knights, but dragged out the situation through negotiations until malaria broke out in the German army. Then they struck. But the minute the situation turned against the Italians, they pulled their claws back in and the soft paws came out. In the Italian cities at the same time, Swabian bureaucrats acting as proconsuls for the Hohenstaufens continued managing the local affairs calmly, objectively, and firmly.[23]

Just as in medieval times, Colonel Scholl, in whose veins the blood of the Hohenstaufen ministers flowed, was the German commandant in Naples. And just like his forefathers, he controlled Naples calmly, objectively, and firmly. He never deviated from the necessary objectives. He was capable of handling all of the political intrigues with his direct and straightforward Swabian attitude. Scholl was a Rittmeister in the 18th Cavalry Regiment when I was a lieutenant. We had never actually been friends, and now with him subordinate to me our meeting in Naples was somewhat reserved. We both must have thought, "My goodness, not him again."

I saw immediately that Scholl during his years serving in Naples had developed such knowledge of the place and the people that he was able to balance the military necessities against the justifiable wishes of the civilian population. Two days after our first meeting I told him, "What is important to me is that we do not end up with a popular uprising here in Naples, and that you maintain the situation until the decisive moment. If you consider orders and directives as not achievable, then execute whatever you consider to be right. I will cover everything you do."

In order to support Scholl and to impress the Neapolitans with our combat power, all damaged tanks and the wounded were moved around (rather than through) Naples. Prisoners, however, we moved directly through the city, sometimes more than once. Refurbished tanks and replacements moved through Naples to the front lines.

One of our main challenges was supplying Naples. As long as the Neapolitans had enough to eat, there was no partisan war. But if they started to go hungry, they would become roaring lions. I directed the procurement of foodstuffs in northern Italy and had them brought down with our own convoys. The supplies were then sold in Naples, because we needed the money to pay for everything. My very capable and decisive corps finance officer immediately and without asking a lot of questions agreed to issue bonds for several million Reichsmarks. It made more sense to me to sell rather than distribute the supplies. In free distribution operations the largest quantity of the supplies quickly dissipates or winds up on the black market. Frequently changing the sellers was also a good idea. This sort of market-based regulation kept the prices down.

Scholl will forever remain a prime example of Clausewitz's harmonious union of strengths. Anybody with a single-track mentality would have failed here. I checked the markets several times personally to ensure that the system was working. I always moved among the people accompanied only by a translator. I always was received in a friendly way and never had the feeling that I was in a hostile environment. I had made it clear to the populace, however, that the supply of food would automatically stop with the smallest hostile act.

The other major challenge was the destruction of Naples's entire infrastructure that could be used to support military operations. We were planning to withdraw from Naples in due time, and it was important to prevent the city's harbors and industrial facilities from falling into the enemy's hands. OKW demanded a complete inventory of everything in the city that was militarily useful, and it also required a daily report of what had been destroyed. Eventually we managed to destroy everything that could have been of any use to the Allies. That action influenced considerably the course of the coming operations and bought us a considerable time advantage to prepare for the Battle of Cassino.

There was an effort to transfer to northern Italy all of the civilian population that was fit for work, but I stopped that operation after only twenty-four hours. It was an impractical task to begin with, and it would only create the conditions for partisan warfare, which we could do without. On the other hand, we were ordered to send all war-essential raw materials back to Germany. A flood of rear echelon staffers of all kinds descended upon Naples. Keeping these people at bay was more than difficult, but Scholl managed everything with a firm hand. Rear echelon elements that had arrived with specific special recovery missions dissolved upon their arrival in Naples. They started plundering, and could only be brought back under control with great difficulty. Finally, I started to press these people into combat service and send them off to the front lines. That helped somewhat, even if I greatly overreached my authority. I always responded to complaints from the senior directorates with, "Just talk to Hitler about it."

Among the string of visitors to Naples was a delegate from Himmler who had the mission of recovering the remains of Conradin von Hohenstaufen.[24] At least the man did not cause any damage and so I let him do his job. He returned the remains safely back to the Hohenstaufen castle in Swabia.

Some of the fascist elements in Naples wanted to raise a volunteer division to fight the Allies. In a city of more than 1 million, 156 men volunteered. They all disappeared as soon as they were told to guard a coastal sector in a harmless place. Thus, I was more than happy when we withdrew from Naples and established our main line of resistance north of the city. We managed to do that with no enemy interference. The Anglo-Americans tried to prevent the destruction of the port of Naples by appealing directly to the population. One propaganda leaflet read: "A ship with food supplies is moored and ready in the port of Salerno. It will arrive immediately as soon as the Germans withdraw from Naples. More will follow as soon as they can be unloaded in the harbor. Therefore, prevent its destruction. Your time of suffering will be over as soon as the port is operating again."

The ground units of the Luftwaffe and navy were a problem. Naples for them was what Capua had been for Hannibal.[25] During the evacuation of the city much valuable equipment was senselessly and unnecessarily destroyed, while the superfluous items that only served individual comforts were carried along. Much of this can be attributed to the fact that the infantry training of these Luftwaffe and navy ground troops had been completely inadequate. They had barely progressed beyond learning how to salute and now they were thrown into a combat environment that they were not prepared for.

During the early 1960s many of us who had served in Naples during the period of the evacuation met during a German film industry-sponsored critique of the 1962 Italian movie *The Four Days of Naples*.[26] It was a pure piece of communist propaganda that had very little to do with reality. Nothing in the film came close to the truth. Initially the movie had not been released in Germany, because of its distortions of the truth. When it was finally released in Germany it was unsuccessful. Undoubtedly, the required trailer stating that it was not historically accurate had something to do with its poor reception.

Withdrawal to the Winter Line

After we broke off the Battle of Salerno on 16 September we withdrew without pressure back to the Winter Line, which ran from Gaeta to Lanciano.[27] The enemy followed very hesitatingly. Clark's Fifth Army had been hit hard at Salerno and Montgomery's Eighth Army had been pulled into the eastern side of the boot. Their extreme caution made it almost impossible for us to conduct counterattacks. It was very hard to lure them into a trap. We were not at all impressed by the enemy. Our recruits were far superior to the older and well-trained British and American battalions. It was interesting to hear what the POWs had to say. Typical comments included: "We do not know why we are fighting against Germany. The war will be over in the fall and then we have to fight against Russia and Japan. It is nonsense. So, why should we even try hard?"

Some Americans said that this war was senseless and that the main enemy was Japan. "England pulled us into this war in Europe. Maybe the Germans will fight with us against Russia." The war was not popular with the Anglo-Americans. This was evident in the way their infantry operated.

When we confronted the English POWs with the air war against the German civilian population and told them about Hamburg, they often flew into a rage and declared that that was an incredulous lie. No Englishman would accept such a vicious conduct of a war.[28]

The enemy air forces were a very difficult problem. As long as we were still fighting at Salerno their airfields were on Sicily. But as they established closer airfields on the Italian mainland their effective combat radius increased accordingly. It was very hard to work with the FLAK[29] units, which were part of the Luftwaffe. I had directed a FLAK battalion to secure a bridge across the Volturno River. The bridge was critical for our rearward movement. They, of course, did not do this and the bridge was destroyed by an Allied air attack. The Luftwaffe hesitated to court-martial the battalion commander. They only did so after I delivered an ultimatum that I would put him on trial in front of an army court that would be flown in from northern Italy, and I would make sure that the battalion commander received an adequate prison term. Göring did everything he possibly could to make things difficult.

There were some bright moments. My corps sector had been extended into the Apennine Mountains. I had one battalion and one battery positioned there on my extreme left flank. I drove out there to ensure that everything was going smoothly. Along the approach route, which the battalion was supposed to block, I ran into the battery, but the officers were gone. The officers supposedly were conducting a reconnaissance forward. I drove on, but still found no trace of the battalion. Nobody was at the position where the battalion headquarters was supposed to be. No one was along the designated main line of resistance. The forward observation posts were nowhere in sight. Where were all these people? Thinking they were perhaps farther forward, I jumped from hill to hill. Before every leap, however, I searched the terrain. Running into the competition was a definite possibility.

Finally, after my third leap forward, I saw a soldier with a large group of mules under a chestnut tree in the valley to my front. Judging from the shape of his steel helmet, he was without a doubt a German soldier. So we headed toward him. The soldier stepped into the middle of the road and signaled for us to halt. When we did so he stepped next to my vehicle and reported: "Obergefreiter[30] Müller, X Company, X Panzergrenadier Regiment. I have the mission to stop all asses here and collect them under the chestnut tree." When I asked him whether I too would have to stand under the chestnut tree, he was a little stunned. As it turned out, the battalion had occupied a position a little forward into the mountains and was collecting pack animals on the road to move its supplies forward.

On 8 October I handed command of the corps back to General Hube. It had been an interesting if not all that satisfying temporary assignment. But it could have been a most successful campaign with far-reaching consequences.

First-rate leaders who had proven themselves on the eastern front were plentifully available. But it was our flawed personnel policies that brought together Kesselring and Rommel in the same theater, where they never should have been. Having them both reporting directly to OKW only exacerbated the command problems in Italy.[31] It was utter nonsense.

On the other hand, nobody had interfered with the way I commanded the corps. There had been no explicit or implicit directives from Hitler. At all times I had total freedom of action, forward as well as rearward. Hitler only got directly involved in the destruction operations in Naples, which did not especially concern me.

In the course of the fighting we had developed a detailed map of the enemy's bombing operations. From it we were able to detect the patterns to his operations that clearly betrayed his intentions. Comparing this intelligence picture with the information broadcast by the enemy's journalists—usually twenty-four hours too early—we were able to develop a good picture of the enemy's situation and intentions and initiate the appropriate countermeasures.

Our betrayal by the Italians naturally colored our attitudes toward the country and the people. Nobody expected the Italians to carry out German policies. The interest of its own people is any government's top priority. But they could have done so with a certain sense of decency, and that was just not there. For the second time in just a few decades Italy had broken a treaty with its allies.[32] One should keep this in mind when it comes to future cooperation.[33] On 22 September I noted in my journal about Mussolini's new government: "Mussolini is now just a straw man. In any case, no one pays notice to any of his actions."[34] The Vatican, on the other hand, was considered pro-German and was making every effort toward peace.[35]

On 9 October I flew back across the Alps. Originally we had been scheduled to fly only to northern Italy because of the weather, but once in flight we were redirected to Prien, near Munich. During the flight across the Alps we had to put on parachutes. A nice Luftwaffe Gefreiter[36] explained how they worked and got me into one, ". . . and then when you, Sir, are far enough from the airplane, you forcefully hit this button with your fist. Like this. . . ."

Demonstrating the required intensity of the hit, his fist slammed into my recently healed ribs and almost broke them again.

Back to the East, 1943

Several beautiful days followed my return to Germany. After our home in Berlin had been bombed out my family found new accommodations in Silesia, in Wildschütz (now Vlčice) near Breslau-Oels (now Wrocław Oleśnica), where we lived in the castle of Count Pfeil. I welcomed the peace and quiet of country life. The old 22nd Jägers, a company of which I had commanded on the eastern front in 1915–1916, put on a nice evening for us in Breslau.

In the middle of November it was time again. I was assigned as the commanding general of the XL Panzer Corps that was holding a bridgehead near Nikopol with two general commands and twelve divisions. I flew first to Field Marshal von Manstein's army group headquarters. After dinner Manstein told me, "I have just spoken on the phone with Schmundt.[37] You will take command of the XLVIII Panzer Corps near Kiev. That's where the point of decision will be and that's where I need the best Panzer leader."

Zhytomyr

On 14 November I took over my new corps. The corps chief of staff was Colonel Friedrich-Wilhelm von Mellenthin, whom I knew from the Chir River battles. It was an extremely "happy marriage," which I now continued with this outstanding General Staff officer.[38] On the Chir we had always communicated efficiently and without a lot of words. Now, after a short meeting every morning, sometimes with only a quick pointing at the map, we were in synch for the rest of the day.

Never during our years of cooperation was there as much as the smallest disagreement between us. We also agreed on the principle of the minimum necessary staff work. We never burdened the troops with a lot of paperwork. We made maximum use of verbal operations orders.[39] We often took turns in visiting the front lines, because a chief of staff can only function if he maintains the closest possible contact with the people in the trenches and he knows the terrain.

The Russians had broken through near Kiev and were advancing in a westerly direction, capturing Zhytomyr in the process. The mass of Army Group South was positioned on the Dnieper River. The XLVIII Panzer Corps held the left flank in a defensive position oriented north. The corps consisted of the 1st and 25th Panzer Divisions and the 1st and 2nd SS Panzer Divisions.[40] Our mission was to retake Zhytomyr from the east, then turn around and take Kiev. The operational plan was written by Colonel General Hermann Hoth, commander of the Fourth Panzer Army. I knew him well from the fighting around Stalingrad. He was one of our most capable Panzer commanders.

I did not like, however, the way the operations order read. I wanted to thrust toward Kiev immediately with everything we had, bypassing Zhytomyr, which would then fall on its own. By attacking Zhytomyr first, we would lose time, and the Russians could use that time to bring up more forces to organize

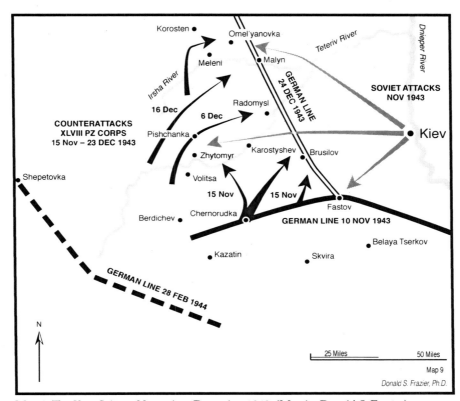

Map 9. The Kiev Salient, November–December 1943. (Map by Donald S. Frazier)

a bridgehead at Kiev, which would then be harder to take. Unfortunately, I was not able to get my assessment across.

We tightly concentrated all forces within the corps and formed the main effort with the 1st Panzer Division and 1st SS Panzer Division. The attack by these two first-rate and fully equipped divisions on 16 November thrust into the left flank of the Russians as they were advancing to the west. The Panzers cut down everything in front of them. On the morning of 17 November we reached the attack route Kiev–Zhytomyr, and I turned the 1st Panzer Division toward Zhytomyr. On my left flank the 7th Panzer Division under the brilliant General Hasso von Manteuffel and the very good 69th Infantry Division moved forward. Zhytomyr fell to the concentric attack of these three divisions on the night of 18–19 November.

During that night I had sent Mellenthin to the 1st Panzer Division to order it to turn toward the east immediately, to make sure that we did not waste a second. The first part of the operation was successful. Unfortunately, we lost five days in the process. But one advantage was that in Zhytomyr we found our own well-stocked supply depots untouched. We destroyed two Soviet divisions in Zhytomyr and three more in the Konstytchev Forest.

Old Acquaintances

Some of my subordinate units were no strangers to me. During the 1940 campaign in the West I had been the commander of the 1st Panzer Division's 1st Infantry Regiment. I was able to greet by name quite a number of old acquaintances among the enlisted troops. The current regimental commander was Lieutenant Colonel von Seydlitz, who in France had been a senior lieutenant and company commander under me. But such moments brought home to me the unbelievable levels of attrition we had experienced. Very few officers of the old cadre were still with the unit; many of them had been killed. Major Feig, with whom I visited, was just minutes later stabbed in the back and killed by a Russian POW he was in the process of interrogating.

The 1st Panzer Division was now commanded by Lieutenant General Walter Krüger, who previously had been my brigade commander. It was not a very comfortable situation, but thanks to a mutual sense of professionalism and the fact that Krüger commanded the division well, it did not cause any problems.

Also assigned to my corps was the 25th Panzer Division. Its commander had been my last peacetime superior, General Adolf von Schell. He stood up the division in Norway in May 1941. Thanks to his connections the unit was well equipped, but the commander and the troops were not used to combat and not yet fully trained. Deployed by the high command to the eastern front in October 1943, the division was thrown hastily into the fight to hold Zhytomyr. There the division was destroyed piece by piece, losing most of its equipment in the process. The troops had lost all confidence and their inner strength, and the unit had to be disbanded. One of my first official duties was to provide an official report about the disaster of the 25th Panzer Division and my old superior, to whom I owed so much and who I admired deeply. In the process of the fighting Schell had become critically ill and developed almost total blindness, so thank God no one could make him bear all the blame for the division's failure.

It is impossible to take a freshly stood-up division that does not have any combat experience, has not completed its training, and is under a commander who also does not have combat experience and throw that unit into the decisive point of a critical fight. It would have been better to reconstitute two or three old combat-proven divisions with the fresh troops, officers, weapons, and equipment. The 3rd, 8th, and 19th Panzer Divisions, which were all attached to my corps a few days later, could have been the decisive factor had they been so reconstituted and then committed.

Another reason for the poor decision to commit the 25th Panzer Division was the fact that we no longer had an army commander in chief who had things firmly under control. Hitler was too overextended to do the job effectively. Consequently, too many issues were resolved through mutual agreements and because of personal relationships instead of one person in charge issuing clear, unambiguous, and objective orders.

There was another lesson to be learned here. No senior officer should assume command without first having been thoroughly examined by an independent medical panel. Hitler was justifiably upset that the medical officers had certified Schell as completely combat ready. His glaucoma and resulting blindness was a decisive factor in the division's catastrophic failure. He had a history of vision problems, but unfortunately the medics cleared him for duty.

Brusilov

The Russians took advantage of the five lost days by assembling a strong concentration of forces near Brusilov. On 17 and 18 November the I Guards Cavalry Corps and V and VII Guards Tank Corps hit our right flank with eight separate attacks near Kotcherovo and four at Brusilov, but they failed to accomplish anything. The destruction of that force was a precondition for our own thrust toward Kiev. After I received three additional divisions we were able to conduct a double envelopment pincer attack. I put the 19th Panzer Division on my right wing and the 1st SS Panzer Division in the middle. In the north I put the 1st Panzer Division, whose left flank was screened by the 7th Panzer Division.

On 20 November we moved out. The Fourth Panzer Army initially wanted me to postpone the attack for one day in order to prepare better. In the end, my insistence on attacking immediately prevailed. One of the advantages of armored warfare is that preparations can be greatly minimized. The fighting was difficult, but the advance went well on both flanks. The not yet reconstituted 7th and 19th Panzer Divisions were both only as strong as a weak battle group, but were commanded very well by Generals Manteuffel and Hans Källner. Both divisions achieved decisive success. What could they have accomplished with the senselessly wasted personnel and equipment of the 25th Panzer Division? In the middle, the 1st SS Panzer Division's attack against a much superior enemy force failed to make headway. They reported in a radio message: "For the first time an attack by the *Leibstandarte* has failed. Morale is down."

Tensions built up. The Fourth Panzer Army wanted to cancel the attack

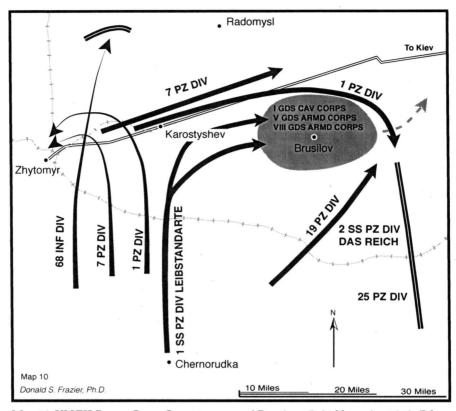

Map 10. XLVIII Panzer Corps Operations around Brusilov, 15–24 November 1943. (Map by Donald S. Frazier)

because they did not believe it could succeed. The 19th and 1st Panzer Divisions had not exploited their success and had stopped moving. With a great deal of effort the attack regained some momentum in the afternoon, only to come to a halt again at nightfall at the two points of the pincer. They were reluctant to continue the attack into the night. After I issued some rather blunt orders, the 1st and 19th Panzer Divisions finally resumed their thrusts into the pitch black night and closed the encirclement just after midnight on 23 November.

The Russians evacuated the Brusilov Pocket that day. They skillfully extracted the staffs and specialists, which they would use to form new units.[41] Many Russian troops escaped at night through our thin and porous lines, but they still left some fat prey for us. The three Russian corps left in the pocket 153 tanks, 70 field guns, 250 antitank guns, more than three thousand dead, and numerous prisoners. The fighting, however, had given the Russians time to establish a new front with additional forces between us and Kiev. Worse still, a horrible thaw made any kind of movement impossible. I had no alternative but to call off the corps attack. Our losses were growing unnecessarily, caused by the fact that nobody wanted to get bogged down in the muddy wet ground made worse by rain, rain, and more rain.

My trips to the front gave me a clear understanding of the impact of the weather conditions. On 26 November, while I was on my way to the northern wing of the corps, I had to be towed three times just to get to the 19th Panzer Division. After that I got into a tracked vehicle, which promptly threw a track in the next village. Then I was able to get a bit farther in a staff car, which finally also got stuck in the mud. Then I hiked on foot to the 1st Panzer Division's headquarters, and finally made it to my destination in another staff car. I made my way back well enough in another tracked vehicle. The trip took me twelve hours, while just a few days earlier the same trip had taken only three hours, including the staff meetings and briefings. The next day I sent Mellenthin forward. He left at 0500 hours, and was still not back by 2200. His car bogged down and he radioed that he was proceeding on foot to the next village.

Radomysl

On 30 November Hoth called me to say that he was going back home for a thorough rest leave. He would be receiving the Swords to the Knight's Cross of the Iron Cross,[42] and he also was mentioned in the Wehrmacht daily report. He had always been at the hot spots since the beginning of the war, giving his all in every situation. His successor was General of Panzer Troops Erhard Raus, who was preceded by a good reputation. He was an Austrian with a quite good military education, a no-nonsense and calm approach, and an infallible military sense. I served for a long time under this great soldier while commanding my XLVIII Panzer Corps. We had a solid working relationship and we developed a real friendship that lasted until his death in 1956.

After our successes at Brusilov the front line ran from south to north approximately to the area of Radomysl, where the XXIV Panzer Corps' area of operations started. At Radomysl the newly arrived XIII Army Corps formed a 90-degree angle toward Zhytomyr. Behind its left flank stood my XLVIII Panzer Corps, with the 1st and 7th Panzer Divisions, the 1st SS Panzer Division, and the 68th Infantry Division. At that point we had not been able to determine the size and kind of forces the Russians had north of Zhytomyr, and whether it was a firm front line or just a screen of partisan forces. We assumed they had been greatly weakened by our attacks at Zhytomyr and Brusilov.

On 23 November 1943 we monitored a British radio broadcast that

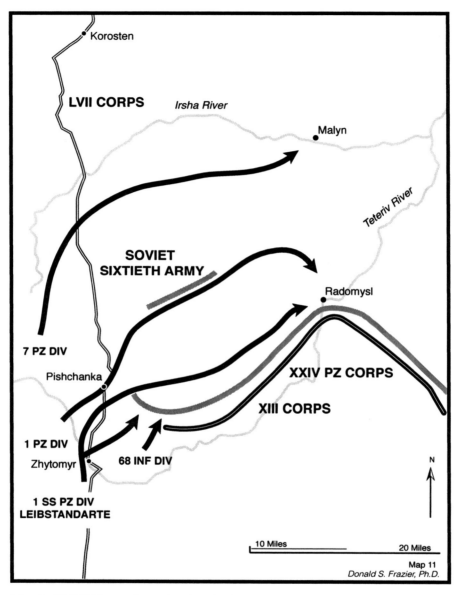

Map 11. XLVIII Panzer Corps Attack on Radomysl, 6–15 December 1943. (Map by Donald S. Frazier)

reported: "The Moscow correspondent of *The Times* writes that the military events in the area west of Kiev have taken on a serious turn. It must be admitted that the Germans in this area are fighting with great skill and that they have superior leadership."

Stalin also commented shortly thereafter that our attacks at Zhytomyr and Brusilov had been the most dangerous of the three offensive thrusts of the XLVIII Panzer Corps. Looking back, the biggest regrets are the failure of our attack at Zhytomyr and the mistakes that were made in deploying and committing the 25th Panzer Division. By late November the corps' divisions were once again fully combat ready. We were uncommitted and ready for future operations.

The situation had developed to the advantage of the Russians. Their Zhytomyr–Radomysl front was an ideal position from which to launch a large-scale envelopment of the Fourth Panzer Army. The threatening position had to be eliminated. During a meeting with General Raus and Field Marshal von Manstein the latter asked me, "Can you roll up the Zhytomyr–Radomysl front from the flank with a surprise pincer move?" Without hesitation I answered immediately, "Yes." Then the work started.

The deception plan was first. We had to assume that every Russian was a spy, and that every movement we made and even every staff meeting was reported immediately. On the other hand, we could not betray our intentions by conducting any kind of reconnaissance. If we wanted to maintain surprise we had to act completely in the dark. The road from Zhytomyr to Korosten led straight away from the western flank of the Russians toward the north, as if it had been drawn with a straightedge. I wanted to cross that road at 0600 hours on 6 December with all divisions moving simultaneously on a broad front.

The 68th Infantry Division and the 1st SS Panzer Division near Zhytomyr would be able to attack right out of their assembly areas. After a short night movement the 1st Panzer Division would be able to position itself to the left of the Leibstandarte without any problem. It would be much more difficult for the 7th Panzer Division, which would have to make a long night march through terrain dominated by partisans. We had to assume that all bridges in that area were destroyed. A night movement to reach the Zhytomyr–Korosten road without preparation was out of the question. It would have involved too many problems. In the end we decided to use the method of motorized infiltration.

On 5 December at noon we pushed forward on all routes possible with our motorized reconnaissance units, followed closely by engineers who repaired the bridges. The recon elements were not supposed to get any closer than three kilometers to the Zhytomyr–Korosten road. The main body of the 7th Panzer Division was to start movement in the dark on the 5th, and by 0600 hours on 6 December would be guided toward the highway so that it could cross on a wide front down to the second. The division was to be the main effort. A PzKpfw-VI Tiger tank battalion that could not follow on the same route was to thrust right through the enemy right flank along the highway.

Only a division with such an outstanding combat record as the 7th Panzer Division, which had a flexible and courageous commander like General von Manteuffel and a top-notch General Staff officer Ia like Major Bleicken, could have been trusted with such a task. For deception purposes we conducted north-south movements during daylight hours. To issue the orders I drove from division to division without my commander's pennant showing on my car. Gatherings of commanders were almost always detected by enemy intelligence and reported.

On 6 December at 0600 hours the weather was favorable, with slight frost and moonshine. All divisions crossed the Zhytomyr–Korosten road exactly on time. The enemy was caught completely by surprise. They had not detected our preparations or movements. The enemy did put up a courageous but uncoordinated resistance. By evening we had rolled up the enemy front a distance of thirty-six kilometers. This operation had gone as they almost never do, without any crisis situation developing.

We were good at intercepting the Russian radio traffic and adapting our actions accordingly. Initially they underestimated our attack completely. Later, they threw in some antitank guns and tanks against us. Then the radio traffic became panicky: "Report immediately what direction the enemy is coming from!"

"Your report is not credible!"

"Ask the devil's grandmother. How the hell should I know what direction the enemy is coming from."

When the devil and his relations were cited in the radio transmissions, we knew we had won the battle. Soon thereafter the radio traffic stopped altogether. The staff of the Russian Sixtieth Army was fleeing. Manteuffel's Panzers rolled right over their command post. The 1st Panzer Division captured the staff of a tank corps, unfortunately without the commanding general.

We had received excellent support from the Luftwaffe. The commander of the VIII Aviation Corps, General of Aviation Hans Seidemann, had his command post right next to mine. We worked often and well with this outstanding aviator. There was never any back and forth, no objections, only the prompt execution of all of our support requests.

On the night of 7 December and the following day my divisions moved another twenty kilometers. On 8 December the 1st SS Panzer Division and the 1st Panzer Division reached the Teterev. The 7th Panzer Division broke into the bridgehead at Malyn. On the right wing the stout 68th Infantry Division kept pace with the Panzer divisions and stormed into Radomysl.

The Russian Sixtieth Army had been swept away. The well-developed road network and the extremely well-stocked ammunition dumps we found made it clear that we also had thwarted the preparations for a large-scale attack. The XIII Army Corps followed behind us and established a frontline position facing east from Radomysl to Malyn. The next few days brought rather diverse fighting. My corps conducted a mobile defense forward of the new positions being established by the XIII Army Corps. The Russians threw anything they had against us in a counterattack, which gave us the opportunity to commit the combined divisions repeatedly against separate Russian elements, encircling and destroying them. We finally succeeded in closing with the 68th Infantry Division near Radomysl by committing the 1st Panzer and 1st SS Panzer Divisions on a narrow front supported by eight artillery and five rocket launcher battalions. The encirclement closed on 12 December, trapping three to four Russian divisions. On 14 December the XLVIII Panzer Corps attacked successfully with everything it had in the opposite direction, toward the north again.

The Wehrmacht daily report of 14 December noted for our area: "From 6 through 13 December the enemy lost 4,400 prisoners, about 11,000 killed, 927 guns, and 254 tanks."

On 13 December I noted in my journal: "Ran into several columns of prisoners today. Fifty percent children, aged between 13 and 17; forty percent Asians; ten percent old people. No young or strong men at all. The Russians too are scraping the bottom of the barrel."

Meleni

The situation that had developed after our successes at Radomysl was similar to the one at Brusilov. The XIII Army Corps was positioned with a front line facing east. On its left wing the front made a sharp turn west toward Korosten. There the front line trace turned again to face east, and the LXII Army Corps held a series of loosely distributed strongpoints with weak forces. Again, the Russians had the opportunity to surround us and advance against the left wing and the rear of the Fourth Panzer Army.

Intercepts of enemy radio traffic and reports from the XIII Army Corps indicated that the Russians were putting fresh forces into the area around Malyn. From there enemy reconnaissance elements were probing deeply into our rear area. That was always a sure indicator of an impending offensive. We immediately deployed a reconnaissance battalion into the area, where it attacked and rolled up the enemy security elements. That helped clarify the intelligence picture. We identified one guards cavalry corps, one rifle division, and an esti-

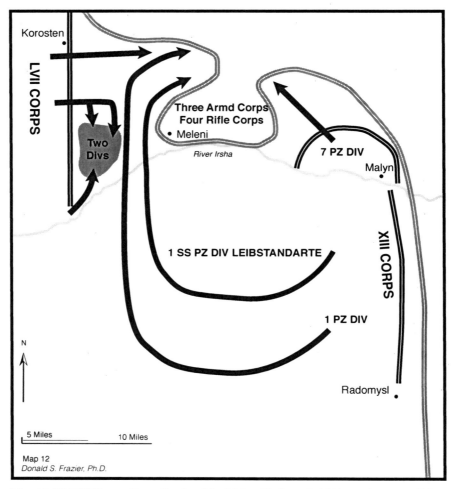

Map 12. XLVIII Panzer Corps Battle of the Meleni Pocket, 12–23 December 1943. (Map by Donald S. Frazier)

mated forty tanks, with additional forces expected. Their preparations were not quite complete yet.

I recommended that we conduct a comprehensive enveloping attack into the enemy forces near Malyn–Meleni. The 7th Panzer Division would attack from Janarka toward the north. The 1st Panzer and 1st SS Panzer Divisions would make night movements toward the area south of Korosten. They would then move across the Irsha River the following morning and dislodge from west to east the enemy's positions at Gosha, pushing them toward the 7th Panzer

Division. Then they would turn and hit from the rear the group that we presumed would be split off near Korosten, and drive them toward the LVII Army Corps. At the end of the operation the XLVIII Panzer Corps would stop in an echeloned position forward of the Fourth Panzer Army's left wing and screen it with local offensive actions.

The difficult part was the nighttime movement of the two divisions and the synchronized attack, all done without conducting reconnaissance while on the march. I went over every detail with both divisions. They believed they could do it. They had long since learned how to make the most impossible maneuvers, and I had complete confidence in them.

On the morning of 18 December both divisions were at the Irsha. Both divisions were committed closely together, operating in a narrow zone. The scheme of maneuver called for the Leibstandarte to attack first, with the 1st Panzer Division's 1st Panzer Brigade attached to it. The force would be supported by all available artillery from the two divisions and the corps artillery—all in all, ten artillery battalions and two rocket launcher regiments. After the attack reached a depth of five kilometers, the fires of the entire artillery would shift in front of the 1st Panzer Division. Then the Panzers of the 1st Panzer Division that had to that point supported the attack of the 1st SS Panzer Division would turn to the west and hit in the rear the enemy forces that were being pinned down by the rest of the 1st Panzer Division. The Leibstandarte, meanwhile, would continue to attack. Unfortunately, the attack was delayed for an hour, and we could not jump off until 1000 hours instead of 0900; but with such complicated maneuvers friction is always inevitable.

Both divisions destroyed the enemy to their fronts with lightning speed, crossed the major Korosten–Malyn highway, and turned toward the east according to plan. The 7th Panzer Division also made good progress. "Hopefully both attack groups will join hands tomorrow morning," I wrote in my journal. To our left the LVII Army Corps had been staged and was encircling the enemy forces that had been separated near Korosten.

The enemy situation was quite clear. New units had not appeared and the ones we suspected were all confirmed. The weakness of their artillery counterfire was quite noticeable. The attack continued on 19 and 20 December. My primary function was to be at the decisive point and to coordinate continually with the 1st Panzer and 1st SS Panzer Divisions to keep their attacks synchronized. On 20 December the Leibstandarte reached the road, crossed south of Inseforka and destroyed forty-six tanks. The 1st Panzer Division was on the left and just as far forward. The 7th Panzer Division was involved in heavy fighting, and I halted its attack. The situation turned on 21 December. From all sides the Russians attacked the spearhead elements of our attacks with superior forces, creating crisis situation after crisis situation. But my courageous troops managed to resolve all the problems.

Around noon on the 21st the fog of battle cleared. We found two maps on a dead Russian major that indicated the enemy's distribution of forces and his intentions. The Russians had prepared to attack Zhytomyr—with three rifle corps on either side of Malyn and three tank corps and a rifle corps in the area of Ischenositschi. From here they intended—as we had assessed correctly—to drive a wide gap into our front. Our attack had caught them in their right flank and had completely thrown them off balance. If we had recognized fully their intentions, who knows if we would have attacked the way we did.

The new situation, however, required a new course of action. I decided to halt the attack and then only establish a linkage between the 1st SS Panzer and the 7th Panzer Divisions in order to prevent the Russian forces from moving south toward Zhytomyr. From radio intercepts we learned that the enemy had scheduled a major orders briefing for 1500 hours on 21 December.

Their most dangerous course of action for us would have been to fight a delaying battle to their front while their main body thrust into the rear of the XIII Army Corps and into Zhytomyr. But the Russians did not do that on 22 December. Instead, they attacked with two tank corps directly against the 1st Panzer Division, which did not yield an inch of ground and destroyed sixty-eight enemy tanks. Meanwhile, an attack by the 1st SS Panzer Division did not make any headway.

I spent all that day with the heavily engaged 1st Panzer Division. Because of the way the front line was shaped, the division's command post was positioned in the forwardmost lines of the infantry division positioned to the left. When I was ready to drive off, somebody yelled "Russian tanks 100 meters in front of the village! Infantry is falling back!" At the entrance of the village I was forced to turn around because Russian tanks were right in front of me. I tried to drive back to the divisional command post, but I was surrounded by withdrawing infantry, horse-drawn wagons, limbers, and motor vehicles, while the Russian tanks were firing constantly. Thank God they were firing while in wild pursuit and not hitting anything. The T-34 had miserable sights. Suddenly, I was in the middle of the Russian tank assault. The Russian tanks were in front of me, to my left and right, and behind me. "Just drive along with them," I yelled to my driver. It must have been the only time that a German commanding general accompanied a Russian tank attack in his Kübel, flying his command pennant. I could not help myself thinking that I would not get out of this mess alive. To the right of us I saw a railroad embankment, and in the distance I noticed an opening. "Head toward the underpass!" We moved past the Russian tanks. Jerking, the Kübel lurched through. A lieutenant with five Panzers from the 1st Panzer Regiment was sitting there on the other side, peacefully and totally unaware. I immediately sent him toward the rear of the Russians and soon thereafter burning T-34s were sitting next to each other. The lieutenant was beaming.

"I cannot believe it was us from the 1st Panzer Regiment that saved our general's butt. That's great."

"Okay, why Lieutenant?"

"Well, Sir, you have criticized us so often, and now this."

Even back in France in 1940 I frequently complained about the 1st Panzer Regiment's practice of moving back to refuel, rearm, and take on rations, instead of moving the gas, ammunition, and mess trucks forward. Many an unnecessary delay had been caused doing things that way. Since then, this marvelous regiment that maintained a level of peak performance until the last day of the war had abandoned this bad practice. But my reputation as a critic of the 1st Panzer Regiment still followed me.

On 23 December we assumed a defensive posture, pulling in all the salients in our line. Even though our attack had not led to the intended destruction of the enemy's forces at Malyn and Meleni, the enemy concentration nonetheless had been hit to the extent where they could no longer attack Zhytomyr. The original Russian intent had been to conduct a double envelopment of our forces in the area around Zhytomyr. They now had to conduct a frontal attack. That, however, would still be bad for us.

The Dnieper Line

Even though we were fully occupied with the back and forth of the daily situation, we still were concerned about other matters, which we discussed in the evenings. The issue that weighed most heavily on us was our loss of the line of the Dnieper River. Why had it collapsed so fast? Why had the Russians succeeded so quickly in crossing that imposing glacial valley with its extremely high and dominating west bank? I had my own thoughts on the matter.

We had a failure in foresight to reinforce the river line defenses in adequate time. Napoleon had made the same mistake on the Elbe in 1813. It was not entirely a failure by the senior military leadership. Hitler had specifically prohibited reinforcing that line, believing that to do so would have a negative psychological influence on the troops who were fighting far forward of that line. He was wrong, however. The draw toward a protective river line remains the same whether it is fortified or not.

Furthermore, we again had neglected the tactical level in favor of the operational level. Our unit-level tactical training had fallen to minimal levels in comparison to World War I. The fight for a river line, however, is a strongly tactical process, and our leadership at the army, corps, and divisional levels could no longer cope with such tactical procedures. We committed forces to secure the bridgeheads over which we withdrew, but that was unnecessary because withdrawing troops secure their own bridgeheads. Meanwhile, the Russians crossed between our crossing points, where we had nobody to stop them. Nor did we establish separate bridgeheads from which to launch counterattacks back to the east side.

The troops hoped that the withdrawal back across the Dnieper would produce miracles and give them some time to rest. But rest is impossible in a protective zone unless one has fought for it. When the troops arrived on the west side of the Dnieper they found the Russians there already. During the subsequent heavy fighting the morale of the leaders and the troops broke down in various sectors. Later in the war I took this psychological factor into account when analyzing other situations in light of the Dnieper experience.

Organization

I took advantage of my good relationship with General Walther Buhle, the chief of army organization at OKW, and frequently wrote to him in detail. Buhle showed these letters to Hitler, who always read them and, as Buhle told me later, often cited certain details. Specific issues I wrote about extensively included:

1. The jumble of the types of motor vehicles had to be reduced to the minimum number possible, using the same engine wherever possible. The automobile industry most likely would have to be nationalized to achieve that objective. Industry was looking too much to future peacetime production and was afraid of the coming competition. Hitler paid especially close attention to this letter.

2. We had to stop over-equipping the divisions with materiel and weapons. The Panzer divisions had to remain flexible enough to be led by any good, average commander. With too many weapons the leadership would drown in the excess and the equipment would sit around uselessly and finally be destroyed or lost. The excess equipment of the Gross-Deutschland Division or any one of the SS Panzer divisions would have been enough to equip an additional division. From a leadership standpoint it was far better to have two highly mobile, easily led divisions than one that was cumbersome and over-equipped. Hitler did not agree at all with this recommendation.

3. We needed a new type of division, equipped largely with motorized anti-tank guns. Such units would be held under the direct control of the senior leadership for commitment against Russian breakthroughs. During its three

battles the XLVIII Panzer Corps had captured such a great number of antitank guns that according to my calculations there were enough to stand up two such strong divisions easily, without burdening the armament industry. With a quick work order the barrels of the captured Russian guns could have been enlarged easily to fit our ammunition. But these precious, captured weapons were now just wasting away.[43]

Such a unique division was later established, but I have no way of knowing if my letter had any influence in the matter. It was designated a *Sturmdivision*,[44] but it was not used as a higher command reserve asset. Rather, it was assigned to hold rigidly an assigned sector of the line, and consequently it was a total failure.

The Leadership

Hitler never interfered in the operations of my corps. I always had complete freedom of action. I was allowed to attack, defend, or withdraw as I thought appropriate. In the usual fashion, army and army group allocated the tasks and objectives without ever getting involved in details.[45]

At the army group level the situation was different. Constrained strictly by Hitler's orders, Army Group South had to hold at all costs in the center and on its right, and thus had no chance to operate independently and maneuver to maintain positional advantage. In his own memoirs Field Marshal von Manstein discusses in detail the restrictions and the incredible stress that resulted. This naturally affected the situation around us and the distribution of forces to my corps. My journal entries at the time are filled with critical comments about the situation.

Evening Conversations

Ever since I had taken command of the 11th Panzer Division I had gotten into the routine of practicing my English for an hour before dinner. It was a good way to balance out the often hectic, exciting, and physically challenging events of the day. It was fascinating how this mental exercise cleared out my brain, distracted me from the daily events, and created the opportunity for me to deal with different matters in the evening. Our evening dinner meal was a custom strictly observed by all the officers of the staff. The effort to reduce staff work to its minimum made it possible. Any visitors to the corps headquarters were also invited. Two conversations with visiting officers still stick in my mind.

One officer had been to Galicia[46] and told us there were no more Jews there. To my question as to where they had gone, he stated that they had been moved and eliminated. I answered skeptically, "Well you better win the war, otherwise

Lord help us." I did not put much weight on his statement, because from my time in Frankfurt I knew what sort of misinformation was going around.

Sometime later another officer traveled through. He had been to Auschwitz and had seen the camps. He described enthusiastically how the Jews there were being prepared for their resettlement. He described the barns, the agriculture, schools, and such. I interjected, "I thought the Galician Jews had all been killed."

"But no, nobody harmed them; they are all well taken care of in Auschwitz."

I thought to myself how unreliable the rumors always were, and how useless it was to listen to such talk. But I mention those two conversations here because they illustrate how little we knew and how devilishly clever the cloak of deception had been. None of what was happening was supposed to filter through to the Wehrmacht.[47]

The Hydra

We had some justification in hoping that the XLVIII Panzer Corps' three offensive thrusts had crippled the Russian ability to attack on a large scale. We knew, of course, that we had not stopped them completely. When on the morning of 23 December General Raus called to inform me that the [XXIV Panzer Corps][48] had been defeated near Brusilov and that my corps was to advance south through Zhytomyr in front of the Russian attack, we knew that the Russians had been able to bring up new strong forces. At least instead of attacking in three places we would have to attack only in one place. The orders were issued quickly. On 25 December my staff was already south of Zhytomyr. A German Panzer corps had been destroyed. The three Panzer divisions of its northern wing, the 8th, 19th, and 2nd SS, now came under my command. Where exactly they were located was unclear.

The 1st Panzer Division was far too slow in arriving to suit my understanding of the overall situation. I immediately moved them onto the major Zhytomyr–Kiev highway and ordered them to attack toward the east. Even though the attack was not a complete success, the stout division still managed to make contact with the main body of the 8th Panzer Division. We tried to pass the 2nd SS Panzer and 19th Panzer Divisions back through our lines. We got Das Reich through, and with it an element of the 8th, but not the 19th. The enemy had managed to move between them and the 1st Panzer Division, which was pushed off toward the south.

The situation became tense. Doing the right thing, Mellenthin immediately established a special radio relay station with the sole mission of establishing and maintaining radio contact with the 19th Panzer Division. "Thirty enemy tanks to my front," was the first radio contact. Then. "We are being attacked by strong tank forces. No fuel. Help, help, help!" After that the radio fell silent and we did not hear anything for hours.

The lead elements of the 1st SS Panzer Division were struggling to get through Zhytomyr. As the individual battalions, tanks, and batteries arrived, we had to decide if we would commit them to the fight piecemeal in an attempt to relieve the 19th Panzer Division. Emotionally, the obligation of comradeship pointed to that course of action. Logic, however, argued against it. The piecemeal commitment of the Leibstandarte could have resulted in the destruction of a first-rate division, without which it would no longer be possible to stop the Russians. The decision to first assemble the 1st SS Panzer Division and then attack was one of the most difficult Mellenthin and I ever had to make. We knew that this decision most likely would mean the end of the 19th Panzer Division.

I sat in my room in a dark mood as the hours passed. Then the door flew open and a beaming Mellenthin stood there holding the most recent radio report from the 19th: "Currently conducting a somewhat orderly withdrawal toward the west." On 27 December we established the linkup. General Källner had brilliantly withdrawn the division, destroyed numerous tanks, and brought back almost all his equipment. The elements of the 8th Panzer Division also looked better than we had hoped. Källner had done it just like the Russians; he avoided the major highways and marched back on secondary roads. It was a marvelous accomplishment.

In the meantime the 1st SS Panzer Division moved forward near Weliza while the 7th Panzer Division followed. We had managed to extract the remnants of the destroyed divisions and then form a new front—for the time being, at least. The Russians were now very strong. They had hundreds of tanks positioned near Zhytomyr.

And then a small "Marne Miracle"[49] occurred. On 27 December the Russians halted. There were several possible explanations why they did so. Perhaps they had become cautious because of the aggressive active defense that the XLVIII Panzer Corps always conducted. Perhaps they had massed too many units on one road. Perhaps they were intimidated by the overwhelming firepower of the 18th Artillery Division.[50] Perhaps they could not redeploy their units fast enough out of the encirclement maneuver and into a main attack. Whatever the reason, the one day reprieve was a blessing.

What had happened to the XXIV Panzer Corps? In one of the Panzer divisions the commander, who was an artillery officer, had used his Panzers as artillery, grouping four tanks into a battery. The Panzers were not trained to fire as artillery and proved worthless. In the process, they gave up their most important weapon, which was their mobility. At least, that was how I saw the situation at the time, without really being able to verify it.[51] The broader reason for the failure can be explained by the lack of tightly managed training, which we had cultivated with such resounding success during World War I. Our habit of committing all our Panzer divisions to the forward front lines certainly compounded the failure. That made it almost impossible for the next higher level of command to detach them and deploy them elsewhere. And that, of course, tied the hands of the higher echelon commanders.

Once Again to Zhytomyr

The traffic hub at Zhytomyr had influenced the course of the recent events in a most unfavorable manner. Countless logistics and supply units were in the town itself. Convoys and supply trains of the XIII Army Corps and one other German corps were pouring in from the east. Simultaneously from the west, the Fourth Panzer Army was sending the newly arrived 18th Artillery Division into the town. It was next to impossible to pull my corps' three divisions through the town toward the south. Any active interference from the enemy would result in a catastrophe.

We started working on the problem immediately. My corps' adjutant obtained an order giving me the authority to establish control in the town and move the three divisions through. He counted no fewer than 327 units concentrated within the town. The main reason for the mess was that all the rear area services had moved together. They did not want to stay out in the villages, where the partisans were. Once inside the town there was no requirement for guard duty and there were plenty of opportunities for horse trading and other similar foolishness.

An artillery division was an absurdity that was established out of valuable army-level artillery units.[52] If this unit had been committed to reinforce troop artillery units, it could have had a decisive influence on the battle. As a division it had an independent combat mission that it could not accomplish, and it was doomed to fail. Reconstituted, the division reappeared later in Galicia. Now—interestingly enough—it was reinforced with an assault gun battalion, and as a result the division was used as a Panzer division. Once again, it failed to meet expectations and it senselessly tied up precious equipment. It was all organizational madness, and it was not only Hitler who was guilty of such nonsense.[53]

Fortunately, I was soon able to return control of Zhytomyr back to the XIII Army Corps. Since the front was stabilizing, no decisive actions were initiated to withdraw from the town. When we were finally forced to abandon it under pressure, we had to torch between six thousand and seven thousand of our vehicles because we could not move them out. Based on the Zhytomyr experience, from that point on I prohibited my units from taking up positions in any of the larger towns and traffic nodes in the rear. Military police made sure that this order was enforced. Between Berdychiv and Graz in 1945 I did not allow a "second Zhytomyr" to develop. With all my supply units positioned in the flatlands or in small villages, the partisans were robbed of their bases of operations. Nonetheless, I was flooded with well thought out and brilliantly analyzed assessments explaining why moving the logistical support units out into the countryside would endanger and even make impossible the overall support of the troops. As the flawlessly reasoned arguments ran, only the towns had the traffic infrastructure necessary for support operations. But I remained firm and never allowed the smallest exception. The predicted grave disadvantages never appeared, but partisans did disappear.

Defensive Battles

We succeeded in pulling the XLVIII Panzer Corps in front of the Russian offensive, establishing contact with our adjacent corps, and developing a somewhat contiguous front line. The Russian tendency to operate hesitantly and methodically played to our advantage. They missed a number of good opportunities. Thank God I had complete freedom to maneuver the corps and I did not receive any orders to hold at all costs. Thus, I was able to conduct mobile defensive operations.

In professional military literature the question has been raised time and again as to which is the strongest form of combat, the attack or the defense? In World War I it was the defense, because barbed wire and machine guns were invincible. But in the age of the Panzer it is the attack. The effect of a dozen soldiers acting with forceful initiative can transmit a psychologically decisive energy to the attack of an entire division. The mass just has to follow through. In the defense, with its extended front lines during World War II, everybody had to perform at full capacity. Sitting in your foxhole by yourself—not a fellow soldier in sight, but everything moving toward you—is a situation that not everyone has the nerves for. As a result, almost all linear and stubbornly defended positions in World War II were penetrated. The defense, therefore, had to be conducted in a mobile and offensive manner, so that the two most precious weapons, initiative and surprise, remained in your own hands and not the enemy's.[54]

This was our operational approach in the following weeks. Our weak and overstretched divisions holding frontline sectors up to forty kilometers long were penetrated at numerous points by strong Russian tank forces. I pulled the corps back into a shorter straight-line position, and in the course of the move we destroyed every Russian tank that stood between and behind our battle groups. Most importantly, my three stalwart divisions took up their new positions confident of victory.

At one point we launched a surprise counterattack along the whole front line after we had evaded the enemy purposely for two days. At another point we concentrated strong Panzer formations and then rolled up the entire Russian advance position parallel to the corps' front. The most important thing was never to repeat our tactics and only to do what would catch the enemy by total surprise. However, my three first-rate divisions were the main pillars of success, and after months of fighting together they had been welded into an effective weapon. Without a lot of back and forth discussion, they executed quickly what was ordered of them, even though at the time they might not fully understand the intent of the corps headquarters. The element of trust we had built slowly was now bearing rich fruit.

The position of the corps command post was especially important during this kind of fighting. Russian tank attacks almost always targeted towns and traffic nodes with pincer movements. If the command post was at the point where the pincers came together, the invariable result was that the staff had to displace and all command and control ceased. That is why near Berdychiv I did not position my command post in the town, but six kilometers behind it. Nor was it on a major road, but three kilometers off, in a small, miserable village with only dirt road access. The radio relay stations upon which the enemy could establish a fix and then determine our exact position were emplaced remotely and well distributed along the perimeter. A robust radio network ensured the uninterrupted flow of the signals traffic. Thus, when the Russians moved into Berdychiv from all sides they only hit a pocket of air. We were able to continue operations and maintain control without interruption.

We always issued orders well in advance, putting them into effect by broadcasting a pre-designated code word. Knowing the orders they would have to execute, the divisions could establish their positions and send all unnecessary equipment and supplies to the rear. If they had to conduct a withdrawal, the divisions had the flexibility to conduct the movement calmly. The use of such preplanned orders also gave the subordinate units the sense that we never acted on snap decisions, that everything was well thought out and planned in advance. The troops appreciated it. The 1st SS Panzer Division was attached to a different corps for a period. When they came back under my command and they received a preplanned order, they responded on the radio, "Hurrah, we again hear the voice of our master!"

During withdrawal movements the higher-level command post must be in communications at all times. We therefore always moved the corps command post well to the rear and then established the signals network. Then, we calmly let the front line move back toward us over the course of a few days. All too often higher-level headquarters were, for reasons of prestige, reluctant to move immediately and stayed too long in the advanced front lines. The consequence was that they had to displace at the critical moments and could not maintain command and control. Catastrophe was often the result. Under our system, I always had the options of rushing forward to a crisis point or of sending a liaison officer.

The Result

The operations of the XLVIII Panzer Corps had prevented the Russians from launching any of their own operations, even though they had superior forces. Next to my troops themselves, the decisive factor in the overall outcome were the army and army group headquarters, both of which gave my corps freedom of action and screened us from all attempted interferences. Such a screen is worth more than a hundred tanks.

Two additional factors gave us strength. We knew that friendly reinforcements were moving forward and we also noticed that the Russians were noticeably running out of steam. From 25 December to 3 January, 396 enemy tanks were destroyed in the corps area of operations. By 18 January the count increased to 530 tanks and our main adversary, the Third Guards Army, was out of tanks. We monitored the enemy closely through our radio intercepts and we knew his daily problems.

The Soviet prisoners left a deep impression on us. The majority seemed to be only eleven to seventeen years old, but there were also a lot of Asians, and very old men. As one of my divisions radioed in after an action, "Another children's crusade done with." Another called it "The Bethlehem Murder of the Innocents."

On 31 December the 1st SS Panzer Division destroyed a tank whose commander had been an armament worker in the Urals. He told his interrogators that on 17 November a decree by Stalin had been read to them, ordering to the front all armament workers who knew how to drive a tank. They apparently had enough tanks now.

Women increasingly appeared among the prisoners. On 16 January we captured a radio relay station. The station chief cooperated willingly and told us everything we wanted to know. Two of the captured radio operators were women. One of them, named Masha, was gravely wounded and later died. We intercepted a radio transmission from a higher-level Russian General Staff officer asking about Masha. He was very concerned about her.

The other female radio operator told us, "I am a communist. I will not say anything. I am not such a disgraceful wimp, like that one," she said, pointing at the station chief. And she stuck to it, earning our respect. We treated her accordingly—we let her escape.

During the fighting of the past few weeks we had become completely convinced that the Russians were scraping the bottom of the barrel. We believed that we could see that bottom. That gave us the strength and confidence to hold out. Again and again I recorded this thought in my journal. We were fighting now to save our homeland. Such was the background to Manteuffel's decision to execute a German soldier for cowardice.[55]

Incidentals

It would take too much space to describe the fighting in every detail. It was a string of crisis situations. Soviet tanks broke through, we chased them down and destroyed them. The Luftwaffe became increasingly successful at intervening in ground combat with tank-destroying attack aircraft. They often provided the decisive support. On 5 January the XLVIII Panzer Corps conducted an especially successful attack on thirty-seven enemy tanks that had established an all-round defensive perimeter behind our front near Sherebin. At the exact same second that the Panzers bore down on the enemy the air support came in, and together they annihilated the enemy in just a few minutes. Some of the bombs, however, landed only five meters in front of the Panzers. Peiper,[56] the courageous commander of the 1st SS Panzer Regiment, later said that they could have finished the fight well enough without air support.

Divisions came and went. The 1st Panzer and 1st SS Panzer Divisions took part in the relief of the Cherkasy Pocket and later the Kamenets–Podolsky Pocket.[57] During various crises, other corps headquarters (for example, XIII Army Corps) were attached to the XLVIII Panzer Corps. Sometimes we had only infantry divisions, sometimes only Panzer divisions under us. When at one point the 1st SS Panzer Division was cut off and the radio contact ceased, a detachment from the corps signal battalion was able to lay a wire right through enemy territory. Just as we had completed issuing the orders to the Leibstandarte, the connection was cut. It was a unique accomplishment. All members of the signal detachment received the Iron Cross 2nd Class, and those who already had one received the Iron Cross 1st Class.[58]

When things calmed down a little I was able to thank the troops. On 20 January I invited two hundred stalwart frontline soldiers to the corps headquarters for two days. After delousing and a bath, they got fresh laundry and new uniforms. Then they watched a comedy movie, heard a lecture, and had a soldiers' night out. After two full nights of sleep they received stationery with air-mail stamps to write home, saw another movie, and then returned to their units. The mood was incredible during the soldiers' night. I sat next to a Gefreiter who had the Knight's Cross of the Iron Cross and eighty-one confirmed tank kills. The situation only became a little touchy when the troops of the 1st SS Panzer Division and the 7th Panzer Division decided to settle the question of which of the two divisions was better. But that situation was eventually resolved with a friendly handshake. Overall the troops were relaxed and friendly. They were quite different from the faces of the soldiers of 1918. The latter had been hard-edged, with sunken cheeks and dogged faces reflecting their problems. The soldiers of this war were well fed, and confidence reflected in their faces. It was an elite force we had assembled there.[59]

Of our division commanders, Manteuffel was reassigned. He was a huge loss. It is hard to describe what it means for a corps when such a division commander leaves, a man who could be given any mission without having to worry about it again. What the 7th Panzer Division was then, Manteuffel had made it. His successor was the commander of the division's 25th Panzer Regiment, Colonel Adelbert Schulz, nicknamed "Diamond Schulz." He was the ninth of only twenty-seven German soldiers to receive the Iron Cross Knight's Cross with Oak Leaves, Swords, and Diamonds.[60] Unfortunately, he died a hero's death all too soon on 28 January. Certainly he would have developed into one of the best Panzer leaders. His successor, Major General Dr. Karl Maus, also received the Diamonds. Including Manteuffel, the 7th Panzer Division had three commanders who earned Germany's highest military decoration.[61]

As January turned into February the situation calmed down. The Russians pulled some of their forces back. The unseasonal rain and resulting mud brought everything to a standstill. The operational pause was a relaxing break for the staff.

Political Strands

An article in the Soviet official newspaper *Pravda* accused England of conducting secret peace negotiations with Germany. The American press picked the story up in a big way, with headlines and commentary about perfidious Albion. As I wrote in my journal at the time:

"How much is true? The war has come to a standstill. The front lines are frozen in place. This is the hour of politics. There are three things the English are afraid of: our retaliatory attacks, their own attack on the Atlantic Wall, and the further expansion of Russia. Paradoxically, any Russian gains strengthen our political position. Since the Russians know no limits to their expansionism and they could grab vital English Mediterranean nerve centers, a rapprochement between England and Germany does not seem impossible. We do not want anything from England and Italy's crazy ambitions no longer mean anything to us. Antwerp? As Napoleon said on St. Helena, *'C'est pour l'Anvers, que je suis ici.'* ['It is because of Antwerp, that I am here.'] That is the critical point. But if neither side can achieve a total victory, both sides will have no choice but to come to an agreement. Maybe 1944 will be a year of politics."

Graf Vitzthum, a General Staff officer, was traveling through my corps' sector. He had left Stalingrad on the last plane, and he told us stories about the heroism and incredible suffering of the troops who held out to the last moment. Ten days before he was flown out they ran out of bread. Countless wounded must have perished in Stalingrad. We were no longer capable of taking care of them, and the Russians just let them die. The Russians claimed ninety-two thousand men as prisoners, which could be somewhat accurate. We never saw many of them again. Most of those captured were totally exhausted and could not have survived the marches. A captured logistics officer who did survive later stated that many who were too weak in the prisoner camps were beaten to death by Italian prisoners. If that is true, it would be consistent with the Bolshevist policies of sowing hatred and discontent. Years later a senior medical officer who survived Stalingrad told me, "Since Stalingrad I again believe in the German as a human being."

The propaganda was now running at full speed, fired along by the National Committee for a Free Germany.[62] It had little effect, however. Interestingly enough, the Russians were now treating their prisoners very well at the time, as people who had escaped from Russian captivity later told us. It seemed that the time was over when the Russians beat all their prisoners to death.

On the Styr River

In mid-February I wrote in my journal: "Overall, the situation on the eastern front is not bad. At Army Groups North and Center it looks relatively good, and Army Group South now seems to be out of the worst of it, thanks to Manstein and to Hitler finally approving withdrawals. [On the right flank of] Army Group Center, however, there is a gap, and nothing to fill it from either side."

No sooner had I written those words than the headquarters and staff of the XLVIII Panzer Corps were pulled out of the line and sent to plug that gap. Initially we deployed without any troop units. We traveled across Galicia. For some reason I can no longer remember we had a twenty-four-hour layover in Lwów. A Ukrainian professor gave me a tour of the city. It was an unexpected sight. Countless cultures over time had left their influence on the city. This temporary excursion into the academic world was an indescribable pleasure after the long military winter.

On 16 February we arrived at our objective in Radekhiv. The Russians in that sector had nothing and we had nothing, but the elusive partisan bands were everywhere. The corps' mission was to close the gap between Army Groups South and Center, push the Russians beyond the Styr, and if possible take Lutsk. Meanwhile, the 7th Panzer Division and half of the 8th Panzer Division were moving up to join us. Near Sokal the newly formed *Generalgouvernement* Infantry Division was assembling.[63] It was uncertain if it had any combat value. At least the newly assigned division commander, General Gustav Harteneck, was an old colleague from my time in the 17th Cavalry Regiment and a proven commander. In and around Kovel there was also a Waffen-SS battle group under Obergruppenführer Erich von dem Bach-Zelewski.[64]

The Russians did not have many units in the area yet. The mass of their forces was near Dubno, with the I Guard Cavalry Corps north of Lutsk and the 2nd Infantry Division farther north. The Fourth Panzer Army favored a frontal attack on Lutsk. I did not think that would produce much effect. My recommended course of action, with which higher headquarters finally concurred, was to take the bridge across the Styr near Rozhysche with the 7th Panzer Division and then advance on the eastern side of the river to take Lutsk from the rear.

We attacked in absolutely horrible weather, as the divisions crept painfully forward in the snow and mud. I was only able to visit my divisions in a Storch. On schedule, the 7th Panzer Division took the bridge across the Styr and Rozhysche on 23 February. Fighting with a recently raised division that he did not know and that did not know him, Harteneck threw the enemy back into Lutsk. Meanwhile, General Joseph von Radowitz with half of the 8th Panzer Division arrived south of Lutsk and crossed the Styr.

So far the operation had gone smoothly. But then the bridge across the Styr near Rozhysche collapsed while a Panzer was crossing it. Then a hastily constructed replacement sank into the mud. It took an additional day before an adequate bridge was ready. The Russians, meanwhile, used the time to close off the breakout point from the bridgehead, and we made no progress on the 24th. On 25 February the Russians broke out of their bridgehead at Lutsk, created some chaos, lost thirty-seven tanks, and then disappeared.

On 27 February it was clear that our operation had ground to a halt. Snow and ice had robbed us of the element of surprise. The Russians also had committed strong air assets against us, which made moving around in a Storch very difficult and risky. We were constantly dodging air attacks. After one such attack, when I had been forced to crawl into the snow, I dug myself out only to be staring into the beaming face of my escort officer from the 7th Panzer Division.

"Looks like you are enjoying the fact that the old man got into this mess."

"Yes, Sir," he responded back happily. Such moments make you forget all the troubles of the day.

The Russians were encircling us on our northern and southern wings with one cavalry division each. Initially we concentrated on the northern division, which only managed to escape back across the Styr by abandoning all of its artillery. The situation in the south was a little more tedious, but we were quite confident. During this fight Kovel was generally calm. I flew into there once, and was favorably impressed with von dem Bach-Zelewski's leadership.

By 2 March we had the entire Styr line north of Lutsk in our hands. The Russians had been thrown back across the river and into the narrow bridgehead at Lutsk. South of Lutsk the operation moved along quite nicely, and we antici-pated that in three to four days we would have firm control of the entire line of the Styr. On the evening of 2 March, General Raus called me and ordered: "Detach your corps headquarters and the 7th Panzer Division immediately and move toward Tarnopol."

It was frustrating. I did not want to leave unfinished work behind, but I had to leave Vladimir–Volynskyi. In 1915 as the commander of a Jäger company I had participated in the attack on that city and then had held it for several days against Russian attacks. I would have liked to visit the old site again, but there was just not enough time.

Tarnopol

Hitler never interfered directly in the combat operations of the XLVIII Pan-zer Corps, and the corps had a totally free hand in the conduct of its missions. Nevertheless, Hitler's order to hold to the last man still affected the corps and its senior headquarters, Army Group South. There were too many forces con-centrated in the bend of the Dnieper River, and the corps was always short one division of consolidating any of its victories. Again and again I was forced to write in my journal, "I stopped the attack." In all these cases we found ourselves lacking that last bit of strength, and we therefore had to settle for lesser results to avoid sacrificing the troops unnecessarily. Manstein's restricted freedom of action will always be a classic example of the limitations of a political war lead-ership and where politics has to bend to the military requirements or the tool will break. That Germany had a military genius in Manstein who was at the right place at the right time and who should have been given a free hand only exacerbated the German tragedy.

So, it was a rather desperate situation that the corps faced as we arrived in the vicinity of Tarnopol. With the 1st SS Panzer and 7th Panzer Divisions we were supposed to close the gap to the left wing of the First Panzer Army, and in the process prevent its encirclement by the Russians, who had positioned their forces from north to south with their right wing in the direction of Tarnopol. Some dark, sixth sense told me to move away from Zbarazh, that we would be in the wrong position. Thus, I moved the command post to Tarnopol. As the corps headquarters elements were displacing from Zbarazh, Russian tanks were already pushing into the town.

The 1st SS Panzer and the 7th Panzer Divisions were positioned along the road from Tarnopol to Proskuriv,[65] but with open flanks on both the left and right. In Tarnopol there were some quick reaction units, three armored railroad trains, and the corps headquarters, and then nothing up to the right flank of XIII Army Corps. Practically speaking, there was nothing available. Even though the Leibstandarte and the 7th Panzer Division had destroyed one hundred tanks in thirty hours, that success by these two marvelous divisions had no meaning whatsoever against the overwhelming Russian masses that were rolling toward us. Things looked bleak in Tarnopol. We had to make something out of nothing.

Hitler had ordered that Tarnopol would be evacuated only on his orders, which in this case was the right decision. In support, the Fourth Panzer Army ordered any available units into Tarnopol, restricting their commitment only to the defense of the city itself. But that was a wrong decision that could only lead to the loss of the town. I relieved the commandant of Tarnopol and gave Major Johannes Erasmus, my corps Ia, the armored trains, an engineer battalion, and some assault guns. I then ordered him to delay the enemy as far north as possible from Tarnopol. For two days Erasmus conducted a heavy but clever fight near Zbarazh against the spearhead of the Russian VI Guards Tank Corps. Erasmus was awarded the Iron Cross Knight's Cross for the extra time he bought us, and the deep mud also helped us spoil the Russian plans. The Fourth Panzer Army, understandably, did not insist on their order to use the few forces that we had only in the city itself. On the evening of 8 March, in accordance with our standing procedures, we displaced the corps command post from Tarnopol to a village south of the city.

Three newly stood-up infantry divisions were ordered forward to come under my operational control, which meant that the worst was over. At the moment, however, I still could not help the 1st SS Panzer and 7th Panzer Divisions that were isolated in forward positions, acting as breakwaters in the onrushing sea. One thing that helped was that the Fourth Panzer Army relieved the corps of the responsibility of commanding Tarnopol and assumed direct command of the town's defense. We had enough responsibilities without Tarnopol.

How were we to continue the operation? The Fourth Panzer Army wanted us to thrust north of Tarnopol into the right flank of the southward advancing Russian forces. Attacking through the mud with only infantry divisions was something I questioned, and I finally was able to get acceptance for my course of action. I wanted to meet the enemy head on, then attack his lead elements, and then move the infantry divisions around south of Tarnopol and thus close the gap with the 7th Panzer Division. It was a simple, unsophisticated solution, dictated by the road net. The mud made any sort of wide-ranging maneuver impossible.

Some tense hours followed. The corps headquarters had been discovered by Russian fighter planes because somebody had found it necessary to establish a landing strip for medical evacuation aircraft right next to us. We were able to move the command post just in time. Immediately after we displaced, the buildings in which we had been located were piles of smoking rubble.

The new infantry divisions finally arrived on 12 March. The 395th Infantry Division was committed north of Tarnopol on the Siret River, plugging at least part of the gap between us and the XIII Army Corps. The 68th and 359th Infantry Divisions were committed to the attack. Supported by assault guns, they made good progress. We continuously monitored Russian radio traffic reporting that an avalanche was coming their way. But nothing moved quite fast enough in the mud, even though the 68th Infantry Division was masterfully led and attacked with incredible energy and the adjacent 359th Infantry Division provided excellent support. By 20 March success was within reach. The VI Guards Mechanized Corps and two Russian infantry divisions were pushed against the left flank of the 7th Panzer Division and encircled.

We were hoping for a decisive success, but things turned out differently. At 0500 hours on 21 March the Russians attacked us on a broad front, supported by countless tanks. Messages with bad news kept piling up. Even though we managed to destroy forty-eight Russian tanks, there were no reserve forces available. I had little option but to withdraw the 7th Panzer and 68th Infantry Divisions back to a rearward line. Several extremely tense days followed. The Russians broke through the gap between the 1st SS Panzer and 7th Panzer Divisions. The 68th Infantry Division positioned on the left moved closer to the 7th Panzer. Farther to the west in the direction of the 359th Infantry Division, the Russians advanced through a huge gap and attacked the 359th from the rear. The 359th Infantry Division, north of Tarnopol, was in dire straits. Between it and the XIII Army Corps the Russians were moving south without opposition.

In such a situation the only viable course of action was to break contact. I pulled the Leibstandarte, the 7th Panzer Division, and the 68th Infantry Division back, and moved the 359th Infantry Division back beyond the Siret River. I also reinforced the 359th by attaching a Tiger[66] tank battalion to it.

The retrograde movements were difficult and crisis-riddled, but they succeeded. I turned the two Panzer divisions over to the First Panzer Army, which considerably reduced my command problems. Only the 359th Infantry Division was still in trouble. Even though it had forty-two Tigers attached to it, it nonetheless had trouble starting its withdrawal. But finally the front stabilized, and the 395th and 359th Infantry Divisions got across the Siret River. The 359th Infantry Division had put up an especially good fight. With five Tigers, one platoon of engineers, and assorted supply clerks they had held two Russian infantry divisions in check, conducting several courageous counterattacks along the division's twenty-kilometer-deep open flank.

Two more new infantry divisions arrived. The 349th Infantry Division was committed in the gap with the XIII Army Corps. Its mission was to attack and establish a link with the corps. They succeeded. The 100th Jäger Division, meanwhile, moved to the corps' right wing, as the 8th Panzer Division now came up from our rear. The 100th Jäger Division took Podlyce, and behind it the II SS Panzer Corps moved up. I watched it moving toward Podlyce and noted that it had marvelous marching discipline, excellent equipment, and impressive people. It was incredible that in the fifth year of the war we could still muster such divisions.

On 10 April we established the link to the withdrawing First Panzer Army. We knew the First Panzer Army's situation was not all that bad from a radio message that the Russians had sent to them on 2 April: "If the First Army does not throw down their weapons today, the leadership will be shot in front of the troops for the unnecessary bloodshed. Signed Zhukov."[67] The Russians typically sent out such broadcasts whenever things were not going their way.

A crisis of the first order had been resolved, but it could have been avoided completely if only Manstein had been given totally free reign, if instead of forming new divisions the new troops and equipment had been integrated into the old units, and if the decision had been made in a timely manner to bring all available reserves from France and give them to Manstein. There would have been sufficient time to shift the reserves to the East and then back to the West to deal with the impending invasion of the western Allies.

Manstein was relieved of his command in early April. His memoirs well reflect how we all felt about that.[68]

The End at Tarnopol

The fortified city of Tarnopol held by about two thousand men was now forward of our front lines. The decision to hold Tarnopol had been a correct one initially. On 1 April I wrote in my journal: "Fortress Tarnopol has withstood the thrust. We owe them our current calm. Without them we would not have been able to hold, and the [encircled] First Panzer Army most likely would have been lost. But the correct moment to order the evacuation of the town has passed. Now the Tarnopol garrison must be relieved."

On 10 April the 8th Panzer Division and the 9th SS Panzer Division[69] were attached to my corps for that relief mission. I wrote in my journal: "Hopefully it is not too late. The garrison force is very much at the end of their strength."

Horrible rain and muddy weather conditions prevailed as we got ready. In the sector of one of the divisions a recently finished bridge sank into the bog. While I was at one of the division's command posts three attacks by Russian fighter-bombers dropped 150 heavy bombs right on top of us. For the first time in my military career I got directly involved in the command of my subordinate units. I went to all the regiments and battalions, personally made sure that fuel was brought forward to the tanks, and stayed with the forwardmost Panzer until it was refueled. My personal intervention provided the necessary jump-start.

On 16 April the Russian air attacks stopped. I later learned the reason when I was in Velykyy Khodachkiv with the leading Panzers. General Egon von Neindorff, the commandant of Tarnopol, had ordered a breakout in three directions. Seventy of the garrison troops reached my location. Neindorff along with his deputy, Colonel von Schönfeld, had been killed on 15 April. With all forces available I continued the attack to reach the remaining encircled troops. The attack gained some momentum, but unfortunately it was now too late. Ten more troops made it to the Panzer spearhead and fifty more reached the 357th Infantry Division. Then the Russians counterattacked our attack wedge from all sides. I issued the order to hold on for another two days, until we were sure that remaining survivors of the breakout had reached us. Then we pulled our attacking forces back, and the Russians did not follow us.

The operation had been less than satisfactory. We only managed to rescue a little more than one hundred out of two thousand. That was not enough. Many of those who had escaped had been allowed to do so by the Russians, hoping to gain a propaganda effect. What had caused the failure? The initial problem was that although the decision to hold Tarnopol was correct initially, we continued to hold it too long after its usefulness had lapsed. The order to break out came far too late. The success of the relief operation was then doubtful at that point because we did not have the necessary forces to reach the encircled troops. By design Tarnopol had been an economy of force position.

When we launched the relief operation the weather turned any kind of combat action into agony of the worst sort and restricted the direction of our advance to our disadvantage. The weather and the terrain dictated where we had to attack, and the enemy could see that as clearly as we could. Once we had managed to link up with the First Panzer Army southeast of Tarnopol, the Russians then had the freedom of action to concentrate all of their forces and air assets against us.

Psychologically we had made another mistake, and Himmler himself was the most likely source. The II SS Panzer Corps had been deployed to Russia to gain combat experience, but with orders to avoid unnecessary losses. As Himmler told them: "Your main mission is not to fight in the East, but to turn back the invasion [in the West]."[70] It does not take a psychologist to understand the consequences of these orders.

The forming of the 9th SS Panzer Division was one of our organizational failures. The proper leadership was not available for the division's marvelous people and equipment. On 17 April I noted in my journal: "The Division Hohenstaufen was, even considering all of its enthusiasm for combat, not at the level of combat readiness necessary to accomplish a quick breakthrough. Everyone in the unit did his best, but that was not the issue. The best man in the division was the Ia, Obersturmbannführer [Walter] Harzer, who deplored the situation and who stated such in the most diplomatic way."

It would be unfair not to add here that the 9th SS Panzer Division later overcame these initial problems and accomplished many good things.[71] Hitler had not put any priority onto the relief of Tarnopol. Beyond that, anything else is speculation.

Between the Storms

The Russians had not succeeded in destroying us. But neither had we succeeded in forcing the enemy into a draw. The result was a forced lull.

Both opponents had to reconstitute their forces. The Russians were now planning to wait to launch their next offensive until our divisions in the West were tied up by the Anglo-American invasion.

Galicia

After the withdrawal, the corps staff was based in the Potocki Palace near Pomorzany, in the beautiful region of Galicia. It was not much of a castle at that point. All the furniture had been plundered. The building was empty except for a preserved crab, the size of a lobster, hanging on the wall in a glass case. It gave us all sorts of culinary ideas, but in its current state it had no value at all.

In contrast to the Ukraine, where our administration had made itself rather unpopular, Galicia had been extremely well administered. At the top of the administration was the governor, *SS-Gruppenführer* Otto Wächter, an old-school Austrian. The district chiefs were considered to be the best examples of the old Prussian county administrators. We formed a complete division from Galician Ukrainian volunteers, and many other Ukrainians fought alongside our divisions. In the later fighting one company of Ukrainian volunteers distinguished itself in very heavy combat. There were many cases of separated German soldiers who were hidden from the Russians and later returned to us. The district chief of Rava-Ruska, a man named Mehring, was protected from the Russians by Ukrainian volunteer troops that hid him in their camp in Germany. When the Russians later forced the Ukrainians into their regiments, they defected to us in large numbers. Galicia will always be a prime example of what Germany could have accomplished with a reasonable eastern policy in the satellite states of Russia.[72]

Partisans

Up until the end of 1943 and the beginning of 1944 there had been almost no partisan activity in Galicia. But as the front line moved farther west, Russian partisans moved into the area. Because the Galicians were quite religious, Russian propaganda proclaimed that no priest had to fear for his life because there was total religious freedom in the Soviet Union. The churches would not be touched. Anything to the contrary was Nazi propaganda.

The Ukrainians had formed their own strong partisan group—the Ukrainian Insurgent Army, or UPA.[73] They were neutral toward us and they fought against the Russians and the Poles. They put most of their efforts into massacring Poles. We had no clear political guidelines for dealing with them. Unlike some other commanders, I did not maintain any contacts with the UPA and I made it clear that I would not tolerate any partisan activity in my area of responsibility. That decision served me well. They avoided my corps sector and every incident of resistance was countered with a direct attack. The Polish bands who called themselves "White Eagle" were especially irksome. Galicia had long been terrorized by the Poles. The "White Eagle" was a right-wing Polish organization that completely misread what was coming at them from the East. They believed they were going to be able to reestablish Poland's prewar eastern border, and therefore terrorized the Ukrainian population in an attempt to reassert control.[74] There were also reports of Jewish partisans, but they never appeared in my corps area.

The local population generally did not support any of the partisan groups, with the exception of the Ukrainian UPA. Initially we could not get a clear picture of the situation. Slowly many leads pointed toward our district headquarters in Zlochzow. Something was wrong there. Too many identification cards from that agency were in circulation. There also seemed to be a connection to a Soviet colonel who was somehow evading capture in our rear area and supposedly was directing the partisans. I finally decided to get involved directly. Early one morning I dissolved the Zlochzow district headquarters. We found the commandant in bed with a Polish woman who was the station's classified documents and official stamps clerk.

An even bigger catch was the station commandant's seemingly loyal assistant and translator. His biography was quite interesting. His parents had emigrated from southern Hungary to Austria. They supposedly were Serbs, or possibly Bunjevci (Catholic Serbs). He himself was an Austrian first lieutenant during World War I. On 4 October 1918 he became an intelligence officer in a clandestine Polish army. When Poland was finally consolidated, he became the owner of a large estate near Rivne in the Polish Ukraine. That was in the part of Poland that the Russians seized in 1939. Claiming to be an ethnic German, he was repatriated to German-controlled Poland and was compensated for his losses in the Ukraine with a large estate near Kutno.

As a Wehrmacht volunteer, he eventually became a first lieutenant and the official translator of the Zlochzow district headquarters. In that capacity he had formed a security guard force from Poles imprisoned at Jarosław and Przemyśl. That force was supposed to guard a lignite mine near Lwów, but it actually pillaged and burned down Ukrainian villages, murdering and raping in the process. Breeding cattle that supposedly were saved from the Russians ended up on his estate in Kutno. His operations were little more than a continuation of the old Polish policies in the Ukraine.

The court-martial proceedings ended in long-term prison sentences for both officers. The president of the court-martial believed that he was not allowed to call Ukrainian witnesses against the two defendants—even though I told him in very clear terms that I would take the full responsibility for violating the policy. Believing that far stiffer punishment was called for, I appealed the sentence. But there was no new trial. The Ukrainian witnesses were no longer available because most of them were now living in Russian-controlled territory.

As long as I was the corps commanding general, I kept the case open. The Polish squire was sent to the Germersheim Fortress on the Rhine. In 1945 he became a prisoner of the Russians, but for some reason they released him early on. I ran into him again in the late 1950s during General von Manteuffel's trial for having a deserter shot. Our Polish hero was still trying to manipulate me even then.[75]

The common soldier generally has a keen sense of when something smells rotten. Accordingly, the dissolution of the Zlochzow district headquarters was met with spontaneous breakouts of applause. Not a very soldierly reaction, perhaps, but a clear indicator that something had been very rotten there. The soldier wants to be protected from such elements, whose activities he has to pay for with his blood.

On 4 May I noted in my journal: "The partisan bands are getting nervous. They are starting to dissolve."

And on 27 May: "For about four weeks now the corps area has been free of partisan bands—a nice supplemental success. I never entered into a pact with anybody. First the UPA helped to destroy the Polish and Russian bands, and then we pressured the UPA to move out."

Our worst enemy was always our own administrative offices. They had no understanding of the big picture. They were incapable of broad thinking, and their enforcement of standards was lax. The rear will always be the rear.[76] You can try to change it by altering its dishonorable name, but the stigma cannot be erased. This is not just a problem in our military.

On 9 June I wrote: "This should be an opportunity to clear up the Ukrainian question. We must face the fact that we have made huge mistakes. We should build on the brilliantly conducted Ukraine policy of the General Government of Poland. We should try to establish peace with the UPA under the condition that they accept German supreme command. The political basis would be a free Ukraine, at best in a real union with Germany. The UPA's military activity in the rear of the Reds causes them a lot of headaches. Hopefully, such a political decision will be made sometime soon. A satisfied neighbor is worth more than a subjugated colony. Any local deal-making by subordinate agencies is a mistake. I kept my area totally free of it and we have no gang activity, neither by the Reds, nor the Poles, nor by the UPA. My corps area is apparently the most pacified of all."

Field Marshal Model

Field Marshal Walther Model, Manstein's successor, visited us on 1 May. That evening I wrote in my journal: "Brief, clear, knows his business. Disadvantage: a little jumpy. In the detail there is sometimes a lack of consistency. But much energy and firm will. Far above average."

On 18 May I wrote: "General Raus, my superior officer, and I talked about Model. On the one hand, in his impulsive, jumpy way he creates a lot of disruption; on the other hand he accomplishes some significant things and he is conducting the defensive preparations at large and in detail very well. Some things you would not accept in more peaceful times are his interference in your responsibilities. Now he carries a huge responsibility and you have to accept some things."

Model's strength was that he put himself on Hitler's good side. He staked out his political position very clearly by making an SS officer his aide-de-camp, which naturally irritated all who were too ignorant to understand what he was doing. The fact that Model got everything he wanted from Hitler, which in turn helped the troops immensely, was a point that went right by his critics. Finally we had a senior leader who was not constantly mistrusted by Hitler. Generals Hans Hube and Eduard Dietl had been able to get along with Hitler, but they unfortunately were killed in airplane crashes. Soon, however, a strong point of disagreement arose between Model and me.

Unlike during World War I, the German Army was no longer a learning and adaptive organization. As a result, we faced the forthcoming defensive battle without a set of clear and consistent tenets. Model so far had succeeded by conducting strong, linear, but well thought out defensive tactics. My deductions from the defensive battles in the East were different, and we were now facing the mass of the Russian shock armies. The Russians had been able to penetrate every linear defense that was based on the holding of the forwardmost lines because they could mass their forces at the decisive point without the risk of being encircled by our weak forces.

In contrast to Model, I wanted to conduct the main defense in the depth, far back from the effective range of the enemy's artillery. Weak advance guards would be used to screen our main positions. The mass of every division was to be positioned in depth, ready to counterattack at any time to retake lost advance guard positions, or as a reserve to be deployed laterally to any developing trouble spot. Ruses were naturally essential, as were strongly manned advance positions at night and demonstrations with strong artillery forces. Assault detachments of tanks strongly supported by artillery would conduct deep raids into the enemy positions. Of course, such tactics would require the troops to conduct a great deal of energy-sapping back and forth movements.

Unlike Model, I never wanted to commit additional Panzerjäger[77] battalions to reinforce the forwardmost lines, but rather to hold them back as a mobile reserve to mass at the decisive point. Although we disagreed, Model still made the decisions and issued the orders, which I carried out. There was never any question on this basic command principle. But Model nonetheless created a lot of turmoil among the troops during his countless visits to the front line. He often gave conflicting orders and did not always use the appropriate tone when speaking to people. The troops did not know how to take him.

Through his adjutant I let Model know that I thought it was necessary to have a face-to-face conversation. He arrived the next day. I told him in no uncertain terms that if he continued to upset already nervous troops prior to a defensive battle, they would then fail in the coming fight. My corps' divisions were in good shape, they had always performed above average, and they would continue to do so in the future. Continuous riling up of the troops would only lead to the opposite.

Model listened to everything quietly, and he agreed with me on a lot of points. He never visited my corps again. He accepted our discussion in the old-fashioned Prussian way by not taking it personally. Quite the contrary, on every appropriate occasion Model was always one of the first to send a friendly congratulatory telegram. I have always given Model great credit for his human and professional conduct. I later wrote in my journal: "Working with Model is not easy on any level. He is very jumpy. He does not listen to anybody and he makes no contact with his subordinates. He is a bad psychologist. His 'Stakhanov System'[78] approach does nothing to develop the leadership traits [of his subordinates]. But he leaves my corps alone since I bared my teeth. The troops found him unbearable."

Innere Führung[79]

The *innere Führung* concept is not a new development of the postwar era. It has always been there, but if it is applied incorrectly the troops will fail. The wisdom of this principle was understood ages ago, and all reasonable military leaders acted accordingly. Some were masters of the principle, others were solid craftsmen, and some were bunglers—as can be expected in any human process. The forms of innere Führung must be adapted to the social conditions of the people. It is only natural that there will be some psychological tensions in any military service designed with young soldiers in mind but led by older superiors. Likewise, there will be similar tensions for older soldiers who were well established in civilian life and now have to serve under much younger superiors. In Germany's past there was an effort to accommodate the older soldiers by forming them into Landwehr[80] divisions under older, calmer leadership, and tasking those units with less strenuous missions. But during World War I the situation made this system impossible, and the young and the old were mixed together in units of every branch. That often created much tension. Many of these tensions were overcome through the sheer force of military authority, but it is far better to avoid such situations if at all possible.

I always considered innere Führung to be one of my particular strengths. Anyone with years of experience as a young lieutenant commanding companies in combat could only have done so by developing a good sense of innere Führung. I believe I had that sense. But innere Führung does not mean being soft and always giving in. The *Landser*[81] would find that quite funny and try to take advantage. It requires toughness where necessary, but also an ability to understand and empathize with the soldier on the line.

The feeling for the troops one develops as a company commander also serve him once he becomes a division commander. You live closely with the troops and know when to tighten up and when to relax a little.[82] At the higher echelons, however, it is a little different. When I took over the corps, I set up a special field post box number to which anyone could write with "ideas for improvement." That, of course, was a euphemism. The real purpose of the post box was to provide an outlet for troops to express their concerns privately. If you can talk or write about something that is bothering you, it becomes easier to bear and sometimes the problem sorts itself out. Everyone who wrote in received a detailed answer that was either signed by my chief of staff, Mellenthin, or in difficult situations by me personally. Using this system, we were able to resolve some especially touchy situations without resort to court-martial or disciplinary action. It was not always easy to convince the division commanders that dealing with those cases head-on with fire and brimstone would not necessarily produce the best results. The concept of working without detailed reports and outside of the military justice system was unfathomable to many. But so long as discipline was tightly maintained, which was the essential precondition, no damage was done in the long run. I used this system with great success right until the end of the war. Fortunately, all my chiefs of staff supported the approach enthusiastically.

We also established a corps rest and relaxation center in a wonderfully located castle. Since we were no longer dealing with partisan actions we had the flexibility to do that. The center did not have an immediate military supervisor, a nun actually managed it. It was only for NCOs and enlisted soldiers, and the rigid formalities of the chain of command were suspended during their stay. We selected those to rotate in and out not by name, but by duty position, such as "machine gunner, 1st Platoon, 3rd Company, X Grenadier Regiment, X Division." This way we ensured that only the frontline troops and not the clerks got to go.

Some objected to the fact that there would be no officer in charge of the center and predicted all sorts of resulting catastrophes. But I had always believed in leave policies based on one's word of honor. The German frontline soldier never once disappointed me. I visited the center often, speaking to the soldiers. The nun never complained about any of the troops and not even the smallest incident ever occurred.

We also established what we called "training sessions" at the corps headquarters. Every four to five days approximately sixty men from all the divisions came in as guests. Their selection was handled like the visits to the rest center.

After they arrived they were given a good meal, a good night's sleep until the next day, a bath, a movie, and an open discussion period. It was a pleasure to see how openly our troops spoke. Everyone also received airmail postage for a special letter home, and in some rare cases a telephone call to family members. I also encouraged the subordinate divisions to establish a rest center for every battalion close behind the front line.

A newly established corps newspaper created an additional channel of communications for the frontline soldiers. In it, tactics and techniques and other matters were discussed that were not always passed along the chain of command to every soldier. We also established contests for such things as the best camouflaged battery position, with the winners receiving an extra ration of comfort items. Such unconventional indirect measures often produced results that could not have been achieved solely through the workings of the chain of command.

Daily visits to the front line were also an element of my approach to innere Führung. I made it a habit after the comfort items were issued to go to the front line and to ask when the last time was that the troops had received them. The simple fact that I was asking about these items in the forwardmost positions invariably ensured their proper distribution without the necessity of having to resort to disciplinary action.

Troop hygiene was always a concern. The general slacking-off also affected the medical officers. The idea of making a daily walk-through of the complete sector checking on hygiene was foreign to some unit surgeons. Venereal disease has been a problem with all the armies of history. My World War I commander, Kirchheim, told me that when he was in Southwest Africa in 1913 the state secretary for colonial affairs visited the country. The local missionaries approached him with complaints about the troops having been issued means of birth control, which they said was contrary to Christian mores and morality. The state secretary sided with the troops.

When cases of venereal disease occurred in my company in 1914 near Łódź, I ordered every man in my platoon to have the appropriate medication with him at all times and enforced this relentlessly. During my entire time as a company commander during World War I, I had only two cases of venereal disease. Years later grateful wives of soldiers still thanked me for the care I gave to my soldiers. Interestingly, when British field marshal Bernard Montgomery was the commander of the 3rd Infantry Division at the start of the war, he had the same policy, but he was forced to rescind his order under pressure from the British bishops.[83]

I often took my corps finance officer and my corps surgeon with me, because it was impossible for those officers to perform their duties without keeping in touch with the forward lines. Just as my divisional surgeon had done in the Gross-Deutschland Division, I wanted to establish a kind of frontline medical school at the corps level. Unfortunately, I ran into stiff resistance and I could not find a capable medical officer to run it, so I had to abandon the project. Since I was not an expert in the field of medicine, I could not do something like that myself.

It was also of the greatest importance that in all the subordinate divisions we established noncommissioned officer academies to train the new NCOs. After almost five long years of war and with approximately fifty thousand officers killed, the leadership layer was wearing thin indeed.

The Enemy and the Overall Situation

We knew little about the enemy at this point. We were certain, however, that an offensive would come. Thanks to the human masses available to the Russians, they had established to our front a human screen that made it difficult for us to determine what they had farther back. We did send reconnaissance probes deep into the enemy's territory, but he usually withdrew immediately before we could reach him. One deep recon probe conducted by two battalions and supported by forty batteries and numerous tanks failed to produce any useful intelligence. Finally, some defectors reported the redeployment of strong forces to Belorussia. When the attack started there, we knew that they would be trying to draw off our reserves. We were certain that the enemy's main effort would be right where we were.[84]

But their attack in Belorussia was a complete success, and as a result Model was reassigned as commander of Army Group Center. He was replaced as commander of Army Group North Ukraine[85] by Colonel General Josef Harpe. Now I finally had a free hand in my defensive tactics. Unfortunately, it was already late to be making major changes quickly without over-stressing the system. Changes had to be made slowly and carefully. Most importantly, I wanted to keep the majority of my infantry out of the effective range of the enemy's artillery. We were able to accomplish that without losing the advance guard positions. All mine laying was done behind the advance post positions throughout the depth of the battle zone. It proved extremely effective.

The morale of the troops was quite extraordinary, especially among the many foreign troops that faithfully and courageously fought alongside us. Everywhere along the forward line German soldiers and local troops from the Caucasus served side by side. We were never disappointed. The troops from Galicia, who were rooted to their home soil, were used initially in the rearward services and supply units. Once they proved themselves, we deployed them farther forward into the combat units. When speaking with any soldier at random, you had to be prepared for an answer in a foreign language. The accomplishments of our armament industry were especially impressive. On 29 May I wrote in my journal: "We had nothing after the winter battle, and now we are stronger than ever."

The coming invasion in the West naturally weighed heavily on us. There were, however, many indicators that they might not come.[86] Somebody supposedly in a position to know reported Hitler as saying: "Everything is ready over there [across the English Channel], however, there is nobody who will take the responsibility and give the order. The responsibility is too heavy. I did not have the courage either in 1940."

When on 6 June the invasion really did take place, the subsequent course of the fighting in the West turned out very disappointing. We definitely understood that the final decisive battle had now started.

The Final Days

Following on the invasion in the West, the large-scale Russian attack in Belorussia was coming as well. Our quiet days were numbered. On 17 May the other side started up its propaganda campaign, targeting our troops with broadcasts of music and "We are coming!" slogans. The effect was restlessness along the whole front.

15 June: "Everything continues to be calm here. The Russians do not seem to be eager to attack yet. From their standpoint that is absolutely understandable. Let the Anglo-Americans rectify the situation initially. Until then Russia can restore order to its severely worn-down army and can come back fresh."

20 June: "The Russians attacked the forward lines of the 375th Infantry Division today, around contour lines 394 to 401.[87] It was tough fighting, during which the hill changed hands several times. Things are getting a little uncomfortable."

22 June: "A defector told us that his division is moving to Belorussia. If that is true, the entire Russian activity in our area is a feint."

5 July: "All signs point at an impending large-scale attack, maybe as soon as tomorrow morning. Difficult decisions must be made—evasive actions, artillery countermeasures, etc. Too early is just as bad as too late. You have to rely on your sixth sense. There is no room for mistakes. We displaced the corps command post from our castle and into a forest."[88]

6 July: "Yesterday it still looked like it was just about to happen, but today everything is quiet. During the night from 5 to 6 July we fired two strong artillery counter-preparations against enemy command posts and lines of departure."

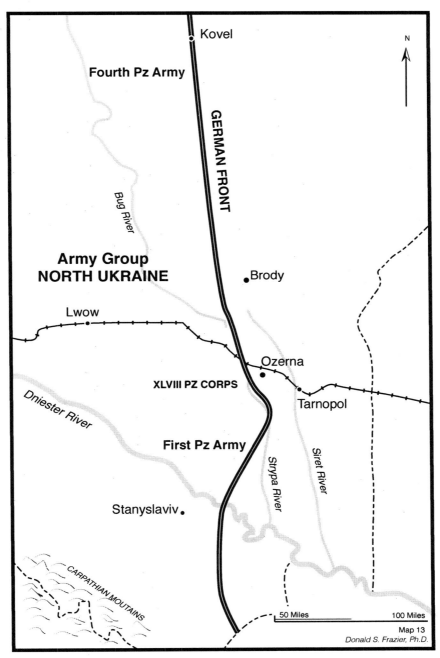

Map 13. Galicia, 13 July 1944. (Map by Donald S. Frazier)

8 July: "It is still quiet. Yesterday the enemy, preceded by a strong artillery barrage, broke through my left flank division. By the evening we had thrown them back, inflicting in the process heavy enemy losses of 136 killed. Prisoners stated that [the offensive] will start on the 10th or 11th. Today it was absolutely quiet, which is an indicator that it will soon begin. Today we again fired from dummy artillery positions to mislead the Russians."

11 July: "Will they come or not? The waiting is horrible. We have made ourselves weak in the front and strong in the rear, but we cannot keep this up forever. Sooner or later the Russians will realize it, and then they will come."

12 July: "A defector reports that the attack is imminent. He had been ordered to clear mines."

13 July: "Attacks in platoon to battalion strength along the whole front. The enemy is filling in his trenches. It looks as if it is really starting now. His main attack will hit my corps squarely. Hopefully, the new main line of resistance we established will come as an effective surprise to the Russians. I am completely confident, fully knowing what will be thrown at us, material-wise."

The Storm Breaks

On 14 July at 0420 hours the Russian infantry charged forward, following a one-hour artillery barrage. The main objective of their attack was the 357th Infantry Division, which was unfortunately not the strongest. The southern flank of the 349th Infantry Division was also affected. While the 349th Infantry Division countered the situation with a swift and decisive counterattack, the 357th attacked too late. Unfortunately, they were also unclear in their reporting. We identified Mshanets and Oliiv as the objectives of the Russian points of main effort. At 0930 while reconnoitering forward I concluded that the 357th Infantry Division by itself could not stop the breakthrough that was imminent.

I requested the commitment of the two divisions of the III Panzer Corps that were positioned behind my front line. Since the two Russian attack axes were predictable, both divisions had clear outlines of their missions. They had reconnoitered and identified their approach routes. The initial commitment was controlled by the III Panzer Corps, after which operational control of the two divisions passed to me. According to plan, the 1st Panzer Division advanced spaced out and away from the major roads. It reached its objective and executed its mission there by pushing back the Russian breakthrough. Everything went differently for the 8th Panzer Division.

The 8th Panzer Division was supposed to reach the enemy's breakthrough points north of Zolochiv by going through the woods to conceal its movements from enemy air. I had put the main highway from Zolochiv to Ibotar to

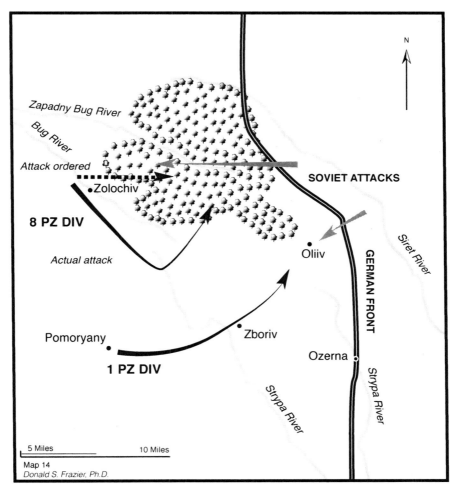

Map 14. Destruction of the 8th Panzer Division, 14 July 1944. (Map by Donald S. Frazier)

Ikclierna off limits because it was obvious that everything that moved on that road would be a target for the Russian Air Force. The town of Zolochiv and all the other towns along that road had been evacuated. After the completion of the evacuation had been reported to me, I had it continuously checked. Thus, I hoped that any attacks by the Russian Air Force would hit empty ground.

Unfortunately, the commander of the 8th Panzer Division decided without my knowledge to advance his division via Zolochiv on the main road, because it would be faster. And as anticipated, the Russian Air Force caught the division on the main road and hit it so hard that it was combat ineffective for the next forty-eight hours. This catastrophe was most likely the result of the chain of command system established by the commanding general of III Panzer Corps.[89]

Following the completely unnecessary destruction of the 8th Panzer Division, the Russians thrust forward through the woods. The 14th SS Volunteer Division, which was positioned perpendicular to the Russian advance, simply dissolved without a fight. They had not been combat ready to begin with, and large numbers of their German cadre personnel were away at various training courses.[90]

Thus, the advancing Russians managed to avoid what was still at that point the fully equipped and manned 8th Panzer Division. They thrust deep into our rear areas and encircled the XIII Army Corps. At the XLVIII Panzer Corps it took us a few hours to recognize the situation. We were assuming that the III Panzer Corps' two divisions would stabilize the situation. The information about the failure of the 8th Panzer Division hit us like a bomb. It was clear to me that there was something wrong at the divisional leadership level. I relieved the division commander and sent my proven chief of staff, Colonel von Mellenthin, to assume command of the 8th Panzer Division and to attack from the south, northward into the Russian flank, and to close the gap to the 349th Infantry Division. It was the only thing that could be done at that point. But that also meant that I had to work in this highly tense situation without a chief of staff.

On 15 July I wrote in my journal: "The battle is raging, that is the only word that comes to mind. There is no other way to describe it. It is a battle of attrition like we have not seen before on the eastern front. So far, everything has gone well. The 357th Division with the support of the 1st Panzer Division managed to halt the breakthrough. At the 349th Division the situation looks worse, but for the time being seems stable. The only breakthrough has been along the boundary between the 349th Division and the 357th Division, but today the 8th Panzer Division will get there and that currently weak defensive line should hold for now. For two days now we have been fighting one of the hardest attritional battles in history, and so far we have prevented a decisive breakthrough. That is a solid accomplishment. If we can continue like this, we can be very proud."

After one of my daily visits to the front line I wrote: "An aerial attack on a scale I have not seen before. Everything is shaking and rolling. In its battle report the 1st Panzer Division wrote that such a massed concentration of materiel, specifically tanks, heavy and super heavy artillery, bombers, fighter aircraft, etc., has been unprecedented up to this point on the eastern front. Hourslong, massed artillery fire is now a daily occurrence. The enemy's air force has restricted us to only nighttime supply movements to our combat units."

16 July: "The situation turned ugly overnight. Only now do we recognize

the full impact of the disaster at the 8th Panzer Division. In order to get the 1st Panzer Division out I moved my two right divisions back across the Strypa River. By the evening we had succeeded. We had not lost an inch of ground. In three days we destroyed 150 enemy tanks and 300 aircraft. We also managed to get the 8th and 1st Panzer Divisions ready to attack north in the direction of Nushche, toward the 349th Infantry Division."

On 17 July the wreck of a human being sat in front of me, the likes of which I have never seen before, nor since. The commander of the 8th Panzer Division had not slept or eaten for three days. He was smoking constantly. It was horrible. Although I would just as soon not write about this, I have my reasons for including it. He was an especially good, very smart, well-educated, and highly qualified officer; a shrewd General Staff officer; an accomplished Panzer leader. He had always received glowing evaluation reports from top Panzer commanders; but he nonetheless was a second-rate man. He himself could not be blamed for his misfortune. He was a victim of the flawed selection system within our General Staff. Although he was full of personal integrity, he did not have that harmonious union of strengths that Clausewitz wrote about. Intelligence with nothing else to support it is a curse.

Unfortunately, during both world wars nobody thought it was necessary to develop a system to test the performance of General Staff officers in order to guide how they were evaluated, how they were assigned, and where and why they were successful or why they failed. The General Staff officer can never become just a pure desk soldier with an automatic claim to the highest command positions. He also must be a good frontline leader with as many years of experience as possible. Part of the flaw in the system was the tendency to fill every possible key position with General Staff officers. They all should have experience serving in the front lines. Periodic administrative assignments are also quite useful for developing line officers. The blood that the troops shed obligates us not to avoid addressing this problem head-on. This, then, is my reason for reopening this old and festering wound. It has not been my intention to condemn and pile the guilt on a perfectly honorable officer who believed that he was doing his best.

20 July 1944

The Seer of Berezhany

During my visits to the front before the Russian attack I observed that people everywhere were on the move. They all wanted to save themselves from the Russians. The roads were full of people heading out on foot and in wagons. The closer you got to Berezhany the thinner the stream became, until it stopped completely near the town. What was the reason? Near Berezhany there lived a wise woman. Long before the First World War she had predicted a decisive battle in eastern Galicia in which four peoples, Germans, Austrians, Hungarians, and Turks, would conquer the Russians. And indeed the Germans, Austrians, Hungarians, and the Turkish I Army Corps did defeat the Russians in 1916–1917 along the Gnila Line and at Solota Lipa. While the woman was first laughed at, her fame grew immensely after her impossible prediction came true. Recently she had made another prophecy: "If the Germans can hold until 20 July, then they will have won the war. On 20 July I see blood, blood, and more blood. It will be a horrible scene in the Kremlin. 20 July will be the turning point to victory." This time everyone believed her. Unfortunately, she had erred in exactly the opposite direction.

The Assassination Attempt

The events of 20 July 1944 struck us all like thunder. We were in the middle of the heaviest fighting, and now there was revolution at home. It could have meant the end of the *Ostheer*.[91] As far as I could tell at the time, there was hardly anybody in the responsible military leadership who would have sympathized with—let alone supported—those who attempted the assassination. When I drove to all my subordinate divisions on 21 July I was greeted almost everywhere with the "*deutscher Gruss.*"[92] Up to that point the Hitler salute had been mandatory for civilians, but optional for the military. We retained the traditional military salute.[93] But anyone who knew how to read the salutes of the soldiers could understand how they felt by their spontaneous use of the Hitler salute. On the outside, at least, the soldiers clearly sided with Hitler. Later, while in Allied captivity, I had a conversation with a colonel who had been a corps chief of staff on the western front. He had been closely connected to the events of 20 July, and he was a staunch opponent of National Socialism. He told me that anyone during those days who would have stood in front of the troops in an attempt to lead them against Hitler would have been killed. But when the coup failed, the domestic political situation was brought under control immediately and stability was restored.

Personalities and Causes

When a dictatorship suffers military or political failures, elements of the population will react against it. When Napoleon suffered his first defeat near Aspern in 1809, the tensions were similar to what the Germany Army experienced in 1944. French minister of police Joseph Fouché sent a message from Paris to the opposition elements in the army: "We cannot start this from here. If you have even twelve determined men, then strangle him in bed, put him in a sack, and throw him in the Danube. Then everything will be good."

The tension between Hitler and the generals had been simmering for a long time. The constraints that Hitler had put on the most capable of our leaders, Field Marshal von Manstein, were seen as the cause for the severe setbacks in the East, and justifiably so. Nonetheless, the number of Hitler's interventions was not nearly as high as popular legend now describes it. I experienced much the same thing on my level. On most of my visits to the front I made a record of all the orders that I had supposedly given, some of which would raise anybody's blood pressure. I also kept a careful record of all cases where Hitler's intervention had restricted my actions. Other commands may have experienced more direct interference because Hitler's mistrust caused him to intervene wherever he could not overcome his lack of confidence in certain commanders. The inability to trust was one of Hitler's key characteristics, and a big handicap.

Leadership means trusting the man on the front line. Unfortunately, that was missing all too often. In all fairness, however, this situation was not completely Hitler's fault. It was a process of action and reaction. While the conditions along the front line were still tolerable, the environment in the circles closest to Hitler was extremely tense and unbearable. The rebellion, therefore, grew out of his immediate military circle, out of the ranks of OKH.

The leadership of the eastern front was hardly involved in the putsch. We were involved in the heaviest fighting of the war and we knew that a putsch would mean the end for Germany. While in captivity after the war a circle of about twenty generals discussed the pros and cons of the attempted coup. I interjected that had the putsch been successful, the eastern front would have collapsed. Then, following good old German practice, everyone would have tried to save his own skin. Half of those gentlemen agreed with me, the other half interjected that the eastern front could have never dissolved because it was tied down by the enemy. Those generals who agreed with me had extensive frontline experience. The ones who disagreed had never or only infrequently commanded on the front line.

While the attitude toward the putsch on the eastern front was for the most part unambiguous, the attitude on the western front was different. Those who clearly could not handle the unique stress on the eastern front were transferred into equivalent key positions on the western front. Some of them did not accept the real reasons for their transfers. I will not, however, say that the policy was a failure. Personal criticisms should stop where the conditions are so difficult that they are beyond the control of those affected. Once out of the stress of the battle, things look much different.

Stauffenberg

I had known Stauffenberg well for a long time. We had been assigned to the same cavalry brigade. I often had many pleasant conversations with this intelligent man who was highly educated in history. It was most interesting when he talked about superstitions and supernatural sensations. Later, when I was general of the mobile troops and Stauffenberg was working in the Organizational Department, we met frequently during duty hours and off duty. Stauffenberg was not at all a second stringer. With his personality he was destined for the highest of positions. He embodied to the utmost what Clausewitz called the harmonious union of strengths.

As long as I was at OKH, Stauffenberg as far as I knew was not an opponent of the system. He was determined, like all of us, to bring matters to a successful conclusion. Ironically, he shared some personal characteristics with Hitler: a certain genius; an interest in history; independent judgment; and last but not least, an obsession with an idea. Their eyes and their somewhat wild hair added to the similarity. Both were caught up in the same mysticism. Hitler was convinced that providence had destined him to save and elevate Germany. Stauffenberg held the somewhat peculiar opinion for a General Staff officer that in every war there is a culminating point, and if you can seize it, you will win the war. In the previous war that point had been Salonika and in this one North Africa. I think that Stauffenberg went to Tunisia as a divisional General Staff officer with a certain missionary zeal.[94] When he was severely wounded he also must have been wounded on the inside, which then resulted in his "Road to Damascus" conversion.[95]

It was certainly a different Stauffenberg after his recovery. I met with him on a visit to Berlin, and we talked briefly in passing. Stauffenberg was now highly critical of the regime. I asked him, "How do you want to turn it off? That can only be done with violence, and there is the danger that the Ostheer will fall into Russian hands or the state into the hands of the SS. We are for better or for worse tied to Hitler."

But like Hitler, Stauffenberg had an eye for the visionary goals, while neglecting those closer to home.

The Situation in Mid-1944

In my opinion there had not been the slightest possibility of the putsch succeeding. No combat units—the only units that mattered—would have marched against Hitler at that point. The conspirators themselves must have understood this well when they attempted to spread the rumor that the SS had mutinied against Hitler. Nor were the conditions right in the foreign policy arena. Although the Anglo-Americans were more than happy to see the treasonous internal events unfold, they had no intention of letting go of their policy of unconditional surrender and the consequent political and economic destruction of an undesirable Germany. They fought against Germany, not against National Socialism.[96]

It is quite possible that the Soviets would have been the beneficiaries of Stauffenberg's action, had he succeeded. And I have my doubts that he could have remained immune against a political sickness called Russophilia that got a hold of many German officers. I speak only of Stauffenberg because of the influence his strong and dynamic personality brought to bear on the heterogeneous senior leadership circles he moved in and which would have swept him to the top quickly.

The Front Line

The front line was completely against the assassination attempt. Not only the act itself, but the way it was carried out, which killed a large number of innocent bystanders.[97] Everyone agreed that strong retaliation was justified, but Hitler, as usual, overreacted. When those involved in the plot were hanged like dishonored criminals, rather than receiving the soldierly bullet from a firing squad, the mood shifted.[98] *"Allzu scharf macht schartig."*[99]

Personal Conviction

Many years have passed since 20 July 1944. Nothing has convinced me yet that my earlier judgment was wrong. Today, I consider myself to have been lucky that I was not drawn into the conspiracy personally and that I was totally unaware of the preparations. In retrospect it became clear to me that General Staff officer Colonel Eberhard Finckh had sounded me out during a series of conversations.[100] These careful probes stopped immediately when I did not respond properly. I must concede, however, that for a man like Stauffenberg, with his education, his personality, his worldview, and his sense of responsibility, he acted as he saw right. I have no way of knowing if his act followed from sober deliberation or from fanaticism and mysticism. The fact that the conspiracy could not be kept secret for much longer must have added to the pressure to act. Germans, unfortunately, are talkative. My opinion of some of the others involved in the conspiracy is not so positive, but I will always hold Stauffenberg in honorable remembrance.[101]

Back to the Everyday Life

Overall, the events of 20 July had only a marginal effect on those of us on the front lines. Our daily situation with its tensions and crises demanded our full attention. The XLVIII Panzer Corps had held its front line well, while conducting a fluid defense. Our losses were sustainable. We were closely tied in with the adjacent units on our right. The most frustrating thing was the gap that had developed with the adjacent unit on our left, the result of the failure of the 8th Panzer Division. The Russians were pouring through the gap with everything available to destroy the XIII Army Corps on our left.

Now under the command of my chief of staff, Mellenthin, the 8th Panzer Division attempted but failed to close the gap. Anticipating this move, the Russians had established an impenetrable antitank defensive line. The Russians had learned their lessons and drew the right conclusions from our earlier tactics. But the enemy pressure was diminishing in our corps sector, so I pulled the front line back in order to unite the 1st and 8th Panzer Divisions, and then support the XIII Army Corps. The following excerpts from my journal illustrate the kinds of problems we had to deal with:

21 July: "The morning was unpleasant. No contact with any of the divisions. In addition, march movements are difficult on the muddy roads. Slowly the picture becomes clearer. The south and the middle are holding. In the north the 8th Panzer Division established contact with the XIII Army Corps. The 1st Panzer Division also made good progress moving north. One group under Major Zahn particularly distinguished itself. Making a bold, energetic move into Peremyshlyany, it cut the supply line of the Russian VIII Motorized Corps."

22 July: "Not a great day. Bad news followed more bad news. The withdrawal through the mountain terrain with its poor roads is extremely difficult for the troops and their leaders. The congestion is horrible. We have too much materiel forward for the available road network. Bringing it all back is an almost unsolvable task. In the afternoon General [Otto] Lasch, commander of the 349th Division, managed to break out with approximately five thousand men and link up with us."

24 July: "The divisions have been compressed into the smallest of areas. No supply lines are open. Only with great difficulty was I able to move through to organize the occupation of the Gnila-Lipa position."

A stream of troops from the XIII Army Corps poured through that position. They had broken out of the encirclement toward the south. The morale of the troops seemed high, but they were completely physically exhausted. Some were without boots and they moved along sluggishly. Some of them pulled dogs along on leashes. Interspersed in the column were Russian kitchen maids wearing steel helmets and carrying hand grenades, who fought courageously right alongside the troops. During the last storm assault the Russians overran everything. All general officers had been in the forward lines at the time. General Arthur Hauffe, the corps commander, was killed along with his chief of staff. Altogether, between fifteen thousand and twenty thousand men seemed to have made it through.

25 July: "All is quiet in our sector. Unfortunately, the adjacent unit to my south caved in, endangering our only supply route. These have been the most difficult situations that I have lived through in war. The many unnecessary frictions make matters worse. The 1st and 8th Panzer Divisions were supposed to be supplied by air. As the aircraft roared in low above us, our own light FLAK guns promptly shot two of them down. The rest of the aircraft dumped our urgently needed fuel over the Russian lines."

26 July: "We have lived through the most difficult of times. We succeeded in supplying the divisions and getting them out of the difficult mountain forest terrain. My hat off to all the General Staff officers. The strain on the nerves has been immense, especially since we knew that the Russians only had to start moving to destroy us. Thank God they remained idle!"

On 28 July the XLVIII Panzer Corps stood unbroken on the west side of the Dniester River. Our losses in men and equipment were bearable. All the subordinate divisions were fully combat ready. We had pulled off the most difficult of operations. We took a deep breath.

To Be or Not to Be

One should never judge matters too early. The XI Army Corps and the Hungarian Second Army to the right of us collapsed. That gravely threatened the Stryi–Skole–Mukachevo road, the main artery of my corps. If the Russians cut that line it would be impossible to withdraw any equipment or to supply the troops. I drove to the adjacent units on my right. The situation there was horrible. The Hungarians were throwing away their weapons without fighting and were going home. Most of their leaders, doing nothing to reverse the situation, were heading home as well.

On the evening of the 28th a Russian shock group, consisting of their 271st Division, advanced through the Carpathian Mountains toward the road from Skole to Mukachevo. An even stronger group advanced on the northern edge of the Carpathian Mountains through Dolina toward the line Stryi–Skole. I immediately pulled back the 8th Panzer Division and the 100th Jäger Division and sent them toward my right flank.

The Fourth Panzer Army had nothing available to help. It ordered the staffs of the XI Army Corps and XLVIII Panzer Corps to exchange sectors. That was, admittedly, proof of a high level of trust in us, but it was also an almost impossible task. The units we were to assume command of included the 357th Infantry Division, which was across from Dolyna, and north of them the 371st Infantry Division, with a huge forested area in its rear. Somewhere forward in an echeloned formation still stood the very capable 1st Infantry Division. We decided to move the German forces back into a rearward line and unite them with the approaching 8th Panzer and 100th Jäger Divisions, and then to attack and destroy the Russians advancing through Dolyna.

Meanwhile, as the Russian 271st Division was moving forward through the Carpathians toward our lines of communication, we formed ad hoc blocking units from the withdrawing human masses of the XIII Army Corps coming across the pass road. They came under the command of the 36th Infantry Division and were committed from all sides across the mountain ranges and against the flanks and the rear of the Russian 271st Division. Artillery support was not necessary in the forested mountain terrain, and besides, the attacking wedge formations committed against the rear of the isolated Red division had to do whatever they could on their own by carrying through the direction of attack.

Battle of the Lions

The 371st Infantry Division was ordered to withdraw through the forested area to its rear, and to secure this difficult terrain forward of their own front lines. The heavily committed 1st Infantry Division, meanwhile, was supposed to break through south of the forested area and move toward us at night through open terrain. Against specific orders to avoid the forest, and without reporting this to us, they broke through the woods and managed to reach friendly lines. The morning after, the following reports came in:

371st Infantry Division: "Strong enemy forces struck the division's withdrawal movement. The division managed to reach the new positions without any loss in personnel or equipment. The enemy suffered heavy losses."

1st Infantry Division: "The division broke through the forested area without losses against strong enemy resistance and is positioned along the designated line. The enemy suffered heavy losses."

As the old story goes: "*Zwei Löwen gingen miteinand' in einem Wald spazoren, da haben beide wutentbrannt einander aufgezohren.*"[102] That can even be the case when two combat-proven and highly accomplished units under the best leadership are involved. "*Interdum dormit Homerus.*"[103]

The Decision

We had hoped to be able to bring everything forward for the counterattack. That all depended on our ability to hold the front with the divisions that were in contact. The ammunition status of the 1st Infantry Division was one of the biggest concerns at this point. We were scheduled to attack at 0500 hours on 31 July. Earlier that night the Russians attacked us, and near daybreak the troops were exhausted. The 8th Panzer and 357th Infantry Divisions reported at the same time and almost verbatim: "It is over. Total collapse." It looked like the fates of the XLVIII Panzer and XI Army Corps were sealed. Unsurprisingly, the Fourth Panzer Army was nervous, which only compounded our tensions.

In such a situation orders must be executed without compromise. I called both division commanders and ordered, ". . . not a single step back. The division staffs into the forwardmost lines." I did not interfere with any other movements. Any initial Russian success could not be taken too seriously. I did not think it was likely that they would try to exploit their success. We attacked on schedule at 0500 hours on the 31st and overran the enemy in and around Dolina. The 100th Jäger Division advanced as far as Wygoda. On 2 August we had passed the crisis. I recorded in my journal: "We can be satisfied. The hopeless situation that I had inherited from the XI Corps has been turned around. The Russian pincer arm has been destroyed. Their 271st Division is encircled near Kalna—a ray of hope in these dismal days."

3 August: "The battle is over. We opened the pocket and cleared it out. The Russian 271st [Division] was destroyed, their entire equipment captured. Surviving troops have fled into the woods. The defeated enemy near Dolna no longer resists. We can conduct all movements without interference."

In addition to 1,860 counted enemy dead, we had destroyed or captured 13 tanks, 120 antitank guns, 61 field guns, 18 mortars, 165 machine guns, 57 motor vehicles, 216 prisoners and defectors, and a complete convoy of more than 200 vehicles. That evening General Raus called me to express his relief. The Fourth Panzer Army later sent us a telegram: "I commend leadership and troops of the XLVIII Panzer Corps for the action in the vicinity Dolina Skola, which turned into a significant victory by adhering to a decision. Signed Raus."

Army Commander in Poland

After the agonies of the last few days I slept deeply. But one should never count the chickens before they hatch. At 0500 hours I received a call from General Raus: "Proceed immediately to OKH in East Prussia." He did not know what was going on.

On the morning of 5 August I took a rather emotional farewell of my staff. I had grown close with every one of them, especially my chief of staff, Colonel von Mellenthin. He had been a never-failing pillar of strength. We were united by the same military and humanist outlook. I went to the Fourth Panzer Army headquarters, where Raus gave me a most touching farewell. Nine months of the heaviest fighting can bring people very close. I thanked him for his incredible trust in me, which allowed the full development of my strengths. He always covered my back.

I went past Mukachevo's high tower, then past Cracow toward East Prussia. I had known for quite a long time both Guderian, the new chief of the General Staff, and his right-hand man, General Walther Wenck. I had a good impression of their working relationship with Hitler, even though I knew that every superior has to appear optimistic toward his subordinates and can never be critical. Otherwise the instrument will break in his hands. When I reached OKH I learned that I was assigned command of the Fourth Panzer Army.

The Situation

I flew to my new command post at the Fourth Panzer Army in Szydłowiec, passing over the burning Warsaw, which was embroiled in an insurgency and the heaviest of fighting.[104] The situation was more than tense. The Russians had broken through on a wide front on both sides of the Upper Vistula River. We had nothing between them and Silesia. They had turned north and were threatening to roll up the Vistula Front from south to north.

In the north the XLII Army Corps under General Hermann Recknagel, an undaunted, courageous, and prudent leader, faced the Russians with the front line facing the south.

On their left flank stood the LVI Panzer Corps under General Johannes Block. That unit was on the far side of the Vistula with its front line facing east. The Russians in that sector had already gained some bridgeheads across the Vistula. Both corps consisted only of infantry divisions. Of my units, the III Panzer Corps was assembling with the 3rd, 8th, and 17th Panzer Divisions, while my old XLVIII Panzer Corps was redeploying with the 1st, 16th, and 23rd Panzer Divisions.

The situation as I found it would have caused a sense of hopelessness in the typical armchair strategist. On closer examination, however, things looked somewhat different. The enemy was at the end of his strength after intense fighting and making enormous advances. His supply lines were not functioning yet, while on our side the supply lines were short and intact. Our supply bases were full and positioned right behind the front lines, and reinforcements were coming in from all directions.

In short order the enemy advance exceeded its culmination point and the situation was now favorable for a counterattack. It was exactly as Clausewitz had described it. The situation was there to exploit, but the psychological strain of what was to come exceeded even what we had experienced in the earlier part of the year.

Initial Fighting

The first thing to do was to hold the front line, and that could be done only by attacking. The XLII Panzer Corps did this very well. In heavy fighting the corps destroyed 120 Russian tanks on 9 August and another fifty-six just a few days later. Russian tanks that had broken through were hunted down and destroyed by pursuit detachments that were committed everywhere on foot, by bicycle, on horseback, and even by *Panzerfaust*-armed[105] troops in motor vehicles. These detachments were composed mostly of the often-derided supply clerks and kitchen police. They performed heroically.

The fighting had its share of drama. For days the 72nd Infantry Division was cut off, but it was able to break out with the support of the 23rd Panzer Division. They lost only one artillery piece in the process. The Russians, however, reported that they had totally destroyed three divisions. They also reported not having taken any prisoners because all the Germans had been killed.

My plane trips to the front lines were also tense affairs, but it was only by using a Storch that I could be at the right place and at the right time. On my first plane trip I was sent off in the wrong direction and came under fire from Russian tanks when we landed. I quickly jumped out of the aircraft when Russian scouts appeared to be firing at the Storch. But then I jumped back in quickly and we took off. We had to start by turning directly toward the Russian tanks. The Storch took five hits, but we got away. The pilot, Feldwebel[106] Moritz, was completely calm throughout.

The events of 20 July had hit the Fourth Panzer Army headquarters staff like a bomb. The chief of staff was involved in the affair, and I was ordered to send him back to Berlin. Upon assuming command I immediately noticed the lax, mechanical, and unmotivated way that staff work was done. I requested and was assigned my old Mellenthin.

Transition to the Large-Scale Attack

In the meantime my two Panzer corps had been assembled and we launched an attack on the Baranov bridgehead. Within just a few days it had been reduced to one third of its original size, but we did not succeed in eliminating it. The

Russian forces were too strong. We estimated their strength at approximately four tank armies and one infantry army, supported by strong air assets. Our own troops were also showing strong signs of wear and exhaustion. The staffs were not leading from the battlefield anymore. Almost all of the staffs had established their combat command posts in buildings. It was understandable, then, that the troops attacked in only the most lax manner. At one division, with a good reputation, I found all of the leaders of an infantry regiment committed to the attack positioned inside houses and commanding by telephone. I had traveled forward on a *Kettenkrad*[107]; I loaded them on it and drove them forward. Then I moved on. But the commander cannot be everywhere all of the time. A newly arrived Tiger battalion lost within twenty-four hours all but three of its forty-five Tigers because of technical breakdowns. Almost daily I noted in my journal entries that the troops no longer understood how to exploit initial successes.

By massing strong artillery fires we managed to eliminate a small Russian bridgehead on our side of the Vistula, destroying a Russian division in the process. Only the division commander reached the eastern bank of the Vistula by swimming back across. The Russians were not the same anymore. They were suffering from the same difficulties we were.

I must at this point pay honor to the memory of one man, the commanding general of the XLVIII Panzer Corps, General of Panzer Troops Fritz-Hubert Gräser. Having previously lost a leg to a severe wound, he commanded on a prosthetic leg. Because he no longer had the agility to take cover quickly, and he always led from the front, a grenade tore off his remaining leg. As soon as he had recovered he kept going on two prosthetic legs and still led under fire in the most forward lines. His leadership was superb. He was my successor at the Fourth Panzer Army, and commanded it until the end of the war.[108]

At the Führer's Headquarters

On 8 and 9 September 1944 I was at the Führer's headquarters, where Hitler awarded me the Diamonds to the Knight's Cross.[109] Hitler was very solicitous toward me, emphasizing repeatedly how satisfied he was with my leadership. "Yes, that's how it should be done," he repeated several times. Later, he personally arranged for me to fly back to my headquarters with a fighter escort. Guderian also said that the fight had been "the first offensively conducted defensive battle."

I spoke with Hitler about the situation and the Russian advance on Bucharest. He said, "Now they are moving toward their old objective, Constantinople, and then it will be our turn, because that will turn England against them."

"If they do that," I responded, "they would have to let go of us and would be gambling away all of their successes of the last years. First, they have to defeat us completely, then Constantinople will fall into their lap by itself. I believe that they are going into Bucharest now in order to finish us off first."

Hitler looked at me for a long time and said: "You do not have the intelligence information that I have."

Later, after the end of the war, I spoke about this with Field Marshal Maximilian von Weichs, who at the time had been the commander of Army Group F in the southeast. He told me, "In effect, the English did not disrupt our withdrawal from Crete. Surfaced English submarines moved alongside our transport ships, with their crews waving at our people. I had the impression that England was glad to see the movement of German divisions toward Bucharest." The interpretation of intelligence is the most difficult of tasks. It is so easy to believe what you want to believe.

I discussed the situation at large with Guderian. I explained that as long as we were fighting in long thin lines and remained in an inflexible defense the Russians would mass incredibly large forces at the points of attack, and we would not be able to hold. Between those attack wedges we had almost nothing; but we were tying down our own major forces in front of these screens. If we were able to shift into an attack posture, they too would have to make themselves strong everywhere, and their attack wedges would have to be dispersed. Guderian essentially agreed with me, but he was not yet clear on how to solve the problem.

The overall situation only became clear to me after the war. In the Courland bridgehead numerically inferior Russian forces tied down our garrison force. The Russians had withdrawn almost everything from the Finnish front, where approximately two hundred thousand Russians faced five hundred thousand Finns. Finnish officers were urging us to take advantage of this situation. Unfortunately, the political dynamics were not right. Finnish leader Carl Mannerheim was looking for a way out of the war, which was understandable from his standpoint. He had no reason to support German policies and in the end his own political path allowed Finland to survive as an independent state.

According to legend, Hitler after 20 July was hermetically sealed off and every visitor, even generals, supposedly had to go through a body search before coming into his presence. I never encountered anything of the sort. It was like it always had been. I was never required to surrender my pistol while visiting Hitler; and if I had decided to use it, nobody could have stopped me.

When I returned to my command post an intense battle was raging all around it. Our Kalmyk Division[110] was slugging it out with partisans. This was the first time that I had heard of this peculiar unit. The fighting methods of the

Kalmyks had not changed since the times of Genghis Khan and Tamerlane, and had actually gotten worse. I asked the commander of the eastern troops, General Ernst-August Köstring, to try to bring the division under control, and shortly thereafter I had them reassigned.

Finale in Poland

On 12 September I wrote in my journal: "[The Fourth Panzer] Army's situation is at this time not at all unfavorable. We have won a defensive battle against the mass of Russian tank forces. The enemy at this time has been weakened to the point that he will most likely not be able to attack again within the next 10–14 days." Actually, the Russians did not resume attacking for another three to four months.

But we also realized that the front—I called it a "pretzel" front because of its shape—could not be held in this manner. During my visit to the Führer Headquarters I recommended to Guderian straightening the front line and moving it back twenty kilometers, which thus would allow us to form all of our mobile forces into a reserve. Guderian concurred, but Hitler vetoed it. So then we decided to straighten the front line by moving forward, which in the process would eliminate the Russians' Vistula bridgehead. That option had definite advantages as well. As a precautionary measure I ordered the improvement of the short line twenty kilometers back and had the area in front of it cleared. According to Guderian's memoirs, this line twenty kilometers to the rear later played a fatal role in the conflict between him and Hitler.[111]

Dorotka

On 12 September we attacked the Dorotka bridgehead. The enemy was between four and six divisions strong. Our attack was conducted with only six battalions, which had been pulled out of the front lines earlier, well rested and especially trained for this mission. Although we committed only a minimum number of infantry, we supported them with an incredible amount of materiel.

The artillery preparation was conducted by the divisional artilleries of the 1st Infantry Division, the 2nd Panzer Division, and the corps artillery units. The artillery assets of two more divisions were pulled out, leaving one gun per battery in position. The withdrawn guns fired in the preparation and then shifted back immediately to their old positions after completion of the preparatory fires. The risk was manageable. The Russians usually did not react that quickly. For the most part, they did not even detect the shifting back and forth of our artillery.

The artillery was augmented by the fires of two rocket launcher brigades. At suitable positions the engineers also dug emplacements for several hundred heavy howitzers. Thank God we had an excellent senior artillery officer who was fully capable of managing all of this.

After a fire strike of unprecedented intensity, the Panzers of two Panzer divisions thrust through the bridgehead and cut it off from the rear. Simultaneously, the six battalions supported by 120 assault guns attacked. We had massed for the attack all the available assault guns in the Fourth Panzer Army.

During the battle we intercepted the following radio traffic:

A: "You will hold your position."

B: "I am finished."

A: "Reinforcements are on the way."

B: "To hell with your reinforcements. I am cut off. Your great reinforcements will not find anybody here."

A: "For the last time. I prohibit you to transmit in the open. I would rather you would shoot your own people than allow the enemy to do that."

B: "Comrade 54, maybe you will grasp my situation when I tell you that there is nobody left to shoot except my radio operator."

It had been one of the most modern, if not the most modern, attack of the war. Here I had for a change the opportunity to draw from the experiences of World War I, which showed that war does not favor repeated patterns. All actions must be based on the immediate situation. In the new positions we established along the Vistula River our daily losses were reduced to a minimum. As soon as the situation had stabilized I took six days of leave to visit my family in nearby Silesia. I had been at home only four days when I received a call: "Report immediately to the Führer Headquarters. Follow-on assignment in the West."

My duties in the East had for now come to an end. But it was a closure in other ways, too. We were now standing along the same line from which we started our attack on Russia in 1941, meaning that we had lost the campaign against the Soviets.

Politics in the East

Wars are won and lost on the political level. Bismarck deserved at least as much credit as Moltke for winning the Wars of German Unification. Within the framework of the miserable Prussian politics of 1805–1806 the courageous Prussian Army had not been able to accomplish anything. And what did the situation look like now? The campaign in the East had been based on a completely false political assumption. Hitler, whose view of the world had been formed by World War I, never moved beyond the mind-set of the infantryman on the western front. He considered the Russians a dumb, amorphous herd, without a sense of technology and who needed a leader and a master who could lead and control the masses.

The cruelties of the Bolshevik Revolution only added to Hitler's misconceptions. The conclusion was that we were a master race, they were subhumans, and the result would be a German imperium in the space of Eastern Europe. Hitler was encouraged by many people who never disagreed with him. Our chances might have been different if our policies had been liberation and independence for the countries on the periphery; no territorial acquisitions; the overthrow of Bolshevism; and all the land to the farmers in a free Russia. In many parts of the East we actually had been welcomed as liberators at first. This had been the case in the Baltic States, in eastern Galicia, and in the Caucuses.

The instant abolition of the Kolkhoz[112] system would have produced favorable results for us too. But our administrators generally were incapable of dealing with the required tasks in a foreign land and under conditions they only vaguely understood. Wherever our administration was good, as in eastern Galicia, the population stood loyally behind us. At times it felt like we were fighting on home territory. If our administration in the Ukraine had been all that poor, the Ukrainian people who fled from the Russians would not have shielded our former area commander of Rava-Ruska, Mehring, for so long, eventually getting him back to safety. General von Pannwitz with his Cossack troops was another example of what might have been possible, had we pursued a reasonable political policy in the East. We could not have won the war by military means alone. Soldiers, politicians, and economists should have worked hand-in-hand based on a reasonable, common concept.

Was the campaign in the East necessary? At the time the situation was not all that clear. Fear was likely a key factor. When after the campaign in the West we redeployed divisions to our eastern borders, the Russians responded by deploying their divisions to their western border, which was then followed by move and countermove. When the deployment was finalized and staged on both sides, it was only a small step until the first shot was fired, as experience shows. Fear of losing the initiative was a strong stimulus.[113]

While Hitler underestimated the Russians, Stalin overestimated us. But we failed to capitalize on the incredible respect and the deference that the average Russian had for Germany.

It would have been ideal if we had managed to maneuver Russia into a conflict with England, and then slowly disengaged to play the role of the *tertius gaudens*.[114] But this only could have worked by letting Russia have Romania and

Bulgaria and allowing them access to the Mediterranean. All that, however, was unacceptable to Hitler.

And Stalin was too smart. There was a reason that he halted the Russian campaign in Finland short of total military and political victory. He did not want a conflict with the West. He wanted to save the role of *tertius gaudens* for himself. Hitler was afraid of Stalin in such a role. Nor did he want a two-front war; therefore, the Soviet Union had to be destroyed before the Anglo-Americans could again attack on land. But in order to avoid a two-front war, Hitler ironically rushed into a two-front war, overlooking the possibility of a triple alliance of Germany-Russia-Japan, which would have been invincible against the Anglo-Americans. Hitler's never-ending mistrust thwarted the possibility of any such plan.

The often repeated argument that war with the Soviet Union was inevitable must be rejected. Nobody can see the future. Even in 1945 certain circles in the United States were playing with the idea of a preventive war against Russia. Since the end of World War II the conflict between Moscow and Peking, which was not foreseeable then, has created a new situation. In politics one must have staying power. But regardless, the soldier has to accept the situation that war brings and he has to make the best of it. "Right or wrong, my country."[115]

Hannibal in Russia

Since the end of the Thirty Years' War Germany stood against a *cauchemar des coalitions*:[116] France-Sweden; France-Turkey; France-Russia; France-Poland; England-Russia; and America-Russia. Militarily this required us to strike before superior forces could be united and massed against us. The problem on the battlefield became one of winning against larger forces.

Our military philosophy, formed in practice by Frederick the Great, theoretically developed by Clausewitz, and advanced to a science by Moltke and Schlieffen, was based on solving that problem. Schlieffen started with Hannibal's victory at Cannae, in which the Carthaginians with a smaller force had been able to destroy the numerically superior Roman legions, led by consuls and lawyers. We got as far as the doctrine of the double envelopment battle, but unfortunately we did not develop from there. Why did the most brilliant military commander, who was at the head of the best army of its time, and who had prepared for war politically in a first-rate manner, lose the war, even though initially there was no equally capable "Roman" facing him as an opponent and he was adding one victorious campaign streamer after another to his battle flag?[117]

We have, unfortunately, never pursued these problems to the end. After Cannae, Hannibal did not march on to Rome, which caused his cavalry commander Marhabal to exclaim, "*Vincere scis, Hannibal, victoria uti nescis.*"[118] Did Hannibal lack military leadership greatness, or did he correctly know the limits of his power? He probably was right because he was vulnerable in human resources and space. Both of these factors were on the side of Rome, as well as decisive maritime dominance.

Germany also achieved legendary victories but in the end succumbed to the human factor, space, and maritime domination, all of which were clearly on the side of Russia. Unfortunately, we did not have the sense of proportion and reality, like the great Carthaginian. Visionary soldiers had recognized the situation. Seeckt once said, "Russia is invincible." Soldiers have no say in politics; that is the realm of politicians. But when things go wrong, naturally the soldier is blamed. That is how it has always been—in 1806, in 1918, in 1945, and so on.[119]

One point that was rarely discussed was what we would have done had we achieved victory? Before the beginning of the war I was called to OKH and asked about one aspect of this issue. Could we use the potentially large numbers of captured Russian tanks to equip our units for the conduct of the expected small-scale wars? Could we maintain our levels of armament production? No one seemed to understand that this was more of a political question than a technical one. Today, with the benefit of hindsight, we can say that we would have ended up like Napoleon in Spain. Our significant postwar historical writings still show significant gaps.[120]

17

Commander in Chief, Army Group G

Hitler's Situational Assessment

I had been home just four days when I received a call from the Führer Head-quarters, "Report immediately! Then proceed to the West." Hitler appointed me as *Oberbefehlshaber*[1] of Army Group G and explained the following:

"Owing to logistical difficulties the Allies will come to a standstill at about their current line. This must be exploited for a counterattack. The Americans have nothing behind them. No reserves. If we break through anywhere they have nothing to throw against us. On the side of the Allies it is a complete campaign of deception. I hope to be able to attack in the middle of November with strong forces, which will include ten Panzer divisions and strong air assets.[2] Assumed preconditions would be muddy ground and foggy weather, so that the enemy air forces and armored forces are either neutralized or at a minimum held in check. We must do it like the Russians, until we are strong again in the air. Until the beginning of the offensive the situation in the West will have developed as follows. On the right wing we will have withdrawn to the Rhine. I hope that we will succeed in pulling all our forces back there. In the middle we will be able to hold the West Wall. Your mission is to do so with as small a force as possible. Under no circumstances can forces that are earmarked for the offensive be drawn off by you. Should you also succeed in holding in Alsace, I would really appreciate that, so I have a security buffer if I need it."

It was a rather sobering and precise situational analysis, which I could endorse absolutely. My mission statement was significantly better defined and more "*generalstabsmässig*"[3] than the one for the German Sixth Army, which fought in the same sector in 1914. Hitler did not know that the Allies could defog their airfields and he overlooked the reality that the American reserves were not in France but in America, from which they could be transported rapidly to where they were needed with modern means of transportation. I, too, did not recognize these two points.

Then Hitler addressed the disciplinary situation in the West that appeared more than gloomy. Some units had retreated in a single bound from Lyon back to Halle on the Saale River.

Hitler gave me complete authority to act, free of all legal restrictions. That was a great deal of power for a single commander, but any western army would have done the same facing a similar situation.[4] Personally, I had the impression that Hitler was completely normal and in full command of his mental faculties. There was no indication at all that anything had changed from before. He was as always friendly and personable toward me and he assured me again and again that I had his full trust.

A glance at the situation map was not discouraging. Three field armies were in position along the line from Luxembourg to Belfort, with approximately fifteen corps headquarters and about fifty divisions. Everything depended on what the reality on the ground looked like.

Probing

I used my stay in Rastenburg to orient myself thoroughly, politically, militarily, and on the new weapons technologies. Militarily, Hitler's statements had been correct. Ten fully equipped Panzer divisions should be able to turn the tide, together with the allocated infantry divisions. The force ratio compared to the Allies was not unfavorable. In France in 1940 we had also only committed about ten Panzer divisions.

Politically, there doubtlessly were weak spots on the enemy side. The Canadians were the best troops the Allies had, but they had exhibited insubordinate conduct during their transport to Europe and the Canadian Parliament had agreed to the troop commitment with only a one-vote majority. A few days later I called on Ambassador Franz von Papen,[5] who lived in the Saarland region, to discuss the political situation with him. During our conversation he said that he did not consider it impossible for us to reach a gentlemen's agreement with the western Allies regarding the Soviet Union.

The questions about the new weapons technologies were of the utmost importance. I had always been of the opinion that superior weapons and equipment were worth more than good operational leadership. From Miltiades[6] to Gaius Duilius[7] and his boarding devices to the Prussian needle gun and the tank, military history teaches this lesson rather clearly. Any military success we might achieve in the West in 1944 would only have a significant effect if it bought us the time to regain weapons technology superiority. If we could do that, then we could at least hope for a draw. From conversations with Armaments Minister Albert Speer, I learned of several innovations that were technically feasible, although Speer was quite somber and did not exhibit much hope or optimism. The new weapons under development included:

Walter's air-independent submarine propulsion system, and a U-boat with an improved snorkel, against which the Allies had no countermeasures.

An acoustically guided FLAK projectile that would home in on the aircraft to the point of impact.

New jet aircraft in sufficiently large numbers.

Tanks with infrared target acquisition systems that would turn night fighting into daytime, leaving the opponent blind. Later in Hungary I commanded the first units so equipped.

Thus, the picture of our situation that emerged was one where these new technologies were our last chance to thwart our enemies' inflexible intent to destroy us. What would come after the called-for unconditional surrender seemed so horrible that it justified any course of action.[8] *We had to fight like a cornered rat.*[9]

First Impressions

While at the Führer Headquarters I requested that Mellenthin, my highly proven chief of staff, be reassigned to me. Hitler agreed. Two men who work well together for so long should not be split up. During World War I in France we had not followed that principle.

I met Mellenthin in Łódź and from Darmstadt on we drove by car to Molsheim, where the Army Group G command post was located. While crossing the Rhine we encountered combat-ready elements of a Panzer division that was moving back toward Baden-Baden, supposedly for reconstitution. In Molsheim the traffic was so bad that I ordered the area commander to report to me immediately. A distinguished older gentleman appeared and reported that he was the personal friend of the previous army group commander in chief, and he could not be held responsible for anything since there was no funding for his activities. Coming from the East, I realized I had entered an alien world.

The overall situation was not unfavorable. Instead of rushing forward toward the Rhine between Lorraine and the Vosges Mountains, the Americans let themselves be drawn toward Metz, where they were fighting stubbornly but without success for the Metz fortresses. That ring of fortresses around the city was courageously and effectively defended by the soldiers of an officer candidate school class. That provided us some time to reconstitute slowly the First Army, which was commanded by my old commanding general and predecessor at the XLVIII Panzer Corps, General von Knobelsdorf. On his left the brilliant Manteuffel commanded the Fifth Panzer Army, which extended as far south as the edge of the Vosges Mountains. Originally, the Fifth Panzer Army was supposed to thrust from the plateau at Langres into the American right flank, but the attack never came off. Fantasies that are not based on reality are seldom achievable.[10] Now the Americans were pushing forward toward the Saar region, along

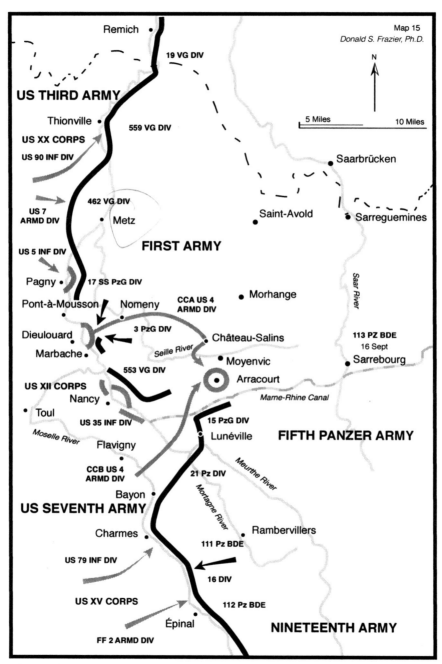

Map 15. Army Group G Situation, 15 September 1944. (Map by Donald S. Frazier)

the boundary between the First Army and the Fifth Panzer Army. There is where I assessed the greatest danger. In preparation for a counterattack I moved everything available there, including my old reliable 11th Panzer Division. The reality we constantly faced was that whenever the flying weather was bad our attacks moved along quickly. As soon as the enemy's air forces were able to bear down on us with little or no opposition, all progress stopped. After consulting with Field Marshal Gerd von Rundstedt, the OB-West,[11] we halted the attacks.

Having established a straight defensive front line, we considered at the time that we had achieved complete success. In reality, however, the situation on the Allied side had been such that Eisenhower stopped Generals Omar Bradley[12] and George Patton[13] because all supplies had been diverted north to capture the Ruhr region before the onset of winter. Nonetheless, it gave us a bitterly needed break.

On the left flank of Manteuffel's Fifth Panzer Army, the Nineteenth Army under General of the Infantry Friedrich Wiese held the line of the Vosges Mountains forward of Belfort all the way to the Swiss border. At the Zhizdra River Wiese had commanded an infantry division adjacent to my division. His army consisted only of a few combat-ready units very thinly deployed. It had conducted a difficult but well-commanded withdrawal from the French Riviera to Belfort, but it was now looking toward future developments with apprehension.[14]

The American spearheads were closing in on the Nineteenth Army's line. I ordered it to attack the points of the American force. Wiese and his chief of staff, General Walter Botsch, looked at me uncomprehendingly and asked, "With what?" Then we pored over the map together and scraped up anything that could be assembled. Only patrols or flimsy screens remained in large sectors of the front line. But the energetic Wiese was finally able to attack the American advance guards and bring them to a halt. The Americans were not good at fighting in wooded terrain, and being on the attack undeniably generates its own magical power. "*Attaquez donc toujours*"[15] the great field commanders always preached. The Americans thought we were stronger than we actually were.

The condition of the Nineteenth Army was pitiful. One division had no artillery at all. Somebody had surrendered the division's artillery and other combat-capable units to an American lieutenant and his twelve men. Now the division's infantry was paying for that with their blood. The Nineteenth Army had been held up for too long on the Langres Plateau to be able to incorporate that withdrawing division and at the same time cover a planned Panzer thrust into the American right flank. That Panzer thrust had to be scrubbed. The Nineteenth Army reached the Vosges Mountains too late and too hastily.

What would happen if the Nineteenth Army were thrown back against the bridgeless upper Rhine did not bear contemplating. Wiese tried to reassure me. One of his staff sections was planning everything for a crossing, with twelve crossing sites being prepared and manned. But when I heard the names of the people in charge of the crossing, I decided to drive there immediately. I expected the worst, and even those expectations were surpassed. Twelve individual pontoons had been distributed along the entire Upper Rhine, without the possibility of actually building a single crossing. The approach routes had not been marked, and some of those responsible were lounging in the warm autumn sun. A crossing of that size required approximately sixteen bridges of two to four pontoons each. There is no telling what these people thought they could do with twelve individual pontoons. If it had come to a rearward surge of the two hundred thousand to three hundred thousand Nineteenth Army troops in Alsace, the result would have been a catastrophe, for which Hitler naturally would have been blamed.

The following day I gave those responsible for the crossing a piece of my mind. Looking into their blank faces, I heard the standard line in such situations: "We have nothing left." But within three to four days everything had been staged. All of a sudden personnel and equipment had become available.

Alsace was full of non-combat-effective units, including the Indian Legion, a Russian SS division that had already mutinied once, Cossack brigades, and the supply trains of several destroyed divisions. Hitler had prohibited the withdrawal across the Rhine of all these elements without his explicit order. If I wanted to avoid a catastrophe, all these people that could not or did not want to fight had to be brought back across the Rhine. After a very difficult, day-long series of arguments, Hitler finally agreed to move these people across the river and into Baden.[16] At that point, we seized the opportunity to bring back across the Rhine anything that had no combat value. That was Mellenthin's work.

What made things even more complicated was that Himmler was now the commander in chief of the *Ersatzheer*.[17] He immediately started to collect up officers who had completely failed with us and reinstate them in positions of responsibility in the Ersatzheer and the new *Volkseinheiten*.[18] He was assured of their complete loyalty to him, but they did not become any more competent. They only created more problems.

Himmler had a penchant for recruiting the delinquents, putting them into good positions, but letting the still-open legal cases dangle in front of them. He also set them up well financially. Not everyone could resist such an opportunity. I knew of one case in which Ernst Schlange[19] had called Reichsminister of Labor Robert Ley a drunkard, and was sentenced to a concentration camp for it. If he agreed to throw in with Himmler, he would be set up as an *SS-*

Brigadeführer.[20] Schlange chose to stay in the concentration camp. My hat is off to such strength of character. Schlange was the younger brother of Hans Schlange-Schoeningen, one of the founders of the Christian Democratic Union.[21]

During these days it became clear to me what Himmler was up to. He was creating SS organizations everywhere to take over the Reich, should the opportunity arise. He already controlled all the police, and he was reaching into the Wehrmacht. The *Volksgrenadier* units were only staffed with officers of his choosing, many of whom had criminal pasts. There was no concern for capability. How he imagined he could accomplish his goal remains unclear—possibly an alliance with Russia and a form of "Brown Bolshevism."[22]

The condition of the troops was abominable for the most part. The newly formed and now ubiquitous Volksgrenadier divisions[23] were not fully trained. Even worse, they were under Himmler's jurisdiction for military justice matters, which created additional unfathomable difficulties. In order to slow down the withdrawal from the West, OKW had instituted a number of special courts-martial with increased summary powers. These courts came directly under Field Marshal Wilhelm Keitel.[24] Order had to be established out of all this chaos. I immediately suspended the special courts-martial and sent them home. That at least reduced the number of court organizations. A number of units, including several Panzer brigades, were not self-supporting. They had insufficient maintenance assets and they were quickly disintegrating, even without enemy action. I disbanded those units and integrated their assets into the Panzer divisions.

The Panzer division that I had run into at the Rhine crossing on its way to reconstitution in Baden-Baden came under especially thorough scrutiny. It had three hundred men on the front line and approximately nine thousand combatants back in Baden-Baden. It was holding a frontline sector of approximately two kilometers. After three days, six thousand men with their weapons were forward again and the division held a sector of twenty-five kilometers.

Almost all the Panzer divisions had repositioned their maintenance assets across the Rhine, mostly to Baden-Baden. The refurbished tanks that were damaged again at the Saverne Gap during the march movement toward the front had to return back to Baden-Baden for repair. That crazy game stopped when I ordered the maintenance units to displace closer to the front, where they were supposed to be.

Every soldier needs rations, uniforms, mail, and rest in order to perform his duty. These were issues that I immediately got involved in. The food supplies were taken from the surrounding country, and that process was under control. Uniform supplies were miserable for the most part. Troops were wearing tropical uniforms in the wet, melting, pre-winter snow of the Vosges Mountains.

Change was needed. My hat is off to those troops who staunchly lived through that and still fought well.

Sadly, I could not offer them any rest, but mail I could. The responsible senior postal official gave me an excellent rundown on how everything worked. All units were designated by their field post numbers, he told me, and everything worked with lightning speed. Unfortunately for him, he did not know me. I had the disconcerting habit of going into the forwardmost positions and asking the last man there when he had received comfort items last and how much he had received. What did he get for rations that day? When was the last time he received mail and how did he send it off? After three days I found out that many units did not have assigned field post numbers and the troops were not getting mail from home.

I had the responsible gentleman report to me. He had to admit everything. The mail from home was routed to a specific location in Baden and it was then regularly destroyed in Allied bombing attacks.

"What have you done to stop this?"

"I am not authorized to interfere there, that is outside of my jurisdiction."

"So, you did nothing."

"I am not authorized to interfere."

What I did find out is that his own office had succeeded in receiving the highest ration priority for itself. When I downgraded the postal activities to the lowest ration priority, order returned to the field postal operation and mail was no longer destroyed by fire. Of course, the said gentleman objected to what he considered an affront to his bruised honor. I countered by saying that I thought his honor was to supply the troops with mail from home, and not to supply his own stomach.

Conclusions

Once I had an understanding of everything, it was time to act. On 10 October I wrote Colonel General Alfred Jodl at OKW a personal letter that I knew he would share with General Buhle, who in turn would show it to Hitler. According to historian Percy Schramm, Hitler concluded from the letter that the conditions of the First Army and the Fifth Panzer Army were passable, and that of the Nineteenth Army was abominable.[25] I wrote: "I have never before commanded such a hodgepodge and poorly equipped bunch of troops. The fact that we were able to correct the situation and finally hand off the 3rd Panzergrenadier Division to the north was only made possible by the poor and hesitant leadership of the Americans and the French, combined with efforts of the troops who managed to put up one hell of a fight despite being grouped into ad hoc units. What has been accomplished here by both general officers and soldiers who often fought side-by-side in the forwardmost lines against forces stronger in both personnel and equipment has been nothing short of incredible."

OKW and Hitler had to know what was and what was not possible here. I chose the format of the personal letter to ensure that the report did not get stuck somewhere, that it would make it to Hitler, and to prevent it from being watered down. It was also the earliest possible time that I could do this, two weeks after taking command and after our initial successes. If I had sent it earlier one could have argued correctly that I should have first developed a better assessment of the situation. When Jodl, as usual, did not answer me, I arranged in coordination with my excellent National Socialist leadership officer (NSFO),[26] Freiherr von Lersener, to forward a similar letter through NSFO channels. According to Schramm, Hitler read both versions.

I had selected Lersener as my NSFO. He was an old officer and former Hessian Guards Dragoon, a little older than me. He was an aristocrat of the best stature. After the war he was awarded the Federal Republic of Germany's Order of Merit for his charitable work.[27]

Rest Period

October brought us a totally unexpected break and we used it well. Army Group G headquarters displaced to Bergzabern because the telephone lines in Molsheim were disrupted every time there was a bombing raid on Strasbourg. Then the organizational tasks started. Units that had no chance of surviving were disbanded, including the entire *Volkssturm*.[28] Those members who were trained soldiers were sent to existing units. Untrained individuals were sent to special training units. Youths were sent home. I also argued fiercely and successfully against a recommendation of one of our highest and most influential generals to use the Hitler Youth in the rear area services as messengers, etc., in order to free up soldiers for the front. Children do not belong in combat and in the rear they only learn how to play truant. Fortunately, the leadership of the Hitler Youth supported me on this.[29]

We formed training units, through which we made every effort to funnel all replacements. We tried hard to avoid sending poorly trained individuals to the front. Back in Germany, fortress battalions had been formed from soldiers suffering from various dyspeptic conditions and hearing loss. When these units were deployed forward to us I seriously questioned their value. Some of those units were sent to Fortress Metz. Some we retrained as mine-laying battalions and then committed to establishing extensive minefield obstacles in the rear areas of the emerging attack zones. Both missions were within the capabilities of the health conditions of those soldiers. Army group headquarters centrally controlled and managed the emplacement of the minefields. Based on operational requirements, we used combinations of live and dummy mines. Thus, these otherwise operationally useless units were able to contribute to stopping the large-scale attacks of the American elite units.[30]

We were especially well supported by Area Command XII, which always understood the importance of sending us additional battalions and batteries. Arriving replacements normally went to the First Army in Lorraine. That was where the decision would be made. The Nineteenth Army in the Vosges Mountains remained the proverbial stepchild for replacements, a fact that makes what it accomplished even more impressive. It was most important to reestablish orderly combat conditions, but a large portion of the senior leadership was not up to that task. Many of the senior commanders in the West had commanded in the East, but not very successfully. They were not much better in the West. Many of them still wanted to command based on the outdated principles of World War I.

It was a continuously repeating process. The Americans would attack some hill and be repulsed. Then they would come back under the protection of a Red Cross flag or a white flag of truce and negotiate a cease-fire to recover their wounded. In the process, they would infiltrate our positions. At that point the local German commander would panic, scrape up what he had available, and throw it against the enemy in a disorganized fashion. That, of course, usually failed and resulted in great losses. I therefore prohibited any cease-fires without my personal approval. There had been nothing like this sort of thing in the East, and during all of World War I we had managed without it, too. But at this stage of the war we could not force the Americans to observe the Geneva and the Hague Conventions. There is no justice without the power to enforce it.[31]

The Americans acted just like they had during the Sioux Wars, which I later learned about while traveling through Indian reservations in the United States. Even before the war I had read such things in novels about the Indians.[32] It is peculiar how an army cannot outgrow the principles upon which it was established.

After a few days I received a report that another hill had been lost after abuse of the cease-fire, followed by a failed counterattack with heavy losses. I court-martialed the responsible commander, but he was acquitted because the court found that the reality was different than what had been indicated in the clear, unambiguous report. With a knowing smile it also was reported to me orally that the "right" judges had been selected. After the war I learned that there had been relatives of the defendant among the judges. But there was nothing more I could do through legal channels. I accepted what I considered to be a wrong finding and reinstated the person in question. A few days later I relieved him again, but then the Nineteenth Army neglected to send him home. He became my fanatical enemy, but there was no one whose low opinion I valued more highly. The eighteen days of rest and relaxation he was given did not make him a better officer.

Normandy

The horrible fighting in Normandy broke the backs of many of the older leadership. We called it the "Normandy Syndrome," much like what in Naples we had called the "Tunis Syndrome," referring to those who had been broken in North Africa. The only way to deal with this problem was through the large-scale replacement of the affected individuals.

The battle in Normandy and the successful Allied invasion was naturally often the topic of conversation. Could the invasion battle have been won? I believe so, although I must beg indulgence for offering the after-the-fact wisdom of a nonparticipant. Two points have emerged in my mind.

First, if you want to win a battle you must first decide whether you want to fight it operationally or tactically. An operational approach equals movement; nothing other than allowing the enemy to approach and then grabbing him in the open field and beating him with the old, proven methods. We would have been well suited for such a solution. Unfortunately, the proponents of this solution overlooked the fact that the enemy's overwhelming air superiority made movement virtually impossible, and therefore operations were not possible. The operational solution was completely untenable even though some key military leaders advocated it.

Victory could have been achieved tactically by layering the defense in depth at the anticipated landing site and keeping the reserves close by on a broad front to thrust automatically and immediately at the first landing attempts. Tactical logistics operations would have to be secured within air defense corridors. Operational moves would have to be reduced to a minimum.

Both solutions were considered without reaching any clear conclusions. Rommel opted for the tactical solution, Rundstedt for the operational. All of the senior leadership positions in the theater should have been filled with confirmed advocates of the tactical solution.[33] Rommel was right there in place. Field Marshals Walther Model and Günther von Kluge would have been equally qualified to execute the tactical solution. The effects of the vagueness of our basic defensive concept and the command assignments can be traced throughout the entire battle.

The second point is a further mistake in our personnel policies. Everyone who had been unsuccessful in the East was transferred into an equivalent position in the West. This created an unhealthy atmosphere that was contrary to the necessary decisive will to win, and without that will victory is impossible. The events surrounding Rommel and Hans Speidel seemed to have had a further negative effect.[34] Future historians should evaluate this closely.

New Formations

It would not have been easy to execute the necessary personnel policies. The continuous establishment of new divisions required a constant drain of the best human resources from the old units, from the NCOs on up. By that point in the war we had suffered six hundred General Staff officers killed, and a casualty rate for general officers that was higher than for combat infantry units.[35] They were difficult to replace. The main bodies of the old divisions remained in existence, and they too required the best leaders we could provide. But by and large the newly raised units were not up to the standards of the old units. Hitler tried to bluff it out by constantly forming new divisions. In war, in the world of hard facts, deception can often produce success; but it cannot do so endlessly and not always in the same manner.

Combat Preparations

We assumed that the attacks by the Americans would resume soon. We assessed three axes of advance as the most likely: two between Metz and the Vosges Mountains and one north of Metz. I ordered every division to keep in reserve one infantry regiment, one assault gun battalion, one artillery battalion, and one antitank company. The artillery, of course, would remain in position and be integrated into the existing fire plans. Each reserve force was to be ready to move immediately. The intent was to commit these tactical reserves from all directions and without delay against any necessary focal point. Thus, we would compensate for our inability to establish operational reserves. An important secondary intention was to thin out the forwardmost lines and thus avoid unnecessary losses.

Almost all my subordinate divisions put up a fierce resistance against this order. Over time it had become a standard practice on both the eastern and western fronts to commit all available forces to make it impossible for higher headquarters to take any units away for commitment elsewhere. Unfortunately, Field Marshal von Kluge had condoned this practice when he was OB-West. The problem with this method is that you are too weak at the focal point and too strong everywhere in between. When the enemy makes a penetration it quickly leads to disaster for the units not at the point of the attack, which will always oppose the detachment of their subordinate units. I personally drove from division to division, tried to convince the commanders, and then issued the order there on the spot. They complied, more or less.

According to my journal, this is how my day typically went:

0300 Hours: Wake up.

0400 Hours: Breakfast, followed by a meeting with my chief of staff and then departure for the front.

1600–1700 Hours: Return from the front, followed by a meeting with the chief of staff and briefings. Aside from members of the key staff, the briefings always included those who were scheduled to go forward to familiarize themselves with the front lines, and those scheduled to go to the rear, so they could carry accurate information on the conditions at the front. These last two groups were particularly important.

1930: Dinner.

2030 or 2100 Hours: Briefings by the army group logistics officer, administrative officer, army group judge advocate, and the IIa.[36]

2200 Hours: Lights out.

I often slept in my car en route. I was fifty years old then, and it was only thanks to my incredibly strong conditioning that I was able to bear the stress.

Naturally, my small dinner circle was resented by those not included. Vainness and curiosity are natural conditions, but the small circle also ensured that as little as possible of the important matters was widely broadcast.

We massed Panzer units behind each of the anticipated American attack axes. The 11th and 21st Panzer Divisions were between Metz and the Vosges Mountains. Between Metz and Diedenhofen I assumed we could call on a battle group of the 25th Motorized Infantry Division that was reconstituting near Trier. That was a grave mistake on my part.

We gave special attention to the formations in the rear. In the event of an American penetration, everyone was expected to defend in place. But we learned some peculiar things. During one alert exercise the defense force of a small town, including its commander, immediately fled to the Rhine. When another town was to be alerted we could not reach it by telephone. The *Ortsgruppenleiter*[37] had initiated the direct sale of the inventory of all local stores without having to present food ration stamps. At that point, everyone in the town including the telephone operators rushed to the stores. It took us quite some time to figure out what was going on there. Rather than imposing legal sanctions, I ordered a series of training courses for the rear area troops in an effort to bring them back into the fold. My NSFO Lersener handled it all.

Up to that point I had conducted almost all the defensive battles by attacking. The attack is easier. The defensive weapons today are hopelessly inferior and nothing results in bigger losses than a failed defense. As a young lieutenant in 1914 I was already reflecting on this. When after a heavy attack we stormed the English positions across a two-kilometer open plain near Fontaine-au-Pire, 50 Jägers of the 10th and 3rd Jäger Battalions were killed, compared to 150 Englishmen. We also captured 250 to 300 unwounded Englishmen. We had no way of estimating the number of enemy wounded that evaded capture. The attack always results in lower losses, assuming that it is well prepared and it succeeds, or is broken off in time. The Americans are learning that lesson in Vietnam now.[38] But large-scale attacks were not a feasible option for us at this point. The distribution of forces was too uneven. The troops were not trained well enough, the enemy air superiority was overwhelming, and our air force in the army group area of operations was nonexistent.

We were supposed to hold the West Wall until the beginning of the offensive, which gave us enough space to conduct a fluid defense. Whenever the opportunity presented itself in various locations, we went on the attack. I was under no extensive restrictions from Hitler, but one problem was Fortress Metz.[39] We fully expected to receive the order to hold Metz, but I wanted to withdraw my front line behind the fortification zone. The fortress in front of us would stall the American advance for a few days, and that extra time at the beginning of the offensive could prove decisive. On that basis, Metz was worth holding. One key factor in our considerations was the assurance that any of our units captured by the Americans at Metz would not share the fate of those captured at Stalingrad.

We emplaced extensive minefields around each of the forts. Garrison troops were selected who were no longer capable of sustaining the continued stress of combat, and therefore had only a low level of combat value or none at all. We also dug in extensively, which up to that point had been neglected. We had to improvise everything. Construction crews were available, but they lacked clear and uniform procedures and standards. The Gauleiter[40] offered up the local citizens as a workforce. It was incredible what they accomplished there. Since there were no supply units available, the local citizens could only be used close to their homes. The people were impressive. I often saw columns of young girls marching to and from work singing.[41] When I drove back in the evenings I offered my car and the accompanying car to women with children, filling them to capacity as a goodwill gesture, albeit on a small scale. On the larger scale we reduced the frontline rations by a certain percentage and gave the excess to the fortress workers as an additional "Thank you!" I visited and talked with them as often as I could. Unfortunately, it was not possible to do much more.

I did have the time to do at least one enjoyable thing. As I mentioned earlier, Hitler had at the conclusion of my division command time awarded me 1,500 marks for a rest period in Czechoslovakia. I now used that money to host for five pleasant days all the soldiers of the 11th Panzer Division who had served under me when I was the commander. All the local civilian and Nazi Party authorities supported me enthusiastically in this endeavor. It was a nice bit of relief for the troops.

By this point we believed that we had done everything possible to delay the enemy attacks until the middle of November, when the offensive in the Ardennes[42] was to start. We had calculated that the Americans would be weak when it came to exploiting success at the operational level, and events proved us correct. But we all realized as well that our castle was built on shifting sands.

Bradley Attacks

On 8 November the Americans attacked, as we had expected. There were no surprises. The imbalance in materiel was horrific. As a typical example, on 12 November in Lorraine thirty of our Panzers and assault guns were fighting against seven hundred American tanks; we had zero German air sorties against approximately twelve hundred on the American side. That was a normal day; other days we faced even less favorable force ratios. The situation was similar for artillery. Increasingly the divisions reported: "Artillery ammunition expended; no ammunition available for tomorrow." It was becoming increasingly impossible to find the correct ammunition for our haphazard assortment of artillery types. At that stage in the war German artillery was composed largely of captured guns from almost all European states, which only compounded the ammunition supply problems. The improvisations and logistical miracles accomplished by our General Staff officers were nothing short of amazing.

Even with the huge imbalance in Lorraine, the outcome of the battle was not catastrophic, and we managed to hold out until the beginning of the Ardennes Offensive. There were multiple reasons contributing to these results. First, the officers and men fought with rare dedication and there was a high level of experience and expertise at all ranks. Second, we managed to maintain and preserve the freedom to conduct a mobile battle. We were not bound by orders to hold at all costs. Third, the obsolescent fortresses of Metz bought us at least five additional days. And finally, the American leadership never understood how to exploit success and how to concentrate their incredible advantages in time and space.

In some of the most desperate situations we were only able to hold out because we knew for certain that there would be no follow-up, the Americans would just stop. That was how it always went without fail. We had the impres-

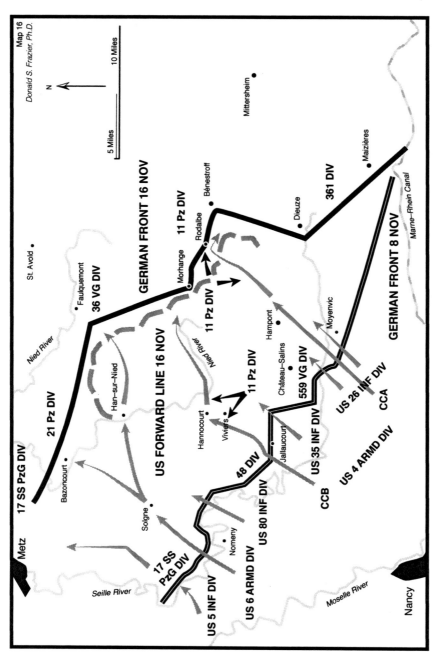

Map 16. U.S. XII Corps Attack, 8–16 November 1944. (Map by Donald S. Frazier)

sion that the American leadership was not at all interested in achieving operational success, but rather intended to destroy our weapons and personnel until we were strangled through attrition. Later as a prisoner of war in American hands I was quite surprised when my captors firmly insisted that the concept of total destruction was far from their intent, and they really had tried to achieve operational success with all the means at their disposal.

The leadership of Army Group G worked to influence the battle by avoiding the total destruction of our own units, while simultaneously shifting constantly from evasive action, to tenacious resistance, to intense counterattacks, all with the purpose of confusing the enemy about our methods and our intentions. Our flexible tactics and stubborn defense of Metz finally succeeded in stopping American general George Patton. But even though we accomplished our broader mission of stalling the enemy until we could launch the Ardennes Offensive, we were only too well aware that each day we stood on the verge of catastrophe. Throughout the battle we were thankful for the energetic support we received from OB-West and Area Command XII. They channeled anything they could scrape up in reserves toward us. Unfortunately, they had no control over the reality that a newly formed and immediately deployed division often had little real combat value.

Commitment of the Operational Reserve

We managed to move the seasoned 11th Panzer Division, superbly commanded by General Wend von Wietersheim, to block the spearhead of the American attack. That eliminated the imminent danger in that sector. The 11th Panzer Division was always far above average, and one of the reasons for its success was its ability to maintain a high operational rate for its Panzers. When I relinquished command of the division in Russia and I was making my final visit to OKH, Lieutenant General Adolf Heusinger[43] asked me how the 11th Panzer Division had always managed to maintain such a high operational rate for its tanks. I had never thought about it. The 15th Panzer Regiment was simply the best. It still was, but now I looked a little more deeply into the matter and I found a most outstanding maintenance NCO. *Oberfeldwebel* Kurt Reuschel was in charge of the maintenance section of the 15th Panzer Regiment's 2nd Battalion. I recommended him for the *Ritterkreuz des Kriegsverdienstkreuzes*,[44] and he received it. But getting a decoration that high for an NCO was not easy, and it required Colonel General Guderian's intervention to push it through. That brave man went missing after his return to his Silesian homeland in May 1945.[45]

My other Panzer division, unfortunately, was in trouble.[46] Their relief by a newly arriving division and subsequent withdrawal from the enemy advance had been delayed far too long. Now they reported that there was no fuel for them to move. We did not understand what was wrong. They had received a fuel resupply in time. But there was no time for deliberations. We scraped up more fuel, and the division finally reached its assigned sector, which up to that time had been covered by the 11th Panzer Division. Once there, they actually accomplished their mission rather well.

About this time my army group judge advocate general showed me a file on a lawsuit against the commander of that Panzer division.[47] I was asked to endorse the findings of his investigation. Seeing the name of the officer under investigation brought me up short. Everything supposedly had been checked, and the judge advocates concluded that there was nothing that justified legal proceedings in the case. Finally I said, "I am not a lawyer, but if you ask me, it is insurance fraud, abuse of authority, and bribery." Then I crossed out the prepared endorsement statement and wrote in the file: "Forward to the army court-martial authority. Investigation cannot be conducted at this location because most of the incidents occurred in the homeland. In my opinion, an offense as [alleged] above did occur."

I should have relieved the commander in question until the matter was resolved. I did not do so because he had commanded the division well during the last few days and at the time we had to be careful with reliefs. We never knew what was coming next. The end was painfully close at hand.

After I relinquished command of Army Group G the division commander was arrested at his command post on order of the military court-martial authority and subsequently received the death penalty. As it was later explained to me, this officer's stored furniture had been grossly overinsured. After it was destroyed in a bombing raid, he took the insurance money and purchased valuable, formerly Jewish-owned furniture in Paris for next to nothing. He again overinsured that furniture and put it in storage near a key train station. Again, his property was destroyed by bombing, and this time he used the money to purchase a castle. (The castle was later confiscated and as far as I know it was given to Field Marshal August von Mackensen[48] when he was forced to flee from the East.) Then that commander moved his division's entire fuel resupply into his new castle. That's why the division was out of fuel and we could not understand how. All this illegal business had been carried out by an officer acting on his orders. Of course, considerable amounts of bribery and alcohol were involved.

Unfortunately, Hitler stayed the death sentence. That officer's ties to the Nazi Party were too strong. When he died in early 1960, it came out that he had spent the last seven years working for the Soviets, spying on German rearmament.[49] My trust in the effectiveness and impartiality of our military justice system suffered considerably from this case. Both the judge advocate and the division commander had been stationed in Paris together. It was quite peculiar how difficult it was to get our military judicial system to act on matters that occurred during the occupation.

We had initially no reserves in the third focal point between Metz and Diedenhofen. In an emergency a battle group of the 25th Motorized Infantry Division, located near Trier, was to move into our sector. The 25th Motorized Infantry Division had been allocated to the Ardennes Offensive. When we did actually need the unit, it took twenty-four hours to get the battle group detached. Then for the next twenty-four hours it just sat because it had no fuel. It finally started arriving in our sector. Right at the beginning of an operation reserves should be assigned to the unit they are supposed to support. That was what had gone wrong with the 8th Panzer Division in Galicia, in the summer of 1944.

Hitler had ordered that the 25th Motorized Infantry Division's battle group was to advance with their right wing forward along the Moselle River and thrust into the northern flank of the American bridgehead. I protested that direction of attack because it would lead the battle group directly onto a steep, rocky ravine that a motorized unit could not cross. The answer I got was that the order of the Führer must be executed. I could not accept that. I tried to call Field Marshal Keitel to tell him that I wanted an order from the Führer telling me what to do when the response force could not get across the ravine. On my second attempt I finally got through directly to Keitel. He told me to do whatever I wanted to do. I cannot prove it, but I am convinced no such Führer Order ever existed. More likely, someone had rushed to the telephone following an incidental remark by Hitler, and that went out as a Führer Order. I seriously doubt that Hitler even knew about my request for a second order. The time between my two telephone calls had been much too short for that.

The Battle for Alsace

Army Group G had moved its center of gravity toward Lorraine. If the front in Alsace collapsed, then any enemy offensive there would initially come to a dead stop along the Rhine. We proceeded accordingly. All arriving replacements were sent to Lorraine. The Nineteenth Army in Alsace received only the most basic necessities. It is a miracle that they held at all. At best it only had two really combat-effective divisions, including the 198th Infantry Division from Württemberg. Despite this, or rather because of it, I continued insisting during my frequent visits to the Nineteenth Army sector that combat operations must be conducted only by attacking. The army commander, General Wiese, and his excellent chief of staff, General Botsch, understood.

The inadequately uniformed and completely overstretched troops accomplished amazing things during the icy snowstorms of early winter in the Vosges Mountains. They completely stopped the Allies' first-rate Moroccan 3rd Mountain Division. In order to free up forces, we had to resort to pulling back from certain sectors to shorten the line. That essentially was what Hindenburg had done in France in 1917.[50]

During the withdrawal every forward position and dugout was destroyed, which stalled the American offensive in the Vosges Mountains that winter. The winter conditions worked to the disadvantage of the French troops from Morocco and the American troops from California of Japanese descent, the Nisei.[51]

We experienced some difficulties with the civilian population. Against existing orders, we had arranged to supply the civilians in the department of Montbéliard with food, baby milk, and medicine from Switzerland to avoid unnecessary casualties. We were in a quandary over what to do with the civilians there. Their fate seemed too uncertain. One option was to evacuate them back to the Reich, but we ruled that out. On the other hand, leaving them in place, especially in the town of Gérardmer, which was directly in front of our line, would have exposed them to high casualties and certain annihilation from our artillery fire.

We decided to hand most of the citizenry of Gérardmer over to the enemy. When our front line was still far to the west of Gérardmer, the population was conducted to an area right behind the front lines and was supplied with food and medical supplies. We also secured medical support for them. Then, after we pulled our front line back, our artillery established a forty-eight-hour no-fire zone in the area. The corps responsible for the area did whatever else was necessary and sent a negotiator to the other side to inform the enemy of our intentions and to initiate the transfer of the civilians. The corps sector from then on was only held by patrol activity. The Americans stopped their advance in this area.

After the war all the German leaders involved at Gérardmer were tried before a French military tribunal. At the time I was in a German prison and the Americans refused to extradite me, because they considered the charges unjustified.[52] All those who appeared before the tribunal were acquitted. I, however, received a sentence of twenty years in prison in absentia. My absence made it easier for the French to acquit those present, especially since during the pretrial depositions I had clearly admitted to the measures we had taken.[53]

Looking back, I can say that the evacuation of Gérardmer had been inevi-

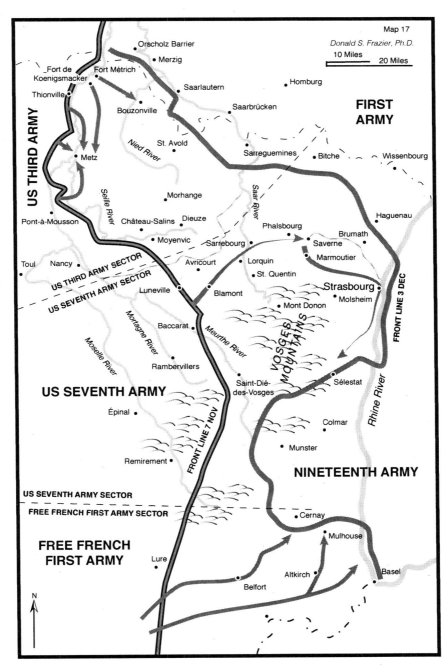

Map 17

Donald S. Frazier, Ph.D.

10 Miles
20 Miles

Orscholz Barrier
Merzig
_Fort de Koenigsmacker
Fort Métrich
Thionville
Saarlautern
Homburg
Bouzonville
Saarbrücken

FIRST ARMY

US THIRD ARMY

St. Avold
Nied River
Sarreguemines
Bitche
Wissenbourg

Metz

Seille River
Morhange
Saar River
Haguenau

Pont-à-Mousson
Château-Salins
Dieuze
Phalsbourg
Brumath
Moyenvic
Sarrebourg
Saverne
Marmoutier

Toul
Nancy
US THIRD ARMY SECTOR
Avricourt
Lorquin
St. Quentin
Strasbourg
Molsheim

US SEVENTH ARMY SECTOR
Luneville
Blamont
Mont Donon

Mortagne River
Baccarat
Meurthe River
VOSGES MOUNTAINS

FRONT LINE 3 DEC

Moselle River
Rambervillers

US SEVENTH ARMY
Saint-Dié-des-Vosges
Sélestat

Épinal
Colmar
Rhine River

Munster

Remiremont
FRONT LINE 7 NOV
NINETEENTH ARMY

US SEVENTH ARMY SECTOR

FREE FRENCH FIRST ARMY SECTOR
Cernay
Mulhouse

FREE FRENCH FIRST ARMY
Lure
Altkirch
Basel
Belfort

N

Map 17. Army Group G Situation, November 1944. (Map by Donald S. Frazier)

table. The town was located directly in front of the planned permanent position that we held for a long time. If the citizens had been left in the town, they would have certainly suffered considerable losses. Situated as it was directly in front of our defensive positions, its destruction was inevitable. There are countless similar situations throughout military history. It was predictable that the French would show no understanding in this case, although they later did exactly the same sort of things in Indochina and Algeria.

The Turenne Maneuver

At the end of 1675, French Marshal Turenne moved into winter quarters near Épinal. Opposing him and using the Vosges Mountains as a screen, the imperial forces under the Great Elector[54] were near Türkheim. Executing a surprise move, Turenne in January 1675 advanced his forces through the Sundgau region, and around the southern pillar of the Vosges. He then thrust northward and surprised the Great Elector in his winter quarters and pushed him out of Alsace. Both the historical precedent and the topography of Alsace made it likely that the Allies would try to repeat this best of Turenne's operations. The key question was whether the thrust would be launched through our positions in the Sundgau, or the very real possibility that it would come through neutral Switzerland. We had to be prepared for both courses of action.

We needed a Panzer unit in the Belfort Gap in the Sundgau, but we did not have one. We tried to compensate by laying mines and constructing very extensive tree obstacles in the forests, where a brigade of Cossacks demonstrated the Russian mastery of axe and timber. Nonetheless, we expected the enemy to succeed there. We therefore withdrew the veteran 198th Infantry Division from Alsace and moved it to the decisive sector in Lorraine. There was no sense in sacrificing this solid division in the looming catastrophe in Alsace.

Perhaps we would have been able to devise a better defense in the Belfort Gap if we had withdrawn our forces from the salient at Belfort itself, and pulled back into a shorter and straighter line. But the local authorities there insisted on keeping the town behind the German line. Our complete lack of aerial reconnaissance assets made matters even more complicated. We did, however, get good results from our signals intelligence and by monitoring the Allied press. The Anglo-American journalists always filed their reports twenty-four hours too early.

On 16 November the French under General Jean de Lattre de Tassigny[55] penetrated our positions near Belfort, and within a matter of days the French 1st Armored Division and 9th Colonial Division reached Mulhouse. General Hans Oschmann, the commander of the 338th Infantry Division in the breakthrough sector, was killed on 16 November. We also received reports that the Allies had violated Swiss neutrality in making the attack. Some seventy to eighty French tanks supposedly bypassed our positions through Swiss territory. The French unit that was cut off near Mulhouse supposedly was supplied through Switzerland. Then, as now, I question the credibility of these reports.[56]

At the same time the American-French forces attacked near Saarburg and caved in a newly raised Volksgrenadier division. The adjacent 553rd Volksgrenadier Division under General Johannes Bruhn held. That division had an incredible combat record. Not only did it master any situation in the most difficult battles, but General Bruhn also managed twice to extract the division with all of its equipment from a looming enemy encirclement, to face the enemy again. The unusual achievements of the 553rd Volksgrenadier Division and the splendid leadership of General Bruhn deserve special recognition in the history of the war.

The direction of the Allied thrust was clearly through Savern–Strasbourg. A double envelopment of the Nineteenth Army in Alsace was looming. I decided to withdraw the Nineteenth Army back across the Rhine and into the Baden region, and from there to hold the Upper Rhine Line with weak forces while moving the army's main body toward Lorraine, which was still the decisive point. In so doing, we could hold the Allied forces in Alsace at an operational dead end, where they could not be committed to the decisive battle.

Unfortunately, Hitler did not endorse this course of action. Because of the serious political and military repercussions involved, I was required to report such an action beforehand. Thus, we now had a very grave situation on our hands. We next recommended eliminating the wedge near Strasbourg to prevent splitting Army Group G. That too was rejected. We received an absolute order to hold and destroy the French force near Mulhouse.

The Nineteenth Army took advantage of the separation of the two French divisions at Mulhouse to thrust toward the south with the reliable 198th Infantry Division, reinforced with Panzers and antitank weapons. Some elements of the division initially ran into terrain difficulties, but they finally reached the Swiss border. For a few days it looked like we would succeed in destroying the French at Mulhouse. Unfortunately, the force ratios were too heavily against us. As always during the final years of the war, we were one division short of achieving full success.[57]

What we were left with was an unfortunate bulge that reached to Belfort and prompted an order from Hitler to hold Belfort. That order could only lead to the destruction of our forces near Belfort, and with that, to catastrophe for the Nineteenth Army. All the access routes into the Belfort Bulge were covered by Allied artillery fire, as I knew only too well from personal experience. There was heavy fighting at Belfort, but we were able to commit for the first time some units that up until then I had held back because they were inadequately trained. But now they were ready, and they managed to destroy some thirty enemy tanks in close combat in the streets of Belfort. Even at this point in time the worn-out German soldiers' unbroken will to fight was still superior to the best of the enemy's troops. Those were days of combat of the first order for the Army Group G staff as well. During a four-day protracted struggle my veteran chief of staff, Mellenthin, managed to push through the evacuation of the Belfort Bulge. Hitler finally gave in.

In the meantime, the French 2nd Armored Division took Strasbourg. We then pulled the Nineteenth Army back into a large bridgehead around Colmar,[58] which stabilized the situation in Alsace. Reinforced by the newly arrived Panzerlehr Division, we conducted a series of attacks against the rear of the enemy forces that broke through toward Strasbourg; but those attacks failed. The enemy was too strong and our troops got mired down fighting piecemeal for towns, instead of bypassing them and moving ahead.

During the fall of Strasbourg there were some ugly incidents in our rear areas. They were shameful. I do not want to go into details and name names, but that information is locked away securely in my personal files. I should, however, mention one of the most pathetic of the bureaucrats. On the evening preceding the French attack onto the Strasbourg city center, he stopped issuing Panzerfaust rocket launchers and ammunition to the troops at 1800 hours because his duty hours were over. When he was ready to resume issuing weapons the next morning at 0900 hours, the French were already standing in his office.

The Final Struggle

While the heavy fighting was going on in Alsace, the crisis-ridden fighting continued in Lorraine. We had to pull our front line back to the east of Metz by withdrawing the two wings of the First Army that tied in with the fortress. On 9 December I wrote in my journal: "Until today I have not written in my journal lately because the situation has been too grave. The French and American breakthroughs near Mulhouse were inevitable. No amount of heroism on the part of the troops will help if in the end the line is so thin that it breaks one day. At that point all the tricks of leadership are too late. It is a miracle that we were able to absorb everything so far. Thank God the Americans helped us by their indecisiveness at exploiting favorable opportunities. And the French no longer have the Napoleonic flourish."

On 11 December the 11th Panzer Division in Lorraine reported the heaviest day of fighting in the West. A new order of battle went into effect that day.

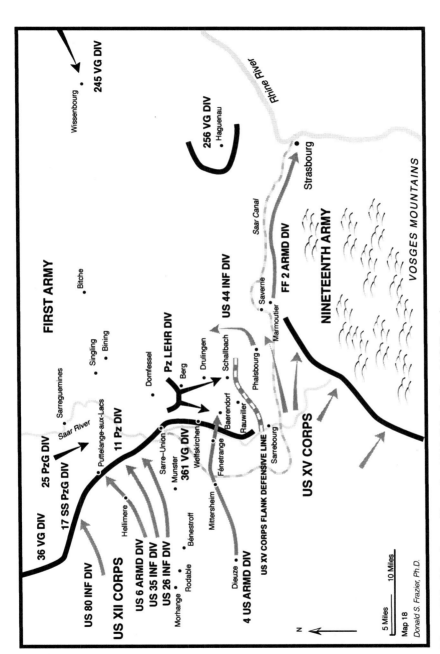

Map 18. Fall of Strasbourg, November 1944. (Map by Donald S. Frazier)

Along the Upper Rhine a special army group was established under Himmler, and the Nineteenth Army was subordinated to him.[59] "Hopefully it will be better supplied now," I wrote. All I had under me now was the First Army and the separate LXXXIX Army Corps in northern Alsace.

We knew that the main body of the enemy forces was near Strasbourg and that they were turning north to throw everything against the First Army in Lorraine. To counter their move I withdrew the First Army back across the Nied River on both sides of Falkenberg. That shortened the line and allowed us to pull divisions out and form reserves. Our move back in one sweep also confronted the Americans with a new situation. They had to readjust, and that took them some time. Having Metz now in front of our lines and the extensive minefields we established also tied up the Americans and gave us another reprieve. Naturally we had no realistic hope of holding Metz. But the fortress did provide us with the five days of delay we had anticipated. The troops remaining in Metz were of the lowest combat rating, but they did their duty. The garrison commander, General Friedrich Kittel, was wounded in the fight.

I wrote in my journal: "Hopefully we will not have to hear again that terrible phrase, 'too late.' The crisis is more than dramatic. Everything depends on our offensive in the Ardennes getting off to a good start. That will only happen if we can hold here. We still have five days until the launch date. (It was actually even more.) Maybe the Americans will dawdle. But you cannot count too much on your enemy's mistakes."

The Gravest Crisis

During this highly tense situation the commanding general of the First Army, Lieutenant General Otto von Knobelsdorff, called me one morning to report that an unbelievable mess had occurred in one of his divisions. The commander of the artillery regiment[60] was totally drunk and the division was at a standstill. Knobelsdorff had halted everything, and some of the division's artillery assets might have been lost. When his division commander had him picked up, the artillery commander was so drunk that he was not even able to stand up by himself.

We immediately halted the Panzer division which was en route to a hot spot on the left wing and moved it behind the stalled division. I then had the facts checked by three independent reporting chains, the command chain, the military justice chain, and the adjutant's chain. All results were the same. The command's judge advocate recommended a death sentence.

That colonel's actions had endangered our frontline troops and our mission worse than anything I had ever seen before, including the disgraceful incidents at Strasbourg. I decided to use my authority and ordered a [summary] execution through command channels. It was a very difficult and agonizing decision, but it was the way all such similar crisis situations had always been handled in wartime. My action was never vacated by a German military court. The language of the German military code of justice covered this situation completely.[61]

It was like a cleansing bolt of lightning. All such similar nonsense stopped immediately. Part of the reasoning in my decision was that any court-martial proceedings in this matter would have come under Himmler's jurisdiction, which would have dragged the affair out and in the end would have acquitted him. He was the type of person that Himmler pulled into his personal orbit. What an event like this means in a situation that consists of one crisis after another can really only be judged by someone who for weeks on end has had to carry personally the leadership burden, the tensions, and the incredible responsibility of straightening these messes out.

The West Wall

We intentionally established a front line as far forward of the West Wall as possible. We still wanted to have maneuver space in depth. I had concerns about the West Wall. Its emplacements were already out of date. Our current antitank guns no longer fit into the gun ports, the dragon's teeth obstacles were no defense against bombing raids, and there were no troops available to man the complex facilities. On top of that, most of the West Wall's weapons had been moved to the Atlantic Wall. Thus, the West Wall had little tactical value other than as a place to quarter the troops. But even that was useful, considering the season and the mud of Lorraine.

The troops naturally expected miracles from the West Wall defenses, especially some respite and an opportunity for rest. Any breaks, however, must be earned through fighting, and that was the big psychological fallacy of the defensive line. I had seen much the same thing at the Dnieper River. There, too, the troops had hoped for miracles as they withdrew behind this enormous obstacle. But when the Russians came across the Dnieper, the result was a psychological breakdown and the loss of the majority of the Dnieper positions.

I was afraid of the same thing happening at the West Wall. I brought in the NSFO organization in an effort to counter it. All the officers that had been trained in passing on National Socialist ideology were given the exclusive mission to prepare the troops for fighting at the West Wall that would offer no respite. They had to expect the heaviest of fighting and understand that any respite could only be had after the enemy was defeated in front of the West Wall.

Correlation of Forces

The uneven fight continued. Ten American infantry divisions, three tank divisions, and incomparable personnel and materiel resources were fighting against eight worn-out, inadequately equipped rumps of German divisions. But those German divisions continued to hold their ground. The daily situation was thirty to seventy German Panzers against seven hundred American tanks. We stood at the map every evening, worrying and counting the days until the start of our Ardennes Offensive.

Individual reinforcements and march battalions[62] trickled in. In one particularly amazing effort, our railroad system transported the newly arriving 36th Infantry Division close to our front line and unloaded it there. But everything that arrived could not replace our losses, and much of what arrived had no combat value at all and was often expended within days and even hours.

Mellenthin Departs

My chief of staff, Mellenthin, was reassigned. The reasons were obvious. Despite his conciliatory personality, Mellenthin had forthrightly supported my command decisions. The clearing of Alsace of the ineffective remnants of troop formations and the withdrawal from the Belfort Bulge were his fine work. He had fought hard for our most recent actions. He had been a chief of staff and a source of support such as you rarely find. For more than a year throughout the worst crises in the East we had stood together and overcome all situations. Here, too, in the West we thought that together we had made the impossible possible.[63]

General Helmut Staedke replaced Mellenthin as my chief of staff. Any General Staff officer who rises to become the chief of staff of an army group is one of the elite. Staedke was no exception. The two weeks that we worked together while I was still in command went without any sort of friction.

Corps Höhne

Throughout our withdrawal in Lorraine we felt that we had maintained the initiative. We withdrew the First Army to the West Wall in a series of short bounds. The situation of Corps Höhne[64] [LXXXIX Army Corps] on our left wing was more difficult. It was located near Hagenau and had been battered during the fighting in the areas of Saverne and Strasbourg. Neither of its flanks was tied into anything, and a double envelopment by the Americans was imminent. Meanwhile, a large number of march battalions and individual batteries had reached the West Wall behind Corps Höhne. Our obvious course of action was to pull the corps back to the West Wall, and there integrate it with the available relief forces. We could expect the Americans to pause in order to prepare for their attack on the West Wall. It made no sense to move the relief forces forward and attempt to integrate them into the corps during the fight for Hagenau. That course of action was bound to fail. It made even less sense to leave the corps at Hagenau and the relief forces sitting in the West Wall. If the corps was left to be destroyed at Hagenau, the corps and divisional staffs we would lose would only make it all that much the easier for the Americans to penetrate the West Wall.

We therefore repositioned the corps back to the West Wall in a series of three jumps. During the first phase nothing happened. During the second phase OB-West got involved and ordered the corps to halt where it stood. But the corps was now three to six kilometers in front of the West Wall and still forward of the reinforcements there. I considered this illogical and I allowed the corps to make the third move into the West Wall. On 16 December at 0300 hours Field Marshal von Rundstedt called me and in the harshest tone ordered me to move Corps Höhne back to its original position immediately. That would have meant the destruction of the corps. When I objected that it was night, that the troops were on the move, and that the order was not executable, Rundstedt responded, "I will report to the Führer that you have disobeyed an order three times in the face of the enemy. You can picture the consequence." That was the end of the conversation.

I immediately called the chief of staff at OB-West, General Siegfried Westphal, and explained that the order was not technically possible to execute. That should have been unquestionably clear among experts. Meanwhile, I let the corps' rearward movement trickle out. Westphal must have somehow set the matter straight. I never heard about it again. It is enough for me to know that my disobedience saved Corps Höhne from certain destruction. I was fully aware of the possible consequences. The obedience of a general is of a different nature than that of a private. My disobedience had saved the lives of many soldiers. If OB-West did not recognize this fact, the Americans certainly did.

Once we had the corps back in the West Wall we were able to combine the reinforcements with it. The American attacks were rebuffed. Shortly thereafter I received a telegram addressed to me personally from Hitler:

> I thank you for the excellent leadership. I expect, however, that you will continue to do everything possible to hold the current line.
> Adolf Hitler

Along with other files, I destroyed the original of the telegram at the end of the war. But its real meaning was obvious—from now on you better follow orders. Even though the position of Army Group G was vindicated in the long run, it had been for me the most difficult crisis during a period of continuous crises.

Background

Hitler's order to hold at all costs was so senseless that long after the war I continued to analyze the pros and cons. The simple answer that the man was crazy is too pat, because it lets everyone else off the hook. Upon closer examination the rationale behind this order is very interesting and sheds much light on the thoughts and principles underlying Hitler's military thought processes.

Armament Minister Speer had concentrated the production of all antitank munitions in Strasbourg. With the fall of Strasbourg, the German army could no longer be supplied with antitank ammunition. It was a simple calculation from that point on as to the day that the last antitank round would be fired, and then all resistance would seize up. Strasbourg, therefore, had to be retaken. But as a result of the order that any leader was not to know more about the situation than he needed to know to accomplish his mission, Speer knew nothing about the operational situation and he therefore did not move the production. We did not know anything about the production of antitank ammunition in Strasbourg, and therefore the role of Strasbourg in Germany's war economy never entered our calculations.

As the Americans were thrusting from Strasbourg to the north with their backs to our Colmar bridgehead, we had a unique operational opportunity. Hitler clearly and correctly recognized it. The only problem was that his correlation of forces calculations were off, as they almost always were. It was impossible to accomplish anything with our one or two newly committed divisions and the few units that Himmler was scraping together. We needed four Panzer divisions at a minimum, and they simply were not available. Thus, as tempting as the operation was, we had to scrap it.

If this operation had been launched, it would have had a greater chance of success if Corps Höhne had started out as close as possible to the Saverne–Strasbourg line, giving it a shorter distance to cover in the attack. Thus, holding Corps Höhne near Hagenau would have been both logical and necessary. But as the corps could not have accomplished that mission since it really was not capable of doing so, we had to do something else. Hitler's gigantic will could not alter the situation, and as a result the instrument broke in his hands. This short example is typical of the basic ideas behind Hitler's concept of command, and why he had to fail in the end.

Conclusion in the West

When our Ardennes Offensive started, the Americans in my sector stopped their attacks two days later and withdrew to the Maginot Line. We sighed a breath of relief. We had held for four weeks longer than expected and felt that we had accomplished the impossible. Looking back, I can say that my time in the West dwarfed everything else I experienced in terms of crises and strained nerves. In my journal I noted, "The task was unimaginably difficult, with troops that were not troops, with a wild collection of artillery that had almost no ammunition, to stop half the American and French army until our [Ardennes] offensive could start. The soldiers were mostly unfit for duty. What the German soldier accomplished here is worthy of a heroic poem."

The Anglo-American side also recognized the effective leadership of Army Group G during the battle.[65]

Change of Command

As I was sitting down to dinner on 23 December I received a telephone call from OKH telling me to report to Zossen immediately. From there I was to move onward by plane and take command at Budapest within twenty-four hours. Danger was looming. Speed was of the utmost importance. I had no time to think about why this change of command was happening. Later, of course, there was a lot of talk. Guderian, who had the best insights into the matter, later wrote that I had fallen victim to Himmler's intrigues. Himmler was no friend of mine. We did not say a word to each other during one meeting in the Baden region, and from several sources I learned that Himmler complained to Hitler that I was too tough on his SS divisions. But that more than likely would have been a reason for Hitler not to give in to Himmler. Personally, I believe that Hitler wanted someone from the West who would follow his orders, and he preferred to use me again in the East. Also, my relations with the OB-West, Field Marshal von Rundstedt, were more than tense. We did not agree at all on our ideas about operational matters. And although Rundstedt was one of the most humanly upstanding men I had ever met, he was militarily still stuck back in World War I. He had not developed in his thinking, and he therefore had to fail like so many others. My overall assessment of Rundstedt is exactly the same as General Hans Speidel's in his book *Invasion 1944*.[66]

On 24 December at 0300 hours I met with Guderian[67] at the OKH in Zossen. As he briefed me on the new situation, I noticed that both the 3rd and 6th Panzer Divisions were fragmented. The armored elements of both divisions were south of the Danube near Budapest, with almost all of their tanks, their

Panzergrenadiers in armored personnel carriers, and their motorized artillery. The mass of their infantry and nonmotorized artillery were north of the Danube. "This must have been done by a real armor expert," I said somewhat sarcastically. The problem, which came about from a misunderstanding between Colonel General Johannes Friessner and OKH, was beyond the point of fixing after Friessner's sudden dismissal as commander of Army Group Southeast on 22 December.

After arriving at my new headquarters[68] I saw that our armored elements dominated the ground during daylight, but at night the Russian infantry marched right through the Panzers. And then the game would start over again. Tactics is the coordinated effect of all arms in space and time onto one objective, with the emphasis being on *all* arms and *one* objective. The armored units on their own could not handle the Russian infantry. One type of arm by itself is doomed to failure, and this iron-clad principle had been violated.

My new chief of staff was Major General Heinrich Gaedcke.[69] The Knight's Cross that he had earned for the breakout from the Korssun–Cherkasy Pocket told me much about the man and his well-rounded, strong personality. As we evaluated the overall situation I decided that the two Panzer divisions would be regrouped immediately, as prescribed in their wartime tables of organization and equipment. Their center of mass would be Budapest. "But Sir," Gaedcke told me, "dividing the units was done under an explicit Führer Order. Without orders from Hitler we are not allowed to change anything."

Everyone at Sixth Army had argued emphatically but unsuccessfully against Hitler's order. I issued the reconsolidation order anyway and added: "We will not ask anybody. If it works, everyone will have to live with it." That sounds like bravado, but I firmly believed that Guderian would support me and that Hitler in the end would accept the fait accompli. Our tactical methods up to this point had been the cause of all our failures. The order went out immediately. After the war the Hungarian historian Peter Gosztony gave Guderian the credit for issuing the order, which I think is incorrect.[70]

Situation Assessment

After issuing the reconsolidation order, I called General Wenck, the chief of the leadership department at OKH. I knew Wenck very well and I consider him one of the most remarkable soldiers we had in World War II. Immediately after my conversation with Wenck I wrote in my journal: "The situation is hellish. Within the next twenty-four hours it will develop as follows:

"The III Panzer Corps will hold. To the north in the Bakony Forest the enemy will infiltrate with strong infantry forces. With only Panzers and no infantry we will not be able to stop them. The enemy will encircle Budapest from the west, and that will threaten us with a new Stalingrad. It is very questionable if we can hold Budapest as a fortress, because we do not have enough infantry there. The Russians can infiltrate into the sea of houses. The city of eight hundred thousand is hungry and is getting restless. A putsch by communist elements is possible at any time. North of the Danube the correlation of forces will be balanced.

"Courses of Action:

a.) Give up Budapest. The Hungarians will cooperate. Then turn the freed-up divisions around and beat the Russians.

b.) Fall back to the inner ring within Budapest. That will free up relatively few forces. It will be necessary to insert new forces. The situation overall is very serious.

"Decision: IV SS Panzer Corps with Viking and Totenkopf Divisions[71] will move to Budapest and hold the outer ring of the city. Meanwhile, one division in Budapest will be detached and sent toward the west."

On 26 December I noted: "Whenever we bring in new forces we must consider if we can get along operationally without them. Once Budapest is under siege (which happened just as I took command) the newly committed forces will most likely be too weak, and their absence elsewhere will be felt."

Besides the Sixth Army, which I commanded directly, I also had operational control of the Hungarian First and Third Armies. Despite any amount of goodwill, the mass of Hungarian soldiers will not fight without decisive political guidance. The only exception was the Saint László Division. But a few days later that division disintegrated without warning. We could not have analyzed the situation any more realistically and unemotionally. The decision was made and we acted accordingly. Looking at the big picture, I understood completely at this point that after our Ardennes Offensive failed the war was lost. Now came the most difficult of all leadership challenges in war—ending it without bigger catastrophes.

Preliminary Operation

The next few days went as expected. Some most difficult crises developed. It was only with a great deal of effort that we managed to extract the LVII Panzer Corps fighting north of the Danube from its almost complete encirclement and bring it back across the Hron River with hardly any losses. We established a new defensive line there. The corps was firmly and surely commanded by General Friedrich Kirchner, my old division commander from the 1940 campaign in France. Kirchner commanded from the front, not from a desk. On 31 December I wrote in my journal: "The front is stabilized, it is actually a miracle. Now comes the relief operation for Budapest."

The First Relief Operation

My chief of staff became pale when he found out that the IV SS Panzer Corps was arriving. "That is [SS-Obergruppenführer Herbert] Gille. I know him from the Cherkasy Pocket." Gaedcke then told about Gille's troublemaking and his disinclination to follow orders. When Gille reported to me he struck me as a strong, egocentric type who had no understanding of operational context and possibilities. Probably he was quite courageous. He was the type of Waffen-SS commander who as a matter of principle always resisted orders from any army officer. Even Rommel had complained about that bitterly. Right until the end the entire leadership structure of the Sixth Army had to deal with this totally unnecessary friction.

One thing was clear: even after the attachment of the IV SS Panzer Corps the correlation of forces was not in our favor. On the German side we had seven Panzer divisions, two cavalry divisions, and four infantry divisions. The Hungarian units, which for the most part could not be counted on for serious missions, included four infantry divisions, one cavalry division, and miscellaneous groups. It was difficult to get an accurate strength picture of the Hungarians. In Budapest itself we had remnants of the 13th Panzer Division and the 60th Panzergrenadier Division, two SS cavalry divisions, and Hungarian-Germans with little training and not much combat value. Overall we had approximately thirty thousand Germans and at best seventy thousand Hungarian soldiers.

On the Russian side we were facing fifty-four rifle divisions, five mechanized corps, three tank corps, two cavalry corps, four air defense divisions, seven antitank brigades, and three rocket launcher brigades. With these force ratios we could only succeed if we either managed to surprise the Russians and unhinge them for a short time, or if we hit them in short order with destructive strikes that inflicted such losses that they would break off the siege. Neither course of action had much chance of succeeding.

The biggest danger was that the enemy would successfully encircle us after one of our strikes and then virtually drown us in his masses. The narrow, twenty-one-kilometer-long corridor that led into Budapest made our task more difficult because it was impossible to secure it, let alone hold it. But we had to hold that access route under all circumstances, at least until we completed the evacu-

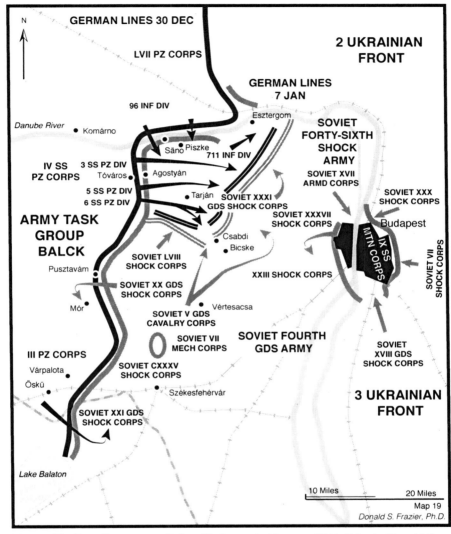

Map 19. The First Operation to Relieve Budapest, 1–6 January 1944. (Map by Donald S. Frazier)

ation of the wounded (at a minimum ten thousand) and the flow of refugees stopped. That could take days.

The simplest operation would have been to thrust straight on to Budapest from the line from Lake Balaton to the Bakony Forest [Transdanubian Mountains]. That would result in a head-to-head clash with the Russian main concentration of forces—and no matter how successful initially, it eventually would bog down. We had to come up with something better. The right flank of the Russian forces was covered by the Danube. They would not expect an attack there. As far as we could tell they only had their supply trains there. If we managed to get across the Danube by surprise, we could take control of the road along the riverbank, thrust along that road with the IV SS Panzer Corps, and then turn south by echelon. If everything went according to plan and if we moved quickly and continuously night and day, we could completely surprise the Russians and pick them apart. We decided on this latter course of action.

The thrust across the Danube and the seizing of the road along the banks of the river was to be done by the 96th Infantry Division under General Hermann Harrendorf, a reserve officer. The division executed its mission superbly. After the main body of the division conducted the crossing on a wide front during the night of 1–2 January, the engines of the assault boats stopped operating because of carbon build-up. On the morning of 2 January the IV SS Panzer Corps without artillery preparation broke through the Russian positions according to plan, marched forward along the riverbank, which now was controlled by the 96th Infantry Division, and turned south by echelon. But after some excellent initial success, the IV SS Panzer Corps' attack on the right stalled in difficult terrain. On the left and in the Pilis Mountains the corps continued to advance swiftly. The follow-on 711th Infantry Division took Esztergom.

The Russians had not thought that we were capable any longer of launching a massive attack of such strength. Meanwhile, we confused them further with a series of simultaneous feint attacks by the III Panzer Corps. That achieved the desired effect, and the Russians hesitated in their reaction. Unfortunately, we had not been fast enough. The Russians were able to still get in front of the IV SS Panzer Corps. Thus, the fate of the operation was sealed. Nevertheless, we continued to advance on the left wing. We managed to move ahead nicely there, relieving a good number of German field hospitals and evacuating thousands of wounded and sick. The attack came as close as twenty-one kilometers to Budapest. Then the Russian countermeasures started to take effect.

That was the end of the operation. Gaedcke wanted to regroup immediately. I still hesitated, hoping to push the Russian front back toward the west far enough to establish contact with the city. Then we would have controlled a road that was secured on one side by the Danube, and only exposed on the other side. Gille at the time thought that a further thrust of the IV SS Panzer Corps was impossible, only to state afterward that he would have gone farther. Hitler finally ended our internal argument and ordered us to regroup. In this case Hitler's intervention was appropriate.

18

North of the Danube

While we were attacking south of the Danube from west to east, the Russian Sixth Guards Tank Army on 6 January broke through north of the Danube and penetrated deeply into the LVII Panzer Corps from east to west. We only managed to stop their penetration at Komorn[1] by committing FLAK batteries. Göring had issued an order forbidding the commitment of FLAK units in the front lines, but the withdrawal of the V FLAK Corps was prevented by the timely intervention of Luftwaffe General Hans-Detlef Herhudt von Rhoden. Guderian was visiting me at the time, and he allowed me to redirect the 20th Panzer Division from Slovakia and commit it to a counterattack.

Hitler, as usual, ordered the 20th Panzer Division to attack into the base of the enemy breakthrough. But as we could have predicted, the attack ran into impenetrable antitank gun blocking positions. Then, based on my experience, I redeployed the Panzers on a 45-degree oblique axis into the Russians' breakthrough salient. Upon further interference by Hitler, I reported that the division was already engaged and achieving initial success. False reporting is the consequence of bad leadership. Even though I was confident, we were greatly relieved when the 20th Panzer Division succeeded on a large scale and the Sixth Guards Tank Army withdrew, completely beaten. On 12 January that episode was over. With the exception of one bridgehead across the Gran River, the breakthrough was eliminated.

The Second Relief Attempt

We wanted to thrust through the enemy between Lake Balaton and Lake Velence, straight onto Budapest with our right wing tied to the Danube. The correlation of forces was now more favorable because our attack had inflicted heavy losses on the enemy and forced him to regroup his entire force toward the north. As a consequence, he was considerably weaker along the front of our planned attack. The danger if we broke through was that the Russians would attack us toward the north from our rear with the very strong forces they had in position between the Danube and Lake Balaton. If that happened, our attacking element would be caught between the Russian masses with little possibility of being extracted. It was thus imperative for us to take advantage of every opportunity to encircle the Russian forces and destroy them. The relief of Budapest would only be possible after all the Russian forces had been defeated.

In order to gain operational space we let the Hungarian Third Army under Colonel General Zoltan Heszlenyi thrust toward the south on the right flank of the attacking IV SS Panzer Corps. The farther southward that attack advanced, the more space and time we would gain for our main effort. Since the Hungarians were much better at attacking than defending, I believed that the Hungarian Third Army would be able to accomplish this task. As "corset stays" and pacesetters for the Hungarians, we attached three motorcycle infantry battalions from the Panzer divisions that were to make the main effort. My intent was to use our less capable allies in a way that exploited their strengths. Unfortunately, I had only three German battalions with which to reinforce them.

We prepared for the attack with great care because, as I had noted on 11 January, I had serious doubts about it. On 13 January I noted: "In the meantime, Budapest is engaged in an unnecessary but desperate struggle. The troops there are fighting magnificently. Our hopes of getting them out are little more than minuscule. Nobody should have any illusions on that point."

The Russians, meanwhile, detected the detachment of the IV SS Panzer Corps, but they interpreted it as a move via Prague toward Silesia. They also assessed that the situation had changed drastically. Rather than expecting a new attack, they now concluded that they had to attack to prevent us from withdrawing troops to reinforce Poland.

Our attack on 18 January surprised the Russians completely. The thrust of four tightly grouped Panzer divisions overwhelmed the Russians, advanced to the Danube, turned north, and reached the Valisz sector. Small elements crossed into it. The IV SS Panzer Corps reported the total destruction of a strong Russian force and the capture of—if I remember correctly—sixty guns and assorted equipment. Unfortunately, not a single word about the destruction of this Russian force was true. The IV SS Panzer Corps simply allowed the Russians to march off and then they continued moving northward. When I later tried to confirm their initial report, I could not find a trace of the sixty captured guns at the reported location. After the end of the war General Herhudt von Rhoden told me that the destruction of the Russian force was a complete lie. He had been the Luftwaffe liaison officer with the IV SS Panzer Corps.

We had to make a tough decision in the Valisz sector. The options were either an immediate advance toward Budapest, which is what Gille wanted to do, or first destroy the large enemy force on our left flank with the IV SS Panzer Corps, supported by the III Panzer Corps. I decided first to destroy the enemy group in our left flank. If we moved on Budapest immediately, we would end

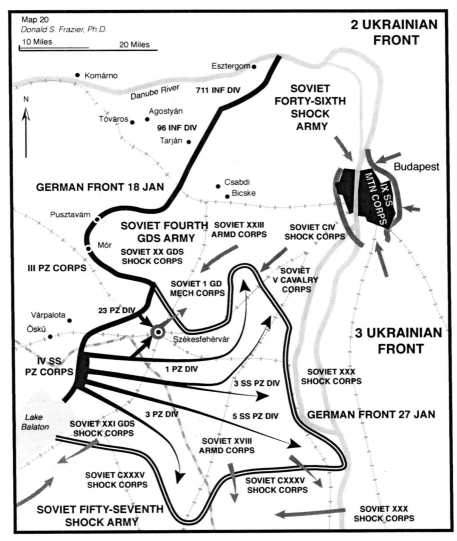

Map 20. The Second Operation to Relieve Budapest, 18–27 January 1944. (Map by Donald S. Frazier)

up with two instead of one SS Corps in the city, but there would be no forces to prevent the surviving Russian units from coming back at us. Gille was incapable of understanding this, which made the situation more difficult and cost us a precious twenty-four hours in delay. By the time we finally launched the new attack it was too late. As I had feared, the Russians that had been pushed toward the south evaded destruction. They were reinforced, they turned around, and they wiped out the Hungarian Third Army.

With that the fate of this relief attempt and the fate of Budapest were sealed. Reluctantly, we had to pull the IV SS Panzer Corps back. Despite heavy fighting we were able to absorb the Russian attack between Lake Balaton and Lake Velence. What would have happened if Gille had continued his move toward Budapest? All the courage of the troops, including the fanatically fighting 3rd and 5th SS Panzer Divisions, and all of the efforts of the leadership had been in vain. The correlation of forces had been tilted too heavily against us.

The casualty numbers indicate the severity of the fighting. Russian losses between 24 December 1944 and 10 February 1945 were 6,532 killed by actual count, 13,600 estimated additional killed, 5,138 captured, 1,981 destroyed tanks, 946 destroyed artillery pieces, 273 destroyed infantry mortars, 1,700 destroyed antitank guns, and 63 aircraft shot down by army units and FLAK units.[2] At the time I thought those numbers were gross exaggerations, but much the same numbers have been reported in Peter Gosztony's *Endkampf an der Donau 1944/45*, based on Russian sources.[3] Our own losses were heavy, too. During the same time period we lost 1,111 officers and 32,997 NCOs and enlisted killed and wounded. Our equipment losses were low.

The Enemy

The Fourth Guards Army had been completely surprised by our advance. Their reserves were positioned behind their right wing. Initially they threw their VII Mechanized Corps at us, which we destroyed in only a few hours. That gave us the time to establish a new front behind the Valisz sector. When the IV SS Panzer Corps reached the Valisz sector they faced the combined V Guards Cavalry Corps, the I Guards Mechanized Corps, the 113th Rifle Division, and a huge amount of artillery. The enemy had two hundred tanks and assault guns, as well as six hundred artillery pieces and infantry mortars. Later the XXIII Tank Corps and the CIV Rifle Corps joined the fight. The Russians, however, overestimated our advance to the south. According to Marshal Fyodor Tolbukhin:[4]

> After the enemy had broken through to the Danube, the troops of the 3rd Ukrainian Front fought under very difficult conditions. Since the southern wing of the breakthrough remained open, there was a threat of encirclement of the Fifty-Seventh Rifle Army and Bulgarian First Army, as well as the Yugoslav XII Corps fighting south of Lake Balaton.
>
> The assault had swept away the crossing points along the Danube.

The frontline staff was located in the town of Paks, where the enemy's armored reconnaissance was already approaching. Frankly, our situation was quite serious and we were forced to decide whether or not it was more practical to give up the bridgehead west of the Danube. Nevertheless, we did not want to withdraw across the Danube, because that would have put Vienna that much farther away for us. We did not have much hope of making another forced crossing of the Danube later because of the enemy's organized resistance. . . . So, in the end we decided to hold the bridgehead.[5]

Tolbukhin estimated that we were trying to encircle all Russian forces in the area of the Danube, Drava, and Lake Balaton by conducting a pincer movement in coordination with the Second Panzer Army, which was positioned south of Lake Balaton. Tolbukhin considered pulling back the Fifty-Seventh Rifle Army and the Bulgarian First Army beyond the Danube. Stalin had already ordered by telephone the withdrawal beyond the Danube. That would have resulted in an unintended but decisive advantage for us, because it would have given us the necessary freedom of action in the Budapest area. Unfortunately, Tolbukhin, and the Fifty-Seventh Rifle Army had strong nerves and ignored Stalin's directive.

That led to the ultimate reversal. By 21 January the Russians had mastered their crisis and now the principle of mass was working in their favor. They now saw very clearly that our main forces were deployed in the north, and not in a southerly direction. Logistics remained a difficult challenge for the Russians. Their supply depots for ammunition and rations were on the eastern banks of the Danube. They had blown the bridges at Dunapentele[6] and Dunaföld-vár when the Hungarian Third Army attacked. The Russian southern group had to be resupplied over a bridge near Csepel, on the southern edge of Budapest. Incredible congestion developed there, which we unfortunately could not exploit because of our weakness in the air. The Russians had to resort to airlifting their ammunition supplies.

Was the relief of Budapest even possible? No, not with our available forces. Then the question becomes one of what additional forces might have been brought in? During the course of the operation we had received the 6th and the 20th Panzer Divisions, as well as one to two infantry divisions. Whether or not they could have been committed earlier is impossible to say now. Hitler was always reluctant to expose other sectors of the front line in order to build up any real concentrations at the focal point. Perhaps an attack by the Second Panzer Army against the 3rd Ukrainian Front could have also brought us some relief and extra time. By the time such an attack was finally launched, it was too late.

Our operations were made much more difficult by the fact that each major Waffen-SS unit had a direct telephone line to Himmler, who routinely interfered in everything and who probably wanted to make Gille the savior of Budapest. During that time all of this was unknown to me, and I later learned about it from Guderian. I just had to straighten out the consequences. It was a totally unacceptable situation. Politicians should not interfere in military leadership matters.

Budapest

The Budapest garrison was commanded by a civilian and by a general who at best was a politician. Neither that general nor his civilian boss were up to the situation. We came to this conclusion after only a few days. Replacing that person was no longer possible.[7] Making matters worse, all the reports that came out of Budapest were biased, to say the least. The regimental commanders who made it out of Budapest later said as much in far more blunt terms. One particular incident sticks in my mind. We tried to establish a supply line by waterway up the Danube. The involved naval personnel gave their utmost and reached the periphery of Budapest. The cargo, as we learned later, also reached the garrison force and was unloaded under the most difficult conditions. But what was reported back to us was that the boat had not reached Budapest.[8] As a consequence, we did not send the second and the third planned shipments. Air drop did not work either. Almost all the supplies were picked up by the civilian population. On one occasion only sixteen out of 371 resupply pallets dropped reached the troops.

Only the remnants of the 13th Panzer Division and the 60th Panzergrenadier Division inside Budapest were actually able and willing to fight. There were two poorly trained SS cavalry divisions inside the city,[9] but one mutinied against their German officers and NCOs,[10] and in the process the Russians took the Orlické Mountains. The Hungarian units, except for a few exceptions, had no combat value and most had no equipment.

Naturally we considered attempting a breakout. In the end we decided against it because we did not trust the leadership in Budapest with the conduct of such an attack. When the garrison commander in Budapest finally did try to break out on his own accord, he only managed to muster about ten thousand men, and the result was a bloodbath, as I had feared. It also was clear to me that in any breakout the wounded, numbering between ten thousand and twenty thousand, could not be transported. We had no illusions about what their fate would be. An order to break out would have been their death sentence.

I have experienced many breakouts from encirclements. The difficulty in such situations lies in the fact that the typical German believes that he can get off the "sinking ship" at the last moment and get himself to safety. In the process, he has a tendency to abandon his unit and throw away his weapon to make it easier to move. As a consequence, a human avalanche develops that charges directly into machine guns and at best breaks out with severe losses. During a breakout, firm leadership with an iron fist is the most important factor.

The exact opposite was done in Budapest. The troops received their orders too late or not at all. No preparatory measures of any kind were initiated. All weapons and communications equipment were destroyed. Then the human mass marched straight into the enemy's fire. For a successful breakout you need tanks, assault guns, self-propelled artillery, antitank guns, sufficient communications equipment, and at least some trucks with fuel. Why they destroyed all of that before they started will remain forever a mystery to me.

The result was predetermined. The troops that assembled for the breakout were destroyed by concentrated Russian fire. Only a few made it out, and their after-action reports are reflected in my above comments. Their reports were for the most part objective, evenhanded, and without exaggeration. They did not make unjust accusations, but they all did emphasize the failings of the garrison commander. All of this is a warning that politicians should keep their hands off military matters and they must never be put in a position of command in the face of the enemy. The soldier pays with his blood, and he is too valuable for that. The fate of those troops who had thrown away their weapons was horrible. They were chased down and killed by the Russian cavalry. The horrors of the Asian-style conduct of war hovered over Budapest.

The Hungarians

I knew the Hungarians well and did not have a lot of confidence in their military abilities. They were effective only when fighting in their homeland, as long as the common soldier understood the goals, and then also only in the attack and less so in the defense. I had been attached to the *Honvéd*[11] for quite a while during World War I as the commander of a Jäger company. We were virtually the only German element in the 11th Honvéd Cavalry Division as it marched through the Pinsk Marshes. During World War II a number of factors complicated the Hungarian situation. The unclear politics of Horthy, who played both sides, resulted in ambiguous orders to the troops. Furthermore, it was expecting too much that in an era of socialism the common man would let himself be beaten to death to defend medieval feudalism. He could only gain from that system's demise.

The territories that had been acquired by Hungary during the war had for the most part only small segments of ethnic Hungarians. Only the die-hard optimists believed that the non-Hungarian elements of these populations would be loyal to the hated Hungarians, and especially when they resumed the "Magyarization" policies. These non-Hungarian peoples had no interest in the current Hungarian state.

The Hungarian equipment was completely inadequate for modern warfare. Today's continuous, large-scale battles fought extensively with materiel make human demands on a scale that the Hungarians are too soft and climate sensitive for. There were signs that the Hungarian 24th Infantry Division was dis-integrating. On the morning of 25 March 1945 the chief of staff of the Eighth Army reported to the Army Group South chief of staff that the commander of an attached Hungarian division declared that he could no longer accept the responsibility of his troops having to fight in such difficult mountain terrain under such difficult logistical challenges.

The senior leadership often tried to do its best. One notable officer was Colonel General Zoltan Heszlenyi,[12] an ethnic German from the Spiš region,[13] whose name was actually Hesslauer.

The new Hungarian head of state, Ferenc Szálasi,[14] came to see me. He was very smart, had good operational knowledge, but he had the blood of too many heterogeneous peoples in him to be reliable.[15] The Arrow Cross Party move-ment, however, had no new political ideas to offer. The old premise in Budapest that the Magyars[16] ruled and dominated the Carpathian region and all others had to knuckle under the Crown of St. Stephan had hardly changed. My Hun-garian liaison officer, Lieutenant Colonel von Moricz, was a pure Magyar—smart, adroit, and decent. He honestly worked to do everything for the best.

You always had to remain on guard to avoid getting sucked in. People mas-terfully attempted all forms of social corruption. I immediately forwarded all presents I received to the field hospitals and thanked the donors in the name of the wounded soldiers. One incorrigible individual, the abbot of the Pannon-halma Arch-Abbey, did not get the message. He incorrectly concluded that the wine he had sent to me was insufficient or not good enough. He sent me a larger and better case of wine. I sent it straight back with a letter, noting my regret that as a German general officer I was neither able to accept gifts nor in a posi-tion to reciprocate. Someone else tried to bribe me with a land grant, but to the frustration of the careful negotiator in the attempted process I pretended that I was too dumb to understand.

The Saint László Division fought exceptionally well. Upon recommenda-tion of the Sixth Army, the division was mentioned in the Wehrmacht dis-patches, and its commander was awarded the Knight's Cross of the Iron Cross.[17] The 1st Hussar Division under Colonel Schell accomplished much in the Bakony Forest, where it was deployed because it was an armor-safe sector. Some of the Hungarian battalions encircled in the city of Budapest also did their duty.

The Hungarians played a large role in Himmler's Waffen-SS.[18] Many of those Hungarian SS units supported *SS-Erfassungskommando* South-East,[19] which established a brutal alternative government and did a lot of damage. I blocked the operations of SS-Erfassungskommando South-East and expelled that unit from my area of responsibility.

The Hungarians were in a horrible situation politically. Some of them hoped that the Soviets would save them; others hoped that we would; and still others pinned their hopes on the western Allies. After we took Esztergom back from the Russians,[20] I sent a liaison officer to the prince primate [archbishop] to ask if we could somehow be of service. "Oh no," we were told, "I was well taken care of under the Russians." And a Countess Esterhazy, who experienced Russian governance for a while, said, "I believe one can live better under Stalin than under Szálasi." An International Red Cross commission that visited the liberated Hungarian villages told a different story.

In March 1941 the Hungarian prime minister, Pál Teleki, sent a cable to the Hungarian embassies in London and Washington outlining Hungary's foreign policy objectives. The most urgent task of Hungarian politics was to preserve the country to the end of the war with its powers intact. Hungary's youth and military power should only be used for the country's own objectives, and no one else's.[21]

That, however, was a recipe for destroying an army without ever even using it. Slovakia provides an interesting contrast to Hungary. After the war, while in captivity, the Slovakian prime minister, Jozef Tiso,[22] told me: "A small state cannot conduct its own politics. It must take one side or the other clearly, and then stick with it. You cannot switch sides."

The Sixth SS Panzer Army

After the conclusion of fighting around Budapest the question then became: Now what? At that point we turned our attention to the deteriorating situation in the West, but we received no political guidance. There were only rumors that the western Allies would fight together with us against the Soviet Union. As I heard from his own mouth, that was one of Hitler's political expectations—or rather illusions. When we learned that the Sixth SS Panzer Army[23] would be arriving from the West, that seemed to confirm the rumors. The mission of the Sixth SS Panzer Army was to throw the Russians back toward the Danube, after which it would be withdrawn for other missions.

Our first impression was that we must still be very strong if in such a highly tense situation in both the East and West we could free up such strong and well-equipped forces. General Otto Wöhler,[24] who commanded all the German forces in Hungary, returned from a visit to Hitler. After he briefed me on what he had learned I noted the following in my journal on 19 February: "The Führer is fresh and confident. He must have something up his sleeve. For this reason it is correct to follow his orders."

Coming directly from Wöhler, who was an upright man and not at all a follower of Hitler and National Socialism, this statement had decisive value. Nonetheless, I argued vehemently against the new offensive that was to follow directly behind our second attempt to relieve Budapest. The then-current mud conditions would drive all of our equipment into the ground in very short order. My only role in the offensive was to support it with the IV SS Panzer Corps and the I Cavalry Corps. General Wöhler told me on the phone, "I agree, but it is useless to present alternate options." I then called General Wenck at OKH and predicted the catastrophe. Unfortunately, my efforts were in vain.

When our offensive started on 5 March it achieved some good initial successes, but then it got stuck in the mud. By the middle of March—as I had predicted—our equipment was exhausted. From that point everything depended on the IV SS Panzer Corps holding between Stuhlweissenburg[25] and the Vértes Mountains. I frequently was forward with the corps and I had requested the relief of its command group, to include the commanding general. They were not up to the operational task. I could not do anything about them through performance evaluations because I could not get around Himmler's irrationality. I tried to get them relieved for health reasons. But when I found out who the incoming commanding general would have been, I put all wheels in motion to retain Gille. We would have been worse off with his replacement.[26] What proved decisive in the end was that Gille's troops had a high level of blind trust in him, and that was capital that had to be valued highly for the coming final operation.

On 20 March the Russians launched their long-expected flank attack against the IV SS Panzer Corps. The situation was too tempting for the Russians. If they broke through, everything we had south of Stuhlweissenburg would be trapped. I personally checked our fire support plans and the deployment of the reserves at the critical point. I specifically ordered the positioning of a reserve force along the boundary with the Hungarian 1st Hussar Division. That was an ideal breakthrough point for the Russians.

I looked forward to the fight with confidence, and in heavy fighting the IV SS Panzer Corps initially absorbed the attack. But contrary to the reports I had received, the reserve force had not been deployed according to my orders. The Russians marched right through the gap along the boundary and unhinged the 1st Hussar Division in the Vértes Mountains. It was another all-too-typical case of Waffen-SS false reporting and disobedience. Now the situation was bad. It also was a classic example of the sort of imponderables senior commanders have to deal with. As another example, I had closed a certain road to all traffic after a rearward movement because it was within the Russians' reach. But ignoring that order, one of Gille's General Staff officers drove down that road and the Russians captured him, complete with the operations orders he was carrying.

The headquarters of the Sixth SS Panzer Army was pulled out and sent in the direction east of the Rába River. I was handed the responsibility for the river bend at Stuhlweissenburg. I was supposed to hold the bend while pulling out all the Sixth SS Panzer Army's divisions, which were then to follow their army headquarters. We immediately pulled out any nonessential vehicles, leaving only the essential equipment with the troops. In so doing we were able to pull the Panzer divisions out more or less intact. In the same manner we withdrew the I Cavalry Corps, which was calmly and confidently commanded by General Gustav Harteneck. Only the 44th Infantry Division[27] was mauled during the process. That was entirely the fault of the 9th SS Panzer Division. Against specific orders, it failed to remain in place and left its positions without orders and without waiting for and orienting its relief force. It just marched off to rejoin the Sixth SS Panzer Army. It took us two days to figure out what had happened there. The commander, SS-Brigadeführer Sylvester Stadler, had not deemed it necessary to orient his relieving division. The 44th Infantry Division paid with the blood of its people. It ceased to exist. It was the only major unit under my command that was destroyed during World War II.

The 9th SS Panzer Division reported instead its own destruction by radio. They also complained of abusive treatment at the hands of my Sixth Army and demanded immediate detachment. OHL had to get deeply engaged in the fight to force the Waffen-SS leadership to obey orders. In the end I was given disciplinary authority over the leadership of all the Waffen-SS units under my command. In all their postwar publications the SS veterans continue to insist that they were always right. They have never passed up an opportunity to criticize me. This is typical of what psychologists call "conversion disorder." People in the wrong become obsessed with a reversed truth and finally believe it themselves. It is an exaggerated defensive measure of the ego.

After several days of continuous crises the bulk of the Sixth Army was again out of immediate danger. We had prevented a catastrophe. The Sixth Army now stood north of Lake Balaton, tied into it with its right flank and with the left flank north of Veszprém. The situation, however, was not a rosy one. Although the Sixth Army was secure for the time being, it was not in good shape. We had saved most of our equipment, but we were out of fuel. The troops were like chickens without heads, and their only concern was to avoid encirclement. That possibly was the reason that the 9th SS Panzer Division acted as it had.

The Sixth SS Panzer Army was even in worse shape. In terms of equipment and personnel strength, they should have been able to stop the Russian thrust without difficulty. But they were falling apart rapidly. Their large numbers of incompetent leaders wrought havoc. As soon as the tension reached a certain level, they had a tendency to send as many troops as possible to the rear for rest and relaxation. Their attitude was one of "let the army take care of the mess." That worked only as long as one Waffen-SS division was integrated with other army divisions. But when six Waffen-SS divisions were committed as an integrated whole, it was a catastrophe waiting to happen, especially when so many of the SS senior leaders had so little understanding of operational issues and the bigger picture.

Near the end of March, I was following behind some elements of the Sixth SS Panzer Army. In the forward positions exceptionally courageous Waffen-SS subordinate commanders with a handful of men consistently fought heroic fights to the death. In the rear areas, meanwhile, entire units with their weapons and equipment were marching off to rest and relax. I called Guderian that evening and requested some help. I had no intention whatsoever of getting sucked into a new and unnecessary catastrophe. I explicitly mentioned locations, times, and unit designations that I had encountered during the withdrawal movement. The war diary of Army Group South recorded the following on 23 March:

> At 0935 the commanding general of Sixth Army called. He reported that the units were no longer fighting as they should. Some are saying that the war is lost anyway and they do not want to get killed before the imminent end of the war. Everyone is afraid of being encircled. The trust that the leadership is capable of mastering the situation has been lost. He wanted to talk to Colonel General Guderian immediately about the situation.

And a later entry:

> Colonel General Guderian told General Wöhler that the assessment of General Balck has been reported to the Führer and to the *Reichsführer-SS* in all urgency. This is the first time that such failure on the part of the SS has been reported. It is a serious indicator, almost like a sign of an impending storm.

Hitler immediately dispatched Himmler and overshot the objective—as usual—by immediately taking away the SS cuff titles from the troops. The troops did not deserve that. They only had been following the orders that they had been given by their leaders, and they were not responsible for Himmler's system of leader selection and his other funny business. Another of the major problems in the Waffen-SS units was the poorly trained replacements they were receiving at the end.

The situation in my sector was getting difficult. As I noted in my journal: "The cavalry corps under Harteneck is fighting bravely and well with no signs of dissolving. It is a different picture with the 5th SS Panzer Division 'Viking.' A stream of troops left their positions and marched back along the side of the main road without the corps intervening. The troops were collected up later and sent back forward, but then they immediately slipped back toward the rear. It is a horrible, recurring cycle behind the courageously but barely held forward lines. On 23 March, 75 percent of the troops at a collection point were SS. Thank God the 1st Mountain Division has arrived and we can still hold the front line intact."

About a year later my old regimental commander Field Marshal Maximilian von Weichs and I were being held in the American prisoner of war camp at Allendorf. He had been with Hitler near the final days of the war. Hitler had complained to him that everyone in Hungary had failed him, and he named the names of the senior army and Waffen-SS leadership. The only man that he had been able to rely upon, he said, had been Balck. Hearing that left me with a bitter and empty feeling. I had never held back, and I was usually right in my assessments, but what good was that praise after the fact when no one listened to me at the time.

My last quarters in Hungary had been in the castle of a feudal count. As I looked out the window I could see on the porch ladies wearing expensive jewelry and low-cut dresses with gentlemen in their magnificent attire of the Hungarian feudal masters. The servants in livery handed out refreshments. It was an image of bygone days that I will never forget. My first reaction was that the Hungarians must have gone totally crazy. The following day, as we continued our withdrawal toward the border of the Reich, we passed a painfully slow ox cart. The count was driving it, dressed like a farmer. The ladies were hunched in the cart, all dressed like farmers' wives. The previous night they had said farewell to a dying era and to all the old splendor and magnificence. Their world was going down in the Red storm, never to rise again. I had stood by at its deathbed.

A foreign army cannot be evaluated superficially on the basis of its societal ways of demeanor, but only based on its own psychological and historical values. Outside observers are fooled all too easily by theatrical pomp. There are distinctions between mountain peoples, civilized peoples, and the peoples of the steppes. The Hungarians were among these latter peoples. Since their appearance on the stage of history they materialized seemingly out of nowhere on horseback, achieved success by the element of surprise, took what they needed, and disappeared just as fast as they came. They never had any interest in covering forces. In 1915, when my 4th Company, 22nd Jägers, was the only German unit attached to the Hungarian 11th Honvéd Cavalry Division, I experienced two such major actions. Similar methods of operating have been reported about Arab troops. In modern large-scale battles such troops using these tactics can easily lead to failure. Another factor explaining the Hungarian failures was the lack of the very important political conviction.

I know of an interesting similar example in Africa. The German colonial protectorate forces wanted to encircle the Hereros at the Waterberg Plateau and destroy them in a Cannae-like double envelopment. By accident there was a gap in the encirclement, through which large numbers of the Hereros escaped with all of their cattle, although the main force was destroyed as intended.[28] The Germans thought they had won a great victory. Not so the leader of the Hottentots, Hendrik Wittboi. One of his companies had fought on the German side. The analysis of the Hottentots' leader was that the Hereros won because they saved all of their cattle. Wittboi, therefore, decided to attack the—as he believed—beaten Germans. Thus the second very difficult part of the South-West Africa campaign began, which eventually ended with the failure of a modern army to win a partisan war. The situation was not unlike what Napoleon experienced in Spain.

The End in Austria: The German Army's Last Successful Envelopment Battle

At the beginning of April, Army Task Group Balck moved back to the border of the Reich, where we occupied prepared positions. The enemy had been shaken off. To the right we were tied in with the Second Panzer Army, but to the left the Sixth SS Panzer Army had not been able to hold.

The mission that I formulated myself from the knowledge that I had of the overall situation was to hold the border until the cease-fire, so that Styria[29] had a chance of falling into western hands. I also had to stay tied in on the right flank to Army Group Southeast, which still had elements deep in the Balkans (Sarajevo), in order to hold open a withdrawal route back into Germany for those units. Finally, I had to withdraw the Sixth Army behind the old border and into Germany proper. Complicating those missions, we were burdened with more than two hundred thousand Hungarian refugees who filled the valleys of Styria in our rear, believing that they were safe there. Mixed in with that mass were the newly formed units of the Hungarian Second Army, which were under my command. The alpine passes in our rear were snowed in and mostly impassable.

We assumed that the enemy would concentrate his main effort on Vienna, which kept us off on the side. For the first time in weeks we took a breath of relief. Our corps had roads and passages to withdraw along. We calmly awaited the next events. The Saint László Division reported its combat readiness by telephone through a German-speaking Hungarian officer. They received their operations order from me personally. Only the fuel situation had been difficult during the last few days. We had to leave behind and destroy a considerable number of operational Panzers.

I was in a fairly upbeat mood when I drove out to the position where the IV SS Panzer Corps was supposed to establish its operations center. I wanted to confirm for myself that everything there and at the Saint László Division was in order. At the designated location I found an SS officer as the advance party, who reported the imminent arrival of the corps staff. I waited. Nothing happened. Then I drove in the direction of the enemy along the corps' withdrawal route. There were no friendly troops in sight, neither the 5th SS Panzer Division nor the Saint László Division. When I returned to my own operations center I found one of the worst possible situations that I had ever encountered.

The IV SS Panzer Corps had decided to turn north, out of its sector of the front line, and made an effort to reach safety beyond the Rába River. In the process, they had gotten onto the withdrawal route of the III Panzer Corps, where everything now was mixed into an insoluble mass of humans and vehicles in the most difficult mountain terrain. All movement had stopped there. At that time, of course, it was impossible to know what reasons had prompted the IV SS Panzer Corps to attempt such an impossible action. Very possibly their decision was linked to what happened to the Saint László Division. Nothing else seemed plausible. We had our hands full trying to rectify the situation. The future was ahead of us, not behind. Today I believe that it was rampant fear of encirclement that resulted in their absurd decision. The corps leadership's complete lack of understanding of the big picture and the available operational options did the rest.

Meanwhile, a Russian tank corps advanced swiftly toward Graz, through the IV SS Panzer Corps' former sector, which was now devoid of any kind of German troops. In the center of our front line the freshly reconstituted Hungarian Saint László Division, which had fought well before, defected to the enemy. They turned their weapons against us, and they were now attacking with the Russians. When the Saint László Division initially had reported its combat-ready status to us, I issued their operations order and handed it to a German-speaking Hungarian officer of German descent, possibly B. Faber. After one or two days that officer called back and reported that the advance party had reached the assigned sector, and the rest of the division would follow in one to two days. After that I did not hear from them again for thirty years.

Along the left flank where the Sixth SS Panzer Army had not established a tie-in with us, five Russian divisions facing only minor resistance marched toward Graz through a gaping hole between Pinkafeld and the Semmering Pass. Meanwhile, the army divisions still positioned along the front line were now showing troubling symptoms of dissolving. In a destroyed Russian command vehicle we found documents indicating that the Russian plan was to thrust through Hatzendorf, Fürstenfeld, Burgau, Hartberg, Riegersburg, Ilz, Gross Steinbach, and Hartberg, effectively encircling the Sixth Army. That could mean the end, not only for us, but for the hundreds of thousands of Hungarian refugees in Styria and for Army Group E, which was still tied into us in the south.[30]

This situation required tough, decisive, and most importantly fast action. The most uncomfortable situation was on my left flank. If the Russians reached Graz we would be cut off from the Reich. Defensive action in such a situation always leads to self-destruction. Only the attack would be effective here. Against those five Russian divisions moving toward Graz we deployed concentrically from the south with the reliable 1st Panzer Division. They were supported by a rocket launcher brigade without launchers and by one officer with five Panzers. They achieved amazing results in the attack. In the defense they certainly would have been annihilated. Then we moved up the 117th Jäger Division, which had been in the rear. It advanced from the north (south of the Semmering Pass) to a position to support the attack of the 1st Mountain Division. All of this took some time, of course.

We scraped up everything we could muster. It was high risk, of course, but we had to accept risk somewhere else. At the Semmering Pass the area commander of Salzburg, General Julius Ringel, started to establish a defensive line and found the right man to do it, Colonel Raithel, the commander of the Mountain Artillery School at Dachstein. There was a danger that the newly forming divisions of the Hungarian First Army would follow the example of the Saint László Division and cut off our line of retreat. I ordered the immediate disarmament of all Hungarian units in Styria. To this day, the Hungarians very much resent that order. But there was no time for negotiations and second guessing. Time was precious, and we also had to take the rescue of huge numbers of Hungarian refugees into consideration.

I kept the disarmed units moving toward Germany proper along secondary roads. They resented that, too, but I had to keep the main roads clear. The required march distances were short, and we still had many horse-drawn vehicles. I commandeered all of their motor vehicles, because that was the most effective way to conserve fuel. The Hungarians never would have followed fuel conservation orders properly, and I could not just let Panzers sit while fuel was being wasted elsewhere.

And the Russian tank corps that was moving toward Graz? I had nothing left. Because of the tangled mess that the IV SS Panzer Corps and the Hungarians caused, we had no ability to extract anybody from the path of the human maelstrom. But the longer the war lasted the more I came to understand that one man often can be worth more than one thousand. I pulled aside Lieutenant Colonel Wolff, a Panzer officer on my staff. I explained the situation to him and told him, "Take a Kübel with two or three men, fill it with Panzerfausts, and drive toward the Russian tank corps and stop them. How? I cannot tell you. Maybe it would be enough to set up a sign 'No thoroughfare for Russian tanks!'"

Wolff said, "Order understood!" and drove off. Directly in front of the Russian armored spearhead he found a German field hospital and the 18th Driver Replacement Detachment from Graz. He got the patients in their blue-and-white-striped gowns out of the hospital, issued them Panzerfausts, and took up the uneven fight. The entire advance stopped as soon as the six lead tanks were blown up. Then the Russians were cooperative enough to wait until we managed to find some more units to throw in front of them. As unlikely as all that might seem today, those were the events as I saw them at the time.

I drove out to where the two corps were insolubly entangled. With a great deal of effort we slowly returned order to this chaos. The fact that the integrity of the tactical units of the IV SS Panzer Corps had not been maintained made things especially complicated. All the NCOs of one company, for example, were together in one vehicle while all the enlisted troops were somewhere else. But we finally got some combat-ready elements moved back into their old sectors.

It took unrelenting harshness to stamp out malingering. Had we not been able to bring that under control within twenty-four hours, all other efforts would have been in vain. We established drumhead courts-martial. After a few stiff sentences were handed out, the troops got the message. At one point a marauding gang of deserters started murdering and plundering summer cottages that were full of fleeing citizens from Vienna. A Volkssturm unit captured them after a fight, during which the deserters killed four Volkssturm troops, all of them fathers of several children. All in all, they were responsible for some ten murders. Their case was handled quickly, and the information spread like wildfire. Within forty-eight hours there were no more deserters. After twenty-four hours had passed, we were able to report that one of the gravest crises had been resolved. If that situation had gotten out of control, the result would have been a catastrophe even by the standards of World War II.

Several days later the 14th SS Volunteer Division[31] showed up. After the experience I had with that unit at Tarnopol, I had mixed feelings at best. This time, however, it did do its duty, although it held down a quiet sector.

It took some time to assemble the divisions for the planned concentric attack south of the Semmering Pass toward Graz, against the advancing Russians. By 16 April we were able to face the enemy with superior forces. On 27 April the operation was completed. Three Russian divisions in the area of Vorau were encircled and destroyed, and the rest were pushed back. We now had established a straight and easily held front line up to the Semmering Pass, where Colonel Raithel threw back the Russians with the troops assembled from General Ringel's Area Command XVII. In the process of the hard fighting at the Semmering Pass, Ringel formed these ad hoc troops into the new 9th Mountain Division, a unique accomplishment. Battle Group Semmering, later designated the 9th Mountain Division, consisted of the following elements:

> Mountain Training NCO School, Mittenwald
> Mountain Artillery School, Dachstein
> SS Mountain Reserve Battalion, Leoben
> Bomber Wing Bölcke
> One FLAK battalion
> One infantry battalion
> Two quick reaction battalions
> Volkssturm personnel used as ammunition and ration porters

The airmen of the 27th Bomber Wing[32] fought exceptionally well, even though they had not been trained for ground combat.

But it was not just the troops of the army and the Waffen-SS that were fighting, the whole country participated. Replacements entered our ranks directly from the civilian population. The Volkssturm stood the test. Even the Nazi Party district leaders fought in the forwardmost lines. When a village near Vorau was recaptured and the local Kreisleiter entered the village with our lead riflemen, the local priest stepped up to him, rendered the Hitler salute, and said "Heil Herr Kreisleiter, I am cured." The experience of the previous eight days under Russian control had been a little too much.

The primary value of the support from the civilians and the party was that we had elements that we could commit to quieter sectors of the front, thus freeing up combat units. General Ringel, the head of Area Command XVII in Salzburg, deserves special recognition. He was everywhere, with his imposing personality and his incredible full beard. Full of energy, he was always where the action was, sometimes in the forwardmost lines, sometimes coordinating. He was the epitome of a general acting and leading purposefully. The only thing else I can add about this true soldier and leader is to repeat the battle cry of his 5th Mountain Division, "Hurrah, the Chamois!"

The Perspective from Today

Once we had established a stable and straight front line at the Lafnitz River, tied in left and right, the retreat route for Army Group E was open from the Balkans to the homeland. The critical Semmering Pass that we had to hold at all costs for the security of the retreat routes into Germany proper was firmly in our hands. We believed that we had mastered the situation with our forceful attack. We credited that success to the troops, who through their unconditional courage and compliance with every order had turned a looming defeat into a resounding victory. The Sixth Army was now ready for its final mission.

The Russians initially tried to encircle us with a two-pronged thrust toward Graz, but that was now no longer their objective. The Stavka[33] shifted gears, pulled back the Russian tank corps that had halted in the Rába Valley, and set it in motion toward Vienna. The Russian 5th Infantry Division that was supposed to move around us in the north and was already in our rear was withdrawn behind the Lafnitz River, just as we were getting ready to attack them. The Stavka, apparently for political reasons, did not commit the strong reserves they still had. They had no political objectives in Styria, and therefore no operational goals. The Russian focus was now on Berlin, Prague, and Vienna. Would they have made the same decisions if they had known how desperate our situation was in the south? Looking at it now in hindsight, we at the time were operating nonetheless under the most unbearable stress, and we had to act. Once again, the basic tenet of "*attaquez donc toujours*" had resolved the crisis.

Politics

As military action comes closer to its end, political action takes priority. Churchill had refused to ally with Germany. But now that the Russian giant was threatening the gates of Europe, Churchill recognized that the wrong pig had been slaughtered.[34] Now that it was too late, he wanted to push the East back with the nuclear threat.[35] But since that effort also required land forces, the significance of those forces increased. German weapons were stored in northern Germany. Pannwitz's Cossack Corps remained intact. Troop units in Hungary were still capable of being formed, especially the Saint László Division.[36] When

Churchill was replaced by the government of Clement Atlee the dream ended and the units designated in the planning were handed over to the Russians. The final fate of the division commander of the Saint László Division speaks volumes. Colonel Zoltan Vitéz Szügyi was an excellent man, still walking free in August 1945 in Hungarian uniform and carrying his weapon. He was extradited to Russia, where he was court-martialed, convicted, and sentenced to a long prison term. Then he was sent back to Hungary, where a people's court convicted and sentenced him to life in prison. Then there was the XV Cossack Cavalry Corps, the last elements of which reached Austrian soil during the night of 13 May. Despite the promises that the British had made to General von Pannwitz, the bulk of the corps was handed over to the Red Army at Judenburg on 28 May 1945.

Quiet Time

The front line was stabilized. The exhausted Russians halted in front of our positions. Now it was time to think things through. The coming weeks could still bring many unwelcome situations, and we had to be prepared for the worst. The first step was to reestablish iron discipline. Only then would we be able to deal with anything that was to come. Presumably we would reach Germany proper at some point. In order to accomplish that, we had to conserve fuel tightly. We therefore made extensive use of bicycles for individual travel and a local bus line for our messenger system. One rear area services official who exchanged gasoline for food in order to sell the food in Germany was court-martialed. In our situation that was a crime worse than cold-blooded murder.

In Graz we geared up fuel production. Even though it produced only small quantities, it still made a huge difference. In order to preserve German infantry ammunition for actual fighting, we reloaded spent German cartridges from captured Russian ammunition. In the villages everywhere close to the front line we established small reloading points. The quartering of troops in the city of Graz itself was prohibited. Any congestion created there would have made any further withdrawal movements impossible. In order to relieve the pressures on the local population, I issued orders on 15 May for all rear area units and their staffs to bivouac in forested areas.[37] This kept the rear services busy and prevented them from getting any stupid ideas.

The political situation was bothersome. We anticipated an Austrian independence movement at any time,[38] which would have made the withdrawal of the Sixth Army impossible. I issued an order for all senior officers to proceed in their duty uniforms to the nearest senior local party official and report in accordance with my orders that they would support him and would not tolerate any disturbances or subversion.[39] Politics and unrest could be dealt with later. We also made extensive preparations to destroy key sites to make Russian pursuit impossible. The release authority for the demolitions was tightly held at Sixth Army headquarters. Meanwhile, we disabled all unnecessary equipment and started improvement work on the selected withdrawal routes. That was especially necessary for the IV SS Panzer Corps, which we wanted to evacuate toward Carinthia.

Hitler

On 30 April we received the news of Hitler's death. The key figure on the German side of this war had vanished. "Criminal" and "crazy" are terms many have used to describe him. Neither term is satisfactory. They both prevent one from critical assessment. The reality of Hitler lies much deeper. The writings of contemporary history are mostly the continuation of the propaganda of the victorious parties, including in this case Germany's external enemies and the internal opponents of National Socialism. Both have vested interests in painting everything as black as possible. I cannot offer a conclusive analysis here; I can only offer some individual insights drawn from my own experiences.

The Treaty of Versailles and subsequently the inevitable failure of the German democratic parties that wore themselves down through internal and external fighting created the fertile ground from which a dictatorship and someone like Hitler had to emerge. Hitler can be most closely compared to Charles XII of Sweden. Both were men of decision, but not of development. Whenever something happened, both immediately reacted with a countermove. That in turn often propelled an event that was in itself insignificant into something large and often insoluble. Both failed through their belief in the principle that no subordinate leader should know the intentions of the senior leadership any earlier than necessary, and no more than what he needed to accomplish his immediate mission. With that approach Hitler destroyed the best of what we had, the independent cooperation of the leaders at all levels.

After achieving a successful breakthrough at the Battle of Poltava,[40] Charles XII was carried off the battlefield wounded and unconscious. Nobody else knew anything about his battle plan. His planned follow-on maneuver to destroy the Russian main body never happened, and in the end the Swedish Army was destroyed. Bismarck's wait-and-see approach, letting events develop and then proceeding as if "carried by the cloak of the Deity," was foreign to Hitler's thinking.

Command requires trust in the man at the point of the action. Hitler was mistrusting by his very nature. This fatal character flaw was exploited by many people in his immediate circle and in the Nazi Party against the leadership of the army. Hitler's greatest fear was that the generals always wanted to operate by withdrawing, then blame him for the failure, and then launch a counter-revolution. He thus gambled away one of the greatest chances he had, the unique operational talents of Germany's generals and the entire officer corps, which were at a level of skill and competence never before achieved by any other army, not even the German Army of 1914.

Lenin once said, "I can only govern if my ministers are at odds with each other." Hitler also ruled according to this principle. The result was widespread duplication of effort and authority. Everybody was at odds with everyone else. That was the only way Hitler felt confident to make decisions. He did not trust the army, so he built the Waffen-SS as a second army. But even there, he placed Oberstgruppenführer Sepp Dietrich[41] right under Himmler's nose as a counter-weight to Himmler's absolute authority. The chief of staff of the 1st SS Panzer Division later told me that when the division was once refitting near Poltava, Himmler announced his arrival, saying that he wanted to talk to the entire leadership of the division at the airfield. When only Dietrich and his Ia[42] were waiting for him at the airfield, the surprised Himmler asked where the division's leadership was. Dietrich replied, "Only the Führer and I talk to the leadership of the Leibstandarte,[43] no one else." That was the end of that.

The reason that Hitler reached down from the level of head-of-state to the military leadership level was largely a function of his deep-seated mistrust of most military leaders. Hitler was shaped and influenced by World War I, but he incorrectly internalized what he saw and experienced. He also drew many incorrect conclusions from what he subsequently read and studied.[44] His opinions on Russia were those of the infantryman of the western front of 1914–1918, which totally underestimated the Russians. If Hitler had fought in the East during World War I, German policies toward the East might have been different. He believed that the real war of 1914–1918 had been fought by the German main forces in the West, while in the East fire brigades had held the line.

Operationally, Hitler had a clear and one might even say an exceptional understanding. He combined this with a rare ability to influence men. He was incapable, however, of judging what could be accomplished with the available forces and when the correlation of forces was completely against him. He believed that he could bridge any gaps with his iron will. That worked during the winter of 1941–1942 because the Russians were exhausted too. Later, when the gap between will and what was realistically possible became larger and larger, Hitler's blind willfulness caused the instrument to break in his hands. The same thing happened to Napoleon during the winter of 1806–1807 at Preussisch Eylau.[45]

The similarities between Hitler and Napoleon lead to questions about the negative effects of strong personalities when they are given free reign without any counterbalance. This is an important question for our democracy. America had similar experiences with Franklin Delano Roosevelt, as the nuclear attack on Hiroshima clearly shows.[46]

From his World War I experiences Hitler believed that a unit that did not want to be pushed out of its defensive position would hold it at all costs. But at that time the defensive weapons, including the machine gun and barbed wire, were superior to all offensive weapons, and German defensive tactics in that war were always a year ahead of the enemy. By World War II the offensive weapons, especially the tank, were superior to the defensive weapons in the thinly stretched divisional sectors. Consequently, our thin defensive lines were almost always broken through whenever we insisted on remaining on the defense. We had to stay on the offensive if we wanted to win, either by advancing or by counterattacking from a retrograde movement. Hitler did not recognize this essential element in Manstein's strategy, and he therefore failed to recognize the great opportunity we still had after Stalingrad. Manstein could have been our savior, but that was what Hitler himself wanted to be.

Instead of conducting operations we held lines and so-called strongpoints. Without doubt that produced some initial success. But since we did not exploit operationally these halts that we imposed upon the enemy, we wound up holding so many wretched pockets. Tactical measures only are successful when they surprise the enemy. If you repeat yourself you end up playing with open cards and handing the advantage to the enemy. The troops will only fight well in a pocket initially; all too soon the fear of encirclement will follow. Once a force is encircled, a disorganized pressure builds for a headlong breakout. At best an unorganized and often unarmed human mass will stampede through the encirclement ring, suffering huge losses and only having to be extracted and reorganized later. The situation becomes even worse when the troops attempting to escape a pocket abandon their equipment. But who can really blame exhausted and overextended soldiers in such situations? It is the responsibility of the leadership not to let an avoidable encirclement happen.

Mistrust and the attempt to shape events according to his own wishes through the immense force of his will led Hitler to interfere with the military leadership continuously, and with serious consequences. But not everything that has been said since the war about Hitler's interference is quite true. All too often the personal shortcomings of military leaders at all levels were blamed on Hitler, "the Ignoramus." Quite often, the label "Führer Order" was attached to purely local orders to give them more force. I have carefully recorded in these pages any interference into my leadership, direct or indirect. Normally Hitler's interference was kept within limits. Of course, toward the end of the war, when we were facing the threat of defeat, the level of interference did increase, as could be expected.

On 23 January 1945 Hitler severely restricted the independence of the senior leaders by issuing a special Führer Order.[47] But that order had no effect whatsoever because it could not have been implemented in the rapidly changing situations. It remained nothing but a piece of printed paper. I cannot remember that it ever played any role in our decisions.

Hitler's interventions became more frequent toward the end of the war, when matters were on the knife's edge. It is tempting here to make comparisons to military leaders in similar situations. Napoleon acted similarly in comparable situations. He sent orders to Spain regulating the movements of individual battalions that were naturally outdated by the time they were received. Churchill from London got involved in the movement of individual tanks on Crete. Ludendorff cheated himself out of a victory at the Battle of Mount Kemmel in April 1918 through his detailed interference. Great men in unfortunate situations.

Hitler thought very logically and followed events to the bitter end. But in doing so he frequently went past the point where reason becomes irrational and things reverse themselves. What he lacked was an audience that he listened to, with whom he could exchange his thoughts. That was difficult, because Hitler only engaged in relationships very reluctantly. He was very sensitive to clumsy reproofs, and the army's personnel department was never able to match him with a counterpart with the appropriate personality. Perhaps Guderian could have managed to do it at the beginning of the war, when Hitler was still quite unsure of himself. But many people considered Guderian too assertive. On the one hand, anyone with a laid-back personality, no matter how intelligent, was immediately overwhelmed by Hitler. On the other hand, there would have been nothing but constant conflict between Guderian and Hitler. I think it might have been possible earlier on for the two of them to learn to work together. After the beginning of the campaign in Russia, however, I think it would have been impossible for anyone to develop a real working relationship with Hitler.

Jodl was right when he said that Hitler was our fate and that we would be victorious or go down with him. Hitler just was not replaceable. His person was the glue that held the people and the Wehrmacht inseparably together. All authority of all leaders at any level and any willingness for sacrifice on the part of the common man were grounded in Hitler. Without him, the Wehrmacht and the state would have collapsed, much the same as it had been with Napoleon and his grenadiers.[48] Throughout the war I carefully monitored the censorship of the letters from the field. With the exception of one case, I prohibited any court-martial action for anything written in a letter. I did not want to shut down this important barometer of what the troops were really thinking. Shortly before Hitler's death in mid-April 1945, 60 percent of the letter writers were still convinced that in the end Hitler would master the deteriorating situation.

It is a standard approach to look for the reasons for any catastrophe in the faults and shortcomings of the leading personality involved. Nonetheless, the fact cannot be obscured that Hitler succeeded in some ways that nobody thought possible. British military historian Basil Liddell Hart described the dismemberment of Czechoslovakia without a fight as a classic example of the coordination of politics and military force. Hitler's intervention in the planning of the 1940 campaign in the West and his salvation of the German Army in front of Moscow were leadership accomplishments of the first order. Certainly, his thinking about the conduct of war was different from that of the General Staff. He did not look at the war exclusively from a military standpoint, but also focused strongly on the economy and the armament industry. He preferred holding static positions to elegant maneuver operations.[49]

These factors serve to explain the rationale behind Hitler's conduct of the war. We achieved our initial large successes because of our superior armaments. Once the Anglo-Americans rearmed and we were now facing superior armaments, we were clearly at a disadvantage. Hitler's intent from that point on was to preserve Germany's economic capacity until we could develop even more advanced weapons systems, such as the Walter U-boat, Panzers with night fire control systems, jet fighters, and FLAK projectiles with acoustic fuses. The Americans believed that they would not win if the war lasted six months longer. They may have been right.[50]

Hitler lost his race. Maybe he would not have if he had pursued a more balanced approach to operations and materiel. He was quite capable of managing the third key factor, morale. The General Staff and Hitler had opposing views on the conduct of the war. Each brought to the table what the other lacked. They could have complemented each other so well. That they did not come together was part of the German tragedy.

Was Hitler insane? That question has been raised over and over again. I want to answer with a decisive no. The opinion I had of Hitler's mental state in September 1944 was essentially the same as that of Colonel General Lothar Rendulic[51] right to the very end of the war. General Wöhler, who saw Hitler in April 1945, also had the same opinion of him. Wöhler was a staunch opponent of Hitler and National Socialism and did not try to hide the fact. Of course, many contrary opinions about Hitler's sanity have been expressed by members of his immediate circle who were involved in the daily, grueling conflicts with him.

The role of Hitler's personal physician, Dr. Theodor Morell, remains a big question mark. While in prison Dr. Karl Brandt[52] told me about the irresponsible regimen of injections that Morell routinely gave Hitler. It is possible that under the influence of the injections Hitler underestimated imponderables, fell prey to illusions, and in the process became mentally impaired. Much seems to point in that direction, but I am not a doctor.[53]

Personally, I got along well with Hitler. I only knew him as well mannered and very formal. His decisions were clear and factual, even if I disagreed with some of them. Whenever I had a conflict with Himmler, Hitler always backed me. I was always able to tell him candidly what I thought, and he always paid attention. He also never held it against me when I did not agree with his orders.

On occasion he played the actor. When I reported to him after my return from the Moscow front, his eyes focused fixedly on my Wound Badge in Gold[54] from World War I and my Iron Cross Knight's Cross. His intention was obvious. On another occasion he stepped up to the map table beside me. When I laid both hands on the table rim, I suddenly felt the pressure of a soft, molding hand. The sensation went through me like an electric shock. He then locked onto me with his eyes and said in a forceful voice, "So, now show me on the map." I never experienced anything like that before or since, and I am generally far too sober an individual to let something like that influence me. When he removed his hand after a few seconds, the formal atmosphere returned.

The image of the *Teppichbeisser*[55] is now a part of the Hitler legend. It has been reported widely that Hitler always screamed at everybody. I have heard that many times, but I do not know anyone who claims to have been screamed at personally by Hitler. I do know of two incidents of screaming involving Hitler, but in both cases it was not Hitler doing the screaming. One was Guderian, the other one Hitler's naval adjutant, Admiral Karl-Jesco von Puttkamer. But despite all my conscious efforts to evaluate Hitler with complete objectivity, I cannot escape the final verdict—he was our downfall. Beware of strong men who do not know the limits of their power.

Before the Final Act

The front line was paralyzed. The Russians pulled out forces and sent them toward Vienna. There was a lull in the action, a deep calm. There was, however, no rest for the staffs. I was on the road almost daily, providing encouragement everywhere and maintaining communications. The picture starting to develop was positive. The roads were empty, with hardly a motor vehicle on them. Discipline clearly was improving, and even the IV SS Panzer Corps returned to its usual level of effectiveness. Of course, unexpected problems continued to pop up. One battery just disappeared—the guns were still in position, but the crews disappeared toward the homeland. Germans always believe that in a crisis situation they can just excuse themselves.

> Then spoke the wicked Ganaleon,
> He said it only sneakily,
> If I got away in one piece,
> May the devil get the rest of you![56]

The fate of my family weighed especially heavily on me. I knew that they were in Silesia, but I had not had any contact with them for a long time. An officer suggested moving them to safety with a military truck. I rejected that suggestion. The Landser on the front line whose family meant just as much to him could not do anything like that, and there should be no such special privileges for the commander. And besides, something like that would have gotten around in a matter of hours, and it would have broken the Sixth Army's back.

In the meantime, things were now working smoothly again with the Nazi Party leadership. The local Gauleiter, Dr. Siegfried Überreither, who was nicknamed Dr. Übereifer,[57] did what he could to defend his Styrian homeland. In the various wars with the Turks eleven members of the Überreither family had lost their lives in battle on the borders of Styria. He was proud of his ancestors.

It was impossible to get a sense of the big picture. One telephonic instruction we received was, "Hold! With the West against the East." But then there was no follow-on clarification. On the night of 6–7 May, I met in Judenburg with Field Marshal Kesselring,[58] but I still gained no clarity. Army Group South sent my chief of staff, General Gaedcke, to negotiate with the Americans. But the Americans at that point refused to negotiate. They were only willing to talk directly with the army group commander, and even then only if he was willing to surrender his armies unconditionally. Gaedcke thought that the entire army group staff was overcome with lethargy. This confirmed the impression I got while listening to a telephone conversation between Kesselring and the army group commander.

Cease-Fire

On 7 May my Sixth Army Ic,[59] Lieutenant Colonel von Czernicki, received the text of the cease-fire conditions via radio. All German units were to be taken prisoner by the side they had last fought against. That meant that we were going to have to turn around and launch a pro forma attack against the Americans to justify surrendering to them rather than the Russians. The big question was whether or not the Americans would play along. We had already thrown quite a few interdiction measures against the Americans.

On the night of 8 May we received instructions to pull back toward the West immediately and surrender to the Americans. We did not have a lot of fuel but it was sufficient. Most importantly, Graz was now empty and there was no danger of getting bogged down in the streets. The orders went out fast. The Austrians were to be released immediately. The *Hiwis*[60] remained in place. The weapons were left behind. Only the rear guards consisting of tanks and antitank guns kept their full complements of equipment. Knowing the terrain, we were confident that the rear guards would be quite capable of keeping the Russians off our backs without having to destroy everything as we withdrew. We also expected that the Russians would not immediately notice our departure and would then react sluggishly.

All movements started immediately, with the exception of the forces at the Semmering Pass. They started withdrawing a little later to prevent the Russians from intercepting our withdrawal on the road from Semmering to Leoben. The IV SS Panzer Corps headed for the English forces in Carinthia; the III Panzer Corps moved via Liezen toward the Americans; and the two mountain divisions moved across the mountains toward Upper Austria. By the morning of 8 May we were certain that everything was running smoothly and everyone was moving. Only then did I start moving with my chief of staff and my IIa.[61] I had sent all my other General Staff officers ahead to the critical points in order to keep the movement flowing.

In Graz, I met one more time with Überreither. He had tried his utmost to defend his Styrian homeland, but he was now overwhelmed by the events. I told him that he could do anything except commit suicide. We were accountable to the German people and could not escape that responsibility. He put away the pistol that he had been considering using. Überreither's wife was the daughter of the German geophysicist Alfred Wegener, known for his continental drift theory. She had the complete set of his posthumous papers. I gave her some advice on how to get those papers back to Germany. Later she used her father's papers to ransom her husband out of American detention and helped him escape to Argentina.

Leaving Graz, we went on to the Enns River. The local leadership there was not up to the challenges of the situation. They had been negotiating for quite a while with an American lieutenant, allowing themselves to be stalled. It was not clear at that point that the Americans would accept us. They had already stopped onward movements and sent German forces that crossed their lines back into the Enns Valley. It was looking more and more like we would be handed off to the Russians. Establishing contact with the American divisional commander via telephone, I was able to arrange an immediate face-to-face meeting. Before leaving for that meeting, I announced that if the Americans refused to accept all of us, I would remain with the Sixth Army.

General McBride

In Kirchdorf we met the American staff. The reception was flawless, the guards stood at attention and saluted. I trooped the line giving the Hitler salute. Concessions in such a situation only backfire, especially with the Anglo-Americans. The reception by the divisional commander, Major General Horace McBride, was rather cool initially.[62]

Throughout the entire war I had devoted an hour a day before dinner to studying English. That was the daily quiet time I needed to clear my head. Now all that time paid off as I was able to conduct the conversation in English. We were just by ourselves. Nobody had to do any posturing in front of a translator. I laid out our situation, our reasons for attacking the Americans, and our fears of Russian imprisonment. McBride and I settled everything in short order. We selected assembly areas and the Americans established a security screen against the Russians that were pursuing us. I issued the necessary orders telephonically to my units on the Enns.

McBride warmed up, and I accepted a cup of coffee from him. He bade me a hearty farewell as I returned to the Enns. My mood was quite different on the return trip. If everything worked out we could save the Sixth Army. Years later an American told me how lucky I had been to encounter McBride. No other American general would have acted contrary to his orders to such an extent. McBride came from an Irish family. A McBride had commanded an Irish brigade against the British in the Boer War, and was executed by the English during World War I. I considered McBride a committed friend of Germany.

Along the Enns

According to the conditions of the cease-fire, all movement had to stop on 9 May at 0100 hours. McBride told me that he would send a guard force at 0800 hours on 9 May to the Liezen Bridge to stop any further traffic. We had to get everything across by then. It was a wild night. We were all on our feet to keep everything moving. From all directions the traffic stream moved toward Liezen. That morning the American guard force arrived at 0900 instead of 0800, but then the GIs leaned against the bridge railings and stared left and right into the river while my troops continued moving right by them. Gradually it began to look like we were going to make it. Every so often the Liezen Bridge was closed and traffic was detoured across other bridges.

By the evening of 9 May, when Russian tanks rolled up to the Enns, we had almost everything across. Remnants still needing to cross veered off into the mountains and used secondary roads. It was difficult to keep the troops moving because they had no idea about the seriousness of the situation. Again and again General Staff officers drove along the convoy lines toward the Russians to keep everything flowing.

There was a bit of humor even in this situation. Instead of getting across the Enns Bridge to safety, some four hundred troops were lolling in the grass on the Russian side, sunning themselves and bathing in the river. As soon as the Russian tanks showed up, the entire four hundred swam the river. Then they reported to me totally naked, urgently requesting clothing I did not have. The only thing to do was to order them to retrieve their uniforms by swimming back across. It worked because the Russians did not have a clear field of observation of that sector of the riverbank.

By that evening we were largely successful, thanks in no small part to the understanding and generosity of General McBride. Another major factor had been the many tireless, young General Staff officers, whose dedication kept things in line and moving, and who fought hard to overcome the lethargy that was now setting in among the men and the officers. One of those key General Staff officers was Colonel Krantz. Although he had an artificial leg, he constantly kept moving on foot through the difficult terrain of the Semmering to organize the flow of the troops from there. I had to use him for that task despite his handicap, because I had no one else available.

The Austrian population acted well. There was trouble only in Leoben, where some local communists had seized control of an 88 mm FLAK gun from the territorial air defense service. However, they picked the wrong unit to quarrel with when they tangled with the 1st Panzer Division. At another location a newly arrived lieutenant from Berlin declared himself a resistance fighter, seized control of a fuel depot, refused to issue fuel to Germans, and intended to hand the depot over to the Russians. The Austrian populace promptly took care of that matter.

The next few days were full of uncertainty. All day long I went from bivouac site to bivouac site, talked to as many troops as possible, and explained the situation to them. I wrote in my journal: "Discipline and morale of the troops are excellent throughout. It was well worth working for these men."

We had other worries as well, not the least of which was rations. All available loading space during the evacuation was supposed to be used for rations. But all sorts of other material got carried along, including sixty tons of cement hauled by one convoy. Moving the wounded was another problem. At the train station in Liezen five or seven trains had stopped with seriously wounded troops. But to reach Upper Austria these trains would have to travel through Russian-controlled territory, which could be a possible death sentence. An American major said that would not happen, because the trains were under American protection. "Do you really think that that would stop the Russians?" I asked. "You do not know them. They will take the trains from you, even with American guards on them."

"We shall see!" Full of anger, the American stormed off. When the trains finally moved out there was a GI on every outside platform, machine guns on the roofs of all the cars, and American flags everywhere. The trains with their several hundred wounded troops reached their destination without incident. The moral of this story is that the surest way to get an American to do something is to tell him that it cannot be done because it is impossible.

Mauerkirchen[63]

The units were continuously pulling back. To the very end the Sixth Army staff remained at the bridge at Liezen. One more time it looked like my staff would be handed over to the Russians. Then it was all finished. We had managed to surrender almost all of the Sixth Army to the Americans. Only somewhat less than one hundred troops from one of the mountain divisions fell into Russian hands. When we reached Upper Austria I was able to take effective command of the Sixth Army once more. Again, I spent day after day going from bivouac to bivouac to talk to the troops, to calm them down, and to reason with them. The average German is impatient. They all wanted to get home as fast as possible, but the smallest element of disorder could have had the gravest consequences. The Americans were very strict and they reacted strongly to any problems.

On 21 May I was ordered to report to the Americans and McBride told me that I was under arrest and relieved of my command because I had not followed American orders. Among the one thousand men that we had reported to be released to Lower Bavaria, there supposedly had been some four hundred that were supposed to go to other destinations. That was more than likely true, but was still a case of hairsplitting. The true reason was Eisenhower's well-known order to mistreat us, which had been issued after Göring was captured. McBride probably had concerns that he had been too accommodating.[64] McBride proved himself to be a good soldier and decent human being after the surrender of the Sixth Army. I thank him for that, not for myself, but for my troops. But Americans' personal courage ends where public opinion starts, which I learned here for the first time.

Saying goodbye to my first-rate staff was painful. I have rarely seen such erect and expressive salutes rendered me. My chief of staff, General Gaedcke, was an outstanding General Staff officer and a soldier's soldier. I remained in close touch with him in later years. Lueder, my adjutant, was not a yes-man. That is why I had selected him. I cannot mention them all individually, but I offer my thanks to every one of them. It was through their earnest and faithful fulfillment of their duty that the accomplishments and in the end the rescue of the Sixth Army had been possible.

19

Looking Back

Politics

The aggressor in any war is always the side that loses. Personally, I am not certain that it really was not English politics that forced Hitler into the war. Some respected voices in America have expressed this opinion, and documents recently made public in England support this argument.[1] Hitler had no intentions in the West.[2] On the contrary, he considered the British Empire a guarantor of the continuation of Western European culture. What is certain is that after our victorious campaign in France in 1940 the hardliners in Churchill's circle blocked any rapprochement with Germany that had been sought by very influential circles in England.[3] There should be no question by now regarding Roosevelt's war policies.[4] After it was too late, Churchill admitted to having slaughtered the wrong pig.

Hitler may not have been quite up to this Anglo-American political game. He never changed his tactics and after the occupation of Prague he played with open cards. He had the disadvantage of not knowing other foreign countries. He misinterpreted English stolidity as decadence. He also did not understand that England opposed any kind of dictatorship in Europe—not for idealistic reasons, but because a dictatorship was unpredictable and the British were uncomfortable dealing with one. This had been their attitude toward Prussia long before World War I. As much as they admired Prussian accomplishments, they did not have any sympathy or understanding for Prussia.[5]

Looking back, one can only regret that Hitler never had taken the opportunity to get to know England and America and the vast Russian lands. Whatever he saw and experienced personally he almost always filed away correctly; but whatever knowledge he acquired indirectly he almost always misinterpreted.

Germany's Allies

Modern wars are coalition wars. We had no understanding of how to manage a coalition politically. We let things drift along. The seeking of mutual consent and agreements on goals and operations never developed adequately, and in the end there was no firm leadership of the coalition. That backfired on us, especially in the case of Japan. We left them unclear about our intentions in Russia. As the result of the usual mistrust, Japan went its own separate way. Italy, well known as militarily weak and ineffective, was given too much freedom of action, which caused us a great deal of damage.

Finland and Japan were valuable and effective allies. Romania, through the loyalty of Ion Antonescu and the stalwartness of its soldiers, had the potential to be an effective ally if there had not been so many Romanian units with obsolescent equipment. We gambled away the support of the militarily excellent and willing Croats by handing them over to the Italians, who were much hated by the Croats. The Hungarians were hardly useful outside of their homeland, as we should have known from our experiences during World War I. Horthy's double-dealing policies were an additional burden on his own troops, and the inferior Hungarian weapons did the rest.

The catastrophe was inevitable when Hungarian, Italian, and Romanian units were committed along hundreds of kilometers of the front line in Russia under the command of their own field army headquarters. The belief that they would be adequate in the defense ignored the reality that modern weaponry made the defense far more difficult than the attack, especially for units inadequately equipped.

To paraphrase the saying about the destruction of the Spanish Armada, *Stalinus afflavit ac dissipati sunt.*[6] Stalin did not even have to blow very hard, and within hours our allies disappeared, hardly putting up a fight. They had no business at the Don and in the steppes of the Kalmyks. The best way to have used those units would have been as reinforced regimental groups within German divisions. But for reasons of national prestige, that never happened, and once again the soldier paid with his blood for what his politicians had wrought.

The Summit

The political constitutions of all peoples run the spectrum from all-inclusive participation to dictatorship. In normal times the former model is the only correct one. A dictatorship is necessary in difficult times.[7] During my travels through middle and southern Africa I encountered examples of both poles in the constitutions of all the African tribes.

The English approach is exemplary, which facilitates the free play of democratic forces in normal times, but in times of crisis the opposition participates in the government and supports all policies without condition. In Germany, of course, such would hardly be thinkable. In time of crisis, then, the national leadership must assume a different form.[8] But our modern economic and social life is so complex that a one-man dictatorship is quite impossible. A small, tightly organized team must lead, but it cannot be the type of war council of the past that votes on every issue.

Even if one recognizes Hitler's above-average capabilities, his one-man dictatorship was beyond even his abilities. The great decisions involving the conflicting interests between politics and the conduct of war were decided by him only. There never was any balanced compromise, no multilateral exchange. When Hitler stepped down from the level of a statesman into the military, economic, and political arena, he was inundated with such a multitude of details that had to be dealt with and decided upon that it overwhelmed him and jeopardized control of the whole. Consequently he overlooked much. Some of his unilateral decisions, like the development of tank construction, were spot-on. Others, like the issues regarding the Luftwaffe, were wrong because he had no team input.

The *Diadochi*[9]

The lack of tight organization at the top and flawed teamwork created a power vacuum that was exploited by various individuals pursuing their own agendas. This was fertile soil in which the destructive influences of Himmler and Göring flourished. The private armies they both tried to muster had only one purpose: to prepare for the power struggle to succeed Hitler. Himmler especially built a state-within-a-state apparatus. The ultimate victim was the goal of successfully concluding the war.

The consequences played out on the battlefield, while Göring and Himmler jealously stood guard over their units to prevent as much as possible their subordination to the army. The only reasonable way of operating was to have a single commander in chief in each theater, who had all the army, Luftwaffe, navy, and Waffen-SS units under him. We never were able to bring ourselves to do that. Heavy friction, absolutely unnecessary losses, and finally the loss of the war were the inevitable consequences. [See Guderian's statement in Appendix 4.]

Strategic Elements

The German ideas about war were derived from the geographical position of Prussia and Germany, which faced superior enemies all around and unsecured borders. In order to survive they had to be faster than their enemies, stay ahead of them, and hit them decisively at a vulnerable point with locally superior forces. Complete victory over a superior enemy was the problem. Frederick the Great solved it at Leuthen; Clausewitz underscored it in theory; Schlieffen made it the focus of his studies of the Battle of Cannae; and Seeckt planted these tenets deeply with us. Thus, operations[10] were at the focal point of our strategic thinking and in the formal education of our officer corps. Never before did an officer corps enter battle with a higher and better level of operational training than the German Army in 1939.

Anglo-American strategy was quite different. One was on an island and the other was an ocean away. They could pick their times to enter into the conflict—when their Continental opponent was exhausted, and when their own armament was distinctly superior.[11] They additionally waged economic warfare to weaken their opponent decisively. They dominated the sea and pushed as many so-called allied states as possible into the war against their main opponent. Once that opponent was decisively weakened, they committed their well-equipped and -trained land forces and delivered the coup de grâce. Any defeats they may have suffered in the early stages of the war were of no consequence. They sat back far from the action and waited.[12] This has been dubbed the "Anaconda Strategy."[13] Our enemies in the East were also masters of psychological warfare, carefully preparing their enemy before delivering the decisive blow. In 1918 psychological warfare was effectively used against us. During World War II the Allied bombing attacks designed to demoralize us failed because of our brilliant leadership, and we stood the test.[14]

The fourth element was superior equipment and armament. The side that holds the stronger club can overcome the many other setbacks that inevitably happen.

Which system was right? To be effective, all four elements must be applied. Exclusive reliance on any one of them will lead to disaster. It required more than just our superior operations to defeat Russia in 1914–1917. We were fortunate that Russia strangled economically in the process. Russia did not receive its fatal blow at Tannenberg, but rather at the Dardanelles. The tsarist regime also committed psychological suicide. If in 1940–1945 we had combined our superior operational capabilities with economic warfare (such as cutting off the Murmansk railroad) and with a solid political approach that offered the people of Russia liberation from the communist yoke, if we had brought Japan into the war against Russia at the decisive moment, and if we had given our tanks superior armor and acquired them in sufficient numbers, things possibly would have turned out differently.

When the Americans supported Nationalist China's Chiang Kai-shek against the Chinese Communists, they believed it was a matter of money and materials, and they failed because they misread the psychological element. All of these factors were clearly present in the American Civil War, the most modern conflict fought between the Napoleonic wars and World War I. Unfortunately, the lessons of that war were never evaluated in Europe. The thought was that whatever might have worked in America could not possibly have been applicable for Europe.

Because we did not understand the combined application of these basic strategic concepts, and we instead focused almost exclusively on the operational level, we lost the war. Hitler all along had had the right ideas about combining all the elements of national power, and he therefore had an aversion to purely operational solutions. But as a politician he had an insufficient background in military matters to bring all these elements together through his directives, and the necessary teamwork was missing to help him to do that.

Bismarck's most effective political chess move was ending the Austro-Prussian War of 1866 before it could expand into a world war that might have destroyed Germany. Hitler did not understand something like that, but even before the outbreak of World War II Guderian told me that he believed that we would lose any drawn-out war. Guderian also understood the psychological factor in war.

I must comment here on the often raised complaint that Hitler did not listen to his generals. During World War I, defensive weapons (especially machine guns and barbed wire) were superior to offensive weapons. Thus, the defense became the effective option. But during World War II offensive weapons, especially the tank, gained superiority over the defense. Therefore, all of those who believed in conducting World War II as World War I were behind the times. Mobility and attack were the only keys to success. Many experienced and proven military leaders failed to grasp this shift, and Hitler himself lacked the basic military training to recognize it and abandon the old ways. Many members of the General Staff also failed to recognize the new situation, especially when the General Staff became full of so many second stringers with top-notch qualifications but few natural leaders. The conduct of war is an art, not a science. Strong academic credentials alone are worthless.

Success in Battle

A battle is conducted on both the operational and tactical levels. Superior armament, good training, and stubborn perseverance are all important factors. While strategic factors must always be taken into consideration, an unbalanced focus on the strategic level can backfire. Battles can only be won by focusing on operational and tactical factors. In conducting a battle you must have a clear idea of which of these factors your efforts will be based upon. There is nothing new in any of this, but did we always act accordingly?

Operationally we were the best in World War II.[15] We always preferred to try to win at the operational level, even when that was the wrong approach, such as the first winter in front of Moscow. That was a situation that only could have been won tactically. We recognized that, but we did not take the necessary actions, especially in the key personnel assignments. Once we were on the defensive in the East, we tried to prevail tactically, when at that point only large-scale operational maneuver could have succeeded. We were not always fully committed to fielding the most superior armament. That led to the crisis near Moscow. We also treated training during the war like something of a stepchild. We started formal training of the more senior leaders far too late. We hardly ever analyzed lessons learned. Compared with World War I we were quite weak in that area. We lost Stalingrad, Africa, and the Caucasus campaign because these campaigns were conducted beyond secured supply lines, and when this error became apparent, we did not abort in time. We only overcame the crisis in front of Moscow through stubborn perseverance. While you must have a clear idea of how you want to win a battle before it starts, the situation can change later by the hour.

In some cases, including the campaign in the West, the crisis in front of Moscow, and armament development, Hitler made the right decisions. In other cases, including the conduct of the defense in Russia and training, his decisions were less than optimal. Despite all of his intuitive genius, he lacked the military training and the support team without which nothing can be achieved today. Even a highly qualified soldier could not have succeeded without an effective support team.[16]

Organizational Matters

Every war is virgin territory compared to the past, which means that the organization is in a constant state of development. The defense against a breakthrough by masses of modern tanks requires highly mobile divisions equipped with a large number of antitank weapons. Such units must remain under the operational control of the higher command echelons, and committed only when a developing breakthrough can no longer be held with local forces. We never did develop such units.

The artillery division equipped with assault guns and assigned infantry battalions was a failure, and even its designation as a division was misleading. The result was its commitment as a Panzer division, and inevitable failure. Artillery brigades without assault guns and infantry units would have been far more effective as fire support assets.

We stood up too many new units. The old divisions were drained in the process.[17] They had to provide the leaders of all grades for the new units, and in the process the esprit de corps, combat experience, and self-confidence of the older units wilted away. Again, Falkenhayn's idea of a "children's corps" haunted us in the form of the Hitler Youths Division.[18] Without the experience of older warriors, unnecessary losses were the result. The Luftwaffe field divisions were initially useless, because the Luftwaffe did not have the leaders with ground combat experience. Göring's pursuit of prestige resulted in a high and unnecessary toll in blood.

There was nothing wrong with the Waffen-SS divisions that were stood up at the beginning of the war. On the contrary, high esprit de corps, good people, and good equipment resulted in highly capable divisions. But as soon as the Waffen-SS leaders tried to exceed their capabilities, the result was considerable damage. Chiefs of police, even if they had been lieutenants in World War I, did not make good generals. Himmler's continual efforts to withdraw his divisions frequently for reconstitution were especially disruptive. The resulting uncertainty in the chain of command developed a leadership vacuum in which the troops did whatever they wanted. Waffen-SS divisions frequently disappeared from the battlefield as they moved piecemeal to reconstitute. Once, I had to order a withdrawing Waffen-SS unit under my command that had already been loaded on railcars to detrain and return to the front. At one point a small part of the 1st SS Panzer Division was fighting in the East while the main body was reconstituting in the West against orders. Enemy intelligence thought that was an intentional bit of deception on our part.

A correctly organized division should be small enough so that even an average leader can command it efficiently. Overstuffing the organization with people and equipment only results in unnecessary losses through enemy action. Guderian conceived the ideal organization for the Panzer division, with additional units required for specific missions attached and detached as needed.

It was a mistake to stand up divisions consisting of foreigners without giving those people a clear and desirable political motive. It was rather naive of us to think that they would gladly die to replace Russian domination with German domination.

All of our organizational structures were overshadowed by the evil spirits of Göring and Himmler. Thanks to them and their obsessions with prestige, we never achieved a reasonable leadership structure at the top and no clear chain of command at the front. Once again we were haunted by the words of Horace: *Quidquid delirant reges, plectuntur Achivi.* The blood of our soldiers was too precious to be spilled for the ambitions of those two ignoramuses.

The Human Factor

Without a doubt we managed to develop a military leadership corps of high moral standing and first-rate operational ability. Tacticians were less in demand. We did not succeed in resolving the problem of second-rate personalities and the correct assignment of such men based on their abilities. Although I could list many more names, three will suffice: Richard Hentsch,[19] Friedrich Paulus, and Wilhelm Keitel. As in Clausewitz's "harmony of forces" concept, intelligence is a curse if it is not supported by a strong personality. This problem has been compounded in modern times as politicians and journalists have expanded their influence and have encountered second-rate men everywhere. While impressed with their cleverness and obliging manners, they fail to recognize their shortcomings, often compounded by a lack of military background and knowledge. French general Maurice Gamelin is a prime example of this problem.[20]

The problem that has always concerned me is the one of how to recognize and remove such a leader before he does too much damage. After the damage has been done it is easy to identify him, but the unnecessarily sacrificed victims cannot be brought back to life. I offer two cases I was involved in. In one case I had developed a suspicion early on that something was wrong. I always had an interest in psychology, but I was reluctant as a nonprofessional to act on my limited knowledge and perhaps do greater damage. I called in a medical officer who was a reservist and a psychiatrist in civilian life, and sent him on a cover mission to observe the individual in question. The medical officer later reported back to me in general terms and without violating medical privacy rights. He told me, "Well, you are right, there is something wrong. It will never have any negative consequences, though." At that point I shifted my concerns to other problems and never regretted it. In the other case the medical officer called me at once and told me to relieve the officer immediately. "Every second counts." On his way to report to me for relief that officer suffered a breakdown.

I adopted this approach to dealing with suspected problem officers after reading the works of the Swiss medical officer Eugen Bircher, who demonstrated that all German leaders who had to make decisions during the Battle of the Marne were stressed to the point where it took a toll on their health. This is not, however, an approach that should be applied widely. It should not, for example, be used for routinely assigning officers within a branch. Otherwise, the medical service's chain of command becomes a kind of parallel authority with all the negative consequences that implies. After the war I learned that the U.S. Navy had developed a similar system.[21]

We constantly complained about the lack of replacements. During the fighting for Tarnopol, Field Marshal von Manstein said to me, "The whole situation along the southern front is a problem of the lack of seventy thousand infantrymen." Did we have them? I believe we did, but we continuously stood up new divisions as a bluff, and in the process we consumed leaders and human beings. Göring and Himmler, and to a lesser degree the *Reichsarbeitsdienst*,[22] tied up far too many of the best men in their overblown organizations. Colonel General Lothar Rendulic estimated the number to be between 2 and 3 million. We also were too slow to replace human beings with machines wherever possible. And finally, our administrative services were unnecessarily bloated in the occupied areas, and we generally had no control over those people.

So what do we conclude from all this? The human being must be the centerpiece of all leadership and all organizational structures. It is better to do something wrong with the right man than to do something right with the wrong man. One man must step into the breach, not humanity as a whole. Whenever Hitler inspected a new weapons system he looked at it from the gunner's perspective: Where does he sit? How does he operate the gun? Only then did he look at the system's technological capabilities. That was the right approach.

Our Cardinal Sins

Political: Let the scholars determine whether or not we started the war. Some Americans incriminate Roosevelt and England quite convincingly. Certainly we started the war under ominous auspices. Hitler never wanted war with the West at all.[23] He assumed that his own opinion about the Bolshevik peril was supported by the western powers. That was his fundamental error. He had a clear political goal for the Russian campaign, but it was in conflict with the more pragmatic goal of liberating the Eastern peoples from the yoke of Bolshevism. The simple fact that nobody in the East wanted to replace Bolshevik domination with German domination was left out of the calculations. That is why we lost the campaign in Russia, which we should not have started to begin with.

Economic: When it became clear that Churchill and his followers would sabotage any English-German rapprochement,[24] we did not draw the conclusion that we would be in a total war.

Armament Technology: We stood up a tank army without the tank factories, thus relegating our best weapon to a skeleton force. In the area of aerial warfare we did not advance the development of fighter aircraft with all means, but shifted significant portions of our fighter production to fighter-bombers. Hitler applied the isolated experience of the Spanish Civil War to a global political war.

Military: Dunkirk was an excusable failure. We overestimated the capabilities of the Luftwaffe. The analysis of war experience is difficult and takes time. What was inexcusable was that when the looming catastrophe at Stalingrad became obvious, we failed to hand complete command authority and freedom to act to the one man capable of exercising it—Manstein.

It was equally inexcusable that while the battle for Naples raged around

Salerno, we left an army sitting inactive in northern Italy instead of committing that force to a war of mobility in the south. A German victory there would have squashed the Anglo-American desire for further invasions. The Americans, however, deny this. We lost the later invasion battle for France both operationally and tactically through the unclearness of our conduct of the battle. Making matters worse, we did not have the right leaders in the right places.

Leadership: We never succeeded in establishing a coherent top leadership organization. Our concentration on the single personality of Hitler was impossible and created vacuums in which characters like Himmler and Göring flourished. We lacked a tightly functioning team with clearly distributed responsibilities.

I cannot agree with the argument that the war was unwinnable. All the proponents of that argument base their conclusion on the comparison of population sizes and industrial capabilities. What really mattered was the masterful control of the means available, and we had enough of those means. Throughout the war our adversaries were not at all clear that they were going to win, although they had made those same calculations.

The End

I will stop my memoirs here. There is still much of interest to report about my activities since the end of the war, about my great travels through Africa and America during which I met many interesting people of all nations. I will, however, offer only a few final comments on how I see the future.

I do not give pacifism a chance; it is too contrary to human nature. No idealist yet has succeeded in leading humanity into a so-called better future. In every case the idealists and fanatics have made sure that everything ended in a bloodbath.[25]

At the beginning of the modern era of history the motives for war were of a confessional nature. This period ended with the Thirty Years' War, which started as a religious war and led into the age of the *Kabinettskriege*,[26] which characterized the period up to the revolutionary and Napoleonic wars. From that point wars were primarily national wars, until the world wars. Following those conflicts we are now in a period of social wars. Confessional, dynastic, and national causes no longer resonate, but even a conscientious objector will take up arms in support of a social agenda.[27]

In the future it will be increasingly important to address military problems with economic tools. The two world wars provide some examples. The first modern war was Hitler's destruction of Czechoslovakia, and what is happening in the world now can be considered the Third World War.[28]

Germany must try to stay out of any involvement. Our losses of the last two world wars and above all the losses of our best and brightest through emigration, which I have observed throughout the world, have taken a substantial toll. On the basis of demographics alone we cannot afford another war. In order to accomplish this we must adjust our policies as follows:

1. No interference in the affairs of other states.
2. Migration laws that prohibit agitation against other states and respect the age-old right of asylum.
3. No foreign development aid without effective birth control programs in the receiving countries. Herein lies the strongest cause for future wars.[29]

All this is only possible on the basis of a justice system supported by police and military forces of total integrity. Never again can a single wild-eyed idealist be allowed to acquire unchecked power. Even then, another global war just might happen in the manner described by General Sir John Hackett in his excellent book *The Third World War.*[30] But we also must prepare ourselves for the possibilities of proxy wars, revolutionary wars, the reversion to the more primitive forms of warfare, or a combination thereof. There are, of course, other undercurrents in the world today, partly of a social nature, partly religious.

So much for my reminiscences. I kept a journal from August 1914 until the end of World War II. I have not changed anything here, even when what I wrote in my journal at the time was wrong. We have plenty of people in the world who see things in perfectly clear hindsight. My intention here is to present the point of view of an officer who was involved in some of the most critical events of both world wars and who acted without regard to whether history would confirm or deny his views.

Despite my considerable experience, it still takes me a good amount of time and thought to evaluate the future. If balance of power is maintained in today's world, the old style of warfare will be impossible because modern weapons developments make it suicidal. But the resolution of tensions and the achievement of far-reaching political goals cannot always be gained at the negotiating table. Therefore, the resort to the more primitive forms of warfare, of which the Russians are masters, will gain increasing importance. The example of Afghanistan should make one think.[31]

The solution to this problem is a free but firmly led democracy that makes human life worth living. Terrorist organizations and chaos mongers of all stripes are dangerous and difficult to combat. In any conflict with such elements the democratic system must prove itself continuously.

Final observations. The German soldier was bound by his oath and had no influence on the large-scale political events. During the course of World War II the necessity to fight with full strength to prevent the apparent and threatening catastrophe was continually reinforced. Consciously and unconsciously, that was our guiding principle. Ending the war through negotiation was apparently never an option. We had to fight until the enemy conceded the impossibility of forcing us to our knees. That we were unsuccessful was not the fault of the soldier, who at all levels of rank from recruit to field marshal accomplished all that was humanly possible.

Appendix 1

Curriculum Vitae of Hermann Balck

Born:	7 December 1893 in Danzig-Langfuhr (now Gdańsk).
Father:	William Balck, Lieutenant General, Knight of the Order *Pour le Mérite*.
Mother:	Mathilde, née Jensen, daughter of District Court President Jensen.
Schools:	Berlin; Lauban (now Lubań); Posen (now Poznań); Hirschberg (now Jelenia Góra); Thorn (now Torun) Humanities Gymnasium.[1]
Military Service:	Entered on 10 April 1913 in Goslar, 2nd Company, 10th Jäger Battalion. Cadet at the Hannover War School, 22 February 1914 to 8 August 1914.

World War I

1914:	Deployed as a platoon leader in the 2nd Company, 10th Jäger Battalion.
10 August:	Commissioned as a Second Lieutenant. Later, adjutant of the 10th Jäger Battalion.
Wounds:	6 August: Grazing shot to right upper arm; remained with unit. 30 October: Shot through left ear; field hospital. 30 October: Rifle shot in the back, grenade splinter in left hip; field hospital.
Decorations:	15 October: Iron Cross 2nd Class. 15 November: Bavarian Order of Military Merit, 4th Class with Swords. 26 November: Iron Cross 1st Class.
Campaign Participation:	Invasion of Belgium and Northern France. Fighting in Tournai and Fontaine-au-Pire. Battle of the Marne. Fighting in Dampierre, Flanders, and Zandvoorde.

1915:	Transferred from 10th Jäger Replacement Battalion to 22nd Reserve Jäger Battalion.
	Company commander of the 4th Company.
Wounds:	28 June: Shrapnel in right shoulder; remained with unit.
Campaign Participation:	Fighting at the Ravka River in Poland.
	Deployment to Serbia.
	Offensive from Lwów to Pinsk.
	Trench warfare in the Rokitno Marshes.
	7 December: Leader of Jagdkommando, 5th Cavalry Division, conducting raids behind the Russian front line.
	Ambush and destruction of a Russian advance party company; unit mentioned in the *Heeresbericht*[2] (without mention of the commander's name).
1916:	Commander of the Machine Gun Company, 22nd Reserve Jäger Battalion.
	9 November: Transferred back to the 10th Jäger Battalion as commander of the Machine Gun Company.
Decorations:	28 February: Austrian Military Order of Merit 3rd Class.
Campaign Participation:	Fighting in Romania from the Turnu Roşu Pass to Focşani.
1917:	
Wounds:	14 August: Grazing shot to the breast and bullet lodged in the left upper arm.
	25 October: Grazing shots above the chest, back, left upper arm, and both hands; remained with the unit.
Decorations:	3 December: Knight's Cross with Swords, Hohenzollern House Order.
Campaign Participation:	Rest leave in Alsace and Transylvania.
	Offensive in Moldova.
	Campaign against Italy.
	Breakthrough at Tolmin.
	Fighting at Monte Tombea.
1918:	Commander, 4th Company, 10th Jäger Battalion.

Wounds:	26 April: Shell splinters to the right upper hip and knee; remained with the unit.
Decorations:	10 May: Wound Badge in Gold.
	October: Recommended for the *Pour le Mérite*.[3]
Campaign Participation:	Fighting in Flanders.
	Assault of Mount Kemmel.
	Fighting in Northern France.
	Withdrawal from Macedonia, Serbia, and Hungary.
	Night ambush on Kruševac; unit mentioned in the *Heeresbericht* (without mention of the commander's name).

Between the World Wars

1919:	Assigned to Border Security, East.
	Commander, 2nd Company, Hannoverian Volunteer Jäger Battalion, under Kirchheim.
	Intense fighting in Poznań Province.
1920:	Accepted into the 100,000-man Reichswehr as the first of all second and first lieutenants from the X and VIII Army Corps.
	Adjutant of Reichswehr 10th Jäger Battalion, later designated the 3rd (Jäger) Battalion, 17th Infantry Regiment.
	Fighting in the Ruhr district and in Central Germany.
1923:	1 January: Assigned to the 18th Cavalry Regiment in Stuttgart-Bad Cannstadt and Ludwigsburg.
	Leader of the Machine Gun Platoon, 18th Cavalry Regiment.
	Commander, 2nd Squadron (Heavy), 18th Cavalry Regiment.
1924:	1 May: Promotion to 1st Lieutenant.
1929:	1 February: Promotion to Rittmeister.[4]
1933:	1 October: Adjutant and General Staff officer IIa, 3rd Cavalry Division, Frankfurt/Oder.[5]

Exchange officer with the Swiss, Finnish, and
Hungarian armies.

1934: 1 April: Adjutant and General Staff officer IIa, 3rd
Cavalry Division, Frankfurt/Oder.

1935: 1 June: Promotion to Major.
25 October: Commander, 1st Bicycle Battalion,
Tilsit.

1938: 1 February: Promotion to Lieutenant Colonel,
assigned to upgrading the Panzer divisions.
3 November: Assigned to OKH Department 3, then
6, responsible for cavalry and motorized troops.

World War II

1939: 1 October: Commander, 1st Rifle Regiment in
Weimar, the first fully armored rifle regiment, most
modern in the army.

1940: 1 August: Promotion to Colonel.
Campaign Participation: Breakthrough at Sedan, mentioned by name in the
Wehrmachtsbericht.[6]
Fighting at Amiens and in Flanders.
Command of the 1st Panzer Brigade.
Breakthrough at the Aisne River.
Surprise attack at Belfort.
Thrust into the Vosges Mountains.
Awards: 12 May: 1939 Clasp to the Iron Cross 2nd Class.
18 May: 1939 Clasp to the Iron Cross 1st Class.
3 June: Knight's Cross of the Iron Cross.
14 October: Panzer Combat Badge in Silver.

1941: Commander of 3rd Panzer Regiment, garrisoned in
Mödling, near Vienna.
6 July: Commander, 2nd Panzer Brigade.
7 July: Detached to OKH with the special mission

of cleaning up the wheeled-vehicle fleet, with full directive authority.

1 November: Assignment as general of mobile forces at OKH.[7]

Campaign Participation: Campaign against Yugoslavia and Greece.
Breakthrough at the Metaxas Line.
Breakthrough at the Vale of Tempe.
Capture of Salonica and Athens.

Decorations: 2 December: Bulgarian Medal of Courage 3rd Class with Swords.

1942: 12 May: Commander, 11th Panzer Division.
1 August: Promotion to Major General.

Campaign Participation: Fighting east of Smolensk.
Breakthrough on the Chir River.
Thrust toward Voronezh.
Defensive battle in the Sukhinichi Salient.
7 December: Fighting around Stalingrad, twice mentioned in the *Wehrmachtsbericht.*
10 December: Destruction of Army Popoff, mentioned in the *Wehrmachtsbericht.*

Decorations: 20 December: Oak Leafs to Knight's Cross of the Iron Cross. (155th award conferred)

1943: 1 January: Promotion to Lieutenant General.
13 March: Assigned to OKH Leaders Reserve.
4 April: Acting Commander of the Gross-Deutschland Division.
2 September: Acting Commander of XIV Panzer Corps.
1 November: Promotion to General of Panzer Troops.
1 November: Commander of XLVIII Panzer Corps.

Campaign Participation: Battle of Salerno.
Defense and attack near Kiev, Zhytomyr, and Berdychiv.
Destruction of Army Brusilov and the Russian Sixtieth Army.

Wounds: 5 September: Plane crash with serious internal injuries; maintained command of the corps.

Decorations:	4 March: Swords to Knight's Cross of the Iron Cross. (25th award conferred)
1944–1945:	5 August 1944: Commander, Fourth Panzer Army. 31 August 1944: Mentioned in *Wehrmachtsbericht*. 20 September 1944: Commander, Army Group G. 24 December 1944: Commander, Sixth Army and Army Task Group Balck. 9 May 1945: Surrender of Sixth Army to U.S. 80th Infantry Division.
Campaign Participation:	Battles near Baranivka. Fighting near Shepetivka and Jampo. Attack battles near Lutsk. Battles at Ternopil, Kovel, and Brody. Lorraine Campaign. Siege of Belfort. Siege of Metz. Battle of the Colmar Pocket. Siege of Budapest. Withdrawal of all German forces from Hungary. Last German encirclement battle east of Graz.
Decorations:	31 August 1944: Diamonds to the Knight's Cross of the Iron Cross. (19th award conferred)

Appendix 2

Excerpts from War Diaries Concerning the Decline of Discipline and Readiness

Excerpt from War Diary, Army Group South, 23 March 1945

At 0945 Commander in Chief, Sixth Army, called the [Army Group South] Chief of Staff. Situational awareness at this time is unsatisfactory because there is no telephone communications with any of the corps. He feels obligated to report that the troops are no longer fighting as they should. Some are stating that the war is lost anyway and that they do not want to be killed shortly before the end. Everyone is afraid of encirclement. The trust that the leadership is capable of getting them out of such a situation has been lost. He wants to talk directly to Colonel General Guderian about this. The chief of the general staff noted that under no circumstances can the cavalry corps be allowed to end up in another cauldron. Commander in Chief, Sixth Army, stated that the troops could not endure such a situation again because they are physically and mentally totally exhausted and handicapped by the lack of ammunition and the condition of rear services.

At 1710 Commander in Chief, Sixth Army, reported to the [army group] Commander in Chief that he had spoken twice with Colonel General Guderian about the crisis within the units that extends all the way to the higher echelons. The situation of the cavalry corps, however, has stabilized. It reported that the leadership has regained control of the troops. The III Panzer Corps has been charged with collecting up withdrawing elements and is authorized to take summary and extrajudicial actions against malingerers. The 9th SS Panzer Division reported by radio that it has been completely destroyed, has been misused to the last man, and requests release from the operational control of Sixth Army and attachment back to the Sixth SS Panzer Army.

TELEX from Sixth Army, 23 March 1945, 2350 hours

Colonel General Guderian, 2 copies.
Chief of General Staff of the Army, 1 copy.
Subject: Waffen-SS

1. It has become apparent once again that our reporting procedures must be improved immediately. As one example, the situation of the 9th SS Panzer Division could not be verified for two days during the attack into Austria. Not enough use is made of tactical radio capabilities. Instead, this division radioed on 23 March 1945 at 1135 to Sixth Army and the SS Panzer Corps, "Division has been completely destroyed, has been misused to the last man, and requests release from the control of Sixth Army and attachment back to the control of Sixth SS Panzer Army. 9th SS Div, Stadler."[1]

I have made it clear beyond any doubt that this division absolutely must follow the orders of its higher headquarters, Sixth Army (Balck).

I have at every opportunity insisted on more frequent and clearer reporting. Before the operational detachment [of the 9th SS Panzer Division] to the Sixth Army I had detailed conversations about this with SS-Oberstgruppenführer Dietrich.[2]

2. It is my opinion that the leadership of 9th SS Panzer Division is too slow. SS-Oberstgruppenführer Dietrich and SS-Oberstgruppenführer Bittrich[3] do not agree and describe *SS-Oberführer* Stadler as a brilliant leader.

Further Dissolution of Hungarian Units

Extracts from the War Diaries of Army Group South

30 March 1945

Under influence of the current crisis the Hungarian allies are defecting in droves to the enemy. Chief of Staff, Sixth Army, reported at 0930 to Chief of Staff [Army Group South] that yesterday for the first time soldiers in Hungarian uniforms and probably of Hungarian nationality faced us on the enemy's side. [Army Group South] Chief of Staff after a conversation at 0950 with Chief of Staff of the Second Panzer Army concurs that Hungarian units that appear to be unstable will be disarmed.

At 2230 the Commander in Chief [Army Group South] reported to General of Infantry Krebs[4] that the attitude of the Hungarians is doubtful except in the artillery units, where they are still exhibiting a German sense of duty. He ordered the relentless disarming of unreliable units and their redesignation as labor battalions.

31 March 1945

Following the loss of the remaining Hungarian territory the Hungarian question must be resolved. As the result of the setbacks, the last Hungarian units are either running away from the front line or over to the enemy. Since 29 March they also have been taking up arms against their own troops.

The Commander in Chief, Sixth Army, in conversation at 1245 with the [Army Group South] Commander in Chief attributed the success of a deep enemy penetration on the left wing of the Sixth Army near Ják (south of Szombathely) to the remnants of a Hungarian division that had fought well previously, but had defected en masse to the enemy. After joining with enemy breakthrough units, they continued to attack together toward the west.

Army Group South Order Ia. Nr. 1190/45, Classified SECRET

1. The subordinate army headquarters are authorized to disarm immediately Hungarian units to prevent weapons and equipment from falling into the enemy's hands in large quantities in all cases where there is a reasonable assumption that such units are about to self-dissolve or defect to the enemy. Disarmed units should be used as labor battalions. When possible, Hungarian units of platoon or company strength should be integrated into German units.

Letter from Major Imre Vitéz Kalándy, Hungarian Army (retired)

Imre Vitéz Kalándy

15 March 1977

14 Mahony Street
Westworthville
WSW 2145
Australia

As first lieutenant of a bicycle company I had the honor of receiving and passing on your directives. At that time I got to know you well. In 1942 you also received me in Wünsdorf, even though it was brief meeting. At that time you reminisced fondly about the large-scale maneuvers in Hungary.

My reason for writing to you today is an article in the newspaper *Welt am Sonntag,* issue number 4, page 5, dated 23 January 1977. The article about you written by Günter Fraschka is titled *"Er siegte in der letzten Kesselschlacht."*[1]

In this article Fraschka states, "... first the IV SS Panzer Corps abandoned its positions, then the Hungarian Saint László Division defected to the Soviets. ..."

The Saint László Division did not defect to the Soviets. The division fought until midnight 9 May. (See attached article from *"Das Ritterkreuz,"* 1968, 2, Gedenkschrift zum Tode von Zoltan Vitéz Szügyi.)[2]

Sir, if you believe that the Saint László Division did defect to the Russians, then I must offer the following evidence to the contrary:

1. In August 1945 the division commander, Zoltan Vitéz Szügyi, was allowed to move around in the British Sector in Hungarian uniform and still carrying his pistol.

2. The Russians court-martialed Zoltan Vitéz Szügyi after he was extradited to them by the English.

3. The Hungarian People's Court convicted him to life in prison after his release from Russian custody. If Zoltan Vitéz Szügyi had really defected to the Russians, he would have been seen as helping to "free" Hungary.

4. Hundreds of members of the Saint László Division still live in the West.

This would have been impossible if they had defected to the Russians. (The division totaled approximately 20,000 troops.)

Sir, I know that based on your assumption that the Saint László Division had defected you on 31 March 1945 issued an order to disarm all Hungarian units in the Sixth Army area, to hand over all Hungarian vehicles to the German Army, and to march all family members on foot to a camp in the rear. You most likely issued this order because Major Lajtos, a General Staff officer on the division staff, defected with a few subordinates to the Russians and announced over the radio that the whole division had defected.

When Major Lajtos returned to Hungary after his rehabilitation he apologized for his actions to the members of Zoltan Vitéz Szügyi's family.

Your order caused great resentment because it was unfair. It brought not only great material damage but also great humiliation upon our soldiers and their families.

Signed
Imre Vitéz Kalandy
Major (ret.)

Appendix 4

Colonel General Heinz Guderian's Sworn Statement

Heinz Guderian   Neustadt, Kreis Marburg
23 November 1947

Sworn Statement

I, Heinz Guderian, at this time residing at Neustadt, Kreis Marburg, born 17 June 1888 in Kulm on Vistula, am fully aware that the following sworn statement will be used in court, i.e. it will serve as sworn evidence in the proceedings of the *Spruchkammer*.[1]

I have never been a member of the National Socialist German Workers Party, nor have I belonged to any of its organizations. I am disinterested in the verdict on Herr Balck, former General of Panzer Troops, in the proceedings of this Spruchkammer. I am not related by blood or marriage to Herr Balck. I have known him since 1919.

I want to make the following statement:

In the fall of 1944 Balck became the commander in chief of an army group in the West on the Vosges Front. After the unfortunate conclusion of the fighting on the invasion front, Hitler established an interception line on the Upper Rhine, which he entrusted to the Reichsführer-SS Himmler under the name of Army Group Upper Rhine. Several meetings between Balck and Himmler followed, during which strong differences of opinion developed which eventually resulted in Balck's relief as commander of his army group. Himmler on several occasions had complained to me about Balck's unyielding attitude, especially after I pressed Hitler for Balck's reassignment as commander in chief of the Sixth Army in the East.

I know Balck as an energetic, judicious, and unusually courageous officer, who especially distinguished himself under my command in 1940 during the campaign in France at the breakthrough of the Maginot Line near Sedan; the breakthrough at the Aisne Front; and the capture of Langres and Belfort. He also commanded the Fourth Panzer Army successfully at Baranov. He had

467

toward Himmler—as I know from Himmler himself—the same forthright attitude that characterized his entire life. He never shied away from conflict.

Signed

Heinz Guderian
Colonel General (Retired)
Final Assignment as Chief of the
General Staff of the Army

Subscribed and sworn to before me
this 2nd day of November 1947.

Signed

Merle F. Finley[2]
Captain, Infantry
Adjutant

Appendix 5

Verdict of Spruchkammer

Central Spruchkammer of Northern Württemberg
Verdict of the Spruchkammer (to become final 19 September 1949)

The hearings yielded the following verdict:

The person concerned [Balck][1] comes from an old officer family. Like his father who was a general in World War I, he also chose to become a career officer. His qualities were absolutely suited for military affairs, without drifting toward the ruinous side of rigid militarism. He had a well-developed soldierly personality which would have been respected and treasured in any country with a good army. He displayed no characteristics or indicators from which could have been deduced any kind of Nazi convictions, in the most negative sense of the definition. Several sworn statements declare convincingly that his whole belief system is based on disciplined order and a sense of duty. He was just and strict toward senior-ranking Nazi Party members in his division. At one point he had a senior-ranking party member locked up for dereliction of duty, just as he would have anybody else. He had to fight the encroachment of the party constantly, and the encroachments of the SS against the Wehrmacht. If Hitler respected him, it was only for reasons of pragmatism and not as a party member. He was not a member of the party or any of its major organizations, and he was relieved from his command at the end by the SS General [Paul] Hauser.

This general officer is liable to prosecution because of the following incident:

In the fall of 1944 he commanded the army group that defended the sector from Belfort to Metz. The troops were under pressure to withdraw and his divisions were involved in constant fighting when it was reported to him by a division commander that a Lieutenant Colonel Schottke had gotten so drunk that he could not stand up when asked to report, and he had no idea where his batteries were located. Through these actions the lives of tens of thousands of soldiers were endangered, as they were deployed at the front line without artillery support. As a result, he [Balck] gave the order to have the derelict officer executed. On the advice of the division commander, [Otto] von Knobelsdorff, he had the facts checked and confirmed one more time the next day. He thus reissued the execution order on the second day, which was then carried out on

469

the morning of the third day. Under pressure of the events he refrained from appointing a drumhead court-martial, which undoubtedly would have rendered the same verdict in the case. It can be assumed that the military laws of all countries, to include the Allied powers, would have issued the death penalty. Even though one can have opposing opinions on the extreme urgency of the situation, nobody can deny that there was a putative emergency situation. In the final analysis, however, this is not the matter for the Spruchkammer to pass judgment on. This court's only purpose is to determine whether or not this action can be judged as a Nazi terror act in the political sense. This clearly is not the case. As clearly delineated above, this lieutenant colonel had accumulated immeasurable guilt. It would have been less objectionable if he had taken all of his artillery batteries and had given himself up to the enemy in order to help end the war. Then one could have attributed his actions to an anti-Nazi conviction; but it is objectionable that his irreparable act exposed uncountable troops to destruction. As noted, the armies of other nations would have acted with similar severity in such a situation. It is, therefore, impossible to reach the conclusion the person concerned [Balck] acted in accordance with National Socialist policies just because the infernal storm of National Socialism had swept over Germany. These proceedings have found no causal connection between this man and National Socialism. The public prosecutor Kischke,[2] who served under the accused, has described him as the most loyal and forthright officer he has ever known, who never could be described as a National Socialist.

If the general court finds that it should charge the defendant with negligence (failure to convene a court-martial), it is a matter for that judicial authority to act upon. Furthermore, if the accused as a general officer should subsequently be formally charged under Directive No. 104[3] these hearings have shown clearly that he only served the Wehrmacht dutifully, and as a consequence he unintentionally supported National Socialism to a lesser degree.

It would be unfair to charge an officer who made no concessions to the National Socialist principles and who was not a member of the NSDAP, only because he was a good and courageous general officer.

He is subject to the [denazification law], but not incriminated as described herein.

Central Spruchkammer
Northern Württemberg

Appendix 6

Letter from Herr Hans Falkenstein

Falkenstein   Christmas 1968
96 Doncaster Road
North Balwyn, 3104
Melbourne, Australia

Dear General Balck,

You most likely will hardly remember me. During the First World War I was a private in the 10th Jäger Battalion, and in 1918 I participated with you as my company commander in the campaign in the West and in Serbia. I always like to remember you as a capable, courageous, and just leader. After I left Goslar in 1918 at the end of the war to go on leave to my hometown, Freiburg im Breisgau, I lost contact with you. Recently I received your address through another German officer.

You have had an astonishing career and I want to congratulate you.

After the war I went into my father's optical business, which I managed until 1938. The political situation under the Nazis was against me because I was branded a non-Aryan. So in 1938 I fled to England, leaving my property behind. But there was grave unemployment there and I was not allowed to work. After the fall of Dunkirk all enemy foreigners were interned and the unmarried ones were deported overseas. After a fortunately unsuccessful attack by a U-boat my ship made it to Australia.

After the war I regained my totally bombed-out property back in Freiburg. I was able to sell it and with the proceeds I started an import business in Melbourne.

In 1964 I retired and then I spent a year traveling around the world with my wife and daughter, visiting the East, Western Europe, the United States, Hawaii, Fiji, and New Zealand.

I have a question for you, although I do not know if you want to answer it. It was never clear to me that upstanding men in leading positions could have allowed the horrors that were committed in Auschwitz without being horrified by them or even trying to stop them. How was this possible? I lost part of my family there.

Please, do not take my asking of this question wrong.[1]

In the meantime, I am happy to have regained contact with you, and it would be nice to hear back from you.

For now, best greetings from your old fellow warrior,

Hans Falkenstein

Appendix 7

The Odyssey of the Journals

In officer families the writing of memoirs was nothing unusual, as these families led rather active lives with frequent reassignments to new garrisons, new tasks, new faces, and especially the experiences during wartime on foreign battlefields. Thus, it was quite natural in our family that my father wrote down his reminiscences from World War I and the period between the wars.

He also collected records, which he kept in a cardboard box. The record collection grew from year to year and moved with the family from garrison to garrison. The collection had already grown to quite some extent by the time we were living in Berlin in 1938. At the breakout of the war and because of the frequent bombing raids on Berlin, the records were stored in an air-raid shelter until 1941, when we had the opportunity to move them to Insterburg in East Prussia.

While we lived in Berlin he continuously sent us new journal entries from foreign locations by way of the *Feldpost*.[1] After our apartment was bombed out, the journals made their way along with the family to a castle outside of Breslau [now Wrocław]. They initially were stored in a deep wine cellar until we discovered that they were showing signs of mold and rats were nesting in them.

Near the end of the war the journals were reunited with the documents that had been stored in Insterburg [now Chernyakhovsk]. During our escape to the West the entire collection was shipped in a small horse-drawn wagon, concealed under bedding and the family silver. At one village the Ortsgruppenleiter refused us permission to pass through without approval from his higher headquarters in Breslau, which had already fled to the West. We succeeded in escaping literally at the last minute under the sound of the fire of the approaching front line. The journals, records, and the family finally moved west by train, under aerial strafing attacks. We ended up in the area of Marburg, where we stored the journals and the few household effects we had managed to salvage.

After the family, minus our father, was reunited in Nördlingen we were allocated a temporary residence in a baroque house. We then sent for the journals and our household goods. The journals ended the war in Nördlingen. As the Americans moved into the area, we hid the journals in the rafters of a ramshackle barn at the rear of the gardens of the house. We had just hidden the journals when we were forced to evacuate the house within an hour so it could be used to billet American soldiers. We had to leave the journals behind, but they remained untouched in the barn. After a few days we were allowed to move back in, and this time we remained there for several months. When we again were forced to evacuate, we were given twelve hours notice that time, and we were able to take the journals along. As we were scrambling through the barn's rafters, the American soldiers watched us with interest and even offered to help us.

Susanne Magirus, née Balck

From Nördlingen the journals made it to Stuttgart, and after a long time back into the hands of the author. Thus, the journals survived. The memoirs of my great grandfather, the Hannoverian General Lütgen, were lost. They included lively and irreplaceable descriptions of the allied troops after the Battle of Waterloo entering Paris amid the incredible jubilation of the population just freed from Napoleonic oppression.

The journals of the last six months of the war (January–May 1945) stayed with me. I was able to get them through all the stages of my American captivity. We managed to smuggle them home during visits from my wife. She arrived skinny and left hefty. Just before being captured I was forced to destroy one file with some especially interesting documents. That was most unfortunate.

Hermann Balck

Notes

Preface

1. William E. Depuy, quoted in *Generals Balck and von Mellenthin on Tactics: Implications for NATO Military Doctrine*, Art of War Colloquium, U.S. Army War College (McLean, Va.: BDM Corporation, 1983), 48.

2. Freeman Dyson, *Weapons and Hope* (New York: Harper and Row, 1984), 151.

3. F.-W. von Mellenthin, *Panzer Battles* (Norman: Univ. of Oklahoma Press, 1956), 252.

4. *Generals Balck and von Mellenthin on Tactics*, 10.

5. Hugh M. Cole, *The Lorraine Campaign: United States Army in World War II* (Washington, D.C.: Center of Military History, 1950), 230.

6. See Appendix 5 in this book.

7. Mellenthin, *Panzer Battles*, 313, n. 3.

8. Dyson, *Weapons and Hope*, 153.

9. Vernor R. Carlson, "Portrait of a German General Staff Officer," *Military Review* (April 1990): 69–81; F-W. von Mellenthin, *German Generals of World War II: As I Saw Them* (Norman: Univ. of Oklahoma Press, 1977), 222.

10. "Translation of Taped Conversation with General Hermann Balck, 12 January 1979" (Columbus, Ohio: Battelle Columbus Laboratories, 1979); "Translation of Taped Conversation with General Hermann Balck, 13 April 1979" (Columbus, Ohio: Battelle Columbus Laboratories, 1979).

11. *Generals Balck and von Mellenthin on Tactics.*

12. See *FM 100-5 Operations* (Washington D.C.: Department of the Army, 20 August 1982), and *FM 100-5 Operations* (Washington D.C.: Department of the Army, 5 May 1986).

13. Soldatentum translates into English as soldiership, but it can also mean military tradition.

14. Dyson, *Weapons and Hope*, 151.

15. This is a very stark contrast to Cole's assessment of Balck.

16. Dyson, *Weapons and Hope*, 154.

17. Ibid., 154–155.

18. Ibid., 155.

19. Ibid., 151.

20. See Appendix 5 in this volume.

21. Ibid.

22. Balck's father's name was William, not the German spelling of Wilhelm, the reasons for which Balck explains in his memoirs.

23. See William Balck, *Development of Tactics—World War*, trans. Harry Bell (Fort Leavenworth, Kans.: General Service Schools Press, 1922).

24. Erwin Rommel, *Attacks*, English translation (Vienna, Va.: Athena Press, 1979). Originally published in Germany in 1937.

25. Bundesarchiv/Militärarchiv, Freiburg, Germany, "Kriegstagebuch Nr. 6 der 11. Panzer Division. Einsatz Russland in der Zeit vom 1.11.1942 bis 31.12.1942.," Files RH27-11/53 and RH27-11/55-59.

26. "Translation of Taped Conversation with General Hermann Balck, 13 April 1979," 15.

27. David Fraser, *Knight's Cross: A Life of Field Marshal Erwin Rommel* (New York: HarperCollins, 1993), 97.

28. Mellenthin, *German Generals of World War II*, 194.

29. Carlson, "Portrait of a German General Staff Officer," 74.

30. Mellenthin, *Panzer Battles*, 252.

31. Mellenthin, *German Generals of World War II*, 194.

32. "Translation of Taped Conversation with General Hermann Balck," 12 January 1979, 20.

33. Heinz Guderian, *Panzer Leader*, trans. Constantine Fitzgibbon (London: Harborough, 1957), 102.

34. See Geoffrey P. Megargee, *War of Annihilation: Combat and Genocide on the Eastern Front 1941* (New York: Rowman and Littlefield, 2006).

35. Dyson, *Weapons and Hope*, 153.

36. The Battle of Maldon took place three weeks before Whitsun in A.D. 991, near Maldon beside the River Blackwater in Essex, England, during the reign of Aethelred the Unready. Earl Byrhtnoth and his thanes led the English against a Viking invasion. The battle ended in an Anglo-Saxon defeat.

Introduction

1. Balck mistakenly reversed the words in this Latin phrase, which is actually "Flecti, non frangi" (to be bent, but not to be broken).

2. An *Oberfinanzrat* is a high-ranking official in the state treasury or revenue service.

3. The Great Northern war ran from 1700 to 1721.

4. This probably was Friedrich Balck.

5. Harry Harvest, *Massloses Russland* (Zurich: Rotapfel Verlag, 1949), 130.

6. The Old Country.

7. Balck Lake.

8. Bailiffs.

9. A *Landrat* is the head of a county, equivalent to a U.S. county commissioner.

10. Many references incorrectly cite the name of Balck's father as Wilhelm. It was actually William.

11. William Balck was a General Staff officer and an instructor at the Kriegsakademie, the school that trained German General Staff officers. Between 1901 and 1903 he published his impressive six-volume study *Tactik*, under the imprint of Verlag von R. Eisenschmidt, Berlin.

12. Rank of the highest judge of a Prussian state court.

13. An officer cadet serving with a unit.

14. Jägers were elite light infantry units. During the first half of the nineteenth century, when most line infantry units were armed with smoothbore muskets, Jägers

were armed with rifles. The Goslar Jägers were known formally as Jäger Battalion Nr. 10.

15. Friedrich Guderian. Heinz Guderian himself started his military career in 1907 in Jäger Battalion Nr. 10.

16. The *Einjährige* or *Mittlere Reife* roughly equates to a high school diploma but does not admit the bearer to a German university.

17. The *Primareife* was a level of secondary civilian education equivalent to today's *Abitur*. It was the level of education necessary for admission to the university, and also for commissioning as an officer.

18. General of Infantry Bodewin Keitel was the brother of Field Marshal Wilhelm Keitel.

19. Nazi Party regional leader.

20. *Einjährig-Freiwilliger* were one-year volunteers, as opposed to two- or three-year conscripts. They served at their own expense, and they were required to have higher levels of civilian education. At the completion of their service they could qualify for commissions as reserve officers.

21. Fähnrich was (and still is in the modern German Army) an officer candidate. It is the next level up from Fahnenjunker.

22. The colors of Imperial Germany.

23. Balck was the last survivor at the time of the publication of his book in Germany in 1981.

1. 1914

1. Britain's King Edward VII, who died in 1910, was the uncle of Kaiser Wilhelm II and the great uncle of Crown Prince Wilhelm.

2. Kaiser Wilhelm II, *Ereignisse und Gestalten 1878–1918* (Leipzig: Koehler Verlag, 1922), 217.

3. Franc-tireurs—literally "free shooters"—were irregular forces, or partisans.

4. An ad hoc brigade.

5. Cavalry lancers.

6. Senior Jäger, roughly equivalent to an American private first class.

7. The French *mitrailleuse* was a volley gun with multiple barrels that could fire either multiple 13 mm rounds simultaneously, or in rapid succession. It had an effective range of thirty-five hundred meters and was a forerunner of the modern machine gun.

8. Balck's unit was part of the II Cavalry Corps, which screened the fronts of the First and Second Armies, on the extreme right end of the German pivot.

9. Lance corporal.

10. There were two branches of German artillery in World War I. The *Fussartillerie* (Foot Artillery) was the branch with the heavy guns and siege howitzers. The *Feldartillerie* (Field Artillery) was the light branch, operating mobile field guns and providing direct support to the infantry and cavalry.

11. A senior sergeant.

12. *Leibgrenadierregiment.*

13. "It is because of Antwerp that I am here."

14. After the German defeat by the Russians at Gumbinnen on 20 August, Moltke ordered two corps withdrawn from the right flank of the western front and sent to the eastern front to reinforce the German Eighth Army. Ironically, those corps arrived too late to contribute to the crushing German victory at Tannenberg on 26–31 August.

15. Colonel General Friedrich Paulus commanded the Sixth Army at Stalingrad. The day before the German position fell, Hitler promoted Paulus to Field Marshal, with the intent that he would commit suicide, because no German Field Marshal had ever been captured. When Paulus surrendered without committing suicide, Hitler was more upset by what he considered Paulus's treason than he was with the loss of an entire German field army.

16. Up through the end of World War I the Bavarian Army was almost a semiautonomous force within the broader German Army. In 1866 Bavaria had fought on the side of Austria against Prussia, and many Germans continued to regard Bavarians with deep suspicion. A certain sense of separatism continues to characterize Bavaria to this day, which still officially calls itself *Freistaat Bayern*—The Free State of Bavaria.

17. A French colonial unit, consisting primarily of native troops and French officers.

18. A German division with troops recruited for Pomerania, in the northeast of Germany.

19. The Sixth Army consisted primarily of Bavarian units and was under the command of Crown Prince Rupprecht of Bavaria.

20. The Landwehr was a territorial militia, originally intended only for home defense.

21. The German sack of the Belgian university town of Leuven and the destruction of the university's magnificent library on 25 August 1914 remains one of the most infamous atrocities of World War I.

22. That was the case in 1914, but by the end of World War I shotguns had become standard weapons for trench warfare.

23. Alpine riflemen.

24. A signal for surrender.

25. The "Grand Tattoo," roughly the German equivalent of the American "Taps" or the British "Last Post."

26. Literally, gold cars.

27. Richard von Kühlmann was Germany's foreign secretary from August 1917 to July 1918.

28. An "NCO Mafia."

2. 1915

1. Literally, a Children's Corps. These units consisted primarily of young volunteers who in many cases left school prematurely in 1914 to join up. After only minimal training, large numbers of these troops were committed to an attack against the professional British Expeditionary Force at the First Battle of Ypres in October–November 1914. The resulting slaughter is known in German history as the *Kindermord,* the Slaughter of the Innocents, a Biblical reference.

2. Karl Eduard, Herzog von Sachsen-Coburg und Gotha, was a grandson of Queen Victoria and Prince Albert, and until 1919 he also held the British title of duke

of Albany. Because he supported Germany during World War I and served as a German general officer, his first cousin, King George V, ordered his name stricken from the register of the Knights of the Garter.

3. Up until 1919 German senior general officers were customarily accorded the honorific of "Excellency."

4. In 1914 the standard German infantry division consisted of two infantry brigades of two infantry regiments each. Most new divisions raised after 1915 had only a single infantry brigade, of three infantry regiments each. The older divisions were slowly converted from the old "square" to the new "triangular" structure. By the end of 1916 that conversion was mostly complete.

5. Then the capital of German Silesia, today Breslau is Wrocław, Poland.

6. Later Lwów, Poland, today Lviv, Ukraine.

7. Balck's comments are rather curious here. Although Falkenhayn at this point was overall chief of the German General Staff, he was focused almost exclusively on the western front. As early as 25 September 1914, Hindenburg had already been designated commander in chief of all German forces on the eastern front, and on 1 November he was designated overall Central Powers commander in chief in the East. In 1916, of course, Hindenburg replaced Falkenhayn as chief of the German General Staff. At this point in 1915 the Ninth Army was commanded by Prince Leopold of Bavaria, who had been brought out of retirement.

8. A crossing point on the Berezina River.

9. A short, braided leather whip used by Cossacks.

10. The Polish Legion was a semi-independent formation of the Austro-Hungarian Army. It was formed in Galicia in August 1914. The officers who served in the Polish Legion later became the backbone of the Polish Army when Poland gained its independence as a result of the Versailles Treaty.

11. North Caucasian ethnic group, originally native to Circassia. They were displaced during the course of the Russian conquest of the Caucasus in the nineteenth century.

12. The *Honvédség* was the Hungarian home defense force of the Austro-Hungarian Army. The equivalent Austrian units were the Landwehr.

13. In these last two sentences Balck is referring to the situation in Germany immediately after the war.

14. Hamilton returned to Sweden in 1919 and became a regimental commander in the Swedish Army. For several weeks each year he served as one of Wilhelm II's adjutants in Doorn, Netherlands, where the ex-Kaiser was in exile. In 1939 Hamilton was made a major general *à la suite* (honorary) in the Wehrmacht.

15. Search and destroy detachments.

16. Wachtmeister was the senior NCO rank in German cavalry and field artillery units. In all other units the rank title was Feldwebel.

3. 1916

1. "I do not know!"—Literal translation from Hungarian. Balck's "Nempte doem" is inaccurate, probably transcribed as he heard it.

2. General Erich von Falkenhayn replaced General Helmuth von Moltke the

Younger as chief of the German General Staff in September 1914, following the failure at the Battle of the Marne. He was replaced by Hindenburg in 1916, largely because of the disastrous results of the Battle of Verdun. Falkenhayn was then assigned as commander of the Ninth Army, and is generally credited with conducting an effective campaign in Romania.

3. Cornmeal boiled into a porridge and eaten directly or baked, fried, or grilled.

4. 1917

1. Kaschau in German.

2. The British naval blockade resulted in severe food shortages in Germany by 1917.

3. The "dual monarchy" refers to Austria-Hungary.

4. Siebenbürgen in German.

5. Balck erroneously spelled it Predeal.

6. Mediasch in German.

7. Schässburg in German.

8. Now Braşov, Romania.

9. Now Vintu de Jos.

10. Although Balck says they offloaded in Alsace, everything he describes in this paragraph is actually on the German side of the Rhine, in the Breisgau region of Baden.

11. The Kaiserstuhl (Emperor's Chair) is an extinct volcanic hill near the east bank of the Rhine. Today it is famous for its vineyards.

12. Rudolph I of Germany was born near Sasbach on 1 May 1218. He reigned as king of the Romans from 1273 to 1291.

13. Lothringen is the German name for Lorraine.

14. A senior NCO holding a position as an acting officer for the duration of the war.

15. At the time of the French Revolution Alsace was technically part of France. Separated from the rest of France by the Vosges Mountains, it was economically, culturally, and linguistically closer to Germany. Alsace passed back to Germany in 1871, after the Franco-Prussian War.

16. The extreme southeast corner of Alsace.

17. *Oberste Heeresleitung,* the German Supreme Army Command in World War I.

18. The Romanian Army had been defeated in 1916 by the forces of the Central Powers in Wallachia and Dobruja.

19. The oddly named German Alpine Corps was really a provisional division of elite mountain troops.

20. Alexander Kerensky was the minister of war in Russia's first revolutionary government. Balck here seems to be echoing the Russian Army's own harsh criticisms of Kerensky's liberal policies.

21. Forage master, responsible for feeding and caring for the horses.

22. The Russian machine guns were mounted on small, wheeled carriages.

23. This is an idiomatic phrase that is difficult to translate into English. "Hammer, do not tap" is one way to translate it. Another is "Pour, do not dribble." They all essentially mean "Do not take half measures."

24. Colonel General Heinz Guderian was the German Army's leading theorist of armored warfare before and during World War II, and one of the most effective Panzer commanders in all military history. Guderian later became one of Balck's mentors and role models.

25. Balck is referring here to the failed Kerensky Offensive, which took place mostly in Galicia in July 1917. Balck's unit was on the southern end of the operation. The Kerensky Offensive was the last major attack launched by the Russian Army in World War I. It broke the back of the Russian Army.

26. Hungarian for "I do not know. Not German, Hungarian." Balck's transliteration "*Nemtedem*" is incorrect.

27. A gorge on the Danube River that forms part of the boundary between Romania and Serbia.

28. Presumably the B.V.G. of 2nd T.L. was a movement control headquarters.

29. Laibach in German.

30. An area of eastern Trentino, in northern Italy, also known as Val Giudicarie and Valli Giudicarie.

31. Balck misspelled it "Zaone."

32. A funicular is a narrow-gauge cable railway for transport up and down steep slopes.

33. "Long live Germany!"

34. German–Krain.

35. Balck's description of the valley in the first and second parts of this paragraph seem oddly contradictory.

36. Tolmein in German.

37. Nickname for the members of the Bavarian Life Guards—*Leib-Regiment.*

38. "Long live Germany! The war is over, the war is over. On to Milan, on to Milan!"

39. A senior NCO who held a reserve commission, and in wartime served in junior officer positions. A Feldwebel Leutnant ranked below a lieutenant, but above an *Offizier-Stellvertreter* (acting officer).

40. "Death unto you, Cadorna." General Luigi Cadorna was the chief of staff of the Italian Army until late October 1917.

41. *Torrente* is Italian for torrent. It also means a stream or a small river with highly variable seasonal flows.

42. The krone was the official currency of the Austro-Hungarian Empire.

43. Veldes in German.

44. Balck incorrectly spelled it "Monte Tomba."

45. Balck misspelled it as "Setti Comuni."

46. Italian—"Mountain of Fear."

47. Howitzers generally fire with a relatively slow muzzle velocity.

48. *Königlicher Hausorden von Hohenzollern*—Royal House Order of Hohenzollern.

49. Tolmin is a town in Slovenia.

50. Most historians today agree that America's April 1917 entry into the war, with its fresh manpower reserves and economic power, tipped the strategic balance irrevocably against Germany.

51. This is a reference to the French efforts to restore military discipline after the widespread mutinies following the disastrous Neville Offensive of 1917.

5. 1918

1. Balck is referring to the great Operation MICHAEL offensive, scheduled to start on 21 March 1918. The intent of the operation was to split the British from the French and drive the British off the continent before the rapidly arriving American forces could tip the strategic balance irrevocably against Germany.

2. For an in-depth analysis of this question, see David T. Zabecki, *The German 1918 Offensives: A Case Study in the Operational Level of War* (London: Routledge, 2006).

3. Balck incorrectly notes the start date. The Operation GEORGETTE offensive started on 9 April 1918.

4. Balck is referring here to Operation GEORGETTE, launched immediately after the failure of Operation MICHAEL farther to the south.

5. Military gas, being heavier than air, settled and concentrated in low areas, such as shell craters, bunkers, and wine cellars.

6. Mount Kemmel was actually near the southern end of a ridge called the Flanders Hills that partially encircled Ypres, stretching from the low Passchendaele Ridge in the south and running to Mount Cassel in the north. Mount Kemmel was 156 meters high, and Mount Cassel 158 meters.

7. The first General Staff officer was also called the General Staff officer Ia. At the corps level and above, he was the operations officer. In German World War I divisions, however, the Ia was the only General Staff officer, and therefore functioned simultaneously as the divisional chief of staff and the operations officer.

8. Kluge served as a field marshal in World War II. In July 1944 he replaced Rundstedt as commander in chief in the West. Several weeks later he committed suicide in order to avoid arrest for suspicion of complicity in the plot to assassinate Hitler.

9. Balck's description here of the operational situation is somewhat simplified. After the failure of Operation GEORGETTE in April, the Germans actually launched three more large-scale but unsuccessful offensives, all three to the south in the sector of the Marne River. Operation BLÜCHER in May, Operation GNEISENAU in June, and Operation MARNESCHUTZ-REIMS in July all had the purpose of drawing the Allied reserves out of Flanders so the Germans could once more attack the British with Operation HAGEN. After the failure of Operation MARNESCHUTZ-REIMS on 15–17 July, Foch on 18 July launched a massive Allied counterattack against the huge German salient north of the Marne. From that point the Germans were on the defensive for the rest of the war, and they never launched Operation HAGEN.

10. *Militär-Wochenblatt* (*Military Weekly*) was the leading German professional military journal between the two wars. It was noted for its robust and dynamic debates, to which even junior officers contributed.

11. Actually, Ludendorff's principal error was to shift the entire direction of the main attack to take Mount Kemmel, which was not an original objective of Operation GEORGETTE. When Ludendorff shifted the attack almost 90 degrees to the right, the lead German forces were within ten kilometers of capturing Hazebrouck, the key rail center in the entire British rail network in the northern half of their sector. Had Hazebrouck fallen, it is almost certain that the entire British logistics system would have

collapsed, producing even more decisive results than those suggested by Balck above. See Zabecki, *The German 1918 Offensives*, 174–205.

12. But none of this was part of the original Operation GEORGETTE operations order. It was all afterthought once the offensive started.

13. See "Der Angriff im Stellungskrieg," in Erich Ludendorff, *Urkunden der Obersten Heeresleitung über ihre Tätigkeit 1916/18* (Berlin: Mittler, 1921).

14. Hohenzollern House Order. The Hohenzollerns were the ruling family of Germany.

15. Ironically, more than ninety-five years after Balck wrote those comments in his diary, the social and political tensions between the Flemish- and French-speaking populations of Belgium remain a volatile and contentious issue.

16. Balck is referring to Operation MARSCHUTZ-REIMS, the last of the five great Ludendorff Offensives of 1918. It was launched on 15 July, and by 17 July it had failed. The Allies counterattacked in the same sector on 18 July.

17. That would have been Operation HAGEN, which was designed to push the British Expeditionary Force off the continent. HAGEN was planned in detail, but never launched.

18. The massive British counterattack at Amiens on 8 August caved in the German lines. It was the start of the Allies' "Hundred Days Campaign" that ended the war. Ludendorff in his memoirs called 8 August 1918 "The Black Day of the German Army."

19. Balck here fails to account for the tens of thousands of fresh American troops that were arriving in Europe each week in 1918. The strategic balance at that point had tipped against Germany, and its final defeat was only a question of time.

20. By that point in the war, of course, the German Army in the persons of Hindenburg and Ludendorff controlled virtually all aspects of the German government and economy.

21. Balck here seems to be ignoring the effects of the severe economic hardships on the German home front caused by the Allied maritime blockade. By 1917 and 1918 civilians in Germany were literally starving from lack of adequate foodstuffs. The winter of 1917–1918 was called "the Turnip Winter," a reference to just about the only food available in many parts of Germany. Although the army and workers in the war industries generally continued to receive adequate rations, soldiers returning to Germany on home leave often had to watch helplessly as their families were starving. Such experiences could not but have negative effects on military morale.

22. The German Army by 1918 had two basic types of divisions: the more mobile and heavily armed *Angriffsdivisionen* (attack divisions), and the static and weaker *Stellungsdivisionen* (trench divisions). The attack divisions, naturally, had the younger and more physically fit troops.

23. The Battle of Épehy was fought on 18 September, when British forces took the outlying positions of the Hindenburg Line.

24. Balck's reference here is to the professional soldiers of the British Expeditionary Force of 1914, who referred to themselves as "The Old Contemptibles."

25. Balck here is referring to the changes at Oberste Heeresleitung in October 1918 when Ludendorff resigned as first quartermaster general of the German Army and was replaced by Wilhelm Groener.

26. *Komitatschis.* During World War I, Chetniks were guerrilla forces in Central Power-occupied Serbia.

27. After World War I, Franz von Epp was a prominent *Freikorps* leader during the early, turbulent days of the Weimar Republic. He later joined the Nazi Party and became a member of the Reichstag.

28. That battle took place on 11 September 1697.

29. This is now Bratislava, the capital of Slovakia.

6. Retrospective on World War I

1. A reference to the huge number of American troops arriving in Europe in 1918.

2. In German *hinten* means rear.

3. Normally, there was only a single General Staff officer assigned to each German division in World War I. The divisional General Staff officer Ia was a captain, and he functioned simultaneously as the division's chief of staff and operations officer. He answered not only to his divisional commander, but also to the chief of staff at the corps level.

4. Whenever a German division, corps, or field army failed to accomplish its mission, the chief of staff normally was replaced even before the commander.

5. Balck qualified as a General Staff officer, but he declined appointment to the General Staff. Unlike Rommel, who also was not a General Staff officer, Balck was never dismissive of the General Staff, and he especially respected those General Staff officers who were assigned to him later in his career. Balck's relationship with Friedrich-Wilhelm von Mellenthin during World War II was one of the most effective commander-chief of staff partnerships of all times.

6. The Prussian General Staff system was instituted in the early nineteenth century during an era when members of the high nobility became senior commanders based on their social/political status, and not necessarily based on any real military experience, ability, or training. This practice continued through World War I, with German's Crown Prince Wilhelm being one of the most notorious examples.

7. In 1878 von der Goltz as a captain was appointed a lecturer in military history at the Kriegsakademie in Berlin. In 1883 he published the book *Rossbach und Jena.* In 1906 he published a new and revised edition as *Von Rossbach bis Jena und Auerstadt.* That same year he also published *Das Volk in Waffen* (*The Nation in Arms*). Both books quickly became military classics.

8. Cavalry captain.

9. The *Zündnadelgewehr* was a highly advanced breech-loading rifle for its day.

10. Prior to the start of the war, Winston Churchill had quite accurately called the German Navy "The Luxury Fleet."

11. Replacement divisions.

12. In 1914 the typical German division was organized on the "square" structure, with two infantry brigades of two infantry regiments each. The divisional artillery brigade consisted of two field artillery battalions. By 1918 almost all German divisions were organized on the "triangular" structure, with a single infantry brigade consisting of three infantry regiments. The divisional artillery command typically consisted of a field artillery regiment and a foot artillery battalion.

13. Technically, of course, Ludendorff was not a field commander. On the eastern front he was Hindenburg's chief of staff. When in 1916 Hindenburg was appointed chief of the General Staff of the German Army, Ludendorff became the first quartermaster general of the German Army, effectively the chief of staff to the chief of the General Staff. In practice, however, Ludendorff exercised a level of real command authority rarely equaled by modern battlefield commanders.

14. Otto Gessler was minister of defense of Germany from 1920 to 1928.

15. Theodor Heuss, *Hitlers Weg: Eine historisch-politische Studie über den Nationalsozialismus* (Leipzig: Olms 1932), 257. Heuss was the president of West Germany from 1949 to 1959. Despite this seemingly positive comment about Hitler, the book was critical of National Socialism. The Nazis burned the book in 1933.

7. 1919

1. Noske became a Social Democratic (SPD) member of the Reichstag in 1906. When the Kiel naval mutiny started in early November 1918, the chancellor, Prince Max von Baden, sent Noske to Kiel to negotiate an end to the revolt. The mutineers welcomed Noske as a Social Democrat, assuming that he was automatically on their side. But within days Noske managed to convince the mutineers to return to duty and restored the authority of the officers. Noske became the first minister of defense of the Weimar Republic, serving from 1919 to 1920.

2. This is a historically questionable statement.

3. Now Poznan, Poland.

4. Now Żagań, Poland.

5. Now Wschowa, Poland.

6. Now Rawicz, Poland.

7. Now Sarnowa, Poland.

8. Guderian was the future father of the German Panzer forces, and one of Balck's most important supporters during World War II.

9. Now Wrocław, Poland.

10. Now Babimost, Poland.

11. Now Zbąszyń, Poland.

12. Now Grójce Wielki, Poland.

13. People's Militia.

14. The Spartacus League was a Marxist revolutionary movement named after Spartacus, leader of the largest slave rebellion of the Roman Republic. The League was organized in Germany during World War I by Karl Liebknecht and Rosa Luxemburg. Following the failure of the general strike and subsequent armed street battles that started in January 1919, the League renamed itself the *Kommunistische Partei Deutschlands* (Communist Party Germany—KPD).

15. For an excellent analysis of the internal debate on this question, see Matthias Strohn, *The German Army and the Defense of the Reich* (Cambridge: Cambridge Univ. Press, 2011).

16. The armistice was signed on 11 November 1918.

17. Heinrich Kirchheim was awarded the Pour le Mérite on 13 October 1918.

18. Under the terms of the Versailles Treaty, Germany was allowed an entire military force of only one hundred thousand.

19. The Reichswehr refused to intervene to stop the Kapp Putsch. But when the putsch started to fail on its own, that triggered uprisings by local communist groups throughout Germany, especially in the Ruhr industrial region. The Reichswehr then intervened forcefully to put down those uprisings.

20. The citizenry, the bourgeoisie.

8. 1920

1. Gisbert Freiherr von Romberg was a famously eccentric Westphalian nobleman of the late nineteenth century. He was the historical model for Josef Winckler's 1923 novel *The Mad Bomberg*.

2. It is sweet and right to die for the fatherland.

3. While the officers just shrugged it off, the soldiers were upset because the injured military personnel received no compensation.

4. On 3 April, Reich president Friedrich Ebert forbade the use of summary trials in the Ruhr. Nine days later von Watter issued the order that from then on "illegal behavior" would be dealt with directly.

5. Voice of the People and Voice of Jupiter.

6. Syndicalism was an economic system proposed as a replacement for capitalism and an alternative to state socialism. It was based on the idea of confederations of collectivized trade and industrial unions.

7. This is a reference to the Russo-Polish War of 1920.

8. A king-military commander.

9. 1921

1. German communist leader Max Hölz was sentenced to life imprisonment for murder in 1921. He was released in 1928, and drowned in Gorky, Russia, in 1933.

2. During World War II, Trettner served as a Luftwaffe officer in paratroop units, finishing the war as a major general. From 1964 to 1966 he served as general inspector of the Bundeswehr, the senior officer in the German armed forces. He was the last living general officer of the Wehrmacht when he died in 2006.

3. Wachtmeister was the highest NCO rank in Reichswehr cavalry and artillery units. Feldwebel was the equivalent rank in infantry and other units.

4. The Präsentiergriff was a type of Prussian salute.

5. A type of Prussian marching step and time.

6. Seeckt was forced to resign after permitting the former Kaiser's grandson, Prince Wilhelm, to participate in military maneuvers in the uniform of the old imperial 1st Foot Guards without first gaining the government's approval.

7. Philipp Scheidemann was the second chancellor of the Weimar Republic, serving briefly from 13 February to 20 June 1919.

8. Eduard David was the Weimar Republic's minister of the interior from 21 June to 3 October 1919.

9. MSPD refers to the *Mehrheitssozialdemokratische Partei Deutschland*, the name for the Social Democratic Party between 1917 and 1919.

10. Franz von Papen was the chancellor of Germany from 1 June to 17 November 1932. He was succeeded by Kurt von Schleicher, who was succeeded by Hitler on 30 January 1933.

11. Steel Helmet was the primary German war veterans' organization.

12. Reich Banner Black-Red-Gold was a coalition organization formed in 1919 by the Social Democratic Party, the German Center Party, and the German Democratic Party to advance liberal parliamentary democracy and the republic. It came to be seen, however, as the SPD's primary paramilitary force.

13. The *Sturmabteilung* (Storm Detachment) was the paramilitary force of the fledgling Nazi Party.

14. Alfred Hugenberg was the leader of the German National People's Party, and he was instrumental in helping Adolf Hitler become chancellor of Germany. Hugenberg served in Hitler's first cabinet in 1933 as minister of economics.

15. The existence of the General Staff had been banned by the Versailles Treaty. The Reichswehr's clandestine General Staff was called the *Truppenamt*. Normally, attendance at the Kriegsakademie (War Academy) was the basic means of qualification for assignment to the General Staff. During the Weimar years, however, the Reichswehr had to use other methods of training and qualification. The General Staff was a separate and highly exclusive career field for German officers. Competition was, and still is, very stiff for the relatively few slots available for new members each year. The fact that Balck was invited to transfer twice and declined is quite unusual. Rommel was never invited to join the General Staff.

10. In the Third Reich

1. Kurt von Schleicher was the last chancellor of the Weimar Republic, serving from 3 December 1932 to 28 January 1933.

2. The chief of staff of the *Sturmabteilung* (SA) was Ernst Rhöm. At the time, the *Schutzstaffel* (SS) was a relatively small subordinate unit of the SA.

3. Ludendorff, of course, had been an early supporter of Hitler and the Nazis in the 1920s. Ludendorff stood trial with Hitler as a codefendant for the 1923 "Beer Hall Putsch" in Munich. Shortly after the trial, Hitler and Ludendorff fell out.

4. The *Kulturkampf* (Culture Struggle) was an 1871–1878 power struggle between Bismarck and the Catholic Church in Germany.

5. Modern Germany evolved from ancient Germanic tribes, whose national characteristics define regional differences in the country to this day. The Prussians, the Swabians, the Bavarians, the Alemanni, the Saxons, and many others still maintain subtle but strong cultural distinctions that for the most part are transparent to almost everyone but the Germans themselves.

6. As a general of infantry, Wietersheim commanded the XIV Panzer Corps during the battle for Stalingrad.

7. Fretter-Pico served as a corps commander during World War II, and briefly commanded the Sixth Army.

8. The Ia was the operations officer at the corps level and above. At the divisional level the Ia was the senior (and usually the only) General Staff officer in the division, and was "dual-hatted" as the chief of staff and the operations officer.

9. Haase commanded the Fifteenth Army in 1941 and 1942 as a colonel general.

10. An SA and SS rank essentially equivalent to an army general of infantry (or artillery, or cavalry, etc.).

11. See the following section.

12. The ruling social, political, and economic elite of Prussia were called the *Junkers.*

13. These were regimental-sized SA units.

14. SA Chief of Staff Ernst Röhm, who had been drummed out of the Reichswehr following the Munich Beer Hall Putsch, envisioned the SA as Germany's primary military force, with the army subordinate to the SA. Röhm, of course, would be the leader of the whole thing, answering only to Hitler.

15. Hitler's suppression of the SA on the night of 30 June 1934 became known as the *Nacht der langen Messer*—Night of the Long Knives. Röhm and his inner circle were arrested in the middle of the night at Bad Wiessee, and then shot a few days later. The army broadly supported the suppression, because it considered the SA a bitter rival. The SS, which up to that point had been a component of the SA, turned against Röhm and provided many of the actual forces used to disarm the SA throughout the country. From that point on, the SA was never a significant force in the Third Reich. Unfortunately for the Wehrmacht, the SS quickly emerged in its own right to become the rival military force that the Wehrmacht had feared. For additional reading on the Night of the Long Knives, see Paul Maracin, *The Night of the Long Knives: 48 Hours That Changed the History of the World* (New York: Lyons Press, 2004).

16. An SS rank equivalent to the army's colonel general.

17. Dietrich commanded the Sixth Panzer Army, which made the main attack during the Battle of the Bulge. A Waffen-SS officer, the historical assessments of Dietrich remain very mixed. Many German generals looked down on him as a Nazi Party hack. Others respected his skill as a tactician, his abilities to relate to the common troops, and his willingness to surround himself with competent staff officers.

18. Fritsch became commander in chief of the army in 1935. He generally supported the Nazis, but he strongly opposed the establishment of rival military forces, such as the SS. Fritsch was forced to resign in February 1938 on a trumped-up charge that he was a homosexual. Although he was later exonerated by a formal court-martial, he was never restored to command. In September 1939 he became the second German general of World War II to be killed in action, while in the front lines in his capacity as honorary colonel of the 12th Artillery Regiment.

19. Wilhelm Kube was the Gauleiter of Brandenburg.

20. The "grosser Zapfenstreich," which is conducted by torchlight after dark, is Germany's premier military honor ceremony. The ceremony dates back to at least 1569, and is still conducted on special occasions by the Bundeswehr today.

21. Streicher was the Gauleiter of Franconia. In 1945 and 1946 he was one of the twenty-two defendants in the Trial of the Major War Criminals before the International Military Tribunal at Nuremberg. He was convicted and executed in October 1946.

22. As a colonel general, Mackensen commanded the Fourteenth Army in Italy during World War II. His father was Field Marshal August von Mackensen.

23. The Nazi Party district leader.

24. Rudolf Nadolny was the German ambassador to Russia and then Turkey.

25. Hugh Wilson was the American ambassador to Germany from March to November 1938.

26. The region of western Czechoslovakia that was largely inhabited by ethnic Germans. The Sudetenland was the proximate cause of the 1938 Munich Crisis.

27. Field Marshal Werner von Blomberg was Germany's minister of war. In January 1938 he was forced to resign when it was revealed that his young second wife had a long police record. A few days later Hitler moved against the commander in chief of the army, General Fritsch. Hitler used what is today known as the Blomberg-Fritsch Affair to consolidate his absolute control over the Wehrmacht. The Ministry of War (*Reichskriegsministerium*) was abolished and replaced with a new organization—the Supreme Command of the Armed Forces (*Oberkommando der Wehrmacht*, or OKW). This move weakened the traditional Army High Command (*Oberkommando des Heeres*, or OKH), which was now subordinated to OKW.

28. Árpád was the leader of the Hungarian conquest of the Carpathian Basin around the year 890.

29. Schell had plenipotentiary powers in this position, which made him effectively the czar of the German automotive industry. He often clashed with General Heinz Guderian, who at the same time held the position of general inspector of mobile troops.

30. Balck's undoubtedly correct assessment runs contrary to what General Heinz Guderian was writing at the time. Although Germany in 1936 accounted for only 4.8 percent of the world's production of motor vehicles—to Britain's 7.8 percent and America's 77.2 percent—Guderian in 1937 nonetheless wrote that Germany was in "a favorable position, which means that in the event of war we will be able to maintain the level of our mechanized forces and our motorized rearward forces." Heinz Guderian, *Achtung—Panzer!* trans. Christopher Duffy (London: Arms and Armour Press, 1992).

31. Field Marshal Walther von Brauchitsch, 1938–1941. When he was dismissed in 1941, Hitler personally assumed direct command of the army.

32. The *Allgemeinen Heeresamtes* consisted of a number of important but partly unrelated branches of the *Oberkommando des Heeres* (Army High Command) that were grouped together for administrative purposes.

33. Balck's rather naive apologist comments here border on the absurd. His assertion that Hitler never wanted a war with Britain simply cannot be reconciled with the reality of the Battle of Britain or the German planning and preparations for Operation SEA LION. There is, however, something to be said about President Roosevelt's intentions leading up to America's entry in the war, particularly the undeclared naval war in the Atlantic between America and Germany in 1941.

34. Again, Balck is completely off base in these comments. He assumes that the senior general in France could have prevented the French government from going to war, when it is certain that no German general could have thwarted Hitler. When in 1938 Colonel General Ludwig Beck resigned as chief of the General Staff in protest of Hitler's plans to prosecute wars of aggression, it did nothing to prevent or even delay World War II.

35. Both times Balck uses this phrase he cites it in English.

36. There is a certain level of validity to what Balck says about Germany's domestic politics during World War I, but not during World War II. Nor does the comparison to Britain hold up. In 1939 Britain was a robust multiparty democracy, while Germany was a repressive single-party dictatorship.

11. World War II

1. There is something to be said for this argument, considering the centuries of animosity between Russia and Poland, which continues to this day. On the other hand, German-Polish animosities go back to at least the 1410 Battle of Tannenberg (known to the Poles as the Battle of Grunwald).

2. See note 33 in the previous chapter. But in other passages in the present chapter Balck seems to contradict himself on this point.

3. Many nonmilitary organizations in the Third Reich wore military-like uniforms, including the Nazi Party, the Reich Labor Service, the Todt construction organization, the *Allgemeine-SS* (General SS, as opposed to the Waffen-SS), the Hitler Youth, and even the German Red Cross.

4. The Maas River in German.

5. More commonly known as Godefroy de Bouillon, a Frankish knight who was one of the leaders of the First Crusade. In 1099 he became the first ruler of the Crusader Kingdom of Jerusalem, although he refused to accept the title of king.

6. Ju-87 dive bomber, an aircraft specifically designed for ground attack.

7. The Grossdeutschland (Greater Germany) was the elite Panzergrenadier regiment of the Germany Army. In 1942 it was converted into a division. Balck briefly commanded the division in 1943.

8. Spahis were light cavalry colonial troops, recruited primarily from the indigenous populations of Algeria, Tunisia, and Morocco. Their officers were French.

9. Édouard Daladier, three times prime minister of France and prime minister at the start of World War II until March 1940; Édouard Herriot, three times prime minister of France between 1924 and 1932; Paul Reynaud, last prime minister of France, from March to June 1940.

10. Here again, Balck tends to ignore the significance of the very nature of the Third Reich, and the impossibility of a vibrant democracy entering into an alliance with a brutal dictatorship.

11. On 17 May 1940, Weygand replaced General Maurice Gamelin as commander of the French Army.

12. Manufactured by Volkswagen, the Kübelwagen (literally Bucket Car) was the German equivalent of the jeep.

13. Sculpted by Frédéric Bartholdi, sculptor of the Statue of Liberty, *The Lion of Belfort* was dedicated in 1880 to symbolize French resistance during the December 1870 to February 1871 Siege of Belfort, in the Franco-Prussian War.

14. France declared war on Germany in 1939 to honor a security commitment to Poland given by both Britain and France. Balck also glosses over the fact that it was Germany that attacked France in May 1940.

15. Now Gdansk, Poland.

16. Again, Balck seems to think that French generals had the ultimate say over national policy, while in Germany the generals certainly had no such power.

17. The French common soldier.

18. One of the leading conspirators in the 20 July 1944 attempt to assassinate Hitler, Witzleben was the designated commander in chief of the Wehrmacht in the post-Nazi regime. He was hanged from a meat hook in Berlin on 7 August 1944.

19. See Heinz Guderian, *Achtung—Panzer! The Development of Armoured Forces, Their Tactics, and Operational Potential,* trans. Christopher Duffy (first published in German in 1937; London: Arms and Armour Press, 1992).

20. Hitler did relieve Brauchitsch as commander in chief of the German Army on 10 December 1941 and assumed that role personally.

21. Three times prime minister of France between 1936 and 1938. Balck's observation here contradicts his earlier assertions that the commander in chief of the French Army could have prevented France from going to war.

22. The Royal Navy fired on the French fleet at Algeria's Mers-el-Kébir harbor on 3 July 1940 to prevent the warships from falling into German hands.

23. This is a peculiar comment. Did Balck physically beat an enlisted soldier? It seems unlikely since the Prussian Army had abandoned summary corporal punishment early in the nineteenth century. Did other soldiers do so on his orders? Or is Balck making a metaphorical reference to the official punishment the offender received?

24. Balck here offers a naively simplistic explanation for the origins of the French resistance, completely ignoring Germany's increasingly draconian occupation policies.

12. Greece

1. Opanci are the traditional leather shoe of the Balkans.

2. Popular belief long attributed this defensive wall to the Romans, built during the reign of the Emperor Trajan. Most recent scholarship, however, largely agrees that the construction was much later, in the last half of the first millennium.

3. Kiep later became a member of the German opposition, associated with the Kreisau Circle. He was executed in August 1944.

4. The Brandenburgers were the Wehrmacht's special forces. The unit started as a battalion in January 1940, was increased to a regiment in June 1940, and to a division in April 1943.

5. This was an unusual and critical omission. The key to the German command system of *Auftragstaktik* (mission-oriented tactics) was the commander's intent (*Absicht*). Subordinate leaders were always supposed to understand why they were being ordered to execute any task. This gave the subordinate commanders the flexibility to use workarounds, when necessary, to achieve the final intent.

6. Johann Wolfgang von Goethe, *Faust: A Tragedy,* trans. Walter Arndt, ed. Cyrus Hamlin (New York: Norton, 2001), part 2, act 2, lines 7118–7119, page 203.

7. Balck's description of the Tempe Valley and the tactical problems it presented echo the Roman historian Livy, writing almost two thousand years earlier. In his Book XLIV, writing about the Third Macedonian War in 169 B.C., Livy describes the passage

of the Roman troops through the valley. By 1941 the described valley was still quite recognizable, with the exception of the railroad line. See Livy, *Rome and the Mediterranean,* trans. Henry Bettenson (London: Penguin Books, 1976), 561–562.

8. Goethe, *Faust,* part 2, act 2, lines 7333–7335, page 209.

9. Ibid., lines 7608–7609, page 217.

10. Lieutenant General Sir Bernard Freyberg, in the introduction to Joseph Cody's *21 Battalion: The Official History of New Zealand in the Second World War, 1939–1945* (Wellington, New Zealand: Historical Publications Branch, 1953), v.

11. Protective spirit of a place.

12. Goethe, *Faust,* part 2, act 3, page 258.

13. Ibid., part 2, act 3, page 259.

14. Ibid., part 2, act 3, page 260.

13. Russia

1. On 3 July 1940, British prime minister Winston Churchill ordered the Royal Navy to open fire on the French fleet at Mers-el-Kébir, Algeria, after the French refused to surrender their warships to the British. The purpose of the attack was to prevent the French fleet from falling into German hands. The incident cast a long shadow over British-French relations for many years after.

2. Known to Germans as the Wars of Liberation or the Wars of Freedom, the Napoleonic War of the Sixth Coalition was fought between 1812 and 1814, culminating in Napoleon's defeat at the Battle of Leipzig and his first exile.

3. Caulaincourt was Napoleon's aide-de-camp.

4. Joseph Victor von Scheffel, "The Trumpeter of Säkkingen: A Song from the Upper Rhine," trans. Francis Bruennow, http://www.gutenberg.org/etext/31314.

5. See Constantine von der Pahlen, *Im Auftrag des Zaren in Turkestan* (Stuttgart: Steingrüben-Verlag, 1969).

6. See Heinz Guderian, *Achtung—Panzer! The Development of Armoured Forces, Their Tactics, and Operational Potential,* trans. Christopher Duffy (first published in German in 1937; London: Arms and Armour Press, 1992), 136–159.

7. Admiral Wilhelm Canaris was the head of the Abwehr, the Wehrmacht's military intelligence organization. He also was a leading member of the opposition to Hitler. He was arrested following the failure of the 20 July 1944 bomb plot to assassinate Hitler, and was executed on 9 April 1945 during the closing days of the war and the collapse of the Third Reich.

8. Actual translation: "Whatever the king's rage is, the Greeks will suffer for it."

9. *Oberkommando des Heeres.*

10. Economization commissioner.

11. Friedrich-Wilhelm Balck was killed in action in June 1941.

12. *General der schnellen Truppen* was a job title, not a rank title. Balck was still a colonel at the time.

13. In late 1941 and early 1942 the Wehrmacht's Panzer Groups were redesignated Panzer Armies.

14. *Panzerkampfwagen*—Armored Fighting Vehicle—the German basic designation for a tank.

15. The 2nd SS Panzer Division.

16. Balck is criticizing Guderian's judgment for letting this information get out before the final decisions were made. The resulting rumors, especially if they failed to be true, could have an overwhelmingly negative effect on the morale of frontline combat troops.

17. Culmination and the culminating point are two of the most important concepts introduced by Carl von Clausewitz in his seminal work, *On War*.

18. The longer the barrel on a gun, the greater the muzzle velocity, and hence, the greater the penetrating power of the projectile.

19. Instead of the traditional *Feldgrau* (field gray) uniforms, the soldiers of the Wehrmacht's Panzer units wore black uniforms, which did not show oil and grease stains as much. As the war progressed, captured Panzer crewmen frequently were mistaken for Waffen-SS troops, and harshly treated.

20. This is a reference to the aborted Operation SEELÖWE (SEA LION).

21. Balck translated this as "The soldier has to suffer for it." The proper translation is "Whatever the king's rage is, the Greeks will suffer for it." The quote is actually from Horace's "Epistolae," 1, 2, 14.

22. A sergeant major in artillery and cavalry units.

23. General of mobile forces was a duty title, not a military rank. Balck was still a colonel at the time.

24. The U.S. Army relearned this hard lesson during the Vietnam War, when it tried to introduce fast-track NCO schools to turn draftees into NCOs in a matter of a few months. Derisively called "shake 'n bakes," the products of the program proved to be a mixed lot at best.

25. Lueder retired from the Bundeswehr in 1966 as a brigadier general.

26. The Wehrmacht's 1st Cossack Division was established on the eastern front in April 1943 by consolidating various units of Don Cossacks who were anticommunists and other Russian POWs willing to serve in the German Army.

27. In early 1945 the 1st and 2nd Cossack Cavalry Divisions were organized under the XV Cossack Corps. In February 1945 all foreign units in the Werhmacht were transferred to the Waffen-SS, and the corps was redesignated the XV SS Cossack Corps. Pannwitz remained in command, although he refused to transfer personally to the Waffen-SS.

28. Pannwitz and most of his officers were executed in Moscow in 1947.

29. Stauffenberg was one of the principal leaders of the 20 July 1944 bomb plot to assassinate Hitler. He personally carried the bomb into Hitler's command bunker. The bomb went off, but it failed to kill Hitler. Stauffenberg was summarily executed in Berlin shortly afterward. The Bundeswehr today considers Stauffenberg one of its greatest heroes and moral role models.

14. 1942

1. The Sacred Road. A somewhat cynical reference to the French Voie Sacrée during the World War I Battle of Verdun.

2. Halder had been chief of the German Army General Staff since 1938. He was dismissed in September 1942 after frequent disagreements with Hitler.

3. Fromm was commander in chief of the Ersatzheer (the Reserve Army). He was responsible for training, personnel replacement, and what today would be called force generation.

4. The Westheer consisted of all German Army forces in Western Europe.

5. Although not identified by Balck, the commander of the 22nd Panzer Division was Lieutenant General Wilhelm von Apell. The division sustained a 30 to 40 percent loss in personnel during its disastrous attack of 20 March.

6. Father, I have sinned.

7. One of the key weaknesses in German staff procedures was that they generally only tried to project and then war-game against the enemy's most dangerous course of action, instead of both his most dangerous *and* his most likely courses of action. In any intelligence assessment the most dangerous course of action is far easier to project than the most likely.

8. Officer candidate.

9. Paulus was commander of the German Sixth Army.

10. *Oberkommando des Heeres,* the High Command of the German Army.

11. Lieutenant General Walter Scheller.

12. Baron.

13. Four gun batteries were the standard at the time for divisional artillery battalions.

14. The 11th Panzergrenadier Brigade of the 11th Panzer Division consisted of the 110th and 112th Panzergrenadier Regiments.

15. Normally the only qualified General Staff officer at the divisional level served as the combined chief of staff and operations officer, with the designation of divisional Ia.

16. In the German Army at the time, the senior General Staff officer at each echelon routinely answered to the senior General Staff officer at the next higher echelon, as well as to his immediate commander.

17. Indispensable, or war effort-essential laborers.

18. Short for Kübelsitzwagen, the German World War II equivalent of the jeep. Manufactured by Volkswagen.

19. The Ju-87 Sturzkampfflugzeug dive bomber.

20. Officer candidates.

21. Their commissions.

22. Katyushas were Soviet field artillery rockets, launched from multiple-barrel launchers. They were nicknamed "Stalin Organs."

23. This refers to the Dieppe Raid.

24. *Oberleutnant.*

25. *Hauptkampflinie.*

26. The Knight's Cross of the Iron Cross.

27. *Obergefreiter.*

28. This was a tank destroyer battalion.

29. In both world wars the Germans were masters of using captured enemy weapons and equipment.

30. A hasty counterattack was a *Gegenstoss,* as opposed to a deliberate counterattack, a *Gegenangriff.*

31. Unfortunately, Balck never mentions his first name.

32. *Beamten*, military administrators.

33. Colonel General Rudolf Schmidt.

34. The German *Sie*, as opposed to the familiar *du*.

35. Holy Simplicity! Or in other words, "What naiveté!"

36. This comment refers to Operation TORCH, the Anglo-American invasion of Northwest Africa starting on 8 November 1942.

37. Wenck finished the war as a general of Panzer troops.

38. Operations officer.

39. State Collective Farm Number 79.

40. General Staff section Ic was intelligence.

41. The Allied Unconditional Surrender Policy had been widely discussed, but not yet adopted at this point. It would be adopted a few weeks later at the Casablanca conference in January 1943.

42. A Luftwaffe Field Division was organized similarly to a standard infantry division, but it was manned entirely by air force personnel and was supposed to operate under Luftwaffe control. The Luftwaffe Field Divisions were huge failures for the most part. The 1st Luftwaffe Field Division was disbanded after being mauled during the Chir River battles.

43. Whatever the king's rage is, the Greeks will suffer for it.

44. Lieutenant Colonel Theodor Graf Schimmelmann von Lindenburg, commander of the 15th Panzer Regiment.

45. 2nd Battalion, 15th Panzer Regiment.

46. Stalin blew and they scattered.

47. Morozovskaya is the name of the nearby railroad station.

48. *Feuerwehren*, fire brigades or rapid reaction forces.

49. The 4th Panzergrenadier Regiment was attached to the 11th Panzer Division from the 6th Panzer Division.

50. Gaius Terentius Varro, the Roman commander defeated at Cannae in 216 B.C.

51. Tank hunter or tank destroyer battalion.

15. 1943

1. Balck declines to identify "G" by name, apparently reluctant to portray a fellow German general officer in a negative light.

2. The concept of active defense is based on instant and continuous counterattacks. It is, as Clausewitz described it, a "shield of blows."

3. In 1944 the 16th Motorized Infantry Division was redesignated the 116th Panzer Division, fighting on the western front.

4. This refers to the period of warfare prior to German unification in 1871.

5. The Bogatyr is a standard character in medieval East Slavic legend, similar to the Western European knight-errant.

6. This was done to prevent their being identified as staff officers in the event they were captured.

7. Balck is referring to the collapse of the Romanian Third Army, Italian Eighth

Army, and Hungarian Second Army, which held some 250 miles of the Axis line north of the German Sixth Army at Stalingrad.

8. Operational art is the body of techniques and procedures at the operational level of warfare, the middle level between the tactical and the strategic.

9. Throughout most of the siege of Stalingrad, Paulus was not a field marshal. Hitler promoted him to that rank just before the final, inevitable collapse. He did so hoping to force Paulus to commit suicide, because by tradition no German field marshal had ever been captured alive. Paulus did not commit suicide, which for days after the surrender infuriated Hitler more than the loss of the Sixth Army.

10. Magyarization was an assimilation or acculturation process under which non-Hungarian nationals came to adopt the Hungarian culture and language voluntarily or through social pressure.

11. The General Staff officer IIa was the division's adjutant and chief administrative officer.

12. Count.

13. After the fact; hindsight.

14. The *Führerreserve* was established in 1939 as a temporary holding pool for senior officers awaiting follow-on assignments. As the war progressed, semi-permanent assignment to the *Führerreserve* became the preferred means of neutralizing incompetent or politically unreliable officers.

15. General Dietrich von Choltitz, who in 1944 was the German general who surrendered Paris to the Allies.

16. In "The Genius for War," the third chapter of Clausewitz's book *On War*, he actually called it "*harmonischer Verein der Kräfte*," or harmonious union of strengths.

17. "Lord stay with us, for evening falls." From *Bach-Werke-Verzeichnis Cantata 6*, Johann Sebastian Bach.

18. Awarding a monetary bonus for senior commanders at the end of a successful combat assignment was a common practice.

16. The Gross-Deutschland Division

1. Lowest priority.

2. A reference to the Atlantic Wall defenses, which ultimately made the Allied assault on the Continent more difficult, but not impossible.

3. By May 1943 the Allies were just turning the tide in the Battle of the Atlantic. On 24 May, Grand Admiral Karl Dönitz suspended U-boat operations in the North Atlantic.

4. Nor would there be. Shortly after Balck wrote this, the Allied air war against Germany went into high gear. Operation POINTBLANK, the Allied air forces' Combined Bomber Offensive, started on 10 June 1943.

5. Balck is referring to Hitler's decision to reinforce German troops in North Africa after the British victory at El Alamein and the Anglo-American landing in Northwest Africa. Virtually all those newly committed forces were lost within a matter of months.

6. Ulrich von Hassell, *The von Hassell Diaries 1938–1944: The Story of the Forces against Hitler inside Germany* (New York: Doubleday, 1947). Ulrich von Hassell was the

German ambassador to Italy and a leading member of the Opposition to Hitler. He was executed in 1944 for his role in the 20 July bomb plot.

7. Hindenburg once referred to Hitler as the "Bohemian Corporal," and Rundstedt continued to think of him as such.

8. The OKH headquarters in Berlin was located at Bendler Strasse.

9. This was especially odd, considering that Kesselring was a Luftwaffe officer.

10. In almost every dispute between Kesselring and Rommel, subsequent events proved Kesselring right.

11. The Hermann Göring Division was a Luftwaffe Panzer division.

12. The three temples at Paestum were built between 550 and 450 B.C. in the part of southern Italy that was then known as Magna Graecia. They remain today some of the most impressive and best preserved ancient Greek temples anywhere in the world. Although there was heavy fighting in the area during the American landings at Salerno, the temples escaped relatively unharmed.

13. The Fieseler Fi 156 Storch (Stork) was Germany's primary single-engine observation and liaison aircraft. It was legendary for its ability to take off and land in tight spaces, which supports Balck's assessment of that particular aircraft and its pilot.

14. An exaggeration to be sure, but not much of one.

15. U.S. Fifth Army in September 1943 consisted of the British X Corps and the U.S. VI Corps.

16. On 21 November 1943, Hitler finally gave Kesselring overall command of the Italian theater. Rommel and the headquarters of Army Group B were transferred to Normandy, France, and given the responsibility for defending the French coast against the long-anticipated Allied invasion.

17. Carl von Clausewitz, "*Wir mögen nichts hören von Feldherren, die ohne Menschenblut siegen,*" in *Vom Kriege,* Book 4, *Das Gefecht* (Berlin: Ferdinand Dümmler, 1832).

18. American military historian Martin Blumenson criticizes Balck for not reinforcing the 16th Panzer Division adequately. "The 16th Panzer Division thus fought alone, taking the full force of the invasion. The six Italian coastal batteries were soon silenced by naval gunfire. Spread thin over a large area, the division launched small counterthrusts by tank-infantry teams." Martin Blumenson, *Salerno to Cassino: United States Army in World War II* (Washington, D.C.: Center of Military History, 1969), 86.

19. There is no reference in the U.S. Navy's official history of World War II to an American cruiser being hit by German artillery fire on 11 September 1943. See Samuel Eliot Morrison, *Sicily-Salerno-Anzio: History of United States Naval Operations in World War II,* vol. 9 (Annapolis, Md.: U.S. Naval Institute Press, 1953).

20. Mark Clark and Martin Blumenson, *Calculated Risk* (New York: Harper Collins, 1950): 164.

21. Ibid., 166.

22. Balck is referring to the power struggle in central and northern Italy between the Papacy and the Holy Roman Empire during the twelfth and thirteenth centuries.

23. The House of Hohenstaufen was a dynasty of German monarchs in the high middle ages. They reigned from 1138 to 1254. Three Hohenstaufens, including Frederick Barbarossa, were crowned Holy Roman Emperors.

24. Conradin (1252–1268) was the last of the Hohenstaufen line. He was the duke

of Swabia (1254–1268) as Conrad IV, the king of Jerusalem (1254–1268) as Conrad III, and the king of Sicily (1254–1268) as Conrad II. He died at the age of sixteen and was buried in Naples, which was then part of the kingdom of Sicily.

25. During the Second Punic War (218–201 B.C.) the city of Capua defected to Hannibal, welcoming his troops and supporting them generously. The Roman historian Livy suggested that the luxurious living conditions contributed to Hannibal's eventual downfall because his troops became soft and demoralized.

26. *Le quattro giornate di Napoli*, directed by Nanni Loy.

27. The Winter Line was a system of German defenses that ran across the Italian peninsula. Its main component was the Gustav Line. Subsidiary lines included the Bernhardt Line in front of the main Gustav positions, and the Hitler Line five miles to the rear.

28. Balck, of course, is ignoring the Luftwaffe's fire bombing raids against London, Coventry, Birmingham, etc.

29. Air defense artillery units. FLAK is an acronym for *Flugzeugabwehrkanone*, an aircraft defense gun.

30. Senior lance corporal.

31. Because of their long-standing hostility to each other, Rommel as the army group commander in northern Italy reported directly to OKW, even though Kesselring as the titular OB-Süd was the official theater commander. After Rommel's transfer to France in November 1943, Kesselring resumed unified command in Italy. Rommel was notorious for his inability to work with his peers, but he was Hitler's favorite.

32. Prior to World War I, Italy was a member of the Triple Alliance, with Germany and Austro-Hungary. Italy refused to join the Central Powers when the war started in 1914. In May 1915 Italy entered the war on the side of the Entente.

33. Balck here appears to be making a not too subtle reference to Italy and NATO.

34. After Italy surrendered and Mussolini was overthrown, he shifted his power base to German-controlled northern Italy and established the pro-fascist Italian Social Republic, in opposition to the government in Rome.

35. The policies of the Vatican under Pope Pius XII during World War II remain a topic of intense historical controversy. Eugenio Pacelli had been the papal nuncio in Germany from 1917 to 1930.

36. Lance corporal.

37. Lieutenant General Rudolf Schmundt was the German Army's chief of personnel. Schmundt was in Hitler's bunker field headquarters on 20 July 1944 and died of injuries he received in the bomb blast.

38. The Germans typically called a good partnership between a commander and his chief of staff a "happy marriage." The Balck-Mellenthin partnership was one of the most successful in all military history. See David T. Zabecki, "Friedrich-Wilhelm von Mellenthin," in *Chief of Staff: The Principal Officers behind History's Great Commanders* (Annapolis, Md.: U.S. Naval Institute Press, 2008). See also F.-W. Mellenthin, *Panzer Battles: A Study of the Employment of Armor in the Second World War* (Norman: Univ. of Oklahoma Press, 1956). See also F.-W. Mellenthin, *German Generals of World War II: As I Saw Them* (Norman: Univ. of Oklahoma Press, 1977).

39. This practice is in sharp contrast to the U.S. Army's predilection for issuing telephone book-sized operations orders.

40. The 1st SS Panzer Division, also called the Leibstandarte SS Adolf Hitler, evolved from Hitler's original SS bodyguard detachment. The 2nd SS Panzer Division was also called Das Reich.

41. The Germans did the same thing on the western front in July 1944 when they managed to extract most of the Seventh Army's senior staffs from the Falaise Pocket in western France. Within a month those staffs had managed to rebuild the Seventh Army.

42. The Swords were awarded only 160 times.

43. During both world wars the Germans excelled over all other armies in modifying and using captured enemy weapons.

44. Assault Division, literally, Storm Division.

45. This is a system of command the Germans call *Auftragstaktik*, or mission-oriented tactics.

46. Galicia is an area that encompasses southeastern Poland and western Ukraine.

47. Like many of the Wehrmacht's senior commanders, Balck too claims to have known little about the scope of the Holocaust for most of the war, even though anyone who lived in Germany after 1933 could not help but know about the Third Reich's virulent anti-Semitic policies. The postwar "Myth of the Clean Wehrmacht" held up for more than forty years after the war. Within the past twenty-five years, however, historical scholarship has exposed a high level of Wehrmacht complicity in the crimes of the Holocaust.

48. Balck does not specifically identify the XXIV Panzer Corps in the German edition of his memoirs, but it was clearly that unit from its subordinate divisions.

49. *Marnewunder* is a very ironic phrase referring to the wholly unexpected French victory at the Battle of the Marne in 1914. Thus, it became something of a buzzword for any unexpected positive reversal in a military action.

50. The 18th Artillery Division was formed at the end of 1943 by reorganizing the 18th Panzer Division. The 18th Artillery Division was the Wehrmacht's only such unit. The division consisted of three artillery regiments and a number of separate battalions and batteries. The Americans and British never had artillery divisions, while the Soviets had as many as fifty such units.

51. Even writing more than thirty years after the war, Balck seems unsure on this point, which is most likely why he did not specify the division or identify its commander. It was almost certainly the 8th Panzer Division, commanded by Major General Gottfried Fröhlich, an artillery officer.

52. See Wolfgang Paul, *Geschichte der 18. Artillerie-Division 1943-1944* (Freiburg: Rintelen, 1975), 291–340.

53. For the unit's organizational structure see ibid., 295.

54. Rommel, however, either ignored or failed to understand this principle when he advocated a rigid forward defense at the beaches in Normandy in June 1944. But as Balck comments later, he agreed with Rommel's tactical solution for Normandy.

55. Although never charged with a war crime by the Allies, Manteuffel was tried by the West German government in 1959 for having a deserter shot in 1944. He was convicted and sentenced to two years, but it was highly controversial. German political leaders lobbied vigorously to overturn the conviction, and he was released after four months. Balck himself in 1948 was tried and convicted of something similar.

56. *SS-Standartenführer* Joachim Peiper later commanded Kampfgruppe Peiper during the Battle of the Bulge, where his troops committed the infamous Malmedy Massacre of American POWs.

57. This is also known as Hube's Pocket, after Colonel General Hans-Valentin Hube, commander of the First Panzer Army.

58. The award of the various grades of the Iron Cross was a progressive process. Almost without exception a German soldier's initial act of heroism was recognized with the Iron Cross 2nd Class regardless of the action. His second act resulted in an Iron Cross 1st Class, and so on up to the Iron Cross Knight's Cross with Gold Oak Leaves, Swords, and Diamonds. That decoration was awarded only once during World War II, to Stuka pilot Hans Ulrich Rudel. One exception to the normal process was the award of the highest level, the Grand Cross of the Iron Cross, which was awarded directly to Hermann Göring in 1940 without his receiving the lower levels. Göring was the only Grand Cross recipient during World War II.

59. For a starkly different picture of the condition of the World War II German soldier on the eastern front, see Guy Sajer, *The Forgotten Soldier: War on the Russian Front—A True Story* (London: Weidenfield and Nicholson, 1971). Guy Sajer is a pseudonym for Guy Mouminoux, the son of a French father and a German mother, who served in the Gross-Deutschland Division.

60. Balck himself was the nineteenth recipient.

61. Curiously, Balck fails to include Rommel in the count. Rommel had commanded the 7th Panzer Division in 1940, during the Battle of France.

62. *Nationalkomitee Freies Deutschland* (NKFD) was an anti-Nazi organization of German POWs in the Soviet Union during World War II.

63. This was an ad hoc division-sized force pulled together on 13 February 1944 from various Wehrmacht units based in the puppet state of the General Government of Poland. The division only existed until 23 February, when it was consolidated with the 72nd Infantry Division.

64. Erich von dem Bach-Zelewski was the SS commander responsible for brutally crushing the Warsaw Uprising in August 1944.

65. Proskuriv is now named Khmelnytsky.

66. This refers to a battalion of heavy PzKpfw-VI Tiger tanks.

67. Marshal Georgy Konstantinovich Zhukov at that time commanded the 1st Ukrainian Front.

68. See Erich von Manstein, *Lost Victories*, ed. and trans. Anthony G. Powell (Chicago: Regnery, 1958). Also see Mungo Melvin, *Manstein: Hitler's Greatest General* (London: Weidenfeld and Nicolson, 2010).

69. The 9th SS Panzer Division also was named *Hohenstaufen.*

70. The II SS Panzer Corps was transferred from Russia to France in January 1944. After reconstituting, it was sent back to Russia, where it was involved in the operation to relieve the encircled First Panzer Army. After that, one of its units, the 9th SS Panzer Division, was attached to Balck's corps for the operation to relieve Tarnopol. Then the II SS Panzer Corps was redeployed to France, where it played a major role in the fighting in Normandy after the Allied D-Day landings.

71. Balck is referring to the 9th SS Panzer Division's performance at the bat-

tle for Caen in Normandy, and later at Arnhem, during the Allies' Operation MARKET-GARDEN.

72. As current events continue to show well into the twenty-first century, there has never been any love lost between the Russians and the western Ukrainians.

73. *Ukrayins'ka Povstans'ka Armiya.*

74. Poland and the Ukraine had been bitter rivals for centuries. In the fifteenth century the Polish-Lithuanian Confederation included most of the Ukraine, and its eastern border reached almost to Moscow. After Poland was resurrected as a nation following World War I, its eastern border was supposed to follow what was known as the "Curzon Line," but Poland seized the West Ukrainian People's Republic during the Polish-Ukrainian War of 1919. Poland's eastern border finally stabilized some 160 miles to the east of the Curzon Line, following the Polish-Soviet War of 1919–1921. During the 1943 Allied Teheran Conference, the Soviets demanded that Poland's postwar eastern border follow approximately the old Curzon Line. Thus, Poland lost some fifty-two thousand square miles of its interwar territory. The Poles were compensated with Silesia, which had been part of Germany. Poland's western border shifted to the line of the Oder and Neisse Rivers.

75. Unfortunately, Balck does not identify the individual, although he almost certainly would have recorded his name in his journal.

76. This has been the lament of all line officers throughout history.

77. Tank destroyers.

78. Model demanded a great deal of himself and his subordinates. This led to his being compared to the Soviet coal miner Alexey Stachanov, who was famous for habitually producing many times his daily quota.

79. Innere Führung, roughly translated as inner leadership, is a concept of leadership based on the principles of the post–World War II German Federal Constitution and one of the founding principles of the Bundeswehr. Intended as an antidote for "Prussian Militarism," the principle of innere Führung is based on the assumption that every soldier is first a citizen of Germany, and thus an integral part of society. He is only secondarily a soldier. If he is first a citizen, then he is also part of the community of values represented through the society to which he belongs.

80. The Landwehr (Territorial Defense) was the Prussian (later German) militia and reserve, intended to augment the regular army in time of war. It was first organized in March 1813, when King Friedrich Wilhelm III decreed universal military service and called upon Prussia to defeat Napoleonic France. The Landwehr was not revived as part of the postwar Bundeswehr.

81. Landser is the German term for the common soldier, the equivalent of the British Tommy or the American GI.

82. Balck is echoed by the American military historian Brigadier General S.L.A. Marshall: "The good general is simply the good company commander in his postgraduate course." S.L.A. Marshall, *Men against Fire: The Problem of Battle Command in Future War* (New York: Morrow, 1947), 177.

83. Alun Chalfont, *Montgomery of Alamein* (London: Weidenfeld and Nicolson, 1976), 110–112.

84. In fact, Operation BAGRATION, launched by the Soviets in Belorussia on 22 June 1944, resulted in the collapse of Army Group Center.

85. Army Group South was renamed Army Group North Ukraine on 1 April 1944.

86. This was sheer wishful thinking, as the following hearsay statement from Hitler indicates.

87. A reference to a hill position on the map.

88. Operation BAGRATION was already two weeks under way in Belorussia at this point.

89. Balck declines to name both commanders. The commander of the 8th Panzer Division was Major General Werner Friebe, whom Balck relieved of his command. The commander of the III Panzer Corps was Commander of Panzer Troops Hermann Breith.

90. Also named "Galicia," the 14th SS Volunteer Division was composed largely of ethnic Ukrainians from the Galicia region.

91. The Ostheer was the German Army on the eastern front. The Westheer was the German Army on the western front.

92. Literally, the German Greeting, the euphemistic name for what outside of Germany was universally called the Hitler salute.

93. The Hitler salute became the required form of German military salute on 24 July 1944, a direct reaction to the assassination attempt.

94. Stauffenberg was the Operations Officer, General Staff officer Ia, of the 10th Panzer Division.

95. This is a reference to Saint Paul's conversion to the Christian cause, as described in the New Testament book Acts of the Apostles, chapters 9, 22, and 26.

96. The conspirators obviously thought otherwise. It is disappointing to see Balck writing this in the late 1970s, considering the Berlin Airlift, the Marshall Plan, the Berlin Wall, NATO, and the economic and political position of the Federal Republic of Germany in postwar Europe.

97. Actually, only three officers and a stenographer died as a result of the blast in the bunker.

98. In the weeks that followed, more than 7,000 people were arrested and 4,980 were executed. Many of them were not connected with the plot. The Gestapo exploited the situation to settle political scores and eliminate other people suspected of disloyalty.

99. "Too severe makes jagged."

100. Finckh was executed on 30 August 1944.

101. Is Balck indulging in self-justifying double-think here? Or is he an essentially honest man struggling to come to terms with the most complex moral dilemma of his lifetime?

102. The correct verse of this old folksong is: *Zwei Löwen gingen einst selband in einem Wald spazoren und haben da, von Wut entbrannt einander aufgezohren. . . .*" "Two lions went for a walk in the forest, and both full of rage tore each other up."

103. "Sometimes even Homer is asleep."

104. The Warsaw Uprising, 1 August to 2 October 1944. Eighty-five percent of Warsaw was destroyed, two hundred thousand civilians were killed, and another seven hundred thousand were expelled from what was left of the city.

105. The Panzerfaust (Panzer Fist) was a shoulder-fired, antitank rocket launcher. It was the prototype of the modern RPG.

106. An NCO roughly equivalent to a U.S. Army staff sergeant. Like the Royal Air Force in World War II, the Luftwaffe had some NCO pilots. Even the postwar Bundesluftwaffe had some NCO pilots in its early years.

107. The SdKfz 2 was a half-tracked motorcycle.

108. Gräser was the recipient of the Knight's Cross of the Iron Cross, with Oak Leaves and Swords.

109. Balck was the nineteenth of only twenty-seven recipients of the Knight's Cross of the Iron Cross, with Oak Leaves, Swords, and Diamonds. The decoration was established in 1941.

110. The Kalmyks were a western Mongol ethnic group in the North Caucasus who in 1942 volunteered to fight in the Wehrmacht. In 1943, Stalin retaliated by declaring the entire Kalmyk population to be German collaborators and had them deported to Siberia, with resulting great loss of life.

111. Heinz Guderian, *Panzer Leader* (New York: Ballantine Books, 1957), 371–376.

112. The Kolkhoz system was the Soviet use of state collective farms.

113. Balck is equivocating here. Although historians are divided on the significance of the 5 November 1937 "Hossbach Memorandum," many nonetheless see this document as direct and compelling evidence of Hitler's intentions to wage a war of aggression and expansion. Balck's own criticisms of Hitler's views of the Russians and the peoples of the East undercut any suggestions that both sides somehow blundered into the war.

114. *Tertius gaudens* (literally the "rejoicing third" in English) refers to a strategy in which one party benefits from a conflict between two others.

115. Again, quoted in the original English.

116. Nightmare of coalitions.

117. This is one of the most puzzling sentences in Balck's memoirs. Is he talking about World War I, or World War II? Exactly who is "the most brilliant military commander"? It cannot be Schlieffen, because he died before World War I started. Balck certainly cannot mean Moltke the Younger or Falkenhayn, and Germany had already lost the war by the time Hindenburg and Ludendorff took over in mid-1916. If Balck is referring to World War II, "the most brilliant military commander" by his own account cannot be Hitler. The only German general of World War II who comes close to that description is Manstein, but he never commanded more than a single army group. And finally, neither World War I nor World War II can possibly be described as having been prepared "politically in a first-rate manner."

118. "You know how to gain a victory, Hannibal, but you do not know how to make use of it."

119. This is a sentiment widely shared by many in the U.S. military about the Vietnam War after the 1975 fall of Saigon.

120. Balck wrote this in the late 1970s. Since then, the Militärgeschichtliches Forschungsamt, the official military history organization of the Bundeswehr, has produced the excellent and unflinching thirteen-volume series *Das Deutsche Reich und der Zweite Weltkrieg* (1990–2008), published in English by Oxford University Press as *Germany and the Second World War.*

17. Commander in Chief, Army Group G

1. Up until 1945 the Germans applied the title of commander in chief to levels of command from field army up. The British and Americans used the title for only the most senior commands. Thus, when Balck was assigned to the western front in 1944 there were at least seven German Army officers with the title Oberbefehlshaber, abbreviated OB.

2. This is a reference to the Ardennes Offensive, the Battle of the Bulge that would be conducted by Army Group B. The mission of Balck's Army Group G was to screen Army Group B from the south and buy time for the build-up.

3. *Generalstabsmässig*—General Staff-like—was a German euphemism for anything that was well thought out and precisely planned.

4. In other words, when the very survival of the nation was threatened.

5. A World War I General Staff officer, Franz von Papen served as chancellor of Germany in 1932 and as vice chancellor under Adolf Hitler from 1933 to 1934. He later served as ambassador to Austria, and then to Turkey. One of the twenty-two major defendants at the International Military Tribunal at Nuremberg, he was one of only three acquitted on all charges. He later was found guilty and sentenced to eight years by a West German Denazification Court. He was also the German military attaché in Washington from 1913 to 1915 and was involved in espionage activity that led to the sinking of the *Lusitania*. Possibly that is why Balck consulted him as an "expert" on the United States.

6. Miltiades the Younger was the Athenian general who defeated the Persians at the Battle of Marathon in 490 B.C.

7. During the First Punic War (264–241 B.C.) the Carthaginians were the masters of naval warfare and the Romans had no maritime tradition. Gaius Duilius invented a combination grappling device and boarding bridge that allowed Roman troops to cross onto the Carthaginian ships and then fight as they did on land, which was always the Roman strength.

8. At the time this was far from an irrational assessment. In 1944 many on the Allied side were giving serious consideration to the Morgenthau Plan, which was based on eliminating Germany's ability to wage war by destroying enough of its industrial capacity to reduce Germany to little more than an agricultural state. During the years immediately after the war the Soviet Union pursued just such a policy in occupied East Germany.

9. This sentence appears in English in the German edition of Balck's memoirs.

10. See Joachim Ludewig, *Rückzug: The German Retreat from France, 1944*, English translation edited by David T. Zabecki (Lexington: Univ. Press of Kentucky, 2012), 233–251.

11. Commander in chief, Western Theater.

12. Commander of the U.S. 12th Army Group.

13. Commander of the U.S. Third Army.

14. See Ludewig, *Rückzug*, 105–129, 176–187.

15. Always attack!

16. Baden was the former German grand duchy along the east bank of the

Rhine River, opposite Alsace. Today Baden is part of the Federal German state of Baden-Württemberg.

17. This was the Reserve Army. Although he was the head of the SS, Himmler had no military training or experience whatsoever.

18. "People's Units," first raised by the Nazi Party in the autumn of 1944 and officially called the Volkssturm. They were hastily organized and ill-trained units consisting of old men and young boys, led by small cadres of veteran soldiers. The Volkssturm is often incorrectly confused with the Volksgrenadier divisions raised by the Wehrmacht about the same time.

19. Ernst Schlange at one time had been the Nazi Party's Gauleiter of Berlin.

20. An SS rank equivalent to major general in the Wehrmacht.

21. The CDU is one of Germany's major political parties today.

22. A combination of Nazi fascism and communism.

23. Raised in 1944, the Volksgrenadier divisions had only six line infantry battalions instead of the nine for the standard infantry divisions. They had relatively few heavy weapons, but large numbers of submachine guns, automatic weapons, and shoulder-fired antitank weapons, like the Panzerfaust.

24. Keitel was chief of OKW, theoretically Germany's senior-ranking military officer. In practice, Hitler viewed Keitel as merely "the man who runs my office."

25. Percy Schramm, *Hitler als militärischer Führer* (Athenäum Verlag: Frankfurt am Main, 1962), 42.

26. *Nationalsozialistischer Führungsoffizier*, the Nazi Party's equivalent of the Soviet political commissars. The position was established in Wehrmacht units down to the divisional level in December 1943. At the regimental and battalion levels the NSFO was an additional duty assignment.

27. *Bundesverdienstkreuz*.

28. This was a local initiative in Army Group G only. By 1945 the Volkssturm was active in fighting on both fronts.

29. This was another temporary victory. By 1945 the *Volkssturm* was routinely drafting Hitler Youth boys as young as twelve.

30. Balck fails to mention here that fuel shortages also contributed significantly to the halt of the U.S. Third Army's advance.

31. Balck's attitude seems incongruous considering that the Wehrmacht was not known for adhering strictly to those conventions.

32. Balck is clearly referring to the books of German novelist Karl May, which have continued to fascinate Germans since the 1880s. His works are still highly popular in Germany today. Unfortunately, May had no personal knowledge of the American West, and his books are all pure fantasy. He was only in the United States once for a very brief period, and even then Buffalo, New York, was as far west as he got.

33. Hitler, in effect, split the difference between Rommel and Rundstedt, virtually guaranteeing that neither approach would work.

34. Rommel's chief of staff at Army Group B, General Hans Speidel, was involved in the opposition to Hitler and part of the inner circle of the July bomb plot. Rommel was in no way connected with the opposition. But after the Gestapo arrested Speidel, Rommel became implicated in Hitler's mind because of the traditional close relation-

ship between German commanders and their chiefs of staff. While imprisoned for seven months, Speidel admitted nothing and implicated no one. He was the only member of the inner circle to survive the war. After the war he served as a general in the Bundeswehr, and from 1957 to 1963 he was the first German officer to serve as NATO's Commander, Allied Land Forces Central Europe.

35. During World War II Germany lost 475 general and flag officers, killed in action, died of wounds, or missing in action.

36. The General Staff officer IIa was the chief of personnel.

37. Local Group Leader, a Nazi Party political rank roughly equivalent to a Wehrmacht captain.

38. Balck's memoirs were published in Germany in 1981, but he obviously wrote this line at least ten years earlier.

39. Fortress Metz was a ring of nineteenth- and early twentieth-century fortresses around the city. Although obsolescent by the standards of the 1940s, they were still formidable obstacles.

40. Regional Leader, one of the highest of the Nazi Party political ranks, equivalent to a Wehrmacht senior general.

41. The picture painted here by Balck is not necessarily as absurd as it might seem. Metz, one of the major cities of Lorraine, had been German from 1871 to 1918, and then again since 1940. Many people in Lorraine still spoke German and identified with Germany rather than France. Many others, of course, continued to identify with France and considered the Germans illegal occupiers.

42. The Ardennes Offensive, known to the Allies as the Battle of the Bulge, was finally launched on 16 December 1944. It was conducted by Model's Army Group B, but, as the Army Group G commander, Balck was one of the few senior officers privy to the plan early on.

43. Heusinger later became the first general inspector of the Bundeswehr, the senior military officer of the Federal Republic of Germany.

44. Knight's Cross of the War Service Cross.

45. Silesia was part of southeastern Germany. It was annexed by Poland following the war. It remains part of Poland today.

46. Army Group G's only other Panzer division at that point was the 21st Panzer Division.

47. Although Balck declines to identify the division and the commander, it was Lieutenant General Edgar Feuchtinger.

48. World War I hero Field Marshal August von Mackensen was Germany's senior-ranking retired military officer at the time. He was the father of Colonel General Eberhard von Mackensen.

49. Feuchtinger worked in the German steel industry after the war. From 1953 until his death in 1960 he passed classified information on German rearmament to Soviet military intelligence.

50. Conducted between 9 February and 15 March 1917, Operation ALBERICH shortened the overall German line by twenty-five miles, and in the process freed up fourteen divisions.

51. The U.S. 442nd Regimental Combat Team was the most highly decorated regiment- or brigade-sized unit in the history of the U.S. Army.

52. In 1948 Balck was put on trial in Stuttgart by the West German government for the summary execution of a German officer under his command. On 28 November 1944 artillery commander Lieutenant Colonel Johann Schottke had been found drunk on duty in his bunker and could not remember the positions of his guns. Balck had him shot without a court-martial. The Stuttgart court ruled the shooting unlawful. Balck was sentenced to three years in prison, and served eighteen months.

53. In 1950 Balck was tried in absentia by a French military court in Paris and held responsible for the destruction of Gérardmer. He was sentenced to twenty years hard labor, but the sentence was never carried out.

54. Friedrich Wilhelm (1620–1688), elector of Brandenburg.

55. Commander of the French First Army, operating under the Allied 6th Army Group.

56. There is no recorded French violation of Swiss territory during the battle for Alsace in 1944. Throughout the war, both the Germans and the Allies routinely violated Swiss airspace. In 1944 and 1945 the Allies mistakenly bombed Schaffhausen, Stein am Rhein, Basel, and Zurich.

57. The American official history is somewhat critical of Balck's actions at this point: "The entire maneuver was exceedingly complicated and Balck only made the situation worse by directing that the armored brigade be committed piecemeal as its various components reached the front. Instead of concentrating the tank brigade for a rapid, powerful thrust, Balck invited the unit's destruction in detail. Not surprisingly, the maneuver was a total failure." Jeffrey J. Clarke and Robert Ross Smith, *Riviera to the Rhine: United States Army in World War II* (Washington, D.C.: Center of Military History, 1993), 427.

58. This was known to the Allies as the Colmar Pocket.

59. Often mistakenly referred to as an army group, *Oberkommando Oberrhein* (Upper Rhine High Command) was not an army group that reported to the theater commander OB-West, but rather an entirely separate entity that reported directly to OKW. Command of the new organization was given to SS chief Heinrich Himmler, who had no military training or command experience whatsoever. The organization was disbanded on 25 January 1945, and responsibility for the sector returned to Army Group G.

60. Lieutenant Colonel Johann Schottke. See note 52.

61. A West German civilian court in 1948 ruled otherwise. See note 52.

62. *Marschbataillon* was a provisional unit made up of companies from various battalions for the purpose of giving them a command structure during their movement.

63. Mellenthin was relieved as chief of staff of Army Group G because he ran afoul of Himmler. Mellenthin was assigned to the Führer Reserve on 30 November 1944. The following day he was promoted to major general, thanks to Guderian's intervention. From 28 December 1944 to sometime in February 1945 Mellenthin commanded the 9th Panzer Division during the Battle of the Bulge. On 5 March 1945 he assumed his last assignment as chief of staff of the Fifth Panzer Army. For further reading, see the chapter "Friedrich-Wilhelm von Mellenthin" in *Chief of Staff: The Principal Officers behind History's Great Commanders*, vol. 2, *World War II to Korea and Vietnam*, ed. David T. Zabecki (Annapolis, Md.: U.S. Naval Institute Press, 2008), 62–74.

64. The Germans routinely referred to their corps by the shorthand version of their commanders' names. Corps Höhne was the LXXXIX Army Corps, commanded by

General of Infantry Gustav Höhne. At this point in the war it was Army Group G's separate corps.

65. See Hugh M. Cole, *The Lorraine Campaign: U.S. Army in World War II* (Washington, D.C.: U.S. Government Printing Office, 1950).

66. Hans Speidel, *Invasion 1944* (Stuttgart: Rainer Wunderlich Verlag, 1950).

67. At that point Guderian was the chief of staff of the German Army, OKH was running the war in the East, and OKW was running the war in the West.

68. Balck was now the commander of the reconstituted German Sixth Army, but he also commanded the ad hoc Army Task Group Balck, which consisted of the Sixth Army and the Hungarian First and Third Armies.

69. Gaedcke later served in the Bundeswehr as a lieutenant general.

70. Peter Gosztony, *Der Kampf um Budapest 1944/45* (Budapest: Hungarian Institute, 1964), 40–42.

71. The 5th SS Panzer and 3rd SS Panzer Divisions, respectively.

18. North of the Danube

1. This is the German name for two towns on the Danube, one on the Hungarian side named Komárom and the other on the Slovakian side named Komárno.

2. Most German FLAK units were under the Luftwaffe, but a few were under the army.

3. Peter Gosztony, *Endkampf an der Donau 1944/45* (Vienna: Molden Verlag, 1978).

4. Commander of the Soviet 3rd Ukrainian Front.

5. P. G. Kuznetsov, ed., *Marshal Tolbukhin Sovetskie Polkovodtsy I Voenachal'niki* (Moscow: Voennoe Izdatel'stvo, 1966), 220–221.

6. This is now Dunaújváros.

7. The overall "civilian" head of Budapest was Obergruppenführer Karl Pfeffer Wildenbruch, an SS police official. He was captured following the siege. The military commander in Budapest was Major General Gerhard Schmidhuber. He was killed during the siege.

8. The implication is that the supplies were siphoned off into the black market.

9. These were the 8th SS Cavalry Division and the 22nd SS Volunteer Cavalry Division.

10. Most of the rank and file troops in these two divisions were ethnic Germans from outside of Germany, mostly Hungary.

11. The Hungarian Army.

12. Heszlenyi was the commander of the Hungarian Third Army.

13. This is in northeastern Slovakia.

14. He was the leader of the fascist Arrow Cross Party.

15. This is a very disappointing comment that betrays Balck's belief in the concept of "ethnic purity," which tragically was far too typical of many Germans and other Europeans of his generation.

16. The Magyars were ethnic Hungarians.

17. Major General Zoltán Szügyi received the Knight's Cross on 12 January 1945. He was one of only forty-three non-German recipients.

18. Eight of the thirty-eight Waffen-SS divisions were composed primarily of Hungarians.

19. This was a tactical collection team to forage for and collect food, animals, war booty, etc.

20. The capital of Hungary from the tenth until the mid-thirteenth century, Esztergom was captured by Soviet troops on 26 December 1944, but they were pushed back by the Germans on 6 January 1945. The Germans were finally ousted on 21 March 1945.

21. Laszlo Zsigmond, *Magyarorszag és a masodik vilaghaboru* (Budapest: Hungarian Academy of Sciences, Történettudományi Intézet Institute of History, 1961), document no. 126, page 321.

22. Tiso was a Slovak Roman Catholic priest and a leading politician of the Slovak People's Party. Between 1939 and 1945 he was the head of the First Slovak Republic, a satellite state of Nazi Germany. After the end of World War II, Tiso was convicted by the Czechoslovak government and hanged for treason.

23. The Sixth Panzer Army made the main effort during the Battle of the Bulge in December 1944. Many accounts incorrectly identify it as the Sixth SS Panzer Army. Although it was commanded by a Waffen-SS officer and had a large number of Waffen-SS units, it was still a Wehrmacht unit. After the Battle of the Bulge the Sixth Panzer Army was transferred to Hungary. It was officially transferred to the Waffen-SS and redesignated the Sixth SS Panzer Army on 2 April 1945.

24. Wöhler was the commander of Army Group South.

25. Székesfehérvár in Hungarian.

26. Unfortunately, Balck does not offer the slightest hint of who that replacement commander might have been.

27. The 44th Infantry Division was also known as the Division *Hoch- und Deutschmeister.*

28. This occurred on 11 August 1904.

29. Styria is in southeastern Austria.

30. Army Group F was in the Balkans. Army Group E was in northern Greece. On 25 March 1945 the two merged as Army Group E.

31. It was also known as the SS Division Galizien.

32. The 27th Bomber Wing was also known as Kampfgeschwader 27 "Boelcke," named for German World War I ace Oswald Boelcke.

33. The Stavka was the High Command of the Soviet Armed Forces.

34. Balck is completely misreading Churchill. Although the British prime minister warned of the threat from Russia early on, he never for a moment considered allying with Germany against Russia.

35. Balck's nuclear comment is anachronistic at best. The first successful detonation of the nuclear weapon was at the Trinity test site on 16 July 1945, more than two months after the end of the war in Europe.

36. What Balck is saying here does not seem to make sense. By this point the Saint László Division had already gone over to the Russians. That is disputed by a Hungarian major in Appendix 3.

37. This was eight days after Germany surrendered.

38. Austria had been annexed by Germany on 12 March 1938.

39. Balck obviously was thinking of the military disintegration and political turmoil he had experienced at the end of World War I.

40. The Battle of Poltava occurred on 27 June 1709.

41. In the late 1920s Dietrich was Hitler's chauffeur and bodyguard.

42. At the divisional level, the operations officer, the General Staff officer Ia, was "dual-hatted" as the chief of staff.

43. This was the honorific title of the 1st SS Panzer Division, which had started out in 1923 as Hitler's bodyguard force.

44. Hitler, in fact, was widely read. His private library totaled sixteen thousand volumes.

45. Preussisch Eylau is now called Bagrationovsk, Russia.

46. Here, too, Balck is completely misreading the American side. Roosevelt was almost the polar opposite of Hitler when it came to micromanaging military operations. During the Battle of the Bulge Hitler incorrectly assumed that Eisenhower would not be able to react for several days because he would have to get Roosevelt's and Churchill's approval for any military actions. Balck is also mistaken on the bombing of Hiroshima, which was authorized by President Harry S. Truman.

47. The order entitled "The Führer Alone Will Determine Strategy" was actually issued on 21 January 1945.

48. Balck may have put his finger squarely on the central irony of the Third Reich.

49. But throughout all this discussion of Hitler's pros and cons, Balck just cannot seem to bring himself to face the reality of Hitler's brutal racial and occupation policies, the inherent corruption of almost all of the social and political institutions of the Third Reich, and the utter barbarism of the Holocaust.

50. Balck was either misreading postwar American literature on the war, or he was reading what he wanted to see. By early 1944, the Soviet Union almost inevitably was going to defeat Germany, regardless of what the western Allies did.

51. Rendulic was the commander of Army Group Courland and then Army Group South at the end of the war.

52. Brandt was an SS doctor who was Hitler's first personal physician. From 1939 on, Brandt ran the Nazi euthanasia program. He was convicted of war crimes and hanged in 1948.

53. Many historians today agree that the injections Morell gave to Hitler contributed to his deteriorating health and probably his mental capability at the end of the war. The injections included combinations of amphetamines, belladonna, atropine, caffeine, cocaine, methamphetamine, morphine, strychnine, potassium bromide, proteins, and lipids derived from animal tissues and fats, sodium barbitone, sulfonamide, testosterone, and vitamins.

54. This was awarded for five or more wounds.

55. A Teppichbeisser is a small dog biting the carpet.

56. From Ludwig Uhland's poem "König Karls Meerfahrt."

57. Dr. Overzealous.

58. After Hitler committed suicide and Admiral Karl Dönitz became president of the Reich on 30 April 1945, Kesselring was appointed as commander in chief of southern Germany, with plenipotentiary powers.

59. The General Staff officer Ic was the head of the intelligence staff section.

60. This is an abbreviation for *Hilfswillige*, the foreign volunteers fighting for the Wehrmacht.

61. The General Staff officer IIa was the head of the personnel section.

62. McBride commanded the U.S. 80th Infantry Division.

63. The town of Mauerkirchen is in northwestern Austria, close to the German border.

64. Eisenhower's "Mistreatment Order" is something of an urban legend that has taken on a life of its own since World War II. It culminated in the publication in 1989 of the book *Other Losses,* by a Canadian novelist named James Bacque. There is no doubt that some American soldiers mistreated German POWs after the war. There is no evidence whatsoever that Eisenhower ever issued such an order, nor that any mistreatment of POWs was systematic and centrally managed. Most historians believe that Bacque's thesis is without merit.

19. Looking Back

1. Balck is overestimating the credibility of the arguments of some western revisionist historians writing in the 1970s and 1980s.

2. Many historians argue that the Hossbach Memorandum of 5 November 1937 shows that Hitler was in fact planning such a war early on. It is hard to take Balck's statement here seriously, considering the conquest of France in the Low Countries in 1940, the Battle of Britain air campaign a few months later, and the planned Operation SEA LION amphibious invasion of Britain. SEA LION was aborted when the Germans failed in the Battle of Britain.

3. The strong support for appeasement policies in Britain was a direct result of the shattering psychological impact of World War I only twenty years earlier, which was supposed to have been "the war to end all wars."

4. Most historians agree that Roosevelt pursued a strongly anti-Germany policy while America was formally neutral during the first two years of World War II. Roosevelt, however, was convinced that America would get drawn into the war sooner rather than later, and that America's situation would be far more difficult if Germany defeated Britain first.

5. Balck overlooks the fact that for more than two hundred years the neutrality of the Belgian coast, the key to the control of the English Channel, was the centerpiece of British foreign policy toward the Continent. The violation of Belgian neutrality was the main reason for Britain's entry into World War I, and a key reason the British could not accept the German occupation of France and Belgium in 1940.

6. The actual quote is *Afflavit deus et dissipati sunt,* which means God blew and they were scattered. It is from Schiller's poem "Die unüberwindliche Flotte" ("The Insurmountable Fleet").

7. Dictatorship in time of crisis was a central element of the constitution of the Roman Republic.

8. Balck seems to overlook the fact that the German dictatorship that started in 1933 was exactly what caused the crisis.

9. Greek for "successors."

10. Operational is the middle level of warfare. The basic level of warfare is the tactical. The highest level of warfare is the strategic. Tactics focus on winning battles; operational art focuses on winning campaigns; strategy focuses on winning wars. Paradoxically, success at one level of warfare does not automatically result in success at the next higher level. It is possible to win all the battles in a war and yet lose that war, as the United States learned in Vietnam.

11. Balck fails to account for the fact that Germany attacked the British Isles in 1940, and on 11 December 1941 it was Germany that unilaterally declared war on America, four days after the Japanese attacked Pearl Harbor, even though neither Hitler nor almost anyone else on the German General Staff was totally sure where Pearl Harbor was.

12. Balck ignores the war at sea, the Battle of the Atlantic, which reached its culmination point in early 1943. When British and American antisubmarine tactics and weapons finally started to turn the tide in the Atlantic, Britain was within weeks of complete economic collapse. Thus, Germany for a while conducted a very effective and aggressive form of the economic warfare that Balck criticizes.

13. The Anaconda Strategy was used by the Union during the American Civil War. It was based on surrounding and isolating the Confederacy by controlling the Atlantic and Gulf Coasts and the Mississippi River. It bears no resemblance to Anglo-American global strategy in World War II.

14. Of course, the Germans did not succeed in doing the exact same thing with aerial attacks against Britain, the Battle of Britain, the "Blitz," and the V-1 and V-2 attacks. Those all failed to demoralize the British population.

15. Many military historians would dispute this claim. The Soviet Army was always inferior to the Wehrmacht on the tactical level, but they won World War II on the operational level.

16. This, of course, was the entire idea behind the institution of the General Staff.

17. The Germans fielded 354 divisions in World War II, compared to 89 for the U.S. Army.

18. This was the 12th SS Panzer Division.

19. Richard Hentsch is the German General Staff officer most associated with the withdrawal of the First and Second Armies in August 1914, leading to the Battle of the Marne.

20. Gamelin was commander in chief of the French Army at the start of World War II.

21. It would be interesting to know if Balck ever read Herman Wouk's *The Caine Mutiny*, a brilliant novel about the stress of command in the U.S. Navy during World War II. The book was translated into German and published in 1953 as *Die Caine war ihr Schicksal*.

22. This was the Reich Labor Service, or RAD, a uniformed and armed paramilitary force that provided six months of pre-military training.

23. Many historians argue that Hitler did intend a war in the West, but only several years later than it actually started. Hitler failed to take into consideration Britain's and France's determination to honor their treaty obligations to Poland. Both those countries

had made it clear in no uncertain terms that they would react militarily to any attack on Poland. It is, therefore, very difficult to give serious consideration to any argument that Hitler did not want a war in the West but was forced into it by Britain and France.

24. What British-German rapprochement could have been possible after Britain extended security guarantees to Poland, and then Germany attacked Poland? Hitler and much of the leadership of Germany naively believed that the western democracies would continue their policy of appeasement at all costs, as they had at Munich in 1938.

25. This certainly would include Hitler.

26. Cabinet Wars, a term referring to the type of limited wars fought in Europe during the period of the absolute monarchies, from the Peace of Westphalia in 1648 to the French Revolution in 1789.

27. By the time Balck was finishing his memoirs in the late 1970s, many historians would have agreed with him on the causes of modern wars. Since the end of the Cold War, however, the world has seen a new surge of religiously inspired sectarian warfare. But the indicators were always there throughout the Cold War. The most prominent of those indicators was the long-running series of Arab-Israeli conflicts.

28. Here he is referring to the Cold War of the 1970s.

29. Uncontrolled illegal immigration and large numbers of appeals for political asylum (some justified, but some under the flimsiest of pretenses) remain one of the major social and political problems in Europe today.

30. John Hackett, *The Third World War* (London: Sidgwick and Jackson, 1978).

31. As Balck wrote this, the Soviet Union was fighting its ten-year failed war in Afghanistan. As of 2015, the United States has been fighting a war in Afghanistan for fourteen years, with no better results and hardly any better prospect of accomplishing anything.

Appendix 1

1. The Gymnasium is the German university-track secondary school. The completion certificate, called the *Abitur*, is the equivalent of an American associate degree.

2. *The Army Report.*

3. The war ended before the award recommendation could be processed.

4. Cavalry Captain.

5. Although not appointed a member of the General Staff, Balck nonetheless served in this position.

6. *The Armed Forces Report.*

7. This was a position title, not a rank.

Appendix 2

1. SS-Brigadeführer Sylvester Stadler was commander of the 9th SS Panzer Division.

2. Josef "Sepp" Dietrich was commander of the Sixth SS Panzer Army.

3. Wilhelm Bittrich was commander of the II SS Panzer Corps.

4. Hans Krebs was the deputy chief of the Army General Staff. On 1 April 1945 he replaced Guderian as chief of the General Staff.

Appendix 3

1. "He won in the last encirclement battle."
2. "The Knight's Cross," 1968, 2, commemorative volume on the death of Zoltan Vitéz Szügyi.

Appendix 4

1. The Spruchkammer was the German civilian denazification court.
2. Guderian gave his sworn statement to the U.S. Army captain who was the adjutant of the U.S. European Command Historical Detachment, which was then located at Neustadt. On 29 April 1948, Captain Finley also took a sworn statement from Colonel General Franz Halder, Guderian's predecessor as chief of the Army General Staff. Both Guderian and Halder cooperated with the U.S. Army's immediate postwar historical program. Balck did not.

Appendix 5

1. Curiously, the court finding does not mention Balck's name, but it is obvious from the text who he is. Perhaps the original document had a heading that identified Balck, but which was not reproduced in his book.
2. This is possibly Major Kurt Kischke.
3. Directive No. 104 was the denazification law in Baden-Württemberg.

Appendix 6

1. Unfortunately, Balck did not include his response to Falkenstein as an attachment to his memoirs. He did think Falkenstein's letter significant enough to include. Balck must have answered, because he continued to correspond with Falkenstein at least until June 1977.

Appendix 7

1. The Feldpost was the German military postal system, similar to the American APO system.

Index

Numbered military units are listed at the beginning of the index, whether designated by arabic numerals, roman numerals, or spelled-out numbers; military units without numerical designations are listed in alphabetical order. Following the German usage of his contemporaries, Hermann Balck often used the term "Russian" in cases in which "Soviet" would have been more accurate. This index substitutes the term "Soviet" when referring to military units that are described as "Russian" in the text. Similarly, "Great Britain" is often substituted for Balck's "England."

CPSIA information can be obtained at www.ICGtesting.com
Printed in the USA
BVOW04*1034160615

404488BV00002B/8/P